THE YORK CORPUS CHRISTI PLAYS

Middle English Texts Series

The Middle English Texts Series is designed for classroom use. Its goal is to make available to teachers, scholars, and students texts that occupy an important place in the literary and cultural canon but have not been readily available in student editions. The series does not include those authors, such as Chaucer, Langland, or Malory, whose English works are normally in print in good student editions. The focus is, instead, upon Middle English literature adjacent to those authors that teachers need in compiling the syllabuses they wish to teach. The editions maintain the linguistic integrity of the original work but within the parameters of modern reading conventions. The texts are printed in the modern alphabet and follow the practices of modern capitalization, word formation, and punctuation. Manuscript abbreviations are silently expanded, and *u/v* and *j/i* spellings are regularized according to modern orthography. Yogh (ȝ) is transcribed as *g*, *gh*, *y*, or *s*, according to the sound in Modern English spelling to which it corresponds; thorn (þ) and eth (ð) are transcribed as *th*. Distinction between the second person pronoun and the definite article is made by spelling the one *thee* and the other *the*, and final *-e* that receives full syllabic value is accented (e.g., *charité*). Hard words, difficult phrases, and unusual idioms are glossed either in the right margin or at the foot of the page. Explanatory and textual notes appear at the end of the text, often along with a glossary. The editions include short introductions on the history of the work, its merits and points of topical interest, and brief working bibliographies.

This series is published in association with the University of Rochester.

Medieval Institute Publications is a program of
The Medieval Institute, College of Arts and Sciences

 WESTERN MICHIGAN UNIVERSITY

THE YORK CORPUS CHRISTI PLAYS

Edited by
Clifford Davidson

TEAMS • Middle English Texts Series

MEDIEVAL INSTITUTE PUBLICATIONS
Western Michigan University
Kalamazoo

Copyright © 2011 by the Board of Trustees of Western Michigan University
Manufactured in the United States of America

This book is printed on acid-free paper.

Library of Congress Cataloging-in-Publication Data

York plays.
  The York Corpus Christi plays / edited by Clifford Davidson.
     p. cm. – (Middle English texts series)
  Includes bibliographical references.
  ISBN 978-1-58044-162-9 (paperbound : alk. paper)
  1. Mysteries and miracle-plays, English–England–York. 2. Christian drama, English
(Middle)–England–York. 3. English drama–To 1500. 4. Bible plays, English. I. Davidson,
Clifford. II. Title.
  PR1261.Y67 2011
  822'.05160802–dc23

                            2011031005

ISBN 978-1-58044-162-9

P   5   4   3   2   1

CONTENTS

In memoriam
Diether Haenicke
*Exemplary friend of scholars
and scholarship*

⚘ ACKNOWLEDGMENTS

In preparing the present edition of the York Corpus Christi plays, I am indebted to more colleagues and friends than can possibly be named here. These include many whose work I have encountered in various venues, including discussions, incisive commentary at conferences, and of course published work in articles, reviews, and monographs. Very important indebtedness must be acknowledged to Pamela King, Richard Rastall, Alexandra Johnston, and the late John Robinson, but I think also of some significant matters brought to my attention, for example, by Sheila White and the Rev. James Croom. Eve Salisbury and her students used portions of the text in her graduate class and provided some comments and corrections. The documents collected in the Records of Early English Drama volumes on York have been invaluable, as have the previous editions of the York plays by Lucy Toulmin Smith (1885) and Richard Beadle (1982). The latter text is now available in a second edition issued by the Early English Text Society, unfortunately not yet published prior to the typesetting of the present book. In addition, the facsimile prepared by Richard Beadle and Peter Meredith has made my work with the manuscript at the British Library much easier.

I need especially to thank Paul A. Johnston, Jr., who, bringing his considerable skill in dialect study to bear on the alliterative long lines as these appear in the plays, has provided a separate section, included here in an Appendix. The encouragements of Barbara D. Palmer, my late wife Audrey, and so many others were vital to the completion of the work. Russell Peck initially urged me to take on the work. I am very much in his debt for his strong support and useful critiques. Alan Lupack's help in reviewing the text and providing suggestions for glosses of the Middle English vocabulary is acknowledged with gratitude. Leah Haught and John H. Chandler were responsible for the typesetting, a formidable task to be sure. The National Endowment for the Humanities provided financial support for publication in the TEAMS series. Finally, I am of course grateful to Medieval Institute Publications for publishing this volume.

At the British Library I was able to work in the comfort of the new manuscript room, where also the staff allowed examination of erasures and faint passages in the manuscript under ultra-violet light. I am likewise grateful to a number of other libraries, first of all the Western Michigan University Library and its Interlibrary Loan staff, but also the Leeds University Library, the York University Library at King's Manor, the York Minster Library, the Warburg Institute Library, and the University of Michigan Libraries. Permission to use the text of the York plays in MS. Add. 35290 was kindly granted by the British Library.

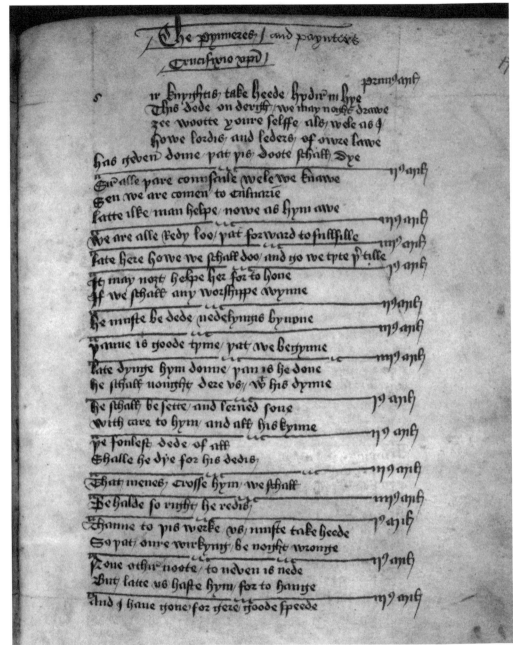

Figure 1. Copyright The British Library Board. London, British Library, MS. Add. 35290, fol. 195 (BL numbering fol. 181), showing the opening of the Pinners' "Crucifixio Christi." Reproduced with permission of the British Library.

❧ INTRODUCTION

For the invisible things of [God], from the creation of the world, are clearly seen, being understood by the things that are made. — Romans 1:20

The feast of Corpus Christi, celebrated annually on Thursday after Trinity Sunday, was devoted to the Eucharist, and the normal practice was to have solemn processions through the city with the Host, the consecrated wafer that was believed to have been transformed into the true body and blood of Jesus.[1] In this way the "cultus Dei"[2] thus celebrated allowed the people to venerate the Eucharistic bread in order that they might be stimulated to devotion and brought symbolically, even mystically into a relationship with the central moments of salvation history. Perhaps it is logical, therefore, that pageants and plays were introduced in order to access yet another way of visualizing and participating in those events of times past that were believed to matter most for the lives of the citizens as well as of other residents and visitors in cities such as York. Thus the "invisible things" of the divine order "from the creation of the world" might be displayed, and this might be done in order to bring these events into the orbit of the collective memory.[3]

There are, however, problems with the popular view that would take York as typical of an entire genre of early civic drama that was supposed to have been generated by the religious feast. The York Corpus Christi plays, contained in London, British Library, MS. Add. 35290 and comprising more than thirteen thousand lines of verse, actually represent a unique survival of medieval theater (see fig. 1).[4] They form the only complete play cycle verifiably associated with the feast of Corpus Christi that is extant and was performed at a specific location in England. Of the Coventry Corpus Christi cycle, texts have survived for only two pageants, the Shearmen and Taylors' and the Weavers' plays, while the Chester plays, though they developed from Corpus Christi drama, are in their present form a Whitsun cycle found

---

[1] For a thorough discussion of the religious feast, see Rubin, *Corpus Christi*.

[2] The term is from an entry dated 1408 in the Register of the Corpus Christi Guild; see *Records of Early English Drama: York*, 1:15 (hereafter *REED: York*).

[3] See Halbwachs, *On Collective Memory*.

[4] British Library, MS. Add. 35290 is of parchment, 8 x 11 inches, and contains 268 leaves. For a full description of the manuscript, see *York Play: A Facsimile*, introd. Beadle and Meredith, pp. xi–xix. The first eight folios are copied by Scribe A. Scribe B, the main scribe, entered the remainder with the exception of the sixteenth-century additions by John Clerke (Scribe C) and the very inferior late addition (not included in the present edition) to the Innholders' pageant, written by Scribe D. The manuscript's contents remained unknown until the middle of the nineteenth century, and were first edited by Lucy Toulmin Smith in 1885.

in the main only in late sixteenth-century and early seventeenth-century transcriptions.[5] The Towneley manuscript, now in the Huntington Library and formerly thought to contain a Corpus Christi cycle from Wakefield in the West Riding of Yorkshire, has been surmised by recent scholarship to be instead a collection of plays, including some of them adapted from York, from which individual pageants might be selected for production on one occasion or another. Their association with Wakefield as its Corpus Christi cycle rested on the authority, now discredited, of a local town historian.[6] The N-Town manuscript is a compilation of separate plays, in this case from East Anglia, connected with Corpus Christi only by the words "The plaie called Corpus Christi" written in a late hand across the top of the first page of the manuscript.[7] In fact, it is no longer possible even to speak of a Corpus Christ tradition of Creation to Doom pageants as the norm, for a "Corpus Christi play" noted in dramatic records of a medieval English town might have been simply a drama *of some kind* presented on this major feast day.[8] York's cycle, then, is of particular interest for its completeness as medieval religious street theater mounted nearly on an annual basis on wagons at stations throughout the city. It was not representative of anything like a national standard for Corpus Christi drama.

Completeness, however, must be seen as relative, since the York cycle as we have it mainly is representative of the pageants as they existed when entered into the Register, or official manuscript maintained by the city Corporation, in c.1463–77.[9] In a manuscript that shows signs of considerable use, it may be no surprise that in some cases leaves have been lost, leaving unfortunate lacunae such as the crucial central segment of the Bakers' *Last Supper*. Notations in the margins, many of them by the John Clerke, "under clerk" to the "common Clerk of this city" between the 1530s and the suppression of the pageants in 1569,[10] indicate that at least in the final years what was played had not always been entered in the Register. The city Corporation was always solicitous of the pageants and concerned about their quality. Auditions had been instituted to remove actors not "sufficiant . . . either in Connyng voice or personne."[11] By 1501 the town clerk or his deputy may have been on hand at the first station, at Holy Trinity Priory gates on Micklegate, to observe the plays.[12] The performances understandably were to be given scrutiny with both the speeches and the pageants' visual appearance in mind, and some discrepancies were duly noted in the Register.

---

[5] *Coventry Corpus Christi Plays*, ed. King and Davidson; and, for convenience, Mills, "Chester Cycle," pp. 125–29.

[6] See Cawley, Forrester, and Goodchild, "References to the Corpus Christi Play in the Wakefield Burgess Rolls"; Palmer, "'Towneley Plays' or 'Wakefield Cycle' Revisited"; and Palmer's conclusion in "Corpus Christi 'Cycles' in Yorkshire," p. 228.

[7] London, British Library, MS. Cotton Vespasian D.VIII, fol. 1; *N-Town Play*, ed. Spector, pp. xiii–xvi, and especially the discussion of N-Town in Fletcher, "N-Town Plays." See also the useful summary in *N-Town Plays*, ed. Sugano, esp. pp. 5–17.

[8] See A. Johnston, "What If No Texts Survived," esp. pp. 11–12; C. Davidson, *Festivals and Plays*, pp. 49–79.

[9] *York Plays*, ed. Beadle, pp. 10–11.

[10] York House Book 13, fol. 14v, as quoted by Meredith, "John Clerke's Hand," pp. 249–51.

[11] *REED: York*, 1:109.

[12] See *REED: York*, 1:187; in 1527 the Clerk's deputy is named for the task (*REED: York*, 1:263).

Further, some pageants were never registered: *The Marriage in Cana* (22A), *The Feast in Simon's House* (23A), and *The Funeral of the Virgin*, or *Fergus* (44A). In 1559 an order was issued to have the text of the Innholders' *Coronation of the Virgin* pageant copied from their "Regynall" or original guild copy into the official Register, either to replace or to supplement the version of the play already present in the manuscript. However, in this instance only a fragment, a text of vastly inferior quality, was entered,[13] while the copying of the *Purification of the Virgin* was not even begun at this time. A subsequent order to John Clerke to copy the *Purification*, the Vintners' *Marriage in Cana*, the Ironmongers' "Marie Magdalene wasshyng the Lordes feete etc." (*The Feast in Simon's House*), and the conclusion of the Tilers' *Nativity* into the "old Registre"[14] was only partially fulfilled, with the *Purification* then being entered by him out of order in the manuscript. Only one pageant, the Scriveners' *Doubting Thomas*, appears both in the Register and also in a guild copy, the damaged Sykes manuscript.[15] No copies of the individual parchment rolls, or parcels, each containing the speeches of an individual character, survive.[16]

The Register likewise will not provide readings of the playtexts as they must once have existed in earliest years before revisions were made to them, in some cases involving radical rewriting. For the state of the playtexts in those years it is necessary to refer, though with great caution, to the cast lists and brief descriptions in the *Ordo paginarum*. This document was designed to designate the content and order of the pageants for the use of the Corporation, which, rather than any ecclesiastical body, had responsibility for the cycle. The *Ordo*, dated 1415, is contained in the *York Memorandum Book A/Y*.[17] It is, unfortunately, extremely problematic on account of damage to the manuscript and also numerous erasures and changes that were made to correct and keep the list up to date.[18] Formerly believed to have been initially written by Roger Burton, the town clerk, Meg Twycross has recently demonstrated that it is in the hand of a different scribe, whose identity is uncertain.[19] When the *Ordo*'s descriptions are not consistent with the playtexts, something nevertheless may be revealed concerning the changes that took place between 1415 and the date of the Register a half century or so later, though again caution must be urged. A second list in the *Memorandum Book A/Y*, apparently by Burton himself and usually dated in c.1422, gives, like the first list, names of responsible guilds, but only provides titles for the plays.[20] This list too was designed to be a record, but much less detailed, of the order of the pageants as they set out

---

[13] For the text of this fragment, see *York Plays*, ed. Beadle, pp. 404–05.

[14] *REED: York*, 1:351.

[15] Cawley, "Sykes MS."

[16] See *MED*, s.v. "parcel" (1c). An example of a parcel, though not from York, is *Dux Moraud*; see Davis, ed., *Non-Cycle Plays*, pp. c–ci, 106–13, pl. IV.

[17] *REED: York*, 1:16–24; see also the facsimile of this heavily damaged record in the *York Memorandum Book A/Y* included by Beadle and Meredith in *York Play: A Facsimile* (fols. 252v–255r).

[18] Twycross, "*Ordo paginarum* Revisited."

[19] Twycross, "*Ordo paginarum* Revisited," p. 121.

[20] *REED: York*, 1:25–26. The titles in this second list have been adapted insofar as possible for the names of the pageants in the present edition. In the Register they are mainly identified by the names of guilds principally responsible for them.

in order to play through the city. It also reveals some amalgamation of pageants as the list was kept up to date.[21]

FROM WHENCE DID THEY COME?

Some of the earliest documentation concerning the York plays are records of pageant houses in which wagon stages were stored, and for the specific stations throughout the city where the pageants were played. The *York Memorandum Book A/Y* notes a structure used to house three Corpus Christi pageant wagons in 1377,[22] and the principal location of such buildings on Toft Green (sometimes called Pageant Green), near the Dominican Friary, was cited in 1387.[23] Already in 1394 there was an order promulgated that "all the pageants of Corpus Christi shall play in the places appointed from ancient times [*in locis antiquitus assignatis*] and not elsewhere."[24] "Ancient times," however, would have been an indefinite period, but perhaps logically should refer to at least one generation in the past, if not longer. No certainty is possible here, except we know that displays on wagons were not invented at York even if performing plays on them possibly was a local or regional innovation.

Trade with the Low Countries would have brought the merchants of York, its most influential citizens, in contact with the tableaux vivants that were paraded on wagons through the streets in cities such as Bruges, Antwerp, Leuven, and Brussels.[25] These were moving wagons, not plays, and where the notion of using wagons originated for setting up and staging drama at fixed locations we cannot tell. It would seem to be too far-fetched to believe that the exception of Lille, which had a procession honoring the Virgin Mary that dated from 1270 and that did in fact develop into plays on various biblical and other subjects on wagons, provided the model.[26] One thing is very clear from the 1394 record, and this is that the York plays in earlier times were not mere tableaux vivants but presentations on wagon stages that stopped at a set number of fixed locations for viewing as designated by the city Corporation. In 1417 these stations were ordered to be marked with banners having the arms of the city.[27] The awareness of movement — the progress of human life as pilgrimage, and history as linear — was a ground against which the pageants were played. Nevertheless, while they could have appeared like iconic "floats" when moving between the places appointed for playing, there is nothing in the records to support such a supposition. When a play had been staged at a specific location, its carriage could simply have been pulled, always by human labor and not impossibly with the accompaniment of minstrels playing, to the next playing station — a task that would have been made easier if the wagons were lightened in weight by not having a cast of actors aboard.

---

[21] See Twycross, "*Ordo paginarum* Revisited," pp. 119–20.

[22] *REED: York*, 1:3, where the date is given as 1376.

[23] *REED: York*, 1:5.

[24] *REED: York*, 1:8; translation from 2:694.

[25] See A. Johnston, "Traders and Playmakers"; Twycross, "Flemish *Ommegang* and Its Pageant Cars"; C. Davidson, *Technology, Guilds*, pp. 17–25.

[26] Knight, "Processional Theatre and Social Unity," and "Manuscript Painting and Play Production."

[27] *REED: York*, 1:8, 29.

French drama cycles are sometimes put forward as models for the York plays. In their sequential presentation of biblical history, these massive productions, acted on fixed stages and often taking several days to perform, had their roots in fourteenth-century community theater.[28] Potential awareness of Continental play cycles by York dramatists and producers still does not reveal precisely how these plays emerged in the form which they adopted.

But one aspect of the development of the York Corpus Christi plays needs especially to be emphasized. Any notion of a clear line of evolutionary development from the Latin liturgical drama must be set aside.[29] There is no evidence that these vernacular plays arose as a result of a process of secularization or dissatisfaction with the clerical control over liturgical plays mounted in the cathedral and churches, like the *Pastores* and the *Magi* in the Christmas and Epiphany seasons at York Minster in the thirteenth century.[30] From the first the Corpus Christi plays arose as an expensive display for the members of the various crafts or guilds of the city who were expected to perform them, even under threat of a hefty fine if they did not — a fact that, however, does not suggest a lack of enthusiasm with the exception, it would appear, of times when the financial burden was felt to be excessive.[31] In no way could the plays have continued to be played for two centuries in a city under the stress of difficult times if the essential good will toward them had not been present.

Speculation concerning the plays' origin, though not explaining the source of using the wagons as stages at fixed locations, at the present seems to favor what has been dubbed the "big bang" theory. This theory, advanced by R. B. Dobson, is based on the supposition that the plays were part of a plan by the mayor and Council to establish an elaborate cycle of plays in order to provide a "mechanism for identifying . . . crafts and their members" — that is, as a way of rationalizing local industry. In so doing, the large amounts assessed the individual craft and mercantile guilds, intended to be based on their ability to pay, could be directed to the activity of play production, which was regarded as a charitable act for the good of the community.[32] It is, nevertheless, difficult to see the hand of the Corporation solely responsible for bringing the pageants into being *ex nihilo*. Their ultimate origin was undoubtedly more complex and surely must have involved wide community support.

There is good reason to suppose that the guilds, or the craftsmen who established such fraternities, were involved at the very beginning. Jeremy Goldberg even suggests not implausibly that the pageants "postdated the origin of the craft gilds," and that there was a desire by them to "give religious meaning to their labours and to participate in this collective manifestation of civic pride, this act of devotion, and this work of mercy that in many cases gave rise

---

[28] Muir, *Biblical Drama*, p. 33.

[29] The notion of evolutionary development from *Minster to Market Place*, to borrow from the title of the book by Canon Purvis, has been considered untenable since the appearance of the seminal chapter on the subject by Hardison, *Christian Rite and Christian Drama*, pp. 1–34.

[30] *REED: York*, 1:1. There was, however, some connection, as yet not fully deciphered, between the York Corpus Christi plays and the Shrewsbury fragments (Davis, ed., *Non-Cycle Plays*, pp. xvii–xix and 3–7).

[31] For recognition of the financial burden already in 1399, see *REED: York*, 1:11, and for the belief that the commons were thus antagonistic to what the Corporation made them do, see Swanson, "Illusion of Economic Structure," p. 44. A refutation of this view is contained in C. Davidson, "York Guilds and the Corpus Christi Plays."

[32] Dobson, "Craft Guilds and the City."

to the gilds."[33] In any case, to be so magnificently successful, the project could hardly have been sustained by the element of coercion alone. This does not mean that some guilds would not have expressed dissatisfaction at times, especially when we keep in mind the levying of fines for hindering the plays and the heavy assessments for their support when in later years the city's economy was declining. But the disorder caused by the Girdlers in tarrying and thus "stoppyng of the rest of the pageantz folowyng and to the disorderyng of the same" for "an wholle hower," for which they were fined 20s in 1554, seems to have been unusual.[34] We should not believe that a "sumptuous" play cycle[35] of the magnitude of the York plays could have been carried on for centuries without the wholehearted enthusiasm of those directly involved. And of magnitude and magnificence the cycle truly seems to have been, attracting watchers and listeners from all around the region. In 1487, when King Henry VII visited York, he saw the plays, but not on Corpus Christi since they were deliberately deferred *at his request* until Lammas day to coincide with his coming to the city.[36]

WAGON STAGES

With one exception, the dramatic records of York are meager with regard to information about the construction and design of the wagon stages but nevertheless point to elaborate structures, many of them likely to have been as large as could be accommodated by the narrow streets of the medieval city.[37] Some details can, however, be surmised from the wagons used in those other cities that used this type of staging, but here too there is a paucity of reliable information. Chester's are described in Rogers' *Breviary*, albeit in a way that has been a source of confusion.[38] Whether of four or (less likely) six wheels, the Chester wagons were large and impressive structures, and, when necessary, they must have accommodated complex and sophisticated equipment in order to achieve spectacular effects in the city's Whitsun plays. At Norwich, the Grocers' wagon, left derelict out-of-doors, had been described in 1564–65 as being "a Howsse of Waynskott paynted and buylded on a Carte with fowre whelys" with "a square toppe" placed overhead on it and having three painted cloths hanging about it. This meager information is accompanied elsewhere in the records by an inventory of the props and

[33] Goldberg, "Craft Guilds, the Corpus Christi Play and Civic Government," p. 148.

[34] *REED: York*, 1:312.

[35] See *REED: York*, 1:42. The description of the plays as "sumptuous" appears in the well-known 1426 entry in the York *Memorandum Book A/Y* in which the Corporation takes account of the recommendations of the friar William Melton, who objected to the disorder that he saw at York on the day of the play. This, he argued, detracted from the spirit of devotion that should have obtained. A large part of the difficulty was that the civic Corpus Christi procession was held on the same day, and virtually along the same route as the plays; Melton firmly recommended that the procession and the plays be separated, with the plays moved to the vigil of the feast. This did not happen, and when there was a change, it was the procession that was transferred. By the time the Register was compiled, the procession had been relegated to the following day, a Friday.

[36] *REED: York*, 1:153–54.

[37] See McKinnell, "Medieval Pageant Wagons at York," pp. 79–99; and also the discussion of pageant wagons in C. Davidson, *Technology, Guilds*, pp. 17–31.

[38] *REED: Chester*, pp. 238–39, 325, 355, and 436.

other accouterments, most famously the "Rybbe Colleryd Redd" for the creation of Eve.[39] But as for the actual wagons, either at York or elsewhere, they have not left a trace behind, not even a drawing or sketch. There is nothing therefore remaining to match the elaborate illustrations of the Flemish tableaux vivants which likely would have set a standard of sumptuousness to which the York producers may have aspired. Attempts such as David Jee's illustration, purporting to show a Chester wagon and elaborated from Rogers' description, in Thomas Sharp's *Dissertation* (1825) reveal more about nineteenth-century preconceptions than about late medieval stages.[40]

The exception to this paucity of information for York appears in a single document, a 1433 inventory of the Mercers' *Doomsday* pageant that remained unknown until 1972.[41] Truly remarkable, this list takes note of such equipment as a device for lowering and raising Jesus at his Second Coming and even puppet angels that run about the heavens.[42] As a prop list this is an essential document, and can profitably be compared with the depiction of similar aspects of Doomsday in the visual arts. Here reference is most fruitfully made to local examples such as the Doomsday illumination in the *Bolton Hours* (1410–20), which has been associated with leading merchant families in the city.[43]

The dramatic records nevertheless, since they are mainly accounts of expenditures, receipts, and enforcement of local ordinances, show very vividly that the making and maintenance of the pageant wagons, their accouterments, and all the other equipment necessary for the plays required wide community effort. The assistance of not only the carpenters, painters, and cloth workers but also other guilds is duly noted in the extant documents, albeit as financial records these are often fragmentary and sporadic. At least we know that the plays were a source of economic gain for some of the citizens, just as musicians brought in to assist were the beneficiaries of payment for their services.[44]

Detailed information at York is, however, available about the stations along the streets at which the pageants were played, for here the records kept by the Corporation are very specific. The entire route can still be traced today since much of the old city remains, albeit with numerous changes (e.g., the shortening of Stonegate to create open space for St. Helen's Square in the eighteenth century).[45] As noted above, each station was to be marked with a banner, and fines were instituted for unauthorized stops for playing. An early sixteenth-century alteration to the official proclamation of the plays entered into the city records ordered that "euery player that shall play be redy in his pagiaunt at convenyant tyme, that is to say at the mydhowre betwix iiij[th] and v[th] of the cloke in the mornyng and then all other pageantes fast followyng ilkon after other as ther course is without Tarieng" on pain of a fine

---

[39] *REED: Norwich 1540–1642*, pp. 52–53.

[40] Sharp, *Dissertation on the Pageants or Dramatic Mysteries*, frontispiece.

[41] See A. Johnston and Dorrell, "York Mercers and Their Pageant of Doomsday."

[42] *REED: York*, 1:55–56.

[43] York Minster Library, MS. Add. 2, fol. 208; reproduced in C. Davidson, *Technology, Guilds*, fig. 93. Compare King, "Corpus Christi Plays and the 'Bolton Hours', 1." Also see the website of the Lancaster University Doomsday project: <http://www.lanc.ac.uk/users/yorkdoom/d06.htm>.

[44] See C. Davidson, *Technology, Guilds*, passim.

[45] See Raine, *Mediaeval York*, p. 123.

of 6s 8d.[46] While this probably does not pertain to the early years of the York plays when a delay would plausibly have been needed to allow for the civic Corpus Christi procession to set out from the same location at Holy Trinity Priory, the 4:30 a.m. starting time is credible after the separation of the procession from the play in the course of the fifteenth century.

We can thus assume that either at a convenient time in earlier years, or in later times around dawn on Corpus Christi, the first of the pageants — the Barkers' (i.e., Tanners') *Creation of the Angels with the Fall of Lucifer* — was being moved away from Toft Green and around to the first station before the gates of Holy Trinity Priory inside Micklegate Bar, the main entrance to the city on the route from London (see figure 2). From there the wagon stages proceeded down Micklegate and over the Ouse River, performing at the specified stations before audiences along the way. On the other side of the river, the stations would be spaced at intervals at the corner of Spurriergate and along Coney Street, Stonegate, Petergate, and the Pavement, the final station and, interestingly, the least popular.[47] In 1417, when the practice of leasing the stations was regularized according to a bid system, twelve stations were specified, the same number that had been awarded in 1398.[48] It appears that the lessees, initially some of the city's most affluent citizens, had financial gain in mind since in turn they were able to set up scaffolds and rent seats as well as to offer concessions to the spectators. This of course does not mean that they were entirely mercenary, if they believed, as surely they did, in the value of the plays as charitable acts to be presented for the general good of the community.

A CHARITABLE DUTY

Much has been made of the theology inherent in the plays, and to be sure this is a part of their civic and religious context that needs to be explained for many modern readers and, when opportunity for seeing actual productions is presented, for viewers. A considerable portion of the Explanatory Notes in the present edition must thus be given over to notice of such matters, which for some scholars are nowadays sometimes treated under the rubric of "ideology," or what was generally assumed more or less by everyone living at that time and in that place.[49] Those who persist in seeing the plays as essentially didactic, as teaching devices focused on doctrine, will be seen to have a generally reductionist view of them. Among other things, they were intended as acts of charity, mnemonic instruments, so to speak, to inspire devotion and bring to mind the totality of the works of God, beginning with the Creation. Like the liturgy, which was to be sure imperfectly accessible to most people since it was in Latin rather than in the vernacular, the Corpus Christi plays were designed to *bring to memory* the events of salvation history. Pamela King's *The York Mystery Cycle and the Worship of the City* is a convincing overview of the deep interconnectedness of the civic drama, under the control of the secular administration of the city, and the content of the liturgy celebrated in parish churches, in York Minster, and in the monasteries and friaries. More directly than through

---

[46] See Twycross, "Forget the 4:30 a.m. Start"; *REED: York*, 1:25.

[47] See Twycross, "'Places to hear the play': Pageant Stations at York, 1398–1572."

[48] *REED: York*, 1:11, 29–30. Placeholders are discussed by Crouch, "Paying to See the Play," and E. White, "Places for Hearing the Corpus Christi Play," as well as, by the same author, "Places to Hear the Play in York."

[49] The term *ideology*, Marxist in origin and as generally used, is a rather rubbery concept.

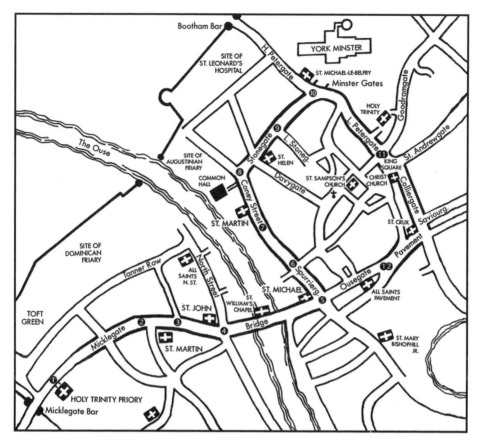

Figure 2. Map of fifteenth-century York, with stations on the pageant route in their most common order numbered.

the Latin liturgy, then, personal and communal engagement with cultural history and tradition through memory—indeed, *charismatic memory*[50]—might be advanced as the most important aspect of the production of the plays. And this was indeed also a communal project designed to bring together the crafts and trades in Christian harmony with each other, however imperfectly this may have been the case.

As religious drama deeply embedded in late medieval "traditional religion"[51] and congruent with the intense spirituality that is found in such writings as Nicholas Love's adaptation of the popular Latin *Meditations on the Life of Christ* (*Meditaciones Vitae Christi*),[52] the plays

---

[50] See Florovsky, "Work of the Holy Spirit," to which Rowan Williams calls attention (*Why Study the Past*, p. 92).

[51] See Duffy, *Stripping of the Altars*.

[52] Love's *Mirror of the Blessed Life of Jesus Christ* as a vernacular work that was given official approval, in part to counter Lollard translations of the Bible, provides perhaps the most useful single tool for interpreting the action of the York Corpus Christi plays in their treatment of the gospel

were designed to promote emotional involvement with the events being staged. Most intensely, the suffering and Crucifixion of Jesus were even to be *felt as necessary* for salvation. Love, who possibly had been prior of the Augustinian friary at York and at the time of his writing was prior of the Carthusian monastery at Mount Grace, is insistent that such identification be felt "inwardly" in one's thoughts through "trewe ymaginacion and inwarde compassion of the peynes and the passion" of the one who died for all humankind.[53] But drama is never quite so simple, even if it stirs strong emotions, such as the York plays must have achieved — very possibly, as the author of the Wycliffite *Treatise of Miraclis Pleyinge* claims to have occurred in response to religious plays, "weping bitere teris."[54] There is also the matter of engaging, whether one will or no, with the characters, even ones representing evil.[55] Leaving aside the matter of *Schadenfreude*, such symbolic participation in plays — for in a deep sense the pageants are symbolic structures representing the essentials of human history — would have had the effect of bringing to life the events of salvation history for late medieval audiences. As such, there is no doubt also that they were consistent with traditional iconography, especially since this would have been not only expected but also demanded in a time when innovation outside the boundaries of the acceptable visual limits was taboo. One could only imagine what the response would have been to the representation of God in an animal mask![56] Jesus' wounds were to be seen bleeding, even after death, and devils were expected to be exceptionally ugly, often hairy and fitted with double (or triple) masks with one of them on the face and another in the groin area.[57] Particular attention to the iconography of the plays, especially with reference to examples in the visual arts at York, will appear in the Explanatory Notes.[58]

AUTHORSHIP AND SOURCES

The authors of the plays, attending to favored iconographic tableaux but not generally as static or fixed scenes that would freeze the action, were of differing talents, and their poetic techniques varied. Richard Beadle argues for the presence of a "basic range of vocabulary,

---

narratives. Its date of composition seems to be c. 1410, for which see the comment of its editor, Michael Sargent (pp. xlv–xlvi); this would imply its availability to those authors and revisers of the York plays who were active after this date.

[53] Love, *Mirror*, p. 161.

[54] *Tretise of Miraclis Pleyinge*, p. 98.

[55] See C. Davidson, *Deliver Us from Evil*.

[56] It seems rather absurd to try to force the York Corpus Christi plays into a pattern of carnival drama, though Martin Stevens has argued that they represent "just such a form" (*Four Middle English Mystery Cycles*, pp. 82–83). However, in another sense they were to be sure festive, and hardly dull, solemn fare. See C. Davidson, *History, Religion, and Violence*, pp. 207–25.

[57] See, for example, Gray, "Five Wounds of Our Lord," and, for an illustration of a hairy devil with masks on head, the genitals, and a knee in the St. Cuthbert window at York Minster, C. Davidson, *Technology, Guilds*, fig. 71.

[58] In the Explanatory Notes, I have made frequent reference to *York Art*, the listing which I prepared in collaboration with David O'Connor many years ago as a rather tentative descriptive index of those scenes depicted locally in the visual arts relevant to the drama. An updated version of this list is available on the web at <http://www.wmich.edu/medieval/resources/edam/york.html>.

often expressed in repeated formulae, which [the dialogue] is guaranteed to share with both its immediate and distant neighbours in the Cycle as a whole."[59] This generalization holds true only in part, since some of the plays introduce vocabulary, including rhyme words, that are not only distinctly Northern but, to many readers, obscure and out of the ordinary. Stylistically, the most unusual plays or segments of plays are those that have been attributed to a "York Realist,"[60] an attribution that is discussed in Paul A. Johnston's Appendix in the present volume. These are plays, and sections of plays, in the long alliterative line, probably otherwise best known through William Langland's *Piers Plowman*.

The poetic forms here differ from those found in Anglo-Saxon practices from which the alliterative technique is ultimately derived. This is particularly true in the choice to use rhyme and in the division into stanzas. While the stanza forms differ, their use of alliteration is "metrically functional" and at the same time provides "a very effective vehicle for dramatic dialogue," as T. Turville-Petre has noted.[61] The manuscript sometimes presents the parts of the long line as two lines, a practice that was followed by Lucy Toulmin Smith in her pioneering edition of 1885 and is generally retained in the present edition. In the manuscript the pageants in the long alliterative line are otherwise some of the most problematic. The handwriting itself suggests that the scribe had considerable difficulty coping with the copies with which he was working, and these portions of the Register are the least well presented on the page in the manuscript.

These and the other pageants in the cycle can firmly be said not to have been written by the guild members themselves. Alexandra F. Johnston has engagingly suggested the involvement in writing these texts of the canons from the Augustinian house next to the Common Hall, for the members of the Corporation were on close and friendly terms with the friary.[62] The York Augustinian friary possessed one of the greatest libraries in the North of England,[63] and was noted for its learning. The plays show signs of knowledge of a wide range of religious literature. The sources are not always evident, but echoes, for example, of the Middle English *Metrical Paraphrase of the Old Testament*, the *Cursor Mundi*, the *Northern Passion*, the *Stanzaic Life of Christ*, and the *Gospel of Nicodemus* are present.[64] The spirit of St. Bernard of Clairvaux is evident. The Franciscan *Meditations on the Life of Christ* was also known to some if not all of the York playwrights, perhaps through the adaptation of Nicholas Love and whose work in any case, as noted above, often provides the most useful explication of passages in the pageants. The *Revelations* of St. Birgitta of Sweden can also be easily traced, most visibly in the *Nativity* where revisions are evident when the play is compared with the earlier description in the *Ordo paginarum*.[65] Other influences, such as Ludolphus of Saxony's *Vita Christi*, are cited by J. W. Robinson in his seminal work, left unfinished at his death and subsequently published as *Studies in Fifteenth-Century Stagecraft*.

---

[59] Beadle, "Verbal Texture and Wordplay," p. 173.

[60] See Reese, "Alliterative Verse in the York Cycle"; Robinson, "Art of the York Realist"; and Craig, *English Religious Drama*, pp. 224–33.

[61] Turville-Petre, *Alliterative Revival*, p. 123.

[62] A. Johnston, "*York Cycle* and the Libraries of York."

[63] For the very extensive catalogue, see Humphreys, *Friars' Libraries*, pp. 11–154.

[64] See *York Plays*, ed. Beadle, pp. 40–41.

[65] C. Davidson, *From Creation to Doom*, pp. 16–18.

The documents excerpted in *Records of Early English Drama: York* fail to give much direct indication of actual re-writing or revision, particularly in the decades about which we would like to know the most. However, in an entry in the *York Memorandum Book A/Y* in c.1422, the Crucifixion was reported to be shortened for the sake of efficiency in playing, herein joining the "stretching out and nailing of Christ on the cross" and "the raising up of the Crucified upon the Mount."[66] Another entry, dated 1432, indicated that further consolidation and regularization elsewhere in the cycle with regard to guild support had taken place. A single pageant was created from the Saucemakers' *Suspencio Judas*, the Tilemakers' *Condemnation of Christ by Pilate*, the Turners, Hayresters, and Bollers' *Flagellation*, and the Millers' *Parting of Jesus' Garments*.[67] These records do not prove that other revisions and rewriting took place between 1422 and 1432, but they can provide a plausible guide for dating alterations that would introduce the long alliterative line into the plays. The second quarter of the fifteenth century still represented a time of prosperity for the city of York, which would later decline both economically and demographically with the flight to the West Riding of the cloth industry and the dramatic reduction of its population, perhaps by the middle of the sixteenth century to a level little more than half of its earlier high point.[68]

MYSTERIES SUPPRESSED

Ironically, when prosperity and population growth began to return in the third quarter of the sixteenth century, the plays, in spite of the desire of the citizens to retain them, would be suppressed. In mid-century disease and other pressures had deterred the city from performing them in some years. In 1551 only ten pageants were ordered to be played at ten stations, and in 1552 the "billettes," written orders issued to the guilds for playing, were called in.[69] Under King Edward VI, who had instituted a process of radical Protestantizing and iconoclasm, the Marian plays of the Death, Assumption, and Coronation of the Virgin were set aside, only to be reinstated under Queen Mary and then suppressed again in 1561.[70]

Pressure on the pageants mounted as the crisis year of 1570 approached, when Catholic rebellion was in the air and Queen Elizabeth was to be excommunicated. The change in archdiocesan politics at York did not bode well for the plays, and in 1569 they were played, on Tuesday during Whitsun week rather than on Corpus Christi, for the last time.[71] In 1579 the Register would be taken to the archbishop and dean "to correcte, if that my Lord Archebisshop doo well like theron," and in 1580 the House Books report that "the Commons did earnestly request of my Lord Mayour and others this worshipfull Assemblee that Corpus

---

[66] *REED: York*, 2:722; for Latin text, see 1:37.

[67] *REED: York*, 1:48; for translation, see 2:733. Compare the second list in the *Ordo paginarum* with the first (corrected) list (1:26, 22).

[68] For demographic decline, see Palliser, *Tudor York*, p. 112, and C. Davidson, "York Guilds and the Corpus Christi Plays," pp. 11–16.

[69] *REED: York*, 1:298, 303, and see 1:9 for noting of billets as early as 1396, when two parchment membranes were purchased for use at Corpus Christi.

[70] *REED: York*, 1:291–92 and 331–32.

[71] *REED: York*, 1:355–56.

christi play might be played this yere,"[72] but to no avail.[73] The plays would not be staged at York again for nearly four centuries.

THE REVIVAL OF THE YORK PLAYS

The revival of the York plays was to be assured only in 1950, when E. Martin Browne, who was known for his successful productions of *Murder in the Cathedral* and other religious plays, was chosen as director.[74] The cycle was mounted the next year in the ruins of St. Mary's Abbey, a spectacular setting but demanding a fixed stage, in this case utilizing mansions more or less modeled on the famous illustration of the 1547 Valenciennes Passion play.[75] Its length too was regarded as a serious problem. Hence the text was condensed to allow only a three-hour production, and it would be done as a single unit, not broken into the segments originally staged as pageants by individual guilds. There also would be considerable modernization of the language, undertaken by Canon J. S. Purvis, who had been enthusiastic about such a project and was in fact the person who initially suggested producing the plays. Even the dialect was standardized to conform with BBC English.[76] For all its value in bringing attention to the York plays as theater, the production was a "heritage" event rather than either an authentic historical experiment or living theater.[77]

Nevertheless, it will surprise many to learn that resistance to the revival emerged from Evangelicals, both within the Church of England and in sectarian protestantism. John R. Elliott, Jr., has noted that even Canon Purvis was nervous about the production, and he quotes the minutes of the York Festival Committee which report his remarks: "There is an enormous and impassable gulf between us and the people who wrote, performed, and watched these plays. . . . The scourging and crucifixion scenes are too realistic for us today. Nobody would dare to put on some of these plays today. They are too shocking."[78] After their successful run of two weeks, the archbishop of York was quoted in the *Yorkshire Post* as having his "misgivings . . . completely removed," but nevertheless argued that there should not be another revival for "a considerable interval — at least five years."[79]

---

[72] *REED: York*, 1:390 and 392–93.

[73] The classic account is H. Gardiner, *Mysteries' End*, though subsequent scholarship has to some extent modified this description of the suppression of the vernacular religious drama.

[74] For the director's account, see E. Browne and Browne, *Two in One*, pp. 183–95. Additional information concerning the revival of the York Corpus Christi plays is found in Margaret Rogerson, *Playing a Part in History: The York Mysteries, 1951–2006* (Toronto: University of Toronto Press, 2009), which was published after the present book was in page proofs.

[75] E. Browne and Browne, *Two in One*, p. 184, and see the illustration in Nagler, *Medieval Religious Stage*, p. 85.

[76] Browne was originally anxious to use the Yorkshire dialect, but quickly cooled to the idea when he found himself unable to understand a countrywoman in the North Riding (E. Browne and Browne, *Two in One*, p. 185). Purvis' modernization is in fact neither Middle English nor Modern English.

[77] Rogerson, "Living History," pp. 12–19.

[78] Elliott, *Playing God*, pp. 76–77.

[79] Quoted in Eliott, *Playing God*, p. 82.

Doctrinal and legal issues also had to be faced in 1951. The Last Supper, being the institution of the Sacrament of the Eucharist, was a sensitive matter, but was retained as an offstage event, and the plays of the Death, Assumption, and Coronation of the Virgin along with other Marian content were omitted as too controversially "Mariolatrous."[80] Legal challenges were only sidestepped because the York cycle antedated the 1737 act for the licensing of plays, which normally allowed the Lord Chamberlain to censor those that were either licentious or blasphemous, with the appearance of representations of God and Jesus on stage falling into the latter category.[81]

Subsequently, the York cycle, in similarly abbreviated versions, continued to be played at intervals in the ruins of the abbey. By the 1970s, emphasis had shifted to spectacle and humor and shied away from religious content as much as possible.[82] In 1976 pageant wagons were introduced onto the stage, but were largely stationary and used for indoor scenes only except for the parody of ceremony at Herod's entrance. The three kings arrived riding horses, and there were sheep, heifers, and donkeys along with "174 extras who somehow managed to make themselves present."[83] Peter Happé's review of the 1980 production reported the choice of "Sumer is icumen in" as a dance at the beginning, and thereafter a selection of mainly familiar music that culminated at Doomsday in the *Old Hundredth* (*English Hymnal*, no. 365), while the text was still so condensed that "there was often little sense of development in individual scenes."[84] In 1992 the plays were moved indoors, and 2000 saw a Millennium production in the Minster. Eventually the success with audiences of Tony Harrison's text (largely derived from York) and Bill Bryden's directing of *The Mysteries* at the National Theatre would influence the staging of the cycle.[85]

However, sporadic attempts to introduce processional wagon staging at York led in 1988 to a four-pageant production in the streets directed by Meg Twycross, whose efforts were a genuine effort to replicate the conditions of late medieval staging.[86] This, like a subsequent production in 1992, was a university production with actors not connected with the city. The plays were returned to community theater in 1994 — a less fragmented version of nine plays, presented by York guilds (see fig. 3).[87] Three of the guilds were still in existence from medieval times, and thus the Butchers could once again play the *Mortificacio Christi*. The production was under the overall direction of Jane Oakshott, who repeated the effort in 1998.[88] By 2002 ten plays, now given over to local control, were able to be mounted

---

[80] Elliott, *Playing God*, pp. 76–77.

[81] See the survey in Elliott, *Playing God*, pp. 14–24.

[82] Elliott, *Playing God*, pp. 97–98

[83] Review by Elliott, in "Census of Medieval Drama Productions," *Research Opportunities in Renaissance Drama* 20 (1977): 97–98.

[84] Review by Happé, in "Census of Medieval Drama Productions," *Research Opportunities in Renaissance Drama* 23 (1980): 91–82.

[85] See Harrison, *Mysteries* and *The Making of The Mysteries* (production booklet, 1985). As for the stage production, Grantley considered it more of "a parody of medieval drama" ("National Theatre's Production of *The Mysteries*," p. 73).

[86] A. Johnston, "Four *York* Pageants Performed in the Streets of York."

[87] Rastall, "Mystery Plays 25 Years On."

[88] Oakshott, "York Guilds' Mystery Plays 1998."

at five stations, running from noon to seven o'clock in the evening and ending, of course, with the Last Judgment, which Margaret Rogerson judged to be appropriately capturing "the spirit of the Middle Ages while linking the message of the play to the present."[89] In 2006 the number of plays had advanced to eleven, but at four stations. In 2008 Oakshott was awarded an MBE for her efforts in community theater — a very encouraging sign of the recognition of this drama for our time.

The productions in York streets have not yet been able to offer a complete cycle, but this had in fact been accomplished elsewhere in academic settings. In 1975, various departments of the University of Leeds, with the leadership of Oakshott who was then a recent graduate, produced thirty-six pageants — not yet a complete cycle, but certainly an historic event.[90] Thereafter, two productions of all forty-seven extant plays were presented on wagons at the University of Toronto in 1977 and 1998 under the

Figure 3. The Harrowing of Hell, directed by Mike Tyler and produced by St. Luke's Church, in 1998 when local guild sponsorship of the York plays in the streets of the city resumed. Courtesy of the York Mystery Plays Archive, The National Centre for Early Music, Walmgate, York YO1 9TL, U.K.

auspices of Poculi Ludique Societas. The 1977 performance, for which David Parry was artistic director, encountered unexpected adversity in the weather, and the performances had to be moved indoors. Nevertheless, David Bevington could praise the effort as one that uniquely gave an incomparable "sense of the vitality and richness of Corpus Christi drama."[91]

The 1998 performance fared much better, and has the advantage of being well documented in both *Research Opportunities in Renaissance Drama* and *Early Theatre*. In this instance, the performances occurred at four stations at Victoria College, and, starting at 6:00 a.m., continued until midnight. The impossibility of staging forty-seven or more pageants at twelve stations widely separated in distance was made evident, resulting in discussion among the participants and spectators concerning the likelihood that some were simply omitted each year

---

[89] Review by Rogerson, in "Census of Medieval Drama Productions," *Research Opportunities in Renaissance Drama* 42 (2003): 165–66.

[90] Rastall, "Mystery Plays 25 Years On."

[91] Review by Bevington, in "Census of Medieval Drama Productions," *Research Opportunities in Renaissance Drama* 20 (1977): 110.

on a regular basis when the Corpus Christi cycle was staged at medieval York.[92] Among other things learned, one of the most important concerned the interaction between actors and audience. In Megan Lloyd's words, "Whatever the intent of individual plays, the effect of the York Cycle . . . was an obscuring of audience and actor, fiction and reality, that helped me feel as though I were participating in the Passion and Christian journey itself. I was not alone in my response."[93] There was also some controversy, as with regard to Handmade Performance's *Doomsday* pageant, a "radical reinterpretation" which struck many as an extreme violation of the ethos of the original play, and certainly it would have been regarded as blasphemous in its own time. The idea that the devil was a classical music lover and that all-powerful God "can play anything he wants," no matter how incompetent musically, was symptomatic of the inversion of values in this "post-modern" production.[94] The 1998 Toronto plays, on account of the very extensive commentary available in print,[95] will continue to be most valuable for future directors, while much can also be learned from the community theater productions at York where they have been reclaimed by the guilds.

EDITORIAL PRINCIPLES

The present edition adheres as closely as feasible to the text of the York Corpus Christi plays as they appear in the Register, London, British Library MS. Add. 35290. However, as is the convention with TEAMS publications, the orthography is lightly modernized with respect to archaic letters. *Thee* is consistently given its modern spelling though normally it appears as *the* in the manuscript. Roman numerals are presented in their arabic equivalents. Emendations introduced by earlier scholars have only been adopted carefully when deemed necessary. In a few instances, however, corrections have been entered into the text from those plays derived from York originals in the Towneley manuscript and from the Sykes manuscript. In the *Mortificacio Christi*, the name *Nichodemus* has been corrected, the manuscript's *Nichomedis* being so obviously a scribal error.

It will be recognized that, in defense of choosing rather conservative principles of editing, there is no perfect *Urtext* available for the plays, nor ever was there one. The Register was

---

[92] The listing of the 1535 receipts in the Chamberlain's rolls for pageant money for thirty-three pageants (as opposed to the full number in the Register) on a year when the "Corpus christi play was not playde" (*REED: York*, 1:260–61) has been suggested as demonstrating the point.

[93] Lloyd, "Reflections of a York Survivor," p. 233.

[94] Johnson, "Last Judgment," pp. 270–71. The impression was of God the Father as a tyrannical ruler, and more in keeping with current earthly tyrants who are able to create their own "reality" at whatever cost to their people. It was a medieval commonplace that God the Creator is synonymous with harmony, as opposed to cacophony and dissonance, in this production recorded and played loudly on a boombox. The oedipal conflict between Father and Son in this pageant, however, would have been even more of a source of displeasure in the fifteenth century. Such an interpretation is precisely opposed to the meaning of both the play and orthodox thought on the subject. Though this interpretation was based on the difference perceived between the sternness of the Semitic Old Testament God and the Christian forgiveness offered by the Son of the New Testament, one can imagine that it would have resulted in a heresy trial had the pageant been staged in this manner by the Mercers in medieval York!

[95] The entire issue of *Early Theatre* 3 (2000), under the title *The York Cycle Then and Now*, was devoted to discussion of the 1998 production.

based on the copies of the plays that had been supplied to the guilds, then subjected to further copying and revision. At times the copies from which the scribes worked in preparing the Register must have looked more like the "foul papers" famously posited for plays of the Shakespeare era. This must particularly have been true for those pageants that adopted the long alliterative line.

THE YORK CORPUS CHRISTI PLAYS

[1. THE CREATION OF THE ANGELS AND THE FALL OF LUCIFER]

The Barkers

[DEUS]   *Ego sum Alpha et O[mega], vita, via,*
        Veritas primus et novissimus.[1]

	I am gracyus and grete, God withoutyn begynnyng,	
	I am maker unmade, all mighte es in me.	
	I am lyfe and way unto welth wynnyng;	
	I am formaste and fyrste, als I byd sall it be.	*foremost; shall*
5	My blyssyng o ble sall be blendyng	*of [my] countenance; dazzling*
	And heldand, fro harme to be hydande,	*pouring out; protecting*
	My body in blys ay abydande	*always abiding*
	Unendande, withoutyn any endyng.	
	Sen I am maker unmade, and most es of mighte,	
10	And ay sall be endeles, and noghte es but I,	
	Unto my dygnyté dere sall diewly be dyghte	*dignity; be made*
	A place full of plenté to my plesyng at ply;	*to design*
	And therewith als wyll I have wroght	
	Many dyvers doynges bedene	*now*
15	Whilke warke sall mekely contene,	*continue*
	And all sall be made even of noghte.	
	But onely the worthely warke of my wyll	*worthy work*
	In my sprete sall enspyre the mighte of me,	*spirit*
	And in the fyrste, faythely, my thoghte to fullfyll,	*truly*
20	Baynely in my blyssyng I byd at here be	*Now; command to be here*
	A blys al beledande abowte me;	*all supporting*
	In the whilke blys I byde at be here	
	Nyen ordres of aungels full clere,	*Nine*
	In lovyng aylastande at lowte me.	*praise everlasting; worship*

---

[1] *I am alpha and omega, life, the way, / Truth first and last*

19

Tunc cantant angeli, Te Deum laudamus, te Dominum confitemur.[1]

25	Here undernethe me nowe a nexile I neven,	*wing (as of building) I name*
	Whilke ile sall be erthe, now all be at ones	*isle*
	Erthe haly and helle, this hegheste be heven;	*wholly*
	And that welth sall welde sall won in this wones.	*wield; dwell in these places*
	This graunte I yowe, mynysters myne,	
30	To whils yhe ar stabill in thoghte,	*As long as you*
	And also to thaime that ar noghte	
	Be put to my presone at pyne.	*in suffering*

	Of all the mightes I have made, moste nexte after me	*powerful ones*
	I make thee als master and merour of my mighte.	*reflector*
35	I beelde thee here baynely in blys for to be,	*set; obediently*
	I name thee for Lucifer, als berar of lyghte.	
	Nothyng here sall thee be derand;	*injuring*
	In this blis sall be yhour beeldyng	*dwelling place*
	And have all welth in youre weledyng,	*will (power)*
40	Ay whils yhe ar buxumly berande.	*humbly behaving*

Tunc cantant angeli, Sanctus, sanctus, sanctus, Dominus Deus Sabaoth.[2]

I ANGELUS SERAPHYN A, mercyfull maker, full mekill es thi mighte		*great*
That all this warke at a worde worthely has wroghte.		
Ay loved be that lufly lorde of his lighte		*praised be*
That us thus mighty has made, that nowe was righte noghte,		
45 In blys for to byde in hys blyssyng.		
Aylastande, in luf lat us lowte hym,		*Everlasting; praise let us worship*
At beelde us thus baynely abowete hym,		*That we flourish; now*
Of myrthe nevermore to have myssyng.		*be lacking*

I ANGELUS DEFICIENS, LUCIFERE All the myrth that es made es markide in me.		
50 The bemes of my brighthode ar byrnande so bryghte,		*radiance; burning*
And I so semely in syghte myselfe now I se,		
For lyke a lorde am I lefte to lende in this lighte.		*exist*
More fayrear be far than my feres,		*fairer; companions*
In me is no poynte that may payre.		*become less*
55 I fele me fetys and fayre,		*fine*
My powar es passande my peres.		

ANGELUS CHERABYN Lord, wyth a lastande luf we love thee allone,		
Thou mightefull maker that markid us and made us,		*ordained*
And wroghte us thus worthely to wone in this wones,		*to dwell in this place*

---

[1] *Then the angels sing, "We praise thee, O God, we acknowledge thee to be the Lord"*

[2] *Then the angels sing, "Holy, holy, holy, Lord God of Hosts"*

60   Ther never felyng of fylth may full us nor fade us.   *befoul; darken*
      All blys es here beeldande aboute us,   *dwelling*
      To whyls we are stabyll in thoughte   *As long as; constant*
      In the worschipp of hym that us wroghte,
      Of dere never thar us more dowte us.   *harm; worry*

II ANGELUS DEFICIENS   O, what I am fetys and fayre and fygured full fytt![1]
66   The forme of all fayrehede apon me es feste.   *beauty; fast (fixed)*
      All welth in my weelde es, I wote be my wytte: *power; understand by; intelligence*
      The bemes of my bryghthede are bygged with the beste.   *as large as*
      My schewyng es schemerande and schynande,   *appearance*
70   So bygly to blys am I broghte.   *surely*
      Me nedes for to noy me righte noghte: *to trouble*
      Here sall never payne me be pynande.   *afflicting*

ANGELUS SERAPHYN   With all the wytt at we welde we woyrschip thi wyll,   *that we*
      Thou gloryus God that es grunde of all grace.
75   Ay with stedefaste steven lat us stande styll,   *voice*
      Lorde, to be fede with the fode of thi fayre face.
      In lyfe that es lely aylastande,   *truly*
      Thi dale, Lorde, es ay daynetethly delande,   *gift; bountifully giving*
      And whoso that fode may be felande,   *experiencing (tasting)*
80   To se thi fayre face es noght fastande.   *fasting*

I ANGELUS DEFECIENS, LUCIFER
      Owe, certes, what I am worthely wroghte with wyrschip, iwys,
      For in a glorius gle my gleteryng it glemes,   *radiance*
      I am so mightyly made my mirth may noghte mys.
      Ay sall I byde in this blys thorowe brightnes of bemes.   *Always shall*
85   Me nedes noghte of noy for to neven.   *harm to mention*
      All welth in my welde have I weledande,
      Abowne yhit sall I be beeldand,   *Above; dwelling*
      On heghte in the hyeste of hewven.

      Ther sall I set myselfe, full semely to seyghte,   *sight*
90   To ressayve my reverence thorowe righte o renowne.   *receive*
      I sall be lyke unto hym that es hyeste on heghte —
      Owe, what I am derworth and defte.   *Oh; worthy; noble*
                Owe, Dewes, all goes downe!   *Deus*
      My mighte and my mayne es all marrande.   *resolve; weakening*
      Helpe, felawes, in faythe I am fallande.   *falling*

II ANGELUS DEFICIENS   Fra heven are we heledande on all hande.   *falling*
96   To wo are we weendande, I warande.   *woe; wending; warrant*

---

[1] *I am handsome and fair and in figure (form) entirely fitting*

LUCIFER, DEIABOLUS IN INFERNO Owte, owte! harrowe!

    Helples, slyke hote at es here!   *[I'm] helpless, such heat*

  This es a dongon of dole that I am to dyghte!   *suffering; condemned*

  Whare es my kynde become, so cumly and clere?   *nature*

100 Nowe am I laytheste, allas, that are was lighte.   *most loathsome; before*

  My bryghtnes es blakkeste and blo nowe;   *dark (discolored)*

  My bale es ay betande and brynande: *misery; beating and burning*

  That gares ane go gowlande and gyrnande.   *makes one; wailing; grimacing*

  Owte, ay walaway! I well enew in wo nowe!   *boil (suffer); enough*

II DIABILUS Owte, owte! I go wode for wo! My wytte es all wente nowe.   *mad*

106 All oure fode es but filth we fynde us beforn.

  We that ware beelded in blys in bale are we brent nowe.   *living*

  Owte on thee, Lucifer, lurdan, oure lyghte has thou lorne!   *rascal; lost*

  Thi dedes to this dole nowe has dyghte us.   *forced*

110 To spill us thou was oure spedar,   *hurt; facilitator*

  For thow was oure lyghte and oure ledar,   *leader*

  The hegheste of heven hade thou hyght us.   *called*

LUCIFER IN INFERNO Walaway, wa es me now, nowe es it war thane it was!   *woe; worse*

  Unthryvandely threpe yhe, I sayde but a thoghte.   *Unthrivingly chide*

II DIABOLUS We, lurdane, thou lost us!   *Alas, rascal; destroyed*

LUCIFER IN INFERNO   Yhe ly, owte, allas!   *You lie*

116 I wyste noghte this wo sculde be wroghte.   *thought*

  Owte on yhow, lurdans, yhe smore me in smoke.   *smother*

II DIABOLUS This wo has thou wroghte us.

LUCIFER IN INFERNO   Yhe ly, yhe ly!

II DIABOLUS Thou lyes, and that sall thou by: *purchase*

120 We, lurdane, have at yowe, lat loke!

ANGELUS CHERUBYN A, Lorde, lovid be thi name that us this lyghte lente

  Sen Lucifer oure ledar es lighted so lawe,   *Since; fallen so low*

  For hys unbuxumnes in bale to be brente,   *lack of humility in sorrow; burned*

  Thi rightewysnes to rewarde on rowe   *in the proper order of things*

125 Ilke warke eftyr is wroghte.   *Each*

  Thorowe grace of thi mercyfull myghte,

  The cause I se itt in syghte,

  Wharefore to bale he es broghte.

DEUS Those foles for thaire fayrehede in fantasyes fell   *fools; beauty*

130 And hade mayne of mi mighte that marked tham and made tham,   *moan (complaint)*

  Forthi efter thaire warkes were, in wo sall thai well,   *Therefore; suffer*

For sum ar fallen into fylthe that evermore sall fade tham	*darken them*
And never sall have grace for to gyrth tham.	*defend*
So passande of power tham thoght tham,	*surpassing*
135 Thai wolde noght me worschip that wroghte tham;	
Forthi sall my wreth ever go with tham.	*wrath*

Ande all that me wyrschippe sall wone here, iwys;	*dwell; I know*
Forthi more forthe of my warke wyrke nowe I will.	*even more*
Syn than ther mighte es for-marryde that mente all omys,[1]	
140 Even to myne awne fygure this blys to fulfyll,	*in my image*
Mankynde of moulde will I make.	*earth*
But fyrste wille I fourme hym before	*before I form him I will*
All thyng that sall hym restore,	*support him*
To whilke that his talente will take.	*ability will take [him]*

145 Ande in my fyrste makyng, to mustyr my mighte,	*show*
Sen erthe es vayne and voyde, and myrknes emel,	*Since; empty; entire darkness*
I byd in my blyssyng yhe aungels gyf lyghte	
To the erthe, for it faded when the fendes fell.	*fiends*
In hell sall never myrknes be myssande,	*absent*
150 The myrknes thus name I for nighte,	*darkness*
The day that call I this lyghte.	
My after warkes sall thai be wyssande.	*known*

Ande nowe in my blyssyng I twyne tham in two,	*divide*
The nighte even fro the day, so that thai mete never,	*meet*
155 But ather in a kynde courese thaire gates for to go;	*each; natural; ways*
Bothe the nighte and the day, does dewly yhour deyver,	*duly your duty*
To all I sall wirke be yhe wysshyng.	*directing*
This day warke es done ilke a dele,	*entirely*
And all this warke lykes me ryght wele,	*pleases me very much*
160 And baynely I gyf it my blyssyng.	*now*

[2. THE CREATION THROUGH THE FIFTH DAY]

Playsterers

DEUS *In altissimis habito,*	
In the heghest hevyn my hame have I,	*home*
Eterne mentis et ego,	
Withoutyn ende aylastandly.	

---

[1] *Since their might is entirely destroyed that meant all amiss*

5   Sen I have wroght thire worldys wyde,   *Since; there*
     Hevyn and ayre and erthe also,
     My hegh Godhede I will noght hyde
     All yf sume foles be fallyn me fro.   *fools (misguided ones)*
     When thai assent with syn of pride   *ascend*
10   Up for to trine my trone unto,   *step up; throne*
     In hevyn thai myght no lengger byde   *abide*
     But wyghtly went to wone in wo;   *immediately; live*
     And sen thai wrange have wroght,   *wrong (error)*
     My lyk ys to lat tham go   *desire (implying will)*
15   To suffir sorowe onsoght
     Syne thai have servid so.

     Thare mys may never be amendid   *error; rectified*
     Sen thai asent me to forsake,   *agreed*
     For all there force non sall thame fende   *defend*
20   For to be fendys foule and blake.
     And tho that lykys with me to lende   *remain*
     And trewly tent to me will take   *give heed to my will*
     Sall wonne in welth withoutyn ende   *live*
     And allway wynly with me wake.   *profitably; keep watch*
25   Thai sall have for thare sele   *profit*
     Solace that never sall sclake.   *slacken*
     This warke methynkys full wele,
     And more now will I make.

     Syne that this world es ordand evyn,   *ordained*
30   Furth well I publysch my power.
     Noght by my strenkyth but by my stevyn   *strength; voice*
     A firmament I byd apere.
     Emange the waterris, lyght so levyn,   *Among; light so bright*
     There cursis lely for to lere,   *courses truly to discover*
35   And that same sall be namyd hewvyn
     With planitys and with clowdis clere.   *planets*
     The water I will be set
     To flowe both fare and nere,
     And than the firmament
40   In mydis to set thame sere.   *midst; them separately*

     The firmament sal nought move,
     But be a mene, thus will I mene,   *mean (intermediate space); order*
     Ovir all the worlde to halde and hove,   *be positioned*
     And be tho tow wateris betwyne.   *those two*
45   Undir the hevyn, and als above
     The wateris serly sall be sene,   *separately*
     And so I wille my post prove   *power*
     By creaturis of kyndis clene.   *by nature*

This warke his to my pay *is; recompense*
50 Righit will, withoutyn wyne. *well; doubt*
Thus sese the secunde day *ends*
Of my doyingys bydene. *now*

Moo sutyll werkys assesay I sall *More subtle; attempt*
For to be set in service sere: *independently*
55 All the waterris grete and smalle
That undir hevyne er ordande here, *are ordained*
Gose togedir and holde yow all
And be a flode festynde in fere *linked together*
So that the erthe, both downe and dale, *hill; valley*
60 In drynesch playnly may apere. *dry land*
The drynes "lande" sall be
Namyd, bothe ferre and nere,
And then I name the "se" *sea*
Geddryng of wateris clere. *Gathering*

65 The erthe sall fostyr and furthe bryng *bring forth*
Buxsumly, as I wyle byde, *Obediently; bid*
Erbys and also othyr thyng *Herbs*
Well for to wax and worthe to wede. *to be fruitful; worthy to be clad*
Treys also tharon sall spryng *Trees*
70 With braunchis and with bowis on brede, *branches; boughs extended*
With flouris fayr on heght to hyng *flowers; hang*
And fruth also to fylle and fede. *fruit; feed (nourish)*
And thane I will that thay
Of themselfe have the sede *seed*
75 And mater that thay may *substance*
Be lastande furth in lede. *in that place (where planted)*

And all ther materis es in mynde
For to be made of mekyl might, *great*
And to be kest in dyveris kynde *cast; diverse species*
80 So for to bere sere burguns bright. *differing blossoms*
And when ther frutys is fully fynde *ripe*
And fayrest semande unto syght, *appearing*
Thane the wedris wete and wynde *weather's rain*
Oway I will it wende full wyght, *Away; go; quickly*
85 And of there sede full sone *seed*
New rotys sall ryse upright. *roots*
The third day thus is done:
Thire dedis er dewly dyght. *named*

Now sene the erthe thus ordand es, *planned*
90 Mesurid and made by myn assent,
Grathely for to growe with gres *Truly; grass*

	And wedis that sone away bese went,	*be gone*
	Of my gudnes now will I ges	*intend*
	So that my werkis no harmes hent,	*experience*
95	Two lyghtis, one more and one lesse,	
	To be fest in the firmament:	*set (firmly)*
	The more light to day	
	Fully suthely sall be sent;	
	The lesse lyght allway	
100	To the nyght sall take entent.	*give (its) attention*
	Thir figuris fayre that furth er fun	*forth are found*
	Thus on sere sydys serve thai sall:	*different*
	The more lyght sall be namid the son,	
	Dymnes to wast be downe and be dale.	*Dimness to lessen on hill*
105	Erbis and treys that er bygune:	
	All sall he governe, gret and smale.	
	With cald yf thai be closid or bun,	*bound*
	Thurgh hete of the sun thai sal be hale.	*healthy*
	Als thei have honours	*gifts*
110	In alkyn welth to wale,	*well-being; select*
	So sall my creaturis	
	Evir byde withoutyn bale.	*sorrow*
	The son and the mone on fayre manere	*sun; moon*
	Now grathly gange in your degré;	*appropriately go [forth]*
115	Als ye have tane youre curses clere	*taken; courses*
	To serve furth loke ye be fre,	*forth (from now on)*
	For ye sall set the sesons sere	*different seasons*
	Kyndely to knowe in ilke cuntré,	*each country*
	Day fro day, and yere fro yere,	
120	By sertayne signes suthly to se.	*definitive; truly*
	The hevyn sall be overhyld	*ornamented*
	With sternys to stand plenté.	*stars*
	The furth day his fulfillid:	*fourth; is*
	This werke well lykys me.	
125	Now sen thir werkis er wroght with wyne,	*joy*
	And fundyn furth be firth and fell,	*founded forth by forest and hill*
	The see now will I set within	*sea*
	Whallis whikly for to dewell,	*Whales actively*
	And othir fysch to flet with fyne,	*swim; fins*
130	Sum with skale and sum with skell,	*shell*
	Of diveris materis more and myn,	
	In sere maner to make and mell.	*many ways; mingle*
	Sum sall be meke and milde	
	And sum both fers and fell:	*fierce; ferocious*

135	This world thus will I eke	*increase*
	Syn I am witt of well.	*well of wit (i.e., wise)*
	Also up in the ayre on hyght	
	I byd now that thore be ordande	*there; ordained*
	For to be foulis fayre and bright,	
140	Dewly in thare degre dwelland,	
	With fedrys fayre to frast ther flight	*feathers; enable*
	For stede to stede whore thai will stande,	*where*
	And also leythly for to lyght	*with ease to alight*
	Whoreso thame lykis in ilke a londe.	*every*
145	Thane fysch and foulis sere	*Then; various*
	Kyndely I you commande	*Consistent with [your] natures*
	To meng on youre manere	*mingle (i.e., copulate); own way*
	Both be se and sande.	
	This materis more yitt will I mende	*improve*
150	So for to fulfill my forthoght	
	With diveris bestis in lande to lende,	*assign*
	To brede and be with bale furth bright.	*breed; pain forth brought*
	And with bestis I wille be blende	*mixed*
	Serpentis to be sene unsoght	
155	And wormis upon thaire wombis sall wende	*snakes; bellies; go*
	To won in erth and worth to noght.	*live; be without value*
	And so it sall be kende	*known*
	How all that eme is oght,	*all that is required*
	Begynnyng, mydes, and ende	*middle*
160	I with my worde hase wrothe.	*wrought*
	For als I byde bus all thyng be	*must*
	And dewly done als I will dresse,	*ordain*
	Now bestys ar sett in sere degré	*beasts; diverse*
	On molde to move, both more and lesse.	*the earth*
165	Thane foulis in ayre and fische in see	
	And bestis on erthe of bone and flesch,	
	I byde ye wax furth fayre plenté	*multiply*
	And grathly growes, als I yow gesse.	*forthwith increase; intend*
	So multiply ye sall	
170	Ay furth in fayre processe:	
	My blyssyng have ye all.	
	The fift day endyd es.	

[3. THE CREATION OF ADAM AND EVE]

Cardmakers

DEUS   In hevyn and erthe duly bedene   *forthwith*
      Of five days werke, evyn onto ende,
      I have complete by curssis clene.   *courses*
      Methynke the space of thame well spende.   *them*

5   In hevyn er angels fayre and brighte,   *are*
      Sternes and planetis ther curssis to ga,   *Stars; go*
      The mone servis onto the nyght,
      The son to lyghte the day alswa.   *sun; also*

      In erthe is treys, and gres to springe,   *trees; grass*
10   Bestis and foulys, bothe gret and smalle,
      Fyschis in flode, all othyr thyng
      Thryffe and have my blyssyng all.   *Thrive*

      Thys werke is wroght now at my will,
      But yet can I no best see   *beast (animal)*
15   That acordys be kynde and skyll   *nature and ability*
      And for my werke myght worschippe me.

      For perfytt werke ne ware it nane   *were it none*
      But ought ware made that myght it yeme,   *Unless something were; care for it*
      For love mad I this warlde alane;   *made; alone*
20   Therfor my loffe sall in it seme.   *love; appear*

      To kepe this warlde bothe mare and lesse
      A skylfull best thane will I make   *rational animal then*
      Eftyr my schape and my lyknes,   *After*
      The wilke sall worschipe to me take.   *which*

25   Off the symplest part of erthe that is here   *Of*
      I sall make man, and for this skylle   *reason*
      For to abate hys hauttande chere,   *haughty*
      Bothe his gret pride and other ille,

      And also for to have in mynde
30   How simpyll he is at hys makyng,
      For als febyll I sall hym fynde   *weak*
      Qwen he is dede at his endyng.   *When; dead*

      For this reson and skyll alane,
      I sall make man lyke onto me.

35	Ryse up, thou erthe in blode and bane,	*bone*
	In schape of man, I commaunde thee.	
	A female sall thou have to fere:	*as companion*
	Her sall I make of thi lyft rybe	*left rib*
	Alane so sall thou nought be here	*Alone*
40	Withoutyn faythefull frende and sybe.	*kin*
	Takys now here the gast of lyffe	*spirit (breath)*
	And ressayve bothe youre saules of me;	*souls*
	The femall take thou to thi wyffe,	
	Adam and Eve your names sall be.	

ADAM A, Lorde, full mekyll is thi mighte,   *great*
46   And that is sene in ilke a syde,   *on all sides*
         For now his here a joyfull syght   *is*
         To se this worlde so lange and wyde.

         Mony diveris thyngis now here es
50   Off bestis and foulis, bathe wylde and tame,   *both*
         Yet is nan made to thi liknes   *none*
         But we alone. A, lovyd be thi name.   *praised*

EVE To swylke a Lorde in all degré
         Be evirmore lastande lovynge,   *praise (worship)*
55   That tyll us swylke a dyngnité   *such a dignity*
         Has gyffyne before all othyr thynge,   *given*

         And selcouth thyngis may we se here   *spectacular*
         Of this ilke warld so lange and brade   *very world; long; broad*
         With bestis and fowlis so many and sere.   *diverse*
60   Blessid be he that us made.

ADAM A, blyssid Lorde, now at thi wille
          Syne we er wroght, wochesaff to telle,   *Since; vouchsafe*
          And also say us two untyll,   *tell*
          Qwate we sall do and whare to dewell?   *What; dwell*

DEUS For this skyl made I yow this day,   *reason*
66   My name to worschip ay whare.   *everywhere*
          Lovys me forthi, and lovys me ay   *Praise me therefore; love (worship)*
          For my makyng, I axke no mare.   *creation; ask; more*

          Bothe wys and witty sall thou be,
70   Als man that I have made of noght.   *nothing*
          Lordschipe in erthe than graunt I thee,
          All thynge to serve thee that I have wroght.

       In paradyse sall ye same wone,   *together live*
       Of erthely thyng get ye no nede;
75   Ille and gude both sall ye kone,   *Evil and good; know*
       I sall you lerne youre lyve to lede.   *teach*

ADAM A, Lorde, sene we sall do nothyng   *since*
       But louffe thee for thi gret gudnesse,   *praise (worship)*
       We sall ay bay to thi biddyng   *always obey*
80   And fulfyll it, both more and less.

EVE His syng sene he has on us sett   *sign since*
       Beforne all othir thyng certayne.
       Hem for to love we sall noght lett   *Him; abandon*
       And worschip hym with myght and mayne.

DEUS At hevyne and erth first I begane,
86   And six days wroght or I walde ryst: *ere I would rest*
       My warke is endyde now at mane.   *man (humankind)*
       All lykes me will, but this is best.   *well*

       My blyssyng have thai ever and ay.
90   The seveynt day sall my restyng be:
       Thus wille I sese, sothely to say,   *cease*
       Of my doying in this degré.

       To blys I sall yow bryng:
       Comys forthe, ye tow, with me.   *two*
95   Ye sall lyffe in lykyng.
       My blyssyng wyth yow be.
       Amen.

[4. THE PROHIBITION OF THE TREE OF KNOWLEDGE]

The Regynall of the Fullers Pagyant

DEUS Adam and Eve, this is the place
       That I have graunte you of my grace
       To have your wonnyng in.   *dwelling*
       Erbes, spyce, frute on tree,   *Herbs*
5   Beastes, fewles, all that ye see   *fowls*
       Shall bowe to you, more and myn.   *less*
       This place hight paradyce;   *is called*
       Here shall your joys begynne,
       And yf that ye be wyse
10   Frome thys tharr ye never twyn.   *need you never separate [yourself]*

All your wyll here shall ye have,
Lykyng for to eate or sayff   *save (maintain)*
Fyshe, fewle, or fee,   *fowl; livestock*
And for to take at your owen wyll
15   All other creatours also theretyll.
Your suggettes shall they bee.   *subjects*
Adam, of more and lesse
Lordeship in erthe here graunte I thee;
Thys place that worthy is,
20   Kepe it in honestye.

Looke that ye yem ytt wetterly,   *attend to; entirely*
All other creatours shall multeply,
Ylke one in tender hower.   *Each; hour*
Looke that ye bothe save and sett
25   Erbes and treys, for nothyng lett,
So that ye may endower   *endeavor*
To susteyn beast and man
And fewll of ylke stature.   *fowls*
Dwell here yf that ye cann:
30   This shall be your endowre.   *living*

ADAM   O Lord, lovyd be thy name,   *praised*
For nowe is this a joyfull hame   *home*
That thowe hais brought us to:
Full of myrthe and solys faughe,   *happy solace*
35   Erbes and trees, frute on haugh   *on hill*
Wyth spysys many one hoo.   *spices; on hill*
Loo, Eve, nowe ar we brought
Bothe unto rest and rowe,   *peace*
We neyd to tayke no thought,
40   But loke ay well to doo.

EVE   Lovyng be ay to suche a Lord   *Praise*
To us hais geven so great reward
To governe bothe great and small,
And mayd us after his owen read   *created; own plan*
.   .   .   [line missing]
45   Emonges these myrthes all.
Here is a joyfull sight
Where that wee wonn in shall.   *live in*
We love thee, mooste of myght,
Great God, that we on call.

DEUS   Love my name with good entent   *Praise (Worship)*
51   And harken to my comaundement,
And do my byddyng buxomly.   *obediently*

      Of all the frute in parradyce
      Tayke ye therof of your best wyse
55   And mayke you right merry.
      The tree of good and yll,
      What tyme you eates of thys
      Thowe speydes thyself to spyll   *hastens; destroy*
      And be brought owte of blysse.

60   All thynges is mayd, man, for thy prowe;   *good*
      All creatours shall to thee bowe
      That here is mayd erthly.
      In erthe I mayke thee lord of all,
      And beast unto thee shall be thrall.
65   Thy kynd shall multeply;
      Therefore this tree alone,
      Adam, this owte take I,   *take out (except)*
      The frute of it negh none,   *approach not*
      For an ye do, then shall ye dye.   *if*

ADAM   Alas, Lorde, that we shuld do so yll,   *ill (wrong)*
71   Thy blyssed byddyng we shall fulfyll
      Bothe in thought and deyd.   *deed*
      We shall no negh thys tre nor the bugh   *not approach; bough*
      Nor yit the fruyte that thereon groweth,
75   Therewith oure fleshe to feyd.   *feed*

EVE   We shall do thy byddyng.
      We have none other neyd;   *needs*
      Thys frute full styll shall hyng,   *hang*
      Lorde, that thowe hays forbyd.   *have*

DEUS   Looke that ye doe as ye have sayd.
81   Of all that there is hold you apayd,   *contented*
      For here is welthe at wyll.
      Thys tre that beres the fruyte of lyfe,
      Luke nother thowe nor Eve thy wyf   *See to it that neither*
85   Lay ye no handes theretyll.
      Forwhy it is knowen   *Since*
      Bothe of good and yll,
      This frute but ye lett hyng   *hang*
      Ye speyd yourself to spyll.   *hasten; destroy*

90   Forthy this tree that I owt tayke,   *disallow*
      Nowe kepe it grathly for my sayke   *truly; sake*
      That nothyng negh it neyre.   *come near it*
      All other at your wyll shall be;
      I owte take nothyng but this tree

95 To feyd you with in feare.   *altogether*
    Here shall ye leyd your lyffe
    With dayntys that is deare.   *dainties (lovely things)*
    Adam and Eve thy wyfe,
    My blyssyng have ye here.

[5. THE FALL]

The Cowpers

Satanas incipit dicens: *Satan begins, saying*

DIABOLUS For woo my witte es in a were   *turmoil*
    That moffes me mykill in my mynde: *moves (distresses); greatly*
    The Godhede that I sawe so cleere
    And parsayved that he shuld take kynde   *take on the nature*
5   Of a degree   *order*
    That he had wrought, and I dedyned   *was offended*
    That aungell kynde shuld it noght be.   *[of] angelic nature*
    And we wer faire and bright,
    Therfore me thoght that he
10 The kynde of us tane myght,   *might take on*
    And therat dedeyned me.   *offended*

    The kynde of man he thoght to take
    And theratt hadde I grete envye,
    But he has made to hym a make   *mate*
15 And harde to her I wol me hye   *quickly; will; go*
    That redy way,
    That purpose prove to putte it by,   *subvert it*
    And fande to pike fro hym that pray.   *try; pick (steal); prey*
    My travayle were wele sette   *effort; well*
20 Myght I hym so betraye,
    His likyng for to lette,   *felicity; spoil*
    And sone I schalle assaye.   *attempt [it]*

    In a worme liknes wille I wende   *serpent's*
    And founde to feyne a lowde lesynge.   *try to invent; lie*
25 Eve, Eve!

EVA   Wha is thare?   *Who*

SATANAS   I, a frende.   *friend*
    And for thy gude es the comynge   *good*
    I hydir sought.   *hither*

       Of all the fruyt that ye se hynge   *hang*
       In paradise, why ete ye noght?   *eat*

EVA We may of tham ilkane   *every one*
31   Take al that us goode thought,
       Save a tree outt is tane,   *Except; is forbidden*
       Wolde do harme to neyghe it ought.   *Would; approach*

SATANAS And why that tree, that wolde I witte,   *would I know*
35   Any more than all othir by?   *nearby*

EVA For oure Lord God forbeedis us itt,
       The frute therof, Adam nor I,
       To neghe it nere.
       And yf we dide we both shuld dye,
40   He saide, and sese our solace sere.   *cease; various joys*

SATANAS Yha, Eve, to me take tente.   *pay attention*
       Take hede and thou shalte here   *hear*
       What that the matere mente   *meant*
       He moved on that manere.

45   To ete therof he you defende   *denied*
       I knawe it wele, this was his skylle;   *reason (purpose)*
       Bycause he wolde non othir kende   *wanted no one else to know*
       Thes grete vertues that longes thertill.   *belongs*
       For will thou see
50   Who etis the frute of goode and ille
       Shalle have knowyng as wele as hee.

EVA Why what kynne thyng art thou   *kind of*
       That telles this tale to me?

SATANAS A worme that wotith wele how   *knows well*
55   That yhe may wirshipped be.

EVE What wirshippe shulde we wynne therby?   *gain*
       To ete therof us nedith it nought;
       We have lordshippe to make maistrie
       Of alle thynge that in erthe is wrought.

SATANAS Woman, do way!
61   To gretter state ye may be broughte   *estate*
       And ye will do as I schall saye.   *If you*

EVE To do is us full lothe   *despicable*
       That shuld oure God myspaye.   *should; anger*

SATANAS   Nay, certis it is no wathe: *danger*
66   Ete it saffely ye maye.

         For perille ryght ther none in lyes
         Bot worshippe and a grete wynnynge,   *gain*
         For right als God yhe shalle be wyse
70   And pere to hym in allkyn thynge.   *equal; all things*
         Ay, goddis shalle ye be,
         Of ille and gode to have knawyng,   *evil and good*
         For to be als wise as he.

EVE   Is this soth that thou sais?   *true; you say*

SATANAS   Yhe, why trowes thou noght me?   *trust*
76   I wolde be no kynnes wayes   *(i.e., in no manner)*
         Telle noght but trouthe to thee.

EVA   Than wille I to thy techyng traste   *trust*
         And fange this frute unto oure foode.   *take*

         Et tunc debet accipere pomum.   *And then she must take the apple*

SATANAS   Byte on boldly, be nought abasshed,
81   And bere Adam to amende his mode   *take [it to]; mood*
         And eke his blisse.

         Tunc Satanas recedet.   *Then Satan slips away*

EVA   Adam, have here of frute full goode.

ADAM   Alas, woman, why toke thou this?
85   Owre Lorde comaunded us bothe
         To tente the tree of his.   *attend to*
         Thy werke wille make hym wrothe.   *angry*
         Allas, thou has don amys.   *[something] wrong*

EVE   Nay, Adam, greve thee nought at it,
90   And I shal saie the reasonne why:
         A worme has done me for to witte   *serpent; caused; know*
         We shalle be as goddis, thou and I,
         Yf that we ete
         Here of this tree; Adam, forthy
95   Lette noght that worshippe for to gete.   *Don't forego; obtain*
         For we shalle be als wise
         Als God that is so grete
         And als mekill of prise;   *value*
         Forthy ete of this mete.   *food*

ADAM To ete it wolde I nought eschewe
101   Myght I me sure in thy saying.

EVE Byte on boldely, for it is trewe,   *is true*
         We shalle be goddis and knawe al thyng.

ADAM To wynne that name
105   I schalle it taste at thy techyng.

         Et accipit et comedit.   *And he takes [the fruit] and eats*

         Allas, what have I done, for shame?
         Ille counsaille, woo worthe thee.   *Evil advisor, a curse on you*
         A, Eve, thou art to blame;
         To this entysed thou me,   *enticed*
110   Me shames with my lyghame,   *body*

         For I am naked, as methynke.

EVE Allas, Adam, right so am I.

ADAM And for sorowe sere why ne myght we synke,   *sorrow sore*
          For we have greved God almyghty
115   That made me man,
          Brokyn his bidyng bittirly.   *cruelly*
          Allas, that ever we it began.
          This werke, Eve, hast thou wrought
          And made this bad bargayne.

EVE Nay, Adam, wite me nought.

ADAM Do wey, lefe Eve, whame than?   *dear; whom*

EVE The worme to wite wele worthy were,
         With tales untrewe he me betrayed.

ADAM Allas, that I lete at thy lare   *took heed of your advice*
125   Or trowed the trufuls that thou me saide.   *trusted; trifling tales*
          So may I byde,
          For I may banne that bittir brayde   *curse; sharp (terrible) act*
          And drery dede that I it dyde.   *evil; did*
          Oure shappe for doole me defes;   *[human] form; misery; overcomes*
130   Wherewith thay shalle be hydde?

EVE Late us take there fygge leves   *fig leaves*
         Sythen it is thus betydde.   *Since this has happened*

ADAM   Ryght as thou sais, so shalle it bee,
          For we are naked and all bare.
135   Full wondyr fayne I wolde hyde me   *gladly*
          Fro my Lordis sight, and I wiste whare,   *if I knew where*
          Where I ne roght!   *Where I should not fear*

DOMINUS   Adam, Adam!

ADAM   Lorde!

DOMINUS   Where art thou, yhare?   *quickly*

ADAM   I here thee, Lorde, and seys thee noght.   *hear; see*

DOMINUS   Say, wheron is it longe,   *what is the reason*
141   This werke, why hast thou wrought?

ADAM   Lorde, Eve garte me do wronge   *made*
          And to that bryg me brought.   *breach*

DOMINUS   Say, Eve, why hast thou garte thy make   *enticed your mate*
145   Ete frute I bad thei shuld hynge stille   *hang yet*
          And comaunded none of it to take?

EVA   A worme, Lord, entysed me therto,   *seduced*
          So welaway
          That ever I did that dede so dill.   *silly (foolish)*

DOMINUS   A wikkid worme, woo worthe thee ay,   *a curse on you always*
151   For thou on this maner
          Hast made tham swilke affraye.   *such trouble*
          My malysoune have thou here   *curse*
          With all the myght I may.

155   And on thy wombe than shall thou glyde   *belly*
          And be ay full of enmyté
          To al mankynde on ilke a side,   *everywhere*
          And erthe it shalle thy sustynaunce be
          To ete and drynke.
160   Adam and Eve alsoo, yhe
          In erthe than shalle ye swete and swynke   *sweat; work*
          And travayle for youre foode.   *struggle*

ADAM   Allas, whanne myght we synke,
          We that haves alle worldis goode?
165   Ful derfly may us thynke.   *grievous*

DOMINUS Now, Cherubyn, myn aungell bryght,
        To middilerth tyte go dryve there twoo.   *quickly*

ANGELUS Alle redy, Lorde, as it is right,
        Syn thy wille is that it be soo,   *Since*
170   And thy lykyng.
        Adam and Eve, do you to goo,
        For here may ye make no dwellyng.
        Goo yhe forthe faste to fare,
        Of sorowe may yhe synge.

ADAM Allas, for sorowe and care,
176   Owre handis may we wryng.

[6. THE EXPULSION FROM THE GARDEN]

The Origenall Perteynyng to the Crafte of Armourers

ANGELUS Alle creatures to me take tent,   *give attention*
        Fro God of heven now am I sent
        Unto the wrecchis that wronge has went   *precipitated*
        Thaymself to woo;   *woe*
5   The joie of heven that thaym was lent
        Is lost thaym froo.

        Fro thaym is loste bothe game and glee.   *From*
        He badde that thei schuld maistirs be
        Over alle kynne thyng, oute tane a tree   *natural things, except*
10   He taught them tille,
        And therto wente bothe she and he
        Agayne his wille.   *Against*

        Agaynst his wille thus have they wrought
        To greeffe grete God gaffe they right noght,   *grieve; gave*
15   That wele wytt ye;   *know*
        And therfore syte is to thaym sought,   *sorrow*
        As ye shalle see.

        The fooles that faithe is fallen fra,   *from*
        Take tente to me nowe or ye ga: *go*
20   Fro God of heven unto yow twa   *two*
        Sente am I nowe
        For to warne you what kynne wa   *type of woe*
        Is wrought for you.

ADAM   For us is wrought, so welaway,
25   Doole endurand nyghte and day;   *Sadness (Sorrow)*
      The welthe we wende have wonnyd in ay   *thought to have lived in always*
      Is loste us fra.   *from*
      For this myscheffe ful wele we may
      Ever mornyng ma.   *mourning make*

ANGELUS   Adam, thyselffe made al this syte,   *sorrow*
31   For to the tree thou wente full tyte   *quickly*
      And boldely on the frute gan byte
      My Lord forbed.   *forbid*

ADAM   Yaa, allas, my wiffe that may I wite,   *blame*
35   For scho me red.   *counseled*

ANGELUS   Adam, for thou trowyd hir tale,   *trusted*
      He sendis thee worde and sais thou shale   *shall*
      Lyffe ay in sorowe,   *Live*
      Abide and be in bittir bale
40   Tille he thee borowe.   *redeem*

ADAM   Allas, wrecchis, what have we wrought!
      To byggly blys we bothe wer brought;   *matchless*
      Whillis we wer thare   *While*
      We hadde inowe; nowe have we noghte.   *enough*
45   Allas, for care.

EVA   Oure cares ar comen bothe kyne and colde,   *sharp*
      With fele fandyngis manyfolde;   *many temptations*
      Allas, that tyraunte to me tolde
      Thurghoute his gyle
50   That we shulde have alle welthis in walde,   *the world*
      Wa worthe the whyle.   *Woe*

ANGELUS   That while yee wrought unwittely   *mindlessly*
      Soo for to greve God Almyghty,
      And that mon ye full dere abye   *dearly abide*
55   Or that ye ga;   *go*
      And to lyffe, as is worthy,   *live*
      In were and wa.   *misery and woe*

      Adam, have this, luke howe ye thynke
      And tille withalle thi meete and drynke   *till [the soil] for; food*
60   For evermore.

ADAM   Allas, for syte why myght I synke,   *sorrow*
      So shames me sore.

EVE   Soore may we shame with sorowes seere   *many*
             And felly fare we bothe in feere.   *with sin burdened; together*
65   Allas, that evyr we neghed it nere,   *approached*
             That tree untill.
             With dole now mon we bye full dere   *must we purchase*
             Oure dedis ille.   *deeds bad*

ANGELUS Giffe, for thou beswyked hym swa,   *If; deceived; so*
70   Travell herto shalle thou ta: *Travail; take (have)*
             Thy barnes to bere with mekill wa,   *children*
             This warne I thee.
             Buxum shalle thou and othir ma   *Obedient; more*
             To man ay be.

EVE   Allas, for doole, what shalle I doo?
76   Now mon I never have rest ne roo.   *may; or peace*

ADAM   Nay, lo, swilke a tole is taken me too   *such a tool; given*
             To travaylle tyte.   *quickly*
             Nowe is shente both I and shoo,   *guilty; she*
80   Allas, for syte.   *sorrow*

             Allas, for syte and sorowe sadde,
             Mournynge makis me mased and madde   *confused; mad*
             To thynke in herte what helpe I hadde,
             And nowe has none.
85   On grounde mon I nevyr goo gladde,   *may*
             My gamys ere gane.   *[Even] my recreation is gone*

             Gone ar my games withowten glee;   *joys*
             Allas, in blisse kouthe we noght bee,   *could*
             For putte we were to grete plenté
90   At prime of the day.   *beginning*
             Be tyme of none alle lost had wee,   *noon*
             Sa welawaye.

             Sa welaway, for harde peyne,
             Alle bestis were to my biddyng bayne;   *obedient*
95   Fisshe and fowle, they were fulle fayne   *eagerly*
             With me to founde,
             And nowe is alle thynge me agayne   *against*
             That gois on grounde.   *goes*

             On grounde ongaynely may I gange   *uneasily; go*
100   To suffre syte and peynes strange: *sorrow*
             Alle is for dede I have done wrange   *[a] deed; wrong*
             Thurgh wykkid wyle.   *wile (trickery)*

On lyve methynkith I lyffe to lange,   *live too long*
Allas the whille.

105   A, Lord, I thynke what thynge is this
      That me is ordayned for my mysse,   *error*
      Gyffe I wirke wronge whom shulde me wys   *If; who; assist*
      Be any waye?   *By*
      How beste wille be, so have I blisse,
110   I shalle assaye.

      Allas, for bale, what may this bee,
      In worlde unwisely wrought have wee;
      This erthe it trembelys for this tree   *trembles*
      And dyns ilke dele.   *makes noise in every manner*
115   Alle this worlde is wrothe with mee,   *angry*
      This wote I wele.   *know I well*

      Full wele I wote my welthe is gone,   *know my well being*
      Erthe, elementis, everilkane,   *everything*
      For my synne has sorowe tane,   *taken*
120   This wele I see.   *well (clearly)*
      Was nevere wrecchis so wylle of wane   *at a loss (distraught)*
      As nowe ar wee.

EVE   We are fulle wele worthy, iwis,
      To have this myscheffe for oure mys,   *sin*
125   For broght we were to byggely blys,   *great*
      Ever in to be.
      Now my sadde sorowe certis is this,
      Mysilfe to see.

ADAM   To see it is a sytfull syghte: *sorrowful sight*
130   We bothe that were in blis so brighte,
      We mon go nakid every ilke a nyghte   *might [in the garden]*
      And dayes bydene.   *indeed*
      Allas, what womans witte was light,   *mind was weak*
      That was wele sene.   *well seen*

EVE   Sethyn it was so me knyth it sore,   *Since; I regret it greatly*
136   Bot sen that woman witteles ware,   *since; were*
      Mans maistrie shulde have bene more
      Agayns the gilte.   *guilt*

ADAM   Nay, at my speche wolde thou never spare;
140   That has us spilte.   *brought us to grief*

EVE	Iff I hadde spoken youe oughte to spill,	
	Ye shulde have taken gode tent theretyll	*attention*
	And turnyd my thought.	*changed my mind*

ADAM	Do way, woman, and neme it noght,	*name*

145	For at my biddyng wolde thou not be,	
	And therfore my woo wyte I thee.	*blame*
	Thurgh ille counsaille thus casten ar we	*Through*
	In bittir bale.	
	Nowe God late never man aftir me	*let*
150	Triste woman tale.	*Trust*

	For certis me rewes fulle sare	*repent; sore*
	That evere I shulde lerne at thi lare,	*lore*
	Thy counsaille has casten me in care,	
	That thou me kende.	*made known*

EVE	Be stille, Adam, and nemen it na mare,	*name it no more*
156	It may not mende.	

	For wele I wate I have done wrange,	*know; wrong*
	And therfore evere I morne emange.	*mourn always*

ADAM	Allas, the whille I leve so lange	*live so long*
160	Dede wolde I be.	*Dead*
	On grounde mon I never gladde gange	*must; go*
	Withowten glee.	

	Withowten glee I ga,	
	This sorowe wille me sla,	*kill*
165	This tree unto me wille I ta	*take*
	That me is sende.	*[to] me*
	He that us wrought wisse us fro wa,	*keep; woe*
	Wharesom we wende.	*Wherever; wander*

[7.] SACRIFICIUM CAYME ET ABELL

The Originall Perteynyng to the Craft of Gloveres

ANGELUS	That Lord of lyffe lele aylastand,	*truly everlasting*
	Whos myght unmesured is to meyne,	*mean*
	He shoppe the sonne, bothe see and sande,	*shaped (created)*
	And wroughte this worlde with worde, I wene.	*believe*
5	His aungell cleere, as cristall clene,	
	Here unto you thus am I sente	

	This tide.	*[At] this time*
	Abell and Cayme, yei both bydeyne,	*now*
	To me enteerly takis entent;	*fully pay attention*
10	To meve my message have I ment,	*move (set forth)*
	If that ye bide.	*abide*

	Allemyghty God of myghtes moste,	
	When he had wrought this world so wide,	
	Nothynge hym thoughte was wroughte in waste	*Nothing; superfluous*
15	But in his blissyng boune to bide.	*was bound to abide*
	Neyne Ordurs for to telle, that tyde,	*Orders; time*
	Of aungeles bryght he bad ther be.	*commanded*
	For pride	
	And sone the tente part it was tried	*soon; tenth; tested*
20	And wente awaye, as was worthye;	*(i.e., as they deserved)*
	They heild to helle alle that meyne,	*fell; company*
	Therin to bide.	

	Thanne made he manne to his liknes	
	That place of price for to restore,	
25	And sithen he kyd him such kyndnes,	*extended to him*
	Somwhat wille he wirke therfore.	
	The tente to tyne he askis, no more,	*tenth to lose (give up)*
	Of alle the goodes he haves you sent,	
	Full trew.	
30	To offyr loke that ye be yore,	*ready*
	And to my tale yhe take entent,	*pay attention*
	For ilke a lede that liffe has lente,	*every man*
	So shalle you ensewe.	

ABELL	Gramercy, God of thy goodnes,	
35	That me on molde has marked thi man.	*earth*
	I worshippe thee with worthynes,	
	With alle the comforte that I can.	
	Me for to were fro warkes wanne	*defend; evil works*
	For to fulfille thy comaundement,	
40	The teynd	*tenth part (tithe)*
	Of alle the gode sen I beganne	*goods since*
	Thow shalle it have, sen thou it sent.	
	Come, brothir Cayme, I wolde we wente	
	With hert ful hende.	*gracious*

CAYM	We, whythir now in wilde waneand?	*insane waning [of moon] (i.e., an inauspicious time)*
46	Trowes thou I thynke to trusse of towne?	*Think; leave town*
	Goo, jape thee, robard jangillande;	*jangling felon*
	Me liste noght nowe to rouk nor rowne.	*I'd prefer; talk [privately]; mumble*

ABELL   A, dere brothir, late us be bowne   *obliged*
50   Goddis biddyng blithe to fulfille,   *happily*
       I tell thee.

CAYME   Ya, daunce in the devil way, dresse thee downe,   *(i.e., out of my way)*
       For I wille wyrke even as I will.
       What mystris thee, in gode or ille,   *Why do you need*
55   Of me to melle thee?   *To meddle with me yourself*

ABELL   To melle of thee myldely I may;
       Bot, goode brothir, go we in haste,
       Gyffe God oure teynde dulye this day;   *Give; tithe*
       He byddis us thus, be nought abassed.   *upset*

CAYME   Ya, devell methynketh that werke were waste,
61   That he us gaffe geffe hym agayne   *gave give*
       To se.
       Nowe fekyll frenshippe for to fraste   *fickle; test*
       Methynkith ther is in hym sarteyne.
65   If he be moste in myghte and mayne,   *with determination*
       What nede has he?

ABELL   He has non nede unto thi goode,   *of your goods*
       But it wille please hym principall
       If thou, myldly in mayne and moode,   *(i.e., willingly)*
70   Grouche noght geve hym tente parte of all.   *Grudge*
       .   .   .   [pages missing]
[**ANGELUS**]   It shall be done evyn as ye bydd,
       And that anone.

BREWBARRET   Lo, maister Cayme, what shaves bryng I,   *sheaves*
       Evyn of the best for to bere seyd,   *seed*
75   And to the feylde I wyll me hye
       To fetch you moo, if ye have neyd.

CAYME   Cume up, sir knave, the devyll thee speyd,   *speed*
       Ye will not come but ye be prayd.   *begged*

BREWBARRET   O, maister Caym, I have broken my to!   *toe*

CAYME   Come up, syr, for by my thryft,
81   Ye shall drynke or ye goo.   *ere*

ANGELUS   Thowe cursyd Came, where is Abell?
       Where hais thowe done thy broder dere?

Cayme   What askes thowe me that taill to tell,
85   For yit his keper was I never?

Angelus   God hais sent thee his curse downe,
   Fro hevyn to hell, *maladictio dei.*   *God's curse [on you]*

Cayme   Take that thyself, evyn on thy crowne,
   Quia non sum custos fratris mei,   *Because I am not my brother's keeper*
90   To tyne.   *To trouble you*

Angelus   God hais sent thee his malyson,   *curse*
   And inwardly I geve thee myne.

Cayme   The same curse light on thy crowne,
   And right so myght it worth and be   *occur*
95   For he that sent that gretyng downe,
   The devyll myght speyd both hym and thee.
   Fowll myght thowe fall.
   Here is a cankerd company;
   Therefore Goddes curse light on you all.

Angelus   What hast thou done? Beholde and heere: *hear*
101   The voice of his bloode cryeth vengeaunce
   Fro erthe to heven, with voice entere,
   This tyde.   *[At] this time*
   That God is greved with thy grevaunce
105   Take hede, I schalle telle thee tydandis,   *tidings*
   Therfore abide.

   Thou shall be curssed uppon the grounde.
   God has geffyn thee his malisonne.   *curse*
   Yff thou wolde tyll the erthe so rounde   *till (plow)*
110   No frute to thee ther shalle be founde.
   Of wikkidnesse sen thou arte sonne,
   Thou shalle be waferyng here and there   *wandering*
   This day.
   In bittir bale nowe art thou boune,   *bound*
115   Outcastyn shal thou be for care.
   No man shal rewe of thy misfare   *feel sorry for*
   For this affraie.   *assault*

Cayme   Allas, for syte, so may I saye,   *sorrow*
   My synne it passis al mercie,
120   For askid thee, Lord, I ne maye;   *ask [it] of you*
   To have it am I nought worthy.
   Fro thee shalle I be hidde in hye,
   Thou castis me, Lorde, oute of my kyth   *kinfolk*

    In lande.
125 Both here and there outecaste am I,
    For ilke a man that metis me with,   *every man*
    They wille slee me, be fenne or ferth,   *kill; swamp or frith (forest)*
    With dynte of hande.   *a blow*

ANGELUS Nay, Cayme, nought soo, have thou no drede.
130 Who that thee slees shalle ponnysshed be   *punished*
    Sevene sithis for doyng of that dede.   *Seven times; deed*
    Forthy a token shal thou see:
    It shalle be prentyd so in thee   *imprinted so on*
    That ilke a man shalle thee knowe full wele.

CAYM Thanne wolle I fardir flee   *further*
136 For shame.
    Sethen I am sette thus out of seill,   *Since; prosperity*
    That curse that I have for to feill,   *know*
    I giffe you the same.   *give*

[8. THE BUILDING OF NOAH'S ARK]

The Shipwrites

DEUS Fyrst qwen I wrought this world so wyde,   *when*
    Wode and wynde and watters wane,   *Wood; waters dark*
    Hevyn and helle was noght to hyde,
    Wyth herbys and gyrse thus I begane.   *grass*
5 In endles blysse to be and byde,
    And to my liknes made I man,
    Lorde and syre on ilke a side   *every side*
    Of all medillerthe I made hym than.   *middle-earth; then*

    A woman also with hym wroght I,
10 Alle in lawe to lede ther lyffe.
    I badde thame waxe and multiplye
    To fulfille this worlde, withowtyn striffe.
    Sythn hays men wroght so wofully   *Since [then] have*
    And synne is nowe reynand so ryffe,   *reigning so completely*
15 That me repentys and rewys forthi   *regrets*
    That ever I made outhir man or wiffe.   *either*

    Bot sen they make me to repente
    My werke I wroght so wele and trewe,
    Wythowtyn seys will noght assente   *ceasing*
20 Bot ever is bowne more bale to brewe.   *bound*
    Bot for ther synnes thai shall be shente   *destroyed*

And fordone hoyly, hyde and hewe. *undone entirely (wholly); hue*
Of tham shal no more be mente,
Bot wirke this werke I wille al newe.

25 Al newe I will this worlde be wroght *made*
And waste away that wonnys therin; *lives*
A flowyd above thame shall be broght *flood*
To stroye medilerthe, both more and myn. *destroy; less*
Bot Noe alon, lefe shal it noght, *leave*
30 To all be sownkyn for ther synne; *sunken (drowned)*
He and his sones, thus is my thoght,
And with there wyffes away sall wynne. *escape*

Nooe, my servand, sad an cleyn, *somber and [morally] clean*
For thou art stabill in stede and stalle, *(i.e., all places)*
35 I wyll thou wyrke, withowten weyn, *will (order); slacking*
A warke to saffe thiselfe wythall. *save*

NOE O, mercy Lorde, qwat may this meyne? *what*

DEUS I am thi Gode of grete and small
Is comyn to telle thee of thy teyn *difficulty (pain)*
40 And qwat ferly sall eftir fall. *marvelous thing shall; happen*

NOE A, Lorde, I lowe thee lowde and still *love (praise)*
That unto me, wretche unworthye,
Thus with thy worde, as is thi will,
Lykis to appere thus propyrly. *Deigns; personally*

DEUS Nooe, as I byd thee, doo fulfill.
46 A shippe I will have wroght in hye;
All yf thou can litill skyll, *have limited ability*
Take it in hande, for helpe sall I.

NOE A, worthy Lorde, wolde thou take heede,
50 I am full olde and oute of qwarte, *physically unfit*
That me liste do no daies dede *would prefer to do; work*
Bot yf gret mystir me garte. *need make me*

DEUS Begynne my werke behoves thee nede,
And thou wyll passe from peynes smerte;
55 I sall thee sokoure and thee spede *succor*
And giffe thee hele in hede and hert. *give; health; head; heart*

I se suche ire emonge mankynde *hostility [to me]*
That of thare werkis I will take wreke, *vengeance*
Thay shall be sownkyn for thare synne; *sunken (drowned)*

60	Therfore a shippe I wille thou make.	
	Thou and thi sonnes shall be therein,	
	They sall be savyd for thy sake.	
	Therfore go bowdly and begynne	*boldly*
	Thy mesures and thy markis to take.	*measurements*

NOE	A, Lorde, thi wille sall ever be wroght	
66	Os counsill gyfys of ilka clerk,	*Us; gives to*
	Bot first of shippecraft can I right noght;	
	Of ther makyng have I no merke.	*mark (ability)*

DEUS	Noe, I byd thee hartely have no thought:	
70	I sall thee wysshe in all thi werke,	*guide*
	And even to itt till ende be wroght;	
	Therfore to me take hede and herke.	

	Take high trees and hewe thame cleyne,	
	All be sware and noght of skwyn,	*square; not at an angle*
75	Make thame of burdes and wandes betwene,	*boards; battens*
	Thus thrivandly and noght over thyn.	*skillfully; thin*
	Luke that thi semes be suttilly seyn	*seams; carefully sealed*
	And naylid wele that thei noght twyne.	*separate*
	Thus I devyse ilk dele bedeyne;	*aspect altogether*
80	Therfore do furthe, and leve thy dyne.	*go forth; (i.e., say nothing more)*

	Three hundred cubyttis it sall be lang	
	And fyfty brode, all for thy blys,	
	The highte of thyrty cubittis strang,	*strong*
	Lok lely that thou thynke on this.	*truly*
85	Thus gyffe I thee grathly or I gang	*give; truly before I go*
	Thi mesures that thou do not mysse.	
	Luk nowe that thou wirke noght wrang;	*wrong*
	Thus wittely sen I thee wyshe.	*intelligently since; direct*

NOE	A, blistfull Lord, that al may beylde,	*defend*
90	I thanke thee hartely both ever and ay,	
	Fyfe hundreth wyntres I am of elde,	*age*
	Methynk ther yeris as yestirday.	
	Ful wayke I was and all unwelde.	*weak; lacking in strength*
	My werynes is wente away,	
95	To wyrk this werke here in this feylde	
	Al be myselfe I will assaye.	*attempt*

	To hewe this burde I wyll begynne,	*board*
	But firste I wille lygge on my lyne.	*lay; line (for measuring)*
	Now bud it be alle in like thynne,	*must; of regular thickness*
100	So that it nowthyr twyne nor twynne.	*separate or warp*

Thus sall I june it with a gynn,   *join; tool*
And sadly sett it with symonde fyne;   *firmly seal; caulk*
Thus schall I wyrke it both more and myne   *less*
Thurgh techyng of God, maister myne.

.   .   .   [line missing]
105   More suttelly kan no man sewe: *skillfully; join [seams]*
It sall be cleyngked ever ilka dele,   *clenched in every part*
With nayles that are both noble and newe;   *rivets*
Thus sall I feste it fast to feele.
Take here a revette and there a rewe,   *rivet; rove*
110   With the bowe ther nowe wyrke I wele.   *[ship's] bow*
This werke I warand both gud and trewe.

Full trewe it is who will take tente,   *pay attention*
Bot faste my force begynnes to fawlde;   *fail*
A hundereth wyntres away is wente
115   Sen I began this werk, full grathely talde,   *Since; truly told*
And in slyke travayle for to be bente   *such effort; engaged*
Is harde to hym that is thus olde.
But he that to me this messages sent,
He wille be my beylde, thus am I bowde.   *supporter; very confident*

DEUS Nooe, this werke is nere an ende
121   And wrought right as I warned thee,   *taught*
Bot yit in maner it must be mende;   *improved*
Therfore this lessoun lerne at me.
For dyverse beestis therin must lende
125   And fewles also in there degree,   *fowls*
And for that thay sall not sam blende,   *mix together*
Dyverse stages must ther be.   *levels (decks)*

And qwen that it is ordand soo   *when; ordered*
With dyverse stawllys and stagis seere,   *various*
130   Of ilka kynde thou sall take twoo,   *every kind (species)*
Bothe male and femalle fare in fere.   *going in company*
Thy wyffe, thy sonnes, with thee sall goo,
And thare thre wyffes, withowten were: *doubt*
There eight bodies withowten moo   *more*
135   Sall thus be saved on this manere.

Therfore to my biddyng be bayne: *obedient*
Tille all be herberd haste thee faste   *harbored (lodged)*
Eftir the seventh day sall it rayne
Tille fowrty dayes be fully paste.   *passed*
140   Take with thee geere, sclyk os may gayne,   *such as may be needed*
To man and beeste thare lyffes to laste.

I sall thee socoure for certeyne
Tille alle thi care awey be kaste.   *(i.e., done with)*

NOE   A, Lorde, that ilka mys may mende,   *failing*
145   I lowe thi lare, both lowde and stille;   *praise thy teaching*
I thanke thee both with herte and hende   *hand*
That me wille helpe fro angrys hill.   *resentfulness*
Abowte this werke now bus me wende   *must; go*
With beestys and fewlys my shippe to fill.   *fowls*
150   He that to me this crafte has kende,   *taught*
He wysshe us with his worthy wille.   *direct*

[9. THE FLOOD]

The Fysshers and Marynars

NOYE   That Lord that leves aylastand lyff,   *lives; everlasting life*
I love thee ever with hart and hande   *praise*
That me wolde rewle be reasonne ryffe,   *by plenteous reason*
Sex hundereth yere to lyffe in lande.   *live*
5   Thre semely sonnes and a worthy wiffe   *handsome*
I have ever at my steven to stande.   *word (command)*
Bot nowe my cares aren keene as knyffe   *troubles*
Bycause I kenne what is commaunde.   *know; commanded*
Thare comes to ilke contré,   *every country*
10   Ya, cares bothe kene and calde.   *sharp; cold (distressing)*
For God has warned me
This worlde wastyd shalle be,   *destroyed*
And certis the sothe I see,   *truth*
As formefadres has tald.   *forefathers; told*

15   My fadir Lamech who, likes to neven,   *appropriate to mention*
Heere in this worlde thus lange gon lende,   *(i.e., lived so long)*
Sevene hundereth yere seventy and sevene,
In swilke a space his tyme he spende.
He prayed to God with stabill stevene   *steady voice*
20   That he to hym a sone shuld sende,   *son*
And at the laste ther come from heven
Slyke hettyng that hym mekill amende   *Such a promise; improved [his status]*
And made hym grubbe and grave,   *delve; dig*
As ordand faste beforne,   *ordained firmly*
25   For he a sone shulde have,
As he gon aftir crave;
And as God vouchydsave   *granted*
In worlde than was I borne.

When I was borne Noye named he me
30   And saide thees wordes with mekill wynne;   *great joy*
"Loo," he saide, "this ilke is he
That shalle be comforte to mankynne."
Syrs, by this wele witte may ye,   *well understand*
My fadir knewe both more and mynne,   *less*
35   By sarteyne signes he couthe wele see   *certain; could well*
That al this worlde shuld synke for synne.
Howe God shulde vengeaunce take,
As nowe is sene sertayne,   *seen definitely*
And hende of mankynde make   *end*
40   That synne wold nought forsake,
And howe that it shuld slake,   *end*
And a worlde waxe agayne.   *rise up*

I wolde God itt wasted were   *were destroyed*
Sa that I shuld nott tente thertille.   *attend thereto*
45   My semely sonnes and doughteres dere,
Takis ye entent unto my skylle.   *notice of; reason*

I FILIUS Fader, we are all redy heere
Youre biddyng baynly to fulfille.   *ready*

NOE Goos calle youre modir, and comes nere,
50   And spede us faste that we nought spille.   *hurry; die*

I FILIUS Fadir, we shal nought fyne   *rest (stop)*
To youre biddyng be done.   *Until*

NOE Alle that leves under lyne,   *lives under linen (i.e., everyone)*
Sall, sone, soner passe to pyne.   *son, sooner; pain (perish)*

I FILIUS Where are ye, modir myne?   *mother*
56   Come to my fadir sone.   *right away*

UXOR What sais thou, sone?

I FILIUS   Moder, certeyne
My fadir thynkis to flitte full ferre.   *flee; far*
He biddis you haste with al youre mayne   *strength*
60   Unto hym that nothyng you marre.   *obstruct*

UXOR Ya, good sone, hy thee faste agayne
And telle hym I wol come no narre.   *nearer*

I FILIUS Dame, I wolde do youre biddyng fayne,   *gladly*
But yow bus wende, els bese it warre.   *must go; it will be worse*

UXOR Werre, that wolde I witte.   *Worse; know*
66   We bowrde al wrange, I wene.   *jest; think*

I FILIUS Modir, I saie you yitte,   *yet*
       My fadir is bowne to flitte.   *determined*

UXOR Now, certis, I sall nought sitte   *(i.e., make speed)*
70   Or I se what he mene.   *Until; means*

I FILIUS Fadir, I have done nowe as ye comaunde:
       My modir comes to you this daye.

NOE Scho is welcome, I wele warrande;
       This worlde sall sone be waste awaye.

UXOR Wher arte thou, Noye?

NOE   Loo, here at hande.
76   Come hedir faste, dame, I thee praye.

UXOR Trowes thou that I wol leve the harde lande   *Think; will leave; dry land*
       And tourne up here on toure deraye?   *go up; such disarray*
       Nay, Noye, I am nought bowne   *obligated*
80   To fonde nowe over there fellis.   *attempt; hills*
       Doo barnes, goo we and trusse to towne.   *children, go*

NOE Nay, certis, sothly than mon ye drowne.   *may*

UXOR In faythe, thou were als goode come downe
       And go do somwhat ellis.

NOE Dame, fowrty dayes are nerhand past
86   And gone sen it began to rayne.   *since*
       On lyffe sall no man lenger laste   *longer*
       Bot we allane, is nought to layne.   *alone; (i.e., this is clear)*

UXOR Now, Noye, in faythe thee fonnes full faste.   *act irrationally*
90   This fare wille I no lenger frayne;   *matter; question*
       Thou arte nere woode, I am agaste.   *almost mad*
       Farewele, I wille go home agayne.

NOE O, woman, arte thou woode?
       Of my werkis thou not wotte;   *do not understand*
95   All that has ban or bloode   *bone*
       Sall be overeflowed with the floode.

UXOR   In faithe, thee were als goode
      To late me go my gatte.   *let; way*

      We owte, herrowe!

NOE   What now, what cheere?

UXOR   I will no nare for no kynnes nede.   *nearer; need*

NOE   Helpe, my sonnes, to holde her here,
102   For tille hir harmes she takes no heede.   *concerning*

II FILIUS   Beis mery, modir, and mende youre chere.   *mood*
      This worlde beis drowned, withouten drede.

UXOR   Allas that I this lare shuld lere.   *lore; learn*

NOE   Thou spilles us all, ille myght thou speede.   *destroy*

III FILIUS   Dere modir, wonne with us,   *remain*
108   Ther shal nothyng you greve.

UXOR   Nay, nedlyngis home me bus,   *I must go home*
110   For I have tolis to trusse.   *[household] equipment; gather*

NOE   Woman, why dois thou thus
      To make us more myscheve?

UXOR   Noye, thou myght have leteyn me wete.   *allowed me [to] know*
      Erly and late thou wente theroutte
115   And ay at home thou lete me sytte
      To loke that nowhere were wele aboutte.   *see*

NOE   Dame, thou holde me excused of itt;
      It was Goddis wille, withowten doutte.

UXOR   What, wenys thou so for to go qwitte?   *free*
120   Nay, be my trouthe, thou getis a clowte.   *blow*

NOE   I pray thee, dame, be stille.
      Thus God wolde have it wrought.

UXOR   Thow shulde have witte my wille   *known my wishes*
      Yf I wolde sente thertille,   *assent*
125   And Noye, for that same skylle,   *reason*
      This bargan sall be bought.

Nowe at firste I fynde and feele   *discover*
Wher thou hast to the forest soght,
Thou shuld have tolde me for oure seele   *happiness*
130   Whan we were to slyke bargane broght.   *such a*

NOE Now, dame, thee thar noght drede a dele,   *dread nothing*
For till accounte it cost thee noght;
A hundereth wyntyr, I watte wele,   *know*
Is wente sen I this werke had wrought.
135   And when I made endyng,
God gaffe me mesore fayre   *measure*
Of every ilke a thyng;
He bad that I shuld bryng
Of beestis and foules yynge,   *young*
140   Of ilke a kynde a peyre.   *each species; pair*

UXOR Nowe, certis, and we shulde skape fro skathe   *escape harm*
And so be saffyd as ye saye here,   *saved*
My commodrys and my cosynes bathe,   *gossips; both*
Tham wolde I wente with us in feere.   *together*

NOE To wende in the watir it were wathe: *perilous*
146   Loke in and loke withouten were.   *(i.e., get in here)*

UXOR Allas, my lyff me is full lath,   *loathly*
I lyffe overelange this lare to lere.   *teaching; learn*

I FILIA Dere modir, mende youre moode,
150   For we sall wende you with.

UXOR My frendis that I fra yoode   *went*
Are overeflowen with floode.   *inundated*

II FILIA Nowe thanke we God al goode
That us has grauntid grith.   *safety*

III FILIA Modir, of this werke nowe wolde ye noght wene *believe*
156   That alle shuld worthe to watres wan.   *pass under; dark*

II FILIUS Fadir, what may this mervaylle mene,
Wherto made God medilerth and man?

I FILIA So selcouthe sight was never non seene   *marvelous*
160   Sen firste that God this worlde began.

NOE Wendes and spers youre dores bedene,   *Go and close (spar); now*
For bettyr counsell none I can.

      This sorowe is sente for synne;
      Therfore to God we pray
165   That he oure bale wolde blynne.   *relieve*

III FILIUS   The kyng of al mankynne
      Owte of this woo us wynne,   *rescue*
      Als thou arte Lorde, that maye.

I FILIUS   Ya, Lorde, as thou late us be borne   *allowed*
170   In this grete bale, som bote us bede.   *sorrow; help us bid (offer)*

NOE   My sonnes, se ye mydday and morne
      To thes catelles takes goode hede.   *animals*
      Keppes tham wele with haye and corne;
      And women, fanges these foules and feede   *care for*
175   So that they be noght lightly lorne   *lost*
      Als longe as we this liffe sall lede.

II FILIUS   Fadir, we are full fayne   *glad*
      Youre biddyng to fulfille.
      Nine monethes paste er playne   *are passed plainly*
180   Sen we wer putte to peyne.   *pain*

III FILIUS   He that is most of mayne   *power*
      May mende it qwen he wyll.   *when*

NOE   O, barnes, itt waxes clere aboute,   *children*
      That may ye see ther wher ye sitte.   *As you may*

I FILIUS   I, leffe fadir, ye loke thareowte   *dear*
186   Yf that the water wane ought yitt.   *recede*

NOE   That sall I do withowten dowte,
      For be the wanyng may we witte.   *by; know*
      A, Lorde, to thee I love and lowte,   *praise and worship*
190   The catteraks I trowe be knytte.   *floodgates [of heaven]; closed*
      Beholde, my sonnes al three,
      The clowdes are waxen clere.

II FILIUS   A, Lorde of mercy free,
      Ay lovyd myght thou be.   *praised*

NOE   I sall assaye the see
196   How depe that it is here.

UXOR   Loved be that Lord that giffes all grace
      That kyndly thus oure care wolde kele.   *suffering; alleviate*

NOE	I sall caste leede and loke the space	*lead*
200	Howe depe the watir is ilke a dele.	
	Fyftene cobittis of highte itt hase	*cubits*
	Overe ilke a hille fully to feylle,	*cover*
	Butte beese wel comforte in this casse,	*be well comforted*
	It is wanand, this wate I wele.	*waning; know well*
205	Therfore a fowle of flight	
	Full sone sall I forthe sende	
	To seke if he have sight	
	Som lande uppon to light;	
	Thanne may we witte full right	*know*
210	When oure mornyng sall mende.	*mourning*
	Of al the fowles that men may fynde,	
	The raven is wighte and wyse is hee.	*strong/white*
	Thou arte full crabbed and al thy kynde,	*sour-tempered*
	Wende forthe thi course, I comaunde thee,	
215	And werly watte and yther thee wynd,	*carefully know; hither make your way*
	Yf thou fynde awdir lande or tree.	*either*
	Nine monethes here have we bene pyned,	*in severe discomfort*
	But when God wyll, better mon bee.	*might it be*
I FILIA	That Lorde that lennes us lyffe,	*gives*
220	To lere his lawes in lande,	
	He mayd bothe man and wyffe,	
	He helpe to stynte oure striffe.	*end*
III FILIA	Oure cares are kene as knyffe,	*sharp*
	God graunte us goode tydand.	
I FILIUS	Fadir, this foule is forthe full lange,	*bird; long*
226	Uppon sum lande I trowe he lende,	*believe; has landed*
	His foode therfore to fynde and fange:	*take up*
	That makis hym be a fayland frende.	*unreliable*
NOE	Nowe, sonne, and yf he so forthe gange	*go*
230	Sen he for all oure welthe gon wende,	*good has gone*
	Then be he for his werkis wrange	
	Evermore weried withowten ende.	*cursed*
	And sertis for to see	
	Whan oure sorowe sall sesse,	
235	Anodyr foule full free	
	Owre messenger sall be.	
	Thou doufe, I comaunde thee,	*dove*
	Owre comforte to encresse.	

A faithfull fewle to sende art thow
240 Of alle within there wanys wyde.   *walls*
Wende forthe, I pray thee, for owre prowe,   *our good*
And sadly seke on ilke a side   *soberly seek everywhere*
Yf the floodes be falland nowe
That thou on the erthe may belde and byde.   *build; abide*
245 Bryng us som tokenyng that we may trowe   *token; rely upon*
What tydandes sall of us betyde.

II FILIA   Goode Lorde, on us thou luke,
And sesse oure sorow sere   *cease; many*
Sen we al synne forsoke
250 And to thy lare us toke.   *teaching*

III FILIA   A twelmothe bott twelve weke   *but (except for)*
Have we be hoverand here.   *been hovering (idle)*

NOE Now barnes, we may be blithe and gladde   *happy and glad*
And lowe oure Lord of hevenes kyng.   *love (praise)*
255 My birde has done as I hym badde,   *bade*
An olyve braunche I se hym brynge.
Blyste be thou fewle that nevere was fayd   *Blessed; deceptive*
That in thy force makis no faylyng.
Mare joie in herte never are I hadde,   *More; before*
260 We mone be saved, now may we synge.   *shall*
Come hedir my sonnes in hye,
Oure woo away is wente.
I se here certaynely
The hillis of Hermony.   *Armenia*

I FILIUS Lovyd be that Lord forthy   *Praised*
266 That us oure lyffes hase lente.   *given*

Tunc cantent Noe et filii sui, etc.   *Then Noe and his sons should sing*

UXOR For wrekis nowe that we may wynne,   *disasters; redeem*
Oute of this woo that we in wore,   *were*
But Noye, wher are nowe all oure kynne
270 And companye we knwe before?   *knew*

NOE Dame, all ar drowned, late be thy dyne,   *(i.e., be quiet)*
And sone thei boughte ther synnes sore.   *recently they paid for*
Gud lewyn latte us begynne   *Good living let*
So that we greve oure God no more;
275 He was greved in degré
And gretely moved in mynde
For synne, as men may see,

Dum dixit "penitet me."   *Then [God] said, "It repenteth me."*
    Full sore forthynkyng was he   *he was sorry*
280   That evere he made mankynde.

    That makis us nowe to tole and trusse,   *toil; heave*
    But sonnes, he saide, I watte wele when,
    Arcum ponam in nubibus,   *I will set the rainbow in the clouds*
    He sette his bowe clerly to kenne   *rainbow; know*
285   As a tokenyng bytwene hym and us   *sign*
    In knawlage tille all Cristen men
    That fro this worlde were fynyd thus,   *ended*
    With wattir wolde he nevere wast yt then.   *destroy*
    Thus has God most of myght
290   Sette his senge full clere   *sign*
    Uppe in the ayre of heght;   *air on high*
    The raynebowe it is right,
    As men may se in sight
    In seasons of the yere.

II FILIUS Sir, nowe sen God oure soverand Syre   *Father*
296   Has sette his syne thus in certayne,   *sign*
    Than may we wytte this worldis empire   *know*
    Shall evermore laste, is noght to layne.   *hide*

NOE Nay, sonne, that sall we nought desire,
300   For and we do we wirke in wane,   *vain*
    For it sall ones be waste with fyre
    And never worthe to worlde agayne.   *(i.e., exist as a world)*

UXOR A, syre, owre hertis are seere   *sore*
    For thes sawes that ye saye here,   *sayings*
305   That myscheffe mon be more.   *may*

NOE Beis noght aferde, therfore,
    Ye sall noght lyffe than yore   *live then so long*
    Be many hundereth yhere.   *years*

I FILIUS Fadir, howe sall this lyffe be ledde
310   Sen non are in this worlde but we?

NOE Sones, with youre wiffes ye salle be stedde   *living together*
    And multyplye youre seede sall ye.
    Youre barnes sall ilkon othir wedde
    And worshippe God in gud degré.   *good*
315   Beestes and foules sall forthe be bredde,
    And so a worlde begynne to bee.
    Nowe travaylle sall ye taste   *travail; experience*

To wynne you brede and wyne,
For alle this worlde is waste.
320   Thez beestes muste be unbraste,   *released*
And wende we hense in haste
In Goddis blissyng and myne.

[10. ABRAHAM AND ISAAC]

The Parchemyners and Bokebynders

ABRAHAM Grett God, that alle this world has wrought
And wisely wote both gud and ille,   *distinguishes*
I thanke hym thraly in my thoght   *fully (without reservation)*
Of alle his lave he lens me tille.   *love; bestows on me*
5   That thus fro barenhede has me broghte,   *barrenness*
A hundereth wynter to fulfille,
Thou graunte me myght so that I mowght   *strength*
Ordan my werkis aftir thi wille,   *Order*
For in this erthely lyffe
10   Ar non to God more boune   *committed*
Then is I and my wyffe,
For frenshippe we have foune.   *found*

Unto me tolde God on a tyde   *God told me once*
Wher I was telde under a tree,   *lodged [in my tent]*
15   He saide my seede shulde be multyplyed
Lyke to the gravell of the see,   *sands*
And als the sternes wer strewed wyde,   *stars*
So saide he that my seede schuld be;
And bad I shulde be circumcicyd   *ordered*
20   To fulfille the lawe: thus lernynde he me.   *taught*
In worlde wherso we wonne   *live*
He sendes us richeys ryve.   *abundant*
Als ferre as schynes the sonne,   *As far as shines*
He is stynter of stryve.   *healer; troubles*

25   Abram first named was I,
And sythen he sette a sylypp ma,   *Then; a syllable more*
And my wiffe hyght Sarae   *was named Sarai*
And sythen was scho named Sara.   *thereafter*

But Sara was uncertan thanne
30   That evere oure seede shulde sagates yelde   *in this manner*
Because hirselfe sho was barrane,
And we wer bothe gone in grete eelde.   *age*
But scho wroght as a wyse woman.

	To have a barne us for to beelde,	*protect (raise)*
35	Hir servand prevely sho wan	*secretly she won*
	Unto my bede my wille to welde.	*bed*
	Sone aftir than befelle	
	When God oure dede wolde dight,	*determine*
	Sho broght forthe Esmaell,	*Ishmael*
40	A sone semely to sight.	*handsome*

	Than aftirward when we waxed alde,	
	My wyffe scho felle in feere for same,	
	Oure God nedes tythynges tyll us talde	*necessarily; tidings; told*
	Wher we wer in oure house at hame,	*home*
45	Tille have a sone we shulde be balde,	*To; bold*
	And Isaak shulde be his name,	
	And his seede shulde springe manyfalde.	*manyfold*
	Gyff I were blythe, who wolde me blame,	*If; happy*
	And for I trowed this tythynge	*trusted*
50	That God talde to me thanne,	*told*
	The grounde and the begynnyng	
	Of trowthe that tyme beganne.	*truth at that time*

	Nowe awe I gretely God to yeelde	*ought; yield up (sacrifice)*
	That so walde telle me his entente,	*would*
55	And noght gaynestandyng oure grete eelde,	
	A semely sone he has us sente.	
	Now is he wight hymselfe to welde	*strong (man)*
	And fra me is all wightnes wente;	*strength*
	Therfore sall he be my beelde.	*support*
60	I lowe hym that this lane has lente,	*love; gift*
	For he may stynte oure stryve	*end our trouble*
	And fende us fro alle ill.	*defend*
	I love hym as my liff	*life*
64	With all myn herte and will.	

ANGELUS Abraham, Abraham!

ABRAHAM   Loo, I am here.

	ANGELUS Nowe bodeword unto thee I brynge:	*message*
	God wille assaye thi wille and cheere,	*test*
	Giffe thou wille bowe tylle his byddyng.	*If*
	Isaak, thi sone, that is thee dere,	*dear*
70	Whom thou loves over alle thyng,	
	To the lande of Vyssyon wende in feere,	*together*
	And there of hym thou make offering.	
	I sall thee shewe fulle sone	
	The stede of sacrifice.	*place*

75	God wille this dede be done,	*wills that*
	And therfore thee avise.	*directs you*

ABRAHAM   Lord God, that lens aylastand light,   *bestows everlasting*
     This is a ferly fare to feele;   *wondrous matter to discover*
     Tille have a sone semely to sight,   *To*
80   Isaak, that I love full wele.
     He is of eelde, to reken right,
     Thyrty yere and more sumdele,   *somewhat*
     And unto dede hym buse be dight: *death he must be put*
     God has saide me so for my seele,   *well-being*
85   And biddis me wende on all wise   *go*
     To the lande of Vysioune
     Ther to make sacryfice
     Of Isaak that is my sone.

     And that is hythyn thre daies jornay,   *hither*
90   The ganeste gate that I gane goo,   *fastest way; may go*
     And sertis, I sall noght say hym nay
     If God commaunde myself to sloo.   *slay [him]*
     Bot to my sone I will noght saye   *say [anything]*
     Bot take hym and my servantis twoo,
95   And with our asse wende forthe our waye.
     As God has said, it sall be soo.
     Isaak, sone, I undirstande
     To wildirnesse now wende will we
     Tharefore to make oure offerand,
100   For so has God comaunded me.

ISAAC   Fadir, I am evere at youre wille,
     As worthy is withowten trayne,   *deception*
     Goddis comaundement to fulfille
     Awe all folke forto be fayne.   *Ought; glad*

ABRAHAM   Sone, thou sais me full gode skille,   *good reason*
106 Bott alle the soth is noght to sayne.
     Go we sen we sall thertille,
     I praye God send us wele agayne.   *[home] well again*

ISAAC   Childir, lede forthe oure asse
110 With wode that we sall bryne;   *wood; burn*
     Even as God ordand has   *ordained*
     To wyrke we will begynne.

I FAMULUS   Att youre biddyng we wille be bowne   *bound (compelled)*
     What way in worlde that ye wille wende.

II FAMULUS   Why, sall we trusse ought forthe a towne   *go out of*
116   In any uncouthe lande to lende?   *strange; remain*

I FAMULUS   I hope tha have in this sessoune   *they; season*
Fro God of hevyn sum solayce sende.   *From; some*

II FAMULUS   To fulfille yt is goode reasoune,
120   And kyndely kepe that he has kende.   *naturally; revealed*

I FAMULUS   Bott what thei mene certayne   *mean*
Have I na knowlage clere.

II FAMULUS   It may noght gretely gayne
To move of swilke matere.

ABRAHAM   No, noye you noght in no degré   *(i.e., don't fuss about this)*
126   So for to deme here of oure dede,   *judge*
For als God comaunded so wirke wille we   *as God commands so we will do*
Untill his tales us bus take hede.   *words we must take heed*

I FAMILIUS   All thos that wille his servandis be,
130   Ful specially he wille thaym spede.   *them prosper*

ISAAC   Childir, with all the myght in me
I lowe that Lorde of ilke a lede   *praise; every man*
And wirshippe hym certayne;
My will is evere unto.   *thereto*

II FAMILIUS   God giffe you myght and mayne   *strength*
136   Right here so for to doo.

ABRAHAM   Sone, yf oure Lord God Almyghty
Of myselfe walde have his offerande,   *would; offering*
I wolde be glade for hym to dye,   *glad in his place*
140   For all oure heele hyngis in his hande.   *well-being hangs*

ISAAC   Fadir, forsuth, ryght so walde I,   *would*
Lever than lange to leve in lande.   *Rather; long*

ABRAHAM   A, sone, thu sais full wele, forthy
God geve thee grace gratthely to stande.   *plainly*
145   Childir, bide ye here still.   *remain*
No ferther sall ye goo,
For yondir I se the hill
That we sall wende untoo.

ISAAC Kepe wele oure asse and all oure gere
150   To tyme we come agayne you till.   *Until; to you*

ABRAHAM My sone, this wode behoves thee bere   *wood; carry*
      Till thou come high uppon yone hill.

ISAAC Fadir, that may do no dere   *harm*
      Goddis comaundement to fullfyll,
155   For fra all wathes he will us were   *dangers; defend*
      Wharso we wende to wirke his wille.   *work*

ABRAHAM A, sone, that was wele saide.
      Lay doune that woode even here
      Tille oure auter be grathide.   *altar; set up*
160   And, my sone, make goode cheere.

ISAAC Fadir, I see here woode and fyre,
      Bot wherof sall oure offerand be?

ABRAHAM Sertis, son, gude God oure suffraynd syre   *good; sovereign*
      Sall ordayne it in goode degré,   *(i.e., in good time)*
165   For sone, and we do his dessyre,
      Full gud rewarde tharfore gette wee.
      In hevyn ther mon we have oure hyre,   *may; reward*
      For unto us so hight has hee.   *promised*
      Therfore, sone, lete us praye
170   To God, bothe thou and I,
      That we may make this daye
      Oure offerand here dewly.   *as is due*

      Grete God that all this worlde has wrought
      And grathely governes goode and ill,   *surely*
175   Thu graunte me myght so that I mowght   *strength; might*
      Thy comaundementis to fullfill.
      And gyffe my flessche groche or greve oght   *if; rebel or grieve*
      Or sertis my saule assentte thertill,   *Even though my soul*
      To byrne all that I hydir broght   *burn; hither*
180   I sall noght spare yf I shulde spille.   *refrain; come to grief*

ISAAC Lorde God, of grete pousté,   *power*
      To wham all pepull prayes,
      Graunte bothe my fadir and me
      To wirke thi wille allweyes.

185   But, fadir, nowe wolde I frayne full fayne   *ask; eagerly*
      Wharof oure offerand shulde be grathid?   *made*

ABRAHAM Sertis, sone, I may no lengar layne,   *longer conceal*
     Thyselfe shulde bide that bittir brayde.   *endure; affliction*

ISAAC Why, fadir, will God that I be slayne?

ABRAHAM Ya suthly, sone, so has he saide.

ISAAC And I sall noght grouche ther agayne;   *complain*
192   To wirke his wille I am wele payed.   *pleased*
     Sen it is his desire
     I sall be bayne to be   *willing*
195   Brittynd and brent in fyre,   *Dismembered; burned*
     And therfore morne noght for me.   *mourn*

ABRAHAM Nay, sone, this gatis most nedis be gone,   *way must be taken*
     My Lord God will I noght gaynesaye,
     Nor never make mornys nor mone   *mourning (weeping); moan*
200   To make offerand of thee this day.

ISAAC Fadir, sen God oure Lorde allane   *alone*
     Vowchesaffe to sende when ye gon praye
     A sone to you whan ye had nane,   *none*
     And nowe will that he wende his waye,   *go [on]*
205   Therfore faynde me to fell   *endeavor; kill*
     Tille offerand in this place,   *For an offering*
     But firste I sall you telle
     My counsaille in this case.

     I knaw myselfe be cours of kynde,   *by course of nature*
210   My flessche for dede will be dredande;   *death; dreading*
     I am ferde that ye sall fynde   *afraid*
     My force youre forward to withstande.   *strength your promise*
     Therfore is beste that ye me bynde
     In bandis faste, boothe fute and hande.
215   Nowe whillis I am in myght and mynde,
     So sall ye saffely make offerrande,
     For fadir, when I am boune   *bound*
     My myght may noght avayle.
     Here sall no fawte be foune   *fault be found*
220   To make youre forward faylle.   *covenant*

     For ye ar alde and alle unwelde,
     And I am wighte and wilde of thoght.   *strong (manly); impetuous*

ABRAHAM To bynde hym that shuld be my beelde,   *defense*
     Outtane Goddis will, that wolde I noght.   *Except for*
225   But loo, her sall no force be felde,   *coercion; felt*

So sall God have that he has soght.
Farewele, my sone, I sall thee yelde
Tylle hym that all this world has wroght.

Nowe kysse me hartely, I thee pray,
230   Isaak, I take my leve for ay,
Me bus thee mys.   *must; miss*
My blissyng have thou enterly,
And I beseke God Allmyghty
He giffe thee his.   *give*

235   Thus aren we samyn assent   *together in agreement*
Eftir thy wordis wise.
Lorde God, to this take tente: *pay attention*
Ressayve thy sacrifice.

This is to me a perles pyne   *unequaled pain*
240   To se myn nawe dere childe thus boune.   *own; bound*
Me had wele lever my lyf to tyne   *rather; lose*
Than see this sight, thus of my sone.
It is Goddis will, it sall be myne,
Agaynste his saande sall I never schone;   *message (command); hesitate*
245   To Goddis cummaundement I sall enclyne
That in me fawte non be foune.   *fault; found*

Therfore my sone so dere,
If thou will anythyng saye,
Thy dede it drawes nere.   *death*
250   Farewele, for anes and ay.   *once*

ISAAC   Now, my dere fadir, I wolde you praye,
Here me thre wordes, graunte me my bone   *Hear; request*
Sen I fro this sall passe for ay.
I see myn houre is comen full sone.
255   In worde, in werke, or any waye
That I have trespassed or oght mysdone,
Forgiffe me, fadir, or I dye this daye,   *before I die*
For his luffe that made bothe sonne and mone.   *love*
Here sen we two sall twynne,   *separate*
260   Firste God I aske mercy
And you in more and myne   *less*
This day or evere I dy.   *ere*

ABRAHAM   Now my grete God Adonay,   *Adonai (Jewish name for God)*
That all this worlde has worthely wroght,
265   Forgyffe the sone, for his mercye,
In worde, in worke, in dede, and thoght.

Nowe, sone, as we ar leryd   *told*
Our tyme may noght myscarie.

ISAAC   Nowe farewele, all medilerth,
270   My flesshe waxis faynte for ferde.   *fear*
Nowe, fadir, take youre swerde,
Methynke full lange ye tarie.

ABRAHAM   Nay, nay, sone, nay, I thee behete   *promise*
That do I noght, withouten were.   *perplexity*
275   Thy wordis makis me my wangges to wete   *cheeks [become] wet*
And chaunges, childe, ful often my cheere.
Therfore lye downe, hande and feete;
Nowe may thou witte thyn oure is nere.   *know; hour is near*

ISAAC   A, dere fadir, lyff is full swete,
280   The drede of dede dose all my dere.   *(i.e., frightens me)*
As I am here youre sone,
To God I take me till.   *(i.e., entrust myself)*
Nowe am I laide here bone,   *bound*
Do with me what ye will.

285   For fadir, I ask no more respete   *delay*
Bot here a worde what I wolde mene: *hear; advise*
I beseke you or that ye smyte   *before*
Lay doune this kyrcheffe on myn eghne.   *eyes*
Than may youre offerand be parfite   *perfect*
290   If ye wille wirke thus as I wene.   *advise*
And here to God my saule I wite,   *my soul I commend*
And all my body to brenne bydene.   *burn now*
Now, fadir, be noght myssyng   *don't fail*
But smyte fast as ye may.

ABRAHAM   Farewele, in Goddis dere blissyng
296   And myn for ever and ay.

That pereles prince I praye   *(i.e., God)*
Myn offerand heretill have it,
My sacryfice this day:
300   I praye the Lorde ressayve it.

ANGELUS   Abraham, Abraham!

ABRAHAM   Loo, here iwys.

ANGELUS   Abraham, abide, and halde thee stille.   *hold*
Sla noght thy sone, do hym no mysse.   *harm*

| | | |
Take here a schepe thy offerand tyll,   *sheep for your offering*
305 Is sente thee fro the kyng of blisse
That faythfull ay to thee is fone.   *found*
He biddis thee make offerrand of this
Here at this tyme, and saffe thy sone.   *save*

ABRAHAM I lowe that Lord with herte entier   *praise; full heart*
310 That of his luffe this lane me lente,   *love; gift*
To saffe my sone, my darlyng dere,
And sente this schepe to this entente   *intent*
That we sall offir it to thee here;
So sall it be as thou has mente.
315 My sone, be gladde and make goode cheere,
God has till us goode comforte sente.   *to*
He will noght thou be dede,
But tille his lawes take kepe.   *care*
And se, son, in thy stede   *place*
320 God has sente us a schepe.

ISAAC To make oure offerand at his wille
All for oure sake he has it sente.
To lowe that Lorde I halde grete skyll   *praise*
That tylle his menye thus has mente.   *company [of heaven]; intended*
325 This dede I wolde have tane me till   *taken*
Full gladly, Lorde, to thyn entent.

ABRAHAM A, sone, thy bloode wolde he noght spill,
Forthy this shepe thus has he sente,
And, sone, I am full fayne
330 Of our spede in this place,   *benefit*
Bot go we home agayne
And lowe God of his grace.   *praise*

ANGELUS Abraham, Abraham!

ABRAHAM   Loo, here indede.
Harke, sone, sum salvyng of our sare.   *some remedy for; sore*

ANGELUS God sais thou sall have mekill mede   *reward*
336 For thys goode will that thou in ware;
Sen thou for hym wolde do this dede
To spille thy sone and noght to spare
He menes to multiplie youre seede
340 On sides seere, as he saide are.   *many; before*
And yit he hight you this   *promises*
That of youre seede sall ryse

Thurgh helpe of hym and his
Overehand of all enmys.   *Above*

345   Luk ye hym love, this is his liste,   *desire*
      And lelly lyff eftir his laye,   *loyally live; law*
      For in youre seede all mon be bliste   *may be blessed*
      That ther bese borne be nyght or day.
      If ye will in hym trowe or triste,   *believe; trust*
350   He will be with you evere and aye.

ABRAHAM   Full wele wer us and we it wiste   *if we it learn*
      Howe we shulde wirke his will alwaye.

ISAAC   Fadir, that sall we frayne   *ask*
      At wyser men than wee,
355   And fulfille it ful fayne
      Indede eftir oure degree.

ABRAHAM   Nowe, sone, sen we thus wele hase spede,
      That God has graunted me thy liffe,
      It is my wille that thou be wedde
360   And welde a woman to thy wyffe;   *wield (have)*
      So sall thy sede springe and be spredde
      In the lawez of God be reasoune ryffe.   *abundantly*
      I wate in what steede sho is stede   *know in what place she lives*
      That thou sall wedde, withowten stryffe.
365   Rabek, that damysell,   *Rebecca*
      Hir fayrer is none fone,   *found*
      The doughter of Batwell   *Bethuel*
      That was my brothir sone.

ISAAC   Fadir, as thou likes my lyffe to spende,
370   I sall assente unto the same.

ABRAHAM   One of my servandis sone sall I sende
      Unto that birde to brynge hir hame.   *lady; home*
      The gaynest gates now will we wende.   *quickest ways*
      My barnes, yee ar noght to blame   *children (young men)*
375   Yeff ye thynke lang that we her lende.   *linger*
      Gadir same oure gere, in Goddis name,   *Gather together*
      And go we hame agayne
      Evyn unto Barsabé.   *Beer-sheba*
      God that is most of mayne
380   Us wisse and with you be.   *direct*

[11. PHARAOH AND MOSES]

The Hoseers

REX PHARAO O pees, I bidde that no man passe		*peace*
But kepe the cours that I comaunde		
And takes gud heede to hym that hasse		*has*
Youre liff all haly in his hande.		*wholly*
5	Kyng Pharo my fadir was,	
	And led the lordshippe of this lande;	
	I am his hayre as elde will asse,	*heir; as seniority will have it*
	Evere in his steede to styrre and stande.	*place; go about; remain*
	All Egippe is myne awne	*own*
10	To lede aftir my lawe;	*lead*
	I will my myght be knawen	*known*
	And honnoured als it awe.	*ought [to be]*
	Therfore als kyng I commaunde pees	
	To all the pepill of this empire,	
15	That no man putte hym fourthe in prees	*(i.e., contradict [me])*
	But that will do als we desire.	
	And of youre sawes I rede you sees,	*sayings; advise; stop*
	And sesse to me, youre sufferayne sire,	*allot; [as] your sovereign*
	That most youre comforte may encrese,	
20	And at my liste lose liffe and lyre.	*wish; body*
I CONSOLATOR My lorde, yf any were		
	That walde not wirke youre will,	*would; do what you wish*
	And we wist whilke thay were,	*know which*
	Ful sone we sall thaym spill.	*soon; destroy (kill)*
REX Thurghoute my kyngdome wolde I kenn		*would I know*
26	And konne tham thanke that couthe me telle	*give; could*
	If any wer so weryd then	*wrongheaded*
	That wolde aught fande owre forse to fell.	*try; power to bring down*
II CONSOLATOR My Lorde, thar ar a maner of men		
30	That mustirs grete maistris tham emell,	*displays great deeds; among*
	The Jewes that wonnes here in Jessen	*live; Goshen (Vulgate: Gessen)*
	And er named the childir of Israell.	*are*
	They multyplye so faste	
	That suthly we suppose	*truly*
35	Thay are like, and they laste,	*likely, if they continue*
	Yowre lordshippe for to lose.	
REX Why, devill, what gawdes have they begonne,		*tricks*
	Er thai of myght to make afrayse?	*Be; attack*

I Consolator   Tho felons folke, sir, first was fonn   *Those; found [in Egypt]*
40   In kyng Pharo youre fadyr dayse.   *father's days*
       Thay come of Joseph, Jacob sonn,
       That was a prince worthy to prayse,
       And sithen in ryste furthe are they run;   *unchecked (increasing)*
       Now ar they like to lose our layse.   *destroy; laws (customs)*
45   Thay sall confounde us clene
       Bot if thai sonner sese.   *Unless; sooner cease*

Rex   What devill ever may it mene
          That they so fast encrese?

II Consolator   Howe they encrese, full wele we kenn,   *know*
50   Als oure elders before us fande;   *discovered*
       Thay were talde but sexty and ten   *counted*
       Whan thei enterd into this lande.
       Sithen have they sojonerd here in Jessen   *sojourned*
       Foure houndereth yere, this we warande,
55   Now are they noumbered of myghty men
       Wele more than thre hundereth thowsande,
       Withowten wiffe and childe   *Aside from*
       And herdes that kepes ther fee.   *herdsmen; livestock*

Rex   So myght we be bygillid,   *beguiled*
60   Bot certis that sall noght be,
       For with qwantise we sall tham qwelle   *trickery; put down*
       That thei sall no farrar sprede.   *further increase*

I Consolator   Lorde, we have herde oure fadres telle   *heard*
       Howe clerkis, that ful wele couthe rede,   *advise (prophesy)*
65   Saide a man shulde wax tham emell   *grow up; among*
       That suld fordo us and owre dede.   *destroy*

Rex   Fy on tham — to the devell of helle!
          Swilke destanye sall we noght drede.
          We sall make mydwayes to spille tham,   *midwives; kill*
70   Whenne oure Ebrewes are borne,   *Hebrews*
       All that are mankynde to kille tham;   *boy children*
       So sall they sone by lorne.   *be destroyed*

       For of the other have I non awe,   *no fear*
       Swilke bondage sall we to tham bede   *bid*
75   To dyke and delfe, beere and drawe,   *dig; delve, bear (carry); pull*
       And do all swilke unhonest dede.   *degrading deeds (tasks)*
       Thus sall the laddis beholden lawe,   *obey the law*
       Als losellis ever thaire lyff to leede.   *wretches*

II CONSOLATOR   Certis, lorde, this is a sotell sawe,   *subtle saying*
80   So sall the folke no farrar sprede.   *further*

REX   Yaa, helpes to halde tham doune
        That we no fantynse fynde.   *deception*

I CONSOLATOR   Lorde, we sall ever be bowne   *compelled*
        In bondage tham to bynde.

MOYSES   Grete God that all this grounde began
86   And governes evere in gud degree,
        That made me Moyses unto man
        And saved me sythen out of the see.   *thereafter; sea*
        Kyng Pharo he comaunded than
90   So that no sonnes shulde saved be,
        Agayns his wille away I wan,   *slipped away*
        Thus has God shewed his myght in me.
        Nowe am I here to kepe,
        Sett undir Synay syde,   *[Mount] Sinai's slope*
95   The bisshoppe Jetro schepe,   *Jethro's sheep*
        So bettir bute to bide.   *boot (fortune) to wait for*

        A, mercy, God, mekill is thy myght,
        What man may of thy mervayles mene!   *marvels reveal*
        I se yondyr a ful selcouth syght   *spectacular*
100   Wherof befor no synge was seene.   *sign*
        A busk I se yondir brennand bright,   *bush; burning*
        And the leves last ay inlike grene;   *without change*
        If it be werke of worldly wight   *earthly man*
        I will go witte withowten wene.   *find out; doubt*

DEUS   Moyses, come noght to nere   *too*
106   Bot stille in that stede dwelle,   *place stay*
        And take hede to me here
        And tente what I thee telle.   *attend to*

110   I am thy Lorde, withoutyn lak,
        To lengh thi liffe even as me list,   *lengthen; desire*
        And the same God that somtyme spak   *spake*
        Unto thyne elders als thei wiste.   *learned*
        But Abraham and Ysaac
        And Jacob, saide I, suld be bliste   *blessed*
115   And multyplye and tham to mak
        So that ther seede shulde noght be myste.   *missed (lost)*
        And nowe kyng Pharo
        Fuls thare childir ful faste.   *Suppresses*

If I suffir hym soo   *allow; [to do] so*
120   Thare seede shulde sone be past.

To make thee message have I mende   *messenger; meant*
To hym that tham so harmed hase,
To warne hym with wordes hende   *gracious*
So that he lette my pepull passe
125   That they to wildirnesse may wende   *wander*
And wirshippe me als whilom was.   *in the past*
And yf he lenger gar them lende,   *cause; to remain*
His sange ful sone sall be "allas."   *soon*

MOYSES   A, Lord, syth, with thy leve,
130   That lynage loves me noght,   *(royal) line*
Gladly they walde me greve,   *would*
And I slyke boodword brought.   *If I such message*

Therfore, Lord, late sum othir fraste   *let some; attempt*
That hase more forse tham for to feere.   *power to make them afraid*

DEUS   Moyses, be noght abaste   *afraid*
136   My bidding baldely to bere.   *boldly*
If thai with wrang ought walde thee wrayste,   *wrong would try to; deceive*
Owte of all wothis I sall thee were.   *dangers; protect*

MOYSES   We, Lord, thai wil noght to me trayste   *trust*
140   For al the othes that I may swere.   *oaths*
To neven slyke note of newe   *To announce such a matter anew*
To folke of wykkyd will,
Withouten taken trewe,   *token (sign)*
They will noght take tente thertill.   *pay attention*

DEUS   And if they will noght undirstande
146   Ne take heede how I have thee sente,   *Nor*
Before the kyng cast downe thy wande
And it sall seme as a serpent.   *appear*
Sithen take the tayle in thy hande
150   And hardely uppe thou itt hente   *boldly; take*
In the firste state als thou it fande: *found*
So sall it turne be myn entent.   *be changed by*
Hyde thy hande in thy barme,   *bosom*
And as a lepre it sall be like,   *leper*
155   Sithen hale withouten harme.   *Then whole (healed)*
Thi syngnes sall be slyke.   *signs; such*

And if he wil not suffre than   *then*
My pepull for to passe in pees,

I sall send vengeaunce nine or ten   *(i.e., plagues)*
160   To sewe hym sararre or I sesse.   *pursue him more sorrily before I cease*
      Bot the Jewes that wonnes in Jessen
      Sall noght be merked with that messe.   *marked (visited) with; suffering*
      Als lange als thai my lawes will kenne
      Ther comfort sal I evere encresse.

MOYSES   A, Lorde, lovyd be thy wille   *praised*
166   That makes thy folke so free.
      I sall tell tham untill   *to them*
      Als thou telles unto me.

      But to the kyng, Lorde, whan I come
170   And he ask me what is thy name
      And I stande stille than, defe and dum,   *then, deaf and dumb*
      How sal I be withouten blame?

DEUS   I saie thus, *Ego sum qui sum,*   *I am who I am*
      I am he that I am the same;
175   And if thou myght not meve ne mum,   *move; speak (whisper)*
      I sall thee saffe fro synne and shame.   *save*

MOYSES   I undirstande this thyng
      With all the myght in me.

DEUS   Be bolde in my blissyng,
180   Thy belde ay sall I be.   *support*

MOYSES   A, Lorde of lyffe, lere me my layre   *teach; lore*
      That I there tales may trewly tell;   *these matters*
      Unto my frendis nowe will I fayre,   *fare (go)*
      The chosen childre of Israell,
185   To telle tham comforte of ther care   *of comfort for*
      And of there daunger that thei in dwell.

      God mayntayne you and me evermare,
      And mekill myrthe be you emell.   *among*

I PUER   A Moyses, maistir dere,
190   Oure myrthe is al mornyng;   *mourning*
      We are harde halden here   *held*
      Als carls under the kynge.   *slaves*

II PUER   Moyses, we may mourne and myne,   *and ponder*
      Ther is no man us myrthes mase,   *makes*
195   And sen we come al of a kynne   *people (tribe)*
      Ken us som comforte in this case.   *Show*

MOYSES	Beith of youre mornyng blyne,	*Be; mourning done*
	God wil defende you of your fays.	*foes*
	Oute of this woo he will you wynne	*save*
200	To plese hym in more plener place.	*open*
	I sall carpe to the kyng	*talk*
	And fande to make you free.	*try*

III PUER	God sende us gud tythyngis,	
	And allway with you be.	

MOYSES	Kyng Pharo, to me take tent.	*pay attention*

REX	Why, what tydyngis can thou tell?	

MOYSES	Fro God of heven thus am I sente	
208	To fecche his folke of Israll;	*Israel*
	To wildirnesse he walde thei wente.	*wished that they*

REX	Yaa, wende thou to the devell of hell!	
211	I make no force howe thou has mente,	*consider irrelevant what*
	For in my daunger sall thei dwelle.	*subjection*
	And faytour, for thy sake,	*liar*
	Thei sall be putte to pyne.	*suffering*

MOYSES	Thanne will God vengeaunce take	
216	On thee and on al thyne.	

REX	Fy on thee, ladde, oute of my lande.	
	Wenes thou with wiles to lose oure laye?	*Think; destroy; law*
	Where is this warlowe with his wande	*(i.e., Who); warlock (wizard)*
220	That wolde thus wynne oure folke away?	

II CONSOLATOR	It is Moyses, we wele warrand,	
	Agayne al Egipte is he ay.	*Against*
	Youre fadir grete faute in hym fande,	*fault; found*
	Nowe will he marre you if he may.	*injure*

REX	Nay, nay, that daunce is done:	
226	That lordan leryd overe late.	*rascal (fool)*

MOYSES	God biddis thee graunte my bone,	*request*
	And late me go my gate.	*let; way*

REX	Biddis God me? Fals lurdayne, thou lyes.	*worthless fellow*
230	What takyn talde he, toke thou tent?	*sign told (revealed); notice*

Moyses Yaa, sir, he saide thou suld despise   *should*
    Botht me and all his comaundement.
    In thy presence kast on this wise   *cast*
    My wande he bad by his assent,   *bade*
235 And that thou shulde thee wele avise   *consider*
    Howe it shulde turne to a serpent.
    And in his haly name
    Here sal I ley it downe —   *lay*
239 Loo, ser, se her the same.

Rex A, dogg, the devyll thee drowne!

Moyses He saide that I shulde take the tayle
    So for to prove his poure playne,   *power*
    And sone he saide it shuld not fayle
    For to turne a wande agayne.
245 Loo, sir, behalde.   *behold*

Rex   Hopp, illa hayle,   *(i.e., Ill luck befall [you])*
    Now certis this is a sotill swayne.   *tricky fellow (trickster)*
    But this boyes sall byde here in oure bayle,   *captivity*
    For all thair gaudis sall noght tham gayne.   *tricks*
    Bot warse, both morne and none   *worse; noon*
250 Sall thei fare for thy sake.

Moyses God sende sum vengeaunce sone,
    And on thi werke take wrake.   *vengeance*

I Egiptius. Allas, allas, this lande is lorne,   *destroyed*
    On lif we may no lenger lende.   *no longer be*

II Egiptius So grete myscheffe is made sen morne,
256 Ther may no medycyne us amende.

I Consolator Sir kyng, we banne that we wer borne;   *curse*
    Oure blisse is all with bales blende.   *sorrow mixed up*

Rex Why crys you swa, laddis, liste you scorne?   *do you ridicule*

I Egiptius Sir kyng, slyk care was nevere kende.   *known*
261 Oure watir that was ordand   *ordained*
    To men and beestis fudde;   *food*
    Thurghoute al Egipte lande
    Is turned to rede blude.   *blood*

265 Full ugly and ful ill is it   *horrible; foul*
    That was ful faire and fresshe before.

REX   This is grete wondir for to witt   *know*
          Of all the werkis that ever wore.

II EGIPTIUS   Nay, lorde, ther is anothir yitt   *yet*
270   That sodenly sewes us ful sore,   *afflicts*
          For tadys and frosshis we may not flitte,   *toads; frogs; move (escape)*
          Thare venym loses lesse and more.   *venom destroys*

I EGIPTIUS   Lorde, grete myses bothe morn and none   *gnats*
          Bytis us full bittirlye,
275   And we hope al by done   *assume all is done*
          By Moyses, oure enemye.

I CONSOLATOR   Lorde, whills we with this menyhe meve   *company move*
          Mon never myrthe be us emange.   *Shall; joy; among*

REX   Go, saie we sall no lenger greve,   *oppress [them]*
280   But thai sall nevere the tytar gange.   *sooner go*

II EGIPTIUS   Moyses, my lord has grauntyd leve   *leave*
          At lede thy folk to likyng lande   *To lead; promised land*
          So that we mende of oure myscheve.

MOYSES   I wate ful wele thar wordes er wrange,
285   That sall ful sone be sene,
          For hardely I hym heete   *boldly; promise*
          And he of malice mene,   *If*
          Mo mervaylles mon he mett.   *will he encounter*

I EGIPTIUS   Lorde, allas, for dule we dye;   *dole*
290   We dar not loke oute at no dore.   *any door*

REX   What devyll ayles yow so to crye?

II EGIPTIUS   We fare nowe werre than evere we fare.   *worse; fared*
          Grete loppis overe all this lande thei flye   *fleas (see note)*
          That with bytyng makis mekill blure.   *lamenting*

I EGIPTIUS   Lorde, oure beestis lyes dede and dry   *dried up*
296   Als wele on myddyng als on more.   *manure pile; moor*
          Both oxe, horse, and asse
          Fallis dede doune sodanly.

REX   Therof no man harme has
300   Halfe so mekill as I.

II CONSOLATOR Yis, lorde, poure men has mekill woo   *poor*
    To see ther catell be out cast.   *destroyed*
    The Jewes in Jessen faren noght soo;
    They have al likyng in to last.   *(i.e., they continue in felicity)*

REX Go, saie we giffe tham leve to goo   *give*
306 To tyme there parellis be overpast,   *Until their perils*
    But or thay flitte overfarre us froo   *ere*
    We sall garre feste tham foure so fast.   *have them bound four times as fast*

II EGIPTIUS Moyses, my lord giffis leve
310 Thy men for to remewe.   *leave*

MOYSES He mon have more mischeff
    But if his tales be trewe.   *Unless*

I EGIPTIUS We, lorde, we may not lede this liffe.

REX Why, is ther grevaunce growen agayne?

II EGIPTIUS Swilke poudre, lord, apon us dryffe,   *powder (ash); drives (blows)*
316 That whare it bettis it makis a blayne.   *boil*

I EGIPTIUS Like mesellis makis it man and wyffe.   *a skin disease (leprosy)*
    Sythen ar they hurte with hayle and rayne
    Oure wynes in mountaynes may noght thryve,   *vines*
320 So ar they threst and thondour-slayne.   *beaten down*

REX How do thay in Jessen,
    The Jewes, can ye aught say?

II EGIPTIUS This care nothyng they ken,   *suffering; show*
    Thay fele no such affray.   *feel; ill-fortune*

REX No, devill, and sitte they so in pees
326 And we ilke day in doute and drede?

I EGIPTIUS My lorde, this care will evere encrese
    Tille Moyses have leve them to lede.   *lead [away]*

I CONSOLATOR Lorde, war they wente, than walde it sese,   *if they; cease*
330 So shuld we save us and oure seede;   *descendants*
    Ellis be we lorne, this is no lese.   *lie*

REX Late hym do fourth, the devill hym spede!   *Allow*
    For his folke sall no ferre   *further*
    Yf he go welland woode.   *raving mad*

II CONSOLATOR Than will itt sone be warre,   *worse*
336   Yit war bettir thai yoode.   *went*

II EGIPTIUS We, lorde, new harme is comon to hande.

REX No, devill, will itt no bettir be?

I EGIPTIUS Wilde wormes is laide overe all this lande;   *locusts*
340   Thai leve no frute ne floure on tree;   *fruit; flower*
       Agayne that storme may nothyng stande.   *Against*

II EGIPTIUS Lord, ther is more myscheff, thynk me,
       And thre daies hase itt bene durand   *enduring*
       So myrke that non myght othir see.   *dark*

I EGIPTIUS My lorde, grete pestelence
346   Is like ful lange to last.   *likely*

REX Owe, come that in oure presence,   *Alas*
       Than is oure pride al past.

II EGIPTIUS My lorde, this vengeaunce lastis lange,
350   And mon till Moyses have his bone.   *shall; wish*

I CONSOLATOR Lorde, late tham wende, else wirke we wrang;   *go away*
       It may not helpe to hover na hone.   *hesitate or delay*

REX Go, saie we graunte tham leve to gange,   *go*
       In the devill way, sen itt bus be done,   *must be*
355   For so may fall we sall tham fang   *it may happen; capture*
       And marre tham or tomorne at none.   *before noon tomorrow*

I EGIPTIUS Moyses, my lorde has saide
       Thou sall have passage playne.

MOYSES And to passe am I paied,   *rewarded*
360   My frendes, bees nowe fayne;   *glad*

       For at oure will now sall we wende   *as we will*
       In lande of lykyng for to lende.   *live (stay)*

I PUER Kyng Pharo, that felowns fende,
       Will have grete care fro this be kende,   *anger; known*
365   Than will he schappe hym us to shende,   *intend; destroy*
       And sone his ooste aftir us sende.   *host (soldiers)*

Moyses   Beis noght aferde, God is youre frende,
      Fro alle oure fooes he will us fende.   *defend*
      Tharfore comes furthe with me,
370   Haves done, and drede yow noght.

II Puer   My Lorde, loved mott thou bee,   *praised*
      That us fro bale has brought.

III Puer   Swilke frenshippe never before we fande,
      But in this faire defautys may fall.   *matter disasters*
375   The Rede See is ryght nere at hande;
      Ther bus us bide to we be thrall.   *must we wait until; captured*

Moyses   I sall make us way with my wande,
      For God hase sayde he save us sall.
      On aythir syde the see sall stande
380   Tille we be wente, right as a wall.
      Therfore have ye no drede
      But faynde ay God to plese.   *strive*

I Puer   That Lorde to lande us lede,   *lead*
      Now wende we all at esse.   *ease*

I Egiptius   Kyng Pharro, ther folke er gane.   *gone*

Rex   Howe nowe, es ther any noyes of newe?   *news*

II Egiptius   The Ebrowes er wente ilkone.   *are gone everyone*

Rex   How sais thou that?

I Egiptius   Ther talis er trewe.   *tales*

Rex   Horse harneys tyte, that thei be tane;   *quickly; taken*
390   This ryott radly sall tham rewe.   *disturbance soon; be sorry*
      We sall not sese or they be slone,   *slain*
      For to the se we sall tham sew.   *pursue*
      Do charge oure charyottis swithe   *quickly*
      And frekly folowes me.   *speedily*

II Egiptius   My lorde, we are full blithe
396   At youre biddyng to be.

II Consolator   Lorde, to youre biddyng we er boune,   *are bound*
      Owre bodies baldely for to bede;   *boldly; offer*
      We sall noght byde but dyng tham doune   *abide; strike*
      Tylle all be dede, withouten drede.

REX Hefe uppe youre hartis ay to Mahownde,   *Heave; Mohammed*
401   He will be nere us in oure nede.
       Owte, ay herrowe, devill, I drowne!   *(cry of distress)*

I EGIPTIUS Allas, we dye, for alle our dede.   *deeds (actions)*

I PUER Now ar we wonne fra waa   *have we escaped from woe*
405   And saved oute of the see.   *the [Red] sea*
       Cantemus domino,   *Let us sing to the Lord*
       To God a sange synge wee.

[12. THE ANNUNCIATION TO MARY AND THE VISITATION]

The Spicers

DOCTOUR Lord God, grete mervell es to mene   *is to tell*
       Howe man was made withouten mysse   *sin*
       And sette whare he sulde ever have bene
       Withouten bale, bidand in blisse,   *sorrow, abiding*
5   And howe he lost that comforth clene
       And was putte oute fro paradys,
       And sithen what sorouse sor warr sene   *then; sorrows sore were*
       Sente unto hym and to al his;
       And howe they lay lange space   *a long time*
10   In helle, lokyn fro lyght,   *locked (shut off)*
       Tille God graunted tham grace
       Of helpe, als he hadde hyght.   *promised*

       Than is it nedfull for to neven   *tell*
       How prophettis all Goddis counsailes kende,   *revealed*
15   Als prophet Amos in his steven   *bidding (voice)*
       Lered whils he in his liffe gun lende: *Taught while he was alive*
       Deus pater disposuit salutem fieri in medio terre, etc.[1]
       He sais thus, God the Fadir in heven
       Ordand in erthe mankynde to mende,   *Ordained*
20   And to grayth it with Godhede even,   *cause it to be*
       His Sone he saide that he suld sende
       To take kynde of mankyn   *the nature*
       In a mayden full mylde.
       So was many saved of syn   *sin*
25   And the foule fende begyled.   *beguiled*

---

[1] *God the Father will grant salvation in the midst of the earth, etc.*

	And for the feende sulde so be fedd	*should*
	Be tyne, and to no treuth take tentt,	*anger; (i.e., be self-deceived)*
	God made that mayden to be wedded	
	Or he his Sone unto hir sentte.	*Before*
30	So was the Godhede closed and cledde	*clad*
	In wede of weddyng whare thy wente,	*wedding garment*
	And that oure blisse sulde so be bredde	*brought about*
	Ful many materes may be mente:	
	Quoniam in semine tuo benedicentur omnes gentes, etc.[1]	
35	God hymself sayde this thynge	
	To Abraham als hym liste:	
	Of thy sede sall uppe sprynge	*seed*
	Wharein folke sall be bliste.	*blessed*
	To prove thes prophetts ordande er,	*ordained before*
40	Als Isay, unto olde and yenge,	*Isaiah; young*
	He moved oure myscheves for to merr,	*spoke of; impair*
	For thus he prayed God for this thynge,	
	Rorate celi desuper,	*Drop down, dew, from heaven*
	Lord, late thou doune at thy likyng	*let; descend*
45	The dewe to fall fro heven so ferre,	
	For than the erthe sall sprede and sprynge	
	A seede that us sall save,	
	That nowe in blisse are bente.	*inclined toward bliss*
	Of clerkis whoso will crave,	*ask*
50	Thus may ther gatis be mente.	*(i.e., matters bespoken of)*
	The dewe to the gode Haly Gaste	
	May be remened in mannes mynde,	*compared*
	The erthe unto the mayden chaste,	
	Bycause sho comes of erthely kynde.	
55	Thir wise wordis ware noght wroght in waste	*were; formed in vain*
	To waffe and wende away als wynde,	
	For this same prophett sone in haste	*soon*
	Saide forthermore, als folkes may fynde,	
	Propter hoc dabit dominus ipse vobis signum, etc.[2]	
60	Loo, he sais thus, God sall gyffe	*give*
	Hereof a syngne to see	*sign*
	Tille all that lely lyffe	*loyally live*
	And this thare sygne sal be,	*sign*
	Ecce virgo concipiett, and pariet filium, etc.[3]	

---

[1] *Because in thy seed shall all the nations be blessed, etc.*

[2] *Therefore the Lord himself shall give you a sign, etc.*

[3] *Behold a virgin shall conceive, and bear a son, etc.*

65 Loo, he sais a mayden mon   *may*
    Here on this molde mankynde omell,   *earth; among*
    Ful clere consayve and bere a Sonne   *Without guilt conceive*
    And neven his name Emanuell.
    His kyngdom that evere is begonne,
70 Sall never sese, but dure and dwell.   *endure*
    On David sege thore sall he wonne,   *David's throne there*
    His domes to deme and trueth to telle: *judgments to pronounce*
    Zelus domini faciet hoc, etc.   *The zeal of the Lord will perform this, etc.*
    He says, luffe of oure Lorde,   *love*
75 All this sall ordan thanne   *ordain*
    That mennes pees and accorde   *intends*
    To make with erthely manne.

    More of this maiden meves me.   *I [will] speak about*
    This prophett sais for oure socoure,
80 *Egredietur virga de Jesse,*   *And there will come forth a rod of [the root of] Jesse*
    A wande sall brede of Jesse boure.   *rod; grow from Jesse's bower (lineage)*
    And of this same also, sais hee,
    Upponne that wande sall springe a floure   *flower*
    Wheron the Haly Gast sall be
85 To governe it with grete honnoure.
    That wande meynes untill us   *signifies for us*
    This mayden, even and morne,   *evening*
    And the floure is Jesus,
    That of that blyst bees borne.   *blessed [maiden] is*

90 The prophet Johell, a gentill Jewe,   *Joel*
    Somtyme has saide of the same thyng:
    He likenes Criste even als he knewe
    Like to the dewe in doune-commyng: *descending*
    Ero quasi ros, et virgo Israell germinabit sicut lilium.[1]
95 The maiden of Israell al newe,
    He sais, sall bere one and forthe brynge
    Als the lelly floure, full faire of hewe,   *lily flower; hue*
    This meynes sa to olde and yenge   *means so; young*
    That the hegh Haly Gaste   *high*
100 Come oure myscheffe to mende   *[Will] come*
    In Marie mayden chaste,
    When God his Sone walde sende.   *would*

    This lady is to the lilly lyke,   *comparable to*
    That is bycause of hir clene liffe,
105 For in this worlde was never slyke   *[anyone] like [her]*

----

[1] *I will be as the dew, Israel shall spring as the lily*

	One to be mayden, modir, and wyffe:	*virgin, mother*
	And hir Sonne, kyng in heven ryke,	*kingdom*
	Als oft es red be reasoune ryfe,	*is advised by; abundant*
	And hir husband bath maistir and meke,	*both; companion*
110	In charité to stynte all striffe.	*to end*
	This passed all worldly witte,	*knowing*
	How God had ordand thaim thanne	
	In hir one to be knytte:	*joined as one*
	Godhed, maydenhed, and manne.	

115	Bot of this werke grete witnes was	
	With formefaders, all folke may tell.	*patriarchs*
	Whan Jacob blyst his sone Judas,	*blessed; Judah*
	He tolde the tale thaim two emell:	*narrative; among*
	Non auferetur septrum de Juda,	
120	*donec veniat qui mittendus est.*[1]	
	He sais the septer sall noght passe	
	Fra Juda lande of Israell,	*Judah*
	Or he comme that God ordand has	*Before he comes*
	To be sente feendis force to fell:	*the fiend's*
125	*Et ipse erit expectacio gencium.*	*And he will be the expectation of the nations*
	Hym sall alle folke abyde	*await*
	And stande unto his steven,	*be obedient to; voice*
	Ther sawes wer signified	*sayings; predicted*
	To Crist, Goddis Sone in heven.	

130	For howe he was sente, se we more,	
	And howe God wolde his place purvay,	*provide*
	He saide, Sonne, I sall sende byfore	
	Myne aungell to rede thee thy way:	*prepare*
	Ecce mitto angelum meum ante faciem	
135	*tuam qui preparabit viam tuam ante te.*[2]	
	Of John Baptist he menyd thore,	*spake there*
	For in erthe he was ordand ay	
	To warne the folke that wilsom wore	*were in error*
	Of Cristis comyng, and thus gon say:	
140	*Ego quidem baptizo in aqua vos, autem*	
	baptizabimini spiritu sancto.[3]	
	Eftir me sall come nowe	*After*
	A man of myghtis mast,	*great power*
	And sall baptis yowe	
145	In the high Holy Gast.	

---

[1] Lines 119–20: *The scepter shall not be taken away from Judah / till he come that is to be sent.*

[2] Lines 134–35: *Behold I send my angel before thy face, / who shall prepare the way before thee.*

[3] Lines 140–41: *I indeed baptize you in water, but / you will be baptized in the Holy Spirit.*

Thus of Cristis commyng may we see
How Sainte Luke spekis in his gospell,
Fro God in heven es sent, sais he,
An aungell is named Gabriell
150 To Nazareth in Galale,   *Galilee*
Where than a mayden mylde gon dwell,   *then; did*
That with Joseph suld wedded be;   *should*
Hir name is Marie, thus gan he telle.   *began; to tell*
How God his grace than grayd   *prepared*
155 To man in this manere,
And how the aungell saide,
Takes hede, all that will here.   *hear*

        Tunc cantat angelus.   *Then the angel shall sing*

ANGELUS Hayle, Marie, full of grace and blysse,
Oure Lord God is with thee
160 And has chosen thee for his.
Of all women blist mot thou be.   *blessed may*

MARIA What maner of halsyng is this   *greeting*
Thus prevely comes to me?   *privately*
For in myn herte a thoght it is,
165 The tokenyng that I here see.   *sign*

        Tunc cantat angelus, Ne timeas, Maria.   *Then the angel shall sing, "Do not fear, Mary"*

ANGELUS Ne drede thee noght, thou mylde Marie,
For nothyng that may befalle,
For thou has fun soveranly   *been found surpassingly*
At God a grace over othir all.   *By God*
170 In chastité of thy bodye
Consayve and bere a childe thou sall.
This bodword brynge I thee, forthy   *message*
His name Jesu sall thou calle.

Mekill of myght than sall he bee;   *then*
175 He sall be God and called God Sonn.
David sege, his fadir free,   *throne; gracious forefather*
Sall God hym giffe to sytte uppon,   *give*
Als kyng forever regne sall hee,
In Jacob house ay for to wonne.   *dwell*
180 Of his kyngdome and dignité
Shall noo man erthly knaw ne con.   *can*

MARIA Thou Goddis aungell, meke and mylde,
Howe sulde it be, I thee praye,

That I sulde consayve a childe
185   Of any man by nyght or daye?
I knawe no man that shulde have fyled   *defiled*
My maydenhode, the sothe to saye.   *truth*
Withouten will of werkis wilde   *uncontrolled behavior*
In chastité I have ben ay.

Angelus   The Holy Gast in thee sall lighte,
191   Hegh vertue sall to thee holde,   *High*
The holy birthe of thee so bright,
God Sonne he sall be calde.
Loo, Elyzabeth, thi cosyne, ne myght
195   In elde consayve a childe for alde;   *because of old age*
This is the sexte moneth full ryght
To hir that baran has ben talde.   *barren; counted*

Maria   Thou aungell, blissid messanger,
Of Goddis will I holde me payde: *rewarded*
200   I love my Lorde with herte clere,
The grace that he has for me layde.   *established*
Goddis handmayden, lo, me here
To his wille all redy grayd,   *prepared*
Be done to me of all manere
205   Thurgh thy worde als thou hast saide.

Now God, that all oure hope is in,
Thur the myght of the Haly Gaste,   *Through*
Save thee, dame, fro sak of synne   *accusation*
And wisse thee fro all werkis wast.   *guide; away from; impure*
210   Elyzabeth, myn awne cosyne,
Methoght I coveyte alway mast   *most*
To speke with thee of all my kynne;
Therfore I comme thus in this hast.

Elizabeth   A, welcome, mylde Marie,
215   Myne aughen cosyne so dere,   *own*
Joifull woman am I
That I nowe see thee here.
Blissid be thou anely
Of all women in feere,   *company*
220   And the frute of thy body
Be blissid ferre and nere.

This is joyfull tydyng
That I may nowe here see
The modyr of my Lord Kyng,   *mother*
225   Thusgate come to me.   *In this way*

Sone als the voyce of thine haylsing   *greeting*
Moght myn neres entreand be   *Might; ears entering*
The childe in my wombe so yenge   *young*
Makes grete myrthe unto thee.

MARIA Nowe, Lorde, blist be thou ay
231   For the grace thou has me lente;
Lorde, I lofe thee, God verray,   *praise*
The sande thou hast me sente.   *message*
I thanke thee nyght and day
235   And prayes with goode entente   *praise*
Thou make me to thy paye,   *liking*
To thee my wille is wentte.

ELIZABETH Blissed be thou grathely grayed   *appropriately ready*
To God thurgh chastité,
240   Thou trowed and helde thee payed   *trusted*
Atte his wille for to bee.
All that to thee is saide
Fro my Lorde so free,   *From*
Swilke grace is for thee layde   *stored up*
245   Sall be fulfilled in thee.

MARIA To his grace I will me ta,   *take*
With chastité to dele,   *(i.e., maintain)*
That made me thus to ga   *go*
Omange his maidens feele.   *Among; many*
250   My saule sall lovyng ma   *praise*
Unto that Lorde so lele,   *true*
And my gast make joye alswa   *spirit; joy always*
In God that es my hele.   *health*

Tunc cantat Magnificat.   *Then she sings "[My soul] doth magnify [the Lord]"*

[13. JOSEPH'S TROUBLES ABOUT MARY]

The Pewteres and Foundours

JOSEPH Of grete mornyng may I me mene   *mourning; speak*
And walke full werily be this way,   *by*
For nowe than wende I best hafe bene   *(i.e., I'd rather have)*
Att ease and reste by reasonne ay.
5   For I am of grete elde,   *age*
Wayke and al unwelde,   *Weak; feeble*
Als ilke man se it maye.   *every man*
I may nowder buske ne belde,   *move easily; stay*

	But owther in frithe or felde.	*wood*
10	For shame what sall I saie,	
	That thusgates nowe on myne alde dase	*in this way; old days*
	Has wedded a yonge wenche to my wiff,	
	And may noght wele tryne over two strase?	*step; straws*
	Nowe, Lorde, how lange sall I lede this liff,	
15	My banes er hevy als lede	*bones; lead*
	And may noght stande in stede	*place*
	Als kende it is full ryfe.	*perceived; in every way*
	Now, Lorde, thou me wisse and rede,	
	Or sone me dryve to dede,	*soon*
20	Thou may best stynte this striffe.	*stop*
	For bittirly than may I banne	*curse*
	The way I in the Temple wente,	
	Itt was to me a bad barganne,	
	For reuthe I may it ay repente.	*shame*
25	For tharein was ordande	
	Unwedded men sulde stande	
	Al sembled at asent,	*assembled as agreed*
	And ilke ane a drye wande	*each one*
	On heght helde in his hand,	*Up high*
30	And I ne wist what it ment.	*knew*
	In mange al othir ane bare I,	*Among; one*
	Itt florisshed faire and floures on sprede,	*bloomed*
	And thay saide to me forthy	
	That with a wiffe I sulde be wedde.	
35	The bargayne I made thare,	
	That rewes me nowe full sare,	*repent; sore*
	So am I straytely sted.	*(i.e., in trouble)*
	Now castes itt me in care,	*conflict*
	For wele I myght everemare	
40	Anlepy life have led.	*A single*
	Hir werkis me wyrkis my wonges to wete.	*doings cause me; cheeks*
	I am begiled, how wate I noght.	*know*
	My yonge wiffe is with childe full grete,	
	That makes me nowe sorowe unsoght.	
45	That reproffe nere has slayne me.	*disgrace nearly*
	Forthy giff any man frayne me	*if; question*
	How this thing might be wroght,	
	To gabbe yf I wolde payne me,	*talk*
	The lawe standis harde agayns me,	
50	To dede I mon be broght.	*death I might*

	And lathe methinketh, on the todir syde,	*loath*
	My wiff with any man to defame	
	And whethir of there twa that I bide,	*which of these two*
	I mon noght scape withouten schame.	*escape*
55	The childe certis is noght myne;	
	That reproffe dose me pyne	*reproof causes me pain*
	And gars me fle fra hame.	*makes; from home*
	My liff gif I shuld tyne,	*if; lose*
	Sho is a clene virgine	
60	For me, withouten blame.	
	But wele I wate thurgh prophicie,	*know*
	A maiden clene suld bere a childe,	
	But it is nought sho, sekirly,	
	Forthy I wate I am begiled.	
65	And why ne walde som yonge man take her?	*wouldn't*
	For certis I thynke over ga hir	*(i.e., to forsake her)*
	Into som wodes wilde.	*woods*
	Thus thynke I to stele fra hir;	*steal away from*
	God childe ther wilde bestes sla hir,	*shield; slay*
70	She is so meke and mylde.	
	Of my wendyng wil I none warne,	*tell*
	Neverethelees it is myne entente	*intention*
	To aske hir who gate hir that barne,	*made her (pregnant with); child*
	Yitt wolde I witte fayne or I went.	*know; before*
75	All hayle, God be hereinne.	

I PUELLA Welcome, by Goddis dere myght.

JOSEPH Whare is that yonge virgine,
Marie, my berde so bright?   *lady*

I PUELLA Certis, Joseph, ye sall undirstande
80   That sho is not full farre you fra.   *very far from you*
        Sho sittis at hir boke full faste prayand   *book*
        For you and us, and for all tha   *those*
        That oght has nede.
        But for to telle hir will I ga
85   Of youre comyng, withouten drede.
        Have done, and rise uppe, dame,
        And to me take gud hede:
        Joseph, he is comen hame.

MARIA Welcome, als God me spede.

90　Dredles to me he is full dere,　　　　　　　　　　　*Doubtless*
　　Joseph my spouse, welcome er yhe.　　　　　　　　*are you*

JOSEPH　Gramercy, Marie, saie what chere,
　　Telle me the soth, how est with thee?　　　　　　*how is it*
　　Wha has ben there?　　　　　　　　　　　　　　*Who*
95　Thy wombe is waxen grete, thynke me;
　　Thou arte with barne, allas, for care.
　　A, maidens, wa worthe you　　　　　　　　　*woe do you deserve*
　　That lete hir lere swilke lare.　　　　　　　　*let her learn such lore*

II PUELLA　Joseph, ye sall noght trowe　　　　　*believe*
100　In hir no febill fare.　　　　　　　　　　*no [moral] weakness*

JOSEPH　Trowe it noght arme? Lefe wenche, do way.　*harm; Leave*
　　Hir sidis shewes she is with childe.
　　Whose ist, Marie?

MARIA　　　　　　　Sir, Goddis and youres.

JOSEPH　　　　　　　　　　　　Nay, nay,
　　Now wate I wele I am begiled,　　　　　　　*I know well*
105　And reasoune why?
　　With me flesshely was thou nevere fylid,　　　*defiled*
　　And I forsake it here forthy.
　　Say, maidens, how es this?
　　Tels me the sothe, rede I,　　　　　　　　　*advise*
110　And but ye do, iwisse,
　　The bargayne sall ye aby.　　　　　　　　　*pay for*

II PUELLA　If ye threte als faste as yhe can,
　　Thare is noght to saie theretill,
　　For trulye her come never no man　　　　　　*here came*
115　To waite her body with non ill　　　　　　　*shame*
　　Of this swete wight.
　　For we have dwelt ay with hir still,
　　And was nevere fro hir day nor nyght.
　　Hir kepars have we bene
120　And sho ay in oure sight,
　　Come here no man bytwene
　　To touche that berde so bright.　　　　　　　*lady*

I PUELLA　Na, here come no man in there wanes,　*walls*
　　And that evere witnesse will we,
125　Save an aungell ilke a day anes　　　　　　　*once*
　　With bodily foode hir fedde has he,
　　Othir come nane.　　　　　　　　　　　　　*none*

	Wharfore we ne wate how it shulde be,	*know*
	But thurgh the Haly Gaste allane.	
130	For trewly we trowe this,	*believe*
	Is grace with hir is gane,	*His grace is with her*
	For sho wroght nevere no mys,	*sin*
	We witnesse evere ilkane.	

JOSEPH   Thanne se I wele youre menyng is:

135	The aungell has made hir with childe.	
	Nay, som man in aungellis liknesse	
	With somkyn gawde has hir begiled,	*trick*
	And that trow I.	*know*
	Forthy nedes noght swilke wordis wilde	*irrational*
140	At carpe to me dissayvandly.	*speak; deceivingly*
	We, why gab ye me swa	*chatter; so*
	And feynes swilk fantassy?	*feign*
	Allas, me is full wa,	*of woe*
	For dule why ne myght I dy?	*dole*

145	To me this is a careful cas.	*sorrowful*
	Rekkeles I raffe, refte is my rede,	*rave; (i.e., my peace is compromised)*
	I dare loke no man in the face,	
	Derfely, for dole why ne were I dede.	*Unhappily*
	Me lathis my liff!	*I loathe*
150	In Temple and in othir stede	*place*
	Ilke man till hethyng will me dryff.	*Each man to scorn; drive*
	Was never wight sa wa,	*man so [full of] woe*
	For ruthe I all to ryff,	*(i.e., am wounded [in heart])*
	Allas, why wroght thou swa,	
155	Marie, my weddid wiffe?	

| **MARIA**   To my witnesse grete God I call, | |
| | That in mynde wroght nevere na mysse. | *error (sin)* |

JOSEPH   Whose is the childe thou arte withall?

MARIA   Youres, sir, and the kyngis of blisse.

JOSEPH Ye, and hoo than?	*how*
161 Na selcouthe tythandis than is this,	*No more marvelous*
	Excuse tham wele there women can.	*(i.e., these)*
	But, Marie, all that sese thee	*see*
	May witte thi werkis ere wan:	*sinful*
165	Thy wombe allway it wreyes thee	*betrays*
	That thou has mette with man.	

Whose is it, als faire mot thee befall?

MARIA Sir, it is youres and Goddis will.

JOSEPH Nay, I ne have noght ado withall.
170 Neme it na more to me, be still. *Name*
Thou wate als wele as I
That we two same flesshly *together carnally*
Wroght never swilk werkis with ill.
Loke thou dide no folye
175 Before me prevely *secretly*
Thy faire maydenhede to spill.

But who is the fader? telle me his name.

MARIA None but youreselfe.

JOSEPH   Late be, for shame. *Let*
I did it nevere, thou dotist, dame, by bukes and belles, *you talk foolishly; books*
180 Full sakles shulde I bere this blame aftir thou telles, *innocent*
For I wroght nevere in worde nor dede
Thyng that shulde marre thy maydenhede
To touche me till.
For of slyk note war litill nede, *such business*
185 Yhitt for myn awne I wolde it fede, *feed*
Might all be still. *kept quiet*
Tharfore the fadir tell me, Marie.

MARIA But God and yhow, I knawe right nane.

JOSEPH A, slike sawes mase me full sarye *such words amaze; sorry*
190 With grete mornyng to make my mane; *moan*
Therfore be noght so balde *bold*
That no slike tales be talde, *told*
But halde thee stille als stane. *stone*
Thou art yonge and I am alde, *old*
195 Slike werkis yf I do walde, *would (be willing to) do*
Thase games fra me are gane. *gone*

Therfore, telle me in privité,
Whos is the childe thou is with nowe?
Sertis, ther sall non witte but we; *know*
200 I drede the law als wele as thou.

MARIA Nowe grete God of his myght,
That all may dresse and dight, *undertake; do*
Mekely to thee I bowe.
Rewe on this wery wight *Have compassion; unhappy man*

205   That in his herte myght light
       The soth to ken and trowe.   *know; trust*

JOSEPH   Who had thy maydenhede, Marie? Has thou oght mynde?   *memory*

MARIA   Forsuth, I am a mayden clene.

JOSEPH   Nay, thou spekis now agayne kynde.   *nature*
210   Slike thing myght nevere na man of mene,   *no; (i.e., assert)*
       A maiden to be with childe!
       Thase werkis fra thee ar wilde,   *mad*
       Sho is not borne, I wene.   *think*

MARIA   Joseph, yhe ar begiled:
215   With synne was I never filid,   *defiled*
       Goddis sande is on me sene.   *message; seen*

JOSEPH   Goddis sande, yha Marie, God helpe,
       Bot certis, that childe was nevere oures twa.   *together*
       But womankynde gif tham list yhelpe,   *if they desire*
220   Yhitt walde thei na man wiste ther wa.   *Yet; know; woe*

MARIA   Sertis, it is Goddis sande,
       .   .   .   [line missing]
       That sall I never ga fra.

JOSEPH   Yha, Marie, drawe thyn hande,   *(i.e., stop talking)*
       For forther yitt will I fande,   *go*
225   I trowe not it be swa.

       The soth fra me gif that thou layne,   *if; conceal*
       The childebering may thou noght hyde;
       But sitte stille here tille I come agayne,
       Me bus an erand here beside.

MARIA   Now, grete God he you wisse   *direct*
231   And mende you of your mysse   *error*
       Of me, what so betyde.
       Als he is kyng of blisse,
       Sende yhou som seand of this,   *message*
235   In truth that ye might bide.

JOSEPH   Nowe, Lord God, that all thing may
       At thyne awne will bothe do and dresse,   *undertake*
       Wisse me now som redy way   *Direct*
       To walke here in this wildirnesse.
240   Bot or I passe this hill,   *But before*

Do with me what God will,
Owther more or lesse;   *Either*
Here bus me bide full stille   *must; abide*
Till I have slepid my fille.   *slept*
245   Myn hert so hevy it is.

ANGELUS   Waken, Joseph, and take bettir kepe
To Marie, that is thi felawe fest.   *fast*

JOSEPH   A, I am full werie, lefe, late me slepe,   *sir, let*
Forwandered and walked in this forest.   *Worn out with wandering and walking*

ANGELUS   Rise uppe and slepe na mare,
251   Thou makist her herte full sare
That loves thee alther best.   *the very best of all*

JOSEPH   We, now es this a farly fare,   *wondrous matter*
For to be cached bathe here and thare,   *pursued both*
255   And nowhere may have rest.

Say, what arte thou, telle me this thyng?

ANGELUS   I, Gabriell, Goddis aungell full even,
That has tane Marie to my kepyng   *taken*
And sente es thee to say with steven   *is; voice*
260   In lele wedlak thou lede thee;   *true wedlock*
Leffe hir noght, I forbid thee,   *Leave*
Na syn of hir thou neven,   *No sin; speak*
But tille hir fast thou spede thee   *to*
And of hir noght thou drede thee,
265   It is Goddis sande of heven.   *message from*

The childe that sall be borne of her,
Itt is consayved of the Haly Gast.
Alle joie and blisse than sall be aftir
And to al mankynde nowe althir mast.   *the very most*
270   Jesus his name thou calle,
For slike happe sall hym fall   *happening to him*
Als thou sall se in haste.
His pepull saffe he sall   *save*
Of evyllis and angris all   *afflictions*
275   That thei ar nowe enbraste.   *surrounded*

JOSEPH   And is this soth, aungell, thou saise?

ANGELUS   Yha, and this to taken right,   *rightly*
Wende forthe to Marie thy wiffe alwayse:

Brynge hir to Bedlem this ilke nyght.   *Bethlehem; same*
280   Ther sall a childe borne be,
       Goddis Sone of heven is hee,
       And man ay mast of myght.   *most*

JOSEPH   Nowe, Lorde God, full wele is me
         That evyr that I this sight suld see;
285   I was never ar so light.   *before*

         For for I walde hir have thus refused   *For since*
         And sakles blame that ay was clere,   *innocent*
         Me bus pray hir halde me excused   *hold*
         Als som men dose with full gud chere.
290   Saie, Marie, wiffe, how fares thou?

MARIA   The bettir, sir, for yhou.
        Why stande yhe thare? Come nere.

JOSEPH   My bakke fayne wolde I bowe
         And aske forgifnesse nowe,
295   Wiste I thou wolde me here.   *hear*

MARIA   Forgiffnesse, sir, late be for shame;   *let*
        Slike wordis suld all gud women lakke.

JOSEPH   Yha, Marie, I am to blame,
         For wordis lang are I to thee spak.   *long (inappropriate) previously*
300   But gadir same nowe all oure gere,   *together*
         Slike poure wede as we were,   *poor clothes; wear*
         And prike tham in a pak.   *press; into*
         Till Bedlem bus me it bere,   *carry*
         For litill thyng will women dere.   *trouble*
305   Helpe up nowe on my bak.

[14. THE NATIVITY]

The Tille Thekers

JOSEPH   All weldand God in Trinité,   *powerful*
         I praye thee, Lord, for thy grete myght,
         Unto thy symple servand see,   *take notice*
         Here in this place wher we are pight,   *placed*
5   Oureself allone;
         Lord, graunte us gode herberow this nyght   *shelter*
         Within this wone.   *place*

For we have sought bothe uppe and doune
Thurgh diverse stretis in this cité;   *streets*
10   So mekill pepull is comen to towne   *many*
That we can nowhare herbered be,   *accommodated*
There is slike prees.   *such a press [of people]*
Forsuthe I can no socoure see
But belde us with there bestes.   *for us to stay; animals*

15   And yf we here all nyght abide
We schall be stormed in this steede;   *exposed to the weather; place*
The walles are doune on ilke a side,
The ruffe is rayved aboven oure hede,   *roof is open; head*
Als have I roo.   *hope to have peace*
20   Say, Marie, doughtir, what is thy rede?   *advice*
How sall we doo?

For in grete nede nowe are we stedde,   *situated*
As thou thyselffe the soth may see,
For here is nowthir cloth ne bedde,   *bedclothes*
25   And we are weyke and all werie   *weary*
And fayne wolde rest.
Now, gracious God, for thy mercie,
Wisse us the best.   *Guide*

MARIA   God will us wisse, full wele witt ye;   *guide; know*
30   Therfore, Joseph, be of gud chere,
For in this place borne will he be
That sall us save fro sorowes sere,   *many*
Bothe even and morne.
Sir, witte ye wele the tyme is nere,   *near*
35   He will be borne.

JOSEPH   Than behoves us bide here stille,   *abide*
Here in this same place all this nyght.

MARIA   Ya, sir, forsuth it is Goddis will.

JOSEPH   Than wolde I fayne we had sum light,   *be glad [if]; some*
40   What so befall.
It waxis right myrke unto my sight   *dark*
And colde withall.

I will go gete us light forthy,
And fewell fande with me to bryng.   *fuel find*

MARIA   All weldand God, yow governe and gy,   *guide*
46   As he is sufferayne of all thyng,   *sovereign*

For his grete myght;
And lende me grace to his lovyng   *praise*
That I me dight.

50   Nowe in my sawle grete joie have I: *soul*
I am all cladde in comforte clere.
Now will be borne of my body
Both God and man togedir in feere.
Blist mott he be.   *Blessed*
55   Jesu, my Sone that is so dere,
Nowe borne is he.

Hayle, my Lord God, hayle prince of pees,   *peace*
Hayle my Fadir, and hayle my Sone,
Hayle sovereyne sege all synnes to sesse,   *man; cease*
60   Hayle God and man in erth to wonne!   *live*
Hayle, thurgh whos myht   *might*
All this worlde was first begonne,
Merknes and light.   *Darkness*

Sone, as I am sympill sugett of thyne,   *humble subject*
65   Vowchesaffe, swete Sone I praye thee,
That I myght thee take in the armys of myne,
And in this poure wede to arraie thee.   *garment to dress*
Graunte me thi bliss
As I am thy modir chosen to be   *mother*
70   In sothfastnesse.   *truth*

JOSEPH   A, Lorde God, what the wedir is colde,   *weather*
The fellest freese that evere I felyd;   *worst freeze; felt*
I pray God helpe tham that is alde   *old*
And namely tham that is unwelde,   *weak*
75   So may I saie.
Now, gud God thou be my bilde,   *support*
As thou best may.

A, Lord God, what light is this
That comes shynyng thus sodenly?
80   I cannot saie, als have I blisse,
When I come home unto Marie
Than sall I spirre.   *ask*
A, here be God, for nowe come I.

MARIA   Ye ar welcum, sirre.

JOSEPH   Say, Marie doghtir, what chere with thee?

MARIA   Right goode, Joseph, as has been ay.

JOSEPH   O, Marie, what swete thyng is that on thy kne?

MARIA   It is my Sone, the soth to saye,   *truth*
89   That is so gud.   *good (healthy)*

JOSEPH   Wele is me I bade this day   *Happy am I*
        To se this foode.   *infant*

        Me merveles mekill of this light   *marvel greatly*
        That thusgates shynes in this place,   *in this manner*
94   Forsuth it is a selcouth sight.   *wondrous*

MARIA   This hase he ordand of his grace,
        My Sone so ying,   *young*
        A starne to be shynyng a space   *star*
        At his bering.   *birth*

        For Balam tolde ful longe beforne   *Balaam*
100   How that a sterne shulde rise full hye,
        And of a maiden shulde be borne
        A Sonne that sall oure saffyng be   *salvation*
        Fro caris kene.   *From cares (suffering) sharp*
        Forsuth it is my Sone so free,
105   Be whame Balam gon meene.   *Of whom; meant*

JOSEPH   Nowe, welcome, floure fairest of hewe,   *flower; hue*
        I shall thee menske with mayne and myght.   *worship*
        Hayle, my maker, hayle Crist Jesu,
        Hayle, riall kyng, roote of all right;   *royal*
110   Hayle, Saveour,
        Hayle, my Lorde, lemer of light,   *source of radiance*
        Hayle, blessid floure.

MARIA   Nowe Lord that all this worlde schall wynne,   *gain*
        To thee my Sone is that I saye,
115   Here is no bedde to laye thee inne;
        Therfore my dere Sone, I thee praye,
        Sen it is soo,
        Here in this cribbe I myght thee lay
        Betwene ther bestis two.   *animals*

120   And I sall happe thee, myn owne dere childe,   *wrap*
        With such clothes as we have here.

JOSEPH   O Marie, beholde thes beestis mylde,
They make lovyng in ther manere   *praise*
As thei wer men.   *were*
125   Forsothe it semes wele be ther chere   *by their*
Thare Lorde thei ken.   *know*

MARIA   Ther Lorde thai kenne, that wate I wele,   *know I well*
They worshippe hym with myght and mayne.
The wedir is colde, as ye may feele,
130   To halde hym warme thei are full fayne   *keep; determined*
With thare warme breth,   *their*
And oondis on hym, is noght to layne,   *breathe; hide*
To warm hym with.

O, nowe slepis my Sone, blist mot he be,
135   And lyes full warme ther bestis bytwene.

JOSEPH   O nowe is fulfillid, forsuth I see,
That Abacuc in mynde gon mene   *Habakkuk; had meant*
And prechid by prophicie.
He saide oure Savyoure shall be sene
140   Betwene bestis lye,   *lying*

And now I see the same in sight.

MARIA   Ya, sir, forsuth the same is he.

JOSEPH   Honnoure and worshippe both day and nyght
Aylastand Lorde, be done to thee   *offered*
145   Allway as is worthy,
And Lord, to thy service I oblissh me   *oblige*
With all myn herte holy.   *heart wholly*

MARIA   Thou mercyfull maker, most myghty,
My God, my Lorde, my Sone so free,
150   Thy handemayden forsoth am I,
And to thi service I oblissh me
With all myn herte entere.   *entirely*
Thy blissing, beseke I thee,   *beseech*
Thou graunte us all in feere.   *together*

[15. THE OFFERING OF THE SHEPHERDS]

The Chandelers

I PASTOR Bredir in haste, takis heede and here		*Brothers; hear*
What I wille speke and specifie;		
Sen we walke thus, withouten were,		*doubt*
What mengis my moode nowe mevyd will I.		*unsettles*
5 Oure formefadres, faythfull in fere,		*forefathers; altogether*
Bothe Osye and Isaye,		*Hosea; Isaiah*
Preved that a prins withouten pere		*Proved; prince; peer*
Shulde descende doune in a lady		
And to make mankynde clerly		*clean (sinless)*
10 To leche tham that are lorne;		*cure*
And in Bedlem hereby		*Bethlehem*
Sall that same barne by borne.		*child be*

II PASTOR Or he be borne in burgh hereby,		*town*
Balaham, brothir, me have herde say,		*heard*
15 A sterne shulde schyne and signifie		*star*
With lightfull lemes like any day.		*bright beams*
And als the texte it tellis clerly		
By witty lerned men of oure lay,		*law*
With his blissid bloode he shulde us by,		*buy [back] (redeem)*
20 He shulde take here al of a maye.		*maid*
I herde my syre saye		*master*
When he of hir was borne,		
She shulde be als clene maye		*clean maid (virgin)*
As ever she was byforne.		*before*

III PASTOR A, mercifull maker, mekill is thy myght		*creator*
26 That thus will to thi servauntes see.		
Might we ones loke uppon that light,		*once*
Gladder bretheren myght no men be.		
I have herde say, by that same light		
30 The childre of Israell shulde be made free,		
The force of the feende to felle in fighte,		*to overcome*
And all his pouer excluded shulde be.		
Wherfore, brether, I rede that wee		*advise*
Flitte faste overe thees felles		*hills*
35 To frayste to fynde oure fee		*try; livestock*
And talke of sumwhat ellis.		*else*

I PASTOR We, Hudde!		*Whee*

II PASTOR We, howe!		*pay attention*

I PASTOR   Herkyn to me!

II PASTOR We, man, thou maddes all out of myght.   *act badly*

I PASTOR We, Colle!

III PASTOR   What care is comen to thee?

I PASTOR Steppe furth and stande by me right   *near me*
41   And telle me than
       Yf thou sawe evere swilke a sight.

III PASTOR I? Nay, certis, nor nevere no man.

II PASTOR Say, felowes, what, fynde yhe any feest,   *feast (revels)*
45   Me falles for to have parte, pardé.   *I ought to have a; by God*

I PASTOR Whe, Hudde, behalde into the heste,   *east*
       A selcouthe sight than sall thou see   *marvelous*
       Uppon the skye.

II PASTOR We, telle me, men, emang us thre,
50   Whatt garres yow stare thus sturdely?   *makes*

III PASTOR Als lange as we have herdemen bene
       And kepid this catell in this cloghe,   *kept; livestock; valley*
       So selcouth a sight was nevere non sene.

I PASTOR We, no Colle, nowe comes it newe inowe   *suddenly*
55   That mon we fynde;
             .   .   .   [pages missing]
[III PASTOR] Itt menes some mervayle us emang,   *omen; among*
       Full hardely I you behete.   *boldly; assure*

I PASTOR What it shulde mene that wate not yee,   *know*
       For all that ye can gape and gone.   *and do*
60   I can synge itt alls wele as hee,
       And on asaie itt sall be sone   *on a try; soon*
       Proved or we passe.   *ere*
       Yf ye will helpe, halde on; late see,   *hold on [to your note]*
       For thus it was.

       Et tunc cantant.   *And then they sing*

II PASTOR Ha, ha, this was a mery note;
66   Be the dede that I sall dye   *death*

I have so crakid in my throte
That my lippis are nere drye.

III Pastor   I trowe thou royse,   *think you talk nonsense*
70   For what it was fayne witte walde I   *gladly know*
      That tille us made this noble noyse.   *to us; musical sound*

I Pastor   An aungell brought us tythandes newe
      A babe in Bedlem shulde be borne,
      Of whom than spake oure prophecie trewe,   *truthfully*
75   And bad us mete hym thare this morne,   *meet*
      That mylde of mode.   *mood*
      I walde giffe hym bothe hatte and horne,   *would give*
      And I myght fynde that frely foode.   *noble child*

III Pastor   Hym for to fynde has we no drede;
80   I sall you telle achesoune why: *reason*
      Yone sterne to that Lorde sall us lede.

II Pastor   Ya, thou sais soth, go we forthy
      Hym to honnour
      And make myrthe and melody
85   With sange to seke oure Savyour.

      Et tunc cantant.   *And then they sing*

I Pastor   Breder, bees all blythe and glad,   *Brothers*
      Here is the burgh ther we shulde be.

II Pastor   In that same steede now are we stadde;   *place; stopped*
      Tharefore I will go seke and see.
90   Slike happe of heele nevere herdemen hadde.   *luck; well-being*
      Loo, here is the house, and here is hee.

III Pastor   Ya, forsothe this is the same,
      Loo! whare that Lorde is layde
      Betwyxe two bestis tame,
95   Right als tha aungell saide.

I Pastor   The aungell saide that he shulde save
      This worlde and all that wonnes therin;   *lives*
      Therfore yf I shulde oght aftir crave
      To wirshippe hym I will begynne.
100   Sen I am but a symple knave,   *peasant*
      Thof all I come of curtayse kynne,   *kinfolk*
      Loo, here slyke harnays as I have,   *such [household] gear*
      A baren broche by a belle of tynne   *poor brooch; tin*

At youre bosom to be,	
105 And whenne ye shall welde all,	*wield (control) all [things]*
Gud Sonne, forgete noght me	*God's (or ?good)*
Yf any fordele falle.	*advantage*

II PASTOR Thou Sonne, that shall save bothe see and sande,	*sea*
Se to me sen I have thee soght,	
110 I am ovir poure to make presande	*overly poor; present*
Als myn harte wolde, and I had ought.	*heart would wish, if*
Two cobill notis uppon a bande,	*hazelnuts*
Loo, litill babe, what I have broght,	
And whan ye sall be Lorde in lande,	
115 Dose goode agayne, forgete me noght,	
For I have herde declared	
Of connyng clerkis and clene	*pure*
That bountith askis rewarde,	*bounty*
Nowe watte ye what I mene.	

III PASTOR Nowe loke on me, my Lorde dere;	
121 Thof all I putte me noght in pres,	*Though I don't mean to push myself forward*
Ye are a prince withouten pere,	*equal*
I have no presentte that you may plees.	*please*
But lo, an horne spone, that have I here,	*spoon*
125 And it will herbar fourty pese;	*contain; peas*
This will I giffe you with gud chere,	
Slike novelté may noght disease.	*displease*
Farewele thou swete swayne,	
God graunte us levyng lange,	*living long*
130 And go we hame agayne	
And make mirthe as we gange.	*go*

[16. HEROD QUESTIONING THE THREE KINGS AND THE OFFERING OF THE MAGI]

The Masonns [and] Goldesmythis

Masons:

HERODES The clowdes clapped in clerenes that ther clematis inclosis,[1]	
Jubiter and Jovis, Martis and Mercurii emyde,	*Mars; amidst*
Raykand overe my rialté on rawe me rejoyses,	*Rushing; row (in order)*
Blonderande ther blastis to blaw when I bidde.	*Whirling about; blow*
5 Saturne, my subgett, that sotilly is hidde,	*subject; subtly*
Listes at my likyng and laies hym full lowe.	*Attends to my desire*

[1] *Clouds wrapped in splendor that their region encloses*

The rakke of the rede skye full rappely I ridde,   *rack [of clouds]; quickly I get rid of*
Thondres full thrallye by thousandes I thrawe   *violently; throw*
When me likis.
10 Venus his voice to me awe   *owes*
    That princes to play in hym pikis.   *picks (chooses)*

    The prince of planetis that proudely is pight   *(i.e., the sun); adorned*
    Sall brace furth his bemes that oure belde blithes;   *radiate; happiness gladdens*
    The mone at my myght he mosteres his myght,   *moon; musters*
15 And kayssaris in castellis grete kyndynes me kythes;   *caesars; affords me*
    Lordis and ladis loo luffely me lithes,   *courteously; attend*
    For I am fairer of face and fressher on folde,   *on earth*
    The soth yf I saie sall, sevene and sexti sithis   *sixty-seven times*
    Than glorius gulles that gayer is than golde   *red (heraldic color)*
20 In price.
    How thynke ye ther tales that I talde,   *told*
    I am worthy, witty, and wyse.

I Miles All kynges to youre croune may clerly comende
    Youre lawe and youre lordshippe as lodsterne on hight.   *guiding star in heavens*
25 What traytoure untrewe that will not attende
    Ye sall lay thaim full lowe, fro leeme and fro light.   *brightness*

II Miles What faitoure, in faithe, that dose you offende,   *false person*
    We sall sette hym full sore, that sotte, in youre sight.   *fool*

Herodes In welthe sall I wisse you to wonne or I wende,   *arrange for you to dwell; go*
30 For ye are wightis ful worthy, both witty and wighte.   *men; strong*

    But ye knawe wele, ser knyghtis, in counsaill full conande, *clever*
    That my regioun so riall is ruled her be rest;   *royal; in peace*
    For I wate of no wighte in this worlde that is wonnande   *living*
    That in forges any feloune, with force sall be fest;   *plans; crime; caught*
35 Arest ye tho rebaldes that unrewly are rownand,   *Arrest; rascals; unruly; speaking*
    Be they kyngis or knyghtis, in care ye thaim cast.   *suffering; them*
    Yaa, and welde tham in woo to wonne, in the wanyand,   *live; waning [of the moon]*
    What browle that is brawlyng his brayne loke ye brest,   *wretch; rioting; smash*
    And dynge ye hym doune.   *strike*

I Miles Sir, what foode in faith will you feese,   *immature person; punish*
41 That sott full sone myselfe sall hym sesse.   *fool; seize*

II Miles We sall noght here doute to do hym disesse,   *fear; discomfort*
    But with countenaunce full cruel we sall crake her his croune.

Herodes My sone that is semely, howe semes thee ther sawes? *handsome; sayings*
45 Howe comely ther knyghtis, thei carpe in this case.   *speak*

FILIUS   Fadir, if thai like noght to listyn youre lawes,   *disloyal; lesson*
            As traytoures ontrewe ye sall teche them a trace,
            For, fadir, unkyndnes ye kythe them no cause.   *have given*

HERODES   Faire falle thee, my faire sone, so fettis of face,   *son; handsome*
50   And knyghtis, I comaunde, who to dule drawes,   *dole (evil)*
            Thas churles as cheveleres ye chastise and chase   *knights*
            And drede ye no doute.   *fear*

FILIUS   Fadir, I sall fell tham in fight,
            What renke that reves you youre right.   *man; robs*

I MILES   With dyntes to dede bes he dight   *strokes; death be; put*
56   That liste not youre lawes for to lowte.   *respect*

―――――

Goldsmiths:

I REX   A, Lorde, that levis, everelastande lyff,   *lives*
            I love thee evir with harte and hande,   *praise*
            That me has made to se this sight
60   Whilke my kynrede was coveytande.   *kinfolk were desiring*
            Thay saide a sterne with lemys bright   *star; beams*
            Owte of the eest shulde stabely stande,   *stand still*
            And that it shulde meffe mekill myght   *move (indicate)*
            Of one that shulde be Lorde in lande,
65   That men of synne shulde saff be;   *sin; saved*
            And certis I sall saye,
            God graunte me happe to have   *luck*
            Wissyng of redy waye.   *Knowledge*

II REX   All weldand God, that all has wroght,   *All powerful*
70   I worshippe thee als is worthye   *praise*
            That with thy brightnes has me broght
            Owte of my reame, riche Arabie.   *realm*
            I shall noght seys tille I have sought   *cease*
            What selcouth thyng it sall syngnyfie,   *wonderful; signify*
75   God graunte me happe so that I myght
            Have grace to gete goode companye
            And my comforte encrese
            With thy sterne schynyng schene.   *brightly*
            For certis, I sall noght cesse   *cease*
80   Tille I witte what it mene.   *means*

III REX   Lorde God, that all goode has bygonne   *created*
            And all may ende, both goode and evyll,
            That made for man both mone and sonne

	And stedde yone sterne to stande stone stille.	*positioned yon star*
85	Tille I the cause may clerly knowe,	
	God wisse me with his worthy wille.	*guide*
	I hope I have her felaws fonde,	*found*
	My yarnyng fathfully to fullfille.	*yearning faithfully*
	Sirs, God yowe saffe ande see,	*save*
90	And were yow evere fro woo.	*defend; from woe*

I REX Amen, so myght it bee,
          And saffe yow, sir, also.

III REX Sirs, with youre wille, I wolde yow praye   *permission*
           To telle me some of youre entent,   *intent*
95   Whedir ye wende forthe in this way   *Whether*
           And fro what contré ye are wente.   *country*

II REX Full gladly, sir, I shall you say,
           A sodayne sight was till us sente,   *sudden*
           A royall sterne that rose or day   *before*
100   Before us on the firmament
           That garte us fare fro home   *caused; to travel from*
           Som poynte therof to preffe.   *prove*

III REX Sertis, syrs, I saw the same
            That makis us thus to moyfe.   *move*

105   For sirs, I have herde saye sertayne   *certain*
           Itt shulde be seyne of selcowthe seere   *sign of many wonders*
           And ferther therof I wolde freyne;   *ask*
           That makis me moffe in this manere.   *move*

I REX Sir, of felashippe are we fayne,   *desirous*
110   Now sall we wende forth all in feere,   *together*
           God graunte us or we come agayne   *ere*
           Som gode hartyng therof to here.   *encouragement; hear*
           Sir, here is Jerusalem,
           To wisse us als we goo,   *direct*
115   And beyonde is Bedleem;   *Bethlehem*
           Ther schall we seke alsoo.

III REX Sirs, ye schall wele undirstande
            For to be wise nowe were it nede,
            Sir Herowde is kyng of this lande
120   And has his lawes her for to leede.   *here; lead*

I REX Sir, sen we neghe now thus nerhand,   *come near; nearby*
           Untill his helpe us muste take heede,

For have we his wille and his warande   *warrant*
Than may we wende withouten drede.

II REX   To have leve of the lorde,
126   That is resoune and skyll.   *sensible*

III REX   And therto we all accorde;
Wende we and witte his wille.   *know*

———

Masons and Goldsmiths:

NUNCIUS   My lorde, ser Herowde, kyng with croune.   *crown*

HERODES   Pees, dastarde, in the develes dispite.   *Peace; malice*

NUNCIUS   My lorde, now note is nere this towne.   *news*

HERODES   What, false harlott, liste thee flight?   *argue*
Go betis yone boy and dyngis hym downe.   *beat; strike*

II MILES   Lorde, messengeres shulde no man wyte,   *blame*
135   It may be for youre awne renoune.   *own reputation*

HERODES   That wolde I here, do telle on tyte.   *hear; quickly*

NUNCIUS   My lorde, I mette at morne
Thre kyngis carpand togedir   *talking*
Of a barne that is borne,
140   And thei hight to come hiddir.   *called (designated)*

HERODES   Thre kyngis, forsoth?

NUNCIUS   Sir, so I say,
For I saw thaim myselffe all fere.   *all together*

I CONSOLATOR   My lorde, appose hym, I you pray.   *interrogate*

HERODES   Say, felowe, are they ferre or nere?   *far or near*

NUNCIUS   Mi lorde, thei will be here this day,
146   That wote I wele, withouten were.   *without question*

HERODES   Do rewle us than in riche array,   *dress; then*
And ilke man make tham mery chere   *each*
That no sembelant be sene   *outward sign; seen*
150   But frendshippe faire and still

    Till we witte what thei mene,   *know; intend*
    Whedir it be gud or ill.

I REX   The lorde that lenes aylastand light   *lends everlasting*
    Whilke has us ledde owte of oure londe,   *Which; land*
155 Kepe thee, ser kynge and comely knyght
    And all thy folke that we her fynde.   *here*

HERODES   Mahounde, my god and most of myght   *Mohammed*
    That has myn hele all in his hande,   *my well-being*
    He saffe you, sirs, semely in sight,   *save*
160 And telle us nowe som new tithand.   *tidings*

II REX   Some sall we saie you, sir.
    A sterne stode us beforne   *star*
    That makis us speke and spir   *ask*
    Of one that is new borne.

HERODES   New borne? That burden halde I bad,   *birth hold*
166 And, certis, unwitty men ye wore   *were*
    To leppe overe lande to laite a ladde.   *hurry; seek*
    Say, whan loste ye hym, ought lange before?   *(i.e., was it long before)*
    All wise men will wene ye madde,   *consider you to be*
170 And therfore moves this never more.   *refer to this*

III REX   Yis, certis, swilke hertyng have we hadde   *encouragement*
    We will not cesse or we come thore.   *cease until*

HERODES   This were a wondir thyng.
    Saie, what barne shulde that be?   *child*

I REX   Forsoth, he sall be kynge
176 Of Jewes and of Jude.   *Judea*

HERODES   Kyng? In the develes name, dogges, fye!
    Nowe se I wele ye roye and rave.   *well you talk nonsense (boast)*
    Be any skemeryng of the skye   *glimmering in*
180 When shulde ye knawe outhir kyng or knave?   *either*

FILIUS   Naye, he is kyng and non but he
    That sall ye kenne if that ye crave,   *know; desire*
    And he is jugge of all Jurie   *judge; Jewry*
    To speke or spille, to saie or saffe.   *defend; condemn; save*

HERODES   Swilke gawdes may gretely greve   *tricks; grieve (offend)*
186 To witnesse that nere was.   *never*

II REX Nowe, lorde, we axe but leve   *ask; permission*
      Be youre poure to passe.   *power (authority)*

HERODES Whedirward, in the develis name,
190   To layte a ladde here in my lande?   *seek*
      Fals harlottis, bot yhe hye you hame   *go; home*
      Ye sall be bette and bune in bande.   *beaten; bound*

II CONSOLATOR Mi lorde, to fell this foule defame,   *put down; disgrace*
      Late alle there hye wordis falle on hande   *Let; their hasty; be put aside*
195   And spere thaim sadly of the same,   *inquire; soberly*
      So sall ye stabely undirstande
      Thaire mynde and ther menyng,   *meaning*
      And takes gud tente therto.   *careful attention*

HERODES I thanke thee of thys thing,
200   And certis so sall I doo.

      Nowe, kyngis, to cache all care awaye   *take (drive)*
      Sen ye are comen oute of youre kyth,   *(i.e., native land)*
      Loke noght ye legge agaynste oure laye,   *allege; law*
      Uppon payne to lose both lymme and lith.   *(i.e., life and limb)*
205   And so that ye the soth will saye
      To come and go I graunte you grith,   *protection*
      And yf youre poyntes be to my paye   *advantage*
      May fall myselfe sall wende you with.   *It may fall out that*

I REX Sir kyng, we all accorde
210   And sais a barne is borne   *Child*
      That sall be kyng and lorde,
      And leche tham that ar lorne.   *heal; lost*

II REX Sir, ye thar mervaylle nothynge
      Of this ilke noote that thusgattes newes,   *note (matter); in this manner is news*
215   For Balaham saide a starne shulde sprynge   *Balaam; star*
      Of Jacob kynde, and that is Jewes.   *Jacob's kin*

III REX Isaie sais a maiden yonge   *Isaiah; young*
      Sall bere a barne emange Ebrewes   *among Hebrews*
      That of all contrees sal be kynge
220   And governe all that on erthe grewes.   *grows*
      Emanuell beiths his name,   *shall be*
      To say, Goddis Sone of hevene.
      And certis this is the same   *certainly*
      That we here to you neven.   *name (identify)*

I REX   Sir, the proved prophete Ossee   *Hosea*
226   Full trewly tolde in towne and toure,   *tower*
A maiden of Israell, forsoth saide he,
Sall bere oone like to lilly floure.
He menes a childe consayved sall be   *conceived*
230   Withouten seede of mannys socoure,   *assistance of a man's seed*
And his modir a mayden free,   *mother*
And he both Sonne and Saveour.

II REX   That fadres talde me beforne   *(i.e., forefathers)*
Has no man myght to marre.   *spoil*

HERODES   Allas, than am I lorne,
236   This wax ay werre and werre.   *worse and worse*

I CONSOLATOR   My lorde, be ye nothyng abast,   *afraid*
This brigge till ende sall wele be broght.   *conflict (situation)*
Byde tham go furth and frendly frayste   *inquire*
240   The soth of this that thei have soght,
And telle it you, soo sall ye traste   *test*
Whedir ther tales be trewe or noght.
Than sall ye waite thaim with a wraste   *wait for them; trick*
And make all waste that thei have wroght.   *destroy*

HERODES   Nowe certis, this is wele saide,
246   This matere makes me fayne.   *happy*
Sir kyngis, I halde me paied   *rewarded*
Off all youre purpose playne.

Wende furth youre forward to fulfill,   *Go; undertaking*
250   To Bedlem is but here at hande,
And speris grathely both gud and ille   *ask plainly*
Of hym that shulde be lorde in lande,
And comes agayne than me untill   *then*
And telle me trulye youre tithande.   *tidings*
255   To worshippe hym than were my will,
This sall ye stabely undirstande.   *firmly*

II REX   Certis, ser, we sall you say
The soth of that same childe,
In all the haste we may.

II CONSOLATOR   Fares wele. Ye be bygilyd.   *Farewell; beguiled*

HERODES   Now, certis, this is a sotell trayne.   *subtle trick*
262   Nowe sall thai truly take there trace   *make their way*
And telle me of that swytteron swayne   *doubtful (of no account) boy*

	And all thare counsaille in this case.	*their*
265	Giffe itt be soth thai shall be slayne,	*If*
	No golde shall gete them bettir grace.	*favor*
	Bot go we tille they come agayne	*until*
	And playe us in som othir place.	
	This holde I gude counsaill,	
270	Yitt wolde I na man wiste;	*no; knew*
	For certis, we shall noght faile	
	To lose tham as us liste.	*lose (kill); we please*

———

Goldsmiths:

Nota: The Harrode passeth and the three kynges commyth agayn to make there offerynges.

I REX   A, sirs, for sight what shall I say,   *sorrow*
Whare is oure syne? I se it noth.   *sign; not*

II REX   No more do I; nowe dar I lay
276   In oure wendyng som wrange is wroght.   *wrong*

III REX   Unto that prince I rede we praye   *advise*
That till us sente his syngne unsoght,   *sign*
That he wysse us in redy way   *direct*
280   So frendly that we fynde hym moght.   *So that lovingly; might*

I REX   A, siris, I se it stande
Aboven where he is borne;
Lo, here is the house at hande.
We have noght myste this morne.   *missed (failed)*

ANCILLA   Whame seke ye, syrs, be wayes wilde   *Whom*
286   With talkyng, travelyng to and froo?
Her wonnes a woman with hir childe,   *Here dwells*
And hir husband; her ar no moo.   *here are*

II REX   We seke a barne that all shall bylde;   *protect*
290   His sartayne syngne hath saide us soo,   *infallible sign; informed us thus*
And his modir, a mayden mylde,
Her hope we to fynde tham twoo.

ANCILLA   Come nere, gud syirs, and see:
Youre way to ende is broght.   *a conclusion*

III REX   Behalde here, syirs, her and se   *hear and see*
296   The same that ye have soght.

I Rex   Loved be that Lorde that lastis aye,   *Praised; exists forever*
        That us has kydde thus curtaysely   *shown*
        To wende by many a wilsom way   *lonely (dangerous) way*
300   And come to this clene companye.   *undefiled*

II Rex   Late us make nowe no more delay   *Let*
        But tyte take furth oure tresurry   *quickly; treasure*
        And ordand giftis of gud aray   *intended gifts [for the Child]*
        To worshippe hym als is worthy.

III Rex   He is worthy to welde   *enjoy*
306   All worshippe, welthe, and wynne;   *felicity*
        And for honnoure and elde,   *age*
        Brother, ye shall begynne.

I Rex   Hayle, the fairest of felde, folke for to fynde,   *(i.e., in the world)*
310   Fro the fende and his feeres faithefully us fende;   *fiend; companions; defend*
        Hayll, the best that shall be borne to unbynde
        All the barnes that are borne and in bale boune.   *bound*
        Hayll, thou marc us thi men and make us in mynde   *mark; keep*
        Sen thi myght is on molde misseis to amende.   *earth sins*
315   Hayll, clene that is comen of a kynges kynde   *undefiled one; lineage*
        And shall be kyng of this kyth, all clergy has kende.   *people; revealed*
        And sith it shall worthe on this wise,   *since; happen this way*
        Thyselffe have I soght sone, I say thee,   *soon*
        With golde that is grettest of price.
320   Be paied of this present, I pray thee.   *Accept*

II Rex   Hayll, foode that thy folke fully may fede;   *child; may nourish*
        Hayll, floure fairest that never shall fade;   *flower*
        Hayll, Sone that is sente of this same sede   *seed*
        That shall save us of synne that oure syris had;   *ancestors*
325   Hayll, mylde, for thou mett to marke us to mede,   *mild one; chose; reward*
        Off a may makeles thi modir thou made.   *maid matchless (without sin)*
        In that gude thurgh grace of thy Godhede,   *good [maid]*
        Als the gleme in the glasse gladly thow glade   *gleam through; glided*
        And sythyn thow shall sitte to be demand,   *then; judging*
330   To helle or to heven for to have us,
        Insens to thi servis is semand.   *Incense; appropriate*
        Sone, se to thi suggettis and save us.   *subjects*

III Rex   Hayll, barne that is best oure balys to bete,   *sorrows to overcome*
        For our boote shall thou be bounden and bett;   *assistance; beaten*
335   Hayll, frende faithfull, we fall to thy feete,
        Thy fadiris folke fro the fende to thee fette.   *fetch*
        Hayll, man that is made to thi men mette   *fitting*
        Sen thou and thy modir with mirthis ar mette;   *Since; joys*

	Hayll, duke that dryves dede undir fete,	*death under [his] feet*
340	But whan thy dedys ar done to dye is thi dette.	*debt*
	And sen thy body beryed shal be,	*buried*
	This mirre will I giffe to thi gravyng.	*myrrh; give; burial*
	The gifte is noght grete of degree,	
	Ressayve it, and se to oure savyng.	

MARIA	Sir kyngis, ye travel not in vayne,	
346	Als ye have ment, hyr may ye fynde,	
	For I consayved my Sone sartayne	*conceived; certainly*
	Withouten misse of man in mynde,	*sin*
	And bare hym here withouten payne	
350	Where women ar wonte to be pynyd.	*to feel pain*
	Goddis aungell in his gretyng playne	
	Saide he shulde comforte al mankynde;	
	Tharfore doute yow no dele	*doubt; entirely*
	Here for to have youre bone;	*wish (desire)*
355	I shall witnesse full wele	
	All that is saide and done.	

I REX	For solas ser now may we synge,	*special*
	All is parformed that we for prayde.	
	But gud barne, giffe us thy blissing,	*give*
360	For faire happe is before thee laide.	*good fortune*

II REX	Wende we nowe to Herowde the kyng,	
	For of this poynte he will be paied	*matter; pleased*
	And come hymselffe and make offeryng	
	Unto this same, for so he saide.	

III REX	I rede we reste a thrawe	*advise; awhile*
366	For to maynteyne our myght,	*stamina*
	And than do as we awe	*ought*
	Both unto kyng and knyght.	

ANGELUS	Nowe curtayse kynges, to me take tent,	*courteous; pay attention*
370	And turne betyme or ye be tenyd,	*without delay; hurt (killed)*
	Fro God hymselfe thus am I sent	
	To warne yow als youre faithfull frende.	
	Herowde the kyng has malise ment	
	And shappis with shame yow for to shende,	*shapes (schemes); destroy*
375	And for that ye non harmes shulde hente	*suffer*
	Be othir waies God will ye wende	*By*
	Even to youre awne contré.	*own country*
	And yf ye aske hym bone,	*a favor*
	Youre beelde ay will he be	*support*
380	For this that ye have done.	

I REX   A, Lorde, I love thee inwardly.   *praise*
         Sirs, God has gudly warned us thre.
         His anungell her now herde have I,
         And how he saide.

II REX   Sir, so did we,
385   He saide Herowde is oure enmye   *enemy*
         And makis hym bowne oure bale to be   *bound*
         With feyned falsed, and forthy   *feigned falsehood*
         Farre fro his force I rede we flee.   *power; advise*

III REX   Syrs, faste I rede we flitte
390   Ilkone till oure contré.   *Each one*
         He that is welle of witte   *the source of knowledge*
         Us wisse, and with yow be.   *direct*

[17. THE PURIFICATION OF THE VIRGIN]

The Hatmakers, Masons, and Laborers

PRISBETER   Almyghty God in heven so hy,   *high*
         The maker of all heven and erth,
         He ordenyd here all thynges evenly,   *properly*
         For man he ment to mend his myrth.   *intended; joy*

5   In nomber, weight, and mesure fyne
         God creat here al thyng, I say.
         His lawes he bad men shulde not tyne,   *bade; break*
         But kepe his commandmentes allway.

         In the mount of Syney full fayre   *Sinai*
10   And in two tabyls to you to tell,   *tables*
         His lawes to Moyses tuke God there   *(i.e., entrusted)*
         To geve to the chylder of Israell,

         That Moyses shull theme gyde alway   *should; guide*
         And lerne theme lely to knowe Goddes wyll,   *teach; truly*
15   And that he shulde not it denay   *deny it*
         But kepe his lawes stable and styll.   *always*

         For payn that he hadd putt therefore,   *distress*
         To stone all theme that kepis it nott
         Utterly to death, both lesse and moore,
20   There shulde no marcy for them be soght.   *mercy*

	Therefore kepe well Goddes commandement	
	And leyd your lyf after his lawes,	*lead*
	Or ells surely ye mon be shent	*may be damned*
	Bothe lesse and moore, ylkone on rawes.	*each one in order*

25	This is his wyll after Moyses lawe:	
	That ye shulde bryng your beistes good	*beasts*
	And offer theme here your God to knawe,	
	And frome your synns to turne your moode.	

	Suche beestes as God hais marked here,	*has*
30	Unto Moyses he spake as I yow tell,	
	And bad hyme boldly with good chere	
	To say to the chylder of Israell	

	That after dyvers seknes seer	*various illnesses*
	And after that dyvers synes alsoo,	
35	Go bryng your beestes to the preest even here	
	To offer theme up in Goddes sight, loo.	

	The woman that hais borne her chylde,	
	She shall comme hether at the forty day	
	To be puryfied where she was fylde	*defiled*
40	And bryng with her a lame, I say,	*lamb*

	And two dove byrdes for her offerand	
	And take them to the preest of lay	*the law*
	To offer theme up with his holy hand.	
	There shulde no man to this say nay.	

45	The lame is offeryd for Goddes honour	
	In sacrefyes all onely dight,	
	And the preistes prayer purchace secure	*advantage*
	For the woman that was fylyd in God sight.	*defiled*

	And yf so be that she be power	*poor*
50	And have no lame to offer, than	
	Two tyrtle doves to Godes honoure	
	To bryng with her for her offrand.	*offering*

	Loo, here am I, preest present alway	
	To resave all offerandes that hydder is broght,	*receive*
55	And for the people to God to pray	
	That helth and lyfe to theme be wroght.	

ANNA PROPHETISSA Here in this holy playce, I say,
    Is my full purpose to abyde   *remain*

	To serve my God bothe nyght and day	
60	With prayer and fastyng in ever ylk a tyde.	*time*

For I have beyn a wyddo this threscore yere   *widow*
And foure yere to, the truthe to tell;
And here I have terryed with full good chere   *tarried*
For the redempcyon of Israell.

65   And so for my holy conversacion
       Grete grace to me hais now God sent
       To tell by profecy for mans redepempcion
       What shall befall by Goddes intent.

       I tell you all here in this place
70   By Godes vertue in prophecy
       That one is borne to oure solace
       Here to be present securely
       Within short space,   *space [of time]*
       Of his owen mother, a madyn free;
75   Of all vyrgens moost chaist suthly,   *chaste*
       The well of mekenes, blyssed myght she be,   *fount*
       Moost full of grace.

       And Symeon, that senyour   *old man*
       That is so semely in Godes sight,   *worthy*
80   He shall hyme se and do honour
       And in his armes he shall hym plight,   *pledge*
       That worthy leyd.   *man*
       Of the Holy Goost he shall suthly
       Take strength and answere when he shall hy   *go*
85   Furth to this Temple and place holy
       To do that deyd.   *deed*

SYMEON   A, blyssed God, thowe be my beylde   *support*
       And beat my baill bothe nyght and day.   *remedy my misery*
       In hevynes my hart is hylde   *held*
90   Unto myself, loo thus I say.
       For I ame wayke and all unwelde,   *weak; feeble*
       My welth ay wayns and passeth away   *wanes*
       Whereso I fayre in fyrth or feylde   *fare [forth] in woods; field*
       I fall ay downe for febyll, in fay.

95   In fay I fall whereso I fayre,   *go*
       In hayre and hewe and hyde I say;   *hair; hue; skin*
       Owte of this worlde I wolde I were.
       Thus wax I warr and warr alway   *grow; worse and worse*
       And my myscheyf growes in all that may.

100	Bot thowe myghty Lorde my mornyng mar,	*grief; destroy (i.e., take away)*
	Mar ye, for it shulde me well pay,	*reward*
	So happy to se hyme yf I warr.	*were*
	Nowe certys then shulde my gamme begynne	*game (joy, mirth)*
	And I myght se hyme, of hyme to tell,	*him*
105	That one is borne withouten synne	
	And for mans kynde mans myrth to mell;	*ameliorate*
	Borne of a woman and madyn fre,	
	As wytnesse Davyt and Danyill,	*David; Daniel*
	Withouten synne or velanye,	*villainy (evil)*
110	As said also Isacheell.	*Ezekiel*
	And Melachiell that proffett snell	*Malachi; wise*
	Hais tolde us of that babb so bright	*baby*
	That he shulde comme with us to dwell	
	In oure Temple as leme of light;	*beam*
115	And other proffettes prophesieth	
	And of this blyssed babb dyd mell	*speak*
	And of his mother, a madyn bright,	
	In prophecy the truth gan tell.	
	That he shulde comme and harro hell	*harrow*
120	As a gyant grathly to glyde	*giant directly to enter (glide into)*
	And fersly the feyndes malles to fell	*malice*
	And putt there poors all on syde.	*powers; aside*
	The worthyest wight in this worlde so wyde	
	His vertues seer no tong can tell,	*many*
125	He sendes all soccour in ylke tyde	
	As redemption of Israell.	
	Thus say they all,	
	There patryarkes and ther prophettes clere:	
	"A babb is borne to be oure fere,	
130	Knytt in oure kynde for all our chere	*nature*
	To grete and small."	
	Ay, well were me for ever and ay	
	If I myght se that babb so bright	
	Or I were buryed here in clay;	*Before*
135	Then wolde my cors here mend in myght	*body; regain its strength*
	Right faithfully.	
	Nowe Lorde, thowe grant to me thy grace	
	To lyf here in this worlde a space	*live*
	That I myght se that babb in his face	
140	Here or I dy.	*ere I die*

A, Lorde God, I thynke may I endure,
Trowe we that babb shall fynde me here.   *Believe*
Nowe certys with aige I ame so power   *age; poor*
That ever it abaites my chere.

145 Yet yf kynde fale for aige in me,   *nature fail*
God yett may length my lyfe suthly   *lengthen*
Tyll I that babb and foode so free   *Until; child*
Have seyn in sight.
For trewly, yf I wyst relesse   *if I [should] know release [from life]*
150 Thare shulde nothyng my hart dyseas.   *disturb*
Lorde, len me grace yf that thowe pleas   *give; please*
And make me light.   *happy*

When wyll thowe comme, babb, let se, have done.
Nay, comme on tyte and tarry nott,   *quickly*
155 For certys my lyf days are nere done,
For aige to me grete wo hais wroght.

Great wo is wroght unto mans harte
Whan he muste want that he wolde have.   *need (desire)*
I kepe no longar to have quarte   *health*
160 For I have seen that I for crave.

A, trowes thowe these two eyes shall see   *think thou*
That blyssed babb or they be owte?
Ye, I pray God so myght it be:
Then were I putt all owte of dowte.   *doubt*

ANGELUS Olde Symeon, Gods servaunt right,
166 Bodworde to thee I bryng, I say,   *Message*
For the Holy Goost moost of myght,
He says thowe shall not dye away
To thowe have seen   *Until*
170 Jesu the babb that Mary bare   *bore*
For all mankynde to slake there care.   *diminish; suffering*
He shall do comforth to lesse and mayr,   *more*
Both morne and even.

SYMEON A, Lorde, gramarcy nowe I say   *(i.e., many thanks)*
175 That thowe this grace hais to me hight   *announced*
Or I be buryed here in clay
To se that semely beam so bright.

No man of molde may have more happ   *earth; luck*
To my solace and myrth allway,
180 Than for to se in Mary lapp

Jesu my joy and Savyour ay.
Blyssyd be his name.
Loo, nowe mon I se, the truth to tell,   *must*
The redempcion of Israell,
185   Jesu my Lorde Emanuell,
Withouten blame.

MARY   Joseph, my husbonde and my feer,   *companion*
Ye take to me grathely entent,   *pay attention truly to my intent*
I wyll you showe in this manere
190   What I wyll do, thus have I ment:
Full forty days is comme and went
Sens that my babb Jesu was borne;   *Since*
Therefore I wolde he were present
As Moyses lawes sais hus beforne,   *say to us*

195   Here in this Temple before Goddes sight
As other women doith in feer,   *altogether*
So methynke good skyll and right
The same to do nowe with good chere,
After Goddes sawe.   *saying*

JOSEPH   Mary, my spowse and madyn clene,
201   This matter that thowe moves to me   *speaks*
Is for all these women bedene   *forthwith*
That hais conceyved with syn fleshely   *carnal sin*
To bere a chylde.
205   The lawe is ledgyd for theme right playn   *affirmed*
That they muste be puryfied agayne,
For in mans pleasoure for certayn
Before were they fylyd.   *defiled*

But Mary, byrde, thowe neyd not soo
210   For this cause to be puryfiede, loo,
In Goddes Temple;
For certys thowe arte a clene vyrgyn
For any thoght thy harte within
Nor never wroght no flesly synne
215   Nor never yll.

MARY   That I my madenheade hais kept styll
It is onely throgh Godds wyll,
That be ye bold;   *very assured*
Yett to fulfyll the lawe ewysse   *iwisse (to be sure)*
220   That God almyghty gon expresse   *did reveal*
And for a sample of mekenesse,   *example*
Offer I wolde.

Joseph   A, Mary, blyssed be thowe ay;
　　　　Thowe thynkes to do after Goddes wyll;
225　As thowe haist said, Mary, I say,
　　　　I will hartely consent theretyll
　　　　Withouten dowte.   *doubt*
　　　　Wherefore we dresse us furth oure way   *undertake; on our way*
　　　　And make offerand to God this day,
230　Even lykwyse as thyself gon say
　　　　With hartes devowte.

Maria   Therto am I full redy dight.
　　　　But one thyng, Joseph, I wolde you meyve.   *point out*

Joseph   Mary, my spouse and madyn bright,
235　Tell on hartely, what is your greyf?   *sorrow*

Maria   Both beest and fewell hus muste neydes have,   *fowl we*
　　　　As a lambe and two dove byrdes also.
　　　　Lame have we none nor none we crave;   *seek*
　　　　Therefore, Joseph, what shall we do,
240　What is your read?   *advice*
　　　　And we do not as custome is,
　　　　We are worth to be blamyd iwysse;
　　　　I wolde we dyd nothyng amys,
　　　　As God me speyd.

Joseph   A, good Mary, the lawe is this:
246　To riche to offer bothe the lame and the byrd,   *rich folk; bird*
　　　　And the poore two tyrtles iwys.   *turtledoves*
　　　　Or two doyf byrdes shall not be fyrd   *dove; rejected*
　　　　For our offerand,   *offering*
250　And, Mary, we have doyf byrdes two
　　　　As falls for hus, therefore we goo.
　　　　They ar here in a panyer, loo,   *basket*
　　　　Reddy at hand.

　　　　And yf we have not both in feer,
255　The lame, the burd, as ryche men have,
　　　　Thynke that us muste present here
　　　　Oure babb Jesus, as we voutsave   *are willing*
　　　　Before Godes sight.
　　　　He is our lame, Mary, kare thee not,   *worry*
260　For riche and power none better soght.
　　　　Full well thowe hais hym hither broght,
　　　　This our offerand dight.

He is the lame of God, I say,
That all our syns shall take away
265 Of this worlde here.
He is the lame of God verray
That muste hus fend frome all our fray,   *Who must defend us*
Borne of thy wombe, all for our pay   *advantage*
And for our chere.

MARIA Joseph, my spowse, ye say full trewe,
271 Than lett us dresse hus furth our way.   *set forth*

JOSEPH Go we than, Mary, and do oure dewe   *duty*
And make meekly offerand this day.
Lo, here is the Tempyll on this hyll
275 And also preest ordand by skyll,
Power havand.   *having*
And Mary, go we thyther forthy,
And lett us both knele devowtly
And offre we up to God meekly
280 Our dewe offrand.   *rightful*

MARIA Unto my God highest in heven
And to this preest ordand by skyll,
Jesu my babb I offer hyme   *him*
Here with my harte and my good wyll
285 Right hartely.
Thowe pray for hus to God on hyght,   *high*
Thowe preest, present here in his myght,
At this deyd may be in his sight,   *deed*
Accept goodly.

JOSEPH Loo, sir, and two doyf byrddes ar here.
291 Receyve them with your holy handes,
We ar no better of power,
For we have neyther rentes ne landes
Trewely.
295 Bott good sir, pray to God of myght
To accepte this at we have dight   *this which we*
That we have offeryd as we arr hight   *are called*
Here hartely.

PRESBITER O God and graunter of all grace,
300 Blyst be thy name both nyght and day,
Accepte there offerand in this place   *their*
That be here present to thee alway.
A, blyssed Lorde, say never nay,   *(i.e., don't refuse)*
But lett thy offerand be boot and beylde   *assistance; comfort*

305 Tyll all such folke lyvand in clay
     That thus to thee mekly wyll heyld.   *incline*

     That this babb, Lord, present in thy sight,
     Borne of a madyns wombe unfylde,   *undefiled*
     Accepte for there specyall gyft
310 Gevyn to mankynde, both man and chylde,
     So specyally,
     And this babb borne and here present
     May beylde us that we be not shent,   *comfort; condemned*
     But ever reddy his grace to hent   *grasp*
315 Here verely.   *truly*

     A, blyssyd babb, welcome thowe be,
     Borne of a madyn in chaistety,
     Thowe art our beylde, babb, our gamme and our glee   *comfort; joy*
     Ever sothly.
320 Welcome oure wytt and our wysdome,
     Welcome our joy all and somme,
     Welcomme *redemptour omnium*   *redeemer of all [the world]*
     Tyll hus hartely.   *To us sincerely*

ANNA PROPHETISSA Welcome blyssed Mary and madyn ay,
325 Welcome mooste meke in thyne array,
     Welcome bright starne that shyneth bright as day,
     All for our blys;
     Welcome, the blyssed beam so bryght,
     Welcome the leym of all oure light,   *(i.e., source)*
330 Welcome that all pleasour hais plight
     To man and wyfe.

     Welcome thowe blyssed babb so free,
     Welcome oure welfayre wyelly   *joyfully*
     And welcome all oure seall, suthly,   *well-being*
335 To grete and small.
     Babb, welcome to thy beyldly boure,   *sheltering bower*
     Babb, welcome nowe for our soccoure,
     And babb, welcomme with all honour
     Here in this hall.

ANGELUS Olde Symeon, I say to thee,
341 Dresse thee furth in thyne array,   *(i.e., Put on your vestments)*
     Come to the Temple, there shall thu see
     Jesus that babb that Mary barre,   *bore*
     That be thowe bolde.   *very certain*

SYMEON A, Lorde, I thanke thee ever and ay,
346 Nowe am I light as leyf on tree;   *leaf*
     My age is went, I feyll no fray,   *gone; feel; trouble*
     Methynke for this that is tolde me
     I ame not olde.

350 Nowe wyll I to yon Temple goo
     To se the babb that Mary bare;
     He is my helth in well and woo   *prosperity; woe*
     And helps me ever frome great care,
     Haill blyssed babb that Mary bare,
355 And blyssed be thy mother, Mary mylde,
     Whose wombe that yeildyd fresh and fayr
     And she a clean vyrgen ay unfyld.

     Haill, babb, the Father of heven own chylde,
     Chosen to chere us for our myschance;
360 No erthly tong can tell fylyd   *[if] defiled*
     What thy myght is in every chance.
     Haill, the moost worthy to enhance,
     Boldly thowe beylde frome all yll,   *protect*
     Withoute thy beylde we gytt grevance   *shelter*
365 And for our deydes here shulde we spyll.

     Haill floscampy and flower vyrgynall,   *flower of the field*
     The odour of thy goodnes reflars to us all;   *rises up*
     Haill, moost happy to great and to small
     For our weyll.   *prosperity*
370 Haill ryall roose, moost ruddy of hewe,   *rose*
     Haill flour unfadyng, both freshe ay and newe,
     Haill the kyndest in comforth that ever man knewe
     For grete heyll.   *health*

     And mekly I beseke thee here where I kneyll   *kneel*
375 To suffre thy servant to take thee in hand,
     And in my narmes for to heve thee here for my weyll,   *arms; take you up*
     And where I bound am in bayll to bait all my bandes.   *bale; release; bonds*

     Nowe come to me, Lorde of all landes,
     Comme myghtyest by see and by sandes,
380 Come myrth by strete and by strandes
     On moolde.   *earth*
     Come halse me, the babb that is best born,   *embrace*
     Come halse me, the myrth of our morne,   *morning*
     Come halse me, for ells I ame lorne   *lost*
385 For olde.

      I thanke the Lord God of thy greet grace
      That thus haith sparyd me a space,   *space [of time]*
      This babb in my narmes for to inbrace   *arms; embrace*
      As the prophecy telles.
390 I thanke thee that me my lyfe lent,
      I thanke thee that me thus seyll sent,   *happiness*
      That this sweyt babb, that I in armes hent   *sweet; carried*
      With myrth my myght alwais melles.   *strength; infuses*

      Mellyd are my myndes ay with myrth,   *thoughts*
395 Full fresh nowe I feyll is my force,   *feel*
      Of thy grace thowe gave me this gyrth   *protection*
      Thus comly to catch here thy corse   *body*
      Moost semely in sight.
      Of helpe thus thy freynd never faills,
400 Thy marcy as every man avaylls   *mercy*
      Both by downes and by daylls;   *hills; dales*
      Thus mervelous and muche is thy myght.

      A, babb, be thow blyssed for ay,
      For thowe art my Savyour, I say,
405 And thowe here rewles me in fay   *rules; faith*
      In all my lyfe.
      Nowe blist be thi name,
      For thowe saves hus fro shame,   *us from*
      And here thou beyld us fro blame   *shelter*
410 And frome all stryfe.

      Nowe care I no moore for my lyfe
      Sen I have seen here this ryall so ryfe,   *royal [child]; (i.e., remarkable)*
      My strength and my stynter of stryfe,   *suppressor*
      I you say.
415 In peace, Lorde, nowe leyf thy servand,   *leave (allow)*
      For myne eys haith seyn that is ordand,
      The helth for all men that be levand   *living*
      Here for ay.

      That helth, Lorde, hais thowe ordand, I say,
420 Here before the face of thy people,
      And thy light hais thowe shynyd this day   *has*
      To be knowe of thy folke that was febyll   *weak*
      For evermore.
      And thy glory for the chylder of Israell
425 That with thee in thy kyngdome shall dwell
      Whan the damnyd shall be drevyn to hell   *When; driven*
      Than with great care.   *Then; suffering*

JOSEPH Mary, my spowse and madyn mylde,
    In hart I marvell here greatly
430 Howe these folke spekes of our chylde.
    They say and tells of great maistry
    That he shall doo.

MARIA Yea certes, Joseph, I marvell also,
    But I shall bere it full styll in mynde.   *bear; quietly*

JOSEPH God geve hyme grace here well to do,
436 For he is comme of gentyll kynde.   *lineage*

SYMEON Harke, Mary, I shall tell thee the truth or I goo.   *ere*
    This was putt here to welde us fro wo,   *protect*
    In redemption of many and recover also,
440 I thee say.
    And the sworde of sorro thy hart shal thryll   *pierce*
    Whan thowe shall se sothly thy Son soffer yll   *suffer ill (evil)*
    For the well of all wrytches, that shall be his wyll   *well (source); riches*
    Here in fay.   *faith*

445 But to be comforth agayn right well thowe may,
    And in harte to be fayne, the suth I thee say,   *happy*
    For his myght is so muche thare can no tong say nay
    Here to his wyll.
    For this babb as a gyant full graythly shall glyde   *giant; truly; glide*
450 And the myghtiest mayster shall meve on ylke syde,   *move*
    To all the wightes that wons in this worlde wyde,   *men; live*
    For good or for yll.

    Tharefore babb, beylde us that we here not spyll   *shelter; come to grief*
    And fayrwell the former of all at thy wyll,
455 Fayrwell starne stabylyst by lowde and be styll,   *star most stable; (i.e., ?constant)*
    In suthfastnes.
    Fayrwell the ryolest roose that is renyng,   *most royal rose; reigning*
    Fayrwell the babb best in thy beryng,   *birth*
    Fayrwell God Son, thowe grant us thy blyssyng
460 To fyne our dystresse.   *end*

[18. THE FLIGHT TO EGYPT]

The Marchallis

JOSEPH Thow maker that is most of myght,
    To thy mercy I make my mone;   *moan*
    Lord, se unto thin symple wight   *thine; man*

That hase non helpe but thee allone.
5 For all this worlde I have forsaken
And to thy service I have me taken *engaged myself*
With witte and will
For to fulfill
Thi commaundement.
10 Theron myn herte is sette; *heart*
With grace thou has me lente, *given*
Thare schall no lede me lette. *person prevent*

For all my triste, Lorde, is in thee *trust*
That made me, man, to thy liknes,
15 Thow myghtfull maker, have mynde on me
And se unto my sympplenes. *sincerity*
I waxe wayke as any wande, *grow weak; wand (stick)*
For febill me faylles both foote and hande, *weakness; fail*
Whatevere it mene,
20 Methynke myne eyne *eyes*
Hevye as leede. *lead*
Therfor I halde it best
A whille her in this stede *place*
To slepe and take my reste.

MARIA Thow luffely Lord that last schall ay,
26 My God, my Lorde, my Sone so dere,
To thy Godhede hartely I pray
With all myn harte holy entere; *entire*
As thou me to thy modir chaas, *chose*
30 I beseke thee of thy grace *beseech*
For all mankynde
That has in mynde
To wirshippe thee.
Thou se thy saules to save,
35 Jesu, my Sone so free,
This bone of thee I crave. *request*

ANGELUS Wakyn, Joseph, and take entent. *pay attention*
My sawes schall seece thy sorowe sare; *words; cease (allay); sore*
Be noght hevy, thi happe is hentte, *sad; fortune; embraced*
40 Tharefore I bidde thee slepe no mare. *more*

JOSEPH A, myghtfull Lorde, whatevere that mente?
So swete a voyce herde I nevere ayre. *before*
But what arte thou with steven so shylle *voice so sweet sounding*
Thus in my slepe that spekis me till?
45 To me appere

And late me here   *let me hear*
What that thou was.

ANGELUS   Joseph, have thou no drede,
Thou shalte witte or I passe;   *understand before I leave*
50   Therfore to me take hede.

For I am sente to thee,
Gabriell, Goddis aungell bright,
Is comen to bidde thee flee
With Marie and hir worthy wight,
55   For Horowde the kyng gars doo to dede   *Herod; plans to kill*
All knave childer in ilke a stede   *male children; place*
That he may ta   *take (capture)*
With yeris twa   *two*
That are of olde.
60   Tille he be dede, away
In Egipte shall ye beelde   *stay*
Tille I witte thee for to saie.   *have informed you*

JOSEPH   Ayelastand Lorde, loved mott thou be   *Everlasting; praised may*
That thy swete sande wolde to me sende.   *messenger*
65   But, Lorde, what ayles the kyng at me?   *vexes; against me*
For unto hym I nevere offende.
Allas, what ayles hym for to spille   *destroy*
Smale yonge barnes that nevere did ille   *Little young boys*
In worde ne dede
70   Unto no lede   *man*
Be nyght nor day.
And sen he wille us schende,   *destroy*
Dere Lorde, I thee praye,
Thou wolde be oure frende.

75   For be he nevere so wode or wrothe,   *mad; angry*
For all his force thou may us fende.   *defend*
I praye thee, Lorde, kepe us fro skathe,   *harm*
Thy socoure sone to us thou sende;   *soon*
For unto Egipte wende we will
80   Thy biddyng baynely to fulfill,   *obediently*
As worthy is
Thou kyng of blisse;
Thi will be wroght.
Marie, my doughtir dere,   *beloved young woman*
85   On thee is all my thought.

MARIA   A, leve Joseph, what chere?   *dear*

JOSEPH The chere of me is done for ay. *My cheer is gone*

MARIA Allas, what tythandis herde have ye?

JOSEPH Now certis, full ille to thee at saye, *(i.e., it is hard to say this)*
90 Ther is noght ellis but us most flee *we must*
Owte of oure kyth where we are knowyn, *native region*
Full wightely bus us be withdrawen, *quickly must*
Both thou and I.

MARIA Leve Joseph, why?
95 Layne it noght, *Conceal*
To doole who has us demed? *dole; judged*
Or what wronge have we wroght
Wherfore we shulde be flemyd? *banished*

JOSEPH Wroght we harme, nay, nay, all wrang,
100 Wytte thou wele it is noght soo; *Know you well*
That yonge page liffe thou mon forgange *boy's life; may surrender*
But yf thou fast flee fro his foo. *Unless; foe*

MARIA His foo, allas, what is youre reede, *advice*
Wha wolde my dere barne do to dede? *Who; death*
105 I durk, I dare, *shrink back, I am afraid*
Whoo may my care
Of balis blynne? *bales (sorrow) put an end*
To flee I wolde full fayne; *gladly*
For all this worlde to wynne
110 Wolde I noght se hym slayne.

JOSEPH I warne thee he is thraly thrette *angrily threatened*
With Herowde kyng, harde harmes to have; *By*
With that mytyng yf that we be mette *small one*
Ther is no salve that hym may save. *remedy*
115 I warne thee wele, he sleeis all *slays*
Knave childir, grete and small,
In towne and felde *field*
Within the elde *age*
Of two yere
120 And for thy Sones sake;
He will fordo that dere, *destroy; dear one*
May that traytoure hym take.

MARIA Leve Joseph, who tolde yow this?
How hadde ye wittering of this dede? *information*

JOSEPH An aungell bright that come fro blisse   *heaven*
126   This tythandis tolde withouten drede,   *fear*
         And wakynd me oute of my slepe
         That comely childe fro cares to kepe,
         And bad me flee
130   With hym and thee
         Onto Egipte.
         And sertis I dred me sore
         To make any smale trippe,   *journey*
         Or tyme that I come thare.   *Ere I come there*

MARIA What ayles thei at my barne
136   Slike harmes hym for to hete?   *Such; threaten*
         Allas, why schulde I tharne   *lose*
         My Sone his liffe so swete.
         His harte aught to be ful sare   *sore*
140   On slike a foode hym to forfare   *such a child; kill*
         That nevir did ill
         Hym for to spill,   *destroy*
         And he ne wate why.   *knows not*
         I ware full wille of wane   *(i.e., I'd be confused about this)*
145   My Sone and he shulde dye,
         And I have but hym allone.

JOSEPH We, leve Marie, do way, late be,   *dear*
         I pray thee, leve of thy dynne   *leave off; clamoring*
         And fande thee furthe faste for to flee   *prepare yourself quickly*
150   Away with hym for to wynne   *rescue*
         That no myscheve on hym betyde,
         Nor none unhappe in no kyn side,   *misfortune anywhere*
         Be way nor strete,
         That we non mete   *no one meet*
155   To slee hym.

MARIA Allas, Joseph, for care.
         Why shuld I forgo hym,   *part with him*
         My dere barne that I bare?

JOSEPH That swete swayne yf thou save,
160   Do tyte, pakke same oure gere   *quickly, pack together*
         And such smale harnes as we have.   *baggage*

MARIA A, leve Joseph, I may not bere.   *bear (carry)*

JOSEPH Bere arme? No, I trowe but small,
         But God it wote I muste care for all,   *God knows*
165   For bed and bak,   *clothes*

And alle the pakke
That nedis unto us.
It fortheres to fene me,   *expedites things if I do not shirk*
This pakald bere me bus,   *package; must*
170   Of all I plege and pleyne me.   *(i.e., Even if I complain about it)*

But God graunte grace I noght forgete
No tulles that we shulde with us take.   *tools*

MARIA   Allas, Joseph, for grevaunce grete,
Whan shall my sorowe slake,   *When*
175   For I wote noght whedir to fare.

JOSEPH   To Egipte talde I thee lang are.   *long ere*

MARIA   Whare standith itt?
Fayne wolde I witt.   *know*

JOSEPH   What wate I?
180   I wote not where it standis.

MARIA   Joseph, I aske mersy;
Helpe me oute of this lande.

JOSEPH   Nowe certis, Marie, I wolde full fayne,
Helpe thee al that I may
185   And at my poure me peyne   *(i.e., I'll do all in my power)*
To wynne with hym and thee away.   *go*

MARIA   Allas, what ayles that feende   *fiend*
Thus wilsom wayes make us to wende?   *lonely (dangerous)*
He dois grete synne,
190   Fro kyth and kynne   *From*
He gares us flee.   *makes*

JOSEPH   Leve, Marie, leve thy grete.   *weeping*

MARIA   Joseph, full wo is me,
For my dere Sone so swete.

JOSEPH   I praye thee, Marie, happe hym warme   *wrap; warmly*
196   And sette hym softe that he noght syle,   *slip down*
And yf thou will ought ese thyn arme,
Gyff me hym, late me bere hym awhile.   *Give; let; bear*

MARIA   I thanke you of youre grete goode dede;
200   Nowe gud Joseph tille hym take hede,   *to*

That fode so free   *infant*
Tille hym ye see   *See that you (attend) to him*
Now in this tyde.   *time*

JOSEPH   Late me and hym allone,   *Let*
205   And yf thou can ille ride
Have and halde thee faste by the mane.

MARIA   Allas, Joseph, for woo,
Was never wight in worde so will.   *man; world; wild (distraught)*

JOSEP[H]   Do way, Marie, and say nought soo,
210   For thou schall have no cause thertill.
For witte thou wele, God is oure frende;
He will be with us wherso we lende;
In all oure nede
He will us spede,
215   This wote I wele;
I love my Lorde of all,
Such forse methynke I fele,   *strength*
I may go where I schall.

Are was I wayke, nowe am I wight,   *Ere; weak; strong*
220   My lymes to welde ay at my wille;   *limbs; wield (move)*
I love my maker most of myght
That such grace has graunte me tille.   *has been granted*
Nowe schall no hatyll do us harme,   *person*
I have oure helpe here in myn arme.
225   He wille us fende   *defend*
Wherso we lende
Fro tene and tray.   *From harm and treachery*
Late us goo with goode chere,
Farewele and have gud day.
230   God blisse us all in fere.

MARIA   Amen as he beste may.

[19. THE MASSACRE OF THE INNOCENTS]

The Gyrdillers and Naylers

HEROD   Powre bewcheris aboute,   *Poor good sirs*
Peyne of lyme and lande,   *Pain; limb*
Stente of youre stevenes stoute,   *Stop; shouting loud*
And stille as stone ye stande,
5   And my carping recorde.   *speaking pay attention to*

	Ye aught to dare and doute,	*fear; worry*
	And lere you lowe to lowte	*learn; bow (reverence)*
	To me, youre lovely lord.	
	Ye awe in felde and towne	*ought*
10	To bowe at my bidding	
	With reverence and renoune,	
	As fallis for swilk a kyng,	*befits*
	The lordlyest on lyve	*alive*
	Who herto is noght bowne,	*obliged*
15	Be allmighty Mahounde,	
	To dede I schall him dryve.	*death*
	So bolde loke no man be,	
	For to aske helpe ne holde	*support*
	But of Mahounde and me	
20	That hase this worlde in welde	*[our] keeping*
	To mayntayne us emell;	*between us*
	For welle of welthe are we,	*fountain (source)*
	And my cheffe helpe is he;	*principal*
	Herto what can ye tell?	

I CONSOLATOR Lord, what you likis to do

26	All folke will be full fayne,	*glad*
	To take entente therto,	*pay attention*
	And none grucche ther agayne.	*complain; against*
	That full wele witte shall ye,	*well know*
30	And yf thai wolde noght soo,	
	We shulde sone wirke tham woo.	*soon work them*

HERODES Ya, faire sirs, so shulde it bee.

II CONSOLATOR Lorde, the soth to saie,

	Fulle wele we undirstande,	
35	Mahounde is god werraye,	*very (true)*
	And ye ar lorde of ilke a lande.	*every*
	Therfore so have I seell,	*well-being*
	I rede we wayte allway,	*advise; watch*
	What myrthe most mende you may.	

HERODES Sertis, ye saie right well.

41	But I am noyed of newe,	*annoyed*
	That blithe may I noght be,	*happy*
	For thre kyngis, as ye knowe,	
	That come thurgh this contré,	*through*
45	And saide thei sought a swayne.	*squire (or knight)*

I CONSOLATOR   That rewlle I hope tham rewe,   *action; regret*
          For hadde ther tales ben trewe
          They hadde comen this waye agayne.

II CONSOLATOR   We harde how thei you hight   *heard; promised*
50   Yf they myght fynde that childe,
          For to have tolde you right,
          But certis thei are begilyd.
          Swilke tales ar noght to trowe,   *trust*
          Full wele wotte ilke a wight,   *knows every man*
55   Ther schalle nevere man have myght
          Ne maystrie unto you.   *over you*

I CONSOLATOR   Tham shamys so, for certayne,   *They are ashamed*
          That they dar mete you no more.   *meet*

HERODES   Wherfore shulde thei be fayne   *glad*
60   To make swilke fare before,   *reveal such matter*
          To saie a boy was borne
          That schulde be moste of mayne?   *power*
          This gadlyng schall agayne   *base fellow (bastard)*
          Yf that the devyll had sworne.

65   For be well never thei wotte,   *whatever they think*
          Whedir thei wirke wele or wrang,   *work good or ill*
          To frayne garte them thusgate,   *ask make; in this manner*
          To seke that gedlyng gane,   *did*
          And swilke carping to kith.   *reveal*

II CONSOLATOR   Nay, lorde, they lered overe latte   *too late*
71   Youre blisse schal nevere abatte,   *slacken*
          And therfore, lorde, be blithe.   *happy*

NUNCIUS   Mahounde withouten pere,   *Mohammed*
          My lorde, you save, and see.

HERODES   Messenger, come nere,
76   And, bewcher, wele thee be.   *good sir, well*
          What tydyngis, telles thou, any?

NUNCIUS   Ya, lorde, sen I was here,
          I have sought sidis seere   *everywhere*
80   And sene merveyllis full many.   *seen marvels*

HERODES   And of mervayles to move,   *perform*
          That wer most myrthe to me.

NUNCIUS Lorde, even as I have seene,

    The soth sone schall ye see,   *soon*

85   If ye wille, here in hye.   *(i.e., straightaway)*

    I mette tow townes betwene   *between two towns*

    Thre kyngis with crounes clene,   *perfect*

    Rydand full ryally.   *Riding; royally*

HERODES A, my blys; boy, thou burdis to brode.   *jest too broadly*

NUNCIUS Sir, ther may no botment be.   *remedy*

HERODES Owe, by sonne and mone,

92   Than tydis us talis tonyght.   *This indicates tales to us*

    Hopes thou thei will come sone

    Hedir, as thei have hight,   *Hither; promised*

95   For to telle me tythande?   *news*

NUNCIUS Nay, lorde, that daunce is done.   *(i.e., that is over and done)*

HERODES Why, whedir are thei gone?

NUNCIUS Ilkone into ther owne lande.   *Each one*

HERODES How sais thou, ladde? Late be.   *Let*

NUNCIUS I saie, for they are past.   *gone*

HERODES What, forthe away fro me?

NUNCIUS Ya, lord, in faitht ful faste,

103   For I herde and toke hede   *took notice*

    How that thei wente, all thre,

105   Into ther awne contré.

HERODES A, dogges, the devell you spede.

NUNCIUS Sir, more of ther menyng   *significance*

    Yitt well I undirstode,

    How thei hadde made offering

110   Unto that frely foode   *noble child*

    That nowe of newe is borne.

    Thai saie he schulde be kyng,

    And welde all erthely thyng.   *have earthly power over*

HERODES Allas, than am I lorne.   *destroyed*

115   Fy on thaym, faytours, fy!   *liars*
       Wille thei begylle me thus?   *beguile*

NUNCIUS   Lorde, by ther prophicy
       Thei named his name Jesus.

HERODES   Fy on thee, ladde, thou lyes.

II CONSOLATOR   Hense tyte, but thou thee hye,   *quickly; go*
121   With doulle her schall thou dye   *misery (dole) here*
       That wreyes hym on this wise.   *proclaims*

NUNCIUS   Ye wyte me all with wrang,   *blame*
       Itt is thus and wele warre.   *much worse*

HERODES   Thou lyes! false traytoure strange,
126   Loke nevere thou negh me nere.   *come near*
       Uppon liffe and lymme   *limb*
       May I that faitour fange,   *deceiver catch*
       Full high I schall gar hym hange,   *cause him to hang*
130   Both thee, harlott, and hym.

NUNCIUS   I am nott worthy to wyte,   *do not deserve to be blamed*
       Bot fareswele, all the heppe.   *crowd (i.e., all of you)*

I CONSOLATOR   Go, in the develes dispite,   *malice*
       Or I schall gar thee leppe,   *make; leap*
135   And dere aby this bro.   *dearly pay for; brew (unsavory business)*

HERODES   Als for sorowe and sighte,
       My woo no wighte may wryte.   *man; write (record)*
       What devell is best to do?

II CONSOLATOR   Lorde, amende youre chere,
140   And takis no nedles noy,   *annoyance*
       We schall you lely lere   *truly teach*
       That ladde for to distroye
       Be counsaille if we cane.   *are able*

HERODES   That may ye noght come nere,
145   For it is past two yere
       Sen that this bale begane.

I CONSOLATOR   Lorde, therfore have no doute
       Yf it were foure or fyve.
       Gars gadir in grete rowte   *Bring together; assembly*
150   Youre knyghtis kene belyve,   *(i.e., all ready without delay)*

And biddis tham dynge to dede	*beat them to death*
Alle knave childir kepte in clowte	*male; swaddling clothes*
In Bedlem and all aboute,	
To layte in ilke a stede.	*seek*

II CONSOLATOR Lorde, save none, for youre seell, *well-being*
156 That are of two yere age withinne,
    Than schall that fandeling felle *bastard feel (perceive)*
    Belyve his blisse schall blynne, *Quickly; end*
    With bale when he schall blede. *bleed*

HERODES Sertis, ye saie right wele *say*
161 And as ye deme ilke dele, *judge*
    Shall I garre do indede. *set out to do*

    Sir knyghtis, curtayse and hende, *worthy*
    Thow ne nott bees nowe all newe, *Though this matter is all new*
165 Ye schall fynde me youre frende,
    And ye this tyme be trewe. *If*

I MILES What saie ye, lorde, lette see.

HERODES To Bedlehem bus ye wende,
    That schorwe with schame to schende *shrew; destroy*
170 That menes to maistir me. *intends; overcome*

    And abowte Bedlehem boght *?both*
    Bus yowe wele spere and spye, *inquire and spy*
    For ellis it will be wathe *a danger*
    That he losis this Jury. *causes the loss of*
175 And certis that were grete schame.

II MILES My lorde, that wer us lathe, *loath*
    And he escapid it wer skathe, *If; harm*
    And we welle worthy blame.

I MILES Full sone he schall be soughte,
180 That make I myne avowe. *pledge*

I CONSOLATOR I bide for hym yow loghte, *bid (request); seize*
    And latte me telle yowe howe *let*
    To werke when ye come there,
    Bycause ye kenne hym noght, *know*
185 To dede they muste be brought,
    Knave childre, lesse and more.

HERODES Yaa, all withinne two yere,
       That none for speche be spared.   *eloquence*

II MILES Lord, howe ye us lere
190   Full wele we take rewarde,   *pay heed*
       And certis we schall not rest.

I MILES Comes furth, felowes, in feere,   *all together*
       Loo, fondelyngis fynde we here   *foundlings (bastards); (see note)*
         . . .   [line missing, see note]
I MULIER Owte on yow theves, I crye!
195   Ye slee my semely sone.   *handsome son*

II MILES Ther browls schall dere abye   *brats; dearly pay*
       This bale that is begonne;
       Therfore lay fro thee faste.   *(i.e., let go the child quickly)*

II MULIER Allas, for doule I dye.   *dole*
200   To save my sone schall I,   *son*
       Aye whils my liff may last.

I MILES A, dame, the devyll thee spede,
       And me, but itt be quytte.   *even*

I MULIER To dye I have no drede,
205   I do thee wele to witte,   *(i.e., I want you to know)*
       To save my sone so dere.   *dear*

I MILES As armes! for nowe is nede,   *To arms*
       But yf we do yone dede,
       Ther quenys will quelle us here.   *queans (harlots); frustrate (destroy)*

II MULIER Allas, this lothly striffe.
211   No blisse may be my bette,   *comfort*
       The knyght uppon his knyffe
       Hath slayne my sone so swette;   *sweet*
       And I hadde but hym allone.

I MULIER Allas, I lose my liffe;
216   Was nevere so wofull a wyffe
       Ne halffe so wille of wone.   *(i.e., distraught)*

       And certis, me were full lotht   *reluctant*
       That thei thus harmeles yede.   *unharmed went*

I MILES The devell myght spede you bothe,
221   False wicchis, are ye woode?   *witches; mad*

II MULIER Nay, false lurdayns, ye lye. *rascals; lie*

I MILES   If ye be woode or wrothe, *mad; angry*
         Ye schall noght skape fro skathe; *escape; harm*
225   Wende we us hense in hye. *Go; haste*

I MULIER   Allas, that we wer wroughte
         In worlde women to be,
         The barne that wee dere bought
         Thus in oure sighte to see
230   Disputuously spill. *Controversially killed*

II MULIER   And certis, ther nott is noght, *their business (i.e., labor) is in vain*
         The same that thei have soughte
         Schall thei nevere come till.

I MILES   Go we to the king;
235   Of all this contek kene *combat sharp*
         I schall nott lette for nothyng *hold back*
         To saie as we have sene. *speak; seen [the events]*

II MILES   And certis, no more shall I.
         We have done his bidding;
240   How so they wraste or wryng, *twist and wring*
         We schall saie sothfastly. *tell truthfully*

I MILES   Mahounde, oure god of myght,
         Save thee, sir Herowde the kyng!

I CONSOLATOR   Lorde, take kepe to youre knyght; *pay attention*
245   He wille telle you nowe thydingis
         Of bordis wher they have bene. *amusing stories [about]*

HERODES   Yaa, and thei have gone right, *if they*
         And holde that thei us hight; *promised*
         Than shall solace be sene.

II MILES   Lorde, as ye demed us to done, *judged; to do*
251   In contrees wher we come . . .

HERODES   Sir, by sonne and mone, *sun; moon*
         Ye are welcome home
         And worthy to have rewarde.
255   Have ye geten us this gome? *caught; man*

I MILES   Wher we fande felle or fone, *found many or few*
         Wittenesse we will that ther was none.

II MILES   Lorde, they are dede ilkone,   *dead every one*
          What wolde ye we ded more?   *killed*

HERODES   I aske but aftir oone   *one (only)*
261   The kyngis tolde of before
          That schulde make grete maistrie.
          Telle us if he be tane.   *taken*

I MILES   Lorde, tokenyng hadde we none   *tokens (signs)*
265   To knawe that brothell by.   *worthless fellow*

II MILES   In bale we have tham brought
          Aboute all Bedleham towne.

HERODES   Ye lye, youre note is nought,   *effort is in vain*
          The develes of helle you droune!
270   So may that boy be fledde,
          For in waste have ye wroght.   *(i.e., you have wasted your time)*
          Or that same ladde be sought,   *Ere*
          Schalle I nevere byde in bedde.

I CONSOLATOR   We will wende with you than
275   To dynge that dastard doune.   *strike; wretch (dullard)*

HERODES   As arme, evere ilke man
          That holdis of Mahounde.   *embraces*
          Wer they a thousand skore,   *(i.e., 20,000)*
          This bargayne schall thai banne   *curse*
280   Comes aftir as yhe canne,
          For we will wende before.

          [20. CHRIST AND THE DOCTORS]

The Sporiers and Lorimers

JOSEPH   Marie, of mirthis we may us mene   *speak*
          And trewly telle betwixte us twoo
          Of solempne sightis that we have sene
          In that cité where we come froo.

MARIA   Sertis, Joseph, ye will noght wene   *believe*
6   What myrthis within my harte I maie
          Sen that oure Sone with us has bene
          And sene ther solempne sightis alswae.   *also*

JOSEPH Hamward I rede we hye   *Homeward; advise; go*
10   In all the myght we maye
         Because of company
         That will wende in oure waye.

         For gode felawshippe have we founde
         And ay so forward schall we fynde.

MARIA A, sir, where is oure semely Sone?
16   I trowe oure wittis be waste as wynde,   *(i.e., we were empty headed)*
         Allas, in bale thus am I boone.   *caught (bound)*
         What ayleth us both to be so blynde?
         To go overe fast we have begonne   *too fast*
20   And late that lovely leve behynde.   *left; loved one*

JOSEPH Marie, mende thy chere,
         For certis whan all is done
         He comes with folke in feere   *in company*
         And will overetake us sone.

MARIA Overetake us sone, sir, certis nay,
26   Such gabbyngis may me noght begyle,   *talk; deceive*
         For we have travelde all this day
         Fro Jerusalem many a myle.

JOSEPH I wende he hadde bene with us aye,   *thought; been*
30   Awaye fro us how schulde he wyle?   *wander away*

MARIA Hit helpis nought such sawes to saie.   *words*
         My barne is lost, allas the whille   *child*
         That evere we wente theroute
         With hym in companye;
35   We lokid overe late aboute,   *too late*
         Full wooe is me forthy.

         For he is wente som wayes wrang   *wrong ways*
         And non is worthy to wyte but wee.   *blame*

JOSEPH Agaynewarde rede I that we gang   *Back again; advise; go*
40   The right way to that same citee
         To spire and spie all men emange,   *inquire; among*
         For hardely homward is he.   *hardly (not likely)*

MARIA Of sorowes sere schal be my sang   *many; song*
         My semely Sone tille I hym see,   *handsome*
45   He is but twelve yere alde.

JOSEPH	What way somevere he wendis,	*soever*
	Woman, we may be balde	*bold*
	To fynde hym with oure frendis.	

I MAGISTER	Maistirs, takes to me intente	*pay attention to me*
50	And rede youre resouns right on rawes,	*expound; rows (in order)*
	And all the pepull in this present,	
	Evere ilke man late see his sawes.	*let; sayings (words)*
	But witte I wolde, or we hens wente,	*know*
	Be clargy clere if we couthe knawe	*could know*
55	Yf any lede that liffe has lente	*man*
	Wolde aught allegge agaynste oure lawe,	*allege (challenge)*
	Owthir in more or lesse.	
	If we defaute myght feele,	*error*
	Dewly we schall gar dresse	*Duly; begin to address*
60	Be dome every ilk a dele.	*By judgment everything completely*

II MAGISTER	That was wele saide, so mot I thee,	*might I thrive*
	Swilke notis to neven methynke wer nede,	*Such evidence to identify; needful*
	For maistirs in this lande ar we	
	And has the lawes lelly to lede,	*truly; read (i.e., teach)*
65	And doctoures also in oure degree	
	That demyng has of ilka dede.	*judging; each deed (thing)*
	Laye fourthe oure bokes belyve, late see	*quickly*
	What mater moste were for oure mede.	

III MAGISTER	We schall ordayne so wele	*ordain so well*
70	Sen we all clergy knawe,	*Since*
	Defaute shall no man fele	*Error*
	Nowdir in dede ne sawe.	*saying*

JESUS	Lordingis, love be with you lentte	*praise; given*
	And mirthis be unto this mené.	*company*

I MAGISTER	Sone, hense away, I wolde thou wente,	
76	For othir haftis in hande have we.	*matters*

II MAGISTER	Sone, whoso thee hedir sente,	
	They were nought wise, that warne I thee,	
	For we have othir tales to tente	*attend to*
80	Than nowe with barnes bordand to be.	*jesting (playing)*

III MAGISTER	Sone, yf thee list ought to lere	*learn*
	To lyve by Moyses laye,	*law*
	Come hedir and thou shalle here	*hear*
	The sawes that we shall saye,	*words*

85   For in som mynde itt may thee brynge
       To here oure reasouns redde by rawes.   *hear; expounded; rows (in order)*

JESUS To lerne of you nedis me nothing,
       For I knawe both youre dedys and sawes.   *sayings*

I MAGISTER Nowe herken yone barne with his bowrdyng,   *jesting*
90   He wenes he kens more than we knawes.   *thinks; knows*
       We, nay, certis sone, thou arte overe yonge   *too young*
       By clergy yitt to knowe oure lawes.   *yet to have knowledge of*

JESUS I wote als wele as yhe   *as well*
       Howe that youre lawes wer wrought.

II MAGISTER Cum, sitte, sone schall we see,   *soon*
96   For certis so semys it noght.

III MAGISTER Itt wer wondir that any wight   *person*
       Untill oure reasouns right schulde reche,   *understand*
       And thou sais thou hast insight
100   Oure lawes truly to telle and teche?

JESUS The Holy Gost has on me light
       And has anoynted me as a leche   *redeemer*
       And geven me pleyne poure and might   *power*
       The kyngdom of hevene for to preche.   *preach*

I MAGISTER Whens evere this barne may be   *(i.e., where is he from)*
106   That shewes ther novellis nowe?   *shows; marvelous things*

JESUS Certis, I was or ye   *existed before you*
       And schall be aftir you.

I MAGISTER Sone, of thy sawes, als have I cele,   *health (well-being)*
110   And of thy witte is wondir thyng,
       But neverethelesse fully I feele
       Itt may falle wele in wirkyng,   *emerge; performance*
       For David demys of ilka dele   *judges in every way*
       And sais thus of childir ying,   *young*
115   And of ther mouthes, he wate full wele   *knew*
       Oure Lord has parformed loving,   *praises*
       But yitt, Sone, schulde thou lette   *forbear*
       Here for to speke overe large,
       For where maistirs are mette   *encountered*
120   Childre wordis are noght to charge.   *(i.e., irrelevant)*

And if thou wolde nevere so fayne   *gladly*
Yf all thee liste to lere the lawe,   *are inclined*
Thou arte nowthir of myght ne mayne   *neither*
To kenne it as a clerke may knawe.   *understand*

JESUS   Sirs, I saie you for sartayne   *certain*
126   That suthfast schal be all my sawe,   *truthful; sayings*
And poure have playnere and playne   *power; complete and without ambiguity*
To say and aunswer as me awe.   *ought*

I DOCTOR   Mastirs, what may this mene?
130   Mervayle methynke have I
Whens evere this barne have bene
That carpis thus connandly.   *speaks; expertly*

II DOCTOR   Als wyde in worlde als we have wente,
Yitt fande we nevere swilke ferly fare,   *found; remarkable matter*
135   For certis I trowe this barne be sente
Full soverandly to salve oure sare.   *remedy; suffering*

JESUS   Sirs, I schall prove in youre present   *presence*
Alle the sawes that I saide are.   *sayings; ere*

III DOCTOR   Why, whilke callest thou the firste comaundement
140   And the moste in Moyses lare?   *lore (teachings)*

JESUS   Sirs, sen ye are sette on rowes,   *rows*
And has youre bokes on brede,   *books opened*
Late se, sirs, in youre sawes
Howe right that ye can rede.   *correctly; expound*

I DOCTOR   I rede this is the firste bidding
146   That Moyses taught us here untill,
To honnoure God overe all thing
With all thy witte and all thi will,
And all thyn harte in hym schall hyng,   *hang*
150   Erlye and late both lowde and still.

JESUS   Ye nedis non othir bokes to bring
But fandis this for to fulfill.   *If [you] attempt*
The secounde may men preve   *prove*
And clerly knawe, wherby
155   Youre neghbours shall ye love
Als youreselffe, sekirly.   *certainly*

This comaunded Moyses to all men
In his ten comaundementis clere,

In ther two biddingis, schall we kene,	*these; commandments; know*
160 Hyngis all the lawe that we shall lere.	*Hangs; must learn*
Whoso ther two fulfilles then	
With mayne and myght in goode manere,	
He trulye fulfillis all the ten	
That aftir folowes in feere.	
165 Than schulde we God honnoure	
With all youre myght and mayne	*power*
And love wele ilke a neghboure	
Right as youreselfe certayne.	

I Doctor Nowe, sone, sen thou haste tolde us two,
160... 170   Whilke ar the eight, can thou ought saye?

Jesus The three biddis whareso ye goo,	
That ye schall halowe the halyday;	*Sabbath*
Than is the fourthe for frende or foo	
That fadir and modir honnoure ay.	
175 The fifth you biddis noght for to sloo	*slay*
No man nor woman by any way.	
The sixth, suthly to see,	
Comaundis both more and myne	
That thei schalle fande to flee	*attempt*
180 All filthes of flesshely synne.	
The seventh forbedis you to stele	*steal*
Youre neghboures goodes, more or lesse,	
Whilke fautez nowe are founden fele	*faults; found [to be] many (common)*
Emang ther folke that ferly is.	*wondrous*
185 The eighth lernes you for to be lele	*teaches; truthful*
Here for to bere no false witnesse.	
Youre neghbours house, whillis ye have hele,	*health*
The ninth biddis take noght be stresse.	*force*
His wiffe nor his women	
190 The tenth biddis noght coveyte.	
Thez are the biddingis ten,	
Whoso will lelly layte.	*faithfully seek*

II Doctor Behalde howe he alleggis oure lawe	*expounds*
And lered nevere on boke to rede.	*(was) taught*
195 Full subtill sawes, methinketh, he saies	
And also trewe, yf we take hede.	

III Doctor Ya, late hym wende fourth on his wayes,
For and he dwelle, withouten drede,
The pepull schall full sone hym prayse
200   Wele more than us for all oure dede.

I DOCTOR   Nay, nay, than wer we wrang;   *wrong [to think thus]*
    Such speking wille we spare.
    Als he come late hym gang,   *let; go*
    And move us nowe no more.

MARIA   A, dere Joseph, what is youre rede?   *advice*
206   Of oure grete bale no bote may be;   *sorrow; help*
    Myne harte is hevy as any lede   *lead*
    My semely Sone tille hym I see.
    Nowe have we sought in ilke a stede,
210   Bothe uppe and doune dayes thre,
    And whedir that he be quyk or dede   *alive*
    Yitt wote we noght, so wo is me.

JOSEPH   Mysese had nevere man more,   *Unease (Discomfort)*
    But mournyng may not mende.
215   I rede forther we fare
    Till God som socoure sende.

    Aboute yone Tempill if he be ought,
    I wolde we wiste this ilke nyght.   *learn*

MARIA   A, sir, I see that we have sought.
220   In worlde was nevere so semely a sight.
    Lo, where he sittis, ye se hym noght
    Emong yone maistiris mekill of myght?

JOSEPH   Now blist be he us hedir brought,
    For in lande was nevere non so light.   *happy*

MARIA   A, dere Joseph, als we have cele,
226   Go furthe and fette youre sone and myne;   *fetch*
    This daye is gone nere ilke a dele,   *nearly over*
    And we have nede for to gang hyne.   *go hence*

JOSEPH   With men of myght can I not mell,   *mix (associate)*
230   Than all my travayle mon I tyne;   *effort; lose*
    I can noght with them, this wate thou wele: *know*
    They are so gay in furres fyne.

MARIA   To tham youre herand for to say   *message*
    Suthly ye thar noght drede no dele;   *not at all*
235   They will take rewarde to you allway   *pay attention*
    Because of elde, this wate ye wele.

JOSEPH   When I come there, what schall I saye?
    I wate nevere, als have I cele.   *health (well-being)*

            Sertis, Marie, thou will have me schamed for ay,
240   For I can nowthir croke nor knele.   *bow or kneel*

MARIA   Go we togedir, I halde it beste,
            Unto yone worthy wysse in wede,   *wise [ones] in garments*
            And yf I see, als have I reste,
            That ye will noght, than bus me nede.   *then must I help*

JOSEPH   Gange on, Marie, and telle thy tale firste.
246   Thy Sone to thee will take goode heede.
            Wende fourth, Marie, and do thy beste;
            I come behynde, als God me spede.

MARIA   A, dere sone Jesus,
250   Sen we love thee allone,
            Why dosse thou thus till us   *do you this to*
            And gares us make swilke mone?   *cause*

            Thy fadir and I betwyxte us twa,
            Son, for thy love has likid ill;   *have been worried*
255   We have thee sought both to and froo,
            Wepand full sore as wightis will.   *Weeping*

JESUS   Wherto shulde ye seke me soo?
            Oftetymes it hase ben tolde you till:
            My Fadir werkis, for wele or woo,   *Father's business*
260   Thus am I sente for to fulfyll.

MARIA   There sawes, als have I cele,
            Can I noght undirstande;
            I schall thynk on tham wele
            To fonde what is folowand.   *discover; following*

JOSEPH   Now sothely, Sone, the sight of thee
266   Hath salved us of all oure sore;   *cured*
            Come furth, Sone, with thi modir and me,
            Att Nazareth I wolde we wore.   *were*

JESUS   Beleves wele, lordis free,
270   For with my frendis nowe will I fare.

I DOCTOR   Nowe, Sone, wher thou schall bide or be,
            Gode make thee gode man evermore.   *[to be a] good*
            No wondir if yone wiffe
            Of his fynding be full fayne;   *glad*
275   He schall, and he have liff,
            Prove till a praty swayne.   *clever squire*

But Sone, loke that thou layne for gud or ill   *be silent*
The note that we have nemed her nowe,   *matter; spoken of here*
And if it like thee to lende her stille,   *remain here*
280   And wonne with us, welcome art thowe.   *dwell*

JESUS   Graunt mercy, sirs, of youre gode will.
No lenger liste me lende with you;   *do I desire to remain*
My frendis thoughtis I wol fulfille
And to ther bidding baynely bowe.   *obediently*

MARIA   Full wele is us this tyde;
286   Nowe maye we make goode chere.

JOSEPH   No lenger will we bide;
Fares wele, all folke in feere.   *in company*

[21. THE BAPTISM OF CHRIST]

The Barbours

JOHANNES   Almyghty God and Lord verray,   *true*
Full woundyrfull is mannys lesyng,   *dishonesty*
For yf I preche tham day be day
And telle tham, Lorde, of thy comyng,
5   That all has wrought,
Men are so dull that my preching
Serves of noght.

When I have, Lord, in the name of thee
Baptiste the folke in watir clere,
10   Than have I saide that aftir me   *Then*
Shall he come that has more powere
Than I to taste;   *feel (show forth)*
He schall giffe baptyme more entire   *complete*
In fire and gaste.   *spirit*

15   Thus am I comen in message right   *correct*
And be forereyner in certayne,   *forerunner*
In wittnesse bering of that light   *bearing*
The wiche schall light in ilka a man
That is comand   *coming*
20   Into this worlde, nowe whoso can
May undirstande.

Thez folke had farly of my fare   *wonder; matter*
And what I was full faste thei spied.   *quickly*

They askid yf I a prophette ware,   *were*
25 And I saide nay, but sone I wreyede;   *revealed*
    High aperte   *openly*
I said I was a voyce that cryede
    Here in deserte.

Loke thou make thee redy, ay saide I,
30 Unto oure Lord God most of myght,
That is that thou be clene haly   *wholly pure*
In worde, in werke, ay redy dight   *prepared*
    Agayns oure Lord,
With parfite liffe that ilke a wight   *perfect life*
35   Be well restored.

For if we be clene in levyng,   *living*
Oure bodis are Goddis tempyll than   *bodies*
In the whilke he will make his dwellyng;   *which*
Therfore be clene, bothe wiffe and man.
40 This is my reed.   *advice*
God will make in yowe haly than   *wholly then*
    His wonnyng steed.   *dwelling place*

And if ye sette all youre delyte
    In luste and lykyng of this liff,   *life*
45 Than will he turne fro yow als tyte   *quickly*
Bycause of synne, boyth of man and wiffe,
    And fro you flee,
For with whome that synne is riffe   *endemic*
    Will God noght be.

I Angelus Thou, John, take tente what I schall saye.   *pay attention to*
51 I brynge thee tythandis wondir gode: *tidings wondrously good*
My Lorde Jesus schall come thys day
Fro Galylee unto this flode   *Galilee; stream (river)*
    Ye Jourdane call,   *Jordan*
55 Baptyme to take myldely with mode   *humbly*
    This day he schall.

John, of his sande therfore be gladde   *message*
And thanke hym hartely, both lowde and still.

Johannes I thanke hym evere, but I am radde   *afraid*
60 I am noght abill to fullfill
    This dede certayne.

II Angelus John, thee aught with harte and will
    To be full bayne   *willing*

	To do his bidding, all bydene;	*forthwith*
65	Bot in his baptyme, John, take tente,	*But*
	The hevenes schalle be oppen sene.	*seen (displayed)*
	The Holy Gost schalle doune be sente	
	To se in sight,	*To be seen*
	The Fadirs voyce with grete talent	*great passion*
70	Be herde full right,	

That schall saie thus to hym forthy

.   .   .   [lacuna, see textual note]

JOHANNES   With wordes fewne   *few*
            I will be subgett nyght and day   *subject*
            As me well awe   *ought*
75   To serve my Lord Jesus to paye   *satisfy*
            In dede and sawe.   *word*

            Bot wele I wote, baptyme is tane   *taken*
            To wasshe and clense man of synne,
            And wele I wotte that synne is none   *I know well*
80   In hym, withoute ne withinne.
            What nedis hym than
            For to be baptiste more or myne
            Als synfull man?

.   .   .   [lacuna, see textual note]

JESUS   John, kynde of man is freele   *nature; frail*
85   To the whilke that I have me knytte,   *joined*
            But I shall shewe thee skyllis twa   *two reasons*
            That thou schallt knawe by kyndly witte   *human intelligence*
            The cause why I have ordand swa,   *ordered so*
            And ane is this: *one*
90   Mankynde may noght unbaptymde go
            Te endless blys.   *To*

            And sithen myselffe have taken mankynde   *man's nature*
            For men schall me ther myrroure make   *example*
            And have my doyng in ther mynde,
95   And also I do the baptyme take.
            I will forthy
            Myselfe be baptiste for ther sake
            Full oppynly.

            Anodir skill I schall thee tell: *Another reason*
100   My will is this, that fro this day
            The vertue of my baptyme dwelle
            In baptyme watir evere and ay,
            Mankynde to taste,   *experience*

| | Thurgh my grace therto to take alway | *receive* |
| 105 | The Haly Gaste. | *Holy Spirit* |

Johannes All myghtfull Lorde, grete is thi grace;
I thanke thee of thi grete fordede. — *preparation*

Jesus Cum, baptise me, John, in this place.

Johannes Lorde, save thy grace that I forbede — *forbid*
110 That itt soo be,
For Lorde, methynketh it wer more nede — *necessary*
Thou baptised me.

That place that I yarne moste of all, — *yearn*
Fro thens come thou, Lorde, as I gesse,
115 How schulde I than, that is a thrall, — *are in subjection*
Giffe thee baptyme, that rightwis is — *righteous*
And has ben evere?
For thow arte roote of rightwissenesse — *righteousness*
That forfette nevere. — *sinned never*

120 What riche man gose from dore to dore
To begge at hym that has right noght? — *from him; absolutely nothing*
Lorde, thou arte riche and I am full poure,
Thou may blisse all, sen thou all wrought. — *bless*
Fro heven come all
125 That helpes in erthe, yf soth be sought, — *truth*
Fro erthe but small. — *little*

Jesus Thou sais full wele, John, certaynly,
But suffre nowe for hevenly mede — *reward*
That rightwisnesse be noght oonlye
130 Fullfillid in worde, but also in dede — *deed*
Thrughe baptyme clere.
Cum, baptise me in my manhed — *manhood*
Appertly here. — *Openly*

Fyrst schall I take, sen schall I preche, — *thereafter*
135 For so behovis mankynde fulfille — *must*
All rightwissenesse, als werray leche. — *as true healer*

Johannes Lord, I am redy at thi will,
And will be ay — *always*
Thy subgett, Lord, both lowde and still, — *subject*
140 In that I may.

A, Lorde, I trymble ther I stande,   *tremble where*
So am I arow to do that dede,   *afraid*
But save me, Lord, that all ordand,   *ordained*
For thee to touche have I grete drede   *dread*
145   For doyngs dark.
Now helpe me, Lorde, thurgh thi Godhede
To do this werk.

Jesus, my Lord of myghtis most,
I baptise thee here in the name
150   Of the Fadir and of the Sone and Holy Gost.
But in this dede, Lorde, right no blame   *apportion*
This day by me,
And bryngis all thase to thy home   *these*
That trowes in thee.

Tunc cantabunt duo angeli Veni creator spiritus.[1]

JESUS   John, for mannys prophete, wit thou wele,
156   Take I this baptyme, certaynely;
The dragons poure ilk a dele   *power in every way*
Thurgh my baptyme distroyed have I,
This is certayne,
160   And saved mankynde, saule and body,
Fro endles payne.

What man that trowis and baptised be
Schall saved be and come to blisse.
Whoso trowes noght, to payne endles
165   He schal be dampned sone, trowe wele this.   *damned soon, trust well*
But wende we nowe   *go*
Wher most is nede the folke to wisse,   *teach*
Both I and you.

JOHANNES   I love thee, Lorde, as sovereyne leche   *healer (savior)*
170   That come to salve men of thare sore;   *heal; their misery*
As thou comaundis I schall gar preche   *(i.e., so shall I go to preach)*
And lere to every man that lare   *teach; lore*
That are was thrall.   *before*
Now, sirs, that barne that Marie bare,   *child; bore*
175   Be with you all.

---

[1] *Then two angels will sing "Come Holy Spirit"*

[22. The Temptation in the Wilderness]

The Smythis

Diabolus Make rome, belyve, and late me gang.	*room, quickly; go*
Who makis here all this thrang?	*noisy crowd*
High thou hense, high myght you hang	*Get*
Right with a roppe.	*rope*
5 I drede me that I dwelle to lang	*fear; too long*
To do a jape.	*jest*
For sithen the firste tyme that I fell	
For my pride fro heven to hell,	
Evere have I mustered me emell	*Always; thus*
10 Emonge mannekynde,	*Among*
How I in dole myght gar tham dwell	*sorrow; make*
Ther to be pynde.	*tormented*
And certis, all that hath ben sithen borne	*born*
Has comen to me, mydday and morne,	
15 And I have ordayned so tham forne,	*on behalf of them*
None may thame fende,	*defend*
That fro all likyng ar they lorne	
Withowten ende.	
And nowe sum men spekis of a swayne	
20 Howe he schall come and suffre payne	
And with his dede to blisse agayne	
Thei schulde be bought.	
But certis this tale is but a trayne,	*trick*
I trowe it noght.	*think*
25 For I wotte ilke a dele bydene	*(i.e., with certainty); indeed*
Of the mytyng that men of mene,	*insignificant person; refer to*
How he has in grete barett bene	*strife*
Sithen he was borne,	
And suffered mekill traye and tene	*great trickery; harm*
30 Bothe even and morne.	
And nowe it is brought so aboute	
That lurdayne that thei love and lowte,	*rascal; venerate*
To wildirnesse he is wente owte	
Withowtyne moo.	
35 To dere hym nowe have I no doute,	*harm*
Betwyxte us two.	

Before this tyme he has bene tent   *been alert*
That I myght gete hym with no glent,   *get (catch); deception*
But now sen he allone is wente
40   I schall assay   *test*
And garre hym to sum synne assente   *cause; some*
If that I may.

He has fastid, that marris his mode,   *affects adversely; mood*
Ther fourty dayes withowten foode;
45   If he be man in bone and bloode
Hym hungris ill;   *greatly*
In glotonye than halde I gude   *hold; good*
To witt his will.   *know*

For so it schall be knowen and kidde   *shown*
50   If Godhed be in hym hidde,
If he will do as I hym bidde
Whanne I come nare,   *near*
Ther was nevere dede that evere he dide   *deed*
That greved hym warre.   *worse*

55   Thou witty man and wise of rede,
If thou can ought of Godhede,
Byd nowe that ther stones be brede   *bread*
Betwyxte us two.
Than may thei stande thyselfe in stede   *[good] stead*
60   And othir moo.   *more*

For thou hast fastid longe, I wene,
I wolde now som mete wer sene   *food*
For olde acqueyntaunce us bytwene,
Thyselve wote howe.   *know*
65   Ther sall no man witte what I mene
But I and thou.

JESUS   My Fadir, that all cytte may slake,   *sorrow*
Honnoure everemore to thee I make
And gladly suffir I for thy sake
70   Swilk velany,
And thus temptacions for to take
Of myn enmy.   *enemy*

Thou weried wight, thi wittis are wode,   *accursed creature; mad*
For wrytyn it is, whoso undirstande,
75   A man lyvis noght in mayne and mode
With brede allone,

But Goddis wordis are gostly fode | *spiritual food*
To men ilkone. | *each one*

Iff I have fastid oute of skill, | *unreasonably*
80 Wytte thou me hungris not so ill
That I ne will wirke my Fadirs will
In all degré;
Thi biddyng will I noght fullfill,
That warne I thee.

DIABOLUS A, slyke carping nevere I kende; | *such talk*
86 Hym hungres noght as I wende. | *thought*
Nowe sen thy Fadir may thee fende | *defend*
Be sotill sleghte, | *By subtle sleight*
Late se yf thou allone may lende | *Let*
90 Ther uppon heghte,

Uppon the pynakill parfitely. | *pinnacle perfectly*

Tunc cantant angeli Veni, creator. | *Then the angels sing "Come, Creator [Spirit]"*

A, ha, nowe go we wele therby;
I schall assaye in vayneglorie | *test [him]*
To garre hym falle, | *cause to fall*
95 And if he be Goddis Sone myghty,
Witt I schall.

Nowe liste to me a litill space: | *listen*
If thou be Goddis Sone, full of grace,
Shew som poynte here in this place
100 To prove thi myght.
Late se, falle doune uppon thi face,
Here in my sight.

For it is wretyn, as wele is kende, | *known*
How God schall aungellis to thee sende,
105 And they schall kepe thee in ther hande
Wherso thou gose
That thou schall on no stones descende
To hurte thi tose. | *toes*

And sen thou may withouten wathe | *danger*
110 Fall and do thyselffe no skathe, | *harm*
Tumbill doune to ease us bathe | *both*
Here to my fete, | *feet*
And but thou do I will be wrothe, | *And if; angry*
That I thee hette. | *promise*

JESUS Late be, warlowe, thy wordis kene,   *warlock; malignant*
116   For wryten it is, withouten wene,   *doubt*
       Thy God thou schall not tempte with tene   *[be] tempted; harm*
       Nor with discorde;
       Ne quarell schall thou none mayntene
120   Agaynste thi Lorde.

       And therfore trowe thou, withouten trayne,   *deception*
       That all thi gaudes schall nothyng gayne,   *tricks*
       Be subgette to thi sovereyne
       Arely and late.   *Early*

DIABOLUS What, this travayle is in vayne,   *effort*
126   Be ought I watte.   *(i.e., For all I know)*

       He proves that he is mekill of price;
       Therfore it is goode I me avise   *advise*
       And sen I may noght on this wise   *in this way*
130   Make hym my thrall,   *slave (captive)*
       I will assaye in covetise
       To garre hym fall,   *cause; [to] fall*

       For certis I schall noght leve hym yitt,   *leave*
       Who is my sovereyne, this wolde I witte.
135   Myselffe ordande thee thore to sitte,   *there*
       This wote thou wele,
       And right even as I ordande itt,   *ordained*
       Is done ilke dele.   *entirely*

       Than may thou se sen itt is soo
140   That I am soverayne of us two,
       And yitt I graunte thee or I goo   *ere*
       Withouten fayle,
       That, if thou woll assente me too,
       It schall avayle.

145   For I have all this worlde to welde,   *govern*
       Toure and toune, forest and felde,   *Tower; field*
       If thou thyn herte will to me helde   *hold (submit [yourself])*
       With wordis hende,   *gracious*
       Yitt will I baynly be thy belde   *willingly; support*
150   And faithfull frende.

       Behalde now, ser, and thou schalt see
       Sere kyngdomes and sere contré;   *many countries*
       Alle this wile I giffe to thee
       For evermore,

155 And thou fall and honour me,
    As I saide are.   *before*

JESUS Sees of thy sawes, thou Sathanas,   *Cease*
    I graunte nothyng that thou me askis;
    To pyne of helle I bide thee passe   *pain; order you to go*
160 And wightely wende   *quickly*
    And wonne in woo, as thou are was,   *dwell; previously*
    Withouten ende.

    Non othyr myght schal be thy mede,   *reward*
    For wretyn it is, who right can rede,   *written*
165 Thy Lord God thee aught to drede   *ought; fear*
    And honoure ay,
    And serve hym in worde and dede
    Both nyght and day.

    And sen thou dose not as I thee tell,
170 No lenger liste me late thee dwell.   *desire; [to] let*
    I comaunde thee thou hy to hell   *go (hurry)*
    And holde thee thar   *(i.e., remain there)*
    With felawschip of fendis fell   *malicious*
    For evermar.

DIABOLUS Owte, I dar noght loke, allas.   *dare*
176 Itt is warre than evere it was;   *worse*
    He musteres what myght he has,   *strength*
    Hye mote he hang.   *High might*
    Folowes fast, for me bus pas   *must pass (be transferred)*
180 To paynes strang.   *strong*

I ANGELUS A, mercy, Lorde, what may this mene?   *signify*
    Me merveyles that ye thole this tene   *endured; affliction*
    Of this foule fende cant and kene,   *cruel and provocative*
    Carpand you till;   *Talking to you*
185 And ye his wickidnesse, I wene,
    May waste at will.   *destroy*

    Methynke that ye ware straytely stedde,   *(i.e., were in a difficult situation)*
    Lorde, with this fende that nowe is fledde.

JESUS Myn aungell dere, be noght adred,
190 He may not greve.   *harass [me]*
    The Haly Goste me has ledde,
    Thus schal thow leve.   *believe*

For whan the fende schall folke see
And salus tham in sere degré,   *assails*
195   Thare myrroure may thei make of me   *Their example*
For to stande still,
For overecome schall thei noght be
Bot yf thay will.

II ANGELUS   A, Lorde, this is a grete mekenesse
200   In yow in whome al mercy is,
And at youre wille may deme or dresse   *judge or direct*
Als is worthy;
And thre temptacions takes expres,   *endure openly*
Thus suffirrantly.   *sovereignly (royally)*

JESUS   My blissing have thei with my hande
206   That with swilke greffe is noght grucchand,   *grief; complaining*
And also that will stiffely stande   *firmly*
Agaynste the fende.
I knawe my tyme is faste command;   *coming*
210   Now will I wende.

[22A. THE MARRIAGE IN CANA]

The Vintenors

ARCHEDECLYNE[1]   Loo, this is a yoyfull day
For me and . . .

[23. THE TRANSFIGURATION]

The Coriours

JESUS   Petir, myne awne discipill dere,
And James and John, my cosyns two,
Takis hartely hede, for ye schall here   *earnestly heed; hear*
That I wille telle unto no moo;
5   And als ye schall see sightis seere   *many*
Whilke none schall see bot ye alsoo,   *but*
Therfore comes forth with me in fere,   *in company*
For to yone mountayne will I goo.
Ther schall ye see a sight
10   Whilk ye have yerned lange.   *long yearned for*

---

[1] *Speech heading: Master of the Feast at Cana*

PETRUS My Lorde, we are full light   *happy*
            And glad with thee to gange.   *go*

JESUS Longe have ye coveyte for to kenne
           My Fadir, for I sette hym before,   *?affirmed*
15   And wele ye wote whilke tyme and when
           In Galylé gangand we were.   *Galilee going*
           "Shewe us thy Fadir," thus saide ye then,
           "That suffice us withouten more."
           I saide to you and to all men,
20   "Who seis me, seis my Fadyr thore."   *there*
           Such wordis to you I spakke   *spake*
           In trewthe to make you bolde,
           Ye cowde noght undyrtake   *[For otherwise] you could not understand*
           The talez that I you tolde.

25   Anodir tyme, for to encresse
           Youre trouthe and worldly you to wys,   *guide*
           I saide, *Quem dicunt homines*
           Esse filium hominis?[1]
           I askid yow wham the pepill chase   *chose*
30   To be mannys Sone, withouten mys;
           Ye answered and saide, "Sum Moyses,"
           And sum saide than, "Hely it is,"   *Elijah*
           And sum saide, "John Baptist."
           Than more I enquered you yitt,   *of you*
35   I askid yiff ye ought wiste   *knew*
           Who I was, by youre witte.

           Thou aunswered, Petir, for thy prowe,   *credit*
           And saide that I was Crist, God Sonne;
           Bot of thyselffe that had noght thowe,   *thou*
40   My Fadir hadde that grace begonne.   *begun*
           Therfore bese bolde and biddis nowe   *be; abide*
           To tyme ye have my Fadir fonne.   *found (seen)*

JACOBUS Lord, to thy byddyng will we bowe
             Full buxumly, as we are bonne.   *obediently; obliged*

JOHANNES Lorde, we will wirke thy will
46   Allway with trew entent.
              We love God lowde and stille
              That us this layne has lente.   *gift*

---

[1] Lines 27–28: *Whom do men say / To be the Son of Man?*

PETRUS Full glad and blithe awe us to be   *ought*
50   And thanke oure maistir, mekill of mayne,
        That sais we schall the sightis see
        The whiche non othir schall see certayne.

JACOBUS He talde us of his Fadir free,
        Of that fare wolde we be full fayne.   *matter; glad*

JOHANNES All that he hyghte us holde will hee;   *promised*
56   Therfore we will no forther frayne,   *question*
        But as he fouchesaffe   *is willing*
        So sall we undirstande.

PETRUS Beholde, her we have nowe in hast
60   Som new tythandys.

HELYAS Lord God, I love thee lastandly   *everlastingly*
        And highly, botht with harte and hande,   *both*
        That me, thy poure prophett Hely,   *poor; Elijah*
        Have stevened me in this stede to stande.   *called*
65   In paradise wonnand am I   *living*
        Ay sen I lefte this erthely lande.
        I come Cristis name to clarifie
        As God his Fadir me has ordand,   *ordained*
        And for to bere witnesse
70   In worde to man and wyffe,
        That this his owne Sone is
        And Lord of lastand liff.   *everlasting life*

MOYSES Lord God, that of all welth is wele,   *well (source)*
        With wille and witte we wirschippe thee,
75   That unto me, Moyses, wolde tell
        This grete poynte of thy pryvyté,   *mystery*
        And hendly hente me oute of hell   *graciously took*
        This solempne syght for I schuld see,
        Whan thy dere darlynges that thore dwell
80   Hase noght thy grace in swilk degree.
        Oure formefadyrs full fayne
        Wolde se this solempne sight
        That in this place thus pleyne   *plain*
        Is mustered thurgh thi myght.   *organized through*

PETRUS Brethir, whatevere yone brightnes be?
86   Swilk burdis beforne was nevere sene.   *marvels*
        It marres my myght, I may not see,
        So selcouth thyng was nevere sene.   *amazing*

JACOBUS What it will worthe, that wote noght wee,   *(i.e., be determined to be)*
90   How wayke I waxe, ye will not wene,   *weak (sleepy)*
     Are was ther one, now is ther thre.   *Before*
     Methynke oure maistir is betwene.

JOHANNES That oure maistir is thare
     That may we trewly trowe;
95   He was ffull fayre beffore,
     But nevere als he is nowe.

PETRUS His clothyng is as white as snowe,
     His face schynes as the sonne.
     To speke with hym I have grete awe,
100   Swilk faire before was nevere fune.   *matter; found*

JACOBUS The tothir two fayne wolde I knawe
     And witte what werke tham hedir has wonne.   *know; hither; transported*

JOHANNES I rede we aske tham all on rowe   *in order*
     And grope tham how this game is begonne.   *interrogate*

PETRUS My bredir, if that ye be come
106 To make clere Cristis name,
     Telles here till us thre,
     For we seke to the same.

HELYAS Itt is Goddis will that we you wys   *inform*
110 Of his werkis, as is worthy.
     I have my place in paradise,
     Ennok my brodyr me by.   *brother [is]*
     Als messenger withouten mys   *sin*
     Am I called to this company
115 To witnesse that Goddis Sone is this,
     Evyn with hym mette and allmyghty.   *equal*
     To dede we wer noght dight,   *death; put*
     But quyk schall we come   *alive*
     With Antecrist for to fyght
120 Beffore the day of dome.   *doom*

MOYSES Frendis, if that ye frayne my name,   *ask*
     Moyses than may ye rede by rawe,   *expound in order*
     Two thousand yere aftir Adam
     Than gaffe God unto me his lawe,   *gave*
125 And sythen in helle has bene oure hame.   *home*
     Allas, Adams kynne, this schall ye knawe:
     Unto Crist come, this is the same   *Until; comes*
     That us schall fro that dongeoun drawe.

	He schall brynge tham to blys	
130	That nowe in bale are bonne;	*bound (captive)*
	This myrthe we may not mys,	
	For this same is Goddis Sonne.	

JESUS My dere discipill, drede you noght,   *dread*
     I am youre soverayne certenly.
135 This wondir werke that here is wrought
     Is of my Fadir almyghty.
     Thire both are hydir brought,
     The tone Moyses, the todir Ely,
     And for youre sake thus are thei sought
140 To saie you, his Sone am I.   *say [to] you*
     So schall bothe heven and helle
     Be demers of this dede,   *judges*
     And ye in erthe schall tell
     My name wher itt is nede.   *necessary*

PETRUS A, loved be thou evere, my Lord Jesus,   *praised*
146 That all this solempne sight has sent
     That fouchest saffe to schew thee thus   *vouchsafe; show*
     So that thi myghtis may be kende.   *known*
     Here is full faire dwellyng for us,
150 A lykand place in for to lende.   *pleasant; remain*
     A, Lord, late us no forther trus,   *go*
     For we will make with herte and hende   *hand*
     A taburnakill unto thee
     Belyve, and thou will bide;   *Forthwith*
155 One schall to Moyses be,
     And to Ely the thirde.

JACOBUS Ya, wittirly, that were wele done,   *wisely*
     But us awe noght swilk case to crave;
     Tham thare but saie and have it sone,
160 Such service and he fouchesaffe.   *if he wills [it]*
     He hetis his men both morne and none   *promises*
     Thare herber high in heven to have;   *[secure] dwelling*
     Therfore is beste we bide hys bone.   *wish*
     Who othir reedis, rudely thei rave.   *advises*

JOHANNES Such sonde as he will sende   *message*
166 May mende all oure mischeve,
     And where hym lykis to lende   *desires; remain*
     We will lende, with his leve.   *leave*

Hic descendunt nubes.   *Here the clouds descend*

PATER IN NUBE Ye ffebill of faithe, folke affraied,

170 Beis noght aferde for us in feere.   *Be*

 I am youre God that gudly grayde   *framed*

 Both erthe and eyre with clowdes clere.   *air*

 This is my Sone, as ye have saide,

 As he has schewed by sygnes sere.

175 Of all his werkis I am wele paied,

 Therfore till hym takis hede and here.   *hear*

 Where he is, thare am I;

 He is myne and I am his:

 Who trowis this stedfastly   *believes*

180 Shall byde in endles blisse.

JESUS Petir, pees be unto thee,

 And to you also, James and John.

 Rise uppe and tellis me what ye see,

 And beis no more so wille of wone.   *be; distraught*

PETRUS A, Lorde, what may this mervayle be?

186 Whedir is this glorious gleme al gone?

 We saugh here pleynly persones thre,   *saw; plainly*

 And nowe is oure Lorde lefte allone.

 This mervayle movis my mynde

190 And makis my flessh affrayed.

JACOBUS This brightnes made me blynde,

 I bode nevere swilke a brayde.   *endured; assault*

JOHANNES Lorde God, oure maker almyghty,

 This mater evermore be ment,   *remembered*

195 We saw two bodis stande hym by   *bodies*

 And saide his Fadir had thame sent.   *them*

PETRUS There come a clowde of the skye,

 Lyght als the lemys on thame lent,   *beams*

 And now fares all as fantasye,

200 For wote noght how thai are wente.   *[we] know*

JACOBUS That clowde cloumsed us clene   *surprised (shocked)*

 That come schynand so clere,   *shining*

 Such syght was never sene,

 To seke all sydis seere.   *seek all around*

JOHANNES Nay, nay, that noys noyed us more   *sound annoyed*

206 That here was horde so hydously.   *heard*

JESUS Frendis, be noght afferde therfore,   *afraid*
   I schall you saye encheson why.   *reason*
   My Fadir wyte how that ye were   *knows*
210 In youre faith fayland and forthy   *failing*
   He come to witnesse ay where,
   And saide that his Sone am I
   And also in this stede   *place*
   To witnesse the same,
215 A quyk man and a dede   *live*
   Come to make clere my name.

PETRUS A, Lord, why latest thou us noght see
   Thy Fadirs face in his fayrenes?

JESUS Petir, thou askis overgrete degree,   *(i.e., too much)*
220 That grace may noght be graunted thee, I gesse.
   In his Godhed so high is he
   As all youre prophetis names expresse,   *proclaim*
   That langar of lyffe schall he noght be
   That seys his Godhede as it is.   *sees*
225 Here have ye sene in sight
   Poyntes of his privité   *mystery*
   Als mekill als erthely wighte
   May suffre in erthe to see.

   And therfore wende we nowe agayne
230 To oure meyné, and mende ther chere.   *company*

JACOBUS Oure felaws ful faste wil us frayne
   How we have faren, al in feere.

JESUS This visioun lely loke ye layne,   *truly; conceal*
   Unto no leffand lede it lere   *living man; reveal*
235 Tille tyme mannys Sone have suffered payne
   And resen fro dede, kens it than clere.   *risen; teach; openly*
   For all that trowis that thyng
   Of my Fadir and me,
   Thay schall have his blessing
240 And myne, so motte it be.

[23A. THE FEAST IN SIMON'S HOUSE]

The Ironmongers

[Not entered. See notes.]

[24. The Woman Taken in Adultery and the Raising of Lazarus]

The Cappemakers and Hatmakers

I Judeus   Steppe fourth, late us no lenger stande   *let*
     But smertely that oure gere wer grayde.   *sharply; equipment; arrayed*
     This felowe that we with folye fande,   *fellow [inferior, or immoral]; found*
     Late haste us fast that she wer flayed.   *punished*

II Judeus   We will bere witnesse and warande
6   How we hir raysed all unarayed   *undressed (nude)*
     Agaynste the lawes here of oure lande
     Wher sche was with hir leman laide.   *lover lying*

I Judeus   Yaa, and he a wedded man,
10   That was a wikkid synne.

II Judeus   That bargayne schall sche banne,   *curse*
     With bale nowe or we blynne.   *before; cease*

I Judeus   A, false stodmere and stynkand strye,   *broodmare; stinking witch*
     How durste thou stele so stille away   *steal*
15   To do so vilaunce avowtry   *wicked adultery*
     That is so grete agaynste oure lay.   *law*

II Judeus   Hir bawdery schall she dere abye,   *dearly pay for*
     For as we sawe, so schall we saye,
     And also hir wirkyng is worthy
20   Sho schall be demed to ded this day.   *judged; death*

I Judeus   The maistirs of the lawe
     Are here even at oure hande.

II Judeus   Go we reherse by rawe
     Hir fawtes as we tham fande.   *faults*

I Judeus   God save you, maistirs, mekill of mayne,   *of great authority*
26   That grete clergy and counsaille cann.   *learning; counsel (wisdom) know*

III Judeus   Welcome, frendis, but I wolde frayne   *ask*
     How fare ye with that faire woman?

II Judeus   A, sirs, we schall you saie certayne
30   Of mekill sorowe sen sche began.
     We have hir tane with putry playne,   *prohibited sex*
     Hirselff may noght gaynesaie it than.

IV JUDEUS What, hath sche done folye
             In fornicacioun and synne?

I JUDEUS Nay, nay, in avowtery   *adultery*
36   Full bolde and will noght blynne.   *cease*

III JUDEUS Avowtery, nemyn it noght, for schame.   *name*
             It is so foule, opynly I it fye.
             Is it sothe that thei saie thee, dame?

II JUDEUS What, sir, scho may it noght denye;
41   We wer than worthy for to blame
             To greve hir, but sche wer gilty.   *harass; unless*

IV JUDEUS Now, certis, this is a foule defame,   *disgraceful situation*
             And mekill bale muste be tharby.

III JUDEUS Ya, sir, ye saie wele thore,   *well there*
46   By lawe and rightwise rede   *correct legal advice*
             Ther falles noght ellis therfore
             But to be stoned to dede.

I JUDEUS Sirs, sen ye telle the lawe this tyde
50   And knawes the course in this contré,
             Demes hir on heght, no lenger hyde,   *Judge; without delay*
             And aftir youre wordis wirke schall we.

IV JUDEUS Beis noght so bryme, bewsheris, abide,   *fast (impatient); good sirs, wait*
             A new mater nowe moves me.
             .   .   .   [pages missing, see note]

III JUDEUS He shewes my mysdedis more and myne;
56   I leve you here, late hym allone.

IV JUDEUS Owe, here will new gaudes begynne;   *sports*
             Ya, grete all wele, saie that I am gone.

I JUDEUS And sen ye are noght bolde,
60   No lengar bide will I.

II JUDEUS Pees, late no tales be tolde
             But passe fourth prevylye.   *unnoticed*

JESUS Woman, wher are tho wighte men went   *those men of authority*
             That kenely here accused thee?
65   Who hase thee dampned, toke thou entent?   *heed*

MULIER Lord, no man has dampned me.

JESUS And for me schall thou noght be schent.   *hurt*
  Of all thy mys I make thee free;   *sin*
  Loke thou no more to synne assentte.

MULIER A, Lord, ay loved mott thou bee.
71 All erthely folke in feere
  Loves hym and his high name
  That me on this manere
  Hath saved fro synne and schame.

I APOSTOLUS A, Lorde, we love thee inwardly
76 And all thi lore, both lowde and still,   *teachings*
  That grauntes thy grace to the gilty
  And spares tham that thy folke wolde spill.   *harm (kill)*

JESUS I schall you saie encheson why,   *reason*
80 I wote it is my Fadirs will
  And for to make tham ware therby   *aware*
  To knawe thamselffe have done more ill.
  And evermore of this same
  Ensample schall be sene: *Example*
85 Whoso schall othir blame,
  Loke firste thamself be clene.

II APOSTOLUS A, maistir, here may men se also
  How mekenes may full mekill amende,   *humility; greatly*
  To forgeve gladly where we goo
90 All folke that hath us oght offende.

JESUS He that will noght forgiffe his foo
  And use mekenesse with herte and hende,   *hand*
  The kyngdom may he noght come too
  That ordande is withouten ende.   *is ordained*
95 And more sone schall we see   *sooner*
  Here or ye forther fare   *before you further*
  How that my Fadir free
  Will mustir myghtis more.   *power greater*

    Lazare mortus.

NUNCIUS Jesu, that es prophett veray,   *very (true)*
100 My ladys Martha and Marie,
  If thou fouchesaffe, thai wolde thee pray   *are willing*
  For to come unto Bethany.
  He whom thou loves full wele alway
  Es seke and like, Lord, for to dye.   *Is sick*

105 Yf thou wolde come, amende hym thou may,
     And comforte all that cumpany.

JESUS   I saie you that sekeness   *sickness*
        Is noght onlye to dede,   *death*
        But joie of Goddis gudnesse   *joy; goodness*
110   Schal be schewed in that stede.   *shown; place*

        And Goddis Sone schall be glorified
        By that sekenesse and signes seere;   *signs various*
        Therfore brethir no lenger bide,   *brother*
        Two daies fully have we ben here;
115   We will go sojourne here beside
        In the Jurie with frendis in feere.   *Jewry (Judea); (i.e., among friends)*

I APOSTOLUS   A, Lorde, thou wote wele ilke a tyde   *know well every time*
        The Jewes thei layte thee ferre and nere   *search for*
        To stone thee unto dede
120   Or putte to pereles payne,   *extreme*
        And thou to that same stede
        Covaites to gange agayne.   *Wish to go*

JESUS   Ye wote by cours wele for to kast,   *well how to compute*
        The daie is now of twelve oures lange,   *hours*
125   And whilis light of the day may last
        It is gode that we grathely gange,   *directly*
        For whan daylight is pleynly past
        Full sone than may ye wende all wrang.   *go astray*
        Therfore takes hede and travayle fast   *labor*
130   Whills light of liffe is you emang.   *life; among*
        And to you saie I more,
        How that Lazar oure frende
        Slepes nowe, and I therfore
        With you to hym will wende.

II APOSTOLUS   We will be ruled aftir thi rede,
136   But and he slepe he schall be save.   *receive salvation*

JESUS   I saie to you, Lazare is dede,
        And for you all grete joie I have.
        Ye wote I was noght in that stede
140   What tyme that he was graved in grave.   *buried*
        His sisteres praye with bowsom beede   *buxom prayer*
        And for comforte thei call and crave;
        Therfore go we togedir
        To make there myrthis more.

I Apostolus Sen he will nedes wende thedir,
146   Go we and dye with hym ther.

Maria Allas, owtane Goddis will allone   *except*
     That I schulld sitte to see this sight.
     For I may morne and make my mone,   *mourn; moan*
150   So wo in worlde was nevere wight.   *[so] strong*
     That I loved most is fro me gone,
     My dere brothir that Lazar hight,   *is called*
     And I durst saye I wolde be slone,   *slain*
     For nowe me fayles both mynde and myght.   *fails; strength*
155   My welthe is wente forevere,   *felicity*
     No medycyne mende me may.
     A, dede, thou do thy dever   *death; duty*
     And have me hense away.

Martha Allas, for ruthe, now may I rave
160   And febilly fare by frith and felde.   *woods; field*
     Wolde God that I wer grathed in grave,   *buried*
     That dede hadde tane me under telde.   *taken; cover [of earth]*
     For hele in harte mon I nevere have   *hale (well-being)*
     But if he helpe that all may welde.   *support*
165   Of Crist I will som comforte crave,
     For he may be my bote and belde.   *help; support*
     To seke I schal noght cesse   *seek; cease*
     Tille I my sovereyne see.
     Hayle, pereles prince of pesse,
170   Jesu, my maistir so free!

Jesus Martha, what menes thou to make such chere?
     . . .   [pages missing, see textual note]
     This stone we schall full sone
     Remove and sette on syde.

Jesus Fadir that is in hevyn on highte,
175   I thanke thee evere overe all thyng
     That hendely heres me day and nyght   *graciously hears*
     And takis hede unto myn askyng:
     Wherfore fouchesaffe of thy grete myght
     So that this pepull, olde and yyng,
180   That standis and bidis to se that sight   *marvel*
     May trulye trowe and have knowyng
     This tyme here or I pas
     How that thou has me sent.
     Lazar, veni foras,   *Lazarus, come forth*
185   Come fro thy monument.

LAZARUS A, pereles prince, full of pitee,
　　　　　Worshipped be thou in worlde alway
　　　　　That thus hast schewed thi myght in me,
　　　　　Both dede and dolven, this is the fourthe day.　　　*dead and buried*
190　　　By certayne singnes here may men see　　　　　　*signs*
　　　　　How that thou art Goddis Sone verray.
　　　　　All tho that truly trastis in thee　　　　　　　*trusts*
　　　　　Schall nevere dye, this dar I saye.
　　　　　Therfore ye folke in fere,　　　　　　　　*all together*
195　　　Menske hym with mayne and myght,　　　　　*Worship*
　　　　　His lawes luke that ye lere;　　　　　　　*look; learn*
　　　　　Than will he lede you to his light.

MARIA Here may men fynde a faythfull frende
　　　　　That thus has covered us of oure care.　　　　*relieved*

MARTHA Jesu, my Lord and maistir hende,
201　　　Of this we thanke thee evermore.

JESUS Sisteres, I may no lenger lende,　　　　　　*delay*
　　　　　To othir folke nowe bus me fare,
　　　　　And to Jerusalem will I wende
205　　　For thyngis that muste be fulfilled there.
　　　　　Therfore rede I you right,　　　　　　　　*advise*
　　　　　My men, to wende with me.
　　　　　Ye that have sene this sight
　　　　　My blissyng with yo be.　　　　　　　　　*you*

[25. THE ENTRY INTO JERUSALEM]

The Skynners

JESUS To me takis tent and giffis gud hede,　　*pay attention; give good heed*
　　　　　My dere discipulis that ben here,
　　　　　I schall you telle that shal be indede;
　　　　　My tyme to passe hense, it drawith nere,
5　　　　And by this skill
　　　　　Mannys sowle to save fro sorowes sere　　　　*many*
　　　　　That loste was ill.　　　　　　　　　　*evilly*

　　　　　From heven to erth whan I dyssende　　　　*descend*
　　　　　Rawnsom to make I made promys,　　　　　*Ransom*
10　　　The prophicie nowe drawes to ende;
　　　　　My Fadirs wille forsoth it is
　　　　　That sente me hedyr.　　　　　　　　　*hither*

Petir, Phelippe, I schall you blisse
And go togedir

15   Unto yone castell that is you agayne,   *near (against)*
Gois with gud harte and tarie noght,   *tarry*
My comaundement to do be ye bayne.   *obedient*
Also I you charge loke it be wrought
That schal ye fynde
20   An asse, this feste als ye had soght,   *fast (tied up)*
Ye hir unbynde

With hir foole, and to me hem bring   *foal; them*
That I on hir may sitte a space
So the prophicy clere menyng   *meaning*
25   May be fulfilled here in this place:
"Doghtyr Syon,
Loo, thi Lorde comys rydand on an asse,
Thee to opon."   *Upon [it] to you*

Yf any man will you gaynesaye,   *object*
30   Say that youre Lorde has nede of tham
And schall restore thame this same day
Unto what man will tham clayme.
Do thus this thyng,
Go furthe ye both and be ay bayne   *obedient*
35   In my blissyng.

PETRUS Jesu, maistir, evyn at thy wille
And at thi liste us likis to doo,   *as you desire we wish*
Yone beste whilke thou desires thee tille.   *animal; [to be brought] to you*
Even at thi will schall come thee too   *to*
40   Unto thin esse.   *ease (convenience)*
Sertis, Lord, we will thedyre all go   *thither*
Thee for to plese.

PHILIPPUS Lord, thee to plese we are full bayne
Bothe nyght and day to do thi will.
45   Go we, brothere, with all oure mayne   *strength*
My Lordis desire for to fulfill,
For prophycye
Us bus it do to hym by skyll   *reason*
To do dewly.   *duly*

PETRUS Ya, brodir Phelipp, behalde grathely,   *plainly behold*
51   For als he saide we shulde sone fynde,
Methinke yone bestis before myn eye,
Thai are the same we schulde unbynde.

	Therfore frely	*freely (willingly)*
55	Go we to hym that thame gan bynde	*did*
	And aske mekely.	

PHILIPPUS The beestis are comen, wele I knawe;   *[held in] common*
        Therfore us nedis to aske lesse leve,   *permission*
        And oure maistir kepis the lawe.
60   We may thame take tyter, I preve,   *readily; (i.e., I say)*
        For noght we lett.   *refrain*
        For wele I watte oure tyme is breve,   *brief*
        Go we tham fett.   *fetch*

JANITOR Saie, what are ye that makis here maistrie   *act authoritatively*
65   To loose thes bestis withoute leverie?   *livery (authority)*
        Yow semes to bolde, sen noght that ye   *too*
        Hase here to do; therfore rede I   *I command*
        Such thingis to sesse,   *cease*
        Or ellis ye may falle in folye
70   And grette diseasse.   *discomfort*

PETRUS Sir, with thi leve hartely we praye   *permission*
        This beste that we myght have.

JANITOR To what intente, firste shall ye saye,
        And than I graunte what ye will crave
75   Be gode resoune?   *For a valid reason*

PHILIPPUS Oure maistir, sir, that all may save,
        Aske by chesoune.   *reason*

JANITOR What man is that ye maistir call
        Swilke privelege dare to hym clayme?

PETRUS Jesus of Jewes kyng, and ay be schall,
81   Of Nazareth prophete the same,
        This same is he,
        Both God and man, withouten blame,
        This trist wele we.   *trust well*

JANITOR Sirs, of that prophette herde I have,
86   But telle me firste playnly, wher is hee?

PHILIPPUS He comes at hande, so God me save.
        That Lorde we lefte at Bephage,   *Bethpage*
        He bidis us there.

JANITOR Sir, take this beste, with herte full free,
91   And forthe ye fare.

And if you thynke it be to don,   *to be done (i.e., necessary)*
I schall declare playnly his comyng
To the chiffe of the Jewes that thei may sone   *chief*
95   Assemble same to his metyng.   *together to meet him*
What is your rede?   *advice*

PETRUS Thou sais full wele in thy menyng,   *intention*
Do forthe thi dede,

And sone this beste we schall thee bring
100   And it restore as resoune will.   *to you*

JANITOR This tydyngis schall have no laynyng   *shall not be hidden*
But to the citezens declare it till
Of this cyté.   *city*
I suppose fully that thei wolle   *will*
105   Come mete that free.   *[good] person*

And sen I will thei warned be,
Both yonge and olde, in ilke a state,   *every condition*
For his comyng I will tham mete
To late tham witte, withoute debate.   *let them know*
110   Lo, wher thei stande,
That citezens cheff, withoute debate,
Of all this lande.

He that is rewler of all right   *ruler*
And freely schoppe both see and sande,   *graciously shaped*
115   He save you, lordyngis, gayly dight,   *arrayed*
And kepe you in youre semelyté   *seemliness*
And all honoure.

I BURGENSIS Welcome, porter, what novelté   *news*
Telle us this owre?   *hour*

JANITOR Sirs, novelté I can you tell
121   And triste thame fully as for trewe;   *true*
Her comes of kynde of Israell   *tribe*
Att hande the prophette called Jesu,
Lo, this same day,
125   Rydand on an asse; this tydandis newe   *Riding*
Consayve ye may.   *Comprehend*

II BURGENSIS   And is that prophette Jesu nere?
          Off hym I have herde grete ferlis tolde: *wonders*
          He dois grete wounderes in contrees seere.
130   He helys the seke, both yonge and olde,   *heals; sick*
          And the blynde giffis tham ther sight;   *gives*
          Both dome and deffe, as hymselffe wolde,   *dumb; deaf*
          He cures thame right.

III BURGENSIS   Ya, five thowsand men with loves fyve   *loaves*
135   He fedde, and ilkone hadde inowe.   *enough*
          Watir to wyne he turned ryve,   *abundantly*
          He garte corne growe withouten plogh   *made wheat*
          Wher are was none;   *ere*
          To dede men als he gaffe liffe,   *gave life*
140   Lazar was one.

IV BURGENSIS   In oure Tempill if he prechid
          Agaynste the pepull that leved wrong,   *lived*
          And also new lawes if he teched
          Agaynste oure lawis we used so lang,   *[old] laws; long*
145   And saide pleynlye   *plainly*
          The olde schall waste, the new schall gang,   *(i.e., fall . . . rise)*
          That we schall see.

V BURGENSIS   Ya, Moyses lawe he cowde ilke dele,   *knew intimately*
          And all the prophettis on a rowe,   *in order*
150   He telles tham so that ilke a man may fele   *expounds; feel (understand)*
          And what thei may interly knowe   *entirely (fully)*
          Yf thei were dyme,   *difficult [to understand]*
          What the prophettis saide in ther sawe,   *sayings*
          All longis to hym.   *applies*

VI BURGENSIS   Emanuell also by right
156   Thai calle that prophette, by this skill,
          He is the same that are was hyght   *ere was identified*
          Be Ysaye befor us till,   *By Isaias*
          Thus saide full clere:
160   Loo, a maydyn that knew nevere ille   *evil (sin)*
          A childe schuld bere.

VII BURGENSIS   David spake of him I wene   *know*
          And lefte witnesse ye knowe ilkone;
          He saide the frute of his corse clene   *body*
165   Shulde royally regne upon his trone,
          And therfore he
          Of David kyn, and othir none,
          Oure kyng schal be.

VIII Burgensis   Sirs, methynketh ye saie right wele,

170   And gud ensampelys furth ye bryng;   *examples*
      And sen we thus this mater fele,   *matter understand [now]*
      Go we hym meete as oure owne kyng,
      And kyng hym call.
      What is youre counsaill in this thyng,
175   Now say ye all?

I Burgensis   Agaynste resoune I will noght plete,   *plead*
      For wele I wote oure kyng he is.
      Whoso agaynst his kyng liste threte,   *wishes to offend*
      He is noght wise, he dose amys.
180   Porter, come nere,
      What knowlage hast thou of his comyng,
      Tels us all here?

      And than we will go mete that free
      And hym honnoure as we wele awe   *well ought*
185   Worthely tyll oure citee,   *to*
      And for oure soverayne Lord hym knawe
      In whome we triste.   *trust*

Janitor   Sirs, I schall telle you all on rowe
      And ye will lyste.   *listen*

190   Of his discipillis two this day,
      Where that I stode, thei faire me grette   *courteously greeted me*
      And on ther maistir halfe gan praye   *behalf began [to]*
      Oure comon asse that thei myght gete
      Bot for a while
195   Wheron ther maistir softe myght sitte   *in comfort*
      Space of a mile.

      And all this mater thai me tolde
      Right haly as I saie to you,   *wholly*
      And the asse thei have right as thei wolde,
200   And sone will bringe agayne, I trowe,   *soon*
      So thai beheste.   *As; promised*
      What ye will doo avise you nowe,   *consider*
      Thus thinke me beste.

II Burgensis   Trewlye as for me, I say,
205   I rede we make us redy bowne   *advise; prepared*
      Hym to mete gudly this day
      And hym ressayve with grete rennowne,
      As worthy is.

        And therfore, sirs, in felde and towne
210   Ye fulfille this.

JANITOR Ya, and youre childer with you take,
        Thoff all in age that thei be yonge;   *Though*
        Ye may fare the better for ther sake
        Thurgh the blissing of so goode a kyng,   *Through*
215   This is no dowte.   *doubt*

III BURGENSIS I kan thee thanke for thy saying,   *do*
        We will hym lowte;   *worship*

        And hym to mete I am right bayne   *willing*
        On the beste maner that I cane,
220   For I desire to se hym fayne
        And hym honnoure as his awne man   *own*
        Sen the soth I see:
        Kyng of Juuys we call hym than,   *Jews*
        Oure kyng is he.

IV BURGENSIS Oure kyng is he, that is no lesse,
226   Oure awne lawe to it cordis will,   *own; accords (agrees) well*
        The prophettis all bare full witnesse   *bore*
        Qwilke full of hym secrete gone telle,   *Which*
        And thus wolde say,
230   "Emang youreselff schall come grete seele   *joy*
        Thurgh God verray."

V BURGENSIS This same is he, ther is non othir,
        Was us beheest full lange before,   *promised*
        For Moyses saide, als oure owne brothir
235   A newe prophette God schulde restore.
        Therfore loke ye
        What ye will do, withouten more:
        Oure kyng is he.

VI BURGENSIS Of Juda come owre kyng so gent,   *Judah; gracious*
240   Of Jesse, David, Salamon,
        Also by his modir kynne take tente,   *mother's lineage pay attention*
        The genolagye beres witnesse on,   *bears*
        This is right playne.
        Hym to honnoure right as I can
245   I am full bayne.

VII BURGENSIS Of youre clene witte and youre consayte   *conceit (intention)*
        I am full gladde in harte and thought,
        And hym to mete withouten latt   *delay*

I am redy and feyne will noght
250 Bot with you same   *together*
To hym agayne us blisse hath brought
With myrthe and game.

VIII Burgensis   Youre argumentis thai are so clere
I can noght saie but graunte you till,
255 For whanne I of that counsaille here,
I coveyte hym with fervent wille   *desire*
Onys for to see;   *Once*
I trowe fro thens I schall
Bettir man be.

I Burgensis   Go we than with processioun
261 To mete that comely as us awe   *gracious one; ought*
With braunches, floures, and unysoune,   *unison (singing)*
With myghtfull songes her on a rawe.   *here*
Our childir schall
265 Go synge before that men may knawe.

II Burgensis   To this graunte we all.

Petrus   Jesu, Lord and maistir free,
Als thou comaunde so have we done:
This asse here we have brought to thee.
270 What is thi wille thou schewe us sone   *soon*
And tarie noght,
And than schall we, withouten hune,   *delay*
Fulfill thi thought.

Jesus   I thanke you, brethere, mylde of mode.
275 Do on this asse youre clothis ye laye
And lifte me uppe with hertis gud   *hearts good*
That I on hir may sitte this daye
In my blissing.

Philippus   Lord, thi will to do allway,
280 We graunte this thing.

Jesus   Now my brethere with gud chere,
Gyves gode entente, for ryde I will   *Pay close attention*
Unto yone cyté ye se so nere.   *see; near*
Ye shall me folowe, sam and still   *all together*
285 Als I are sayde.   *previously*

Philippus   Lord, as thee lyst we graunte thee till,
And halde us payde.   *well-rewarded*

	Tunc cantant.	*Then they sing*

CECUS   A, Lorde, that all this world has made,
      Bothe sonne and mone, nyght and day,
290   What noyse is this that makis me gladde?   *music (singing)*
      Fro whens it schulde come I can noght saye
      Or what it mene.   *signifies*
      Yf any man walke in this way,
      Telle hym me bedene.   *Let him tell; quickly*

PAUPER   Man, what ayles thee to crye?   *causes*
296   Where wolde thou be, thou say me here?

CECUS   A, sir, a blynde man am I,
      And ay has bene of tendyr yere
      Sen I was borne;
300   I harde a voyce with nobill chere   *heard*
      Here me beforne.   *before me*

PAUPER   Man, will thou oght that I can do?   *do [for you]*

CECUS   Ya, sir, gladly wolde I witte   *know*
      Yf thou couthe oght declare me to;   *(i.e., explain)*
305   This myrthe I herde, what mene may it   *music*
      Or undirstande?

PAUPER   Jesu, the prophite full of grace,
      Comys here at hande,

      And all the cetezens thay are bowne   *en route*
310   Gose hym to mete with melodye,
      With the fayrest processioun
      That evere was sene in this Jury.   *Jewry*
      He is right nere.

CECUS   Sir, helpe me to the strete hastely
315   That I may here

      That noyse, and also that I myght thurgh grace
      My syght of hym, to crave I wolde.

PAUPER   Loo, he is here at this same place.
      Crye faste on hym, loke thou be bolde
320   With voyce right high.   *loud*

CECUS   Jesu, the Sone of David calde,   *called*
      Thou have mercy!

Allas, I crye, he heris me noght. *hears*
He has no ruthe of my mysfare, *pity; misfortune*
325 He turnes his herre, where is his thought? *ear*

PAUPER Cry somwhat lowdar, loke thou noght spare,
So may thou spye.

CECUS Jesu, the salver of all sare, *healer; misery*
To me giffis gode hye! *eye (i.e., heal my blindness)*

PHELIPPUS Cesse, man, and crye noght soo.
331 The voyce of the pepill gose thee by.
Thee aghe sette still and tente giffe to, *ought to sit; pay attention*
Here passez the prophite of mercye.
Thou doys amys. *amiss (wrong)*

CECUS A, David Sone, to thee I crye,
336 The kyng of blisse!

PETRUS Lorde, have mercy and late hym goo.
He can noght cesse of his crying; *cease*
He folowes us both to and froo.
340 Graunte hym his boone and his askyng, *request*
And late hym wende. *go [on his way]*
We gette no reste or that this thyng *unless*
Be broght to ende.

JESUS What wolde thou man I to thee dede? *for you did (performed)*
345 In this present, telle oppynly.

CECUS Lorde, my syght is fro me hydde,
Thou graunte me it, I crye mercy;
This wolde I have.

JESUS Loke uppe nowe with chere blythely: *gladly*
350 Thi faith shall thee save.

CECUS Wirschippe and honnoure ay to thee
With all the service that can be done.
The kyng of blisse loved mote he be *praised might*
That thus my sight hath sente so sone
355 And by grete skill.
I was are blynde as any stone,
I se at wille.

CLAUDUS A, wele wer tham that evere had liffe,
Olde or yonge whedir it were,

360 Might welde ther lymmes withouten striffe;	*wield (move); limbs*
Go with this mirthe that I see here	
And contynewe,	*continue*
For I am sette in sorowes sere	*many*
That ay ar newe.	

365 Thou, Lord, that schope both nyght and day,	*formed*
For thy mercy have mynde on me	
And helpe me, Lorde, as thou wele may.	
. . .	[line missing]
I may noght gang,	*walk*
For I am lame, as men may se,	
370 And has ben lang.	

For wele I wote, as knowyn is ryffe,	*(i.e., everywhere)*
Bothe dome and deffe thou grauntist tham grace,	*dumb; deaf*
And also the dede that thou havyst geven liff;	*dead*
Therfore graunte me, Lord, in this place	
375 My lymbis to welde.	

JESUS My man, ryse and caste the crucchys gode space	*crutches a good distance*
Her in the felde,	*Here; field*
And loke in trouthe thou stedfast be	
And folow me furth with gode menyng.	*intent*

CLAUDUS Lorde, lo, my crouchis whare thei flee	
381 Als ferre as I may late tham flenge	*fling*
With bothe myn hende;	*hands*
That evere we have metyng	
Now I defende.	*forbid*

385 For I was halte both lyme and lame,	*lame both limb and body*
And I suffered tene and sorowes inowe.	*torment; enough*
Aylastand Lord, loved be thi name,	
I am als light as birde on bowe.	*happy; bough*
Ay be thou blist,	
390 Such grace hast thou schewed to me,	
Lorde, as thee list.	

ZACHÉ Sen firste this worlde was made of noght	
And all thyng sette in equité,	
Such ferly thyng was nevere non wroght,	*wonderful*
395 As men this tyme may see with eye.	
What it may mene?	
I can noght saye what it may be,	
Comforte or tene.	*misfortune*

And cheffely of a prophete new	*chiefly*
400 That mekill is profite, and that of latte,	*put forward*
Both day and nyght thai hym assewe,	*follow*
Oure pepill same thurgh strete and gatte,	*street*
. . .	[line missing, see textual note]
Oure olde lawes as nowe thei hatte	*hate*
And his kepis yare.	*readily*
405 Men fro deth to liffe he rayse,	*raises*
The blynde and dome geve speche and sight,	
Gretely therfore oure folke hym prayse	
And folowis hym both day and nyght	
Fro towne to towne.	
410 Thay calle hym prophite be right,	
As of renowne.	
And yit I mervayle of that thyng,	
Of puplicans sen prince am I	*publicans since I am*
Of hym I cowthe have no knowyng.	
415 Yf all I wolde have comen hym nere,	*near*
Arly and late,	*Early*
For I am lawe, and of myne hight	*low (short); of my height*
Full is the gate.	*street*
Bot sen no bettir may befalle,	
420 I thynke what beste is for to doo.	
I am schorte, ye knawe wele all;	
Therfore yone tre I will go too	
And in it clyme.	*climb*
Whedir he come or passe me fro,	
425 I schall se hym.	
A nobill tree, thou secomoure,	*sycamore*
I blisse hym that thee on the erthe broght.	
Now may I see both here and thore	
That undir me hid may be noght;	
430 Therfore in thee	
Wille I bidde in herte and thought	*abide*
Till I hym se.	
Unto the prophete come to towne,	
434 Her will I bide whatso befalle.	

JESUS   Do, Zaché, do fast come downe.   *Zacheus*

ZACHÉ   Lorde, even at thi wille hastely I schall,
       And tarie noght.

To thee on knes, Lord, here I shall
For synne I wroght.

440   And welcome, prophete, trast and trewe,   *trusted*
       With all the pepull that to thee langis.   *belong*

JESUS Zaché, thi service new
       Schall make thee clene
       Of all the wrong that thou haste done.

ZACHÉ Lorde, I lette noght for this thrang   *(i.e., I'm not intimidated by); throng*
446   Her to say sone,

       Me schamys with synne, but noght to mende;   *(i.e., I'm ashamed of my)*
       I synne forsake: therfore I will
       Halve my gud I have unspendid   *Half; goods*
450   Poure folke to geve it till,   *Poor*
       This will I fayne;   *gladly*
       Whom I begylyd to hym will I   *cheated*
       Make asith agayne.   *restitution*

JESUS Thy clere confessioun schall thee clense:
455   Thou may be sure of lastand lyffe.   *everlasting*
       Unto thi house, withouten offense,
       Is graunted pees withouten striffe.   *peace*
       Farewele, Zaché.

ZACHÉ Lord, thee lowte ay man and wiffe,   *worship*
460   Blist myght thou be.

JESUS My dere discipulis, beholde and see,
       Unto Jerusalem we schall assende.   *go up*
       Man Sone schall ther betrayed be   *Man's Son*
       And gevyn into his enmys hande   *enemy's*
465   With grete dispitte.   *malevolence*
       Ther spitting on hym ther schall thei spende
       And smertly smyte.   *hit*

       Petir, take this asse me fro
       And lede it where thou are it toke.   *before; took*
470   I murne, I sigh, I wepe also
       Jerusalem on thee to loke;
       And so may thou
       That evere thou thi kyng forsuke
       And was untrewe.

475   For stone on stone schall none be lefte
      But doune to the grounde all schal be caste;
      Thy game, thi gle, al fro thee refte,   *taken away*
      And all for synne that thou done hast,
      Thou arte unkynde.
480   Agayne thi kyng thou hast trespast,   *trespassed (sinned)*
      Have this in mynde.

PETRUS   Porter, take here thyn asse agayne;
      At hande my Lorde comys on his fette.   *on foot*

JANITOR   Behalde, where all thi burgeis bayne   *[prominent] citizens*
485   Comes with wirschippe hym to mete.
      Therfore I will
      Late hym abide here in this strete
      And lowte hym till.   *venerate*

I BURGENSIS   Hayll, prophette, preved withouten pere,   *proven [to be]; peer*
490   Hayll, prince of pees schall evere endure,
      Hayll, kyng comely, curteyse and clere,
      Hayll, soverayne semely, to synfull sure,   *worthy; a sure help*
      To thee all bowes.
      Hayll, Lorde lovely, oure cares may cure,
495   Hayll, kyng of Jewes.

II BURGENSIS   Hayll, florisshand floure that nevere shall fade,   *flower*
      Hayll, vyolett vernand with swete odoure,   *blooming*
      Hayll, marke of myrthe, oure medecyne made,   *sign of joy*
      Hayll, blossome bright, hayll, oure socoure.
500   Hayll, kyng comely.
      Hayll, menskfull man, we thee honnoure   *exalted*
      With herte frely.

III BURGENSIS   Hayll, David sone, doughty in dede,   *strong; deeds*
      Hayll, rose ruddy, hayll birrall clere,   *beryl*
505   Hayll, welle of welthe may make us mede;   *source of well-being; reward*
      Hayll, salver of oure sores sere,   *healer; many*
      We wirschippe thee.
      Hayll, hendfull, with solas sere,   *courteous [one]; special*
      Welcome thou be.

IV BURGENSIS   Hayll, blisfull babe, in Bedleme borne,   *Bethlehem*
511   Hayll, boote of all oure bittir balis,   *help; miseries*
      Hayll, sege that schoppe bothe even and morne,   *man; formed*
      Hayll, talker trystefull of trew tales.   *teller reliable*
      Hayll, comely knyght,

515 Hayll, of mode that most prevayles   *a disposition*
      To save the tyght.   *imprisoned ones*

V BURGENSIS   Hayll, dyamaunde with drewry dight,   *diamond; ornamented*
      Hayll, jasper gentill of Jury,   *Jewry*
      Hayll, lylly lufsome lemyd with lyght,   *lily worthy of love gleaming*
520 Hayll, balme of boote, moyste and drye,   *assistance*
      To all has nede.   *all who are needy*
      Hayll, barne most blist of mylde Marie,   *child*
      Hayll, all oure mede.   *reward*

VI BURGENSIS   Hayll, conquerour, hayll, most of myght,
525 Hayll, rawnsoner of synfull all,   *ransomer*
      Hayll, pytefull, hayll, lovely light,   *the one who pities*
      Hayll to us welcome be schall.
      Hayll, kyng of Jues,   *Jews*
      Hayll, comely corse that we thee call   *body*
530 With mirthe that newes.   *renews*

VII BURGENSIS   Hayll, sonne ay schynand with bright bemes,   *shining*
      Hayll, lampe of liff schall nevere waste,   *decline*
      Hayll, lykand lanterne luffely lemys,   *fair; lovely beams*
      Hayll, texte of trewthe the trew to taste.   *experience*
535 Hayll, kyng and sire,
      Hayll, maydens chylde that menskid hir most,   *honored*
      We thee desire.

VIII BURGENSIS   Hayll, domysman dredful, that all schall deme,   *(n.) judge; (v.) judge*
      Hayll, quyk and dede that all schall lowte,   *reverence*
540 Hayll, whom worschippe moste will seme,   *befit*
      Hayll, whom all thyng schall drede and dowte.   *fear*
      We welcome thee,
      Hayll, and welcome of all abowte
      To owre cité.

            Tunc cantant.   *Then they sing*

[26. THE CONSPIRACY]

The Cuttelores

PILATUS   Undir the ryallest roye of rente and renowne,   *most royal king; revenue*
      Now am I regent of rewle this region in reste,   *rule; peace*
      Obeye unto bidding bud busshoppis me bowne,   *commands; must; oblige*
      And bolde men that in batayll makis brestis to breste. *burst*
5   To me betaught is the tent this towre begon towne,   *entrusted; care; turreted*

For traytoures tyte will I taynte, the trewthe for to triste,   *quickly; attaint; trust*
The dubbyng of my dingnité may noght be done downe,   *my status (by right of title)*
Nowdir with duke nor dugeperes, my dedis are so dreste.[1]
My desire muste dayly be done
10   With thame that are grettest of game,   *(i.e., most skillful)*
And ther agayne fynde I but fone,   *few*
Wherfore I schall bettir ther bone.   *petitions*
But he that me greves for a grone,   *grieves me with a groan*
Beware, for wyscus I am.   *vicious (see note)*

15   Pounce Pilatt of thre partis   *Pontius*
    than is my propir name.
I am a perelous prince
    to prove wher I peere.   *appear*
Emange the philosofers firste
    ther fanged I my fame,   *achieved*
Wherefore I fell to affecte   *aspire*
    I fynde noght my feere.   *peer*
He schall full bittirly banne   *curse*
    that bide schall my blame,   *endure*
20   If all my blee be as bright   *countenance*
    as blossome on brere.   *briar*
For sone his liffe shall he lose,
    or left be for lame,
That lowtes noght to me lowly   *reverences*
    nor liste noght to leere.   *learn*
And thus sen we stande in oure state
Als lordis with all lykyng in lande,   *felicity*
25   Do and late us wete if ye wate   *let us know if you know (hear)*
Owthir, sirs, of bayle or debate,   *Either; bale*
That nedis for to be handeled full hate   *severely*
Sen all of youre helpe hanges in my hande.

CAIPHAS   Sir, and for to certefie the soth in youre sight,
30   As to you for oure soverayne semely we seke.   *handsome*

PILATUS   Why, is ther any myscheve that musteres his myght
Or malice thurgh meene menn us musters to meke?   *mean (low); subdue*

ANNA   Ya, sir, ther is a ranke swayne   *rebellious*
    whos rule is noght right,
For thurgh his romour in this reme   *realm*
    hath raysede mekill reke.   *riot (commotion)*

---

[1] *Neither with duke nor knights, my deeds are so undertaken*

PILATUS I here wele ye hate hym,   *hear*
    youre hartis are on heght,   *(i.e., you are excited)*
36   And ellis if I helpe wolde   *else*
    His harmes for to eke.   *aggravate*
    But why are ye barely thus brathe?   *so angry*
    Bees rewly, and ray fourth youre reasoune.   *Be calm (Behave); set forth*

CAIPHAS Tille us, sir, his lore is full lothe.   *very hateful*

PILATUS Beware that we wax noght to wrothe.   *too angry*

ANNA Why, sir, to skyfte fro his skath   *escape; malice*
42   We seke for youre socoure this sesoune.   *(i.e., at this time)*

PILATUS And if that wrecche in oure warde   *custody*
    have wrought any wrong,
    Sen we are warned we walde witte   *would know*
    and wille or we wende;   *ere*
45   But and his sawe be lawfull,   *sayings*
    legge noght to lange,   *allege; too long*
    For we schall leve hym if us list   *believe*
    with luffe here to lende.   *in peace; allow*

I DOCTOR And yf that false faytor   *deceiver*
    youre fortheraunce may fang,   *favor; gain*
    Than fele I wele that oure folke   *feel*
    mon fayle of a frende.   *may fail*
    Sir, the strengthe of his steven ay still is so strange   *voice always; strong*
50   That but he schortely be schent, he schappe us to schende.[1]
    For he kennes folke hym for to call   *teaches*
    Grete God Son, thus greves us that gome,   *man*
    And sais that he sittande be schall   *sitting*
    In high heven, for there is his hall.

PILATUS And frendis if that force to hym fall,   *should belong*
56   It semes noght ye schall hym consume.   *destroy*

    But that hymselfe is the same
    ye saide schulde descende,
    Youre seede and you then all for to socoure.   *(i.e., descendants)*

CAYPHAS   A, softe sir, and sese,   *cease*
    For of Criste when he comes
    no kynne schall be kenned;   *known*

---

[1] *Unless he soon is condemned, he will cause us to be destroyed*

60 But of this caytiffe kynreden   *rascal's kindred*
   we knawe the encrese.
He lykens hym to be lyke God,
   aylastand to lende,
To lifte uppe the laby to lose or relesse.   *burden*

PILATUS His maistreys schulde move you,
   youre mode for to amende.

ANNA Nay, for swilke mys fro malice   *error from malice*
   we may noght us meese,   *restrain*
65 For he sais he schall deme us, that dote,   *judge; fool*
And that tille us is dayne or dispite.   *to; insult; malice*

PILATUS To noye hym nowe is youre noote,   *persecute; note (i.e., task)*
But yitt the lawe lyes in my lotte.   *province*

I DOCTOR And yf ye will witt, sir, ye wotte,   *understand; know*
70 That he is wele worthy to wyte.   *blame*

For in oure Temple has he taught
   by tymes moo than tenne
Where tabillis full of tresoure lay
   to telle and to trye   *count; sort out*
Of oure cheffe mony changers;
   butte, curstely to kenne,   *maliciously; reveal*
He caste tham overe, that caystiffe,   *rascal*
   and counted noght therby.

CAYPHAS Loo, sir, this is a perjurye
   to prente undir penne,   *inscribe*
76 Wherfore make ye that *appostita*,   *apostate*
   we praye you, to plye.   *submit*

PILATUS Howe mene ye?

CAYPHAS Sir, to mort hym for movyng of men.   *kill; influencing*

PILATUS Than schulde we make hym to morne
   but thurgh youre maistrie.
Latte be, sirs, and move that no more
80 But what in youre Temple betyde?   *happened*

I MILES We, thare, sir, he skelpte oute of score   *beat outrageously*
That stately stode selland ther store.   *stood selling; goods*

PILATUS Than felte he tham fawte before   *at fault*
    And made the cause wele to be kydde.   *known*

85   But what taught he that tyme
      swilk tales as thou telles?

I MILES Sir, that oure Tempill is the toure   *tower*
    of his troned sire,   *enthroned father*
    And thus to prayse in that place
      oure prophettis compellis,
    Tille hym that has posté   *power*
      of prince and of empire.
    And thei make *domus Domini*   *house of the Lord*
      that deland thare dwellis,   *dealing*
90   The denn of the derfenes   *sacrilege*
      and ofte that thei desire.

PILATUS Loo, is he noght a madman
    that for youre mede melles?   *benefit is involved*
    Sen ye ymagyn amys,   *amiss*
      that makeles to myre,   *matchless; ensnare*
    Youre rankoure is raykand full rawe.   *rancor; rashly evident*

CAYPHAS Nay, nay, sir, we rewle us but right.   *rule*

PILATUS Forsothe, ye ar over cruell to knawe.

CAYPHAS Why, sir, for he wolde lose oure lawe
97   Hartely we hym hate as we awe,   *ought [to]*
    And therto schulde ye mayntayne oure myght.

    For why, uppon oure Sabbott day
      the seke makes he saffe   *sick; sound*
100   And will noght sesse for oure sawes   *cease; sayings (complaints)*
      to synke so in synne.

II MILES Sir, he coveres all that comes   *relieves*
    recoveraunce to crave,   *recovery*
    But in a schorte contynuaunce   *time*
      that kennes all oure kynne.   *knows*
    But he haldis noght oure haly dayes —   *keeps; holy*
      harde happe myght hym have —   *luck*
    And therfore hanged be he
      and that by the halse.   *neck*
PILATUS   A, hoo, sir, nowe, and holde in.
105   For thoff ye gange thus gedy   *though; proceed; precipitously*
    hym gilteles to grave   *bury*

Withouten grounde yow gaynes noght, *justification*
  swilke greffe to begynne. *grief*
And loke youre leggyng be lele *allegations be true*
Withowtyn any tryfils to telle. *silly stories*

ANNA For certayne owre sawes dare we seele. *sayings (charges); certify*

PILATUS And than may we prophite oure pele. *put forward; accusation*

CAYPHAS Sir, bot his fawtes wer fele, *faults; many*
112 We mente noght of hym for to melle. *become involved*

For he pervertis oure pepull
  that proves his prechyng,
And for that poynte ye schulde prese
  his poosté to paire. *power; reduce*

II DOCTOR Ya, sir, and also that caytiff
  he callis hym oure kyng,
116 And for that cause our comons are casten in care. *cast into worry*

PILATUS And if so be, that borde to bayll will hym bryng *joke; sorrow*
  And make hym boldely to banne the bones that hym bare. *curse*
For why that wrecche fro oure wretthe schal not wryng, *Therefore; wrath; escape*
120 Or ther be wrought on hym wrake. *destruction*

I DOCTOR   So wolde we it ware, *were*
  For so schulde ye susteyne youre seele *sense of well-being*
And myldely have mynde for to meke you. *make mild of mind*

PILATUS Wele witte ye this werke schall be wele,
  For kende schall that knave be to knele. *taught; kneel*

II DOCTOR And so that oure force he may feele,
126 All samme for the same we beseke you. *Together*

JUDAS *Ingenti pro injuria*, hym Jesus, that Jewe, *Because of a great injury*
  Unjust unto me, Judas, I juge to be lathe, *loathsome*
For at oure soper as we satte, the sothe to pursewe *supper*
130 With Symond Luprus full sone, *Simon Leprous*
  my skiffte come to scathe. *conspiracy; harm*
Tille hym ther brought one a boyste *To; box*
  my bale for to brewe,
That baynly to his bare feete *obediently*
  to bowe was full braythe. *eager*

Sho anoynte tham with an oynement
 that nobill was and newe,
But for that werke that sche wrought
 I wexe woundir wrothe.   *became very angry*
135 And this, to discover, was my skill,   *reason*
For of his penys purser was I,   *pence (money) treasurer*
And what that me taught was untill
The tente parte that stale I ay still.   *stole*
But nowe for me wantis of my will   *lacks*
140 That bargayne with bale schall he by.   *buy (purchase)*

That same oynement, I saide,
 might same have bene solde
For silver penys in a sowme   *sum*
 thre hundereth, and fyne   *approximately*
Have ben departid to poure men   *given; poor*
 as playne pité wolde.   *pity*
But for the poore ne thare parte   *not for their part*
 priked me no peyne,
145 But me tened for the tente parte,   *grieved; tenth*
 the trewthe to beholde,
That thirty pens of three hundereth
 so tyte I schulde tyne.   *quick (sharp); lose*
And for I mysse this mony
 I morne on this molde,   *earth*
Wherfore for to mischeve   *harm*
 this maistir of myne,
And therfore faste forthe will I flitte
150 The princes of prestis untill   *priests*
And selle hym full sone or that I sitte
For therty pens in a knotte knytte.   *bargain made*
Thusgatis full wele schall he witte   *In this manner; know*
That of my wretthe wreke me I will.   *anger revenge*

155 Do open, porter, the porte of this prowde place *door*
That I may passe to youre princes
 to prove for youre prowe.   *benefit*

JANITOR Go hense, thou glorand gedlyng, *glowering gadling (rascal)*
 God geve thee ille grace.
Thy glyfftyng is so grymly   *glaring*
 thou gars my harte growe. *make; to swell (i.e., become terrified)*

JUDAS Goode sir, be toward this tyme,
 and tarie noght my trace,   *hinder; course of action*
For I have tythandis to telle.

JANITOR　　　Ya, som tresoune I trowe,　　　　　　　　　　　　　　*treason*
161　For I fele by a figure in youre fals face　　　　　　　　*by the expression*
　　　It is but foly to feste affeccioun in you;　　　　　　　　　　　*fasten*
　　　For Mars he hath morteysed his mark　　　　　　　　　*fixed; sign*
　　　Eftir all lynes of my lore,　　　　　　　　　　　　　　　　*indication*
165　And sais ye are wikkid of werk
　　　And bothe a strange theffe and a stark.　　　　　　　*(i.e., a reprobate)*

JUDAS　Sir, thus at my berde and ye berk　　　　　　　*beard; bark (shout)*
　　　It semes it schall sitte yow full sore.

JANITOR　Say, bittilbrowed bribour,　　　　　　　　　*beetle-browed briber*
　　　　why blowes thou such boste?　　　　　　　　　　　　*boasting*
170　Full false in thy face in faith can I fynde;
　　　Thou arte combered in curstnesse　　　　　　　　*encumbered by malice*
　　　　and caris to this coste.　　　　　　　　　　　　　*come; place*
　　　To marre men of myght　　　　　　　　　　　　　　　*hurt*
　　　　haste thou marked in thy mynde.　　　　　　　　　*determined*

JUDAS　Sir, I mene of no malice
　　　　but mirthe meve I muste.　　　　　　　　　　*I'd rather choose mirth*

JANITOR　Say, onhanged harlott,
　　　　I holde thee unhende.　　　　　　　　　　　　　*ungracious*
175　Thou lokist like a lurdayne　　　　　　　　　　　　　*rascal*
　　　　his liffelod hadde loste.　　　　　　　　　　　　*livelihood*
　　　Woo schall I wirke thee away but thou wende.　　　*unless you go*

JUDAS　A, goode sir, take tente to my talkyng this tyde,
　　　For tythandis full trew can I telle.

JANITOR　Say, brethell, I bidde thee abide,　　　*brothel (worthless person)*
180　Thou chaterist like a churle that can chyde.

JUDAS　Ya, sir, but and the truthe schulde be tryed,　　　*but if*
　　　Of myrthe are ther materes I mell.

　　　For thurgh my dedis youre dugeperes　　　　　　　*leaders*
　　　　fro dere may be drawen.　　　　　　　　　　　　*from harm*

JANITOR　What, demes thou till oure dukes　　　　　*judge*
　　　　that doole schulde be dight?　　　　　　　　　*[to] dole; put*

JUDAS　　　　Nay, sir, so saide I noght;
185　If I be callid to counsaille
　　　　that cause schall be knawen

Emang that comely companye,
  to clerke and to knyght.

JANITOR Byde me here, bewchere, — *Await*
    or more blore be blowen, — *boasting*
  And I schall buske to the benke — *hurry; bench*
    wher baneres are bright,
  And saie unto oure sovereynes
    or seede more be sawen — *ere; sowed*
190 That swilke a seege as thiselff — *man*
    sewes to ther sight. — *sues (requests an audience)*
  My lorde nowe, of witte that is well,
  I come for a cas to be kydde. — *made known*

PILATUS We, speke on, and spare not thi spell.

CAYPHAS Ya, and if us mystir te mell, — *need to stir*
195 Sen ye bere of bewté the bell, — *Since; bear; beauty*
  Blythely schall we bowe as ye bidde.

JANITOR Sir, withoute this abatyng, — *hesitation*
    ther hoves, as I hope, — *hovers*
  A hyve helte full of ire, for hasty he is. — *hive full up to hilt; anger*

PILATUS What comes he fore?

JANITOR   I kenne hym noght, but he is cladde in a cope; — *know; cloak*
200 He cares with a kene face uncomely to kys. — *goes about with*

PILATUS Go, gete hym that his greffe — *grievance*
    we grathely may grope — *directly; examine*
  So no oppen langage be goyng amys. — *open (careless)*

JANITOR Comes on bylyve to my lorde, — *quickly*
    and if thee liste to lepe, — *(i.e., go quickly)*
  But uttir so thy langage — *speak thus*
    that thou lette noght thare blys. — *disturb; their calm*

JUDAS That lorde, sirs, myght susteyne youre seele — *happiness*
206 That floure is of fortune and fame. — *flower*

PILATUS Welcome, thy wordis are but wele.

CAYPHAS Say, harste thou, knave, can thou not knele? — *hearest*

PILATUS Loo, here may men faute in you fele.   *fault*
210   Late be, sir, youre scornyng, for schame.   *Leave aside*

       Bot, bewshere, be noght abayst to byde at the bar.   *But; afraid; wait*

JUDAS Before you, sirs, to be brought
            abowte have I bene,
         And allway for youre worschippe.   *honor*

ANNA   Say, wotte thou any were?   *know; danger*

JUDAS Of werke, sir, that hath wretthid you,   *endangered*
            I wotte what I meene.
215   But I wolde make a marchaundyse   *agreement*
            youre myscheffe to marre.

PILATUS And may you soo?

JUDAS   Els madde I such maistries to meve.   *(i.e., assertions to allege)*

ANNA Than kennes thou of som comberaunce   *know; trouble*
            oure charge for to chere?   *concern; cheer (alert)*
         For, cosyne, thou art cruell.

JUDAS   My cause, sir, is kene,
220   For if ye will bargayne or by,   *purchase*
         Jesus this tyme will I selle you.

I DOCTOR My blissing, sone, have thou forthy.
            Loo, here is a sporte for to spye.   *find out*

JUDAS And hym dar I hete you in hye   *promise; quickly*
            If ye will be toward I telle you.   *in sympathy with what I*

PILATUS What hytist thou?   *are you called*

JUDAS   Judas Scariott.

PILATUS   Thou art a juste man
226   That will Jesus be justified   *Who wishes; brought to justice*
            by oure jugement.
         But howe gates bought schall he be?   *by what means*
            Bidde furthe thy bargayne.

JUDAS But for a litill betyng   *reward*
            to bere fro this bente.   *place*

PILATUS   Now, what schall we pay?

JUDAS   Sir, thirti pens and plete, no more than.   *pence; in full*

PILATUS   Say, ar ye plesid of this price
              he preces to present?   *presses*

II DOCTOR   Ellis contrarie we oure consciens   *Else against*
                consayve sen we can   *understand*
232   That Judas knawes hym culpabill.   *responsible*

PILATUS   I call you consent,   *agreed*
              But Judas, a knott for to knytt,
              Wilte thou to this comenaunt accorde?   *covenant agree*

JUDAS   Ya, at a worde.

PILATUS   Welcome is it.

II MILES   Take therof, a traytour, tyte.   *quickly*

I MILES   Now leve, ser, late no man wete   *leave; know*
238   How this losell laykis with his lord.   *scoundrel plays*

PILATUS   Why, dwellis he with that dochard   *fool*
              whos dedis has us drovyd?   *deeds; angered*

I MILES   That hase he done, ser, and dose,   *does*
              no dowte is this day.

PILATUS   Than wolde we knawe why this knave
              thus cursidly contryved.   *plotted*

II MILES   Enquere hym sen ye can best   *of him*
               kenne if he contrarie.   *find; offend*

PILATUS   Say, man, to selle thi maistir
              what mysse hath he moved?   *(i.e., what has he done)*

JUDAS   For of als mekill mony he made me delay;   *much; withheld from me*
245   Of you, as I resayve, schall but right be reproved.   *receive; redressed*

ANNA   I rede noght that ye reken us
           oure rewle so to ray,   *rule; take seriously*
           For that the fales fende schall thee fang.   *false fiend; take*

I MILES   When he schall wante of a wraste.   *lack; trick*

I DOCTOR   To whome wirke we wittandly wrang.   *knowingly wrong*

II DOCTOR   Tille hym bot ye hastely hang.

III DOCTOR   Youre langage ye lay oute to lang,   *spin out too much*
252   But Judas, we trewly thee trast.   *trust*

    For truly thou moste lerne us   *must teach*
      that losell to lache,   *catch*
    Or of lande, thurgh a lirte,   *trick*
      that lurdayne may lepe.   *rascal may slip off*

JUDAS   I schall you teche a token   *sign*
    hym tyte for to take   *quickly*
256   Wher he is thryngand in the thrang,   *pressed; throng*
    withouten any threpe.   *dispute (question)*

I MILES   We knawe hym noght.

JUDAS   Take kepe than that caytiffe to catche   *Take care*
    The whilke that I kisse.

II MILES   That comes wele thee, corious, I cleepe.   *becomes you well, curious, I say*
    But yitt to warne us wisely,
      allwayes muste ye wacche.   *watch*
    Whan thou schall wende forthwith
      we schall walke a wilde hepe,   *in a large crowd*
260   And therfore besye loke now thou be.   *busy look*

JUDAS   Yis, yis, a space schall I spie us
    Als sone as the sonne is sette, as ye see.

I MILES   Go forthe, for a traytoure ar ye,

II MILES   Ya, and a wikkid man.

I DOCTOR   Why, what is he?

II DOCTOR   A losell, ser, but lewté shuld lye us,   *scoundrel; loyalty; belie*

267   He is trappid full of trayne the truthe for to trist.   *stuffed full; deception*
    I holde it but folye his faythe for to trowe.

PILATUS   Abide in my blyssing,
    and late youre breste,   *stop; complaints*
270   For it is beste for oure bote   *remedy*
    in bayle for to bowe.   *bale; submit*

            And Judas, for oure prophite   *profit*
                we praye thee be prest.   *quick*

JUDAS   Yitt hadde I noght a peny
                to purvey for my prowe.   *put forth; comfort*

PILATUS   Thou schalte have delyveraunce,
                belyve at thi list,   *as you wish*
            So that thou schall have liking   *(i.e., a reason)*
                oure lordschipp to love.
275   And therfore, Judas, mende thou thy mone   *complaint*
            And take ther thi silvere all same.   *altogether*

JUDAS   Ya, nowe is my grete greffe overegone.   *grief gone away*

I MILES   Be lyght than.   *happy then*

JUDAS   Yis, latte me allone,   *leave*
            For tytte schall that taynte be tone,   *quickly; criminal; taken*
280   And therto jocounde and joly I am.

PILATUS   Judas, to holde thi behest   *promise*
                be hende for oure happe,   *worthy; good luck*
            And of us helpe and upholde
                we hete thee to have.   *expect*

JUDAS   I schall bekenne you his corse   *show; body*
                in care for to clappe.

ANNA   And more comforte in this case
                we coveyte not to crave.

I MILES   Fro we may reche that rekeles,   *seize; reckless one*
                his ribbis schall we rappe
286   And make that roy, or we rest,   *person*
                for rennyng to raffe.   *(i.e., trying to avoid us); rave [in pain]*

PILATUS   Nay, sirs, all if ye scourge hym
                ye schende noght his schappe,   *injure; body*
            For if the sotte be sakles   *fool; guiltless*
                Us sittis hym to save.   *sits (as a judge)*
290   Wherfore when ye go schall to gete hym,   *get (entrap)*
            Unto his body brew ye no bale.

II MILES   Oure liste is fro lepyng to lette hym,   *desire; fleeing; prevent*
            But in youre sight sownde schall ve sette hym.   *we*

PILATUS   Do flitte nowe forthe till ye fette hym,   *fetch*
295   With solace all same to youre sale.   *well-being; hall*

[27. THE LAST SUPPER]

The Baxsteres

JESUS   Pees be both be day and nyght   *Peace*
            Untill this house and till all that is here.   *To; to all*
            Here will I holde as I have hight   *promised*
            The feeste of Paas with frendis in feere.   *Paschal feast; all together*

MARCELUS   Maistir, we have arayed full right
6   Servise that semes for youre sopere: *befits*
          Oure lambe is roste, and redy dight
          As Moyses lawe will lely lere.   *truly teach*

JESUS   That is, ilke man that has
10   Pepill in his awne posté   *[patriarchal] power*
          Shall roste a lambe at Paas
          To hym and his meyné.   *company*

ANDREAS   Maistir, the custome wele we knawe
            That with oure elthers ever has bene,   *elders (forefathers)*
15   How ilke man with his meyné awe   *family ought*
            To roste a lambe and ete it clene.   *eat; entirely*

JESUS   I thanke you sothtly of youre sawe,   *truly; words*
            For ye saye as youreselffe has sene;
            Therfore array you all on rawe,   *in order*
20   Myselfe schall parte itt you betwene.
            Wherfore I will that ye
            Ette therof evere ilkone;   *Eat; everyone*
            The remelaunt parted schall be   *remnant (leftovers)*
            To the poure that purveyse none.   *poor; [can] provide*

25   Of Moyses lawes here make I an ende
          In som party, but noght in all;   *part*
          My comaundement schall othirwise be kende   *known*
          With tham that men schall craftely call.   *wisely*
          But the lambe of Pasc that here is spende,   *dispensed with*
30   Whilke Jewes uses grete and small,
          Evere forward nowe I itt deffende   *forbid*
          Fro Cristis folke whatso befall.
          In that stede schall be sette   *place*
          A newe lawe us bytwene,

35	But who therof schall ette	
	Behoves to be wasshed clene.	*Should be*
	For that new lawe whoso schall lere,	
	In harte tham bus be clene and chaste.	*must be pure*
	Marcelle, myn awne discipill dere,	
40	Do us have watir here in hast.	

MARCELUS Maistir, it is all redy here,
And here a towell clene to taste.   *for use*

JESUS Commes forthe with me, all in feere;
My wordis schall noght be wrought in waste.   *futilely*
45   Settis youre feete fourth, late see: *forth*
They schall be wasshen sone.   *washed soon*

PETRUS A, Lorde, with thi leve, of thee
That dede schall noght be done.

I schall nevere make my membres mete   *ready*
50   Of my soverayne service to see.

JESUS Petir, bott if thou latte me wasshe thi feete,   *unless; allow me to*
Thou getis no parte in blisse with me.

PETRUS A, mercy, Lorde and maistir swete,
Owte of that blisse that I noght be,
55   Wasshe on, my Lorde, to all be wete,
Both hede and hande, beseke I thee.

JESUS Petir, thou wotiste noght yitt   *know; yet*
What this werke will bemene.   *signify*
Hereaftir schall thou witte,
60   And so schall ye all, bedene.   *soon*

Tunc lavat manus.   *Then he washes his hands*

Youre Lorde and maistir ye me call,
And so I am, all welthe to welde.   *wield (control)*
Here have I knelid unto you all
To wasshe youre feete as ye have feled.   *perceived*
65   Ensaumple of me take ye schall   *Example*
Ever for to yeme in youthe and elde,   *give heed to*
To be buxsome in boure and hall,   *obedient; bower*
Ilkone for to bede othir belde.   *Each one; offer others support*
For all if ye be trewe
70   And lele of love ilkone,   *truly*

Ye schall fynde othir ay newe
To greve whan I am gone.

    grieve

JACOBUS Now sen oure maistir sais he schall
Wende and will not telle us whedir,
75   Whilke of us schall be princepall,
Late loke now whils we dwell togedir.

JESUS I wotte youre will, both grete and small,

    know

And youre high hartis I here tham hedir,

    proud; hither

To whilke of you such fare schulde fall;

    matter

80   That myght ye carpe when ye come thedir

    talk (discuss)

Where it so schulde betyde

    happen

Of such materes to melle.
But first behoves you bide
Fayndyngis full ferse and felle.

    Trials; fierce; cruel

85   Here schall I sette you for to see
This yonge childe for insaumpills seere.

    examples many

Both meke and mylde of harte is he
And fro all malice mery of chere,
So meke and mylde but if ye be

   . . .

    [pages missing, see note]

[JESUS] *Quod facis fac cicius,*

    That which thou doest do quickly

91   That thou schall do, do sone.

THOMAS Allas, so wilsom wightis as we

    confused men

Was nevere in worlde walkand in wede;

    clothing

Oure maistir sais his awne meyné

    company

95   Has betrayed hym to synfull seede.

    (i.e., sinful folk)

JACOBUS MAJOR A, I hope, sen thou sittist nexte his kne,
We pray thee spire hym for oure spede.

    inquire [of]; assistance

JOHANNES *Domine, quis est qui tradit te?*

    Lord, who is the one who has betrayed you?

Lord, who schall do that doulfull dede?
100   Allas, oure playe is paste,

    passed

This false forward is feste;

    [If] this; agreement; certain

I may no lenger laste,
For bale myn herte may breste.

    burst

JUDAS Now is tyme to me to gang,
105   For here begynnes noye all of newe.

    trouble

My fellows momellis thame emang

    mumble among themselves

That I schulde alle this bargayne brewe,
And certis thai schall noght wene it wrang.

    consider it wrong

To the prince of prestis I schall pursue,

110   And thei schall lere hym othir ought long   *instruct; otherwise*
       That all his sawes sore schall hym rewe.   *rue (be sorry for)*
       I wotte whedir he removes   *whither; goes*
       With his meyné ilkone,
       I schall telle to the Jewes
115   And tyte he schalle be tane.   *quickly; arrested*

JESUS   I warne you nowe, my frendis free,
       Sese to ther sawes that I schall say: *Pay attention to the words*
       The fende is wrothe with you and me,   *fiend; angry*
       And will you marre if that he may;
120   But Petir I have prayed for thee
       So that thou schall noght drede his dray;   *dread; assault*
       And comforte thou this meyné
       And wisse hem whan I am gone away.   *direct*

PETRUS   A, Lorde, where wilte thou lende?   *be (dwell)*
125   I schall lende in that steede,   *place*
       And with thee schall I wende
       Evermore in lyffe and dede.   *death*

ANDREAS   No wordely drede schall me withdrawe   *worldly dread; restrain*
       That I schall with thee leve and dye.   *(i.e., From) That; living and dying*

THOMAS   Certis, so schall we all on rawe,   *in order*
131   Ellis mekill woo were we worthy.

JESUS   Petir, I saie to thee this sawe,
       That thou schalte fynde no fantasie.
       This ilke nyght or the cokkys crowe   *ere*
135   Shall thou thre tymes my name denye
       And saye thou knewe me nevere
       Nor no meyné of myne.   *company*

PETRUS   Allas, Lorde, me were lever   *rather*
       Be putte to endles pyne.

JESUS   As I yow saie, so schall it bee;
141   Ye nedis non othir recours to crave.
       All that in worlde is wretyn of me   *written*
       Shall be fulfilled, for knyght or knave.
       I am the herde, the schepe are ye,   *shepherd; sheep*
145   And whane the herde schall harmes have,
       The flokke schall be full fayne to flee
       And socoure seke thameselffe to save.   *seek*
       Ye schall whan I am slayne   *slain*
       In grete myslykyng lende,   *unhappiness be*

150   But whanne I ryse agayne,
       Than schall youre myrthe be mende.   *restored*

       Ye have bene bowne my bale to bete,   *obliged; relieve*
       Therfore youre belde ay schall I be;   *support*
       And for ye did in drye and wete
155   My comaundementis in ilke contré.
       The kyngdome of heven I you behete   *promise*
       Even as my Fadir has highte itt me.   *promised it to me*
       With gostely mete there schall we mete,   *spiritual food (sustenance)*
       And on twelffe seeges sitte schall ye,   *thrones*
160   For ye trewlye toke yeme   *heed*
       In worlde with me to dwell,
       There shall ye sitte bydene   *all together*
       Twelve kyndis of Israell.   *tribes*

       But firste ye schall be wille of wone,   *distraught*
165   And mo wathes then ye of wene   *more dangers; expected*
       Fro tyme schall come that I be tone;   *taken*
       Than schall ye turne away with tene.   *grief*
       And loke that ye have swerdis ilkone,
       And whoso haves non you bytwene   *none*
170   Shall selle his cote and bye hym one: *buy*
       Thus bidde I that ye do bedene.
       Satcheles I will ye have   *Satchels (Small bags)*
       And stones to stynte all striffe   *stop*
       Youreselffe for to save
175   In lenghyng of youre liff.   *lengthening*

ANDREAS Maistir, ye have here swerdis twoo
       Us with to save on sidis seere.   *(i.e., on all sides)*

JESUS Itt is inowe, ye nedis no moo,   *more*
       For fro all wathis I schall you were.   *(i.e., I shall help you)*
180   Butt ryse now uppe, for we will goo,
       By this owre enemyes ordand are.   *intended (planned)*
       My Fadir saide it schall be soo;
       His bidding will I noght forbere.   *command*
       Loke ye lere forthe this lawe   *teach (proclaim)*
185   Als ye have herde of me:
       Alle that wele will itte knawe,
       Ay blessed schall thei bee.

[28. THE AGONY AND BETRAYAL]

The Cordewaneres

JESUS	Beholde, my discipulis that deyne is and dere,	*worthy; dear*
	My flesshe dyderis and daris for doute of my dede.	*trembles; shakes; fear*
	Myne enemyes will newly be neghand full nere	*soon*
	With all the myght if thei may to marre my manhede.	*manhood*
5	But sen ye are forwakid	*tired with watching*
	and wanderede in were,	*perplexity*
	Loke ye sette you doune rathely	*promptly*
	and reste youe, I reede.	*advise*
	Beis noght hevy in youre hertis	
	but holde yow even here	
	And bidis me a stounde	*abide with me; time*
	stille in this same steede.	*place*
	Beeis witty and wyse in youre wandyng	*thoughts*
10	So that ye be wakand alway,	*waking*
	And lokis nowe prestely ye pray	*urgently*
	To my Fadir, that ye falle in no fandyng.	*temptation*
PETRUS	Yis, Lorde, at thy bidding	
	full baynly schall we abide,	*obediently*
	For thou arte boote of oure bale	*remedy*
	and bidis for the best.	*abide*
JOAHNNES	Lorde, all oure helpe and oure hele,	*well-being*
	that is noght to hyde,	
16	In thee, oure faythe and oure foode,	
	all hollye is feste.	*wholly; fast (firm)*
JACOBUS	Qwat way is he willid	*What; gone*
	in this worlde wyde?	
	Whedir is he walked,	
	estewarde or weste?	
PETRUS	Yaa, sirs, I schall saye you,	
	sittis us doune on every ilka side,	
20	And late us nowe rathely here take oure reste;	*let; quickly*
	My lymmys are hevy as any leede.	*limbs; lead*
JOHANNES	And I muste slepe, doune muste I lye.	
JACOBUS	In faithe, felawes, right so fare I.	
	I may no lenger holde uppe my hede.	*head*

PETRUS Oure liffe of his lyolty   *truth*
    his liffe schall he lose,
26 Unkyndely be crucified
    and naylyd to a tree.

JESUS Baynly of my blissing,   *Obediently*
    youre eghen ye unclose   *eyes; open*
So that ye falle in no fandyng   *temptation*
    for noght that may be,
But prayes fast.

JOHANNES Lorde, som prayer thou kenne us   *instruct*
31 That somwhat myght mirthe us or mende us.   *cheer; improve*

JACOBUS Fro all fandyng unfaythfull thou fende us,   *defend*
Here in this worlde of liffe whille we laste.

JESUS I schall kenne you and comforte you
    and kepe you from care;
35 Ye schall be broughte, wete ye wele,   *know; well*
    fro bale unto blisse.

PETRUS Yaa, but Lorde, and youre willis were   *will*
    witte wolde we more,   *know would*
Of this prayer so precious late us noght mys,
We beseke thee.

JOHANNES For my felows and me alle in feere,
40 Some prayer that is precious to lere.   *learn*

JACOBUS Unto thy Fadir that moste is of poure   *power*
Some solace of socoure to sende thee.
   . . .   [pages missing, see textual note]
[JESUS] The nowys that me neghed   *information*
    hase, it nedis not to neven,   *say*
For all wate ye full wele   *know*
    what wayes I have wente.
45 Instore me and strenghe   *Restore; strengthen*
    with a stille steven,   *voice*
I pray thee interly thou take entent   *wholly*
Thou menske my manhed with mode.   *honor; strength of will*
My flessh is full dredand for drede,   *dreading; dread*
For my jorneys of my manhed.   *undertakings*
50 I swete now both watir and bloode.

Thes Jewes hase mente in ther mynde full of malice   *intended*
And pretende me to take   *propose*

    withouten any trespasse,
    But, Fadir, as thou wate wele,   *know well*
        I mente nevere amys;
    In worde nor in werk
        I never worthy was.
55 Als thou arte bote of all bale and belder of blisse   *reward; support*
    And all helpe and hele in thy hande hase,   *health*
    Thou mensk thy manhede,   *honor*
        thou mendar of mysse;   *error*
    And if it possible be
        this payne myght I overpasse.
    And, Fadir, if thou se it may noght,
60 Be it worthely wrought
    Even at thyne awne will
    Evermore both myldely and still
    With worschippe allway be it wroght.

    Unto my discipillis will I go agayne
65 Kyndely to comforte tham   *By nature*
        that kacchid are in care.   *caught*
    What, are ye fallen on slepe
        now everilkone,   *everyone*
    And the passioun of me in mynde hase no more?   *in [your] thoughts*
    What, wille ye leve me thus lightly
        and latte me allone   *let*
    In sorowe and in sighyng
        that sattillis full sore?   *sinks deeply in the mind*
70 To whome may I meve me   *move (express) myself*
        and make nowe my mone?   *lament*
    I wolde that ye wakened, and your will wore;   *if it were*
    Do, Petir, sitte uppe now, late se.
    Thou arte strongly stedde in this stoure,   *struggle*
    Might thou noght the space of an owre   *hour*
75 Have wakid nowe mildely with me?   *meekly*

PETRUS Yis, Lorde, with youre leve
        nowe wille we lere,
    Full warely to were you   *vigilantly; defend*
        fro alle wandynge?   *uncertainty*

JESUS Beeis wakand and prayes faste all in fere
        To my Fadir, that ye falle in no fanding,   *temptation*
80 For evelle spiritis is neghand full nere
    That will you tarie at this tyme with his temtyng.   *tempting*
    And I will wende ther I was withouten any were,   *perplexity*
    But bidis me here baynly in my blissing.   *obediently*
    Agayne to the mounte I will gang   *go*

85	Yitt eftesones where I was ere,	
	But loke that ye cacche yow no care,	
	For lely I schall noght dwelle lange.	*truly; long*
	Thou, Fadir, that all formed hase with fode for to fill,	*sustenance*
	I fele by my ferdnes my flessh wolde full fayne	*fear; gladly*
90	Be torned fro this turnement and takyn thee untill,	*tournament (battle)*
	For mased is manhed in mode and in mayne.	*bewildered; strength*
	But if thou se sothly that thi Sone sill	*shall*
	Withouten surffette of synne thus sakles be slayne,	*innocent*
	Be it worthly wroght even at thyne awne will,	*own*
95	For Fadir, att thi bidding am I buxum and bayne.	*humble; obedient*
	Now wightely agayne will I wende	*quickly (boldly)*
	Unto my disciplis so dere.	
	What, slepe ye so faste all in fere?	
	I am ferde ye mon faile of youre frende.	*afraid; may; friend*
100	But yitt will I leve you and late you allone,	
	And eftesones there I was agayne will I wende.	*where*
	Unto my Fadir of myght now make I my mone:	*lament*
	As thou arte salver of all sore som socoure me sende.	
	The passioun they purpose to putte me uppon,	
105	My flesshe is full ferde and fayne wolde defende,	*avoid*
	At thi wille be itt wrought worthely in wone.	*place*
	Have mynde of my manhed my mode for to mende,	
	Some comforte me kythe in this case,	*make known*
	And Fadir, I schall dede taste	*death*
	I will it noght deffende.	*resist*
110	Yitt yf thy willis be	
	spare me a space.	
	[And seis . . . yght	
	With rappes . . . the rode rente.]	*blows; cross torn asunder*
	ANGELUS Unto the maker unmade	
	that moste is of myght,	
	Be lovyng aylastand in light that is lente.	
115	Thy Fadir that in heven is moste,	
	he uppon highte,	*high*
	Thy sorowes for to sobir	*alleviate*
	to thee he hase me sente.	
	For dedis that man done has	
	thy dede schall be dight,	
	And thou with turmentis be tulyd.	*attacked*
	But take nowe entente:	
	Thy bale schall be for the beste	
120	Thurgh that mannys mys schall be mende;	*original sin*

Than schall thou withouten any ende
Rengne in thy rialté full of reste.   *Reign; royalty; peace*

JESUS Now if my flesshe ferde be,   *afraid*
    Fadir, I am fayne
That myne angwisshe and my noyes   *trouble*
    are nere at an ende.
125   Unto my discipilis go will I agayne,
    Kyndely to comforte tham
      that mased is in ther mynde.   *upset*
Do slepe ye nowe savely,   *certainly*
    and I schall you sayne.   *sign (make sign of the cross)*
Wakyns uppe wightely   *quickly*
    and late us hens wende,
For als tyte mon I be taken   *soon must*
    with tresoune and with trayne,   *deceit*
130   My flesshe is full ferde
    and fayne wolde deffende.   *protect [myself]*
Full derfely my dede schall be dight,   *cruelly; death*
And als sone as I am tane   *taken*
Than schall ye forsake me ilkone   *everyone*
And saie nevere ye sawe me with sight.

PETRUS Nay, sothely, I schall nevere my sovereyne forsake,
136   If I schulde for the dede darfely here dye.   *deed; cruelly*

JOHANNES Nay, such mobardis schall nevere man us make,   *villainous fools*
    Erste schulde we dye all at onys.

JACOBUS   Nowe in faith, felows, so shulde I.

JESUS Ya, but when tyme is betydde,   *come*
    thanne men schalle me take.
140   For all youre hartely hetyng   *boldly promising*
    ye schall hyde you in hy: *quickly*
Lyke schepe that were scharid   *sheep; sheared*
    away schall ye schake.   *flee*
Ther schall none of you be balde   *bold [enough]*
    to byde me than by.   *abide with me then*

PETRUS Nay, sothely, whils I may vayle thee,   *serve*
I schall were thee and wake thee,   *guard; watch*
145   And if all othir forsake thee,
I schall nevere fayntely defayle thee.   *desert*

JESUS A, Petir, of swilke bostyng   *boasting*
    I rede thou late bee,   *let be*

For all the kene carpyng
   full kenely I knawe.
For ferde of myne enmyse   *enemies*
   thou schalte sone denye me
150 Thries yitt full thraly   *Thrice; completely*
   or the cokkes crowe.   *ere*
For ferde of my fomen   *foes*
   full fayne be for to flee,
And for grete doute of thi dede   *fear; death*
   thee to withdrawe.

ANNA Sir Cayphas, of youre counsaille,
   do sone, late us now see,
For lely it langes us to luke   *longs; look*
   unto oure lawys.
155 And therfore, sir, prestely I pray you,   *urgently*
   Sen that we are of counsaille ilkone
That Jesus that traytoure wer tane,   *should be taken*
   Do sone late se, sir, I pray you.   *soon let see [it done]*

CAYPHAS   In certayne, sir, and sone schall I saye you,

160 I wolde wene by my witte
   this werke wolde be wele.
Late us justely us june   *Let; join*
   tille Judas the gente,   *with; gracious*
For he kennes his dygnites   *authority*
   full duly ilke a dele,   *lawful*
Ya, and beste wote, I warande,   *knows; warrant (certify)*
   what wayes that he is wente.   *has gone*

ANNA Now this was wisely saide
   als ever have I seele.   *health*
165 And sir, to youre saiyng,
   I saddely will assente;
Therfore take us of oure knyghtis   *take; [those] of*
   that is stedfast as stele,   *steel*
And late Judas go lede tham belyffe   *allow; lead them without delay*
   wher that he laste lente.   *passed*

CAYPHAS   Full wele, sir.
   Nowe, Judas, dere neghbour,
     drawe nere us.
170 Lo, Judas, thus in mynd have we ment,
   To take Jesus is oure entent,
For thou muste lede us and lere us.   *teach (inform)*

JUDAS Sirs, I schall wisse you the way   *guide*
          even at youre awne will,
          But loke that ye have
          many myghty men
175   That is both strang and sterand   *athletic*
          and stedde hym stone stille.   *hold*

ANNA Yis, Judas, but be what knowlache   *by*
          schall we that corse kenne?

JUDAS Sirs, a tokenyng in this tyme   *sign*
          I schall telle you untill,
          But lokis by youre lewty   *loyalty*
          no liffe ye hym lenne.   *grant*
          Qwhat man som I kys,   *What; whom*
          that corse schall ye kyll,   *body (person)*
180   And also beis ware   *be on guard*
          that he wil not away.   *escape*
          I schrew you all thenne.   *curse*

CAYPHAS   Why, nay, Judas,
          We purpose the page schall not passe.   *boy*
          Sir knyghtis, in hy!   *come here quickly*

I MILES   Lorde, we are here.

CAYPHAS Calles fourth youre felaws in feere
185   And gose justely with gentill Judas.   *deal*

I MILES Come, felaws, by youre faith,
          come forthe all faste
          And carpis with Sir Cayphas: *talk*
          he comaundis me to call.

II MILES I schrewe hym all his liffe,   *curse*
          that loves to be last.

III MILES Go we hens than in hy   *in haste*
          and haste us to the halle.

IV MILES Lorde, of youre will worthely
          wolde I witte what wast?   *(i.e., what do you want)*

CAYPHAS To take Jesus, that sawntrelle,   *pretender*
          all same, that ye schall.   *together*

I Miles   Lorde, to that purpose,
       I wolde that we paste.   *passed*

Anna   Ya, but loke that ye be armed wele all,
194   The moste gentill of the Jury schalle gyde you.   *Jewry; guide*

Cayphas   Ya, and every ilke a knyght in degré   *in order*
       Both armed and harneysed ye be   *in armor*
       To belde you and baynely go byde you.   *comfort; obediently; abide (i.e., await)*

Anna   Ya, and therfore, Sir Cayphas, ye hye you,   *go quickly*
       Youre wirschippe ye wynne in this cas.   *gain*
200   As ye are a lorde most lofsom of lyre   *attractive body*
       Undir Sir Pilate that lyfis in this empire,   *lives*
       Yone segger that callis hymselffe a sire   *braggart; lord*
       With tresoure and tene sall we taste hym.   *harm; test (try)*
       Of yone losell his bale schall he brewe.   *knave; cause*
205   Do trottes on for that traytoure apas   *traitor; apace*
       In hast.

Cayphas   Nowe, sirs, sen ye say my poure is moste beste
       And hase all this werke
          thus to wirke at my will,
       Now certayne I thinke not to rest
210   But solempnely youre will to fulfille
       Right sone.

       Full tyte the traytoure schall be tane.   *quickly*
       Sirs knyghtis, ye hye you ilkone,   *hurry*
       For in certayne the losell schall be slane.   *slain*
215   Sir Anna, I praye you have done.

Anna   Full redy tyte I schal be boune
       This journay for to go till.
       Als ye are a lorde of grete renoune,
       Ye spare hym not to spill,   *destroy (kill)*
220   The devill hym spede.
       Go we with oure knyghtis in fere,
       Lo, thay are arrayed and armed clere.
       Sir knyghtis, loke ye be of full gud chere: *good*
       Where ye hym see, on hym take hede.   *heed*

I Judeus   Goode tente to hym, lorde, schall we take: *attention*
226   He schall banne the tyme that he was borne.   *curse*
       All his kynne schall come to late;   *too*
       He schall noght skape withouten scorne   *escape*
       Fro us in fere.   *all together*

II JUDEUS We schall hym seke both even and morne,
231   Erly and late, with full gode chere,
       Is oure entente.

III JUDEUS Stye nor strete we schall spare none,   *Path*
       Felde nor towne, thus have we mente,
235   And boune in corde.   *accord*

CAYPHAS Malcus!

MALCUS   A, ay, and I schulde be rewarde,
       And right als wele worthy were,
       Loo, for I bere light for my lorde.   *a lantern*

CAYPHAS A, sir, of your speche lette, and late us spede   *leave off; allow us to hurry*
240   A space, and of oure speche spare;
       And Judas, go fande thou before   *find the way*
       And wisely thou wisse tham the way,   *guide*
       For sothely sone schall we saye   *truthfully soon*
       To make hym to marre us no more.

JESUS Now will this oure be neghand full nere   *hour; nighing*
246   That schall certefie all the soth that I have saide.   *truth*

CAYPHAS Go, fecche forth the freyke for his forfette.   *bold man; punishment*

JUDAS All hayll, maistir, in faith,
       and felawes all in fere,
       With grete gracious gretyng
       on grounde be ye graied.   *given*
250   I wolde aske you a kysse,
       maistir, and youre willes were,   *(i.e., consent)*
       For all my love and my likyng
       is holy uppon you layde.   *wholly*

JESUS Full hartely, Judas, have it even here,
       For with this kissing is mans Sone betrayed.

I MILES Whe, stande, traytoure, I telle thee for tane.   *apprehended*

CAYPHAS Whe, do knyghtis, go falle on before.   *proceed*

II MILES Yis, maistir, move thou no more,
257   But lightly late us allone.   *quickly*

III MILES Allas, we are loste for leme of this light.   *radiance*

JESUS Saye ye here, whome seke ye?
    do saye me, late see.

I JUDEUS One Jesus of Nazareth
    I hope that he hight.   *is [so] named*

JESUS Beholdis all hedirward, loo,   *(i.e., Look this way)*
    here, I am hee.

I MILES Stande, dastarde, so darfely   *cruelly*
    thy dede schall be dight;   *put down*
263   I will no more be abasshed
    for blenke of thy blee.   *radiance; countenance*

I JUDEUS We, oute, I ame mased almost   *amazed*
    in mayne and in myght.

II JUDEUS And I am ferde, be my feyth,
    and fayne wolde I flee,
    For such a sight have I not sene.

III JUDEUS This leme it lemed so light,   *radiance; shone; brightly*
    I saugh never such a sight:
269   Me mervayles what it may mene.

JESUS Doo, whame seke ye all same, yitt I saye?

I JUDEUS One Jesus of Nazareth,
    hym wolde we neghe nowe.   *approach*

JESUS And I am he sothly.

MALCUS   And that schall I asaie,   *test (check out)*
    For thou schalte dye, dastard,
      sen that it is thowe.

PETRUS And I schall fande be my feythe thee for to flaye,   *try by; faith; put to flight*
275   Here with a lusshe, lordayne, I schalle thee allowe.   *blow*

MALCUS We, oute, all my deveres are done.   *deeds*

PETRUS   Nay,
    Traytoure, but trewly I schall trappe thee, I trowe.

JESUS Pees, Petir, I bidde thee;   *Peace*
    Melle thee nor move thee no more,   *Stir about*
280   For witte thou wele   *well*

    and my willis were,   *will*
    I myght have poure grete plenté.   *power*

    Of aungellis full many
        to mustir my myght;
    Forthy putte uppe thi swerde
        full goodely agayne,
    For he that takis vengeaunce
        all rewlid schall be right,   *governed*
285 With purgens and vengeaunce   *purging*
        that voydes in vayne.   *renders ineffectual*
    Thou man that is thus derede   *hurt*
        and doulfully dyght,
    Come hedir to me savely   *safely*
        and I schalle thee sayne.   *sign (bless)*
    In the name of my Fadir
        that in hevene is most upon hight,
    Of thy hurtis be thou hole   *whole*
        in hyde and in hane, *in field and in enclosure (i.e., everywhere)*
290 Thurgh vertewe thi vaynes be at vayle. *veins; healed*

MALCUS What, ille hayle, I hope that I be hole. *whole (healed)*
    Nowe I schrewe hym this tyme that gyvis tale, *curse; (i.e., considers it worthwhile)*
    To touche thee for thi travayle.

I JUDEUS Do felaws, be youre faithe,
    late us fange on in fere,   *proceed*
295 For I have on this hyne. . . .   *[lower-class] man*

II MILES And I have a loke on hym nowe; *lock*
    howe, felawes, drawe nere.

III MILES Yis, by the bonys that this bare, *bones; bore*
    this bourde schall he banne.   *jest; curse*

JESUS Even like a theffe heneusly   *heinously*
    hurle ye me here.
    I taught you in youre Tempill,
        why toke ye me noght thanne?
300 Now haves mekenes on molde   *earth*
    all his power.

I JUDEUS Do, do, laye youre handes
    belyve on this lourdayne.   *quickly; rascal*

III JUDEUS We, have holde this hauk in thi handis. *hawk*

Malcus Whe, yis, felawes, be my faith he is fast.

IV Judeus Unto Sir Cayphas I wolde that he passen.   *be passed on*
305   Farewell, for, iwisse, we will wenden.

[29. The Trial before Cayphas and Anna]

The Bowers and Flecchers

Cayphas Pees, bewshers, I bid no jangelyng ye make,   *good sirs*
        And sese sone of youre sawes and se what I saye,   *cease; sayings (talking)*
        And trewe tente unto me this tyme that ye take,   *full attention*
        For I am a lorde lerned lelly in youre lay.   *truly; law*

5   By connyng of clergy and casting of witte   *skill; applying of intelligence*
        Full wisely my wordis I welde at my will,   *wield*
        So semely in seete me semys for to sitte,   *seemly; seat; seems*
        And the lawe for to lerne you and lede it by skill,   *teach*
        Right sone.

10   What wyte so will oght with me   *man; have ought [to do]*
        Full frendly in feyth am I foune;
        Come of, do tyte, late me see   *off, do quickly*
        Howe graciously I shall graunte hym his bone.   *request*

        Ther is nowder lorde ne lady lerned in the lawe,   *neither*
15   Ne bisshoppe ne prelate that preved is for pris,   *proved; value*
        Nor clerke in the courte that connyng will knawe
        With wisdam may were hym in worlde is so wise.   *perplex him*

        I have the renke and the rewle of all the ryall,   *sovereignty; kingdom*
        To rewle it by right als reasoune it is;
20   All domesmen on dese awe for to dowte me   *judges; dais ought to fear*
        That hase thaym in bandome in bale or in blis;   *bondage*
        Wherfore takes tente to my tales and lowtis unto me.   *give reverence (bow)*

        And therfore, sir knyghtis . . .

                    Tunc dicunt:
[**Milites**]   Lorde

[**Cayphas**] I charge you chalange youre rightis
25   To wayte both be day and by nyghtis
        Of the bringyng of a boy into bayle.   *fellow; misery*

I MILES Yis, lorde, we schall wayte if any wonderes walke,   *keep watch; are about*
        And freyne howe youre folkis fare that are furth ronne.   *question; run out*

II MILES We schall be bayne at youre bidding and it not to balke   *obedient*
30   Yf thei presente you that boy in a bande boune.   *bonds bound (tied up)*

ANNA Why, syr, and is ther a boy that will noght lowte to youre biding?   *bow (submit)*

CAYPHAS Ya, sir, and of the coriousenesse of that karle ther is carping,[1]
        But I have sente for that segge halfe for hethyng   *man partly; enjoyment*

ANNA What wondirfull werkis workis that wighte?   *man*

CAYPHAS Seke men and sori he sendis siker helyng,   *Sick; unhappy; gives secure healing*
36   And to lame men, and blynde he sendis ther sight.

        Of croked crepillis that we knawe   *cripples*
        Itt is to here grete wondering   *hear*
        How that he helis thame all on rawe,   *heals; in order*
40   And all thurgh his false happenyng.   *happenstance*

        I am sorie of a sight that egges me to ire;   *urges; anger*
        Oure lawe he brekis with all his myght,   *violates*
        That is moste his desire.

        Oure Sabott day he will not safe   *observe*
45   But is aboute to bringe it downe
        And therfore sorowe muste hym have.
        May he be kacched in felde or towne   *caught; field*
        For his false stevyn.   *speaking*
        He defamys fowly the Godhed
50   And callis hymselffe God Sone of hevene.

ANNA I have goode knowlache of that knafe.   *knave*
        Marie me menys, his modir highte,   *mean; is called*
        And Joseph his fadir, as God me safe,   *save*
        Was kidde and knowen wele for a wrighte.   *recognized; carpenter*

55   But o thyng me mervayles mekill overe all   *one*
        Of diverse dedis that he has done.

CAYPHAS With wicchecrafte he fares withall,   *witchcraft*
        Sir, that schall ye se full sone.

---

[1] *Yes, sir, and of the cleverness of that knave there is talk*

	Oure knyghtis thai are furth wente	*gone forth*
60	To take hym with a traye;	*trickery*
	By this I holde hym shente.	*defeated*
	He cannot wende away.	

ANNA	Wolde ye, sir, take youre reste,	
	This day is comen on hande,	
65	And with wyne slake youre thirste?	
	Than durste I wele warande	*dare; warrant (promise)*

	Ye schulde have tithandis sone	*tidings soon*
	Of the knyghtis that are gone	
	And howe that thei have done	
70	To take hym by a trayne,	*deception*

	And putte all thought away	
	And late youre materes reste.	*matters (business)*

CAYPHAS	I will do as ye saie,	
	Do gette us wyne of the best.	

I MILES	My lorde, here is wyne	
	that will make you to wynke;	*sleep*
76	Itt is licoure full delicious,	
	my lorde, and you like.	
	Wherfore I rede drely	*advise earnestly*
	a draughte that ye drynke,	
	For in this contré, that we knawe,	
	iwisse ther is none slyke,	*nothing else like it*
	Wherfore we counsaile you,	
	this cuppe saverly for to kisse.	*confidently*

CAYPHAS	Do on dayntely and dresse me on dees	*graciously; dais*
81	And hendely hille on me happing,	*kindly cover; with bedclothes*
	And warne all wightis to be in pees,	*persons*
	For I am late layde unto napping.	*(i.e., I am ready to sleep)*

ANNA	My lorde, with youre leve, and it like you, I passe.	*am going*

CAYPHAS	Adiew be unte, as the manere is.	*unto you*

MULIER	Sir knyghtys, do kepe this boy in bande,	*bonds*
87	For I will go witte what it may mene,	*discover*
	Why that yone wighte was hym folowand	*following*
	Erly and late, morne and ene.	*evening*

90 He will come nere, he will not lette;   *stop*
    He is a spie, I warand, full bolde.

III MILES It semes by his sembland he had levere be sette   *appearance; wished to; seated*
    By the fervent fire to fleme hym fro colde.   *escape*

MULIER Ya, but and ye wiste as wele as I   *know*
95 What wonders that this wight has wrought,
    And thurgh his maistir sorssery   *through; sorcery*
    Full derfely schulde his deth be bought.   *cruelly*

IV MILES Dame, we have hym nowe at will
    That we have longe tyme soughte;
100 Yf othir go by us still,   *slip by*
    Therfore we have no thought.

MULIER Itt were grete skorne that he schulde skape   *escape*
    Withoute he hadde resoune and skill,
    He lokis lurkand like an nape;   *looks [as if] lurking; ape*
105 I hope I schall haste me hym tille.

    Thou caytiffe, what meves thee stande   *moves you to*
    So stabill and stille in thi thoght?
    Thou hast wrought mekill wronge in londe   *great; land*
    And wondirfull werkis haste thou wroght.

110 A, lorell, a leder of lawe,   *beggar (fool); expositor*
    To sette hym and suye has thou soght.   *accompany; sue*
    Stande furth and threste in yone thrawe,   *push into; crowd*
    Thy maistry thou bryng unto noght.   *great deeds*

    Wayte nowe, he lokis like a brokke,   *badger*
115 Were he in a bande for to bayte,   *bonds (tied up); bait (in sport)*
    Or ellis like an nowele in a stok   *owl; stump*
    Full prevaly his pray for to wayte.   *privily; prey*

PETRUS Woman, thy wordis and thy wynde thou not waste,   *breath*
    Of his company never are I was kende.   *ere; known*
120 Thou haste thee mismarkid, trewly be traste;   *mistaken; be assured*
    Wherfore of thi misse thou thee amende.   *error*

MULIER Than gaynesaies thou here the sawes that thou saide,   *contradict; words*
    How he schulde clayme to be callid God Sonne,
    And with the werkis that he wrought
125 Whils he walketh in this flodde,   *flood*
    Baynly at oure bydding alway to be bonne.   *Willingly; bound (loyal)*

PETRUS I will consente to youre sawes;   *words*
  what schulde I saye more?
For women are crabbed,
  that comes them of kynde.   *nature*
But I saye as I firste saide,
  I sawe hym nevere are;   *before*
130 But as a frende of youre felawschippe
  schall ye me aye fynde.   *always*

MALCHUS Herke, knyghtis, that are knawen
  in this contré as we kenne,   *believe*
Howe yone boy with his boste   *boast*
  has brewed mekill bale: *great misery*
He has forsaken his maistir
  before yone womenne.
But I schall preve to you pertly   *demonstrate; openly*
  and telle you my tale.

135 I was presente with pepull
  whenne prese was full prest   *crowd; urgently [desired]*
To mete with his maistir,
  with mayne and with myght,   *strength*
And hurled hym hardely   *dragged; fiercely*
  and hastely hym arreste,
And in bandis full bittirly   *ropes*
  bande hym sore all that nyght.   *bound*

And of tokenyng of trouth schall I telle yowe,   *truth*
140 Howe yone boy with a brande   *sword*
  brayede me full nere   *chopped*
(Do move of thez materes emelle yowe),   *speak; among*
For swiftely he swapped of my nere.   *cut off; ear*

His maistir with his myght helyd me all hole,   *healed; whole*
That by no syne I cowthe see no man cowthe it witten   *sign; recognize*
145 And than badde hym bere pees in every ilke bale,   *bade; every bad situation*
For he that strikis with a swerde with a swerde schall be streken.   *struck down*

Latte se whedir grauntest thou gilte.   *you admit your guilt*
Do speke oon and spare not to telle us   *on*
Or full faste I schall fonde thee flitte,   *(i.e., make you flee)*
150 The soth but thou saie here emelle us.

Come of, do tyte, late me see nowe,   *quickly*
In savyng of thyselffe fro schame,
 . . .   *[line missing]*
Ya, and also for beryng of blame.   *bearing*

PETRUS   I was nevere with hym in werke that he wroght
155   In worde nor in werke, in will nor in dede;   *deed*
        I knawe no corse that ye have hidir brought,   *body (person)*
        In no courte of this kith, if I schulde right rede.   *region*

MALCHUS   Here, sirs, howe he sais and has forsaken
        His maistir to this woman here twyes,   *twice*
160   And newly oure lawe has he taken;   *perverted*
        Thus hath he denyed hym thryes.   *thrice*

JESUS   Petir, Petir, thus saide I are   *before*
        When thou saide thou wolde abide with me
        In wele and woo, in sorowe and care,   *prosperity*
165   Whillis I schulde thries forsaken be.   *(i.e., denied)*

PETRUS   Allas, the while that I come here,
        That evere I denyed my Lorde in quarte,   *alive*
        The loke of his faire face so clere
        With full sadde sorowe sheris my harte.   *pierces (cuts)*

III MILES   Sir knyghtis, take kepe of this karll and be konnand;   *care; knave; clever*
171   Because of Sir Cayphas we knowe wele his thoght.
        He will rewarde us full wele, that dare I wele warand,
        Whan he wete of oure werkis how wele we have wroght.   *knows*

IV MILES   Sir, this is Cayphas halle here at hande;
175   Go we boldly with this boy that we have here broght.

III MILES   Nay, sirs, us muste stalke to that stede and full still stande,   *place*
        For itt is nowe of the nyght, yf thei nappe oght.   *(i.e., midnight); sleep*
        Say, who is here?

I MILES   Say, who is here?

III MILES   I, a frende,
        Well knawyn in this contré for a knyght.   *known*

II MILES   Gose furthe, on youre wayes may yee wende,
181   For we have herbered enowe for tonyght.   *(i.e., taken in enough)*

I MILES   Gose abakke, bewscheres, ye both are to blame,   *Go away*
        To bourde whenne oure busshopp is boune to his bedde.   *jest; bishop; gone to*

IV MILES   Why, sir, it were worthy to welcome us home;
185   We have gone for this warlowe and we have wele spedde.   *warlock*

II MILES   Why, who is that?

II Miles   The Jewes kyng, Jesus by name.

I Miles A, yee be welcome, that dare I wele wedde,   *wager*
    My lorde has sente for to seke hym.   *seek*

IV Miles   Loo, se here the same.

II Miles Abidde as I bidde and be noght adreed.   *afraid*
190   My lorde, my lorde, my lorde, here is layke, and you list.   *sport, if you wish*

Cayphas Pees, loselles, leste ye be nyse?   *are you fools*

I Miles My lorde, it is wele and ye wiste.

Cayphas What, nemen us no more, for it is twyes.   *call; twice*

    Thou takist non hede to the haste   *heed; urgency*
     that we have here on honde;   *at hand*
195   Go frayne howe oure folke faris   *ask; fare*
     that are furth ronne.   *forth run*

II Miles My lorde, youre knyghtis has kared   *proceeded*
    as ye thame commaunde,   *commanded*
  And thei have fallen full faire.   *into good luck*

Cayphas   Why, and is the foole fonne?   *discovered*

I Miles Ya, lorde, thei have brought a boy in a bande boun.   *rope bound*

Cayphas Where nowe, Sir Anna, that is one and able to be nere?   *near*

Anna My lorde, with youre leve me behoves to be here.

Cayphas A, sir, come nere and sitte we bothe in fere.   *together*

Anna Do, sir, bidde tham bring in that boy that is bune.   *bound*

Cayphas Pese now, Sir Anna, be stille and late hym stande,
204   And late us grope yf this gome be grathly begune.   *interrogate; game; properly*

Anna Sir, this game is begune of the best;
    Nowe hadde he no force for to flee thame.   *them*

Cayphas Nowe, in faithe, I am fayne he is fast;   *glad; captured*
    Do lede in that ladde, late me se than.

II MILES Lo, sir, we have saide to oure sovereyne,
210   Gose nowe and suye to hymselfe for the same thyng.   *proceed*

III MILES Mi lorde, to youre bidding we are buxom and bayne,   *humble; obedient*
       Lo, here is the belschere broght that ye bad bring.   *gentleman; bade [us]*

IV MILES My lorde, fandis now to fere hym.   *seek; frighten*

CAYPHAS   Nowe I am fayne,
       And felawes, faire mott ye fall for youre fynding.   *(i.e., blessings on you)*

ANNA Sir, and ye trowe thei be trewe
             withowten any trayne,   *deception*
216   Bidde thayme telle you the tyme of the takyng.   *circumstances; capture*

CAYPHAS Say, felawes, howe wente ye so nemely by nyght?   *nimbly*

III MILES My lorde, was there no man to marre us ne mende us.[1]

IV MILES My lorde, we had lanternes and light,
220   And some of his company kende us.   *recognized*

ANNA But saie, howe did he, Judas?

III MILES   A, sir, full wisely and wele:
       He markid us his maistir emang all his men
       And kyssid hym full kyndely his comforte to kele   *cool (detract from)*
       Bycause of a countenaunce that karll for to kenne.   *rascal; know*

CAYPHAS And thus did he his devere?   *duty*

IV MILES   Ya, lorde, evere ilke a dele: *each and every way*
226   He taughte us to take hym
             the tyme aftir tenne.   *ten o'clock*

ANNA Nowe, be my feith, a faynte frende myght he ther fynde.   *weak (poor) friend*

III MILES Sire, ye myght so have saide
             hadde ye hym sene thenne.   *seen*

IV MILES He sette us to the same that he solde us   *directed*
230   And feyned to be his frende as a faytour;   *deceiver*
       This was the tokenyng before that he tolde us.   *sign*

---

[1] *My lord, was there no man to prevent or hinder us*

Cayphas   Nowe, trewly, this was a trante of a traytour.   *trick*

Anna   Ya, be he traytour or trewe geve we never tale,   *(i.e., give we no thought)*
      But takes tente at this tyme and here what he telles.   *pay attention; hear*

Cayphas   Now sees that oure howsolde be holden here hole   *household; kept together*
236   So that none carpe in case but that in court dwellis.

III Miles   A, lorde, this brethell hath brewed moche bale.   *worthless fellow; much sorrow*

Cayphas   Therfore schall we spede us to spere of his spellis.   *inquire; sayings*
      Sir Anna, takis hede nowe and here hym.   *hear*

Anna   Say, ladde, liste thee noght lowte to a lorde?   *bow before*

IV Miles   No, sir, with youre leve, we schall lere hym.   *teach*

Cayphas   Nay, sir, noght so, no haste.
      Itt is no burde to bete bestis that are bune,   *sport; beat; tied up*
      And therfore with fayrenes firste we vill hym fraste   *will; question*
245   And sithen forther hym furth as we have fune.   *proceed; further; found*
      And telle us som tales, truly to traste.

Anna   Sir, we myght als wele talke
      tille a tome tonne.   *empty barrel*
    I warande hym witteles
      or ellis he is wrang wrayste,   *(i.e., defective of mind)*
    Or ellis he waitis to wirke
      als he was are wonne.   *ere accustomed*

III Miles   His wonne was to wirke mekill woo   *custom*
251   And make many maystries emelle us.   *(powerful) deeds*

Kayphas   And some schall he graunte or he goo,   *tell [us] before*
      Or muste yowe tente hym and telle us.   *attend to*

IV Miles   Mi lorde, to witte the wonderes that he has wroght,   *begin to know*
255   For to telle you the tente it wolde oure tonges tere.   *tenth; tear out*

Kayphas   Sen the boy for his boste is into bale broght,   *boasting*
      We will witte or he wende how his werkis were.   *explore (know) ere*

III Miles   Oure Sabott day we saye
      saves he right noght
    That he schulde halowe and holde   *keep holy; observe*
      full dingne and full dere.   *worthy; precious*

IV MILES No, sir, in the same feste   *feast*
    als we the sotte soughte,   *fool*
261 He salved thame of sikenesse   *cured; sickness*
    on many sidis seere.   *on all sides*

CAYPHAS What than, makes he thame grathely to gange?   *truly to go*

III MILES Ya, lorde, even forthe in every ilke a toune
    He thame lechis to liffe after lange.   *heals; [being] long [dead]*

CAYPHAS A, this makes he by the myghtis of Mahounde.   *power*

IV MILES Sir, oure stiffe Tempill, that made is of stone,   *strong*
267 That passes any paleys of price for to preyse,   *palace; praise*
    And it were doune to the erth and to the gronde gone,   *If it were*
    This rebalde he rowses hym rathely to rayse.   *scoundrel; boasts; quickly; raise*

III MILES Ya, lorde, and othir wonderis he workis grete wone,   *in great quantity*
271 And with his lowde lesyngis he losis oure layes.   *deceptions; undermines laws*

CAYPHAS Go, lowse hym, and levis than and late me allone,   *loosen [his bonds]; leave then*
    For myselfe schall serche hym and here what he saies.

ANNA Herke, Jesus of Jewes will have joie
275 To spille all thy sporte for thy spellis.   *mar; words*

CAYPHAS Do meve, felawe, of thy frendis that fedde thee beforne,   *move (speak); kin*
    And sithen, felowe, of thi fare forther will I freyne. *business; ask*
    Do neven us lightly — his langage is lorne.   *tell; quickly; ability to speak; gone*

III MILES My lorde, with youre leve, hym likis for to layne,   *remain silent*
280 But and he schulde scape skatheles it wer a full skorne,   *unscathed*
    For he has mustered emonge us full mekil of his mayne. *power*

IV MILES Malkus, youre man, lord, that had his ere schorne,   *ear*
    This harlotte full hastely helid it agayne.

CAYPHAS What, and liste hym be nyse for the nonys,   *foolish*
285 And heres howe we haste to rehete hym.   *hasten; rebuke*

ANNA Nowe, by Beliall bloode and his bonys,
    I holde it beste to go bete hym.   *beat*

CAYPHAS Nay, sir, none haste, we schall have game or we goo.   *before*
    Boy, be not agaste if we seme gaye;   *fearful; seem impressive [in dress]*
290 I conjure thee kyndely and comaunde thee also   *engage*

By grete God that is liffand and laste schall ay,   *living; (i.e., everlastingly)*
Yf thou be Criste, Goddis Sonne, telle till us two.

Jesus Sir, thou says it thiselffe, and sothly I saye
That I schall go to my Fadir that I come froo
295 And dwelle with hym wynly in welthe allway.   *worthily; state of bliss*

Cayphas Why, fie on thee, faitoure untrewe.
Thy fadir haste thou fowly defamed,
Now nedis us no notes of newe,   *(i.e., nothing more)*
Hymselfe with his sawes has he schamed.

Anna Nowe nedis nowdir wittenesse ne counsaille to call,   *neither*
301 But take his sawes as he saieth in the same stede: *place*
He sclaunderes the Godhed and greves us all,
Wherfore he is wele worthy to be dede.   *dead*
And therfore, sir, saies hym the sothe.

Cayphas   Sertis, so I schall.
305 Heres thou not, harlott?   *Hear*
     Ille happe on thy hede.   *head*
Aunswere here grathely to grete and to small,   *fittingly*
And reche us oute rathely som resoune, I rede.   *give; quickly*

Jesus My reasouns are not to reherse,
Nor they that myght helpe me are noght here nowe.

Anna Say, ladde, liste thee make verse?   *do you desire to*
311 Do telle on, belyff, late us here nowe.   *quickly; hear*

Jesus Sir, if I saie the sothe, thou schall not assente
But hyndir or haste me hynge.   *slander; hasten; [to] hang*
I prechid wher pepull was moste in present
315 And no poynte in privité to olde ne yonge.   *secret*
And also in youre Tempill I tolde myne entente,
Ye myght have tane me that tyme for my tellyng   *arrested*
Wele bettir than bringe me with brondis unbrente,   *swords unsheathed*
And thus to noye me be nyght and also for nothyng.   *annoy*

Cayphas For nothyng? Losell, thou lies,
321 Thy wordis and werkis will have a wrekyng.   *punishment*

Jesus Sire, sen thou with wrong so me wreyes,   *betray*
Go, spere thame that herde of my spekyng.   *inquire of; heard*

Cayphas A, this traitoure has tened me   *angered*
     with tales that he has tolde,

325 Yitt hadde I nevere such hething   *mockery*
        as of a harlott as hee.

I MILES What, fye on thee, beggar,
        who made thee so bolde
     To bourde with oure busshoppe?   *jest*
        Thy bane schall I bee.   *slayer*

JESUS Sir, if my wordis be wrange or werse than thou wolde,
        A wronge wittenesse I wotte nowe ar ye,   *false*
330 And if my sawes be soth thei mon be sore solde,   *be expensive*
        Wherfore thou bourdes to brode for to bete me. *jests too hastily*

II MILES My lorde, will ye here, for Mahounde?   *hear*
        No more now for to neven that it nedis.   *to say; is needed*

CAYPHAS Gose, dresse you and dyng ye hym doune,   *strike*
335 And deffe us no more with his dedis.   *deafen; deeds*

ANNA Nay, sir, than blemysshe yee prelatis estatis;   *dishonor; authority (dignity)*
        Ye awe to deme no man to dede for to dynge.   *ought; judge; in order to beat [him]*

CAYPHAS Why, sir, so were bettir than be in debate;   *dispute*
        Ye see the boy will noght bowe for oure bidding.

ANNA Nowe, sir, ye muste presente this boy unto Sir Pilate,
341 For he is domysman nere and nexte to the king,   *judge near*
        And late hym here alle the hole, how ye hym hate   *hear; whole*
        And whedir he will helpe hym or haste hym to hyng.

I MILES My lorde, late men lede hym by nyght,
345 So schall ye beste skape oute o skornyng.   *escape from scorn (scandal)*

II MILES My lorde, it is nowe in the nyght;
        I rede ye abide tille the mornyng.

CAYPHAS Bewschere, thou sais the beste, and so schall it be,
        But lerne yone boy bettir to bende and bowe.   *teach*

I MILES We schall lerne yone ladde, be my lewté,   *faith*
351 For to loute unto ilke lorde like unto yowe.   *reverence*

CAYPHAS Ya, and felawes, wayte that he be ay wakand.   *watch; always awake*

II MILES   Yis, lorde, that warant will wee.
        Itt were a full nedles note to bidde us nappe nowe.   *needless advice*

III Miles Sertis, will ye sitte, and sone schall ye see
355   Howe we schall play popse for the pages prowe.   *a game (see note); [worthless] man's benefit*

IV Miles Late see, who stertis for a stole?   *goes; stool*
       For I have here a hatir to hyde hym.   *cloth (rag), hood*

I Miles Lo, here is one full fitte for a foole;
       Go gete it, and sette thee beside hym.

II Miles Nay, I schall sette it myselffe and frusshe hym also.   *beat*
361   Lo, here a shrowde for a shrewe, and of shene shappe.   *shroud; evil one; of fair*

III Miles Playes faire in feere, and ther is one and ther is — two;
       I schall fande to feste it with a faire flappe,   *attempt to make fast*
       And ther is — three, and there is — four.
365   Say, nowe, with an nevill happe,   *evil*
       Who negheth thee nowe? Not o worde, no.   *comes near*

IV Miles Dose noddill on hym with neffes   *hit; fists*
       That he noght nappe.   *So that he doesn't fall asleep*

I Miles Nay, nowe to nappe is no nede,
       Wassaille, wassaylle!
          I warande hym wakande.

II Miles Ya, and bot he bettir bourdis can byde,   *unless; jests; abide*
371   Such buffettis schall he be takande.   *receiving*

III Miles Prophet, I saie, to be oute of debate,
       Quis te percussit, man? Rede giffe thou may.   *Who smote you; Answer if*

IV Miles Those wordes are in waste,   *useless*
          what wenes thou he wate?   *what do you think he understands*
375   It semys by his wirkyng   *behavior*
          his wittes were awaye.   *are gone*

I Miles Nowe late hym stande as he stode
          in a foles state,   *fool's estate*
       For he likis noght this layke,   *game*
          my liffe dare I laye.   *wager*

II Miles Sirs, us muste presente this page to Ser Pilate,
       But go we firste to oure soverayne
          and see what he saies.

III Miles My lorde, we have bourded with this boy   *sported*
381   And holden hym full hote emelle us.   *pursue him vigorously among*

CAYPHAS   Thanne herde ye some japes of joye?   *jests (jokes)*

IV MILES   The devell have the worde, lorde, he wolde telle us.

ANNA   Sir, bidde belyve, thei goo and bynde hym agayne   *quickly*
385   So that he skape noght, for that were a skorne.   *escapes*

CAYPHAS   Do telle to Sir Pilate oure pleyntes all pleyne   *complaints; plainly*
     And saie, this ladde with his lesyngis has oure lawes lorne;   *lies*
     And saie this same day muste he be slayne   *slain*
     Because of Sabott day that schal be tomorne.
390   And saie that we come oureselffe for certayne,
     And for to fortheren this fare, fare yee beforne.   *advance; matter*

I MILES   Mi lorde, with youre leve, us muste wende,
     Oure message to make as we maye.

CAYPHAS   Sir, youre faire felawschippe
     we betake to the fende.   *fiend*
395   Goose onne nowe and daunce forth in the devyll way.

[30. THE FIRST TRIAL BEFORE PILATE]

The Tapiteres and Couchers

PILATUS   Yhe cursed creatures that cruelly are cryand,   *crying (shouting)*
     Restreyne you for stryvyng
     for strengh of my strakis;   *for fear of my strokes*
     Youre pleyntes in my presence   *complaints*
     use plately applyand,   *plainly appealing*
     Or ellis this brande in youre braynes,   *sword*
     schalle brestis and brekis.   *burst; break*
5   This brande in his bones brekis,
     What brawle that with brawlyng me brewis,   *brawler; brews (produces)*
     That wrecche may not wrye fro my wrekis,   *turn; vengeance*
     Nor his sleyghtis noght slely hym slakis,   *slyly; slackens*
     Latte that traytour noght triste in my trewys.   *trust; truth (good faith)*

10   For Sir Sesar was my sier   *Caesar; sire*
     and I sothely his sonne,
     That exelent emperoure exaltid in hight   *on high*
     Whylk all this wilde worlde with wytes had wone;   *wits (intelligence); conquered*
     And my modir hight Pila that proude was o plight,   *of demeanor*
     O Pila that prowde, and Atus hir fadir he hight.   *was called*
15   This Pila was hadde into Atus,
     Nowe renkis, rede yhe it right?   *men*

For thus schortely I have schewid you in sight
Howe I am prowdely preved Pilatus.   *proudly proved [to be called]*

Loo, Pilate I am, proved a prince of grete pride;
20   I was putte into Pounce the pepill to presse,   *Pontius; repress*
And sithen Sesar hymselffe with exynatores be his side,   *senators*
Remytte me to ther remys, the renkes to redresse.   *Sent; realms; people to reform*
And yitte am I graunted on grounde, as I gesse,
To justifie and juge all the Jewes.   *execute justice*
25   A, luffe, here lady, no lesse?   *love*
Lo, sirs, my worthely wiffe, that sche is;
So semely, loo, certayne scho schewys.   *lovely; she appears*

Uxor Pilati   Was nevir juge in this Jurie of so jocounde generacion,   *Jewry; happy lineage*
Nor of so joifull genologie to gentrys enjoyned,   *aristocracy joined*
30   As yhe, my duke doughty, demar of dampnacion   *judge*
To princes and prelatis
     that youre preceptis perloyned.   *put aside*
Who that youre preceptis pertly perloyned,   *boldly*
With drede into dede schall ye dryffe hym.   *death; drive*
By my trouthe, he untrewly is troned   *falsely; enthroned*
35   That agaynste youre behestis hase honed;   *delayed*
All to ragges schall ye rente hym and ryve hym.   *shreds; tear*

I am dame precious Percula, of prynces the prise,
Wiffe to Ser Pilate, here prince withouten pere,   *peer*
All welle of all womanhede I am, wittie and wise.   *source*
40   Consayve nowe my countenaunce so comly and clere.   *Perceive*
The coloure of my corse is full clere,   *body*
And in richesse of robis I am rayed.   *arrayed*
Ther is no lorde in this londe, as I lere,
In faith, that hath a frendlyar feere   *companion*
45   Than yhe my lorde,
     myselffe thof I saye itt.   *though*

Pilatus   Nowe saye itt may ye saffely,
     for I will certefie the same.

Uxor Pilati   Gracious lorde, gramercye, youre gode worde is gayne.   *good; pleasing*

Pilatus   Yhitt for to comforte my corse, me muste kisse you, madame.   *Yet*

Uxor   To fulfille youre forward, my fayre lorde, in faith I am fayne.   *promise; glad*

Pilatus   Howe, howe, felawys, nowe in faith I am fayne
51   Of theis lippis so loffely are lappid,   *lovely; enclosed*
In bedde is full buxhome and bayne.   *willing*

DOMINA Yha, sir, it nedith not to layne,   *hide*
 All ladise we coveyte than
  bothe to be kyssid and clappid.   *hugged*

BEDELLUS My liberall lorde, o leder of lawis,   *expositor*
56 O schynyng schawe that all schames escheues,   *show (appearance); shames shuns*
 I beseke you, my soverayne, assente to my sawes
 As ye are gentill juger and justice of Jewes.   *judge*

DOMINA Do herke, howe you javell jangill of Jewes.   *brawler; chatter*
60 Why, go bette horosonne boy, when I bidde thee.   *go away whoreson*

BEDELLUS Madame, I do but that diewe is.   *what is due*

DOMINA But yf thou reste of thy resoune thou rewis,   *(i.e., stop talking); will be sorry*
 For all is acursed, carle, hase in, kydde thee.   *churl, go away, behave yourself*

PILATUS Do mende you, madame, and youre mode be amendand,
65 For me semys it wer sittand to se what he sais.   *is appropriate*

DOMINA Mi lorde, he tolde nevir tale that to me was tendand,   *tending (i.e., about me)*
 But with wrynkis and with wiles to wend me my weys.[1]

BEDELLUS Gwisse, of youre wayes to be wendand,   *Certainly*
 itt langis to oure lawes.   *belongs (is in accord with)*

DOMINA Loo, lorde, this ladde with his lawes,
70 Howe thynke ye it prophitis wele   *profits well*
  his prechyng to prayse?

PILATUS Yha, luffe, he knawis all oure custome,   *love (dear)*
 I knawe wele.

BEDELLUS My seniour, will ye see nowe the sonne in your sight,   *My lord; sun*
 For his stately strengh he stemmys in his stremys;   *reduces; beams*
75 Behalde ovir youre hede how he holdis fro hight
 And glydis to the grounde with his glitterand glemys.   *glides; radiant gleams*
 To the grounde he gois with his bemys
 And the nyght is neghand anone.   *near at hand*
 Yhe may deme aftir no dremys,   *judge; dreams*
80 But late my lady here   *let*
  with all her light lemys   *beams*
 Wightely go wende till her wone,   *Quickly; dwelling*

---

[1] *But with twistings and with deceptions to make me change my ways*

For ye muste sitte, sir, this same nyght of lyfe and of lyme; *limb*
Itt is noght leeffull for my lady *lawful*
  by the lawe of this lande
In dome for to dwelle *place of judgment*
  fro the day waxe ought dymme, *dim (at nightfall)*
85 For scho may stakir in the strete *stumble*
  but scho stalworthely stande.
  . . . [line missing]
Late hir take hir leve whill that light is. *leave*

PILATUS Nowe, wiffe, than ye blythely be buskand. *going*

DOMINA I am here, sir, hendely at hande. *seemly*

PILATUS Loo, this renke has us redde als right is. *man; advised as*

DOMINA Youre comaundement to kepe to kare for thee I caste me;[1]
91 My lorde, with youre leve, no lenger I lette yowe. *hinder*

PILATUS Itt were a repreve to my persone *rebuke*
  that prevely ye paste me, *secretly you left*
  Or ye wente fro this wones *place*
  or with wynne ye had wette yowe. *before; wet yourself (i.e., became drunk)*
Ye schall wende forthe with wynne *joy*
  whenne that ye have wette yowe.
95 Gete drinke, what dose thou, have done!
Come, semely, beside me and sette yowe. *sit*
Loke, nowe it is even here that I are behete you, *ere promised*
Ya, saie it nowe sadly and sone.

DOMINA Itt wolde glad me, my lorde, if ye gudly begynne. *goodly*

PILATUS Nowe I assente to youre counsaille, so comely and clene;
101 Nowe drynke, madame; to deth all this dynne. *noise*

DOMINA Iff it like yowe, myne awne lorde, I am not to lere; *learn*
  This lare I am not to lere. *lore; (i.e., do not need to)*

PILATUS Yitt efte to youre damysell, madame. *also*

DOMINA In thy hande, holde nowe, and have here.

ANCILLA Gramarcy, my lady so dere.

---

[1] *To obey your command to proceed (go) from you I prepare myself*

PILATUS Nowe fareswele, and walke on youre way.

   .   .   .   *[two lines missing]*

DOMINA Now farewele the frendlyest, youre fomen to fende.   *foes; fend [off]*

PILATUS Nowe farewele, the fayrest figure that evere did fode fede,   *food eat*

110   And farewele, ye damysell, indede.

ANCILLA My lorde, I comande me to youre ryalté.   *commend; royalty*

PILATUS Fayre lady, here is schall you lede.
    Sir, go with this worthy indede,
    And what scho biddis you doo,   *she*
    Loke that buxsome you be.   *obedient*

FILIUS I am prowde and preste to passe on apasse,   *prepared to go; apace*

116   To go with this gracious hir gudly to gyde.   *guide*

PILATUS Take tente to my tale, thou turne on no trayse,[1]
    Come tyte and telle me yf any tythyngis betyde.   *quickly*

FILIUS Yf any tythyngis my lady betyde,

120   I schall full sone, sir, witte you to say.   *(i.e., tell you)*
    This semely schall I schewe by hir side,
    Belyffe, sir, no lenger we byde.   *Quickly; abide*

PILATUS Nowe fareswele, and walkes on youre way.

    Nowe wente is my wiffe, yf it wer not hir will,   *even if*

125   And scho rakis tille hir reste as of nothyng scho rought.   *goes; cared about*
    Tyme is, I telle thee, thou tente me untill,   *paid attention to*
    And buske thee belyve, belamy, to bedde that I wer broght,   *hurry; my friend*
   .   .   .   *[line missing]*
    And loke I be rychely arrayed.   *see that I am*

BEDELLUS Als youre servaunte I have sadly it sought,

130   And this nyght, sir, newe schall ye noght,   *annoyed*
    I dare laye, fro ye luffely be layde.   *wager, when you*

PILATUS I comaunde thee to come nere, for I will kare to my couche;   *go*
    Have in thy handes hendely and heve me fro hyne,   *graciously; hence*
    But loke that thou tene me not with thi tastyng, but tendirly me touche,[2]

BEDELLUS A, sir, yhe whe wele.   *weigh well (i.e., are heavy)*

---

[1] *Pay attention to my command, do not deviate*

[2] *But see that you don't anger me with your handling, but touch me gently*

PILATUS   Yha, I have wette me with wyne.

  . . .   *[line missing]*

136 Yhit helde doune and lappe me even here, *cover*

      For I will slelye slepe unto synne. *slyly (surreptitiously); later*

      Loke that no man nor no myron of myne *retainer*

      With no noyse be neghand me nere. *coming near*

BEDELLUS Sir, what warlowe yow wakens *warlock*

        with wordis full wilde,

141 That boy for his brawlyng

        were bettir be unborne.

PILATUS Yha, who chatteres, hym chastise,

        be he churle or childe, *knight*

      For and he skape skatheles *if; unhurt (unscathed)*

        itt were to us a grete skorne.

      Yf skatheles he skape, it wer a skorne. *escape*

145 What rebalde that redely will rore, *menial fellow; shout*

      I schall mete with that myron tomorne, *lazy person*

      And for his ledir lewdenes hym lerne to be lorne. *harmful misbehavior; destroyed*

BEDELLUS Whe, so sir, slepe ye, and saies no more. *say*

DOMINA Nowe are we at home, do helpe yf ye may,

150 For I will make me redye and rayke to my reste. *go*

ANCILLA Yhe are werie, madame, forwente of youre way, *exhausted from; journey*

      Do boune you to bedde, for that holde I beste. *Do go*

FILIUS Here is a bedde arayed of the beste.

DOMINA Do happe me, and faste hense ye hye. *cover; go away quickly*

ANCILLA Madame, anone all dewly is dressid.

FILIUS With no stalkyng nor no striffe be ye stressed. *sneaking around; bothered*

DOMINA Nowe be yhe in pese, both youre carpyng and crye. *talking; shouting*

DIABOLUS Owte, owte, harrowe! Into bale am I brought.

      This bargayne may I banne, *curse*

      But yf I wirke some wile, in wo mon I wonne. *But unless; trick; dwell*

160 This gentilman Jesu of cursednesse he can, *maliciousness*

      Be any syngne that I see, this same is Goddis Sonne, *By; sign*

      And he be slone, oure solace will sese. *slain; cease*

      He will save man saule fro oure sonde *from our safekeeping*

      And refe us the remys that are rounde. *take from; realms; around*

165	I will on stiffely in this stounde	*firmly; time*
	Unto Ser Pilate wiffe pertely, and putte me in prese.	*boldly; endeavor*
	O woman, be wise and ware, and wonne in thi witte	*aware; comprehend*
	Ther schall a gentilman, Jesu, unjustely be juged	
	Byfore thy husband in haste, and with harlottis be hytte;	*struck (beaten)*
170	And that doughty today to deth thus be dyghted,	*good fellow; put*
	Sir Pilate, for his prechyng, and thou	
	With nede schalle ye namely be noyed:	*need (deprivation); specifically annoyed*
	Youre striffe and youre strenghe schal be stroyed,	*?striving; destroyed*
	Youre richesse schal be refte you that is rude	*taken from; great*
175	With vengeaunce, and that dare I avowe.	

DOMINA	A, I am drecchid with a dreme full dredfully to dowte.	*tormented; fear*
	Say, childe, rise uppe radly and reste for no roo;	*quickly; rest (peace)*
	Thow muste launce to my lorde and lowly hym lowte:	*rush; bow*
	Comaunde me to his reverence, as right will I doo.	*Commend*

FILIUS	O, what, schall I travayle thus tymely this tyde?	*at this early time*
181	Madame, for the drecchyng of heven,	*tormenting*
	Slyke note is newsome to neven,	*Such a matter is a nuisance to say*
	And it neghes unto mydnyght full even.	*is nearly*

DOMINA	Go bette, boy, I bidde no lenger thou byde,	*quickly*
	And saie to my sovereyne, this same is soth that I send hym.	*true*
	All naked this nyght as I napped	
	With tene and with trayne was I trapped	*trouble; deception*
	With a swevene that swiftely me swapped	*dream; struck*
	Of one Jesu, the juste man the Jewes will undoo.	

190	She prayes tente to that trewe man, with tyne to be noght trapped,[1]	
	But als a domesman dewly to be dressand	*judge; endeavoring*
	And lelye delyvere that lede.	*acquit; man*

FILIUS	Madame, I am dressid to that dede,	*prepared*
	But firste will I nappe in this nede,	
195	For he hase mystir of a morne slepe that mydnyght is myssand.	*need; missed*

ANNA	Sir Cayphas, ye kenne wele	*know*
	this caytiffe we have cached	
	That oftetymes in oure Tempill	
	has teched untrewly,	
	Oure meyné with myght	*people*

---

[1] *She asks attention to that true man, with affliction not to be entrapped*

	at mydnyght hym mached	*set upon*
	And hase drevyn hym till his demyng	*driven; judgment*
	for his dedis undewly.	*wrong*
200	Wherfore I counsaile that kyndely we carie	*by custom; proceed*
	Unto Ser Pilate, oure prince, and pray hym	
	That he for oure right will arraye hym,	*provide for*
	This faitour, for his falsed to flay hym	*deceiver; falsehood; punish*
	For fro we saie hym the soth	
	I schall sitte hym full sore.	*(i.e., make things go badly for him)*

CAYPHAS Sir Anna, this sporte have ye spedely aspied,   *seen*
206   As I am pontificall prince of all prestis.   *(i.e., the high priest)*
       We will prese to Ser Pilate and presente hym with pride   *press*
       With this harlott that has hewed owre hartis fro oure brestis   *torn*
       Thurgh talkyng of tales untrewe;
210   And therfore, ser knyghtis . . .

MILITES   Lorde.

CAYPHAS Sir knyghtis, that are curtayse and kynde,
       We charge you that chorle be wele chyned.   *churl; chained*
       Do buske you and grathely hym bynde   *immediately*
       And rugge hym in ropes, his rase till he rewe.   *harshly pull; behavior; rue*

I MILES Sir, youre sawes schall be served schortly and sone,   *words (sayings); obeyed*
216   Yha, do felawe, be thy feith, late us feste this faitour full fast.   *tie up*

II MILES I am douty to this dede, delyver, have done,   *bold; hurry*
       Latte us pulle on with pride till his poure be paste.   *strength*

I MILES Do have faste and halde at his handes.

II MILES For this same is he that lightly avaunted,   *boasted*
221   And God Sone he grathely hym graunted.   *boldly; admitted to*

I MILES He bese hurled for the highnes he haunted;   *dragged along; pride; pretended*
       Loo, he stonyes for us, he stares where he standis.   *is astonished*

II MILES Nowe is the brothell boune for all the boste that he blowne,   *[has] vented*
225   And the Laste Day he lete no lordyngs myght lawe hym.   *thought; overthrow*

ANNA Ya, he wende this worlde had bene haly his awne   *wholly; own*
       Als ye are dowtiest today   *boldest*
          tille his demyng ye drawe hym,   *pull*
       And than schall we kenne
          how that he canne excuse hym.   *himself*

I MILES Here, ye gomes, gose a-rome, giffe us gate;   *men, make room; way*
230   We muste steppe to yone sterne of astate.   *star; estate*

II MILES We muste yappely wende in at this yate,   *nimbly; gate*
       For he that comes to courte, to curtesye muste use hym.

I MILES Do rappe on the renkis   *men*
          that we may rayse with oure rolyng;   *agitating*
       Come forthe, sir coward,
          why cowre ye behynde?

BEDELLUS O, what javellis are ye that jappis with gollyng?   *brawlers; behave foolishly; shouting*

I MILES A, goode sir, be noght wroth, for wordis are as the wynde.   *angry*

BEDELLUS I saye, gedlynges, gose bakke with youre gawdes.   *gadlings (rascals); tricks*

II MILES Be sufferand, I beseke you,   *patient*
239   And more of this matere yhe meke yowe.   *humble yourself*

BEDELLUS Why, unconand knaves, an I cleke yowe,   *stupid; catch*
       I schall felle yowe,   *knock down*
          be my faith, for all youre false frawdes.

PILATUS Say, childe, ill cheffe you,   *let evil overtake*
          what churlles are so claterand?   *noisy*

BEDELLUS My lorde, unconand knaves, thei crye and thei call.   *ignorant*

PILATUS Gose baldely beliffe, and thos brethellis be batterand,   *Go boldly quickly; beating*
245   And putte tham in prisoune uppon peyne that may fall.
       Yha, spedely spir tham yf any sporte can thei spell,   *inquire; speak of*
       Yha, and loke what lordingis thei be.

BEDELLUS My lorde, that is luffull in lee,   *praiseworthy; tranquility*
249   I am boxsom and blithe to your blee.   *countenance*

PILATUS And if they talke any tythyngis
          come tyte and me tell.   *quickly*

BEDELLUS My felawes, by youre faith,
          can ye talke any tythandis?

I MILES Yha, sir, Sir Cayphas and Anna ar come both togedir
       To Sir Pilate o Pounce and prince of oure lawe,
       And thei have laughte a lorell   *caught a rogue*
          that is lawles and liddir.   *wicked*

BEDELUS My lorde, my lorde!

PILATUS Howe?

BEDELLUS My lorde, unlappe yow belyve wher ye lye. *uncover (i.e., get up)*
257 Sir Cayphas to youre courte is caried *come*
And Sir Anna, but a traytour hem taried; *delayed*
Many wight of that warlowe has waried, *cursed*
260 They have brought hym in a bande, his balis to bye. *bonds (ropes); sorrow to purchase*

PILATUS But are thes sawes certayne in soth that thou saies? *words*

BEDELLUS Yha, lorde, the states yondir standis, *estates (magnates)*
for striffe are they stonden.

PILATUS Now than am I light as a roo *buck*
and ethe for to rayse; *easy*
264 Go bidde tham come in both,
and the boye they have boune.

BEDELLUS Siris, my lorde geves leve
inne for to come.

CAYPHAS Hayle, prince that is pereles in price,
Ye are leder of lawes in this lande,
Youre helpe is full hendely at hande. *graciously*

ANNA Hayle, stronge in youre state for to stande, *estate*
270 Alle this dome muste be dressed at youre dulye devyse. *addressed; legal deposition*

PILATUS Who is there? My prelates?

CAYPHAS Yha, lorde.

PILATUS Nowe be ye welcome, iwisse.

CAYPHAS Gramercy, my soverayne,
but we beseke you all same; *beseech; together*
Bycause of wakand you unwarly *waking; unexpectedly*
be noght wroth with this,
274 For we have brought here a lorell, *rogue*
he lokis like a lambe.

PILATUS Come byn, you bothe, and to the benke brayde yowe. *in; bench hurry*

CAYPHAS Nay, gud sir, laugher is leffull for us. *lower (i.e., more humble); suitable*

PILATUS A, Sir Cayphas, be curtayse yhe bus.   *must be*

ANNA Nay, goode lorde, it may not be thus.

PILATUS Sais no more, but come sitte you beside me
    in sorowe, as I saide youe.

FILIUS Hayle, the semelieste seeg undir sonne sought,   *man; found*
281   Hayle, the derrest duke and doughtiest in dede.   *boldest*

PILATUS Now bene veneuew, beuscher,   *welcome, good sir*
    what boodworde haste thou brought?   *message*
    Hase any langour my lady newe laught in this leede?   *illness; latched (caught); place*

FILIUS Sir, that comely comaundes hir youe too   *commends; to you*
285   And sais, al nakid this nyght as sche napped,
    With tene and with traye was sche trapped   *trouble; deception*
    With a swevene that swiftely hir swapped   *dream*
    Of one Jesu, the juste man the Jewes will undo.

    She beseches you as hir soverayne that symple to save;   *innocent person*
290   Deme hym noght to deth, for drede of vengeaunce.

PILATUS What, I hope this be he that hyder harlid ye have.   *hither dragged*

CAYPHAS Ya, sir, the same and the selffe,
    but this is but a skaunce;   *joke (deception)*
    He with wicchecrafte
    this wile has he wrought.
    Some feende of his sand has he sente   *fiend; message*
295   And warned youre wiffe or he wente.   *informed; before*

PILATUS Yowe, that schalke schuld not shamely be shente.   *fellow; unjustly be destroyed*
    This is sikir in certayne, and soth schulde be sought.   *secure*

ANNA Yha, thurgh his fantome and falshed and fendes craft   *guile*
    He has wrogth many wondir
    where he walked full wyde,
300   Wherfore, my lorde, it wer leeffull   *lawful*
    his liffe were hym rafte.   *reft (taken away)*

PILATUS Be ye nevere so bryme, ye bothe bus abide,   *angry*
    But if the traytoure be taught for untrewe   *Unless; shown to be*
    And therfore sermones you no more,   *speak*
    I will sekirly sende hymselffe fore
305   And se what he sais to thee sore.   *urgently*

Bedell, go brynge hyme,
    for of that renke have I rewthe.   *man; pity*

BEDELLUS   This forward to fulfille   *henceforth*
    am I fayne in myn herte moved.
  Say, Jesu, the juges and the Jewes
    hase me enjoyned
  To bringe thee before tham
    even bounden as thou arte,   *bound (in bonds)*
310   Yone lordyngis to lose thee   *untie*
    full longe have thei heyned.   *waited*
  But firste schall I wirschippe thee
    with witte and with will:
  This reverence I do thee forthy
  For wytes that wer wiser than I;
  They worshipped thee full holy on hy,   *high*
315   And with solempnité sange *Osanna* till.

I MILES   My lorde that is leder of lawes in this lande,
  All bedilis to youre biding schulde be boxsome and bayne,   *beadles*
  And yitt this boy here before yowe
    full boldely was bowand   *bowing*
  To worschippe this warlowe;   *warlock*
    methynke we wirke all in vayne.

II MILES   Yha, and in youre presence he prayed hym of pees   *peace*
321   In knelyng on knes to this knave;
  He besoughte hym his servaunte to save.

CAIPHAS   Loo, lord such arrore amange them thei have   *error among*
  It is grete sorowe to see, no seeg may it sese.   *man; stop it*

325   It is no menske to youre manhed that mekill is of myght   *honor*
  To forbere such forfettis that falsely are feyned,   *allow; offenses*
  Such spites in especiall wolde be eschewed in your sight.   *insults; should be*

PILATUS   Sirs, moves you noght in this matere
    but bese myldely demeaned,   *mild of manner*
  For yone curtasie I kenne had som cause.   *courtesy*

ANNA   In youre sight, sir, the soth schall I saye,
331   As ye are prince, take hede, I you praye,
  Such a lourdayne unlele, dare I laye,   *rascal disloyal; wager*
  Many lordis of oure landis
    might lede fro oure lawes.

PILATUS Saye, losell, who gave thee leve
    so for to lowte to yone ladde *bow (reverence)*
335 And solace hym in my sight
    so semely, that I sawe?

BEDELLUS A, gracious lorde, greve you noght *grieve*
    for gude case I hadde.
  Yhe comaunded me to care
    als ye kende wele and knawe, *understand well*
  To Jerusalem on a journay, with seele, *good fortune*
  And than this semely on an asse was sette *handsome one*
340 And many men myldely hym mette.
  Als a God in that grounde thai hym grette, *greeted*
  Wele semand hym in waye with worschippe lele. *singing psalms to him; true*

  Osanna thei sange, "the sone of David,"
  Riche men with thare robes, thei ranne to his fete,
345 And poure folke fecched floures of the frith *flowers; forest*
  And made myrthe and melody this man for to mete.

PILATUS Nowe, gode sir, be thi feith,
    what is *Osanna* to saie?

BEDELLUS Sir, constrew it we may
    be langage of this lande as I leve,
  It is als moche to me for to meve,
350 Youre prelatis in this place can it preve, *explain*
  Als "Oure Saviour and soverayne,
    thou save us, we praye."

PILATUS Loo, senioures, how semes yow? — *lords*
    the sothe I you saide.

CAYPHAS Yha, lorde, this ladde is full liddir, be this light, *wicked, by*
  Yf his sawes wer serchid and sadly assaied, *sayings; assessed*
355 Save youre reverence,
    his resoune thei rekenne noght with right.
  This caytiffe thus cursedly can construe us.

BEDELLUS Sirs, trulye the trouthe I have tolde
  Of this wighte ye have wrapped in wolde. *(i.e., arrested)*

ANNA I saie, harlott, thy tonge schulde thou holde
360 And noght agaynste thi maistirs to meve thus.

PILATUS Do sese of youre seggyng, and I schall examyne full sore.[1]

ANNA Sir, demes hym to deth, or dose hym away.   *condemn*

PILATUS Sir, have ye saide?

ANNA   Yha, lorde.

PILATUS   Nowe go sette you with sorowe and care,   *sit*
     For I will lose no lede that is lele to oure law.   *man; loyal*
365 But steppe furth and stonde uppe on hight   *high*
     And buske to my bidding, thou boy,
     And for the nones that thou neven us a noy.   *nonce; proclaim; cry [of "Oyez"]*

BEDELLUS I am here at youre hande to halow a *hoy*;   *shout "hear ye" ("Oyez")*
369 Do move of youre maister, for I schall melle it with myght.   *(i.e., do it)*

PILATUS Cry *Oyas.*

BEDELLUS   Oyas!

PILATUS   Yit efte, be thi feithe.   *again*

BEDELLUS   Oyes!   [*Alowde*

PILATUS Yit lowdar
     that ilke lede may lithe,   *man; pay attention*
     Crye pece in this prese uppon payne theruppon,   *peace; press (crowd)*
     Bidde them swage of ther sweying   *stop; noise*
        bothe swiftely and swithe,   *quickly*
     And stynt of ther stryvyng and stande still as a stone.   *stop; unruliness*
375 Calle Jesu, the gentill of Jacob, the Jewe,
     Come preste and appere,   *quickly*
     To the barre drawe thee nere
     To thi jugement here,
     To be demed for his dedis undewe.   *illegal*

I MILES Whe, harke how this harlott he heldis oute of harre,   *is out of order*
381 This lotterelle liste noght my lorde to lowte.   *scoundrel; to reverence*

II MILES Say, beggar, why brawlest thou? Go boune thee to the barre.   *take yourself*

I MILES Steppe on thy standyng so sterne and so stoute.   *place for standing [in court]*

---

[1] *Do cease of your speaking, and I shall examine very carefully*

II MILES Steppe on thy standyng so still.

I MILES Sir cowarde, to courte muste yhe care.   *go*

II MILES A lessoune to lerne of oure lawe.

I MILES Flitte fourthe, foule myght thou fare.

II MILES Say, warlowe, thou wantist of thi will.   *have lost your mind*

FILIUS O Jesu ungentill, thi joie is in japes;   *lowborn*
390   Thou cannot be curtayse, thou caytiffe I calle thee.   *worthy*
      No ruthe were it to rug thee and ryve thee in ropes.   *pity; tug; tear*
      Why falles thou noght flatte here, foule falle thee,
      For ferde of my fadir so free?   *fear; liberal*
      Thou wotte noght his wisdome, iwys;   *know*
395   All thyne helpe in his hande that it is,
      Howe sone he myght save thee fro this.
      Obeye hym, brothell, I bidde thee.

PILATUS Now, Jesu, thou art welcome ewys, as I wene,
      Be noght abasshed but boldely boune thee to the barre.   *take*
400   What seyniour will sewe for thee sore, I have sene.   *argue against you*
      To wirke on this warlowe, his witte is in waste.   *lost*
      Come preste, of a payne, and appere,   *quickly; pain [of punishment]*
      And sir prelatis, youre pontes bes prevyng,   *charges to prove*
      What cause can ye caste of accusyng?   *produce*
405   This mater ye marke to be meving   *undertaken*
      And hendly in haste late us here.   *hear*

CAYPHAS Sir Pilate o Pounce, and prince of grete price,
      We triste ye will trowe oure tales thei be trewe   *trust; believe*
      To deth for to deme hym with dewly device,   *lawful judgment*
410   For cursidnesse yone knave hase in case, if ye knew,   *in [this] case*
      In harte wolde ye hate hym in hye.   *high (greatly)*
      For if it wer so,
      We mente not to misdo;   *offend*
      Triste, ser, schall ye therto,
415   We hadde not hym taken to thee.

PILATUS Sir, youre tales wolde I trowe   *believe*
          but thei touche none entente.   *not the point*
      What cause can ye fynde
          nowe this freke for to felle?   *man; cast down (condemn)*

ANNA Oure Sabbotte he saves not, but sadly assente   *observes; solemnly offers*
      To wirke full unwisely, this wote I right wele,

. . .   *[line missing]*

420 He werkis whane he will, wele I wote,   *when*
     And therfore in herte we hym hate.
     Itt sittis you to strenghe youre estate   *strengthen*
     Yone losell to louse for his lay.   *lose (i.e., kill); customs*

PILATUS   Ilke a lede for to louse for his lay is not lele.   *man; customs (lifestyle); lawful*
425 Youre lawes is leffull, but to youre lawis longis it   *lawful; belongs*
     This faitoure to feese wele with flappes full fele,   *deceiver; punish; blows; many*
     And woo may ye wirke hym be lawe,
        for he wranges it.   *wrongs*
     Therfore takes unto you full tyte   *quickly*
     And like as youre lawes will you lede   *lead (demand)*
430 Ye deme hym to deth for his dede.

CAYPHAS   Nay, nay sir, that dome muste us drede;

. . .   *[line missing]*

     It longes noght till us no lede for to lose.   *belongs; man (man's life)*

PILATUS   What wolde ye I did thanne? —
        the devyll motte you drawe.   *draw [as in an execution]*
     Full fewe are his frendis, but fele are his fooes.   *many*
435 His liff for to lose thare longes no lawe,   *(i.e., is not legal)*
     Nor no cause can I kyndely contryve
     That why he schulde lose thus his liffe.

ANNA   A, gude sir, it raykes full ryffe   *happens; rife (everywhere)*
     In steedis wher he has stirrid mekill striffe   *places*
440 Of ledis that is lele to youre liffe.   *men; loyal*

CAYPHAS   Sir, halte men and hurte he helid in haste,   *lame; healed*
     The deffe and the dome he delyvered fro doole   *deaf; dumb; sorrow*
     By wicchecrafte, I warande; his wittis schall waste,   *decline*
     For the farles that he farith with —   *marvels; busied himself with*
        loo, how thei folowe yone fole,   *fool*
445 Oure folke so thus he frayes in fere.   *dismays (frightens) all together*

ANNA   The dede he rayses anone,   *dead*
     This Lazare that lowe lay allone
     He graunte hym his gates for to gone   *ways; go*
     And pertely thus proved he his poure.   *cleverly; power*

PILATUS   Now goode siris, I saie, what wolde yhe?

CAIPHAS   Sir, to dede for to do hym or dose hym adawe.   *do; to death*

PILATUS Yha, for he dose wele his deth for to deme?
453   Go layke you sir, lightly,   *play [the fool]*
    wher lerned ye such lawe?
    This touches no tresoune, I telle you;   *treason*
    yhe prelatis that proved are for price,
455   Yhe schulde be bothe witty and wise
    And legge oure lawe wher it lyse,   *allege; lies*
    Oure materes ye meve thus emel you.   *amongst*

ANNA Misplese noght youre persone,
    yhe prince withouten pere.
460   It touches to tresoune, this tale I schall tell.
    Yone briboure, full baynly he bed to forbere   *briber; readily; bid (said); withhold*
    The tribute to the emperoure, thus wolde he compell
    Oure pepill thus his poyntis to applye.

CAYPHAS The pepull, he saies, he schall save,
465   And Criste garres he calle hym, yone knave,   *makes (them) call*
    And sais he will the high kyngdome have.
    Loke whethir he deserve to dye.

PILATUS To dye he deserves yf he do thus indede,
    But I will se myselffe what he sais.
470   Speke, Jesu, and spende nowe thi space for to spede.   *space of time*
    Thez lordyngis thei legge thee thou liste noght leve on oure lawes.[1]
    They accuse thee cruelly and kene,
    And therfore, as a chiftene I charge thee,
    Iff thou be Criste that thou telle me,
475   And God Sone thou grughe not to graunte thee,   *grudge*
    For this is the matere that I mene.

JESUS Thou saiste so thiselve, I am sothly the same,   *in truth*
    Here wonnyng in worlde to wirke al thi will.   *dwelling*
    Mi Fadir is faithfull to felle all thi fame;   *cast down*
480   Withouten trespas or tene am I taken thee till.   *trouble*

PILATUS Loo, busshoppis, why blame ye this boye?
    Me semys that it is soth that he saies.
    Ye meve all the malice ye may
    With youre wrenchis and wiles to wrythe hym away   *twist*
485   Unjustely to juge hym fro joie.

CAYPHAS Nought so, sir, his seggyng is full sothly soth,   *saying; truly true*
    It bryngis oure bernes in bale for to bynde.   *people; sorrow*

---

[1] *These lords, they allege that you wish not to live by our laws (customs)*

ANNA   Sir, douteles we deme als dewe the deth   *deserving*
    This foole that ye favour, great fautes can we fynde
490   This daye for to deme hym to dye.

PILATUS   Saie, losell, thou lies be this light;   *by*
    Naie, thou rebalde, thou rekens unright.

CAYPHAS   Avise you, sir, with mayne and with myght,
494   And wreke not youre wrethe nowe forthy.   *avenge; wrath*

PILATUS   Me likes noght his langage so largely for to lye.   *out-of-bounds to be*

CAIPHAS   A, mercy, lorde, mekely, no malice we mente.

PILATUS   Noo done is it douteles, balde be and blithe,   *Now; bold*
    Talke on that traytoure and telle youre entente.
    Yone segge is sotell, ye saie;   *man; subtle*
500   Gud sirs, wer lerned he such lare?   *where; lore (knowledge)*

CAYPHAS   In faith, we cannot fynde whare.

PILATUS   Yhis, his fadir with some farlis gan fare   *wonders began to entertain*
    And has lered this ladde of his lare.   *taught; lore*

ANNA   Nay, nay, sir, he was but a write, that we wiste;   *carpenter*
505   No sotelté he schewed that any segge sawe.

PILATUS   Thanne mene yhe of malice to marre hym of myght,   *out of malice; by your might*
    Of cursidnesse convik no cause can yhe knawe;   *[to] convict*
    Me mervellis ye malyngne o mys.   *accuse falsely amiss*

CAYPHAS   Sir, fro Galely hidir and hoo   *Galilee*
510   The gretteste agayne hym ganne goo,   *[numbers of people] to him began to*
    Yone warlowe to waken of woo,   *incite to*
    And of this werke beres witnesse, ywis.

PILATUS   Why, and hase he gone in Galely, yone gedlyng ongayne?   *gadling bothersome*

ANNA   Yha, lorde, ther was he borne,
    yone brethelle, and bredde.

PILATUS   Nowe withouten fagyng, my frendis, in faith I am fayne,   *deception; glad*
516   For now schall oure striffe full sternely be stede.   *firmly be fixed (settled)*
    Sir Herowde is kyng ther, ye kenne;
    His poure is preved full preste   *power*
    To ridde hym or reve hym of rest.   *clear (free); deprive*

520   And therfore, to go with yone gest,   *stranger*
       Yhe marke us oute of the manliest men.

CAYPHAS Als witte and wisdome youre will schal be wroght;
       Here is kempis full kene to the kyng for to care.   *strong soldiers; go*

PILATUS Nowe, seniours, I saie yow sen soth schall be soght,
525   But if he schortely be sente it may sitte us full sore.   *Unless; be worse for us*
       And therfore, sir knyghtis . . .

MILITES   Lorde.

PILATUS Sir knyghtis that are cruell and kene,
       That warlowe ye warrok and wraste,   *bind; drag away*
       And loke that he brymly be braste;   *roughly; beaten*
       .   .   .   [line missing]
530   Do take on that traytoure you betwene.

       Tille Herowde in haste with that harlott ye hye,   *go quickly*
       Comaunde me full mekely unto his moste myght,   *Commend*
       Saie the dome of this boy, to deme hym to dye,   *judgment concerning; judge*
       Is done upponne hym dewly, to dresse or to dight,   *duly; ordain; do*
535   Or liffe for to leve at his liste.   *live*
       Say ought I may do hym indede,   *if there is anything; to him*
       His awne am I worthely in wede.   *(i.e., I am Herod's own man); livery*

I MILES My lorde, we schall springe on a-spede;
       Come thens to me, this traitoure full tyte.

PILATUS Bewe sirs, I bidde you ye be not to bolde,   *too*
541   But takes tente for oure tribute full trulye to trete.   *pay attention*

II MILES Mi lorde, we schall hye this beheste for to halde   *hurry along; hold*
       And wirke it full wisely in wille and in witte.

PILATUS So, sirs, me semys itt is sittand.   *fitting (legally appropriate)*

I MILES Mahounde, sirs, he menske you with myght.   *honor (bless)*

II MILES And save you, sir, semely in sight.

PILATUS Now in the wilde vengeaunce ye walke with that wight,
548   And fresshely ye founde to be flittand.   *vigorously; proceed; departing*

[31. The Trial before Herod]

The Lytsteres

REX Pes, ye brothellis and browlys, in this broydenesse inbrased,[1]	
And freykis that are frendely your freykenesse to frayne,	*men; manliness inquire into*
Youre tounges fro tretyng of triffillis be trased,	*speaking; trifles; suppressed*
Or this brande that is bright schall breste in youre brayne.	*sword; smash*
5 Plextis for no plasis, but platte you to this playne,	*Plead; places; fall down; plain*
And drawe to no drofyng, but dresse you to drede,	*riot; behave in fear*
With dasshis.	*blows*
Traveylis noght as traytours that tristis in trayne	*Work; rely on deception*
Or by the bloode that Mahounde bledde, with this blad schal ye blede.	*blade*
10 Thus schall I brittyn all youre bones on brede	*hack; (i.e., every one)*
Yae, and lusshe all youre lymmys with lasschis.	*beat; lashes*
Dragons that are dredfull schall derke in ther denne	*lurk*
In wrathe when we writhe or in wrathenesse ar wapped;	*anger are wrapped*
Agaynste jeauntis ongentill have we joined with ingendis,[2]	
15 And swannys that are swymmyng to oure swetnes schall be suapped,	*smitten*
And joged doune ther jolynes oure gentries engenderand.	*cut; nobles begetting*
Whoso repreve oure estate we schall choppe tham in cheynes.	*challenge; clap*
All renkkis that are renand to us schall be reverande.	*men; reigning; revering*
Therfore I bidde you sese or any bale be	*cease ere; misery*
20 That no brothell be so bolde boste for to blowes,	*boasting; vent*
And ye that luffis youre liffis, listen to me	*loves; lives*
As a lorde that is lerned to lede you be lawes.	
And ye that are of my men and of my menye,	*company (family)*
Sen we are comen fro oure kyth as ye wele knawe	*region*
25 And semlys all here same in this cyté,	*assembled; together*
It sittis us in sadnesse to sette all oure sawes.	*seriousness to set forth; sayings (ideas)*
I DUX My lorde, we schall take kepe to youre call	*pay attention*
And stirre to no stede but ye steven us,	*place; call*
29 Ne grevaunce to grete ne to small.	*too; too*
REX Ya, but loke that no fawtes befall.	*mistakes*
II DUX Lely, my lord, so we shall;	*Truly (Loyally)*
Ye nede not no more for to nevyn us.	*tell*

---

[1] *Peace, you reprobates and brawlers, in this broad space surrounded*

[2] *Against giants ungentle have we joined (gone to battle) with weapons*

I DUX   Mounseniour, demene you to menske in mynde what I mene   *may you please; honor*
                And boune to youre bodword, for so holde I best,   *remain obliged; command*
35   For all the comons of this courte bene avoyde clene,   *are all gone away*
                And ilke a renke, as resoune as, are gone to ther reste;   *all men; as reason requires*
                Wherfore I counsaile, my lorde, ye comaunde you a drynke.

REX   Nowe certis, I assente as thou sais,
                Se ych a qwy is wente on his ways   *each man*
40   Lightly withouten any delayes.   *Quickly*
                Giffe us wyne wynly and late us go wynke   *pleasantly; sleep*
                And se that no durdan be done.   *noise*

                            Tunc bibit Rex.   *Then the king drinks*

I DUX   My lorde, unlase you to lye,   *unlace*
                Here schall none come for to crye.

REX   Nowe spedely loke that thou spie
46   That no noyse be neghand this none.   *nearing; midnight*

I DUX   My lorde, youre bedde is new made;
                you nedis noght for to bide it.   *wait [for]*

REX   Ya, but as thou luffes me hartely,   *love*
                laye me doune softely,
                For thou wotte full wele   *know*
                that I am full tendirly hydid.   *have very tender skin*

I DUX   Howe lye ye, my goode lorde?

REX   Right wele, be this light,
51   All holé at my desire,   *(i.e., wholly as I wish)*
                Wherfore I praye Ser Satan, oure sire,
                And Lucifer moste luffely of lyre,   *figure*
                He sauffe you all, sirs, and giffe you goode nyght.   *save; give*

I MILES   Sir knyght, ye wote we are warned to wende,   *told*
56   To witte of this warlowe what is the kyngis will.   *learn; warlock*

II MILES   Sir, here is Herowde all even here at oure hende,   *Herod's hall; hand*
                And all oure entente tyte schall we tell hym untill.   *very soon*

I MILES   Who is here?

I DUX   Who is there?

I Miles   Sir, we are knyghtis kende   *known*
60   Is comen to youre counsaill this carle for to kill.   *churl*

I Dux   Sirs, but youre message may myrthis amende,
            Stalkis furthe be yone stretis, or stande stone still.   *Sneak forth by*

II Miles   Yis, certis, ser, of myrthis we mene;   *good news*
            The kyng schall have matteres to melle hym.   *concern*
65   We brynge here a boy us betwene,
            Wherfore have worschippe, we wene.   *honor; believe*

I Dux   Wele, sirs, so that it turne to no tene,   *mischief*
            Tentis hym and we schall go telle hym.   *Attend to*

            My lorde, yondir is a boy boune that brought is in blame;   *bound; as one blamed*
70   Haste you in hye, thei hove at youre gates.   *quickly; wait*

Rex   What, and schall I rise nowe, in the devyllis name
          To stighill amang straungeres in stales of astate?   *intervene; in court*
          But have here my hande, halde nowe,   *hold*
          And se that my sloppe be wele sittande.   *overgarment; not askew*

I Dux   My lorde, with a goode will I wolde youe,
76   No wrange will I witte at my wittande.   *(i.e., will I wish to know of)*

            But, my lorde, we can tell you of uncouthe tythandes.   *novel (outlandish)*

Rex   Ya, but loke ye telle us no tales but trewe.

II Dux   My lorde, thei bryng you yondir a boy boune in a bande   *bonds (ropes)*
80   That bodus outhir bourdyng or bales to brewe.   *bodes either entertainment; trouble*

Rex   Thanne gete we some harrowe full hastely at hande.   *turmoil*

I Dux   My lorde, ther is some note that is nedfull to neven you of new.   *news; mention*

Rex   Why, hoppis thou thei haste hym to hyng?   *expect; hang*

II Dux   We wotte noght ther will nor ther wenyng,   *their intent*
85   But boodword full blithely thei bryng.   *message*

Rex   Nowe do than and late us se of there sayng.

II Dux   Lo, sirs, ye schall carpe with the kyng
            And telles to hym manly youre menyng.   *properly (courteously)*

I Miles   Lorde, welthis and worschippis be with you alway.   *wealth*

REX What wolde thou?

II MILES A worde, lorde, and youre willes were. *if it were your will*

REX Well, saye on, than.

I MILES My lorde, we fare foolys to flay, *make fools to [be] punished*
92 Yt to you wolde forfette. *offend*

REX We, faire falle you therfore. *(i.e., may you prosper)*

I MILES My lorde, fro ye here what we saie, *hear*
94 Itt will heffe uppe youre hertis. *heave*

REX Ya, but saie what heynde have ye thore? *creature (person)*

II MILES A presente fro Pilate, lorde, the prince of oure lay. *law*

REX Pese in my presence, and nemys hym no more. *Peace; name*

I MILES My lorde, he woll worschippe you faine. *gladly*

REX I consayve ye are ful foes of hym.

II MILES My lorde, he wolde menske you with mayne, *honor; [all his] strength*
100 And therfore he sendis you this swayne. *man*

REX Gose tyte with that gedlyng agayne *gadling*
And saie hym a borowed bene sette I noght be hym. *borrowed bean set; by*

I DUX A, my lorde, with youre leve, thei have faren ferre, *come from afar*
And for to fraiste of youre fare was no folye. *discover; opinion*

II DUX My lorde, and this gedlyng go thus it will greve werre, *if; grieve worse*
106 For he gares growe on this grounde grete velanye. *causes (to)*

REX Why, menys thou that that myghtyng schulde my myghtes marre? *insignificant fellow*

I DUX Nay, lorde, but he makis on this molde mekill maystrie. *earth; deeds*

REX Go ynne, and late us see of the sawes ere,
110 And but yf thei be to oure bordyng, *enjoyment*
thai both schalle abye. *abide*

II MILES My lorde, we were worthy to blame
To brynge you any message of mysse. *evil*

Rex Why, than can ye nemyn us his name? *name (tell)*

I Miles Sir, Criste have we called hym at hame. *home*

Rex O, this is the ilke selve and the same.
116   Nowe, sires, ye be welcome, ywisse.

    And in faith I am fayne he is fonne, *glad; found*
    His farles to frayne and to fele, *marvels; question; experience*
119   Nowe thes games was grathely begonne. *directly*

II Miles Lorde, lely that likis us wele. *truly*

Rex Ya, but dar ye hete hartely that harlott is he? *dare; promise honestly*

I Miles My lorde, takis hede, and in haste ye schall here howe. *hear*

Rex Ya, but what menys that this message was made unto me? *means [it]*

II Miles My lorde, for it touches to tresoune, I trowe. *think*

I Miles My lorde, he is culpabill kende in oure contré *known [to be]; country*
126   Of many perillus poyntis, as Pilate preves nowe. *proves*

II Miles My lorde, when Pilate herde he had gone thurgh Galyle, *Galilee*
    He lerned us that that lordschippe longed to you, *informed; belonged*
    And or he wiste what youre willis were, *until he knew*
130   No ferther wolde he speke for to spille hym. *condemn*

Rex Thanne knawes he that oure myghtis are the more? *greater*

I Miles Ya, certis sir, so saie we thore.

Rex Nowe, sertis, and oure frenschippe therfore
    We graunte hym, and no grevaunce we will hym.

135   And sirs, ye are welcome, ywisse, as ye wele awe, *ought [to be]*
    And for to wende at youre wille I you warande, *permit*
    For I have coveite kyndely that comely to knawe, *wished naturally; comely person*
    For men carpis that the carle schulde be konnand. *say; churl; cunning*

II Miles My lorde, wolde he saie you soth of his sawe,
140   Ye saugh nevir slik selcouth, be see nor be sande. *saw; such wonders; sea*

Rex Nowe gois abakke both, and late the boy blowe, *let; give vent*
    For I hope we gete some harre hastely at hande. *matter of significance*

I MILES   Jerusalem and the Jewes may have joie
  And hele in ther herte for to here hym.   *well-being*

REX   Saie, beene-venew in bone fay,   *welcome in good faith*
146 Ne plesew et a parle remoy?   *(i.e., Doesn't it please you to speak with me)*

II MILES   Nay, my lorde, he can of no bourdyng, this boy.   *joking around*

REX   No, sir, with thi leve we schall lere hym.   *teach*

I FILIUS   Mi lorde, se ther knyghtis that knawe and are kene
150 How thai come to youre courte withoutyn any call.

REX   Ya, sone, and musteris grete maistries,   *perform; deeds*
  what may this bymene?   *suggest*

I DUX   My lorde, for youre myghtis are more than thei all,
  They seke you as soverayne and sertis that is sene.   *certainly; seen (obvious)*

REX   Nowe certis, sen ye saie so, assaie hym I schall,   *test*
155 For I am fayner of that freyke then othir fiftene.   *more interested in; man than [any]*
  Yae, and hym that first fande, faire myght hym fall.   *found*

I MILES   Lorde, lely we lereth you no legh,   *tell; lie*
  This liffe that he ledis will lose hym.   *leads*

REX   Wele, sirs, drawes you adrygh   *stand aside*
160 And, bewscheris, bryngis ye hym nygh,
  For yif all that his sleghtis be slye,
  Yitte or he passe we schalle appose hym.   *ere; question*

  O, my harte hoppis for joie
  To se nowe this prophette appere.
165 We schall have goode game with this boy;
  Takis hede, for in haste ye schall here.

  I leve we schall laugh and have likyng   *believe*
  To se nowe this lidderon her he leggis oure lawis.   *wicked fellow; expounds*

II DUX   Harke, cosyne, thou comys to karpe with kyng;   *cousin*
170 Take tente and be conande, and carpe as thou knowis.   *Pay attention; cunning*

I DUX   Ya, and loke that thou be not a sotte of thy saying,   *fool for*
  But sadly and sone thou sette all thi sawes.   *set forth; words (sayings)*

REX   Hym semys full boudisch, that boy that thei bryng.   *sullen*

II DUX Mi lorde, and of his bordyng grete bostyng men blawes. *idle talk; boasting; give vent*

REX Whi, therfore have I soughte hym to see,
176 Loke, bewscheris, ye be to oure bodis boune. *good men; orders obedient*

I DUX Knele doune here to the kyng on thy knee.

II DUX Naye, nedelyngis yt will not be. *of necessity*

REX Loo, sirs, he mekis hym no more unto me *humbles himself*
180 Thanne it were to a man of ther awne toune. *own*

I DUX Whe, go lawmere, and lerne thee to lowte *fool; reverence (bow)*
Or thai more blame thee to bring.

REX Nay, dredeles withouten any doute *surely; doubt*
He knawes noght the course of a kyng, *protocol*

185 And her beeis in oure bale, bourde or we blynne. *custody, entertain [us]; put an end*
Saie firste at the begynnyng withall, where was thou borne?
Do, felawe, for thy faith, latte us falle ynne. *(i.e., Speak); begin*
Firste of thi ferleis, who fedde thee beforne? *marvels; fed (raised)*
What, deynes thou not? Lo, sirs, he deffis us with dynne. *deign; deafens; din*
190 Say, whare ledde ye this lidrone? His langage is lorne. *rascal; lost*

I MILES My lorde, his mervaylis to more and to myne, *less*
Or musteres emange us both mydday and morne. *musters (shows)*

II MILES Mi lorde, it were to fele *too many*
Of wonderes, he workith tham so wightely. *frequently*

I MILES Whe, man, momelyng may nothyng avayle; *mumbling*
196 Go to the kyng and tell hyme fro toppe unto tayle.

REX Do bringe us that boy unto bale, *custody*
For lely we leffe hym noght lightly. *(i.e., judge)*

I DUX This mop menyes that he may marke men to ther mede;[1]
200 He makes many maistries and mervayles emange. *deeds*

II DUX Five thousand folke faire gon he feede
With fyve looffis and two fisshis to fange. *partake of*

REX Howe fele folke sais thou he fedde? *many*

---

[1] *This simpleton claims that he may assign men to [their] reward*

II DUX   Five thousand, lorde, that come to his call.

REX   Ya, boye, howe mekill brede he them bedde?   *offered*

I DUX   But five looffis, dare I wele wedde.   *wager*

REX   Nowe, be the bloode that Mahounde bledde,
      What, this was a wondir at all.

II DUX   Nowe, lorde, two fisshes blissid he efte,   *also*
210   And gaffe thame and ther none was forgetyn.

I DUX   Ya, lorde, and twelve lepfull ther lefte   *baskets*
      Of releve whan all men had eten.   *leftovers*

REX   Of such anodir mangery no man mene may.   *meal; speak*

II DUX   Mi lorde, but his maistries that musteris his myght.   *deeds [are] what show*

REX   But saie, sirs, ar ther sawis soth that thei saie?   *sayings true*

II MILES   Ya, lorde, and more selcouth were schewed to oure sight. *wonders*
217   One Lazar, a ladde that in oure lande lay,
      Lay loken undir layre fro lymme and fro light,   *locked; earth; leam (gleam)*
      And his sistir come rakand in rewfull arraye;   *rushing in distress*
220   And lorde, for ther raryng he raysed hym full right   *roaring (lamenting)*
      And fro his grath garte hym gang   *up from; grave made; go*
      Evere forthe, withouten any evill.

REX   We, such lesyngis lastis to lange.   *lies; too long*

I MILES   Why, lorde, wene ye that wordis be wronge?   *believe*
225   This same ladde levys us emang.   *lives*

REX   Why, there hope I be dedis of the devyll.

      Why schulde ye haste hym to hyng   *hang*
      That sought not newly youre newys?   *until recently; (i.e., annoyance)*

II MILES   My lorde, for he callis hym a kyng
230   And claymes to be a kyng of Jewis.

REX   But saie, is he kyng in his kyth where he come froo?   *region*

I MILES   Nay, lorde, but he callis hym a kyng his caris to kele.   *cares to alleviate*

REX	Thanne is it litill wondir yf that he be woo,	*woeful (depressed)*
	For to be weried with wrang sen he wirkis wele;	*cursed; wrong; performs good deeds*
235	But he schalle sitte be myselfe sen ye saie soo.	*if you*
	Comes nerre, kyng, into courte. Saie, can ye not knele?	
	We schalle have gaudis full goode and games or we goo.	*sports; ere*
	Howe likis tha? Wele, lorde. Saie — what, devyll nevere a dele?	*deal (i.e., no speaking)*
	I faute in my reverant in otill moy,	*(i.e., am not honored)*
240	I am of favour, loo, fairer be ferre.	*appearance; by far*
	Kyte oute yugilment. Uta, oy, oy!	*(see note to lines 239–45)*
	Be any witte that I watte it will waxe werre.	*I fear; worse*

	Servicia primet,	*Duty demands*
	Such losellis and lurdaynes as thou, loo.	*dull fellows; rascals*
245	*Respicias timet,*	*Let him be wary and fear*
	What the devyll and his dame schall I now doo?	

	Do carpe on, carle, for I can thee cure,	*assist*
	Say, may thou not here me? Oy, man, arte thou woode?	*hear; mad*
	Nowe telle me faithfully before howe thou fore;	*fared*
250	Forthe, frende, be my faith, thou arte a fonde foode.	*[Come] forth; foolish person*

| I DUX | My lorde, it astonys hym, youre steven is so store; | *astonishes; voice; strong* |
| | Hym had levere have stande stone still ther he stode. | *rather; where he stood* |

| REX | And whedir the boy be abasshid of Herrowde byg blure, | *big bluster* |
| | That were a bourde of the beste, be Mahoundes bloode. | |

| II DUX | My lorde, I trowe youre fauchone hym flaies | *falchion; frightens* |
| 256 | And lettis hym. | *hinders him [from speaking]* |

REX	Nowe lely I leve thee,	
	And therfore schall I waffe it away,	*wave*
	And softely with a septoure assaie.	*try (test)*
	Nowe, sir, be perte I thee pray,	*alert*
260	For none of my gromys schall greve thee.	*retainers; grieve*

	Si loqueris tibi laus,	
	Pariter quoque prospera dantur;	
	Si loqueris tibi fraus,	
	Fell fex et bella parantur.[1]	
265	Mi menne, ye go menske hym with mayne	*honor; strength*
	And loke yhow that it wolde seme.	

---

[1] Lines 261–64: *If you utter praise concerning yourself, / Likewise success will be granted; / If you speak deceptively to yourself, / Poison, dregs, and war will follow*

I DUX Dewcus, fayff, ser, and sofferayne.

II DUX Sir Udins, amangidre demayne.

REX Go, aunswer thaym grathely agayne.   *courteously*
270   What, devyll, whedir dote we or dremys.

I MILES Naye, we gete noght o worde, dare I wele wedde,   *get not a; wager*
    For he is wraiste of his witte or will of his wone.   *wrested; distraught*

REX Ye saie he lakkid youre lawis as ye that ladde ledde.   *found fault with*

II MILES Ya, lorde, and made many gaudis as we have gone.   *jests (tricks)*

REX Nowe sen he comes as a knave and as a knave cledde,   *clad*
276   Wherto calle ye hym a kyng?

I DUX   Nay, lorde, he is none,
    But an harlotte is hee.

REX   What devyll, I ame harde stedde,   *pressed*
    A man myght as wele stere a stokke as a stone.   *bestir*

I FILIUS My lorde, this faitour so fouly is affrayde,   *deceiver; afraid*
280   He loked nevere of lorde so langly allone.   *looked at; for so long alone*

REX No, sone, the rebalde seis us so richely arayed,   *son*
    He wenys we be aungelis evere ilkone.   *thinks*

II DUX My lorde, I holde hym agaste of youre gaye gere.   *gear (clothes)*

REX Grete lordis augh to be gay;   *ought; finely dressed*
285   Here schall no man do to thee dere,   *harm*
    And therfore yit nemyne in my nere,   *speak; ear*
    For by the grete God, and thou garre me swere   *cause*
    Thou had nevere dole or this day.   *misery before*

289   Do carpe on tyte, karle, of thy kynne.

I DUX Nay, nedelyngis he nevyns you with none.   *necessarily; speaks [to]; nothing*

REX That schalle he bye or he blynne.   *pay for; concludes*

II DUX A, leves lorde.   *leave (enough of this)*

REX   Lattis me allone.

I Dux   Nowe, good lorde, and ye may, meve you no more;
  Itt is not faire to feght with a fonned foode,   *fight; fond fool*
295   But gose to youre counsaille and comforte you there.

Rex   Thou sais soth, we schall see yf so will be goode,
  For certis oure sorowes are sadde.   *solemn*

II Filius   What a devyll ayles hym?
  Mi lorde, I can garre you be gladde,   *make*
300   For in tyme oure maistir is madde;
  He lurkis, loo, and lokis like a ladde.
  He is wode, lorde, or ellis his witte faylis hym.   *mad; fails*

III Filius   Mi lorde, ye have mefte you as mekill as ye may,   *tried*
  For yhe myght menske hym no more, were he Mahounde;   *honor*
305   And sen it semys to be soo, latte us nowe assaie.   *test [him]*

Rex   Loke, bewscheris, ye be to oure bodis boune.   *commands bound (obliged)*

I Dux   Mi lorde, how schulde he dowte us? He dredis not youre drays.   *fear; threats*

Rex   Nowe do fourthe, the devyll myght hym droune,   *go forth; drown*
  And sen he freyms falsed and makis foule frayes,   *frames (makes) falsehood; riots*
310   Raris on hym rudely, and loke ye not roune.   *Roar; mutter*

I Filius   Mi lorde, I schall enforce myselffe sen ye saie soo.   *attempt*
  Felawe, be noght afferde nor feyne not therfore,   *hold back*
  But telle us nowe some truffillis betwene us twoo,   *trifles*
  And none of oure men schall medill tham more.   *concern themselves*
315   And therfore by resoune array thee,   *prepare*
  Do telle us some poynte for thy prowe.   *point (detail); profit*
  Heris thou not what I saie thee?   *Hear*
  Thou mummeland myghtyng, I may thee   *mumbling*
  Helpe and turne thee fro tene, as I trowe.   *trouble*

II Filius   Loke uppe, ladde, lightly and loute to my lorde here,   *bow (kneel)*
321   For fro bale unto blisse he may nowe thee borowe.   *save you*
  Carpe on, knave, kantely, and caste thee to corde here,   *boldly; accord*
  And saie me nowe somwhat, thou sauterell, with sorowe.   *wretch (hypocrite)*
  Why standis thou as stille as a stone here?
325   Spare not, but speke in this place here,
  Thou gedlyng, it may gayne thee some grace here.

III Filius   My lorde, this faitour is so ferde in youre face here,   *deceiver; afraid of*
  None aunswere in this nede he nevyns you with none here.   *speaks to; (i.e., at all)*
  Do, bewsheris, for Beliall bloode and his bonys,   *bones (relics)*
330   Say somwhat or it will waxe werre.   *worse*

I FILIUS   Nay, we gete nought one worde in this wonys.

II FILIUS   Do crie we all on hym at onys,   *once*

AL CHYLDER   Oyes, Oyes, Oyes!

REX   O, ye make a foule noyse for the nonys.   *nonce*

III FILIUS   Nedlyng, my lorde, it is nevere the nerre.   *Necessarily; nearer*

I FILIUS   Mi lorde, all youre mutyng amendis not a myte,   *disputing; mite*
336   To medill with a madman is mervaille to mene;   *wonder*
       Comaunde youre knyghtis to clothe hym in white
       And late hym carre as he come to youre contré.   *go*

REX   Lo, sirs, we lede you no lenger a lite.   *detain; longer a little (time)*
340   Mi sone has saide sadly how that it schuld be;   *solemnly*
       But such a poynte for a page is to parfite.   *too perfect (i.e., difficult)*

I DUX   Mi lorde, fooles that are fonde, thei falle such a fee.   *fail; reward*

REX   What, in a white garmente to goo
       Thus gayly girde in a gowne?

II DUX   Nay, lorde, but as a foole forcid hym froo.

REX   How saie ye, sirs, schulde it be soo?

AL CHYLDER   Ya, lord.

REX   We, than is ther no more
348   But boldely bidde tham be boune.   *bound*

       Sir knyghtis, we caste to garre you be gladde,   *try to cause*
350   Oure counsaile has warned us wisely and wele:
       White clothis we saie fallis for a fonned ladde,   *are appropriate; foolish*
       And all his foly in faith fully we feele.   *see (perceive)*

I DUX   We will with a goode will for his wedis wende,   *clothes*
       For we wotte wele anowe what wedis he schall were.   *wear*

II DUX   Loo, here is an haterell here at youre hende,   *garment; hands*
356   All faciound therfore foolis to feere.   *fashioned; befit*

I MILES   Loo, here a joppon of joie,   *jupon (tunic)*
       All such schulde be gode for a boy.   *good*

I Dux   He schalle be rayed like a roye   *arrayed; king*
360   And schall be fonne in his folie.   *found (shown)*

II Dux   We, thanke tham, evyll motte thou thee.   *thrive*

I Miles   Nay, we gete noght a worde, wele I warand.

II Miles   Man, mustir some mervaile to me.   *create*

I Dux   What, wene ye he be wiser than we?
365   Leffe we and late the kyng see   *Heave [off]*
      Howe it is forcyd and farand.   *faring*

      Mi lorde, loke yf ye be paied,   *pleased*
      For we have getyn hym his gere.   *clothing*

Rex   Why, and is this rebalde arayed?
370   Mi blissing, bewscheris, ye bere.

      Gose, garre crye in my courte   *announce*
         and grathely garre write   *appropriately cause to be written*
      All the dedis that we have done in this same degré.
      And who fyndis hym greved   *aggrieved*
         late hym telle tyte;
      And yf we fynde no defaute   *guilt*
         hym fallis to go free.   *[it] befalls him*

I Dux   Oyes. Yf any wight with this wriche any werse wate,   *man; wretch; worse knows*
376   Werkis, beris wittenesse who so wirkis wrang,   *bears*
      Buske boldely to the barre, his balis to abate,   *Come; miseries*
      For my lorde, be my lewté, will not be deland.   *faith; judging*
      My lorde, here apperes none to appeyre his estate.   *challenge*

Rex   Wele thanne, fallis hym goo free.
381   Sir knyghtis, thanne grathis you goodly to gange   *prepare*
      And repaire with youre present and saie to Pilate   *return*
      We graunte hym oure frenschippe all fully to fang.   *take (have)*

I Miles   My lorde, with youre leve this way schall we lere,   *leave; take*
385   Us likis no lenger to abide here.

II Miles   Mi lorde, and he worthe ought in were,   *(i.e., if he acts suspiciously)*
      We come agayne with goode chere.

Rex   Nay, bewscheris, ye fynde us not here;
      Oure leve will we take at this tyde

390   And rathely araye us to reste,   *quickly*
      For such notis has noyed us or nowe.   *matters; annoyed; ere*

I Dux   Ya, certis, lorde, so holde I beste,
      For this gedlyng ungoodly has greved you.

II Dux   Loke ye bere worde as ye wotte,
395   Howe wele we have quitte us this while.   *acquitted ourselves*

I Miles   We, wise men will deme it we dote,   *judge; [act] foolish*
      But if we make ende of oure note.   *Unless*

Rex   Wendis fourth, the devyll in thi throte.
      We fynde no defaute hym to slee.   *slay*

400   Wherfore schulde we flaye hym or fleme hym   *punish; condemn*
      We fynde noght in rollis of recorde.   *legal rolls*
      And sen that he is dome, for to deme hym,   *dumb; condemn*
      Ware this a goode lawe for a lorde?   *Is*

      Nay, losellis, unlely ye lerned all to late,   *disloyally; too*
405   Go lere thus lordingis of youre londe such lessons to lere.   *teach; learn*
      Repaire with youre present and saie to Pilate   *company*
      We graunte hym oure poure all playne to appere,   *power; fully*
      And also oure grevaunce forgeve we algate,   *in all respects*
      And we graunte hym oure grace with a goode chere.
410   As touchyng this brothell that brawlis or debate,   *disputes*
      Bidde hym wirke as he will, and wirke noght in were.   *suspiciously*
      Go telle hym this message fro me,
      And lede fourth that mytyng, evyll motte he thee.   *small (insignificant) fellow*

I Miles   Mi lorde, with youre leve, late hym be,
415   For all to longe ledde hym have we.   *too*

II Miles   What, ye sirs, my lorde, will ye see?

Rex   What, felawes, take ye no tente what I telle you   *attention*
      And bid you, that yoman ye yeme?   *yeoman; look after*

II Miles   Mi lorde, we schall wage hym an ill way.   *reward*

Rex   Nay, bewscheris, be not so bryme,   *impatient*
421   Fare softely, for so will it seme.

I MILES   Nowe sen we schall do as ye deme,
     Adewe, sir.

REX   Daunce on, in the devyll way.

[32. THE REMORSE OF JUDAS]

The Cokis and Watirlederes

PILATUS Pees, bewscheres, I bidde you, that beldis here aboute me,		*dwell*
And loke that ye stirre with no striffe but stande stone still,		
Or, by the Lorde that me liffe lente, I schall garre you lowte me,		
And all schall byde in my bale that wirkis noght my will.		*custody*
5 Ye rebaldis that regnys in this rowte,		*prevail; crowd*
Ye stynte of youre stevenyng so stowte,		*stop (cease); shouting*
Or with this brande that dere is to doute,		*sword; dangerous; fear*
All to dede I schall dryve you this day.		*death*

For Sir Pilate of Pounce as prince am I preved,	*proved*
10 As renke moste royall in richeste array,	*man*
Ther is no berne in this burgh has me aboute hevyd,	*boy; raised up*
But he sekis me for sovereyne, in certayne I saie,	
To knawe,	
Therfore take hede to youre lordis estate	
15 That none jangill or jolle at my gate,	*jostle*
Nor no man to grath hym no gate	*(see note)*
Tille I have seggid and saide all my sawe.	*spoken*

For I ame the luffeliest lappid and laide	*covered*
With feetour full faire in my face,	*features*
20 My forhed both brente is and brade	*high is and broad*
And myne eyne thei glittir like the gleme in the glasse;	

And the hore that hillis my heed	*hair; covers; head*
Is even like to the golde wyre;	
My chekis are bothe ruddy and reede,	*red*
25 And my coloure as cristall is cleere.	

Ther is no prince prevyd undir palle	*proved (acknowledged); royal robe*
But I ame moste myghty of all to behold,	
Nor no kyng but he schall come to my call,	
Nor grome that dare greve me for golde.	*man; grieve*

30 Sir Kayphas, thurgh counsaill thi clergy is kid,	*known*
For thy counsaille is knowyn for connand and clere,	*intelligence; clarity*
And Sir Anna, thyn aunswer aught not to be hidde,	

	For thou is one and is abill and aught to be nere	
	In Parlament playne.	*plainly*
35	And I am prince pereles, youre poyntis to enquere.	
	How saie ye, Jues, of Jesus that swayne?	*Jews*
	Have done, sirs, sais on youre sawis,	*sayings*
	What tytill nowe have ye unto hym?	*claim*
	And lely ye loke uppon youre lawes,	
40	Saye, why sente ye so sone for to spille hym?	*destroy*

ANNA   Sir, that is prince and lorde of oure laye, *law*
     That traitour untrewe that ye of telle us,
     Nowe certayne and sone the soth schall I saie:
     It is Jesus that japer that Judas ganne selle us. *scoffer; did*
45   He marres oure men in all that he may,
     His merveylis full mekill is mustered emelle us, *great; are manifested among*
     That faitoure so false. *deceiver*
     He dois many derffe dedis on oure Sabotte day, *evil*
     That unconnand conjeon he castis hym to quelle us; *unwise idiot*
50   Fro man onto man he will compelle us
     And undo you and ourselffe als.
     Youreselffe he will fordo
     And he halde furth this space, *If; hold*
     And all this Jurie to *too*
55   Yf that ye graunte hym grace.

PILATUS   Sir Anna, this aunswere allow I nothyng,
     I halde it but hatereden, this artikill hale, *malicious; whole*
     And therfore, ser busshoppe, at my biddyng,
     Do telle me nowe trewly the texte of this tale.
60   Do termyne it trewly and tyte *pronounce; quickly*
     And lely ye lede it by the lawe, *truly; uphold*
     Felonye or falsed evyn here I defie it; *falsehood*
     Saie me sadly the soth, for love or for awe. *solemnly*

KAYPHAS   Sir Pilate, the talis the traitoure has tolde, *stories*
65   It hevys us in harte full haly to here tham: *grieves; wholly to hear*
     The warlowe with his wilis he wenys tham to wolde, *wiles; to wield (control)*
     The ladde with his lesyngis full lightly gan lere tham. *lies; teach*
     Full tyte will he take tham untill hym *quickly; to*
     And he thus forth go with his gaudis *tricks*
70   Or speche oversprede; ya, bettir is to spille hym, *spread out; kill*
     The faitoure is so felle with his false fraudis. *wicked*

PILATUS   Youre aunsweres is hedouse and hatefull to here. *hideous*
     Hadde I not herde hym and myselfe had hym sene,
     Yitt ye myght have made me to trowe you intere, *believe; entirely (sincerely)*
75   But faute in hym I fynde none, but conande and clene. *fault; wisdom; purity*

For conande and clene can I clepe hym,   *call*
No faute can I fynde to reffuse hym;   *condemn*
I hope yitt in haste ye schall here hym
Whanne he comys to racleyme; than may ye cuse hym.   *returns when summoned; accuse*

I Miles   Lorde, fele of his ferles in faith have we fonne,   *many; marvels; discovered*
81   Yone harlotte hevys oure hartis full of hate ire,   *(i.e., fills our hearts)*
He sais hymselffe that he is Goddis Sone
And schall sitte on the right hande beside his awne sire.

II Miles   Ther talis is full trewe that we telle.   *tales*
85   On the raynebowe the rebalde it redis,   *interprets*
He sais he schall have us to hevene or to hell
To deme us a day aftir oure dedis.   *judge; one day*

Pilatus   To deme us? In the devyll name!
Say whedir, saie whedir to the devyll?
90   What dastardis, wene ye be wiser than we?

I Miles   Mi lorde, with youre leve, we neven it for non ill,   *mention*
He has mustered his mervayles to mo than to me.
Mi soverayne lorde, yone sauterell he sais   *babbler*
He schall caste doune oure Tempill, noght for to layne,   *not to be concealed*
95   And dresse it uppe dewly within thre daies   *raise it up again*
As wele as it was, full goodely agayne.

Anna   Ya, sir, and on oure awne Sabott day,
Thanne werkis he werkis full wele.

Pilatus   We, fye on hym, faitour, for ay,
100   For thei are darke dedis of the devyll.

Kayphas   Sir, a noysomemare note newly is noysed,   *more noisome matter; heard*
That grevis me more than any kynne thyng;   *sort of*
He claymes hym clerly till a kyngdome of Jewes
And callis hymselffe oure comeliest kyng.

Pilatus   Kyng, in the devillis name — we, fye on hym, dastard!
106   What, wenys that woode warlowe overewyn us thus lightly?   *crazy warlock to defeat; easily*
A begger of Bedlem, borne as a bastard,   *Bethlehem*
Nowe, by Lucifer lath I that ladde, I leve hym not lightly.   *loathe*

Anna   Sir, the harlotte is at Heroudes hall evyn her at your hande.

Pilatus   I sente to hym that warlowe, the devyll myght hym wery.   *harass (trouble)*

KAIPHAS It langis to youre lordschippe be lawe of this land,   *belongs*
112   As soverayne youreselffe, to sitte of enquery.   *to preside at a court of inquiry*

ANNA Sir, the traitoure has tolde us mo trufullis truly   *nonsense*
        Wolde tene you full tyte and we you tham tolde.   *displease you quickly if*

PILATUS Nowe, be Beliall bonis, that boy schall abie   *bones; pay (the penalty)*
116   And bring on his bak a burdeyne of golde.   *If [he]*

I FILIUS Mi lorde that is ledar of lawis of this lande,
            Ye sente hym youreselfe to Herowde the kyng
            And sais, "The dome of that doge lies holy in your hande   *prince*
120   To deme hym or lose hym at youre likyng."

            And thus ye comaunded youre knyghtis for to saie,
            For Sir Heroude will serche hym full sore   *interrogate*
            So that he wende with no wilis away;   *tricks (deceptions)*
            And therfore, my goode lorde, move you no more.

KAIPHAS Nowe, certis, this was wele saide,
126   But sir, wille ye sese nowe, and we schall se syne.   *cease; later*

PILATUS Sir Kayphas and Anna, right so nowe I thynke,
            Sittis, in Mahoundis blissing, and aske us the wyne,
            Ye knyghtis of my courte, comaundis us to drynke.

JUDAS Allas, for woo that I was wrought
131   Or evere I come be kynde or kynne;
        I banne the bonys that me furth brought,   *curse*
        Woo worthe the wombe that I bredde ynne,
        So I may bidde.
135   For I so falsely did to hym
        That unto me grete kyndnesse kidde.   *did*

        The purse with his spens aboute I bare,   *pence*
        Ther was none trowed so wele as I.   *trusted*
        Of me he triste no man mare,   *had confidence*
140   And I betrayed hym traytourly
        With a false trayne.   *deception*
        Sakles I solde his blessid body   *Innocent*
        Unto Jues for to be slayne.

        To slaa my sovereyne assente I,   *slay*
145   And tolde them the tyme of his takyng;
        Shamously myselfe thus schente I   *Shamefully; was guilty*
        So sone for to sente to his slayng.   *assent*
        Nowe wiste I howe he mygth passe that payne

To loke that howe beste bote myght be.   *remedy (redemption)*
150 Unto the Jues I will agayne
To save hym he myght passe free,
This ware my will.   *is*
Lorde, welthe and worschippe mot with yow be.   *may*

Pilatus What tythandis, Judas, tellis thou us till?

Judas My tydyngis are tenefull, I telle you,   *grievous*
156 Sir Pilate, therfore I you praye;
My maistir that I gune selle you,   *did*
Gode lorde, late hym wende on his way.

Kaiphas Nay, nedelyngis, Judas, that we denye;   *necessarily*
160 What mynde or mater has moved thee thus?

Judas Sir, I have synned full grevously,
Betraied that rightwisse bloode, Jesus,   *righteous*
And maistir myne.

Kayphas Bewscher, what is that till us?
165 The perill and the plight is thyne.   *guilt*

Thyne is the wronge, thou wroughte it,   *did*
Thou hight us full trulye to take hym,   *assured*
And oures is the bargayne: we bought hym.
Loo, we are alle sente for to slee hym.

Judas Allas, that may me rewe full ill,
171 Giffe ye assente hym for to slaa.   *If*

Pilatus Why, what wolde thou that we did thertill?

Judas I praie you, goode lorde, late hym gaa,   *go*
And here is of me youre paymente hale.   *whole*

Kayphas Naie, we will noght so.
176 We bought hym for he schulde be slayne.

To slee hym thiselffe thou assente it.   *agreed (to)*
This wate thou wondirly wele.   *know*
What right is nowe to repente?
180 Thou schapist thiselffe unseele.   *create misery for yourself*

Anna Do waie, Judas, thou dose for noght.
Thy wordis I warne thee are in waste;
Thyselffe to selle hym whanne thou us sought,

    Thou was agaynste hym thanne the moste
185   Of us ilkan.

KAYPHAS We schall be venged on hym in haste,
    Whedir that evere he will or none.

PILATUS Ther wordis that thou nevys noght nedis it,   *name*
    Thou onhanged harlott, harke what I saie: *not yet put to (the) death (you deserve)*
190   Spare of thy spekyng, noght spedis it,   *Refrain from*
    Or walke oute at the dore, in the devill way.

JUDAS Why will ye thanne noght latte hym passe
    And have of me agayne youre paie?   *payment*

PILATUS I telle thee, traytoure, I wille it noght.

JUDAS Allas, thanne am I lorne,
196   Bothe bone and bloode;
    Allas the while, so may I saie,
    That evere I sente to spille his bloode.

    To save his bloode, sirs, I saie youe,
200   And takes you thare youre payment hole.   *return to you*
    Spare for to spille hym, I praye youe,
    Ellis brewe ye me full mekill bale.   *sorrow*

PILATUS Nay, heriste thou, Judas, thou schall agayne,
    We will it nought, what devyll art thou?
205   When thou us sought thou was full fayne   *extremely happy*
    Of this money. What aylis thee nowe
    For to repente?

JUDAS Agayne, sirs, here, I giffe it you,
    And save hym that he be noght schent.   *killed*

PILATUS To schende hym thyselfe has thee schamed. *destroy*
211   Thou may lathe with thi liffe that thou ledis,   *hate your life*
    Fondely as a false foole thiselffe has famed;   *been made a celebrity*
    Therfore the devyll thee droune for thy darfe dedis. *wicked deeds*

JUDAS I knawe my trespasse and my gilte.
215   It is so grete it garres me grise,   *causes; to shudder in terror*
    Me is full woo he schulde be spilte.
    Might I hym save of any wise,
    Wele were me than;
    Save hym, sirs, to youre service
220   I will me bynde to be your man.

Youre bondeman, lorde, to be
Nowe evere will I bynde me,
Sir Pilate, ye may trowe me,
Full faithfull schall ye fynde me.

PILATUS   Fynde thee faithfull? A, foule mot thee falle   *befall*
226   Or thou come in oure companye,   *Ere*
For, by Mahoundes bloode, thou wolde selle us all.
Thi service will we noght for it   *(i.e., even if)*
Thou art unknowen.   *You were*
230   Fals tiraunte, for thi traitoury   *villain; betrayal*
Thou art worthi to be hanged and drawen.

Hanged and drawen schulde thou be knowen
And thou had right, by all goode reasoune.
Thi maistirs bloode thou biddist us save,
235   And thou was firste that did him treasoune.

JUDAS   I cry you mercy, lorde, on me rewe,
This werryd wight that wronge has wrought;   *accursed man*
Have mercy on my maistir trewe
That I have in youre bandome brought   *power*
.   .   .   [line missing]
PILATUS   Goo, jape thee, Judas, and neven it noght   *play the jester; say*
241   Nor move us of this matere more.

ANNA   No more of this matere thou move thee,
Thou momeland mytyng emell;   *mumbling insignificant person*
Oure poynte expresse her reproves thee   *as expressed here convicts*
245   Of felonye falsely and felle.   *sharply*

KAIPHAS   He grucchis noght to graunte his gilte,
Why schonnys thou noght to schewe thi schame?   *shuns; show*
We bought hym for he schulde be spilte,
All same we were consente to the same
250   And thiselffe als.   *also*
Thou feyned noght for to defame,   *hesitated; denounce*
Thou saide he was a traytoure fals.

PILATUS   Yaa, and for a false faitoure   *deceiver*
Thyselffe full fully gon selle hym;
255   O, that was a trante of a traytour   *trick*
So sone thou schulde goo to begile hym.

I MILES   What, wolde thou that we lete hym ga?
Yon weried wight that wrought such wronge,   *wicked man*
We will noght lose oure bargayne swaa,   *so*

260   So lightely for to late hym gang;   *(i.e., release him)*
       And reson why
       Latte we that lotterell liffe ought long,   *scoundrel live any longer*
       It will be fonde, in faith, foly.   *foolish; folly*

II MILES Yone folte, for no foole schall he fynde us,   *fool (idiot)*
265   We wotte all full wele howe it was,
       His maistir whanne he gune bringe us,   *began [to]*
       He praied yow, my goode lord, late hym not passe.

PILATUS Nay, sertis, he schalle noght passe free
       That we for oure mony has paied.

JUDAS Take it agayne that ye toke me,
271   And save hym fro that bittir braide,   *torment*
       Than were I fayne.   *glad*

ANNA Itt serves of noght that thou has saide,
       And therfore takis it tyte agayne.

PILATUS Tyte agayne, traytoure, thou take it,
276   We wille it noght welde within oure wolde;   *have within our power*
       Yitt schalte thou noght, sawterell, thus sune forsake it,   *babbler (hypocrite); soon*
       For I schall sers hym myselffe sen thou has hym solde.   *search (examine)*

KAIPHAS Forsake it, in faith, that he ne schall,
280   For we will halde hym that we have;   *hold*
       The payment chenys thee withall,   *obliges*
       Thee thar no nodir comenaunte crave,   *other agreement*
       .   .   .   [line missing]
JUDAS Sen ye assente hym for to slaa,
       Vengeaunce I crie on you ilkone!

285   Ilkane I crie, the devill fordo youe,
       And that myghte I both here and see   *hear*
       Herde hevenyng here I unto youe,   *Hard vengeance*
       For sorowe onsought ye on me se.

KAIPHAS Whe, fye on thee, traytoure attaynte, at this tyde;   *convicted*
290   Of treasoune thou tyxste hym that triste thee for trewe.   *charged; trusted*
       Do buske thee henne, brothell, no lenger thou abide,   *hence*
       For if thou do, all thi respouns sare schall thee rewe.   *(miserable) answers; rue*
       Say wote thou noght who is I?   *know you not who I am*
       Nowe be my nociens, myght I negh nere thee,   *by; inclinations; come near*
295   In certayne, ladde, yitt schulde I lere thee   *teach*
       To lordis to speke curtaisely.

PILATUS   Go thy gatis, geddlyng, and greve us no more,   *way*
     Leffe of thi talke, the devill mot thee hange.   *Leave off*

JUDAS   That att ye toke me, take it you there,
300   Ther with youre maistrie make yowe emange   *(i.e., share it among you)*
     And clayme it you clene,
     Me lathes with my liff, so liffe I to lang.   *I hate my; too long*
     My traitourfull torne he turment my tene.   *traitorous act; torments; rage*

     Sen for my treasoune have I tane unto me,   *Since; taken*
305   Me thare aske no mercy, for none mon I gete;
     Therfore in haste myselffe schall fordo me.   *commit suicide*
     Allas, the harde while that evere ete I meete.   *ate; meat (food)*
     Thus schall I marke my mytyng meede   *little reward*
     And wirke me wreke with harte and will,   *vengeance*
310   To spille myselffe nowe wille I spede,   *kill*
     For sadly have I servyd thertill.
     So walaway
     That evere I was in witte or wille
     That tristy trewe for to betraye.   *trusty true [one]*

315   Allas, who may I meve to?   *speak*
     Shall I me take non othir reede?   *advice*
     Miselffe in haste I schall fordoo,
     And take me nowe unto my dede.

KAIPHAS   Have done, nowe, Sir Pilate, late se what ye saie
320   As touchyng this money that we here have
     That Judas in a wreth has wavyd away   *anger*
     And keste us crabbidly, that cursed knave.   *thrown; bad-naturedly*
     Howe saie ye therby?

ANNA   Sir, sen he it slang, we schall it save.   *threw*

KAYPHAS   Tite truste it tille oure tresorie.   *Quickly*

PILATUS   Nay, sir, noght soo.

KAIPHAS   Why, sir, how than?

PILATUS   Sir, it schall nought combre us;   *encumber*
     nor come in oure corbonan.   *treasury*

KAYPHAS   No, tille oure tresory certayne;   *to*
     farther schall it nought.

PILATUS And se youreselffe soth certayne and skill,   *fitting*
330   It is price of the bloode that we with it boght;
      Therfore some othir poynte I purpose it till,
      And thus I devyse.
      A spotte of erthe for to by, wayte nowe I will,   *buy*
      To berie in pilgrimes that by the wey dies.

335   Pilgrimes and palmeres to putte there,
      Sir Kaiphas and Anna, assente ye therto?
      And othere false felons that we forfare.   *execute*

ANNA As ye deme, lorde, so wille we doo.

ARMIGER Hayle, Sir Pilate, perles and prince of this empire;   *peerless*
340   Haile, the gaiest on grounde, in golde ther ye glide;   *move gracefully*
      Haile, the louffeliest lorde of lyme and of lyre   *limb; body*
      And all the soferans semely that sittith thee beside.   *sovereigns*

PILATUS What wolde thou?

ARMIGER   A worde, lorde, and wende.

PILATUS Nowe thou arte welcome, iwisse.

345   But delyvere thee lightly withouten any lette,   *delay*
      We have no tome all day to tente onto thee.   *time; attend*

ARMIGER A place here beside, lorde, wolde I wedde sette.   *mortgage*

PILATUS What title has thou therto? Is it thyne awne free?

ARMIGER Lorde, fre be my fredome me fallis it.   *free on account of*
350   This tale is full trewe that I telle you,
      And Calvary locus men callis it;   *place*
      I wolle it wedde sette, but not for to selle you.   *mortgage it*

PILATUS What wolde thou borowe, bewshire, belyve, late me se?[1]

ARMIGER If it ware youre lekyng, my lorde, for to lene it,   *desire; bestow*
355   Thirty pens I wolde ye lente onto me.

KAYPHAS Yis, bewshire, that schall thou have.

PILATUS Shewe us thi dedis and have here thi mony.   *deed [to property]*

---

[1] *What amount do you wish to borrow, quickly, let me see*

ARMIGER Have her, gode lord, but loke ye thame save.

PILATUS Yis, certis, we schall save thame full soundely,
360   And ellis do we noght dewly oure devere.   *duty*
       Faste, freke, for thy faith, on thy fote fonde thee,   *man; feet go*
       For fro this place, bewschere, I soile thee for evere.   *assoil (release)*

ARMIGER Now sorowe on such socoure as I have soght,
       For all my tresoure thurgh tresoune I tyne.   *have lost*

365   I tyne it untrewly by tresoune,
       Therfore nowe my way will I wende,
       For ye do me no right nor no resoune
       I betake you all to the fende.   *fiend*

PILATUS Nowe, certis, we are served att all,
370   This place is purchesed full propirly;
       The Felde of Bloode loke ye it call,
       I comaunde ilkone forthy.

KAIPHAS Sir, as ye comaunde us, call it schall we soo,
       But my lorde, with youre leve, we may lende her no lengar   *remain here no longer*
375   But faste late us founde to fang on oure foo,   *seize*
       Yone gedlyng ongodly has brewed us grete angir.   *ungodly*

ANNA Do way, sir busshoppe, and be not abaste,   *afraid*
       For loste is all oure lekyng, lepe he so light.   *liking (hope), escape*

KAIPHAS Nay, sir, he schall not trusse so tite, and that he ye traste,   *go so quickly*
380   For it wynnes us no worschippe the werkis of yone wight,
       But grete angir.
       Forthy late us dresse us his deth for to dite,   *accomplish*
       And late we this lotterell leve her no lengar.   *scoundrel live*

PILATUS Sir Kayphas, thurgh counsaile comaunde we oure knyghtis
385   To wacche on yone warlowe   *watch for*
       What way that he wendis,
       Do dresse you nowe dewly
       To yone doderon you dightis,   *wretch; go*
       And lette noght to laite hym   *fail; seek*
390   In lande where he lendis,   *dwells*
       Nor levys hym noght lightly.   *lives*

II MILES In faith, we schall fette hym   *fetch*
       Full farre fro his frendis.

PILATUS Nowe walkis on in the wanyand,   *waning [of the moon] (i.e., an evil time)*
395   And wende youre way wightely.   *briskly*

[33. THE SECOND TRIAL BEFORE PILATE]

The Tyllemakers

PILATUS Lordyngis that are lymett to the lare of my liaunce,   *bound; law; allegiance*
        Ye schappely schalkes and schene for to schawe,   *handsome men; fair; appear*
        I charge you as your chiftan that ye chatt for no chaunce,   *jabber in no wise*
        But loke to youre lord here and lere at my lawe.   *learn*
5   As a duke I may dampne you and drawe.   *damn; (i.e., execute)*
        Many bernys bolde are aboute me,   *knights*
        And what knyght or knave I may knawe
        That list noght as a lord for to lowte me,   *desires; reverence*
        I sall lere hym   *teach*
10   In the develes name, that dastard, to dowte me.   *fear*
        Ya, who werkis any werkes withoute me,
        I sall charge hym in chynes to chere hym.   *shall put; chains; (i.e., punish)*

        Tharfore, ye lusty ledes within this lenght lapped,   *men; space enclosed*
        Do stynte of youre stalkyng and of stoutnes be stalland;   *Stop; moving about must cease*
15   What traytoures his tong with tales has trapped,   *ensnared*
        That fende for his flateryng full foull sall be falland.   *falling*
        What broll overebrathely is bralland   *wretch very noisily; brawling*
        Or unsoftely will sege in ther sales,   *loudly; men; halls*
        That caysteffe thus carpand and calland   *caitiff; talking; calling*
20   As a boy sall be broght unto bales.   *custody (misery)*
        Therfore
        Talkes not nor trete not of tales,   *treat*
        For that gome that gyrnes or gales,   *man; grins; complains*
        I myself sall hym hurte full sore.

ANNA Ye sall sytt hym full sore, what sege will assay you.   *(i.e., he will be sorry); man; challenge*
26   If he like not youre lordshippe, that ladde, sall ye lere hym
        As a pereles prince full prestly to pay you,   *quickly to please*
        Or as a derworth duke with dyntes sall ye dere hym.   *worthy; blows; harm*

CAYPHAS Yaa, in faythe ye have force for to fere hym,   *make him fear*
30   Thurgh youre manhede and myght bes he marred;   *is he hurt*
        No chyvalrus chiftan may chere hym,
        Fro that churll with charge ye have charred   *punishment; chastised*
        .   .   .   *[line missing, see textual note]*
        In pynyng payne bees he parred.   *tormenting; flayed*

ANNA Yaa, and with schath of skelpys yll scarred   *injury; blows*
35 Fro tyme that youre tene he have tasted.   *anger*

PILATUS Now certes, as me semes, whoso sadly has soght you,   *solemnly*
Youre praysyng is prophetable, ye prelates of pees;   *beneficial; peace*
Gramercy, youre goode worde, and ungayne sall it noght you,   *unbeneficial; [be for] you*
That ye will say the sothe and for no sege cese.   *man*

CAYPHAS Elles were it pité we appered in this prees,   *press (assembly)*
41 But consayve how youre knyghtes ere command.   *see; are coming*

ANNA Ya, my lord, that leve ye no lese,   *believe; lie*
I can telle you, you tydes sum tythandis   *are owed some*
Ful sadde.   *serious*

PILATUS Se, they bring yoone brolle in a bande.   *wretch (brawler); bonds (tied up)*
46 We sall here nowe, hastely at hand,   *hear*
What unhappe before Herowde he had.   *misfortune*

I MILES Hayll, lovelyest lorde that evere lawe led yitt,   *expounded until now*
Hayll, semelyest undre sylke on evere ilka syde,   *each and every*
50 Hayll, stateliest on stede in strenghe that is sted yitt,   *place [in this world]; established yet*
Hayll, liberall, hayll, lusty to lordes allied.   *liberal person*

PILATUS Welcome, what tydandis this tyde,   *at this time*
Late no langgage lightly nowe lette you.   *hold you back*

II MILES Sir Herowde, ser, it is noght to hyde,
55 As his gud frende grathely he grete yowe   *good; courteously; greets*
Forevere,
In what manere that evere he mete you,   *(should) meet*
By hymselfe full sone wille he sette you
And sais that ye sall not dissever.   *separate*

PILATUS I thanke hym full thraly, and ser, I saie hym the same,   *sincerely*
61 But what mervelous materes dyd this myron ther mell?   *lazy fellow; reveal*

I MILES For all the lordis langage his lipps, ser, wer lame.
For any spirringes in that space no speche walde he spell,   *questions; speak*
Bot domme as a dore gon he dwell.   *dumb; door; remain*
65 Thus no faute in hym gon he fynde   *fault; could*
For his dedis to deme hym to qwell,   *condemn*
Nor in bandis hym brathely to bynde.   *painfully*
And thus
He sente hym to yourself, and assynde   *assigned*
70 That we, youre knyghtis, suld be clenly enclyned,   *inclined*
And tyte with hym to you to trus.   *quickly; go*

PILATUS Syrs, herkens, here ye not what we have oppon hand?
          Loo, howe there knyghtes carpe that to the kyng cared.   *went*
          Syr Herowde, thai say, no faute in me fand,   *fault; found*
75   He fest me to his frenschippe, so frendly he fared.
          Moreover, sirs, he spake, and noght spared,
          Full gentilly to Jesu, this Jewe,
          And sithen to ther knyghtis declared
          How fawtes in hym fande he but fewe   *faults; found*
80   To dye.
          He taste hym, I telle you for trewe,   *tested*
          For to dere hym he demed undewe,   *harm; not warranted*
          And sirs, thee sothly saie I.

CAIPHAS Sir Pilate, oure prince, we prelatis nowe pray you,
85   Sen Herowde fraysted no ferther this faitour to flaye,   *endeavored; deceiver; punish*
          Resayve in your sall ther sawes that I saie you;   *hall; words*
          Late bryng hym to barre and at his berde sall we baye.   *beard; bay (shout)*

ANNA Ya, for and he wende thus by wiles away,   *escape*
          I wate wele he wirke will us wondre;   *[some] marvel*
90   Oure menye he marres that he may,   *company*
          With his seggynges he settes tham in sondre   *sayings; at odds*
          With synne.
          With his blure he bredis mekill blondre;   *bluster; breeds; dissension*
          Whills ye have hym, nowe haldes hym undir,
95   We sall wery hym away yf he wynne.   *curse; flee*

CAYPHAS Sir, no tyme is to tarie this traytour to taste,   *test*
          Agayne Ser Cesar hymselfe he segges and saies   *Against; he speaks*
          All the wightis in this world wirkis in waste   *futilely*
          That takis hym any tribute, thus his teching outrayes.   *gives him; injures [us]*
100   Yitt forther he feynes slik affraies   *such outrages*
          And sais that hymself is God Son;
          And ser, oure lawe leggis and layes   *alleges; establishes*
          In what faytour falsed is fon   *falsehood; found*
          Suld be slayne.

PILATUS For no schame hym to shende will we shon.   *kill; hesitate*

ANNA Sir, witnesse of this wanes may be wonne,   *matter; discovered*
107   That will tell this withowten any trayne.   *trick (deception)*

CAYPHAS I can reken a rable of renkes full right   *call up; crowd; good men*
          Of perte men in prese fro this place ar I pas   *clever; a crowd; ere*
110   That will witnesse, I warande, the wordis of this wight,   *fellow*
          How wikkidly wrought that this wrecche has:
          Simon, Yarus, and Judas,

Datan and Gamaliell,
Neptalim, Levi, and Lucas,
115 And Amys this maters can mell   *consider*
Togithere.
Ther tales for trewe can they telle
Of this faytour that false is and felle   *deceiver; evil*
And in legyng of lawes ful lithre.   *expounding; wicked*

PILATUS Ya, tussch, for youre tales, thai touche not entente;   *(i.e., are irrelevant)*
121 Ther witnesse I warande that to witnesse ye wage,   *reward (bribe)*
Some hatred in ther hartis agaynes hym have hent   *has taken hold*
And purpose be this processe to putt doun this page.   *boy (peasant)*

CAIPHAS Sir, in faith us fallith not to fage;   *deceive*
125 Thai are trist men and true, that we telle you.   *trusted*

PILATUS Youre swering, seris, swiftely ye swage,   *stop*
And no more in this maters ye mell you,   *concern*
I charge.

ANNA Sir, dispise not this speche that we spell you.   *speak [to]*

PILATUS If ye feyne slike frawdis, I sall felle you,   *feign such; punish*
131 For me likis noght youre langage so large.   *excessive*

CAYPHAS Oure langage is to large, but youre lordshipp releve us,   *too; assist*
Yitt we both beseke you, late brynge hym to barre;   *(i.e., have him brought)*
What poyntes that we putte forth, latt your presence appreve us;   *let; approve*
135 Ye sall here how this harlott heldes out of herre.   *acts; order*

PILATUS Ya, butt be wise, witty, and warre.   *alert; aware*

ANNA Yis, sir, drede you noght for nothyng we doute hym.   *we fear nothing [concerning] him*

PILATUS Fecche hym, he is noght right ferre;
Do, bedell, buske thee abowte hym.   *(i.e., get about it)*

PRECO I am fayne,
141 My lorde, for to lede hym or lowte hym,   *reverence*
Uncleth hym, clappe hym, and clowte hym;   *Unclothe; beat; clout*
If ye bid me, I am buxhome and bayne.   *obedient; willing*

Knyghtis, ye er commaundid with this caityf to care   *rascal (reprobate); go*
145 And bryng him to barre, and so my lord badd.   *ordered*

I MILES Is this thy messege?

PRECO   Ya, sir.

I MILES   Than move thee no mare,   *urge; more*
    For we ar light for to leppe and lede forthe this ladd.   *go quickly; lead*

II MILES Do steppe furth, in striffe ert thou stadde,   *in trouble are; placed*
    I uphalde full evyll has thee happed.   *insist great; occurred*

I MILES O, man, thy mynde is full madde   *mad*
151 In oure clukis to be clowted and clapped,   *clutches; beaten; struck*
    And closed.   *held*

II MILES Thou bes lassched, lusschyd, and lapped.   *lashed, beaten; surrounded*

I MILES Ya, rowted, russhed, and rapped,   *shouted at; struck violently; hit*
155 Thus thy name with noye sall be noysed.   *annoyance; broadcast*

II MILES Loo, this sege her, my soverayne, that ye for sente.   *fellow here*

PILATUS Wele, stirre noght fro that stede, but stande stille thare;   *spot*
    Bot he schappe som shrewdnesse, with shame bese he shente,   *Unless he fashions; trick*
159 And I will frayst, in faith, to frayne of his fare.   *try; question; practices*

CAIPHAS We, outte, stande may I noght, so I stare.   *am astonished*

ANNA Ya, harrowe, of this traytour with tene.   *anger (violence)*

PILATUS Say, renkes, what rewth gars you rare?   *fellows; affliction causes; roar*
    Er ye woode or wittles, I wene,   *Are; mad*
164 What eyles you?   *ails*

CAYPHAS Out, slike a sight suld be sene.   *[that] such*

ANNA Ya, allas, conquered ar we clene.   *entirely*

PILATUS We, ere ye fonde, or youre force fayles you?   *are; mad; strength fails*

CAYPHAS A, ser, saugh ye noght this sight, how that ther schaftes schuke   *shafts shook*
    And thez baneres to this brothell thai bowde all on brede? *worthless fellow; on every side*

ANNA Ya, ther cursed knyghtes by crafte lete them croke   *bow down*
171 To worshippe this warlowe unworthy in wede.   *clothes*

PILATUS Was it dewly done thus, indede?

CAIPHAS Ya, ya, sir, oureselfe we it sawe.

PILATUS We, spitte on them, ill mott thai spede.   *spit*

175 Say, dastardes, the devyll mote you drawe,   *(i.e., draw and quarter)*

How dar ye   *dare*

Ther baners on brede that her blawe   *on every side; blow (wave)*

Lat lowte to this lurdan so lawe?   *bow; rascal; low*

O, faytouris, with falshed, how fare ye?   *deceivers; falsehood*

III Miles We beseke you and tho seniouris beside you, sir, sitte,

181 With none of oure governaunce to be grevous and gryll,   *angry*

For it lay not in oure lott ther launces to lett,   *power; prevent*

And this werke that we have wrought it was not oure will.

PILATUS Thou lise, harstow, lurdan? Full ille,   *lie, hear you, rascal (fool)*

185 Wele thou watte if thou witnes it walde.   *would admit it*

IV Miles Sir, oure strengh myght noght stabill tham stille,   *hold them*

They hilded for ought we couthe halde,   *tipped over; hold*

Oure unwittyng.   *Unknown to us*

V Miles For all oure fors, in faith, did thai folde   *strength*

190 As this warlowe worschippe thai wolde,

And us semid, forsoth, it unfittyng.   *seemed*

CAIPHAS A, unfrendly faytours, full fals is youre fable;   *deceivers*

This segge with his sutteltè to his seett hath you sesid.   *man; subtlety; sect; seized*

VI Miles Ye may say what you semes, ser, bot ther standerdes to stabill,

195 What freyke hym enforces full foull sall he be fesid.   *man; attempts; discomfitted*

ANNA Be the devyllis nese, ye ar doggydly diseasid,   *nose; infected*

A, henne harte, ill happe mot you hente.   *chicken heart*

PILATUS For a whapp so he whyned and whesid,   *blow; wheezed*

And yitt no lasshe to the lurdan was lente,

200 Foul fall you.

III Miles Sir, iwisse, no wiles we have wente.   *tried [to perform]*

PILATUS Shamefully you satt to be shente,   *allowed yourselves; overcome*

Here combred caystiffes, I call you.   *unhappy (fainthearted) caitiffs*

IV Miles Sen you lykis not, my lord, oure langage to leve,   *believe*

205 Latte bryng the biggest men that abides in this land

Propirly in youre presence ther poustè to preve;   *strength; prove*

Beholde that they helde nott fro thei have thaim in hand.   *(i.e., bowed not once)*

PILATUS   Now ye er ferdest that evere I fand,   *most fearful; found*
              Fy on youre faynte hertis in feere;   *altogether*
210   Stir thee, no langer thou stande,   *longer*
              Thou bedell, this bodworde thou bere   *message; bear*
              Thurgh this towne.
              The wyghtest men unto were   *strongest; danger*
              And the strangest ther standerdis to stere,   *(i.e., hold up)*
215   Hider blithely bid tham be bowne.   *eagerly; bound*

PRECO   My soverayne, full sone sall be served youre sawe,   *obeyed; words (command)*
            I sall bryng to ther baneres right bigg men and strange; *strong*
            A company of kevellis in this contré I knawe   *big (strong) men*
            That grete ere and grill, to the gomes will I gange.   *are; fierce; men; go*
220   Say, ye ledis botht lusty and lange,   *lads; tall*
            Ye most passe to Ser Pilate apace.   *must*

I MILES   If we wirke not his wille it wer wrang;
              We are redy to renne on a race   *(i.e., hurry)*
              And rayke.   *rush (proceed)*

PRECO   Then tarie not, but tryne on a trace   *quickly; the way*
226   And folow me fast to his face.

II MILES   Do lede us; us lykes wele this lake.   *game (sport)*

PRECO   Lorde, here are the biggest bernes that bildis in this burgh,   *men; live; town*
            Most stately and strange if with strenght thai be streyned.   *fierce; assailed*
230   Leve me, ser, I lie not, to loke this lande thurgh,   *Believe*
            Thai er myghtiest men with manhode demened.   *endowed*

PILATUS   Wate thou wele, or ellis has thou wenyd?   *Know; [only] thought [so]*

PRECO   Sir, I wate wele, withoute wordis moo.   *more*

CAIPHAS   In thy tale be not taynted nor tenyd.   *suspect; deceptive*

PRECO   We, nay, ser, why shuld I be soo?

PILATUS   Wele than,
237   We sall frayst er they founde us fer fro.   *ask ere; (i.e., go away)*
              To what game thai begynne for to go,
              Sir Cayphas, declare tham ye can.

CAIPHAS   Ye lusty ledis, nowe lith to my lare: *lads; listen; orders*
241   Schappe you to ther schaftis that so schenely her schyne,   *Take up; brightly; shine*
              If yon barnes bowe the brede of an hare,   *persons; breadth; hair*
              Platly ye be putte to perpetuell pyne.   *Immediately; pain*

I Miles I sall holde this as even as a lyne. *line*

Anna Whoso schakis, with schames he shendes. *shakes; (i.e., is disgraced)*

II Miles I, certayne, I saie as for myne,
247   Whan it sattles or sadly discendis *settles; sinks down*
   Whare I stande,
   When it wryngis or wronge it wendis. *twists; moves*
250   Outher bristis, barkis, or bendes, *shatters, bursts*
   Hardly lat hakke of myn hande. *let my hand be hacked off*

Pilatus Sirs, waites to ther wightis that no wiles be wrought, *attend*
   Thai are burely and brode, thare bost have thai blowen. *boast; vented*

Anna To neven of that nowe, ser, it nedis right noght, *speak; there is no need*
255   For who curstely hym quytes, he sone sall be knawen. *abominably; repays him*

Cayphas Ya, that dastard to dede sall be drawen, *death; drawn [and quartered]*
   Whoso fautis, he fouly sall falle. *fails*

Pilatus Nowe knyghtis, sen the cokkis has crowen,
   Have hym hense with hast fra this halle *[away] from*
260   His wayes; *On his way*
   Do stiffely steppe on this stalle, *staunchly; (i.e., to the dock)*
   Make a crye and cautely thou call, *loudly*
   Evene like as Ser Annay thee sais.

        [They cry] Oyes.

Anna Jesu, thou Jewe of gentill Jacob kynne,
265   Thou nerthrist of Nazareth, now nevend is thi name, *lowest; called*
   Alle creatures thee accuses; we commaunde thee comme in
   And aunswer to thin enemys, deffende now thy fame. *reputation*

     Et Preco, semper post Annam, recitabit "judicatur Jesus."[1]

Cayphas We, out! we are shente alle for shame,
269   This is wrasted all wrange, as I wene. *twisted; wrong*

Anna For all ther boste, yone boyes are to blame.

Pilatus Slike a sight was nevere yit sene.
   Come sytt,
   My comforth was caught fro me clene,

---

[1] *And Preco will recite after Anna, "Let Jesus be judged"*

        I upstritt, I my myght noght abstene   *rose up; in my might [could]*
275   To wirschip hym in wark and in witte.   *deed; mind*

CAYPHAS   Therof mervayled we mekill what moved you in mynde
        In reverence of this ribald so rudely to ryse.   *rascal; discourteously*

PILATUS   I was past all my powre, thogh I payned me and pynd;   *made a huge effort*
        I wrought not as I wolde in no maner of wise.
280   Bot syrs, my spech wele aspise,   *consider*
        Wightly his wayes late hym wende;   *Quickly; let; go*
        Thus my dome will dewly devyse,   *verdict; properly prescribe*
        For I am ferde hym in faith to offende   *afraid*
        In sightes.   *(i.e., to behold [publicly])*

ANNA   Than oure lawe were laght till an ende   *brought*
286   To his tales if ye treuly attende.
        He enchaunted and charmed oure knyghtis.

CAYPHAS   Be his sorcery, ser, youreselffe the soth sawe,   *By*
        He charmes oure chyvalers and with myscheffe enchaunted.
290   To reverence hym ryally we rase all on rowe,   *royally; rose*
        Doutles we endure not of this dastard be daunted.   *intimidated*

PILATUS   Why, what harmes has this hatell here haunted?   *person*
        I kenne to convyk hym no cause.   *know; convict*

ANNA   To all gomes he God Son hym graunted,   *men*
295   And liste not to leve on oure lawes.   *believe (respect)*

PILATUS   Say, man,
        Consayves thou noght what comberous clause   *serious allegation*
        That this clargye accusyng thee knawse?   *clergy*
        Speke, and excuse thee if thou can.

JESUS   Every man has a mouthe that made is on molde   *of earth*
301   In wele and in woo to welde at his will,   *well-being; wield*
        If he governe it gudly like as God wolde
        For his spirituale speche hym not to spill.   *die*
        And what gome so governe it ill,   *man*
305   Full unhendly and ill sall he happe: *evilly; fare*
        Of ilk tale thou talkis us untill   *(i.e., accuse me of)*
        Thou accounte sall, thou cannot escappe.

PILATUS   Sirs myne,
        Ye fonne, in faithe, all the frappe,   *are mad; entire crowd*
310   For in this lede no lese can I lappe,   *man; lying; perceive*
        Nor no poynte to putt hym to pyne.   *suffering*

CAIPHAS Withoute cause, ser, we come not this carle to accuse hym, *churl*
      And that will we ye witt as wele is worthy. *we want you to know*

PILATUS Now I recorde wele the right, ye will no rathere refuse hym *never release*
315   To he be dreven to his dede and demed to dye; *Until*
      But takes hym unto you forthe
      And like as youre lawe will you lere,
      Deme ye his body to abye. *pay [the penalty]*

ANNA O, Sir Pilate, withouten any pere, *peer*
320   Do way;
      Ye wate wele withouten any were *question*
      Us falles not, nor oure felowes in feere, *We are not allowed*
      To slo no man, yourself the soth say.

PILATUS Why suld I deme to dede than withoute deservyng in dede?
325   But I have herde al haly why in hertes ye hym hate. *entirely; [your] hearts*
      He is fautles, in faith, and so God mote me spede;
      I graunte hym my gud will to gang on his gate. *go; way*

CAIPHAS Nought so, ser, for wele ye it wate, *well you know it*
      To be kyng he claymeth with croune,
330   And whoso stoutely will steppe to that state *haughtily*
      Ye suld deme, ser, to be dong doune *struck down*
      And dede. *killed*

PILATUS Sir, trulye that touched to tresoune,
      And or I remewe, he rewe sall that reasoune *ere; go; be sorry [for]*
335   And or I stalke or stirre fro this stede. *walk; place*

      Sir knyghtis that ar comly, take this caystiff in keping;
      Skelpe hym with scourges and with skathes hym scorne; *Whip; blows*
      Wrayste and wrynge hym to, for wo to he be wepyng, *Twist; too; until*
      And than bryng hym before us as he was beforne.

I MILES He may banne the tyme he was borne; *curse*
341   Sone sall he be served as ye saide us. *Soon*

ANNA Do wappe of his wedis that are worne. *tear off; clothes*

II MILES All redy, ser, we have arayde us,
      Have done.
345   To this broll late us buske us and brayde us *wretch (brawler); hurry*
      As Ser Pilate has propirly prayde us.

III MILES We sall sette to hym sadly sone.

IV MILES Late us gete of his gere, God giffe hym ille grace.   *take off; gear (clothes); give*

I MILES Thai ere tytt of tite, lo, take ther his trasshes.   *are pulled off quickly; ragged garments*

III MILES Nowe knytte hym in this corde.

II MILES   I am cant in this case.   *eager*

IV MILES He is bun faste, nowe bete on with bittir brasshis.   *bound; blows*

I MILES Go on, lepis, harye, lordingis, with lasshes   *leap (i.e., be vigorous); harry (beat)*
And enforce we this faitour to flay hym.   *set out; deceiver*

II MILES Late us driffe to hym derfly with dasshes,   *move in on him cruelly; blows*
355   Alle rede with oure rowtes we aray hym   *red; blows*
And rente hym.   *tear*

III MILES For my parte I am prest for to pay hym.

IV MILES Ya, sende hym sorow, assaye hym.   *assault*

I MILES Take hym that I have tome for to tente hym.   *time*

II MILES Swyng to this swyre, to swiftely he swete.   *neck, until; sweats*

III MILES Swete may this swayne for sweght of oure swappes.   *force; blows*

IV MILES Russhe on this rebald and hym rathely rehete.   *fiercely assail*

I MILES Rehete hym, I rede you, with rowtes and rappes.   *Attack; blows*

II MILES For all oure noy, this nygard he nappes.   *annoyance; niggard; naps*

III MILES We sall wakken hym with wynde of oure whippes.

IV MILES Nowe flynge to this flaterer with flappes.   *strike at; blows*

I MILES I sall hertely hitte on his hippes
And haunch.

II MILES Fra oure skelpes not scatheles he skyppes.   *blows; unscathed; goes*

III MILES Yitt hym list not lyft up his lippis,
371   And pray us to have pety on his paunch.   *pity*

IV MILES To have petie of his paunche he propheres no prayere.   *pity; offers*

I MILES Lorde, how likis thou this lake and this lare that we lere you? *game; lore*

II MILES Lo, I pull at his pilche, I am prowd payere. *garment; payer*

III MILES Thus youre cloke sall we cloute to clence you and clere you. *hit*

IV MILES I am straunge in striffe for to stere you. *strong; strife; bestir*

I MILES Thus with choppes this churll sall we chastye. *blows; chastise*

II MILES I trowe with this trace we sall tere you. *course [of action]; tear*

III MILES All thin untrew techyngis thus taste I, *your; test*
380   Thou tarand. *?chameleon (tarandre)*

IV MILES I hope I be hardy and hasty.

I MILES I wate wele my wepon not wast I.

II MILES He swounes or sweltes, I swarand. *is overcome; swear [to you]*

III MILES Late us louse hym lightyly, do lay on your handes. *untie*

IV MILES Ya, for and he dye for this dede, undone ere we all. *die; deed; are*

I MILES Nowe unboune is this broll, and unbraced his bandes. *wretch; bonds (ropes)*

II MILES O, fule, how faris thou now, foull mott thee fall. *fool; befall*

III MILES Nowe because he oure kyng gon hym call, *himself*
389   We will kyndely hym croune with a brere. *briar*

IV MILES Ya, but first this purpure and palle *purple (royal) garment; pall*
And this worthy wede sall he were *garment*
For scorne.

I MILES I am prowd at this poynte to apper.

II MILES Latte us clethe hym in ther clothes full clere *clothe*
395   As a lorde that his lordshippe has lorne. *lost*

III MILES Lange or thou mete slike a menye as thou mett with this morne.[1]

IV MILES Do sette hym in this sete as a semely in sales. *halls (i.e., at court)*

---

[1] *It will be a long [time] before you meet such company as you met this morning*

I MILES   Now thryng to hym thrally with this thikk thorne.   *thrust; vigorously*

II MILES   Lo, it heldes to his hede, that the harnes out hales.   *brains; come*

III MILES   Thus we teche hym to tempre his tales,   *modify*
401   His brayne begynnes for to blede.

IV MILES   Ya, his blondre has hym broght to ther bales;   *stirring up of strife; sorrows*
     Now reche hym and raught hym in a rede   *seize; give; reed*
     So rounde,
405   For his septure it serves indede.   *scepter*

I MILES   Ya, it is gode inowe in this nede,
     Late us gudly hym grete on this grounde.   *greet*

     Ave, riall roy and *rex Judeorum*!   *Hail, royal king; king of the Jews*
     Hayle, comely kyng, that no kyngdom has kende;   *known*
410   Hayll, undughty duke, thi dedis ere dom,   *weak; dumb (worthless)*
     Hayll, man unmyghty, thi menye to mende.   *company*

III MILES   Hayll, lord without lande for to lende,
     Hayll, kyng, hayll knave unconand.   *unwise*

IV MILES   Hayll, freyke, without forse thee to fende,   *fellow; strength*
415   Hayll, strang, that may not wele stand   *strong*
     To stryve.

I MILES   We, harlott, heve up thy hande,   *heave*
     And us all that thee wirschip are wirkand   *[mock] worship; working (striving)*
     Thanke us, ther ill mot thou thryve.

II MILES   So late lede hym belyve and lenge her no lenger,   *let lead; quickly; stay here*
421   To Ser Pilate, oure prince, oure pride will we prayse.

III MILES   Ya, he may synge or he slepe of sorowe and angir,   *ere*
     For many derfe dedes he has done in his dayes.   *evil*

IV MILES   Now wightly late wende on oure wayes,   *quickly let*
425   Late us trusse us, no tyme is to tarie.   *depart*

I MILES   My lorde, will ye listen oure layes?   *stories*
     Here this boy is ye bade us go bary   *beat*
     With battis.

II MILES   We ar combered his corpus for to cary,   *burdened; body; cause suffering*
430   Many wightis on hym wondres and wary.   *are astonished and curse*
     Lo, his flessh al be beflapped that fat is.   *beaten (bruised)*

PILATUS	Wele, bringe hym before us as he blisshes all bloo.	*blushes; livid*
	I suppose of his seggyng he will cese evermore.	*speaking; cease*
	Sirs, beholde upon hight and *ecce homoo*,	*high; behold the man*
435	Thus bounden and bette and broght you before.	*beaten*
	Me semes that it sewes hym full sore,	*afflicts*
	For his gilte on this grounde is he grevyd,	*grieved*
	If you like for to listen my lore.	
	In race	*(see note)*

. . .   [missing pages]

[PILATUS]	For propirly by this processe will I preve	
441	I had no force fro this felawshippe this freke for to fende.	*strength; man; defend*

PRECO	Here is all, ser, that ye for sende;	
	Wille ye wasshe whill the water is hote?	

Tunc lavat manus suas.   *Then he washes his hands*

PILATUS	Nowe this Barabas bandes ye unbende,	*bonds (ropes); untie*
445	With grace late hym gange on his gatis	*way*
	Where ye will.	

BARABAS	Ye worthy men, that I here wate,	*know*
	God encrece all youre comely estate,	
	For the grace ye have graunt me untill.	*granted to me*

PILATUS	Here the jugement of Jesus, all Jewes in this stede:	*Hear; place*
451	Crucifie hym on a crosse and on Calverye hym kill.	
	I dampne hym today to dy this same dede;	*damn; death*
	Therfore hyngis hym on hight uppon that high hill;	*hang*
	And on aythir side hym I will	
455	That a harlott ye hyng in this hast.	*criminal; hang; haste*
	Methynkith it both reasoune and skill	
	Emyddis, sen his malice is mast,	*Amidst; most*
	Ye hyng hym.	
	Then hym turmente, som tene for to tast.	*torment; pain; experience*
460	Mo wordis I will not nowe wast,	*waste*
	But blynne not to dede to ye bryng hym.	*do not stop until*

CAIPHAS	Sir, us semys in oure sight that ye sadly has saide.	*solemnly*
	Now knyghtis that are conant with this catyf ye care,	*wise; go*
	The liffe of this losell in youre list is it laide.	*rascal; as you desire*

I MILES	Late us alone, my lorde, and lere us na lare.	*teach; no lore*
466	Siris, sette to hym sadly and sare,	
	All in cordis his coorse umbycast.	*cords; body bind*

II MILES	Late us bynde hym in bandis all bare.	

II MILES   Here is one, full lange will it laste.

IV MILES   Lay on hande here.

V MILES   I powll to my poure is past.   *pull until; strength*
472   Nowe feste is he, felawes, ful fast;   *fast (secure)*
      Late us stere us, we may not long stand here.   *stir*

ANNA   Drawe hym faste hense, delyvere you, have done.
475   Go, do se hym to dede withoute lenger delay,
      For dede bus hym be nedlyng be none.   *necessarily*
      All myrthe bus us move tomorne that we may;
      Itt is sothly oure grette Sabott day,
      No dede bodis unberid sall be.   *dead bodies unburied*

VI MILES   We see wele the soth ye us say.
481   We sall traylle hym tyte to his tree,   *drag; quickly; cross*
      Thus talkand.   *talking*

IV MILES   Farewele, now wightely wende we.

PILATUS   Nowe certis, ye are a manly menye.   *company*
485   Furth in the wylde wanyand be walkand.   *waning [of moon]; walking*

[34. THE ROAD TO CALVARY]

The Shermen

PRIMUS MILES INCIPIT   Pees, barnes and bachillers that beldis here aboute,[1]
      Stirre noght ones in this stede but stonde stone stille,   *once*
      Or, be the lorde that I leve on, I schall gar you lowte.   *by; believe; make you to pay homage*
      But ye spare when I speke youre speche schall I spille   *(i.e., refrain from speaking)*
5   Smertely and sone.
      For I am sente fro Sir Pilate with pride
      To lede this ladde oure lawes to abide,
      He getis no bettir bone.   *reward*

      Therfore I comaunde you on evere ilke a side
10   Uppon payne of enprisonment that no man appere
      To suppowle this traytoure, be tyme ne be tyde,   *support*
      .   .   .   [line missing]
      Noght one of his prees,   *company*
      Nor noght ones so hardy for to enquere,

---

[1] *Peace, knights and retainers who remain here about*

| | But helpe me holly, alle that are here, | *wholly* |
| 15 | This kaitiffe care to encrees. | *caitiff's discomfort (pain)* |

	Therfore make rome and rewle you nowe right	
	That we may with this weried wight	*accursed man*
	Wightely wende on oure wayes.	*Quickly*
	He napped noght of all this nyght	
20	And this daye schall his deth be dight,	*effected*
	Latte see who dare saie naye.	
	Because tomorne is provyde	*(i.e., will be)*
	For oure dere Sabbott day,	
	We will no mysse be moved	*wish no mishap to occur*
25	But mirthe in all that evere men may.	

	We have bene besie all this morne	
	To clothe hym and to croune with thorne,	
	As falles for a fole kyng,	*befits; fool*
	And nowe methynkith oure felawes skorne,	
30	They highte to have ben here this morne,	*promised*
	This faitour forthe to bring.	
	To nappe nowe is noght goode.	
	We! howe! high myght he hyng.	*hang*

II Miles Pees, man, for Mahoundes bloode.
35   Why make ye such crying?

I Miles Why wotte thou noght als wele as I,   *know*
        This carle burde unto Calvery   *churl must go*
        And there on crosse be done?

II Miles Sen dome is geven that he schall dy,   *Since the verdict*
40   Late calle to us more companye,   *Let's*
        And ellis we erre oure fone.   *Or else we are too few*

I Miles Oure gere behoves to be grayde   *ready*
        And felawes sammed sone,   *together*
        For Sir Pilate has saide
45   Hym bus be dede be none.   *must; noon*

        Wher is Sir Wymond, wotte thou oght?

II Miles He wente to garre a crosse be wroght   *cause; made*
        To bere this cursed knave.

I Miles That wolde I sone wer hyder broght,   *hither*
50   For sithen schall othir gere be soght   *then*
        That us behoves to haffe.   *we need to have*

II MILES Us bus have sties and ropes   *ladders*
            To rugge hym tille he rave,   *pull [with violence]; screams*
            And nayles and othir japes   *tricks*
55   If we oureselve wille save.

I MILES To tarie longe us were full lathe,   *unwilling*
            But Wymond come, it is in wathe   *Unless; there is danger*
            But we be blamed all three.
59   We, howe, Sir Wymond waytesskathe.   *troublemaker*

II MILES We, howe, Sir Wymond, howe.

III MILES   I am here, what saie ye bathe,   *both*
            Why crye ye so on me?
            I have bene garre make   *charged to make*
            This crosse, as yhe may see,
            Of that laye over the lake;
65   Men called it the kyngis tree.

I MILES Nowe sekirly I thought the same,   *surely*
            For that balke will no man us blame   *timber*
            To cutte it for the kyng.

II MILES This karle has called hym kyng at hame,
70   And sen this tre has such a name,
            It is accordyng thyng   *appropriate*
            That his rigge on it may reste   *back*
            For skorne and for hethyng.   *mocking*

III MILES Methoughte it semyd beste
75   Tille this bargayne to bryng.   *undertaking*

I MILES It is wele warred, so motte I spede,   *knotty (strong)*
            And it be lele in lenghe and brede;   *If; true*
            Than is this space wele spende.   *Then; amount of time*

III MILES To loke theraftir it is no nede.
80   I toke the mesure or I yode,   *ere; went*
            Bothe for the fette and hande.

II MILES Beholde howe it is boorede
            Full even at ilke an ende;   *at each end*
            This werke will wele accorde,
85   It may not be amende.   *improved*

III MILES Nay, I have ordande mekill more,   *planned (executed)*
            Yaa, thes theves are sente before

That beside hym schall hyng,
And sties also are ordande thore   *ladders*
90 With stalworthe steeles as mystir wore,   *rungs; need*
Bothe some schorte and some lang.

I Miles   For hameres and nayles,
Latte see sone who schall gang.

II Miles   Here are bragges that will noght faile   *large nails*
95 Of irnne and stele full strange.   *iron; steel; strong*

III Miles   Thanne is it as it aweth to bee,   *ought*
But whiche of yowe schall beere this tree   *bear*
Sen I have broughte it hedir?

I Miles   Be my feithe, bere it schall hee
100 That theron hanged sone schall bee,
And we schall teeche hym whedir.   *inform*

II Miles   Uppon his bakke it schalle be laide,
For sone we schall come thedir.

III Miles   Loke that oure gere be grayede,   *readied*
105 And go we all togedir.

Johannes   Allas, for my maistir that moste is of myght,
That yister-even late, with lanternes light,
Before the busshoppe was brought.
Bothe Petir and I we saugh that sight,   *saw*
110 And sithen we wente oure wayes full wight,   *quickly*
When the Jewes wondirly wrought:
At morne thei toke to rede   *counsel*
And soteltes upsoght   *subtleties sought out*
And demed hym to be dede
115 That to tham trespassed noght.   *against*

Allas, for syte, what schall I saie,   *sorrow*
My worldly welthe is wente for ay;
In woo evere may I wende.
My maistir, that nevere lakke in lay   *[knowledge or practice] of the law*
120 Is demed to be dede this day,
Ewen in hys elmys hende.   *Even; enemies' hands*
Allas, for my maistir mylde
That all mennys mysse may mende   *sins*
Shulde so falsely be filed   *defiled*
125 And no frendis hym to fende.

Allas, for his modir and othir moo,
Mi modir and hir sisteres alsoo,
Sittes samen with sighyngis sore.   *Sit together*
Thai wate nothyng of all this woo;   *know*
130   Forthy to warne tham will I goo
Sen I may mende no more.   *redress (events)*
Sen he schall dye as tyte   *so quickly*
And thei unwarned wore,
I ware worthy to wite,   *honored to know*
135   I will to faste therfore.

But in myn herte grete drede have I
That his modir for dole schall dye
When she see ones that sight.   *once*
But certis I schal not wande forthy   *delay*
140   To warne that carefull company
Or he to dede be dight.   *Before; put*
.   .   .   [pages missing, see textual note]

MARIA SANCTA   Sen he fro us will twynne   *be separated*
I schall thee nevere forsake.
Allas, the tyme and tyde,
145   I watte wele the day is come
That are was specified   *before*
Of prophete Symeoun in prophicie:
The swerde of sorowe schulde renne
Thurghoute the herte sotelly.   *mysteriously*

II MARIA   Allas, this is a sithfull sight.   *sorrowful*
151   He that was evere luffely and light   *beloved; righteous*
And Lorde of high and lawe,   *low*
Oo, doulfully nowe is he dight
In worlde is none so wofull a wighte
155   Ne so carefull to knawe.   *full of care (sorrow)*
Thei that he mended moste   *helped*
In dede and als in sawe,   *word*
Now have they full grete haste
To dede hym for to drawe.   *death*

JESUS   Doughteres of Jerusalem cytté,
161   Sees, and mournes no more for me   *Cease*
But thynkes uppon this thyng;
For youreselfe mourne schall yee,
And for the sonnes that borne schal be
165   Of yowe, bothe olde and yonge.
For such fare schall befalle   *matter (events)*
That ye schall giffe blissyng   *give*

To barayne bodies all   *barren*
That no barnes forthe may brynge.   *children*

170   For certis ye schall see suche a day
That with sore sighyng schall ye saye
Unto the hillis on highte,
"Falle on us, mountaynes, and ye may,
And covere us fro that felle affraye   *terrible assault*
175   That on us sone schall light."
Turnes home the toune untill   *Go home to*
Sen ye have seen this sight,
It is my Fadirs will,
Alle that is done and dighte.   *determined*

III Maria   Allas, this is a cursed cas.
181   He that alle hele in his hande has   *well-being*
Shall here be sakles slayne.   *innocent*
A, Lorde, beleve lete clense thy face.   *quickly*
Behalde howe he hath schewed his grace,
185   Howe he is moste of mayne.   *power*
This signe schalle bere witnesse
Unto all pepull playne
Howe Goddes Sone here gilteles
Is putte to pereles payne.   *unparalleled*

I Miles   Saie, wherto bide ye here aboute,
191   Thare quenys, with ther skymeryng and ther schoute,   *whores; agitating*
Wille noght ther stevenis steere?   *voices control*

II Miles   Go home, casbalde, with thi clowte   *?bald fellow; cloth*
Or, be that lorde we love and loute,   *reverence*
195   Thou schall abye full dere.   *pay; dearly*

III Maria   This signe schall vengeaunce calle
On yowe holly in feere.

III Miles   Go, hye thee hense withalle
199   Or ille hayle come thou here.   *ill health*

Johannes   Lady, youre gretyng greves me sore.

Maria Sancta   John, helpe me nowe and everemore
That I myght come hym tille.

Johannes   My lady, wende we forthe before
To Calvery when ye come thedir;
205   Than schall ye saie what ye will.

I MILES   What a devyll is this to saye,
         How longe schall we stande stille?
         Go, hye you hens awaye,
         In the devylis name, doune the hill.

II MILES   Ther quenes us comeres with ther clakke;   *shrew; annoys; outcry*
211   He schall be served for ther sake
         With sorowe and with sore.

III MILES   And thei come more such noyse to make,   *If*
          We schall garre lygge thame in the lake   *cause them to lie; dungeon*
215   Yf thei were halfe a skore.

I MILES   Latis nowe such bourdyng be.   *Put aside; jesting (playing)*
         Sen oure tooles are before
         This traitoure and this tree;
         Wolde I full fayne were thore.

II MILES   We schall no more so stille be stedde,   *positioned*
221   For nowe ther quenes are fro us fledde
         That falsely wolde us feere.

III MILES   Methynkith this boy is so forbledde   *(i.e., lost so much blood)*
          With this ladde may he noght be ledde.   *strap*
225   He swounes, that dare I swere.

I MILES   It nedis noght harde to harle   *drag*
         Sen it dose hym slike dere.   *harm*

II MILES   I se here comes a karle   *churl*
         Shall helpe hym for to bere.   *bear*

III MILES   That schall ye see sone one assaye.   *to take up*
231   Goode man, whedir is thou away?
         Thou walkis as thou were wrothe.   *vexed*

SYMON   Sir, I have a grete journay
         That bus be done this same day,
235   Or ellis it may do skathe.   *great harm*

I MILES   Thou may with litill payne
         Eease thyselffe and us bathe.

SYMON   Goode sirs, that wolde I fayne,   *gladly*
         But to dwelle were me lathe.   *loath*

II MILES Nay, beuscher, thou shall sone be spedde.
241 Loo, here a ladde that muste be ledde
     For his ille dedis to dye.

III MILES And he is brosid and all forbledde,   *bruised*
     That makis us here thus stille be stedde;   *be unable to move*
245 We pray thee, sir, forthy,
     That thou wilte take this tree
     And bere it to Calverye.

SYMON Goode sirs, that may nought be,
     For full grete haste have I.

250 My wayes are lang and wyde,
     And I may noght abide,
     For drede I come to late;   *too*
     For sureté have I hight   *bond (legal obligation)*
     Muste be fulfillid this nyght
255 Or it will paire my state.   *impair (reduce); estate*
     Therfore, sirs, by youre leve,
     Methynkith I dwelle full lang.   *long*
     Me were loth you for to greve,
     Goode sirs, ye late me gang;

260 No lenger here now may I wone.   *stay*

I MILES Nay, certis, thou schalte noght go so sone,
     For ought that thou can saye.
     This dede is moste haste to be done,
     For this boy muste be dede by none,   *noon*
265 And nowe is nere myddaye.
     Go helpe hym in this nede
     And make no more delaye.

SYMON I praye yowe dose youre dede
     And latis me wende my waye.

270 And sirs, I schall come sone agayne
     To helpe this man with all my mayne,   *strength*
     And even at youre awne will.

II MILES What, wolde thou trusse with such a trayne?   *get away with; trick*
     Nay, faitour, thou schalte be fayne
275 This forwarde to fullfille,
     Or, be myghty Mahounde,
     Thou schalte rewe it full ille.

III MILES Late dyng this dastarde doune,   *beat*
          But he goo tyte thertill.   *Unless*

SYMON Sertis, sir, that wer nought wisely wrought
281   To bete me but I trespassid ought   *though*
          Outhir in worde or dede.   *Either*

I MILES Uppon his bakke it schall be brought
          To bere it, whedir he wille or noght.
285   What, devyll, whome schulde we drede?
          Go, take it uppe belyve   *quickly*
          And bere it forthe goode spede.

SYMON It helpis noght here to strive;
          Bere it behoves me nede.

290   And therfore, sirs, as ye have saide,
          To bere this crosse I holde me paied
          Right as ye wolde it wore.   *were [done]*

II MILES Yaa, nowe are we right arraied;
          Loke that oure gere be redy grayed   *made ready*
295   To wirke whanne we come thore.

III MILES I warand all redy
          Oure tooles bothe lesse and more;
          Late hym goo hardely
          Forthe with the crosse before.

I MILES Sen he has his lade, nowe late hym gang,   *load*
301   For with this warlowe wirke we wrang,   *wrong*
          And we thus with hym yode.   *go forth*

II MILES And nowe is noght goode to tarie lang;
          What schulde we done more us emang?   *among*
305   Say, sone, so mote thou spede.

III MILES Neven us no nodir noote   *Speak*
          Tille we have done this dede.

I MILES Weme, methynke we doote,   *(i.e., I'm astonished); act foolishly*
          He muste be naked nede.

310   All yf he called hymselffe a kyng,
          In his clothis he schall noght hyng
          But naked as a stone be stedde.

II Miles   That calle I accordand thyng,
 But tille his sidis I trowe thei clyng,
315   For bloode that he has bledde.

III Miles   Wheder thei clynge or cleve,
 Naked he schalle be ledde,
 And for the more myscheve
 Buffettis hym schall be bedde.   *given*

I Miles   Take of his clothis beliffe, latte see.   *off*
321   Aha, this garment will falle wele for mee,
 And so I hope it schall.

II Miles   Nay, sir, so may it noght be;
 Thame muste be parte amonge us thre,
325   Take even as will fall.

III Miles   Yaa, and Sir Pilate medill hym,   *if; concerns himself (with)*
 Youre parte woll be but small.

I Miles   Sir, and ye liste, go telle hym
 Yitt schall he noght have all

330   Butte even his awne parte and no more.

II Miles   Yaa, late thame ligge still here in stoore   *lie; storage*
 Untill this dede be done.

III Miles   Latte bynde hym as he was before
 And harle on harde that he wer thore,   *drag*
335   And hanged or it be none.

I Miles   He schall be feste as fee   *domestic animal*
 And that right sore and sone.

II Miles   So fallis hym for to be,
 He gettis no bettir bone.   *reward*

II Miles   This werke is wele nowe, I warand,
341   For he is boune as beeste in bande   *beast; bonds (ropes)*
 That is demed for to dye.

I Miles   Thanne rede I that we no lenger stande   *advise*
 But ilke man feste on hym a hande
345   And harle hym hense in hye.   *drag*

II MILES Yaa, nowe is tyme to trusse   *depart*
      To alle oure companye.

III MILES If anye aske aftir us,
      Kenne thame to Calvarie.   *Show*

[35.] CRUCIFIXIO CHRISTI

The Pynneres and Paynters

I MILES Sir knyghtis, take heede hydir in hye: *haste*
      This dede on dergh we may noght drawe.   *in [length of] time; draw out*
      Yee wootte youreselffe als wele as I   *know*
      Howe lordis and leders of owre lawe   *leaders of (authorities on)*
5   Has geven dome that this doote schall dye.   *judgment; fool*

II MILES Sir, alle thare counsaile wele we knawe.
      Sen we are comen to Calvarie
      Latte ilke man helpe nowe as hym awe.   *(i.e., he ought to)*

III MILES We are alle redy, loo,
10   That forward to fullfille.   *agreement*

IV MILES Late here howe we schall doo,
      And go we tyte thertille.   *quickly*

I MILES It may noght helpe her for to hone,   *delay*
14   If we schall any worshippe wynne.

II MILES He muste be dede nedelyngis by none.   *necessarily; noon*

III MILES Thanne is goode tyme that we begynne.

IV MILES Late dynge hym doune, than is he done;   *strike*
      He schall nought dere us with his dynne.   *harm*

I MILES He schall be sette and lerned sone,   *set (secured); taught*
20   With care to hym and all his kynne.   *sorrow; people*

II MILES The foulest dede of all
      Shalle he dye for his dedis.

III MILES That menes crosse hym we schall.

IV MILES Behalde so right he redis.   *understands*

II MILES   Thanne to this werke us muste take heede
26   So that oure wirkyng be noght wronge.

II MILES   None othir noote to neven is nede,   *matter; speak of*
     But latte us haste hym for to hange.

III MILES   And I have gone for gere goode speede,   *equipment*
30   Bothe hammeres and nayles large and lange.

IV MILES   Thanne may we boldely do this dede.
     Commes on, late kille this traitoure strange.   *strong (determined)*

I MILES   Faire myght ye falle in feere
     That has wrought on this wise.

II MILES   Us nedis nought for to lere   *(i.e., We already know how)*
36   Suche faitoures to chastise.   *deceivers*

III MILES   Sen ilke a thyng es right arrayed,   *everything is*
     The wiselier nowe wirke may we.

IV MILES   The crosse on grounde is goodely graied,   *prepared*
40   And boorede even as it awith to be.   *bored; ought*

I MILES   Lokis that the ladde on lenghe be layde,
     And made me thane unto this tree.   *(i.e., then fastened); cross*

II MILES   For alle his fare he schalle be flaied,   *practices; punished*
     That one assaie sone schalle ye see.   *undertaking*

III MILES   Come forthe, thou cursed knave,
46   Thy comforte sone schall kele.   *cool (extinguish)*

IV MILES   Thyne hyre here schall thou have.   *pay*

I MILES   Walkes oon, now wirke we wele.

JESUS   Almyghty God, my Fadir free,
50   Late this materes be made in mynde:
     Thou badde that I schulde buxsome be,   *bade; obedient*
     For Adam plyght for to be pyned.   *Adam's guilt*
     Here to dede I obblisshe me   *oblige*
     Fro that synne for to save mankynde,
55   And soveraynely beseke I thee   *above all beseech*
     That thai for me may favoure fynde,   *because of me*
     And fro the fende thame fende   *fiend themselves defend*
     So that ther saules be saffe

In welthe withouten ende.   *well-being*
60   I kepe nought ellis to crave.

I MILES We, herke sir knyghtis, for Mahoundis bloode,
        Of Adam kynde is all his thoght.   *descendants*

II MILES The warlowe waxis werre than woode;   *warlock; worse; mad*
        This doulfull dede ne dredith he noght.   *doleful deed*

III MILES Thou schulde have mynde, with mayne and moode,
66   Of wikkid werkis that thou haste wrought.

IV MILES I hope that he hadde bene as goode
        Have sesed of sawes that he uppe sought.   *ceased; sayings (words); invented*

I MILES Thoo sawes schall rewe hym sore
70   For all his saunteryng sone.   *babbling soon*

II MILES Ille spede thame that hym spare
        Tille he to dede be done.

III MILES Have done belyve, boy, and make thee boune,   *quickly; prepared*
        And bende thi bakke unto this tree.

IV MILES Byhalde, hymselffe has laide hym doune   *Behold*
76   In lenghe and breede as he schulde bee.

I MILES This traitoure here teynted of treasoune,   *convicted*
        Gose faste and fette hym than, ye thre.   *?fetter*
        And sen he claymeth kyngdome with croune,
80   Even as a kyng here hange schall hee.

II MILES Nowe, certis, I schall noght feyne   *stop*
        Or his right hand be feste.   *Ere; fastened*

III MILES The lefte hande thanne is myne.
        Late see who beres hym beste.   *bears himself*

IV MILES Hys lymmys on lenghe than schalle I lede,   *lead*
86   And even unto the bore thame bringe.   *bore hole*

I MILES Unto his heede I schall take hede,   *head; heed*
        And with myne hande helpe hym to hyng.

II MILES Nowe sen we foure schall do this dede,
90   And medill with this unthrifty thyng,   *involve [ourselves]*

Late no man spare for speciall speede   *hold back*
Tille that we have made endyng.

III Miles This forward may not faile.   *plan*
            Nowe are we right arraiede.

IV Miles This boy here in oure baile   *custody*
96   Shall bide full bittir brayde.   *endure; torment*

I Miles Sir knyghtis, saie, howe wirke we nowe?

II Miles Yis, certis, I hope I holde this hande.
          And to the boore I have it brought,   *bore hole*
100   Full boxumly withouten bande.   *eagerly*

I Miles Strike on than harde, for hym thee boght.

II Miles Yis, here is a stubbe will stiffely stande,   *short nail; securely*
          Thurgh bones and senous it schall be soght.   *sinews*
          This werke is wele, I will warande.

I Miles Saie, sir, howe do we thore.
106   This bargayne may not blynne.   *process; leave off*

III Miles It failis a foote and more,
            The senous are so gone ynne.   *contracted*

IV Miles I hope that marke amisse be bored.   *think; measurement*

II Miles Than muste he bide in bittir bale.   *abide; misery*

III Miles In faith, it was overe skantely scored;   *(i.e., drilled in the wrong spot)*
112   That makis it fouly for to faile.

I Miles Why carpe ye so? Faste on a corde   *complain; Fasten*
          And tugge hym to, by toppe and taile.

III Miles Ya, thou comaundis lightly as a lorde.
116   Come helpe to haale, with ille haile.   *pull*

I Miles Nowe certis, that schall I doo,
          Full suerly as a snayle.   *snail*

III Miles And I schall tacche hym too,   *attach*
120   Full nemely with a nayle.   *nimbly*

This werke will holde, that dar I heete,   *dare; promise*
For nowe are feste faste both his handis.   *fastened firmly*

IV MILES   Go we all foure thanne to his feete,   *then*
So schall oure space be spedely spende.   *our time; well spent*

II MILES   Latte see, what bourde his bale myght beete,   *jest; suffering; assuage*
126   Tharto my bakke nowe wolde I bende.

IV MILES   Owe, this werke is all unmeete.   *wrong*
This boring muste all be amende.   *improved*

I MILES   A, pees, man, for Mahounde,   *peace*
130   Latte no man wotte that wondir.   *Let; marvel*
A roope schall rugge hym doune   *pull violently*
Yf all his synnous go asoundre.   *sinews pull apart*

II MILES   That corde full kyndely can I knytte,   *appropriately; tie*
The comforte of this karle to kele.   *cool*

I MILES   Feste on, thanne, faste that all be fytte;   *Fasten; ready*
136   It is no force howe felle he feele.   *no matter; horrible*

II MILES   Lugge on ye both a litill yitt.   *Pull*

III MILES   I schalle nought sese, as I have seele.   *cease; happiness*

IV MILES   And I schall fonde hym for to hitte.   *attempt*

II MILES   Owe, haylle!

IV MILES   Hoo, nowe, I halde it wele.

I MILES   Have done, dryve in that nayle
142   So that no faute be foune.   *fault; found*

IV MILES   This wirkyng wolde noght faile,
Yf foure bullis here were boune.   *bound*

I MILES   Ther cordis have evill encressed his paynes
146   Or he wer tille the booryngis brought.   *Ere; bore holes*

II MILES   Yaa, assoundir are bothe synnous and veynis   *sinews; veins*
On ilke a side, so have we soughte.

III MILES   Nowe all his gaudis nothyng hym gaynes;   *tricks*
150   His sauntering schall with bale be bought.   *babbling; sorrow*

IV MILES   I wille goo saie to oure soveraynes   *masters*
            Of all this werkis howe we have wrought.

I MILES   Nay, sirs, anothir thyng
            Fallis firste to youe and me,
155   Thei badde we schulde hym hyng
            On heghte that men myght see.

II MILES   We woote wele so ther wordes wore,   *know*
            But sir, that dede will do us dere.   *deed (act); harm*

I MILES   It may not mende for to moote more: *(i.e., change anything); argue*
160   This harlotte muste be hanged here.

II MILES   The mortaise is made fitte therfore.   *mortise; suitable*

III MILES   Feste on youre fyngeres than, in feere.   *Fasten; together*

IV MILES   I wene it wolle nevere come thore   *there*
            We foure rayse it noght right to-yere.   *this year*

I MILES   Say, man, whi carpis thou soo?   *say you*
166   Thy liftyng was but light.

II MILES   He menes ther muste be moo   *more [men]*
            To heve hym uppe on hight.   *heave; high*

III MILES   Now, certis, I hope it schall noght nede
170   To calle to us more companye.
            Methynke we foure schulde do this dede
            And bere hym to yone hille on high.

I MILES   It muste be done, withouten drede,   *never fear*
            No more, but loke ye be redy.   *[Say] no more; look*
175   And this parte schalle I lifte and leede;   *lead*
            On lenghe he schalle no lenger lie.   *length*
            Therfore nowe makis you boune: *bound*
            Late bere hym to yone hill.   *Let us bear*

IV MILES   Thanne will I bere here doune
180   And tente his tase untill.   *pay attention; toes*

II MILES   We twoo schall see tille aythir side,   *to either*
            For ellis this werke wille wrie all wrang.   *go awry*

III MILES   We are redy.

IV MILES   Gode sirs, abide,
184   And late me first his fete up fang.   *feet lift up*

II MILES   Why tente ye so to tales this tyde?   *pay attention; tales (stories)*

I MILES   Lifte uppe!

IV MILES   Latte see!

II MILES   Owe, lifte alang!

III MILES   Fro all this harme he schulde hym hyde
        And he war God.   *If he were*

IV MILES   The devill hym hang!

I MILES   For grete harme have I hente: *experienced*
190   My schuldir is in soundre.   *out of joint*

II MILES   And sertis I am nere schente,   *(i.e., at the end of my strength)*
        So lange have I borne undir.   *long*

III MILES   This crosse and I in twoo muste twynne   *part*
        Ellis brekis my bakke in sondre sone.   *break; asunder*

IV MILES   Laye downe agayne and leve youre dynne.   *(i.e., complaints)*
196   This dede for us will nevere be done.

I MILES   Assaie, sirs, latte se yf any gynne   *Try (make an effort); mechanism*
        May helpe hym uppe, withouten hone,   *delay*
        For here schulde wight men worschippe wynne,   *strong; obtain*
200   And noght with gaudis al day to gone.   *jests; spend*

II MILES   More wighter men than we   *stronger*
        Full fewe I hope ye fynde.   *expect*

III MILES   This bargayne will noght bee,
        For certis me wantis wynde.   *breath*

IV MILES   So wille of werke nevere we wore,   *(i.e., deficient)*
206   I hope this carle some cautellis caste.   *believe; churl; spells [has] cast*

II MILES   My bourdeyne satte me wondir soore,   *burden*
        Unto the hill I myght noght laste.

I MILES   Lifte uppe, and sone he schall be thore;
210   Therfore feste on youre fyngeres faste.   *fasten*

III MILES   Owe, lifte!

I MILES   We, loo!

IV MILES   A litill more.

II MILES   Holde thanne!

I MILES   Howe nowe!

II MILES   The werste is paste.   *worst*

III MILES   He weyes a wikkid weght.   *weighs*

II MILES   So may we all foure saie,
215   Or he was heved on heght   *Ere*
      And raysed in this array.   *manner*

IV MILES   He made us stande as any stones,
      So boustous was he for to bere.   *heavy (awkward); carry*

I MILES   Nowe raise hym nemely for the nonys   *nimbly; nonce*
220   And sette hym be this mortas heere,   *mortise*
      And latte hym falle in alle at ones,
      For certis that payne schall have no pere.   *equal*

III MILES   Heve uppe!

IV MILES   Latte doune, so all his bones
      Are asoundre nowe on sides seere.

I MILES   This fallyng was more felle   *painful*
226   Than all the harmes he hadde.
      Nowe may a man wele telle   *count*
      The leste lith of this ladde.   *(i.e., the smallest part of his body)*

III MILES   Methynkith this crosse will noght abide,   *(i.e., be secure)*
230   Ne stande stille in this morteyse yitt.   *(i.e., it wobbles)*

IV MILES   Att the firste tyme was it made overe wyde,
      That makis it wave, thou may wele witte.

I MILES   Itt schall be sette on ilke a side
      So that it schall no forther flitte;   *move*
235   Goode wegges schall we take this tyde   *wedges*
      And feste the foote, thanne is all fitte.   *make fast*

II Miles   Here are wegges arraied
      For that, both grete and smale.

III Miles   Where are oure hameres laide
240   That we schulde wirke withall?

IV Miles   We have them here even atte oure hande.

II Miles   Gyffe me this wegge: I schall it in dryve.

IV Miles   Here is anodir yitt ordande.   *ready*

III Miles   Do take it me hidir belyve.   *Give it to me quickly*

I Miles   Laye on thanne faste.   *then*

III Miles   Yis, I warrande.
246   I thryng thame same, so motte I thryve.   *press; together; might*
      Nowe will this crosse full stabely stande;   *firmly*
      All yf he rave thei will noght ryve.   *Even if; split (break apart)*

I Miles   Say, sir, howe likis thou nowe
250   This werke that we have wrought?

IV Miles   We praye youe sais us howe   *tell*
      Ye fele, or faynte ye ought?

Jesus   Al men that walkis by waye or strete,
      Takes tente ye schalle no travayle tyne.   *Pay attention; suffering; lose*
255   Byholdes myn heede, myn handis, and my feete,   *head*
      And fully feele nowe, or ye fyne,   *experience; before you pass away*
      Yf any mournyng may be meete   *equal*
      Or myscheve mesured unto myne.
      My Fadir, that alle bales may bete,   *sorrows; cure*
260   Forgiffis thes men that dois me pyne.   *cause; pain*
      What thai wirke wotte thai noght.
      Therfore, my Fadir, I crave
      Latte nevere ther synnys be sought,   *(i.e., visited upon them)*
      But see their saules to save.

I Miles   We, harke, he jangelis like a jay.

II Miles   Methynke he patris like a py.   *patters; magpie*

III Miles   He has ben doand all this day   *doing [so]*
268   And made grete meuyng of mercy.   *much referring to*

IV MILES Es this the same that gune us say   *did*
270   That he was Goddis Sone almyghty?

I MILES Therfore he felis full felle affraye,   *[this] very evil assault*
    And demyd this day for to dye.   *is judged*

II MILES *Vath, qui destruit templum.*   *Vah, thou that destroyest the Temple of God*

III MILES His sawes wer so, certayne.

IV MILES And sirs, he saide to some
276   He myght rayse it agayne.

I MILES To mustir that he hadde no myght,   *perform; power*
    For all the kautelles that he couthe kaste,   *spells; cast*
    All yf he wer in worde so wight,   *strong*
280   For all his force nowe he is feste.   *secure*
    Als Pilate demed is done and dight;   *As; judged*
    Therfore I rede that we go reste.   *advise*

II MILES This race mon be rehersed right
    Thurgh the worlde both este and weste.

III MILES Yaa, late hym hynge here stille   *hang*
286   And make mowes on the mone.   *make faces at the moon*

IV MILES Thanne may we wende at wille.

I MILES Nay, goode sirs, noght so sone,

    For certis us nedis anodir note.   *(i.e., there is another matter)*
290   This kirtill wolde I of you crave.   *gown*

II MILES Nay, nay, sir, we will loke be lotte   *by lot*
    Whilke of us foure fallis it to have.

III MILES I rede we drawe cutte for this coote,   *straws; coat*
    Loo, se howe sone, alle sidis to save.   *(i.e., everyone's interests to preserve)*

IV MILES The schorte cutte schall wynne, that wele ye woote,
296   Whedir itt falle to knyght or knave.

I MILES Felowes, ye thar noght flyte,   *need not argue*
    For this mantell is myne.   *garment with open sides*

II MILES Goo we thanne hense tyte;   *quickly*
300   This travayle here we tyne, etc.   *effort; waste*

[36.] MORTIFICACIO CHRISTI

The Bocheres

PILATUS	Sees, seniours, and see what I saie,	*Cease*
	Takis tente to my talkyng enteere.	*entirely*
	Devoyde all this dynne here this day,	*Stop*
	And fallis to my frenschippe in feere.	*altogether*
5	Sir Pilate, a prince withowten pere,	*peer*
	My name is full nevenly to neven	*plainly; mention*
	And domisman full derworth in dede.	*judge; worthy; deed*
	Of gentillest Jewry full even	*(i.e., certainly)*
	Am I.	
10	Who makis oppressioun	
	Or dose transgressioun,	
	Be my discressioun	*By*
	Shall be demed dewly to dy.	*judged; die*
	To dye schall I deme thame, to dede,	*death*
15	Tho rebelles that rewles thame unright.	*rules (controls) themselves*
	Who that to yone hill wille take heede	
	May se ther the soth in his sight,	*truth*
	Howe doulfull to dede thei are dight	*death; put*
	That liste noght owre lawes for to lere.	*care (desire); learn*
20	Lo, thus be my mayne and my myght	
	Tho churles schalle I chasteise and cheere	*(i.e., punish)*
	Be lawe.	
	Ilke feloune false	*Each felon*
	Shall hynge be the halse,	*neck*
25	Transgressours als	*also*
	On the crosse schalle be knytte for to knawe.	*bound; teach*
	To knawe schall I knytte thame on crosse;	
	To schende thame with schame schall I shappe,	*destroy; attempt*
	Ther liffis for to leese is no losse,	*lives; lose*
30	Suche tirrauntis with teene for to trappe.	*malefactors; misery*
	Thus leelly the lawe I unlappe	*loyally; reveal*
	And punyssh thame pitously.	
	Of Jesu I holde it unhappe	*unlucky*
	That he on yone hill hyng so hye	*high*
35	For gilte.	
	His bloode to spille	
	Toke ye you till,	*Took upon yourselves*
	Thus was youre wille	
	Full spitously to spede he were spilte.	*destroyed*

CAIPHAS To spille hym we spake in a speede,   *hurry*
41   For falsed he folowde in faie,   *falsehood; faith*
        With fraudes oure folke gan he feede   *did*
        And laboured to lere thame his laye.   *teach; lore*

ANNA Sir Pilate, of pees we youe praye,
45   Oure lawe was full lyke to be lorne.   *destroyed*
        He saved noght oure dere Sabott daye,
        And that for to scape it were a scorne,   *escape*
        By lawe.

PILATUS Sirs, before youre sight
50   With all my myght
        I examynde hym right,
        And cause non in hym cowthe I knawe.   *none; could*

CAIPHAS Ye knawe wele the cause, sir, in cace: *[this] case*
        It touched treasoune untrewe.
55   The tribute to take or to trace   *seek out*
        Forbadde he, our bale for to brewe.   *sorrow; stir up*

ANNA Of japes yitt jangelid yone Jewe,   *jests*
        And cursedly he called hym a kyng.
        To deme hym to dede it is diewe,   *due*
60   For treasoune it touches that thyng
        Indede.

CAIPHAS Yitt principall
        And worste of all,
        He garte hym call   *caused; to be called*
65   Goddes Sonne, that foulle motte hyme speede.   *might*

PILATUS He spedis for to spille in space,   *die; space [of time] (i.e., soon)*
        So wondirly wrought is youre will;
        His bloode schall youre bodis enbrace,   *(i.e., be on your head)*
        For that have ye taken you till.

ANNA That forwarde ful fayne to fulfille   *purpose; eagerly*
71   Indede schall we dresse us bedene;   *undertake; forthwith*
        Yone losell hym likis full ille,   *wretch*
        For turned is his trantis all to teene,   *trickery; misery*
        I trowe.   *think*

CAYPHAS He called hym kyng,
76   Ille joie hym wring.   *torture*
        Ya, late hym hyng,   *hang*
        Full madly on the mone for to mowe.   *moon to make faces*

ANNA To mowe on the moone has he mente.

80   We, fye on thee, faitour in faye!   *deceiver; faith*
      Who trowes thou to thi tales toke tente?   *trusts; pay attention*
      Thou saggard, thiselffe gan thou saie,   *sagging one*
      The Tempill distroie thee todaye,   *[If] the; were destroyed*
      Be the thirde day ware done ilka dele,   *were; every way*
85   To rayse it thou schulde thee arraye.   *arrange*
      Loo, howe was thi falsed to feele,   *manifest [itself]*
      Foule falle thee!
      For thy presumpcyoune
      Thou haste thy warisoune;   *reward*
90   Do faste come doune,
      And a comely kyng schalle I calle thee.

CAYPHAS I calle thee a coward to kenne   *know*
      That mervaylles and mirakills made.
      Thou mustered emange many menne,   *among*
95   But, brothell, thou bourded to brade.   *jested too broadly*
      Thou saved thame fro sorowes, thai saide:
      To save nowe thiselffe late us see;
      God Sonne if thou grathely be grayde,   *truly; were made to be*
      Delyvere thee doune of that tree   *off*
100   Anone.
      If thou be funne   *found*
      Thou be Goddis Sonne,
      We schall be bonne   *obliged*
      To trowe on thee trewelye, ilkone.   *trust; truly, each one*

ANNA Sir Pilate, youre pleasaunce we praye,   *good will*
106   Takis tente to oure talkyng this tide   *at this time*
      And wipe ye yone writyng away:
      It is not beste it abide.
      It sittis youe to sette it aside,   *substitute*
110   And sette that he saide in his sawe,
      As he that was prente full of pride,   *marked*
      "Jewes kyng am I," comely to knawe,
      Full playne.

PILATUS *Quod scripci, scripci.*   *What I have written, I have written*
115   Yone same wrotte I;
      I bide therby,
      What gedlyng will grucche there agayne.   *gadling (scoundrel); grudge*

JESUS Thou man that of mys here has mente,   *sin; intended*
      To me tente enteerly thou take.   *attention entirely*
120   On roode am I ragged and rente,
      Thou synfull sawle, for thy sake.

For thy misse amendis will I make.   *sin*
My bakke for to bende, here I bide;
This teene for thi traspase I take.   *suffering; trespasses*
125 Who couthe thee more kyndynes have kydde   *shown*
     Than I?
     Thus for thy goode
     I schedde my bloode.
     Manne, mende thy moode,
130 For full bittir thi blisse mon I by.   *I will purchase*

MARIA Allas, for my swete Sonne I saie,
     That doulfully to dede thus is dight.
     Allas, for full lovely thou laye
     In my wombe, this worthely wight.   *man*
135 Allas, that I schulde see this sight
     Of my Sone so semely to see.   *handsome*
     Allas, that this blossome so bright
     Untrewly is tugged to this tree,   *attached*
     Allas!
140 My lorde, my leyffe,   *dear one*
     With full grete greffe   *grief*
     Hyngis as a theffe.   *thief*
     Allas, he did never trespasse.

JESUS Thou woman, do way of thy wepyng,   *stop*
145 For me may thou nothyng amende;
     My Fadirs wille to be wirkyng,
     For mankynde my body I bende.

MARIA Allas, that thou likes noght to lende,   *remain*
     Howe schulde I but wepe for thy woo?
150 To care nowe my comforte is kende.   *distress; given*
     Allas, why schulde we twynne thus in twoo   *part*
     Forevere?

JESUS Womanne, instede of me,
     Loo, John thi sone schall bee.   *son*
155 John, see to thi modir free,
     For my sake do thou thi devere.   *duty*

MARIA Allas, Sone, sorowe and sighte   *Son; grief*
     That me were closed in clay,
     A swerde of sorowe me smyte,
160 To dede I were done this day.   *death*

JOHANNES A, modir, so schall ye noght saie,
     I praye youe be pees in this presse,   *calm; crowd*

For with all the myght that I maye
Youre comforte I caste to encresse
165 Indede.
Youre sone am I,
Loo, here redy,
And nowe forthy
I praye yowe hense for to speede.

MARIA My steven for to stede or to steere,   *voice; stabilize; control*
171 Howe schulde I such sorowe to see:
My Sone that is dereworthy and dere   *worthy*
Thus doulfull a dede for to dye.

JOHANNES A, dere modir, blynne of this blee;   *stop (amend); attitude*
175 Youre mournyng it may not amende.

MARIA CLEOPHE A, Marie, take triste unto thee,   *hope*
For socoure to thee will he sende
This tyde.

JOHANNES Fayre modir, faste
180 Hense latte us caste.   *go away*

MARIA To he be paste   *Until; passed (away)*
Wille I buske here baynly to bide.   *try; humbly*

JESUS With bittirfull bale have I bought,
Thus, man, all thi misse for te mende,   *sins; to*
185 On me for to looke lette thou noght   *refrain*
Howe baynly my body I bende.   *obediently*
No wighte in this worlde wolde have wende   *(i.e., endured)*
What sorowe I suffre for thy sake.
Manne, kaste thee thy kyndynesse be kende,   *attempt to show*
190 Trewe tente unto me that thou take   *attention*
And treste.   *trust*
For foxis ther dennys have thei,   *dens*
Birdis hase ther nestis to paye,   *satisfy [them]*
But the Sone of Man this daye
195 Hase noght on his heed for to reste.   *head*

LATRO A SINISTRIS If thou be Goddis Sone so free,   *THIEF ON THE LEFT*
Why hyng thou thus on this hille?   *hang*
To saffe nowe thyselffe late us see,   *save; let*
And us now, that spedis for to spille.   *(i.e., soon will be killed)*

LATRO A DEXTRIS Manne, stynte of thy steven and be stille,   *cease; speaking*
201 For douteles thy God dredis thou noght;   *you dread not*

Full wele are we worthy thertill.
Unwisely wrange have we wrought,   *wrong*
Iwisse.
205   Noon ille did hee   *No evil*
Thus for to dye.
Lord, have mynde of me
Whan thou art come to thi bliss.

JESUS   Forsothe, sonne, to thee schall I saie,
210   Sen thou fro thy foly will falle,   *part*
With me schall dwelle nowe this daye
In paradise place principall.
Heloy! heloy!
My God, my God, full free,
215   *Lama zabatanye,*
Wharto forsoke thou me,   *Why*
In care?   *misery*
And I did nevere ille
This dede for to go tille,   *undergo*
220   But be it at thi wille.
A, me thirstis sare.   *sorely*

GARCIO   A drinke schalle I dresse thee indede,   *prepare (for)*
A draughte that is full dayntely dight,   *carefully*
Full faste schall I springe for to spede.
225   I hope I schall holde that I have hight.   *shall do as; promised*

CAYPHAS   Sir Pilate, that moste is of myght,
Harke, "Heely" now harde I hym crye;   *Elijah*
He wenys that that worthely wight
In haste for to helpe hym in hye
230   In his nede.

PILATUS   If he do soo,
He schall have woo.

ANNA   He wer oure foo   *foe*
If he dresse hym to do us that dede.   *try; perform; deed*

GARCIO   That dede for to dresse yf he doo,
236   In sertis he schall rewe it full sore.   *repent*
Neverethelees, if he like it noght, loo,
Full sone may he covere that care.   *be released from*
Now swete sir, youre wille yf it ware,   *were*
240   A draughte here of drinke have I dreste   *prepared*
To spede for no spence that ye spare,   *expense*
But baldely ye bib it for the beste   *boldly; drink*

Forwhy
Aysell and galle   *Vinegar*
245   Is menged withalle.   *mingled*
Drynke it ye schalle.
Youre lippis, I halde thame fulle drye.

JESUS   Thi drinke it schalle do me no deere,   *harm*
Wete thou wele, therof will I none.   *Know; well*
250   Nowe, Fadir, that formed alle in fere,   *all together*
To thy moste myght make I my mone.   *moan (lament)*
Thi wille have I wrought in this wone.   *place*
Thus ragged and rente on this roode,   *cross*
Thus doulffully to dede have thei done.
255   Forgiffe thame be grace that is goode,
Thai ne wote noght what it was.
My Fadir, here my bone,   *hear; request*
For nowe all thyng is done.
My spirite to thee right sone
260   Comende I *in manus tuas*.   *into your hands*

MARIA   Now, dere Sone, Jesus so jente,   *gentle (gracious)*
Sen my harte is hevy as leede,   *lead*
O worde wolde I witte or thou wente.   *know ere*
Allas, nowe my dere Sone is dede.
265   Full rewfully refte is my rede.   *cruelly lost; advisor (supporter)*
Allas, for my darlyng so dere.

JOHANNES   A modir, ye halde uppe youre heede   *hold; head*
And sigh noght with sorowes so seere,   *many (painful)*
I praye.

MARIA CLEOPHE   It dose hir pyne   *pain*
271   To see hym tyne.   *die*
Lede we her heyne,   *Lead; away*
This mornyng helpe hir ne maye.   *[we] may not*

CAIPHAS   Sir Pilate, parceyve, I you praye,   *perceive*
275   Oure costemes to kepe wele ye canne.   *customs; well*
Tomorne is our dere Sabott daye,
Of mirthe muste us meve ilke a man.   *move every*
Yone warlous nowe waxis full wan,   *sorcerer; pale*
And nedis muste thei beried be.
280   Delyver ther dede, sir, and thane   *Hasten; death*
Shall we sew to oure saide solempnité   *pursue*
Indede.

PILATE It schalle be done,
    In wordis fone.   *few*
285 Sir knyghtis, go sone
    To yone harlottis you hendely take heede.   *in a seemly manner*

    Tho caytiffis thou kille with thi knyffe;   *Those*
    Delyvere, have done, thei were dede.

MILES Mi lorde, I schall lenghe so ther liffe   *lengthen; lives*
290 That tho brothelles schall nevere bite brede.   *bread*

PILATUS Ser Longeus, steppe forthe in this steede.   *place*
    This spere, loo, have halde in thy hande,   *hold*
    To Jesus thou rake fourthe I rede   *go; advise*
    And sted nought but stiffely thou stande   *delay; boldly*
295 A stounde.   *while (space of time)*
    In Jesu side
    Schoffe it this tyde;   *Shove*
    No lenger bide,
    But grathely thou go to the grounde.   *directly; location*

LONGEUS LATUS O, maker unmade, full of myght.
301 O, Jesu so jentill and jente,
    That sodenly has lente me my sight.   *given*
    Lorde, louyng to thee be it lente.   *praise*
    On rode arte thou ragged and rente   *cross*
305 Mankynde for to mende of his mys.   *amend; sin*
    Full spitously spilte is and spente   *maliciously*
    Thi bloode, Lorde, to bringe us to blis
    Full free.
    A, mercy my socoure,
310 Mercy, my treasoure,
    Mercy my Savioure,
    Thi mercy be markid in me.

CENTERIO O, wondirfull werkar iwis,
    This weedir is waxen full wan,   *weather; dark*
315 Trewe token I trowe that it is   *sign*
    That mercy is mente unto man.
    Full clerly consayve thus I can   *conceive*
    No cause in this corse couthe thei knowe,   *could*
    Yitt doulfull thei demyd hym than   *judged*
320 To lose thus his liffe be ther lawe,
    No righte.   *(i.e., illegally)*
    Trewly I saie,
    Goddis Sone verraye

	Was he this daye	
325	That doulfully to dede thus is dight.	*death; put*

JOSEPH [OF ARIMATHEA] That Lorde lele aylastyng in lande,	*truly everlasting*
Sir Pilate, full preste in this presse,	*bold; crowd*
He save thee be see and be sande,	
And all that is derworth on deesse.	*worthy; dais*

PILATUS Joseph, this is lely no lesse;	*loyally*
331	To me arte thou welcome iwisse.	
	Do saie me the soth or thou sesse,	*cease*
	Thy worthyly wille what it is	
	Anone.	

JOSEPH To thee I praye,	
336	Giffe me in hye	*Give*
	Jesu bodye	
	In gree it for to grave al alone.	*suitable manner*

PILATUS Joseph, sir, I graunte thee that geste.	*man*
340	I grucche noght to grath hym in grave.	*grudge; bury*
	Delyver, have done he were dreste,	*Hasten, endeavor*
	And sewe, sir, oure Sabott to saffe.	*proceed; save*

JOSEPH With handis and harte that I have	
	I thanke thee in faith for my frende.	
345	God kepe thee thi comforte to crave,	
	For wightely my way will I wende	*quickly*
	In hye.	
	To do that dede	
	He be my speede,	
350	That armys gun sprede,	*were*
	Mannekynde be his bloode for to bye.	*by; purchase*

NICHODEMUS Weill mette, ser; in mynde gune I meffe	*Well met; was I moved*
	For Jesu that juged was unjente.	*was judged to be not noble*
	Ye laboured for license and leve	*permission*
355	To berye his body on bente?	*in a place*

JOSEPH Full myldely that matere I mente,	
And that for to do will I dresse.	

NICHODEMUS Both same I wolde that we wente	*together*
	And lette not for more ne for lesse,	
360	Forwhy	*Since*
	Oure frende was he,	
	Faithfull and free.	

JOSEPH   Therfore go we
          To berie that body in hye.   *quickly*

365   All mankynde may marke in his mynde
      To see here this sorowfull sight.
      No falsnesse in hym couthe thei fynde
      That doulfully to dede thus is dight.

NICHODEMUS   He was a full worthy wight,   *man*
370   Nowe blemysght and bolned with bloode.   *disfigured; swollen*

JOSEPH   Ya, for that he mustered his myght.   *manifested*
          Full falsely thei fellid that foode,   *destroyed; (dear) person*
          I wyne,   *believe*
          Bothe bakke and side
375   His woundes wide;
          Forthi this tyde
          Take we hym doune us betwene.

NICHODEMUS   Betwene us take we hym doune,
          And laie hym on lenthe on this lande.   *ground*

JOSEPH   This reverent and riche of rennoune,   *holy one*
381   Late us halde hym and halse hym with hande.   *hold; embrace*
      A grave have I garte here be ordande   *cause; ordered*
      That never was in noote, it is newe.   *use*

NICHODEMUS   To this corse it is comely accordande   *properly suitable*
385   To dresse hym with dedis full dewe   *[those] acts due [to him]*
      This stounde.   *(i.e., now)*

JOSEPH   A sudarye   *shroud*
          Loo here have I,
          Wynde hym forthy,
390   And sone schalle we grave hym in grounde.   *bury*

NICHODEMUS   In grounde late us grave hym and goo;
          Do liffely, latte us laie hym allone.   *quickly, let us*
          Nowe Saviour of me and of moo,   *more*
          Thou kepe us in clennesse ilkone.   *purity*

JOSEPH   To thy mercy nowe make I my moone,   *lament*
396   As Saviour be see and be sande,
      Thou gyde me that my griffe be al gone;   *guide; grief*
      With lele liffe to lenge in this lande   *righteous; (i.e., dwell)*
      And esse.   *ease*

NICHODEMUS   Seere oynementis here have I   *Many*
401   Brought for this faire body.
      I anoynte thee forthy
      With myrre and aloes.   *myrrh*

JOSEPH   This dede it is done ilke a dele,
405   And wroughte is this werke wele iwis.
      To thee, Kyng, on knes here I knele
      That baynly thou belde me in blisse.   *readily; shelter*

NICHODEMUS   He highte me full hendely to be his   *promised; graciously*
      A nyght whan I neghed hym full nere.   *approached*
410   Have mynde, Lorde, and mende me of mys,   *[my] transgressions*
      For done is oure dedis full dere   *dear*
      This tyde.   *time*

JOSEPH   This Lorde so goode
      That schedde his bloode,
415   He mende youre moode
      And buske on this blis for to bide.   *hurry to; abide*

[37. THE HARROWING OF HELL]

The Sadilleres

JESUS   Manne on molde, be meke to me   *earth; obedient*
      And have thy Maker in thi mynde,
      And thynke howe I have tholid for thee   *worked (suffered)*
      With pereles paynes for to be pyned.   *unequaled; suffered*
5   The forward of my Fadir free   *covenant*
      Have I fulfillid, as folke may fynde;
      Therfore aboute nowe woll I bee   *go about*
      That I have bought for to unbynde.
      The feende thame wanne with trayne   *won by trickery*
10   Thurgh frewte of erthely foode;   *fruit*
      I have thame getyn agayne   *(i.e., in my control)*
      Thurgh bying with my bloode.   *purchasing*

      And so I schall that steede restore   *place*
      For whilke the feende fell for synne;
15   Thare schalle mankynde wonne evermore   *dwell*
      In blisse that schall nevere blynne.   *end*
      All that in werke my werkemen were,
      Owte of thare woo I wol thame wynne,   *win [back]*
      And some signe schall I sende before
20   Of grace to garre ther gamys begynne.   *cause; mirth*

A light I woll thei have
To schewe thame I schall come sone.
My bodie bidis in grave   *remains*
Tille alle thes dedis be done.   *deeds*

25   My Fadir ordand on this wise   *ordained*
     Aftir his will that I schulde wende
     For to fulfille the prophicye
     And als I spake my solace to spende.   *disburse*
     My frendis that in me faith affies   *(i.e., has faith)*
30   Nowe fro ther fois I schall thame fende,   *foes; defend*
     And on the thirde day ryght uprise
     And so tille heven I schall assende.
     Sithen schall I come agayne
     To deme bothe goode and ill   *judge*
35   Tille endles joie or peyne;
     Thus is my Fadris will.

         Tunc cantent.   *Then they sing*

ADAME   Mi bretheren, harkens to me here:
     Swilke hope of heele nevere are we hadde.   *well-being; ere*
     Foure thowsande and sex hundereth yere
40   Have we bene heere in this stedde.   *place*
     Nowe see I signe of solace seere,
     A glorious gleme to make us gladde,
     Wherfore I hope oure helpe is nere
     And sone schall sesse oure sorowes sadde.   *cease*

EVA   Adame, my husband hende,   *gracious*
46   This menys solas certayne;   *means*
     Such light gune on us lende   *did; (i.e., shine)*
     In paradise full playne.

ISAIAH   Adame, we schall wele undirstande;
50   I, Ysaias as God me kende,   *instructed*
     I prechid in Neptalym, that lande,   *Naphtali*
     And Zabulon even untill ende.
     I spake of folke in mirke walkand   *darkness walking*
     And saide a light schulde on thame lende.
55   This lered I whils I was levand;   *living*
     Nowe se I God this same hath sende.
     This light comes all of Criste,
     That seede to save us nowe;   *progeny [of the Father]*
     Thus is my poynte puplisshid,   *proclaimed*
60   But Symeon, what sais thou?

SYMEON   This, my tale of farleis feele,   *wonders many*
          For in the Temple his frendis me fande.   *found*
          I hadde delite with hym to dele
          And halsed homely with my hande.   *held [him] affectionately*
65   I saide, "Lorde, late thy servaunt lele
          Passe nowe in pesse to liffe lastand,   *in peace; everlasting*
          For nowe myselfe has sene thy hele,
          Me liste no lengar to liffe in lande."   *desire; longer*
          This light thou has purveyed
70   To folkes that liffis in leede,   *land*
          The same that I thame saide   *to them*
          I see fulfillid in dede.   *deed*

JOHANNES BAPTISTA   Als voyce criand to folke I kende   *crying; taught*
          The weyes of Criste als I wele kanne;   *could*
75   I baptiste hym with bothe my hande
          Even in the floode of flume Jordanne.   *river*
          The Holy Goste fro hevene discende
          Als a white dowue doune on hym thanne;   *dove*
          The Fadir voice, my mirthe to mende,
80   Was made to me even als manne;
          "This is my Sone," he saide,
          "In whome me paies full wele."   *I am pleased*
          His light is on us laide,
          He comes oure cares to kele.   *cool (assuage)*

MOYSES   Of that same light lernyng have I;
86   To me, Moyses, he mustered his myght
          And also unto anodir, Hely,   *Elijah*
          Wher we were on an hille on hight.
          Whyte as snowe was his body
90   And his face like to the sonne to sight;   *sun*
          No man on molde was so myghty
          Grathely to loke agaynste that light.   *Directly*
          That same light se I nowe
          Shynyng on us sarteyne,   *certainly*
95   Wherfore trewly I trowe   *believe*
          We schalle sone passe fro payne.   *soon*

I DIABOLUS   Helpe, Belsabub, to bynde ther boyes,
          Such harrowe was never are herde in helle.   *turmoil; before*

II DIABOLUS   Why rooris thou soo, Rebalde? Thou royis,   *shout; talk nonsense*
100   What is betidde, canne thou ought telle?

I DIABOLUS   What, heris thou noght this uggely noyse?   *hear*
          Thes lurdans that in lymbo dwelle,

Thei make menyng of many joies   *mention*
And musteres grete mirthe thame emell.

II Diabolus   Mirthe? Nay, nay, that poynte is paste;
106   More hele schall thei never have.   *health (well-being)*

I Diabolus   Thei crie on Criste full faste
And sais he schal thame save.

Belsabub   Ya, if he save thame noght, we schall,
110   For they are sperde in speciall space;   *imprisoned*
Whils I am prince and principall
Schall thei never passe oute of this place.
Calle uppe Astrotte and Anaball
To giffe ther counsaille in this case,
115   Bele-Berit and Belial,
To marre thame that swilke maistries mase.   *perform such outrages*
Say to Satan oure sire
And bidde thame bringe also
119   Lucifer, lovely of lyre.   *body*

I Diabolus   Al redy, lorde, I goo.

Jesus   *Attollite portas principes,*   *Lift up your gates, O princes*
Oppen uppe, ye princes of paynes sere,   *many*

Et elevamini eternales,   *And be ye lifted up, O eternal gates*
124   Youre yendles gatis that ye have here.   *everlasting*

Sattan   What page is there that makes prees   *upstart; press (commotion)*
And callis hym kyng of us in fere?   *altogether*

David   I lered levand, withouten lees,   *learned [while] living*
He is a kyng of vertues clere,
A Lorde mekill of myght
130   And stronge in ilke a stoure,   *every struggle*
In batailes ferse to fight   *fierce*
And worthy to wynne honnoure.

Sattan   Honnoure, in the devel way, for what dede?   *deed*
All erthely men to me are thrall.   *subject*
135   The lad that calles hym Lorde in leede   *in man*
Hadde never yitt herberowe, house, ne halle.   *lodging*

I Diabolus   Harke, Belsabub, I have grete drede,   *dread*
For hydously I herde hym calle.

BELLIALL We, spere oure gates, all ill mot thou spede,   *bar; prosper*
140   And sette furthe watches on the wall.
      And if he calle or crie
      To make us more debate,
      Lay on hym than hardely   *vigorously*
      And garre hym gange his gate.   *make; go [on]; way*

SATTAN Telle me what boyes dare to be so bolde
146   For drede to make so mekill draye.   *racket*

I DIABOLUS Itt is the Jewe that Judas solde
      For to be dede this othir daye.

SATTAN Owe, this tale in tyme is tolde;
150   This traytoure traveses us alway.   *attacks (contradicts)*
      He schall be here full harde in holde,   *captivity*
      Loke that he passe noght, I thee praye.

II DIABOLUS Nay, nay, he will noght wende
      Away or I be ware;
155   He shappis hym for to schende   *plans; destroy*
      Alle helle or he go ferre.   *ere; far*

SATTAN Nay, faitor, therof schall he faile,   *deceiver*
      For alle his fare I hym deffie.   *defy*
      I knowe his trantis fro toppe to taile;   *tricks*
160   He levys with gaudis and with gilery.   *lives; tricks; guile*
      Therby he brought oute of oure bale   *custody*
      Nowe late Lazar of Betannye;   *Bethany*
      Therfore I gaffe to the Jewes counsaille   *gave*
      That thei schulde alway garre hym dye.   *cause*
165   I entered in Judas
      That forwarde to fulfille;   *promise*
      Therfore his hire he has   *reward (punishment)*
      Allway to wonne here stille.   *dwell*

BELSABUB Sir Sattanne, sen we here thee saie   *since*
170   That thou and the Jewes wer same assente,   *together agreed*
      And wotte he wanne Lazar awaye,   *won*
      That tille us was tane for to tente,   *taken; (i.e., guard)*
      Trowe thou that thou marre hym maye,
      To mustir myghtis what he has mente?   *(i.e., such might as he has)*
175   If he nowe deprive us of oure praye   *prey*
      We will ye witte whanne thei are wente.   *tell when*

SATTAN I bidde you be noght abasshed
      But boldely make youe boune   *obliged*

       With toles that ye on traste,   *tools; trust*
180   And dynge that dastard doune.   *down*

JESUS *Principes, portas tollite,*   *Princes, open your gates*
       Undo youre gatis, ye princes of pryde,
       Et introibit rex glorie,   *And the king of glory shall enter in*
       The kyng of blisse comes in this tyde.   *at this time*

SATTAN Owte, harrowe, what harlot is hee
186   That sais his kyngdome schall be cryed.   *proclaimed*

DAVID That may thou in my Sawter see   *Psalter*
       For that poynte of prophicie
       I saide that he schuld breke   *break*
190   Youre barres and bandis by name   *[metal] bands*
       And on youre werkis take wreke;   *vengeance*
       Nowe schalle ye see the same.

JESUS This steede schall stonde no lenger stoken: *place; closed*
       Opynne uppe and latte my pepul passe.

I DIABOLUS Owte, beholdes, oure baill is brokynne,   *jail*
196   And brosten are alle oure bandis of bras.   *burst*
       Telle Lucifer alle is unlokynne.   *unlocked*

BELSABUB What, thanne, is lymbus lorne, allas?   *limbo lost*
       Garre Satan helpe that we were wroken;   *Make; [so] that we may be revenged*
200   This werke is werse than evere it was.

SATTAN I badde ye schulde be boune   *ordered; bound (tied up)*
       If he made maistries more.
       Do dynge that dastard doune
       And sette hym sadde and sore.

BELSABUB Ya, sette hym sore, that is sone saide,
206   But come thiselffe and serve hym soo;
       We may not bide his bittir braide: *attack*
       He wille us marre, and we wer moo.   *if; more*

SATTAN What, faitours, wherfore are ye ferde?   *afraid*
210   Have ye no force to flitte hym froo?   *flee*
       Belyve loke that my gere be grathed,   *Quickly; prepared*
       Miselffe schall to that gedlyng goo.
       Howe, belamy, abide,
       With al thy booste and bere,   *crying out*
215   And telle to me this tyde
       What maistries makes thou here?

JESUS I make no maistries but for myne,   *exercise no mastery (power)*
    Thame wolle I save, I telle thee nowe.   *shall*
    Thou hadde no poure thame to pyne   *power; torment*
220 But as my prisonne for ther prowe.   *profit*
    Here have thei sojorned, noght as thyne
    But in thy warde, thou wote wele howe.   *custody*

SATTAN And what devel haste thou done ay syne   *since*
    That never wolde negh thame nere or nowe?   *approach; near ere*

JESUS Nowe is the tyme certayne
226 Mi Fadir ordand before
    That they schulde passe fro payne
    And wonne in mirthe evermore.   *dwell*

SATTAN Thy fadir knewe I wele be sight;
230 He was a write his mette to wynne,   *carpenter; food; earn*
    And Marie me menys thi modir hight,   *was called*
    The uttiremeste ende of all thi kynne.
    Who made thee be so mekill of myght?

JESUS Thou wikid feende, latte be thy dynne;   *noisemaking*
235 Mi Fadir wonnys in heven on hight   *dwells; high*
    With blisse that schall nevere blynne.   *end*
    I am his awne Sone,
    His forward to fulfille,   *promise*
    And same ay schall we wonne,   *together*
240 And sundir whan we wolle.   *part*

SATTAN God Sonne, thanne schulde thou be ful gladde
    Aftir no catel neyd thowe crave.   *animals (humans) need*
    But thou has leved ay like a ladde   *lived*
    And in sorowe as a symple knave.

JESUS That was for hartely love I hadde   *great*
246 Unto mannis soule it for to save,
    And for to make thee mased and madde.   *bewildered; insane*
    And by that resoune thus dewly to have   *duly*
    Mi Godhede here I hidde
250 In Marie modir myne,
    For it schulde noght be kidde   *known*
    To thee nor to none of thyne.

SATTAN A, this wolde I were tolde in ilk a toune.   *town*
    So sen thou sais God is thy sire,
255 I schall thee prove be right resoune   *by; reason*
    Thou motes his men into the myre.   *you argue*

        To breke his bidding were thei boune,   *bound*
        And, for they did at my desire,   *since*
        Fro paradise he putte thame doune
260   In helle here to have ther hyre.   *reward*
        And thyselfe, day and nyght,
        Has taught al men emang
        To do resoune and right,
        And here werkis thou all wrang.   *(i.e., argue illogically)*

JESUS   I wirke noght wrang, that schal thou witte,
266   If I my men fro woo will wynne;
        Mi prophetis playnly prechid it,   *preached*
        All this note that nowe begynne.
        Thai saide that I schulde be obitte,   *dead*
270   To hell that I schulde entre in
        And save my servauntis fro that pitte
        Wher dampned saulis schall sitte for synne.   *sin*
        And ilke trewe prophettis tale   *story (prophecy)*
        Muste be fulfillid in mee,
275   I have thame boughte with bale,   *purchased; suffering*
        And in blisse schal thei be.

SATTAN Nowe sen thee liste allegge the lawes,   *wish [to] expound*
        Thou schalte be atteynted or we twynne,   *convicted*
        For tho that thou to wittenesse drawes,
280   Full even agaynste thee will begynne.
        Salamon saide in his sawes   *Solomon; sayings*
        That whoso enteres helle withynne
        Shall never come oute, thus clerkis knawes;
        And therfore, felowe, leve thi dynne.
285   Job, thi servaunte also,
        Thus in his tyme gune telle   *began [to]*
        That nowthir frende nor foo
        Shulde fynde reles in helle.   *release from*

JESUS   He saide full soth, that schall thou see,
290   That in helle may be no reles,
        But of that place than preched he
        Where synffull care schall evere encrees.   *suffering; increase*
        And in that bale ay schall thou be
        Whare sorowes sere schall never sesse,   *many; cease*
295   And for my folke therfro wer free;
        Nowe schall thei passe to the place of pees.   *peace (rest)*
        Thai were here with my wille,   *permission*
        And so schall thei fourthe wende,   *forth go*
        And thiselve schall fulfille
300   Ther wooe withouten ende.

SATTAN   Owe, thanne se I howe thou movys emang   *intend all the while*
   Some mesure with malice to melle,   *mix*
   Sen thou sais all schall noght gang
   But some schalle alway with us dwelle.

JESUS   Yaa, witte thou wele, ellis were it wrang,   *or else*
306 Als cursed Cayme that slewe Abell
   And all that hastis hemselve to hange   *hasten*
   Als Judas and Archedefell,   *Achitophel*
   Datan and Abiron,   *Dathan; Abiram*
310 And alle of thare assente
   Als tyrantis everilkone
   That me and myne turmente.   *torment*

   And all that liste noght to lere my lawe
   That I have lefte in lande nowe newe,   *on earth recently*
315 That is my comyng for to knawe   *incarnation*
   And to my sacramente pursewe.
   Mi dede, my rysing, rede be rawe,   *(i.e., understood rightly)*
   Who will noght trowe, thei are noght trewe.   *believe*
   Unto my Dome I schall thame drawe   *[Last] Judgment*
320 And juge thame worse thanne any Jewe.
   And all that likis to leere   *learn*
   My lawe and leve therbye   *believe*
   Shall nevere have harmes heere   *here*
   But welthe as is worthy.   *well-being (bliss)*

SATTAN   Nowe here my hande, I halde me paied,   *paid (rewarded)*
326 This poynte is playnly for oure prowe.   *profit*
   If this be soth that thou hast saide
   We schall have moo thanne we have nowe.   *more [souls]*
   This lawe that thou nowe late has laide   *just now; proclaimed*
330 I schall lere men noght to allowe,
   Iff thei it take thei be betraied,   *accept*
   For I schall turne thame tyte, I trowe.   *corrupt; quickly*
   I schall walke este and weste
   And garre thame werke wele werre.   *cause; much worse*

JESUS   Naye, feende, thou schall be feste   *fast (confined)*
336 That thou schalte flitte not ferre.   *far*

SATTAN   Feste, that were a foule reasoune;
   Nay, bellamy, thou bus be smytte.   *must; struck*

JESUS   Mighill, myne aungell, make thee boune   *Michael; bound*
340 And feste yone fende that he noght flitte.   *fasten*

And Devyll, I comaunde thee go doune
Into thy selle where thou schalte sitte.   *cell*

SATTAN   Owte! Ay, herrowe — helpe, Mahounde!
Nowe wex I woode oute of my witte.   *wax; mad*

BELSABUB   Sattan, this saide we are,   *before*
346   Nowe schall thou fele thi fitte.   *experience; punishment*

SATTAN   Allas, for dolle and care,   *dole*
I synke into helle pitte.

ADAME   A, Jesu Lorde, mekill is thi myght
350   That mekis thiselffe in this manere   *humble*
Us for to helpe as thou has hight   *promised*
Whanne both forfette, I and my feere.   *offended; companion (Eve)*
Here have we levyd withouten light
Foure thousand and six hundreth yere;
355   Now se I be this solempne sight
Howe thy mercy hath made us clene.   *pure (free from sin)*

EVE   A, Lorde, we were worthy
Mo turmentis for to taste,   *More; experience*
But mende us with mercye
360   Als thou of myght is moste.

BAPTISTA   A, Lorde, I love thee inwardly
That me wolde make thi messengere
Thy comyng in erth for to crye
And teche thi faith to folke in feere,   *all together*
365   And sithen before thee for to dye   *then*
And bringe boodworde to thame here   *message*
How thai schulde have thyne helpe in hye.   *soon*
Nowe se I all thi poyntis appere   *acts*
Als David, prophete trewe,
370   Ofte tymes tolde untill us;   *to*
Of this comyng he knewe
And saide it schulde be thus.

DAVID   Als I have saide, yitt saie I soo,   *yet*
Ne derelinquas, Domine,
375   *Animam meam in inferno,*[1]
Leffe noght my saule, Lorde, aftir thee
In depe helle where dampned schall goo,

---

[1] Lines 374–75: *Because, Lord, Thou wilt not leave / my soul in hell.*

Ne suffre nevere saules fro thee be,   *dwell*
The sorowe of thame that wonnes in woo
380   Ay full of filthe, that may repleye.   *redeem*

ADAME   We thanke his grete goodnesse
He fette us fro this place;   *brought*
Makes joie nowe more and lesse.

OMNIS   We laude God of his grace.

          Tunc cantent.   *Then they sing*

JESUS   Adame and my frendis in feere,
386   Fro all youre fooes come fourth with me;
Ye schalle be sette in solas seere   *apart*
Wher ye schall nevere of sorowes see.
And Mighill, myn aungell clere,   *bright*
390   Ressayve thes saules all unto thee   *Receive*
And lede thame als I schall thee lere   *direct*
To paradise with playe and plenté.   *joy*
Mi grave I woll go till,
Redy to rise upperight,
395   And so I schall fulfille
That I before have highte.   *promised*

MICHILL   Lord, wende we schall aftir thi sawe,
To solace sere thai schall be sende,
But that ther develis no draught us drawe,   *(i.e., do not trick us)*
400   Lorde, blisse us with thi holy honde.   *bless; hand*

JESUS   Mi blissing have ye all on rawe.   *in order*
I schall be with youe wher ye wende,
And all that lelly luffes my lawe,   *truly love*
Thai schall be blissed withowten ende.

ADAME   To thee, Lorde, be louyng   *praise*
406   That us has wonne fro waa.   *won; woe*
For solas will we syng,
Laus tibi cum gloria, etc.   *Praise to you with glory*

          [38. THE RESURRECTION]

The Carpenteres

PILATUS   Lordingis, listenys nowe unto me:
I comaunde you in ilke degré   *each rank*

Als domesman chiffe in this contré   *judge chief; country*
For counsaill kende,   *known*
5   Atte my bidding you awe to be   *ought*
And baynly bende.   *without delay oblige*

And Sir Cayphas, chiffe of clergye,
Of youre counsaill late here in hye,   *quickly*
By oure assente sen we dyd dye   *cause to die*
10   Jesus this day,
That we mayntayne and stande therby
That werke allway.

CAYPHAS Yis, sir, that dede schall we mayntayne;
By lawe it was done all bedene,   *accordingly*
15   Ye wotte youreselve, withouten wene,   *a doubt*
Als wele as we.
His sawes are nowe uppon hym sene,   *(i.e., come back upon him)*
And ay schall be.

ANNA The pepull, sirs, in this same steede,   *place*
20   Before you saide with a hole hede   *(i.e., without any dissent)*
That he was worthy to be dede
And therto sware.
Sen all was rewlid by rightis rede,   *reason*
Nevyn it no more.   *Say*

PILATUS To nevyn me thinketh it nedfull thyng.   *speak*
26   Sen he was hadde to beriyng   *burying*
Herde we nowthir of olde ne ying   *neither*
Thithynges betwene.

CAYPHAS Centurio, sir, will bringe thidings
30   Of all bedene.

We lefte hym there for man moste wise;
If any rebelles wolde ought rise
Oure rightwise dome for to dispise
Or it offende,
35   To sese thame till the nexte assise   *seize; court session*
And than make ende.

CENTURIO A, blissed Lorde, Adonay,
What may thes mervayles signifie
That her was schewed so oppinly
40   Unto oure sight,
This day whanne that the man gune dye   *did*
That Jesus highte?   *was named*

	Itt is a misty thyng to mene;	*portent; mention*
	So selcouth a sight was nevere sene	*wondrous*
45	That oure princes and prestis bedene	*forthwith*
	Of this affray	
	I woll go weten withouten wene,	*reveal; doubt*
	What thei can saye.	

	God save you, sirs, on ilke a side,	
50	Worschippe and welthe in worldis wide.	
	With mekill mirthe myght ye abide	
	Boght day and nyght.	*Both*

PILATUS Centurio, welcome this tide,
Oure comely knyght.

55   Ye have bene miste us here among.   *missed*

CENTURIO God giffe you grace grathely to gang.   *worthily to go*

PILATUS Centurio, oure frende full lang,   *long*
What is your will?

CENTURIO I drede me that ye have done wrang
60   And wondir ill.

CAYPHAS Wondir ill, I pray thee, why?
Declare it to this company.

CENTURIO So schall I, sirs, telle you trewly
Withowten trayne.   *deception*
65   The rightwise mane thanne mene I by   *just man; mean*
That ye have slayne.

PILATUS Centurio, sesse of such sawe.   *cease; words*
Thou arte a lered man in the lawe,   *learned*
And if we schulde any witnes drawe
70   Us to excuse,
To mayntayne us evermore thee awe,   *ought*
And noght reffuse.   *refuse*

CENTURIO To mayntayne trouthe is wele worthi.   *truth*
I saide you, whanne I sawe hym dy,
75   That he was Goddis Sone almyghty
That hangeth thore.
Yitt saie I soo, and stande therby
For evermore.

CAYPHAS Ya, sir, such reasouns may ye rewe;   *rue*
80   Ye schulde noght neveyn such note enewe,   *say (raise); matter anew*
      But ye couthe any tokenyngis trewe   *signs*
      Unto us tell.

CENTURIO Such woundirfull cas nevere yitt ye knewe
      As now befell.

ANNA We praye thee telle us of what thyng.

CENTURIO All elementis, both olde and ying,
87   In ther maneres thai made mornyng   *ways; lamenting*
      In ilke a stede,
      And knewe be countenaunce that ther Kyng
90   Was done to dede.

      The sonne for woo he waxed all wanne,   *dark*
      The mone and sterres of schynyng blanne,   *stopped*
      The erthe tremeled, and also manne   *(see note)*
      Began to speke;
95   The stones that never was stered or thanne   *moved ere then*
      Gune asondir breke,   *Did*

      And dede men rose, both grete and small.

PILATUS Centurio, beware withall,
      Ye wote oure clerkis the clipsis thei call   *eclipse*
100   Such sodayne sight,   *sudden*
      Both sonne and mone that sesoune schall   *season*
      Lak of ther light.

CAYPHAS Ya, and if dede men rose bodily,
      That myght be done thurgh socery;   *sorcery*
105   Therfore we sette nothyng therby
      To be abaiste.   *abashed*

CENTURIO All that I tell for trewthe schall I
      Evermore traste.   *trust*

      In this ilke werke that ye did wirke
110   Nought allone the sonne was mirke,
      But howe youre vaile raffe in youre kirke,   *veil was rent asunder; church*
      That witte I wolde.

PILATUS Swilke tales full sone will make us irke   *angry*
      And thei be talde.   *If; told*

ANNA Centurio, such speche withdrawe;
116 Of all thes wordes we have none awe.   *no respect*

CENTURIO Nowe sen ye sette noght be my sawe,
    Sirs, have gode day.
    God graunte you grace that ye may knawe
120 The soth alway.   *truth*

ANNA Withdrawe thee faste, sen thou thee dredis,   *you are afraid*
    For we schall wele mayntayne oure dedis.

PILATUS Such wondir reasouns as he redis   *wondrous; tells*
    Was nevere beforne.

CAIPHAS To neven this noote no more us nedis,   *speak of; matter; need*
126 Nowthere even ne morne.   *evening*

    Therfore loke no manne make ille chere;
    All this doyng may do no dere,   *harm*
    But to beware yitt of more were   *suspicion*
130 That folke may fele,
    We praye you, sirs, of these sawes sere
    Avise you wele.   *Advise*

    And to this tale takes hede in hye,   *quickly*
    For Jesu saide even opynly
135 A thyng that greves all this Jury,   *Jewry*
    And righte so may:
    That he schulde rise uppe bodily
    Within the thirde day.

    And be it so, als motte I spede,
140 His lattar deede is more to drede
    Than is the firste, if we take hede
    Or tente therto.   *attend*
    To nevyn this noote methynke moste nede   *mention; matter*
    And beste to do.

ANNA Ya, sir, if all that he saide soo,
146 He has no myght to rise and goo
    But if his menne stele hym us froo   *steal*
    And bere away.   *bear [him]*
    That were tille us and other moo
150 A foule fraye,   *disturbance*

    For thanne wolde thei saie, evere ilkone,
    That he roose by hymselffe allone;

Therfore latte hym be kepte anone   *let; anon*
With knyghtes hende   *worthy*
155 Unto thre daies be comen and gone
And broght till ende.

PILATUS   In certayne, sirs, right wele ye saie,
For this ilke poynte nowe to purvaye   *arrange*
I schall ordayne if I may.
160 He schall not ryse,
Nor none schalle wynne hym thens away
On nokyns wise.   *In no wise*

Sir knyghtis, that are in dedis dowty,   *deeds bold*
Chosen for chiffe of chevalrye,
165 As we ay in youre force affie   *always; trust*
Bothe day and nyght,
Wendis and kepis Jesu body
With all youre myghte.

And for thyng that evere be maye
170 Kepis hym wele to the thirde day
And latis no man takis hym away   *let*
Oute of that stede;   *place (grave)*
For and thei do, suthly I saie,
Ye schall be dede.

I MILES   Lordingis, we saie you for certayne,
176 We schall kepe hym with myghtis and mayne;
Ther schall no traitoures with no trayne   *trickery*
Stele hym us froo.
Sir knyghtis, takis gere that moste may gayne   *equipment; be helpful*
180 And lates us goo.

II MILES   Yis, certis, we are all redy bowne,   *bound (prepared)*
We schall hym kepe till oure rennowne.   *for our reputation*
On ilke a side latte us sitte doune
Nowe all in fere,   *all together*
185 And sone we schall crake his croune
Whoso comes here.

Tunc Jhesu resurgente.   *Then Jesus being risen*

Tunc angelus cantat Resurgens.   *Then the angel sings "[Christ] is arisen"*

I MARIA   Allas, to dede I wolde be dight,
So woo in werke was nevere wight;   *[experienced by] a person*
Mi sorowe is all for that sight

190   That I gune see,   *have seen*
       Howe Criste my maistir, moste of myght,
       Is dede fro me.

       Allas, that I schulde se his pyne,   *pain*
       Or yit that I his liffe schulde tyne;   *suffer (the loss of)*
195   Of ilke a myscheve he is medicyne
       And bote of all,   *remedy*
       Helpe and halde to ilke a hyne   *hold (support); person*
       That hym on wolde call.

II Maria   Allas, who schall my balis bete   *sorrows lessen*
200   Whanne I thynke on his woundes wete?
       Jesu, that was of love so swete
       And nevere did ill,
       Es dede and graven under the grete   *buried; earth*
       Withouten skill.

III Maria   Withowten skill the Jewes ilkone
206   That lovely Lorde has newly slayne,
       And trespasse did he nevere none
       In nokyn steede.   *(i.e., anywhere)*
       To whome nowe schall I make my mone
210   Sen he is dede?

I Maria   Sen he is dede, my sisteres dere,
       Wende we will on mylde manere
       With oure anoynementis faire and clere
       That we have broght
215   To noynte his wondis on sides sere
       That Jewes hym wroght.

II Maria   Goo we same my sisteres free.   *together*
       Full faire us longis his corse to see,   *we desire; body*
       But I wotte noght howe beste may be,
220   Helpe have we none.
       And who schall nowe here of us thre
       Remove the stone?

III Maria   That do we noght but we wer moo,
       For it is huge and hevy also.

I Maria   Sistirs, a yonge childe as we goo
226   Makand mornyng,   *Making mourning*
       I see it sitte wher we wende to
       In white clothyng.

II Maria   Sistirs, sertis, it is noght to hide:
230   The hevy stone is putte beside.

III Maria   Sertis, for thyng that may betyde   *for whatever*
      Nere will we wende,
      To layte that luffely and with hym bide   *seek; loved one*
      That was oure frende.

Angelus   Ye mournand women in youre thought,
236   Here in this place whome have ye sought?

I Maria   Jesu, that to dede is brought,
      Oure Lorde so free.

Angelus   Women, certayne here is he noght,
240   Come nere and see.

      He is noght here, the soth to saie,
      The place is voide that he in laye.
      The sudary here se ye may
      Was on hym laide.
245   He is resen and wente his way,   *risen*
      As he you saide.

      Even as he saide so done has hee:
      He is resen thurgh grete poostee.   *power*
      He schall be foune in Galilé   *found*
250   In flesshe and fell.   *(i.e., physically present)*
      To his discipilis nowe wende ye
      And thus thame tell.

I Maria   Mi sisteres dere, sen it is soo
      That he is resen dede thus froo
255   As the aungell tolde me and yow too,
      Oure Lorde so fre,
      Hens will I never goo
      Or I hym see.   *Ere*

II Maria   Marie, us thare no lenger lende,   *[need] there; stay*
260   To Galilé nowe late us wende.

I Maria   Nought tille I see that faithfull frende,
      Mi Lorde and leche;   *healer*
      Therfore all this, my sisteres hende,   *gracious*
      That ye forth preche.

III MARIA As we have herde, so schall we saie,
266   Marie oure sistir, have goode daye.

I MARIA Nowe, verray God as he wele maye,
       Man moste of myght,
       He wisse you, sisteres, wele in youre waye   *direct*
270   And rewle you right.

       Allas, what schall nowe worthe on me?
       Mi kaytiffe herte will breke in three   *miserable (unhappy) heart*
       Whenne I thynke on that body free
       How it was spilte.
275   Both feete and handes nayled tille a tre
       Withouten gilte.   *guilt*

       Withouten gilte the trewe was tane,   *true one; taken*
       For trespas did he nevere none.
       The woundes he suffered many one
280   Was for my misse.   *sins*
       It was my dede he was for slayne   *deed*
       And nothyng his.

       How might I but I loved that swete,
       That for my love tholed woundes wete   *suffered*
285   And sithen be graven undir the grete,   *buried; earth*
       Such kyndnes kithe?   *revealed*
       There is nothing to that we mete   *except that; meet*
       May make me blithe.   *happy*

I MILES What, oute allas! What schall I saie?
290   Where is the corse that herein laye?   *body*

II MILES What ayles thee, man? Is he awaye
       That we schulde tent?   *attend*

I MILES Rise uppe and see.

II MILES   Harrowe! For ay,
       I telle us schente.   *believe we are destroyed*

III MILES What devill is this, what aylis you twoo,   *ails*
296   Such noyse and crye thus for to make too?

II MILES Why, is he gone?

III MILES Allas, whare is he that here laye?

IV MILES   Whe, harrowe! Devill, whare is he away?

III MILES   What, is he thusgatis fro us wente,   *in this way*
301   That fals traitour that here was lente?   *placed*
    And we trewly here for to tente   *watch*
    Had undirtane.
    Sekirlie, I telle us schente,
305   Holy ilkane.   *Entirely*

I MILES   Allas, what schall we do this day
    That thus this warlowe is wente his waye?   *warlock*
    And savely, sirs, I dare wele saie   *certainly*
    He rose allone.

II MILES   Witte Sir Pilate of this affraye,   *[If] learns*
311   We mon be slone.   *slain*

III MILES   Why, canne none of us no bettir rede?   *advise*

IV MILES   Ther is not ellis, but we be dede.   *otherwise*

II MILES   Whanne that he stered oute of this steede   *stirred*
315   None couthe it kenne.   *could*

I MILES   Allas, harde happe was on my hede,
    Amonge all menne.

    Fro Sir Pilate witte of this dede,
    That we were slepande whanne he yede,   *sleeping; went [away]*
320   He will forfette withouten drede
    All that we have.

II MILES   Us muste make lies, for that is nede
    Oureselve to save.

III MILES   Ya, that rede I wele, also motte I goo.   *advise; go (prosper)*

IV MILES   And I assente therto alsoo.

II MILES   An hundereth, schall I saie, and moo   *more*
327   Armed ilkone   *each one*
    Come and toke his corse us froo,
    And us nere slayne.

I MILES   Nay, certis, I halde there none so goode
331   As saie the soth even as it stoode:
    Howe that he rose with mayne and mode   *(i.e., supernatural power)*

And wente his way.
To Sir Pilate if he be wode,   *even if; angered*
335   This dar I saie.

II MILES   Why, dare thou to Sir Pilate goo
With thes tydingis and saie hym soo?

I MILES   So rede I, if he us sloo   *slay*
We dye but onys.   *once*

III MILES   Nowe, he that wrought us all this woo,
341   Woo worthe his bonys.   *(i.e., Woe upon him)*

IV MILES   Go we thanne, sir knyghtis hende,
Sen that we schall to Sir Pilate wende;
I trowe that we schall parte no frendes
345   Or that we passe.   *Ere*

I MILES   And I schall hym saie ilke worde tille ende,
Even as it was.

Sir Pilate, prince withouten pere,
Sir Cayphas and Anna in fere
350   And all ye lordyngis that are here
To neven by name,   *identify*
God save you all, on sidis sere,
Fro synne and schame.

PILATUS   Ye are welcome, oure knyghtis kene,
355   Of mekill mirthe nowe may ye mene;   *tell*
Therfore some tales telle us betwene
Howe ye have wroght.

I MILES   Oure wakyng, lorde, withouten wene,   *watching; doubt*
359   Is worthed to noght.   *Comes to naught*

CAYPHAS   To noght? Allas, sesse of such sawe.   *cease; words*

II MILES   The prophete Jesu that ye wele knawe
Is resen and gone, for all oure awe,   *awe (fear)*
With mayne and myght.

PILATUS   Therfore the devill hymselffe thee drawe,
365   Fals recrayed knyght.   *recreant*

Combered cowardis I you call;   *Encumbered (Miserable)*
Have ye latten hym goo fro you all?   *allowed*

III Miles   Sir, ther was none that did but small   *little*
           When that he yede.   *went forth*

IV Miles   We wer so ferde downe ganne we falle,
371   And dared for drede.   *stupefied; fear*

Anna   Hadde ye no strenghe hym to gaynestande?   *withstand*
           Traitoures, ye myght have boune in bande   *bound; bonds (ropes)*
           Bothe hym and thame that ye ther fande   *found*
375   And sessid thame sone.   *seized*

I Miles   That dede all erthely men levand
           Myght noght have done.

II Miles   We wer so radde ever ilkone   *terrified*
           Whanne that he putte beside the stone,
380   We wer so stonyed we durste stirre none   *astonished*
           And so abasshed.

Pilatus   What, rose he by hymselfe allone?

I Miles   Ya, sir, that be ye traste.   *may you trust*

IV Miles   We herde never sen we were borne,
385   Nor all oure faderes us beforne,
           Suche melodie, mydday ne morne
           As was made there.

Cayphas   Allas, thanne is oure lawes lorne
           For everemare.

II Miles   What tyme he rose good tente I toke.   *attention (heed)*
391   The erthe that tyme tremylled and quoke,   *quaked*
           All kyndely force than me forsoke   *natural strength*
           Tille he was gone.

III Miles   I was aferde, I durste not loke,
395   Ne myght had none,   *strength*

           I myght not stande, so was I starke.   *stiff (with fear)*

Pilatus   Sir Cayphas, ye are a connyng clerke;   *intelligent*
           If we amysse have tane oure merke,   *taken; mark (aim)*
           I trowe same faile;   *[we] together*
400   Therfore what schalle worthe nowe of this werke,   *shall become*
           Sais your counsaille?

CAYPHAS To saie the beste forsothe I schall,
That schall be prophete to us all;   *profitable*
Yone knyghtis behoves there wordis agayne call   *must; call back*
405   Howe he is miste.
We nolde for thyng that myght befall   *would not*
That no man wiste.   *knows*

ANNA Now, Sir Pilate, sen that it is soo
That he is resynne dede us froo,   *risen*
410   Comaundis youre knyghtis to saie wher thei goo
That he was tane
With twenty thousand men and mo,   *more*
And thame nere slayne.   *nearly slain*

And therto of oure tresorie   *treasury*
415   Giffe to thame a rewarde forthy.

PILATUS Nowe of this purpose wele plesed am I,
And forther thus;
Sir knyghtis, that are in dedis dowty,   *bold*
Takes tente to us,

420   And herkenes what that ye schall saie   *harken*
To ilke a man both nyght and daye,
That ten thousand men in goode araye
Come you untill,
With forse of armys bare hym awaye   *arms*
425   Agaynst your will.

Thus schall ye saie in ilke a lande,
And therto on that same comenaunde   *agreement*
A thousande pounde have in youre hande
To your rewarde;
430   And frenschippe, sirs, ye undirstande
Schall not be spared.

CAIPHAS Ilkone youre state we schall amende,
And loke ye saie as we you kende.   *we instructed you*

I MILES In what contré so ye us sende,
435   Be nyght or daye,
Wherso we come, wherso we wende,
So schall we saie.

PILATUS Ya, and whereso ye tarie in ilke contré,
Of oure doyng in no degré
440   Dois that no manne the wiser be,   *Allow*

Ne freyne beforne, *ask*
Ne of the sight that ye gonne see *have seen*
Nevynnes it nowhere even ne morne. *Speak*

For we schall mayntayne you alwaye,
445 And to the pepull schall we saie
It is gretely agaynste oure lay *law*
To trowe such thing. *believe*
So schall thei deme, both nyght and day,
All is lesyng. *lying*

450 Thus schall the sothe be bought and solde,
And treasoune schall for trewthe be tolde.
Therfore ay in youre hartis ye holde
This counsaile clene,
And fares nowe wele, both yonge and olde,
455 Haly bedene. *Wholly indeed*

[39. THE APPEARANCE OF CHRIST TO MARY MAGDALEN]

The Wynedrawers

MARIA Allas, in this worlde was nevere no wight *person*
Walkand with so mekill woo. *Walking; great woe*
Thou dredfull Dede, drawen hythir and dight *Death*
And marre me as thou haste done moo. *put an end to; to others*
5 In lame is it loken, all my light, *earth; locked (shut up)*
Forthy on grounde onglad I goo. *unhappy*
Jesus of Nazareth he hight, *is named*
The false Jewes slewe hym me froo.

Mi witte is waste nowe in wede; *decayed; madness*
10 I walowe, I walke, nowe woo is me,
For laide nowe is that lufsome in lede: *loved one; lead (i.e., coffin)*
The Jewes hym nayled untill a tree. *cross*
My doulfull herte is evere in drede,
To grounde nowe gone is all my glee;
15 I sporne ther I was wonte to spede. *stumble where*
Nowe helpe me, God, in persones three.

Thou lufsome lede in ilke a lande, *person*
As thou schope both day and nyght, *shaped (created)*
Sonne and mone both bright schynand, *sun; moon; shining*
20 Thou graunte me grace to have a sight
Of my Lorde, or ellis his sande. *also; messenger*

JESUS   Thou wilfull woman in this waye,
     Why wepis thou soo als thou wolde wede,   *[go] mad*
     Als thou on felde woulde falle doune faie?   *As if; dead*
25   Do way, and do no more that dede.   *deed*
     Whome sekist thou this longe daye?
     Say me the sothe, als Criste thee rede.   *direct*

MARIA   Mi Lorde Jesu and God verray   *very (true)*
     That suffered for synnes his sides bleede.

JESUS   I schall thee saie, will thou me here,   *hear*
31   The soth of hym that thou hast sought.
     Withowten drede, thou faithfull fere,   *companion*
     He is full nere that mankynde bought.

MARIA   Sir, I wolde loke both ferre and nere
35   To fynde my Lorde, I se hym noght.

JESUS   Womane, wepe noght, but mend thy chere;
     I wotte wele whedir that he was brought.   *whither*

MARIA   Swete sir, yf thou hym bare awaye,
     Saie me the sothe and thedir me leede   *Tell; thither lead me*
40   Where thou hym didde; withouten delay   *did [put him]*
     I schall hym seke agayne goode speede.

     Therfore, goode gardener, saie thou me,
     I praye thee for the prophetis sake
     Of thez tythyngis that I aske thee.
45   For it wolde do my sorowe to slake   *assuage*
     Wher Goddis body founden myght be
     That Joseph of the crosse gonne take.   *did*
     Might I hym fange unto my fee,   *take; keeping*
     Of all my woo he wolde me wrake.   *free*

JESUS   What wolde thou doo with that body bare
51   That beried was with balefull chere?
     Thou may noght salve hym of his sare,   *suffering*
     His peynes were so sadde and seere.   *many*
     But he schall cover mankynde of care,   *deliver; from cares*
55   That clowded was he schall make clere,
     And the folke wele for to fare
     That fyled were all in feere.   *defiled; altogether*

MARIA   A, myght I evere with that man mete
     The whiche that is so mekill of myght,

60   Drye schulde I wype that nowe is wete:
      I am but sorowe of worldly sight.   *full of grief*

JESUS Marie, of mournyng amende thy moode
       And beholde my woundes wyde.
       Thus for mannys synnes I schedde my bloode
65   And all this bittir bale gonne bide.   *suffering did endure*
       Thus was I rased on the roode
       With spere and nayles that were unride.   *monstrous*
       Trowe it wele, it turnes to goode
       Whanne men in erthe ther flessh schall hyde.   *be concealed*

MARIA A, Rabony, I have thee sought,   *Rabbi (teacher)*
71   Mi maistir dere, full faste this day.

JESUS Goo awaye, Marie, and touche me noght,
       But take goode kepe what I schall saie.
       I ame hee that all thyng wroght
75   That thou callis thi Lorde and God verraye.
       With bittir dede I mankynde boght,   *death; purchased*
       And I am resen as thou se may.   *risen*

       And therfore, Marie, speke nowe with me
       And latte thou nowe be thy grette.   *stop; weeping*

MARIA Mi Lorde Jesu, I knowe nowe thee;
81   Thi woundes thai are nowe wette.   *fresh*

JESUS Negh me noght, my love, latte be,   *Touch*
       Marie, my doughtir swete;
       To my Fadir in Trinité
85   Forthe I stigh noght yette.   *go up*

MARIA A, mercy, comely conquerour,
       Thurgh thi myght thou haste overcome dede.   *death*
       Mercy, Jesu, man and Saveour:
       Thi love is swetter thanne the mede.   *sweeter; mead (honey drink)*
90   Mercy, myghty confortour,
       For are I was full wille of rede.   *ere; (i.e., at a loss)*
       Welcome, Lorde, all myn honnoure,
       Mi joie, my luffe, in ilke a stede.

JESUS Marie, in thyne harte thou write
95   Myne armoure riche and goode:
       Myne actone covered all with white   *jerkin*
       Als cors of man behewede   *body (i.e., skin); colored*
       With stuffe goode and parfite   *perfect*

Of maydenes flessh and bloode;
100   Whan thei ganne thirle and smyte   *did pierce*
Mi heede for hawberke stoode.   *military tunic, esp. neck armor*

Mi plates wer spredde all on brede   *plates [of armor]; outspread*
That was my body uppon a tree;
Myne helme covered all with manhede,   *hidden; manhood*
105   The strengh therof may no man see;
The croune of thorne that garte me blede,   *made; bleed*
Itt bemenes my dignité.   *signifies*
Mi diademe sais, withouten drede,   *reveals*
That dede schall I nevere be.   *dead*

MARIA   A, blessid body that bale wolde beete,   *misery; relieve*
111   Dere haste thou bought mankynne.   *Dearly*
Thy woundes hath made thi body wete
With bloode that was thee withinne.
Nayled thou was thurgh hande and feete,
115   And all was for oure synne.
Full grissely muste we caitiffis grete,   *sorrowfully; wretches weep*
Of bale howe schulde I blynne?   *stop*

To se this ferly foode   *wondrous man*
Thus ruffully dight,   *pitifully*
120   Rugged and rente on a roode,   *Pulled violently*
This is a rewfull sight,
And all is for oure goode
And nothyng for his plight.
Spilte thus is his bloode
125   For ilke a synfull wight.   *every; person*

JESUS   To my God and my Fadir dere,
To hym als swithe I schall assende,   *swiftly (soon)*
For I schall nowe noght longe dwelle here;
I have done als my Fadir me kende,   *directed*
130   And therfore loke that ilke man lere   *learn*
Howe that in erthe ther liffe may mende.
All that me loves I schall drawe nere
Mi Fadirs blisse that nevere schall ende.

MARIA   Alle for joie me likes to synge,
135   Myne herte is gladder thanne the glee,   *(i.e., overjoyed)*
And all for joie of thy risyng
That suffered dede upponne a tree.
Of luffe nowe is thou crouned kyng,   *love*
Is none so trewe levand more free.   *living*

140   Thy love passis all erthely thyng.
      Lorde, blissed motte thou evere bee.   *must*

JESUS   To Galilé schall thou wende,
      Marie, my doghtir dere,
      Unto my brethir hende;   *brethren courteous*
145   Ther thei are all in fere.   *all together*
      Telle thame ilke worde to ende   *(i.e., tell them everything)*
      That thou spake with me here.
      My blissing on thee lende,
      And all that we leffe here.   *leave*

[40. THE TRAVELERS TO EMMAUS]

[The Woolpackers and Woolbrokers]

I PERIGRINUS   That Lorde that me lente this liffe for to lede,
      In my wayes thou me wisse thus will of wone;   *direct; [being] distraught*
      Qwen othir men halfe moste mirthe to ther mede,   *When; have; reward*
      Thanne als a mornand manne make I my mone,   *mourning; moan*
5   For douteles nowe may we drede us.   *may we dread*
      Allas, thei have refte us oure rede,   *taken away; counselor*
      With doole have thei dight hym to dede,   *dole; put; death*
      That Lorde that was leeffe for to lede us.   *beloved*

II PERIGRINUS   He ledde us full lelly, that Lorde, nowe allas   *truly*
10   Mi Lorde for his lewté his liffe has he lorne.   *loyalty*

I PERIGRINUS   Saye, who comes there claterand?   *chattering*

II PERIGRINUS   Sir, I, Cleophas.
      Abide, my leffe brothere, to bale am I borne,   *dear; carried*
      But telle me whedir thou bounes?   *wither; are going*

I PERIGRINUS   To Emax, this castell beside us;   *Emmaus*
15   Ther may we bothe herber and hyde us;
      Therfore late we tarie at no townes.   *let us*

II PERIGRINUS   Atte townes for to tarie take we no tent,   *intent*
      But take us tome at this tyme to talke of sume tales   *time; (i.e., reminisce)*
      And jangle of the Jewes and of Jesu so gente,   *talk*
20   Howe thei bette that body was bote of all bales.   *beat; remedy; sorrows*
      With buffettis thei bete hym full barely;   *to the extreme*
      In Sir Cayphas hall garte thei hym call
      And hym before Sir Pilate in his hall,
      On the morne than aftir, full arely.   *afterward; early*

I PERIGRINUS   Full arely the juggemen demed hym to dye.   *judges*
26   Both prestis and prelatis to Pilate made preysing,   *flattering*
        And alls cursid caytiffis and kene on Criste gan thei crie   *as; maliciously; to cry*
        And on that lele Lorde made many a lesyng.   *true; lie*
        Thei spitte in his face to dispise hym,
30   To spoile hym nothyng thei spared hym,   *despoil (strip)*
        But natheles baynly thei bared hym,   *nonetheless readily; stripped*
        With scourges smertly goyng thei smote hym.   *in movement*

II PERIGRINUS   Thei smotte hym full smertely that the bloode oute braste,   *burst*
        That all his hyde in hurth was hastely hidde.   *injury (wounds)*
35   A croune of thorne on his heede full thraly thei thraste,   *violently; thrust*
        Itt is grete dole for to deme the dedis thei hym dide.   *sorrow; judge; deeds*
        With byndyng unbaynly and betyng,   *cruelly; beating*
        Thane on his bakke bare he thame by
        A crosse unto Calvery,
40   That swettyng was swemyd for swetyng.   *beloved one; overcome; sweating (toil)*

I PERIGRINUS   For all the swette that he swete with swyngis thei hym swang,[1]
        And raffe hym full rewfully with rapes on a rode,   *pulled him apart; ropes; cross*
        Than hevyd thei hym highly on hight for to hang;
        Withouten misse of this man, thus mensked thai his mode[2]
45   That evere has bene trewest in trastyng.   *trusting (faith)*
        Methynkith myn herte is boune for to breke
        Of his pitefull paynes when we here speke,
        So frendfull we fonde hym in fraistyng.   *loyal (loving); [his] trial (testing)*

II PERIGRINUS   In fraisting we fonde hym full faithfull and free,   *found*
50   And his mynde mente he nevere mysse to no man.   *sin (hostility)*
        Itt was a sorowe, forsoth, in sight for to see
        Whanne that a spetyffull spere unto his harte ranne.   *cruel spear*
        In baill thus his body was beltid,   *custody; enclosed*
        Into his harte thraly thei thraste;   *violently*
55   Whan his piteffull paynes were paste,
        That swett thyng full swiftely he sweltid.   *sweet; was overcome (died)*

I PERIGRINUS   He sweltid full swithe in swonyng, that swette.   *quickly; swooning*
        Allas, for that luffely that laide is so lowe,   *loved one*
        With granyng full grissely on grounde may we grette,   *lamenting; sorrowfully; weep*
60   For so comely a corse canne I none knowe.   *body*
        With dole unto dede thei did hym
        For his wise werkis that he wroght thame,   *them*

---

[1] *For all the sweat that he perspired with whips (blows) that they directed [at] him*

[2] *He being without sin, thus they honored his spirit*

Thes false folke whan thei bethoughte thame,   *contrived*
That grette unkyndynesse thei kidde hym.   *showed*

II Perigrinus Unkyndynesse thei kidde hym, tho caistiffis so kene,   *showed, cruel*
66   And als unwitty wightis wrought thei hym wreke.   *unwise men; violence*

Jesus What are thes mervailes that ye of mene
And thus mekill mournyng in mynde that ye make,
Walkyng thus wille by thes wayes?   *distraught*

II Perigrinus Why, arte thou a pilgryme and haste bene
71   At Jerusalem, and haste thou noght sene   *observed*
What dole has ben done in thes daies?

Jesus In ther daies, dere sir, what dole was ther done?
Of that werke wolde I witte, and youre will were,   *if it is your wish*
75   And therfore I pray you telle me now sone.
Was ther any hurlyng in hande? Nowe late me here.   *violence; let; hear*

I Perigrinus Why herde thou no carpyng nor crying   *talking*
Att Jerusalem ther thou haste bene
Whenne Jesu of Nazarene   *Nazareth*
80   Was doulfully dight to the dying?   *sorrowfully put to death*

II Perigrinus To the dying thei dight hym that defte was and dere,   *gentle*
Thurgh prokering of princes that were ther in prees.   *provoking (plotting); assembly*
Forthy as wightis that are will thus walke we in were,   *distraught; confusion*
For pechyng als pilgrymes that putte are to pees.   *fear of accusation; made to be quiet*
85   For mornyng of oure maistir thus morne wee   *mourning; mourn*
As wightis that are wilsome thus walke we,   *confused (bewildered)*
Of Jesus in telling thus talke we;
Fro townes for takyng thus turne we.   *[possibility of] capture*

I Perigrinus Thus turne we fro townes, but take we entent   *notice*
90   How thei mourthered that man that we of mene;
Full rewfully with ropis on rode thei hym rente
And takkid hym thertill full tyte in a tene,   *fastened; (i.e., in an angry fit)*
Upperightis full rudely thei raised hym.
Thanne myghtely to noye hym withall,   *annoy*
95   In a mortaise faste lete hym fall,   *mortice*
To pynne hym thei putte hym and peysed hym.   *nail; pushed; pressed him down*

II Perigrinus Thei peysed hym to pynne hym, that pereles of pese,   *peace*
Thus on that wight that was wise wroght thei grete wondir,
Yitt with that sorowe wolde thei noght sesse;   *cease*

100 They schogged hym and schotte hym his lymes all in sondir,[1]
     His braynes thus brake thei and braste hym.   *crushed*
     A blynde knyght, such was his happe,   *luck*
     Inne with a spere poynte atte the pappe   *breast*
     To the harte full thraly he thraste hym.   *violently*

I PERIGRINUS Thei thraste hym full thraly, than was ther no threpyng;   *disputing*
106 Thus with dole was that dere unto dede dight.
     His bak and his body was bolned for betyng: *swollen from*
     Itt was, I saie thee forsoth, a sorowfull sight.
     But oftesithes have we herde saie,   *oftentimes*
110 And we trowe as we herde telle,   *believe*
     That he was to rawsoune Israell;   *ransom*
     But nowe is this the thirde daye.

II PERIGRINUS Thes dayes newe owre wittis are waxen in were,   *confusion*
     For some of oure women for certayne thei saide
115 That thai sawe in ther sightis solas full seere,
     Howe all was lemand light wher he was laide.   *gleaming*
     Thei called us, as ever myght thei thriffe,   *thrive*
     For certayne thei saugh it in sight,   *saw*
     A visioune of aungellis bright,
120 And tolde thame ther Lorde was alyve.

I PERIGRINUS On lyve tolde thei that Lorde leved hir in lande,
     Thez women come lightly to warne, I wene.   *quickly; believe*
     Some of oure folke hyed forthe and faste thei it fande   *hurried; found*
     That all was soth that thei saide that sight had thei sene.   *true*
125 For lely thei loked ther he laye,   *truly*
     Thei wende ther that foode to have fonne.   *man; found*
     Thanne was his toumbe tome as a tonne;   *empty; barrel*
     Thanne wiste thei that wight was away.

II PERIGRINUS Awaye is that wight that wonte was us for to wisse.   *man; teach*

JESUS A, fooles, that are fauty and failes of youre feithe,   *fallible; faith*
131 This bale bud hym bide and belde thame in blisse;   *pain must he abide; support*
     But ye be lele of youre laye, youre liffe holde I laith.   *Unless your story is true; loath*
     To prophetis he proved it and preched,
     And also to Moyses gan he saie
135 That he muste nedis die on a day,
     And Moyses forth talde it and teched,

     And talde it and teched it many tymes than.

---

[1] *They shook him and jerked him until his limbs were all asunder*

I PERIGRINUS A, more of this talking we pray you to telle us.

II PERIGRINUS Ya, sir, be youre carping full kyndely we kenne,   *readily*
140   Ye meene of oure maistir of whome that we melle us.   *mean (speak); associated ourselves*

I PERIGRINUS Ya, goode sir, see what I saie you,
        See ye this castell beside her?   *[us] here*
        All nyght we thynke for to bide here.
        Bide with us, sir pilgrime, we praye you,

145   We praye you, sir pilgrime, ye presse noght to passe.   *beg; pass [on]*

JESUS Yis, sir, me bus nede.   *must [go on]*

I PERIGRINUS   Naye, sir, the nyght is over nere.

JESUS And I have ferre for to founde.   *far to go*

II PERIGRINUS   I hope wele thou has.

I PERIGRINUS We praye thee, sir, hartely, all nyght holde thee here.

JESUS I thanke youe of this kyndinesse ye kydde me.   *offer*

I PERIGRINUS Go in, sir, sadly and sone.   *solemnly; soon*

II PERIGRINUS Sir, daunger dowte noght, have done.   *doubt not*

JESUS Sir, I muste nedis do as ye bid me:

153   Ye bidde me so baynly I bide for the beste.

I PERIGRINUS Lo, her is a sege, goode sir, I saie you.   *seat*

II PERIGRINUS With such goode as we have glad we oure geste.   *entertain; guest*

I PERIGRINUS Sir, of this poure pitaunce take parte now, we pray yow.
  . . .   *[two lines missing]*
JESUS Nowe blisse I this brede that brought is on the borde;   *board*
        Fraste theron faithfully, my frendis, you to feede.   *Taste*

I PERIGRINUS . . . unterly have we tane entent.   *?entirely*
160   Ow, I trowe some torfoyr is betidde us.   *calamity; happen (to)*
        Saie, wher is this man.

II PERIGRINUS   Away is he wente,
        Right now satte he beside us.

I PERIGRINUS Beside us we both sawe him sitte,
  And by no poynte couthe I parceyve hym passe.

II PERIGRINUS Nay, be the werkis that he wrought full wele myght we witte   *know*
166   Itt was Jesus hymselffe, I wiste who it was.

I PERIGRINUS Itt was Jesus thus wisely that wrought,
  That raised was and rewfully rente on the rode;   *sorrowfully torn; cross*
  Of bale and of bittirnesse has he us boght,   *purchased*
170   Boune was and betyn that all braste on bloode.   *Bound; beaten; ?splattered with*

II PERIGRINUS All braste on bloode, so sore was he bette
  With ther wickid Jewes that wrethfull was evere,   *wrathful*
  With scourges and scharpe thornes on his heede sette,   *head*
  Suche torfoyr and torment of telle herde I nevere.   *disaster*

I PERIGRINUS Of telle herde I nevere of so pitefull peynes
176   As suffered oure soverayne, hyngand on highte.   *hanging high*
  Nowe is he resen with myght and with mayne;   *power*
  I telle for sikir, we saugh hym in sight.   *surely*

II PERIGRINUS We saugh hym in sight, nowe take we entent,
180   Be the brede that he brake us so baynly betwene,   *bread; broke; readily*
  Such wondirfull wais as we have wente   *ways; traveled*
  Of Jesus the gente was nevere none seene.

I PERIGRINUS Sene was ther nevere so wondirfull werkes,
  Be see ne be sande, in this worlde so wide,   *By sea nor by*
185   Menskfully in mynde thes materes now merkis,   *Fittingly remembers these matters*
  And preche we it prestly on every ilke side.   *without delay; each and every*

II PERIGRINUS On every ilke side prestely prechis we;
  Go we to Jerusaleme thes tydingis to telle;
  Oure felawes fro fandyng nowe fraste we.   *temptation; urge*
190   More of this mater her may we not melle.   *be concerned*

I PERIGRINUS Here may we notte melle more at this tyde,   *mingle; time*
  For prossesse of plaies that precis in plight;[1]
  He bringe to his blisse on every ilke side,
  That sofferayne Lorde that moste is of myght.

---

[1] *On account of the right order (progression) of plays that press on urgently*

[41. DOUBTING THOMAS]

The Escreveneres

PETRUS   Allas, to woo that we wer wrought!
    Hadde never no men so mekill thought
    Sen that oure Lorde to dede was brought   *Since; death*
    With Jewes fell.   *malicious*
5   Oute of this steede ne durst we noght,   *place; dare [go]*
    But here ay dwelle.

JOHANNES   Here have we dwelte with peynes strang.   *strong*
    Of oure liffe us lothis, we leve to lange,   *we (find) loathsome; live too long*
    For sen the Jewes wrought us that wrong
10   Oure Lorde to sloo,   *slay*
    Durste we nevere come thame emang,   *among*
    Ne hense to goo.

JACOBUS   The wikkid Jewes hatis us full ille
    And bittir paynes wolde putte us till;
15   Therfore I rede that we dwelle stille   *advise*
    Here ther we lende,   *where we dwell*
    Unto that Criste oure Lorde us wille
    Some socoure sende.

DEUS   Pees and reste be with yowe.

PETRUS   A, brethir dere, what may we trowe,   *believe*
21   What was this sight that we saughe nowe   *saw*
    Shynand so bright,   *Shining*
    And vanysshed thus and we ne wote how,   *know not*
    Oute of oure sight?

JOHANNES   Oute of oure sight nowe is it soghte;   *(i.e., gone)*
26   Itt makith us madde, the light it broght.
    What may it be?

JACOBUS   Sertis I wotte noght
    But sekirly   *certainly*
    Itt was vanyté in oure thought,   *illusion*
30   Nought ellis trowe I it be.   *else trust*

DEUS   Pees unto yowe evermore myght be,
    Drede you noght, for I am hee.   *Dread*

PETRUS   On Goddis name, *benedicité*,   *Praise God (or: Bless you)*
    What may this mene?

JACOBUS Itt is a sperite, forsothe thynketh me,   *ghost*
36   That dose us tene.   *harm*

JOHANNES A sperite it is, that trowe I right,
         All thus appered here to oure sight;
         Itt makis us madde of mayne and myght,   *power*
40   So it us flaied,   *frightened*
         Yone is the same that broughte the light
         That us affraied.   *frightened us*

DEUS What thynke ye, madmen, in youre thought?
         What mournyng in youre hertis is brought?   *hearts*
45   I ame Criste, ne drede you noght,
         Her may ye se
         The same body that has you bought   *purchased*
         Uppon a tre.   *cross*

         That I am comen you here to mete,
50   Behalde and se myn handis and feete,
         And grathely gropes my woundes wete   *directly touch*
         Al that here is;
         Thus was I dight youre balis to beete   *put [to death] your misery; relieve*
         And bring to blis.

55   For yowe thusgatis thanne have I gone;   *in that manner*
         Felys me grathely everilkone,   *Touch; everyone*
         And se that I have flessh and bone.
         Gropes me nowe,   *Examine (i.e., Touch)*
         For so ne has sperite none,
60   That schall ye trowe.

         To garre you kenne and knowe me clere,   *cause; to know; with certainty*
         I schall you schewe ensaumpillis sere;   *examples many*
         Bringe nowe forthe unto me here
         Some of youre mette,   *food*
65   If ye amange you all in fere   *company*
         Have ought to ete.   *eat*

JACOBUS Thou luffand Lorde that laste schall ay,   *loving; always (forever)*
         Loo, here is mette that thou ete may:
         A hony kombe the soth to saye,   *honeycomb*
70   Roste fecche thertill;   *Roast fish*
         To ete therof here we thee praie   *beg*
         With full goode will.

DEUS Nowe sen ye have broughte me this mete,
         To make youre trouthe stedfast and grete   *truth*

75	And for ye schall wanhope forgete	*despair*
	And trowe in me,	*believe*
	With youe than here wol I ete,	
	That ye schalle see.	

75 And for ye schall wanhope forgete   *despair*
And trowe in me,   *believe*
With youe than here wol I ete,
That ye schalle see.

Nowe have I done, ye have sene howe,
80 Boldely etyng here with youe,
Stedfastly loke that ye trowe
Yitt in me efte,   *Still; hereafter*
And takis the remenaunte sone to you   *leftovers soon*
That her is lefte.   *here*

85 For youe thus was I revyn and rayst;   *torn; wounded*
Therfore some of my peyne ye taste   *experience*
And spekis now nowhare my worde waste,   *diminish*
That schall ye lere;   *learn*
And unto you the Holy Goste
90 Releffe you here.   *Relieve (Assist)*

Beis now trewe and trowes in me,   *Be; believe*
And here I graunte youe in youre poste: *power*
Whome that ye bynde bounden schall be   *bind bound*
Right at youre stevene,   *word*
95 And whome that ye lesid losed schal be   *loosened absolved*
Evermore in hevene.

THOMAS   Allas for sight and sorowes sadde,
Mornyng makis me mased and madde;   *Mourning; distraught*
On grounde nowe may I gang ungladde,   *go*
100 Bothe even and morne.
That hende that I my helpe of hadde   *courteous one*
His liffe has lorne.   *lost*

Lorne I have that lovely light
That was my maistir moste of myght;
105 So doulfully as he was dight   *dolefully; put [to death]*
Was never no man.
Such woo was wrought of that worthy wighte   *man*
With wondis wan.   *dark*

Wan was his wondis and wonderus wette,
110 With skelpis sore was he swongen, that swette,   *blows (lashes); dear one*
All naked nailed thurgh hande and feete.
Allas, for pyne,
That bliste, that beste my bale myght bete,   *blessed one; misery; defeat*
His liffe schulde tyne.   *end*

115	Allas, for sorowe myselffe I schende	*exhaust*
	When I thynke hartely on that hende;	
	I fande hym ay a faithfull frende,	*found*
	Trulie to telle.	
	To my brethir nowe will I wende	*brethren; go*
120	Wherso thei dwell.	

So wofull wightis was nevere none;
Oure joie and comforte is all gone,
Of mournyng may we make oure mone   *complaint*
In ilka lande.   *every nation*
125   God blisse you, brether, bloode and bone,
Same ther ye stande.   *Together*

Petrus   Welcome, Thomas, where has thou bene?
Wete thou wele withouten wene,   *Know; doubt*
Jesu oure Lorde than have we sene
130   On grounde her gang.   *here walking*

Thomas   What saie ye, men? Allas, for tene,
I trowe ye mang.   *are confused*

Johannes   Thomas, trewly it is noght to layne: *conceal*
Jesu oure Lorde is resen agayne.

Thomas   Do waie, thes tales is but a trayne   *trick*
136   Of fooles unwise.
He that was so fully slayne,
Howe schulde he rise?

Jacobus   Thomas, trewly he is on lyve   *alive*
140   That tholede the Jewes his flessh to riffe;   *suffered; tear (wound)*
He lete us fele his woundes fyve,
Oure Lorde verray.

Thomas   That trowe I nought, so motte I thryve,
Whatso ye saie.

Petrus   Thomas, we saugh his woundes wette,
146   Howe he was nayled thurgh hande and feete;
Hony and fisshe with us he eette,
That body free.

Thomas   I laye my liff it was some sperit   *wager*
150   Ye wende wer hee.   *mistook for him*

JOHANNES Nay, Thomas, thou haste misgone,   *mistaken*
  Forwhy he bad us everilkon   *asked*
  To grope hym grathely, bloode and bone   *directly*
  And flessh to feele.
155 Such thyngis, Thomas, hase sperite none,   *ghost*
  That wote ye wele.

THOMAS What, leve felawes, late be youre fare.   *leave (cease); matter (argument)*
  Till that I see his body bare
  And sithen my fyngir putte in thare
160 Within his hyde   *skin*
  And fele the wounde the spere did schere   *shear (cut)*
  Right in his syde,

  Are schalle I trowe no tales betwene.   *Before*

JACOBUS Thomas, that wounde have we seene.

THOMAS Ya, ye wotte nevere what ye mene,
166 Youre witte it wantis;   *lacks*
  Ye muste thynke no syne me thus to tene   *sin; be roused*
  And tule with trantis.   *assail; deceptions*

DEUS Pees, brethir, be unto you,
170 And Thomas, tente to me takis thou: *attention*
  Putte forthe thy fyngir to me nowe,
  Myn handis thou see,
  Howe I was nayled for mannys prowe   *benefit*
  Uppon a tree.

175 Beholde my woundis are bledand,   *bleeding*
  Here in my side putte in thi hande
  And fele my woundis and undirstande
  That this is I,
  And be no more mistrowand   *unbelieving*
180 But trowe trewly.   *believe*

THOMAS Mi Lorde, my God, full wele is me,
  A, blode of price, blessid mote thou be.   *[high] value*
  Mankynd in erth, behold and see
  This blessid blode.
185 Mercy nowe, Lorde, ax I thee,   *ask*
  With mayne and mode.   *(i.e., supernatural power)*

DEUS Thomas, for thou haste sene this sight
  That I am resen as I thee hight,
  Therfore thou trowes it, but ilka wight,

190   Blissed be thou evere,
         That trowis haly in my rising right   *believes wholly*
         And saw it nevere.

         My brethir, fonde nowe forthe in fere,   *go forth; company*
         Overe all in ilke a contré clere;   *every country*
195   My rising both ferre and nere   *far*
         And preche it schall ye.
         And my blissyng I giffe you here
         And my menghe.   *people (household)*

[42. THE ASCENSION]

The Tailoures

PETRUS O mightfull God, how standis it nowe,
         In worlde thus will was I nevere are;   *perplexed; before*
         Butte he apperes, bot I ne wote howe,   *know not*
         He fro us twynnes whanne he will fare.   *separates when; go*
5   And yitt may falle that for oure prowe   *benefit*
         And alle his wirkyng lesse and mare.   *working (efforts)*
         A, kyng of comforte, gudde arte thou,   *good*
         And lele and likand is thy lare.   *true; felicitous; lore (teaching)*

JOHANNES The missing of my maistir trewe
10   That lenghis not with us lastandly,   *remains; always*
         Makis me to morne ilke a day newe   *mourn; every; anew*
         For tharnyng of his company.   *lack*
         His peere of gudnes nevere I knewe,   *equal; goodness*
         Of myght ne wisdome yit any.

PETRUS That we hym tharne sore may us rewe,   *lose; be sorry*
16   For he luffed us full faithfully.   *loved*

         Bot yitt in all my mysselykyng,   *sorrow*
         A worde that Christe saide comfortis me;
         Oure hevynes and oure mournyng
20   He saide to joie turned schuld be.
         That joie he saide in his hetyng,   *promise*
         To reve us none schulde have no posté,   *deprive; power*
         Wherfore aboven all othir thyng
         That joie me longis to knowe and see.   *I long*

MARIA Thou, Petir, whanne my Sone was slayne
26   And laide in grave, ye wer in were   *doubt*
         Whedir he schulde rise, almoste ilkane,   *each one*

But nowe ye wotte thurgh knowyng clere.
Some that he saide schulde come is gane   *Some [things]; would happen have happened*
30 And some to come, but ilkane sere,   *each one separately*
Whedir it be to come or none,
Us awe to knowe it all in fere.   *ought; all together*

Jesus Almyghty God, my Fadir free,
In erthe thi bidding have I done
35 And clarified the name of thee,   *revealed*
To thyselffe clarifie the Sone.   *glorify*
Als thou haste geven me pleyne posté
Of ilke a flesh, graunte me my bone   *request*
That thou me gaffe myght lyffand be   *gave; living*
40 In endles liffe and with thee wonne.   *to live*

That liffe is this that hath none ende,
To knawe thee, Fadir, moste of myght,
And me thy Sone, whame thou gon sende   *whom; did*
To dye for man withouten plight;
45 Mankynde was thyne whome thou bekende   *called (summoned)*
And toke me to thi yemyng right.   *care*
I died for man, mannes misse to mende,
And unto spitous dede was dight.   *spiteful death; put*

Thy wille unto them taughte have I
50 That wolde unto my lare enclyne;   *law incline*
Mi lare have they tane buxsomly,   *taken obediently*
Schall none of them ther travaile tyne.   *harm*
Thou gaffe them me but noght forthy,   *gave; [to] me*
Yitt are they thyne als wele as myne;
55 Fleme them not fro oure companye   *Banish*
Sen thyne are myne and myne er thyne.   *Since; are yours*

Sen they are oures, if thame nede ought   *anything*
Thou helpe them, if it be thy will,
And als thou wate that I thame boght,   *know; purchased*
60 For faute of helpe latte them not spill.   *lack; bring to ruin*
Fro the worlde to take them pray I noght,
But that thou kepe thame ay fro ill,
All thois also that settis thare thoght   *are firm in their*
In erthe my techyng to fulfill.

65 Mi thythandis tane has my menghe   *tidings received; company*
To teche the pepull wher they fare.
In erthe schall thei leve aftir me   *live*
And suffir sorowes sadde and sare.
Dispised and hatted schall thei be   *hated*

70   Als I have bene, with lesse and mare,
      And suffered dede in sere degré,   *death in many ways*
      For sothfastnesse schall none them spare.   *loyalty to truth*

      Thou halowe thame, Fadir, forthy,   *bless*
      In sothfastnes so that thei may
75   Be ane as we ar, thowe and I,   *one*
      In will and werke, both nyght and day,
      And knawe that I am verilye
      Both sothfastnes and liffe alway.   *truth; life eternal*
      Be the whilke ilke man that is willy   *willing*
80   May wynne the liffe that laste schall ay.   *(i.e., everlasting life)*

      Bot ye, my postelis all bedene,   *apostles; forthwith*
      That lange has wente abowte with me,   *for a long time*
      In grete wanne trowyng have ye bene   *weakness in trusting*
      And wondir harde of hartis ar ye.   *wondrous; hearts*
85   Worthy to be reproved, I wene,
      Ar ye forsothe, and ye will see
      In als mekill als ye have sene
      My wirkyng proved and my posté.   *power*

      Whan I was dede and laide in grave,
90   Of myne upryse ye were in doute,   *resurrection*
      And some for myne uprysing strave   *argued*
      When I was laide als undir clowte   *ground*
      So depe in erthe, but sithen I have
      Ben walkand fourty daies aboute,
95   Eten with you, youre trouthe to save,   *Eaten*
      Comand emange you inne and oute.   *Coming among*

      And therfore beis no more in were   *confusion*
      Of myne upperysing, day nor nyght;
      Youre misbeleve leves ilkone seere,   *disbelief everyone abandons*
100   For witte ye wele, als man of myght
      Over whome no dede may have poure,   *death; power*
      I schall be endles liffe and right.   *eternal life; righteousness*
      But for to schewe you figure clere,   *[by] sign*
      Schewe I me thusgatis to youre sight,   *in this manner*

105   Howe man by cours of kynde schall ryse   *nature*
      Allthough he be roten ontill noght;   *decayed to nothing*
      Oute of his grave in this same wise
      At the daye of dome schall he be broght   *Last Judgment*
      Wher I schall sitte as trewe justise
110   And deme man aftir he has wroght: *judge; according to [what]*

The wikkid to wende with ther enmyse,   *enemies*
The gode to blisse thei schall be broght.   *good*

Anodir skill forsoth is this: *reason*
In a tre man was traied thurgh trayne,   *tree; betrayed; trick*
115 One man, forthy, to mende that misse   *lapse (sin)*
On a tree boght mankynde agayne.   *purchased*
In confusioune of hym and his
That falsely to forge that frawde was fayne   *ready*
Mankynde to bringe agayne to blisse,
120 His foo the fende till endles peyne.   *foe; fiend; pain*

The thirde skille is, trewly to tell,
Right als I wende als wele will seme,
So schall I come in flessh and fell   *(i.e., bodily)*
Atte the day of dome whan I schall deme
125 The goode in endles blisse to dwell,
Mi fomen fro me for to fleme   *foemen (enemies); banish*
Withouten ende in woo to well.   *suffer*
Ilke levand man here to take yeme.   *living; heed*

But intill all the worlde wendand   *going*
130 The gospell trewly preche schall ye   *preach*
Tille ilke a creatoure liffand.   *To every; living*
Who trowes, if that he baptised be,   *believes*
He schall, als yhe schall undirstande,
Be saved and of all thraldome free;   *bondage*
135 Who trowis it not, as mistrowand,   *disbelieving*
For faute of trouthe dampned is he.   *lack*

But all ther tokenyngis bedene   *signs altogether*
Schall folowe tham that trowis it right,   *believes*
In my name devellis crewell and kene   *sharp*
140 Schall thei oute caste of ilka wight,   *expel each man*
With newe tongis speke, serpentes unclene
Fordo, and if thei day or nyght
Drinke venym wik, withouten wene,   *venom deadly*
To noye thame schall it have no myght.   *annoy them*

145 On seke folke schall thei handes lay   *sick*
And wele schall thei have sone at welde;   *health; in keeping*
This poure schall thei have alway,   *power*
My menghe, bothe in towne and felde.   *company*
And witte ye wele, so schall thei
150 That wirkis my wille in youthe or elde,
A place for thame I schall purveye   *provide*
In blisse with me ay in to belde.   *dwell*

Nowe is my jornay brought till ende,
Mi tyme that me to lang was lende.   *too long*
155   To my Fadir nowe uppe I wende,
And youre Fadir that me doune sente:
Mi God, youre God, and ilk mannes frende
That till his techyng will consente   *to*
Till synneres that no synne thame schende,   *To; overcomes*
160   That mys amendis and will repente.   *sin*

But for I speke thes wordis nowe
To you, youre hartis hase hevynes,
Fullfillid all be it for youre prowe   *benefit*
That I hense wende, als nedful is.   *go*
165   And butte I wende, comes noght to yowe   *unless*
The comforteoure of comforteles.
And if I wende, ye schall fynde howe
I schall hym sende, of my goodnesse.

Mi Fadirs will fullfillid have I;
170   Therfore fareswele, ilkone seere.
I goo make youe a stede redye   *place ready*
Endles to wonne with me in feere.   *dwell*
Sende doune a clowde, Fadir, forthy
I come to thee, my Fadir deere.
175   The Fadir blissing moste myghty
Giffe I you all that leffe here.   *Give; live*

Tunc cantat angelus Ascendo ad patrem meum.[1]

MARIA   A, myghtfull God, ay moste of myght,
A selcouth sight is this to see,   *wondrous*
My Sone thus to be ravisshed right
180   In a clowde wendande uppe fro me.   *ascending up from*
Bothe is my herte hevy and light,
Hevy for swilke twynnyng schulde be   *such separation*
And light for he haldis that he hight   *holds [to] what; promised*
And thus uppe wendis in grette posté.

185   His hetyngis haldis he all bedene   *promises; forthwith*
That comfortis me in all my care,
But unto whome schall I me mene?   *address (speak)*
Thus will in worlde was I nevere   *confused; (before)*
To dwelle amonge thes Jewes kene,
190   Me to dispise will thei not spare.

---

[1] *Then the angel sings "I ascend to my Father"*

JOHANNES All be he noght in presens seene,	*Even if he is*
Yitt is he salve of ilka sare;	*remedy; every affliction*
But, lady, sen that he betoke	*since*
Me for to serve you as youre sonne,	
195 You nedis nothyng, lady, but loke	
What thyng in erthe ye will have done.	
I ware to blame if I forsoke	*am*
To wirke youre wille, midday or none,	
Or any tyme yitt of the woke.	*week*
MARIA I thanke thee, John, with wordis fune;	*?fond*
201 Mi modirhed, John, schall thou have,	*motherhood*
And for my sone I wolle thee take.	
JOHANNES That grace, dere lady, wolde I crave.	
MARIA Mi Sone sawes will I nevere forsake.	*Son's words (sayings)*
205 Itt were not semand that we strave	*appropriate; argue*
Ne contraried noght that he spake.	*contradicted*
But John, tille I be broght in grave,	
Schall thou never see my sorowe slake.	*diminish*
JACOBUS Owre worthy Lorde, sen he is wente	
210 For us, lady, als is his will,	
We thanke hym that us thee hath lente	*left behind*
With us on lyve to lenge her stille.	*remain here*
I saie for me with full concente,	*consent*
Thi likyng all will I fulfille.	*desires*
ANDREAS So wille we all with grete talent,	*resolution*
216 Forthy, lady, giffe thee noght ill.	
I ANGELUS Ye men of the lande of Galilé,	
What wondir ye to hevene lokand?	*looking*
This Jesus whome ye fro youe see	
220 Uppetane, ye schall wele undirstande,	*Ascended*
Right so agayne come doune schall he	*down*
When he so comes with woundes bledand,	*bleeding*
Who wele has wrought full gladde may be,	
Who ill has leved full sore dredand.	*dreading*
II ANGELUS Ye that has bene his servauntis trewe	
226 And with hym lengand, nyght and day,	*dwelling*
Slike wirkyng als ye with hym knew,	*Such*
Loke that ye preche it fourthe alway.	*forth*

	Youre mede in hevene beis ilke day newe,	*reward; is*
230	And all that servis hym wele to paye;	*satisfy*
	Who trowes you noght, it schall thame rewe,	*trusts; be sorry*
	Thei mon have peyne encresand ay.	*increasing always*

JACOBUS Loved be thou, Lorde, ay, moste of myght   *Praised*
    That thus, in all oure grete disease,   *discomfort (misery)*
235 Us comfortist with thyne aungellis bright.
    Nowe aught ther Jewes thare malise meese   *malice assuage*
    That sawe thameselve this wondir sight
    Thus nere thame wroght undir ther nose.
    And we have mater day and nyght,   *matter*
240 Oure God more for to preyse and plese.

ANDREAS Nowe may ther Jewes be all confused
    If thai onthinke thame inwardly   *reflect on them*
    Howe falsely thei have hym accused
    And sakles schente thurgh ther envy.   *innocent killed*
245 Ther falsed, that thei long have used,   *falsehood*
    Nowe is it proved here opynly.
    And they were of this mater mused,   *conscious*
    Itt schulde thame stirre to aske mercy.   *encourage*

PETRUS That wille thei noght, Andrewe, late be,
250 For thei are full of pompe and pride.
    Itt may noght availe to thee ne me,
    Ne none of us with thame to chide.
    Prophite to dwelle can I none see,   *Profitable; dwell [among them]*
    Forthy late us no lenger bide   *let; longer abide*
255 But wende we unto seere contré   *various countries*
    To preche thurgh all this worlde so wide.

JOHANNES That is oure charge, for that is beste
    That we lenge nowe no lenger here,   *remain; longer*
    For here gete we no place of reste   *have*
260 To lenge so nere the Jewes poure.   *dwell*
    Us to fordo thei will thame caste,   *attempt*
    Forthy come forthe, my lady dere,
    And wende us hense, I am full preste   *(i.e., in haste)*
    With you to wende with full goode chere.

265 Mi triste is nowe ever ilk a dele   *trust; entirely*
    In yowe to wirke aftir youre counsaill.

JACOBUS Mi lady dere, that schall ye fele   *experience*
    In oght that evere us may availe;

	Oure comforte, youre care to kele	*assuage*
270	Whill we may leve we schall not faile.	*live*

MARIA Mi brethir dere, I traste itt wele,   *trust (believe)*
Mi Sone schall quyte you youre travaile.   *requite; [for] your effort*

PETRUS To Jerusalem go we agayne
And loke what fayre so aftir fall;   *events; befall (happen)*
275   Oure Lorde and maistir moste of mayne,
He wisse youe and be with youe all.   *direct*

[43. PENTECOST]

The Potteres

PETRUS Brethir, takes tente unto my steven,   *Brethren; pay attention; speech*
Thanne schall ye stabily undirstande   *firmly*
Oure maistir hende is hente to hevyn   *gracious; received into*
To reste there on his Fadirs right hande.
5   And we are leved alyve, ellevyn,   *left alive, eleven*
To lere his lawes lely in lande.   *teach; faithfully*
Or we begynne us muste be even   *Before; an even [number]*
Ellis are owre werkis noght to warande.   *Or; matter*
For parfite noumbre it is none,   *perfect*
10   Off elleven for to lere,   *inquire*
Twelve may be asoundir tone   *apart taken*
And settis in parties seere.   *several*
Nobis precepit Dominus predicare populo et testificare
quia prope est judex vivorum et mortuorum.[1]

15   Oure Lord comaunded us, more and lesse,
To rewle us right aftir his rede;   *rule (control); advice*
He badde us preche and bere wittenesse   *bear*
That he schulde deme bothe quike and dede.   *living and dead*
To hym all prophettis prevys expresse   *prove explicitly*
20   All tho that trowis in his Godhede,   *those; believes*
Off synnes thei schall have forgiffenesse;
So schall we say mekill rede.   *great counsel*
And senne we on this wise   *since*
Schall his counsaile discrie,   *proclaim*
25   Itt nedis we us avise   *advise*
That we saye noght serely.   *differently*

---

[1] Lines 13–14: *The Lord commanded us to teach to the people, and to testify / that he will be judge of the living and the dead.*

JOHANNES   Serely he saide that we schulde wende   *Surely*
  In all this worlde his will to wirke,
  And be his counsaile to be kende   *known*
30 He saide he schulde sette haly kirke.   *establish holy Church*
  But firste he saide he schulde doune sende
  His sande, that we schuld noght be irke,   *messenger; oppressed*
  His Haly Gaste on us to lende
  And make us to melle of materes mirke.   *be concerned with; obscure*
35 Us menis he saide us thus   *We remember*
  Whan that he fared us froo: *went away from*
  Cum venerit paraclitus
  Docebit vos omnia.[1]

JACOBUS   Ya, certaynely, he saide us soo,
40 And mekill more thanne we of mene: *(i.e., have known)*
  Nisi ego abiero,   *Unless I go away*
  Thus tolde he oftetymes us betwene.
  He saide forsoth, "But if I goo
  The Holy Goste schall not be sene
45 *Et cum assumptus fuero*;   *And after I have ascended*
  Thanne schall I sende you comforte clene."
  Thus tolde he holy howe   *entirely*
  That oure dedis schulde be dight.   *done*
  So schall we trewly trowe   *believe*
50 He will holde that he us highte.   *promised*

IV APOSTOLUS   He highte us fro harme for to hyde
  And holde in hele both hede and hende   *well-being; head; hand*
  Whanne we take that he talde that tyde,   *told; time*
  Fro all oure foois it schall us fende.   *foes; defend*
55 But thus in bayle behoves us bide   *misery*
  To tyme that sande till us be sende.   *messenger*
  The Jewis besettis us in ilke a side   *assail*
  That we may nowdir walke nor wende.   *neither*

V APOSTOLUS   We dare noght walke for drede
60 Or comforte come us till;
  Itt is moste for oure spede   *benefit*
  Here to be stokyn still.   *stock*

MARIA   Brethir, what mene ye you emelle   *thus*
  To make mournyng at ilk a mele?   *continually*
65 My Sone that of all welthe is well,
  He will you wisse to wirke full wele.   *direct*

---

[1] Lines 37–38: *Whereas the Paraclete will come / to teach you all things.*

	For the tente day is this to telle	*tenth; count*
	Sen he saide we schull favoure fele.	*experience*
	Levys wele that lange schall it not dwell,	*Relieve; long [in time]*
70	And therfore drede you nevere a dele,	
	But prayes with harte and hende	*pray*
	That we his helpe may have;	
	Thanne schall it sone be sende,	*soon*
	The sande that schall us save.	*messenger*

I DOCTOR Harke, maistir, for Mahoundes peyne,
76 Howe that thes mobbardis maddis nowe;   *fools (villains) rave*
Ther maistir that oure men have slayne
Hase garte thame on his trifullis trowe.   *made; lies trust*

II DOCTOR The lurdayne sais he leffis agayne;   *rascal; lives*
80 That mater may thei nevere avowe,   *assert*
For as thei herde his prechyng pleyne,   *plain*
He was away, thai wiste noght howe.   *know not*

I DOCTOR They wiste noght whenne he wente;
Therfore fully thei faile
85 And sais tham schall be sente   *to them*
Grete helpe thurgh his counsaille.

II DOCTOR He myghte nowdir sende clothe nor clowte;   *piece of cloth*
He was nevere but a wrecche alway.
But samme oure men and make a schowte,   *gather; shout*
90 So schall we beste yone foolis flaye.   *frighten*

I DOCTOR Nay, nay, than will thei dye for doute.
I rede we make noght mekill dray   *riot (disturbance)*
But warly wayte when thai come oute   *surreptitiously*
And marre thame thanne, if that we may.   *harm*

II DOCTOR Now, certis, I assente thertille,
96 Yitt wolde I noght thei wiste;   *knew*
Yone carles than schall we kill   *churls (peasants)*
But thei liffe als us liste.   *Unless; live; wish*

Angelus tunc cantare Veni creator spiritus.[1]

MARIA Honnoure and blisse be ever nowe
100 With worschippe in this worlde alwaye
To my soverayne Sone, Jesu,

---

[1] *Then the angel shall sing "Come Holy Spirit"*

	Oure Lorde allone that laste schall ay.	*be everlasting*
	Nowe may we triste his talis ar trewe	*believe; stories (narratives)*
	Be dedis that here is done this day.	*deeds*
105	Als lange as ye his pase pursue	*As long; steps*
	The fende he fendis yow for to flay.	*[From] the fiend; prevents; flee*
	For his high Hali Gaste	*Holy Ghost*
	He lattis here on you lende,	*allows; to give*
	Mirthis and trewthe to taste	*experience*
110	And all misse to amende.	*sin (error)*

PETRUS All mys to mende nowe have we myght, *power*
This is the mirthe oure maistir of mente;
I myght noght loke, so was it light, *it was so*
A, loved be that Lorde that itt us lente.
115 Now hase he holden that he us highte, *kept; promised*
His Holy Goste here have we hente, *received*
Like to the sonne itt semed in sight, *sun*
And sodenly thanne was itt sente.

II APOSTOLUS Hitt was sente for oure sele, *spiritual health*
120 Hitt giffis us happe and hele; *It gives; good fortune; health*
Methynke slike forse I fele, *such power*
I myght felle folke full feele. *many; overcome*

III APOSTOLUS We have force for to fighte in felde
And favour of all folke in feere, *all together*
125 With wisdome in this worlde to welde, *wield (use)*
Be knowing of all clergye clere. *By knowledge; clearly*

IV APOSTOLUS We have bewteis to be oure belde *virtues; protection*
And langage nedis us none to lere *learn*
That Lorde us awe yappely to yelde *ought readily; yield up*
130 That us has yemed unto this yere. *guarded; year*

V APOSTOLUS This is the yere of grace
That musteris us emang, *manifests; among*
As aungellis in this place
That sais thus in ther sange. *song*

I APOSTOLUS In thare singing saide thei thus
136 And tolde ther talis betwene them two,
Veni creator spiritus,
mentes tuorum visita.[1]
Thei praied the Spirite come till us

---

[1] Lines 137–38: *Come, Holy Spirit, / visit the souls of your own [people].*

140 And mende oure myndis with mirthis ma, *joys more*
That lered thei of oure Lorde Jesus, *taught*
For he saide that itt schulde be swa.

II APOSTOLUS He saide he schulde us sende
His Holy Goste fro hevyn
145 Oure myndis with mirthe to mende:
Nowe is all ordand evyn. *come to pass*

III APOSTOLUS Even als he saide schulde to us come,
So has bene schewid unto oure sight, *been shown*
Tristicia implevit cor vestrum, *Sorrow will fill your heart*
150 Firste sorowe in herte he us hight; *promised*
Sed convertetur in gaudium; *But will be converted into joy*
Sen saide he that we schulde be light. *Then; without care*
Nowe that he saide us, all and summe, *told; some*
Is mefid emange us thurgh his myght. *occurred among*

IV APOSTOLUS His myght with mayne and mode *(i.e., strength of will)*
156 May comforte all mankynde.

I DOCTOR Harke, man, for Mahoundes bloode,
Ther men maddis oute of mynde. *are insane*

Thei make carpyng of ilke contré *talk; every country*
160 And leris langage of ilk a lande. *have learned*

II DOCTOR They speke oure speche als wele as we
And in ilke a steede it undirstande. *place; understand it*

I DOCTOR And alle are noght of Galilee
That takis this hardinesse on hande. *presumptuous action*
165 Butt thei are drounken, all these menghe, *drunk; company of men*
Of muste or wyne, I wolle warande. *new wine; warrant*

II DOCTOR Nowe certis this was wele saide,
That makis ther mynde to marre;
Yone faitours schall be flaied *deceivers; punished*
170 Or that thei flitte aught ferre. *Before; flee; any farther*

IV APOSTOLUS Harke, brethir, waites wele aboute,
For in oure fayre we fynde no frende. *affair (matter)*
The Jewes with strengh are sterne and stoute
And scharpely schapes them us to schende. *intends*

I APOSTOLUS Oure maistir has putte alle perellis oute *perils*
176 And fellid the falsed of the fende. *destroyed; falsehood*

Undo youre dores and haves no doute,
For to yone warlowes will we wende.   *warlocks; go*

II APOSTOLUS   To wende have we no drede,
180   Nought for to do oure dette,   *if for; debt (obligation)*
      For to nevyn that is nede   *say; needful*
      Shall none on lyve us lette.   *alive; prevent*

PETRUS   Ye Jewez that in Jerusalem dwelle,
           Youre tales are false, that schall ye fynde.
185   That we are dronken we here you telle
      Because ye hope we have bene pynnyd.   *tormented*
      A prophette preved, his name is Johell,   *proved; Joel*
      A gentill Jewe of youre awne kynde,   *own tribe*
      He spekis thus in his speciall spell   *discourse*
190   And of this matere makis he mynde.   *he brings to mind*
      Be poyntis of prophicie
      He tolde full ferre before,   *long*
      This may ye noght denye,
      For thus his wordis wore: *were*
195   *Et erit in novissimus diebus, dicit dominus,*
      effundam de spiritu meo super omnem carnem.[1]

III APOSTOLUS   Loo, losellis, loo, thus may ye lere   *wretches; learn*
            Howe youre elders wrotte alway.   *wrote*
            The Holy Goste have we tane here   *received*
200   As youre awne prophettis prechid ay.   *own*

IV APOSTOLUS   Hitt is the myght of oure maistir dere,
            All dedis that here are done this daye: *deeds*
            He giffis us myght and playne power   *gives*
            To conclude all that ye can saie.

I DOCTOR   There men hase mekill myght
206   Thurgh happe thei here have tone.   *taken (received)*

II DOCTOR   Wende we oute of ther sight
            And latte them even allone.   *leave*

I APOSTOLUS   Nowe, brethir myne, sen we all meffe   *go forth*
210   To teche the feithe to foo and frende,
      Oure tarying may turne us to mischeffe,

---

[1] Lines 196–96: *And it shall come to pass, in the last days, saith the Lord, / I will pour out of my Spirit upon all flesh.*

    Wherfore I counsaille that we wende
    Untille Oure Lady and take oure leve.

II Apostolus Sertis so woll we with wordis hende.
215   Mi Lady, takis it noght to greve;
    I may no lenger with you lende.   *remain*
    .   .   .   [four lines missing]

Maria Nowe, Petir, sen itt schall be soo
    That ye have diverse gatis to gang,   *ways; go*
    Ther schall none dere you for to doo   *harm*
220   Whils my Sone musteris you emang.   *manifests*
    Butt John and Jamys, my cosyns twoo,
    Loke that ye lenge not fro me lange.   *linger; long*

Johannes Lady, youre wille in wele and woo,   *well-being*
    Itt schall be wroght, ellis wirke we wrang.   *or else; wrong*

Jacobus Lady, we bothe are boune   *obliged*
226   Atte youre biddyng to be.

Maria The blissing of my Sone
    Be boith with you and me.

[44. The Death of Mary]

The Draperes

Gabriel Hayle, myghtfull Marie, Godis modir so mylde,
    Hayle be thou, roote of all reste, hayle be thou ryall.   *royal*
    Hayle floure and frewte noght fadid nor filyd,   *flower; fruit; defiled*
    Haile, salve to all synnefull; nowe saie thee I schall,   *remedy*
5   Thy Sone to thiselve me has sente
    His sande, and sothly he saies,   *messenger; truthfully*
    No lenger than ther thre dayes
    Here lefte thee this liffe that is lente.   *life; given*

    And therfore he biddis thee loke that thou blithe be,   *glad*
10   For to that bigly blisse that berde will thee bring   *great; Lord*
    There to sitte with hymselve, all solas to see,
    And to be crowned for his quene and he hymselve kyng
    In mirthe that evere schall be newe.   *joy*
    He sendis to thee worthely, iwis,
15   This palme oute of paradise
    In tokenyng that it schall be trewe.   *sign; true*

MARIA   I thanke my Sone semely of all his sandis sere;   *many messages*
    Unto hym lastandly be ay lovyng   *everlastingly; praising*
    That me thus worthely wolde menske on this manere   *honor*
20 And to his bigly blisse my bones for to bringe.   *perfect*
    But, gode ser, nevenes me thi name?   *say to me*

GABRIELL   Gabriell, that baynly ganne bringe   *did*
    The boodworde of his bering,   *message; bearing*
    Forsothe, Lady, I ame the same.

MARIA   Nowe, Gabriell, that sothly is fro my Sone sent,
26 I thanke thee ther tythyngis thou tellis me untill,
    And loved be that Lorde of the lane that has me lente,   *gift; given*
    . . .   [line missing]
    And dere Sone, I beseke thee,   *beseech*
    Grete God, thou graunte me thi grace,
30 Thyne appostelis to have in this place
    That thei at my bering may be.   *burial (funeral)*

GABRIELL   Nowe, foode faireste of face, most faithfull and fre,   *person*
    Thyne askyng thi Sone has graunte of his grace,   *[For] your asking; has granted*
    And saies all same in sight ye schall see   *together*
35 All his appostelis appere in this place
    To wirke all thi will at thi wending.   *passing away*
    And sone schall thi peynes be paste   *finished*
    And thou to be in liffe that schall laste
    Evermore withouten any ending.

JOHANNES   Marie, my modir, that mylde is and meke
41 And cheffe chosen for chaste, nowe telle me, what chere?   *chief; chastity*

MARIA   John, sone, I saie thee forsothe I am seke;   *sick*
    My swete Sone sonde I hente, right nowe it was here   *message; received*
    And douteles he saies I schall dye.   *without doubt*
45 Within thre daies, iwis,
    I schall be beldid in blisse   *sheltered*
    And come to his awne company.   *own*

JOHANNES   A, with thi leve, Lady, thou nevene it me noght,   *speak*
    Ne telle me no tydingis to twynne us in two,   *separate*
50 For be thou, blissid birde, unto bere broght   *Lady; bier*
    Evermore whils I wonne in this worlde will me be full woo;   *dwell*
    Therfore lete it stynte, and be still.   *cease*

MARIA   Nay John, sone, myselve nowe I see.   *son*
    Atte Goddis will moste it nedis be;
55 Therfore be it wroght at his will.

JOHANNES A, worthy, when thou art wente will me be full woo,

But God giffe the appostelis wiste of thi wending.   *knowledge*

MARIA Yis John, sone, for certayne schall it be so.   *Yes*

All schall thei hardely be here at myne ending.   *forthwith*

60   The sonde of my Sone saide me thus,   *messenger*

That sone schall my penaunce be paste   *soon*

And I to be in liffe that evere schall laste,

Than baynly to belde in that blisse.   *willingly; dwell*

PETRUS O God, omnipotent, the giffer of all grace,

65   *Benedicite Dominus*, a clowde now full clere   *Praise God*

Umbelappid me in Jude prechand as I was,   *Encircled; Judea preaching*

And I have mekill mervayle how that I come here.

JACOBUS A, sesse, of this assemelyng can I noght saie   *cease; assembling*

Howe and in what wise that we are here mette,

70   Owthir myrthe or of mornyng mene wele it maye   *Either joy; mourning*

For sodenly in sight here sone was I sette.

ANDREAS A, bredir, be my wetand and iwisse so wer we   *so far as I know*

In diverse landes lely I wotte we were lente,

And how we are semelid thus can I noght see   *assembled*

75   But as God of his sande has us same sente.   *message; together*

JOHANNES A, felawes, late be youre fare,   *matter*

For as God will it moste nedis be,

That pereles is of posté,   *peerless; power*

His myght is to do mekill mare.   *much more*

80   For Marie, that worthy, schall wende now, I wene,

Unto that bigly blisse that high barne baynly us boght   *person; willingly us purchased*

That we in hir sight all same myght be sene   *together; seen*

Or sche dissever us froo, hir Sone sche besoght.   *Ere; separate herself*

And thus has he wroght atte hir will

85   Whanne sche shal be broght on a bere   *bier*

That we may be neghand hir nere   *coming near her*

This tyme for to tente hir untill.   *attend*

MARIA Jesu, my darlyng that ding is and dere,   *worthy*

I thanke thee my dere Sone of thi grete grace

90   That I all this faire felawschip atte hande nowe has here,

That thei me some comforte may kythe in this case.   *show*

This sikenes it sittis me full sare;   *sickness; sore*

My maidens, take kepe nowe on me

And caste some watir uppon me.

95   I faynte, so febill I fare.

I ANCILLA   Allas, for my Lady that lemed so light   *shone; brightly*
    That evere I leved in this lede thus longe for to lende,   *lived; place (land)*
    That I on this semely schulde se such a sight.   *beautiful one*

II ANCILLA   Allas, helpe, sche dyes in oure hende.   *hands*
100   A, Marie, of me have thou mynde
    . . .   [line missing]
    Some comforte us two for to kythe,
    Thou knowes we are comen of thi kynde.   *people*

MARIA   What ayles yow women for wo thus wynly to wepe?   *excessively*
    Yhe do me dere with youre dynne, for me muste nedis dye.   *harm; crying*
105   Yhe schulde, whenne ye saw me so slippe and slepe,   *(i.e., go to sleep)*
    Have lefte all youre late and lette me lye.   *your fuss*
    John, cosyne, garre thame stynte and be still.   *make; to stop*

JOHANNES   A, Marie, that mylde is of mode,   *mood*
    When thi Sone was raised on a rode,   *cross*
110   To tente thee he toke me thee till,   *attend*

    And therfore at thi bidding full bayne will I be.   *ready*
    Iff ther be oght, modir, that I amende may,
    I pray thee, myldest of mode, meve thee to me,   *speak*
    And I schall, dereworthi dame, do it ilke a daye.   *excellent; this same day*

MARIA   A, John, sone, that this peyne were overe paste.   *passed over (concluded)*
116   With goode harte ye alle that are here
    Praies for me faithfully in feere,   *Pray; all together*
    For I mon wende fro you as faste.   *must go*

I JUDEUS   A, foode fairest of face, moste faithfull to fynde,   *person*
120   Thou mayden and modir that mylde is and meke,   *humble*
    As thou arte curtaise and comen of oure kynde   *courteous*
    All oure synnes for to sesse thi Sone thou beseke   *cease; beseech*
    With mercy to mende us of mys.   *sin (error)*

II JUDEUS   Sen thou, Lady, come of oure kynne,
125   Thou helpe us nowe, thou veray virginne,
    That we may be broght unto blisse.

MARIA   Jesu, my Sone, for my sake beseke I thee this,
    As thou arte gracious and grete God, thou graunte me thy grace.
    Thei that is comen of my kynde and amende will there mys,   *people*
130   Nowe specially thou thame spede and spare thame a space,   *assist*
    And be ther belde, if thi willis be;   *their defender*
    And dere Sone, whane I schall dye,

I pray thee than, for thi mercy,
The fende thou latte me noght see.   *fiend*

135 And also, my blissid barne, if thi will be,
I sadly beseke thee, my Sone, for my sake,   *solemnly*
Men that are stedde stiffely in stormes or in see   *steadfast; sea*
And are in will wittirly my worschippe to awake   *willing wisely*
And thanne nevenes my name in that nede,   *call on*
140 Thou late thame not perissh nor spille;   *allow them; perish*
Of this bone, my Sone, at thi will,   *request*
Thou graunte me specially to spede.

Also, my bliste barne, thou graunte me my bone,
All that are in newe or in nede and nevenes me be name,   *trouble; call on me by*
145 I praie thee, Sone, for my sake, thou socoure thame sone,
In alle ther schoures that are scharpe thou shelde thame fro schame.   *troubles; shield*
And women also in thare childing,   *their childbirth*
Nowe speciall thou thame spede,
And if so be thei die in that drede,   *dread*
150 To thi blisse thane baynly thou thame bringe.

JESUS   Marie, my modir, thurgh thee myght nowe of me
For to make thee in mynde with mirthe to be mending,
Thyne asking all haly here heete I nowe thee.   *wholly; promise*
But modir, the fende muste be nedis at thyne endyng
155 In figoure full foule for to fere thee;   *form; frighten*
Myne aungelis schall than be aboute thee.
And therfore, dere dame, thou thar noght doute thee,   *worry yourself*
For douteles thi dede schall noght dere thee.   *death; harm*

And therfore, my modir, come myldely to me,
160 For aftir the Sonne my sande will I sende,   *messenger*
And to sitte with myselfe all solas to se
In aylastand liffe in likyng to lende.   *everlasting; bliss to dwell*
In this blisse schall be thi bilding,   *dwelling*
Of mirth schall thou nevere have missing
165 But evermore abide in my blissing.
All this schall thou have at thi welding.   *wielding (control)*

MARIA   I thanke thee, my swete Sone, for certis I am seke.
I may noght now meve me, for mercie almoste   *move (speak)*
To thee, Sone myne that made me, thi maiden so meke,
170 Here thurgh thi grace, God Sone, I giffe thee my goste.   *through; spirit*
Mi sely saule I thee sende   *simple*
To hevene that is highest on heghte;
To thee, Sone myne, that moste is of myght,
Ressayve it here into thyne hande.   *Receive*

JESUS Myne aungellis lovely of late, lighter than the levene,		*aspect; brighter; lightning*
176	Into the erthe wightly I will that ye wende	*humanly*
	And bringe me my modir to the highest of hevene	
	With mirthe and with melody hir mode for to mende,	
	For here schall hir blisse never be blynnande.	*ceasing*
180	Mi modir schall myldely be me	*meekly by*
	Sitte nexte the high Trinité	
	And nevere in two to be twynnand.	*separated*

I ANGELUS Lorde, atte thi bidding full bayne will I be,		*ready*
	That floure that nevere was fadid full fayne will we fette.	*flower; gladly; bring*

II ANGELUS And atte thi will, gode Lorde, wirke will we		
186	With solace on ilke side that semely umsitte.	*of that lovely one be seated around*

III ANGELUS Latte us fonde to hir faste hir fors to deffende,		*go; strength*
	That birde for to bringe unto this blis bright.	*Lady*
	Body and sawle we schall hir assende	
190	To regne in this regally be regentte full right.	*reign; dominion*

IV ANGELUS To blisse that birde for to bringe,		*Lady*
	Nowe Gabriell, late us wightly be wendand;	*let; going*
	This maiden mirthe to be mendand	*joy; mending*
	A semely song latte us sing.	*let*

Cum uno diabolo.   *With one devil*

Et cantant antiphona, scilicet, Ave regina celorum.[1]

[44A. THE FUNERAL OF THE VIRGIN ("FERGUS")]

The Lynwevers

[Text not entered in Register]

[45. THE ASSUMPTION OF THE VIRGIN (THOMAS APOSTOLUS)]

The Wefferes

THOMAS In waylyng and weping, in woo am I wapped,		*engulfed*
	In site and in sorowe, in sighing full sadde,	*In sadness*
	Mi Lorde and my luffe, loo, full lowe is he lapped:	*love; brought low*

---

[1] *And they shall sing an antiphon, for example, "Hail, queen of heaven"*

That makes me to mourne nowe full mate and full madde. *distraught*

5 What harling and what hurlyng that hedesman he hadde, *buffeting; violence; leader*

What breking of braunches ware brosten aboute hym, *breaking; were broken*

What bolnyng with betyng of brothellis full badde. *swelling; beating; worthless fellows*

Itt leres me full lely to love hym and lowte hym, *teaches; worship*

That comely to kenne. *gracious one; know*

10 Goddis Sone Jesus,

He died for us;

That makes me thus

To mourne amange many men. *among*

Emange men may I mourne for the malice thei mente *intended*

15 To Jesus, the gentillest of Jewes generacioun. *lineage*

Of wisdome and witte were the waies that he wente

That drewe all tho domesmen derffe indignacioun, *those judges' hostile*

For douteles full dere was his diewe dominacioun. *costly; rightful*

Unkyndely thei kidde them ther kyng for to kenne *showed; know*

20 With carefull comforth and colde recreacioun, *grievous; unhappy*

For he mustered his miracles amonge many men, *performed*

And to the pepull he preched.

But the Pharases fers *fierce*

All his resouns revers, *turn around*

25 And to ther hedesmen rehers *leaders report*

That untrewe were the tales that he teched.

He teched full trewe, but the tirauntes were tened, *tyrants; angry*

For he reproved ther pride, thai purposed thame preste *planned them quickly*

To mischeve hym, with malis in ther mynde have thei menyd, *harm; meant*

30 And to accuse hym of cursednesse the caistiffis has caste. *wickedness; endeavored*

Ther rancoure was raised, no renke might it reste, *man*

Thai toke hym with treasoune, that turtill of treuthe; *turtledove; truth*

Thei fedde hym with flappes, with fersnesse hym feste, *blows; [held] fast*

To rugge hym, to riffe hym: ther reyned no rewthe. *pull violently; tear; was found; mercy*

35 Undewly thei demed hym, *Unjustly; judged*

Thei dusshed hym, thei dasshed hym, *struck; hit violently*

Thei lusshed hym, thei lasshed hym, *beat*

Thei pusshed hym, thei passhed hym, *smashed*

All sorowe thei saide that it semed hym. *befitted*

40 Itt semed hym all sorowe, thei saide in ther seggyng. *saying*

Thei skippid and scourged hym, he skapid not with scornes. *escaped*

That he was leder and Lorde in there lawe lay no leggyng,[1]

But thrange on and thristed a croune of thik thornes. *pressed; thrust down*

Ilk tag of that turtill so tatterid and torne es *tiny piece; turtledove*

---

[1] *That he was leader and Lord in their law made no difference*

45   That that blissid body blo is and bolned for betyng,   *livid; swollen; beating*
     Yitt the hedesmen to hynge hym with huge hydous hornes   *rulers; hang; hideous*
     As brothellis or bribours were belyng and bletyng.   *swindlers; bellowing; bleating*
     "Crucifie hym," thei cried.
     Sone Pilate in parlement   *Soon*
50   Of Jesus gaffe jugement,   *gave*
     To hynge hym the harlottis hym hente;   *took hold*
     Ther was no deide of that domesman denyed.   *deed (hit); not executed*

     Denyed not that domesman to deme hym to dede,
     That frendly faire foode that nevere offended.   *person*
55   Thei hied thame in haste than to hynge uppe there heede,   *hurried; head (leader)*
     What woo that thei wroghte hym no wyght wolde have wende it.   *man; thought*
     His true titill thei toke thame no tome for to attende it,   *legal rights; time; consider*
     But as a traitour atteynted thei toled hym and tuggid hym;   *convicted; pulled*
     Thei schonte for no schoutis his schappe for to schende it,   *held back; figure; injure*
60   Thei rasid hym on rode als full rasely thei rugged hym.   *cross; brutally*
     Thei persed hym with a spere   *pierced; spear*
     That the blode riall   *royal*
     To the erthe gun fall,   *did*
     In redempcion of all
65   That his lele lawes likis to lere.   *true; learn*

     To lere he that likis of his lawe that is lele
     Mai fynde in oure frende here full faithfull feste,   *feast (spiritual)*
     That wolde hynge thus on hight to enhaunce us in hele   *hang; improve; well-being*
     And by us fro bondage by his bloode that is beste.   *buy*
70   Than the comforte of oure companye in kares were keste,   *cares; plunged*
     But that Lorde so allone wolde not leffe us full longe.   *leave*
     On the thirde day he rose right with his renkis to reste;   *men*
     Both flessh and fell fersly that figour gon fange   *in the body; figure did take*
     And to my brethir gonne appere.   *brethren; did appear*
75   Thai tolde me of this,
     Bot I leved amys;   *believed amiss (wrongly)*
     To rise flesshly, iwis,
     Methought that it paste mans poure.   *passed; power*

     But the poure of that prince was presiously previd   *expensively proved*
80   Whan that soverayne schewed hymselffe to my sight.
     To mene of his manhode my mynde was all meved,   *think; moved*
     But that reverent redused me be resoune and be right.   *disabused*
     The woundes full wide of that worthy wight,
     He frayned me to fele thame, my faith for to feste,   *asked; secure*
85   And so I did douteless, and doune I me dight;   *(i.e., reverenced)*
     I bende my bak for to bowe and obeyed hym for beste.
     So sone he assendid   *soon; ascended*
     Mi felaus in feere   *all together*

	Ware sondered sere,	[sent] apart
90	If thai were here	
	Mi myrthe were mekill amended.	

	Amendid were my mirthe with that meyné to mete,	company
	Mi felaus in fere for to fynde woll I fonde;	fellows; attempt
	I schall nott stedde in no stede but in stall and in strete,	remain; place; street
95	Grath me be gydis to gette thame on grounde.	Directly; guides; come to them
	O soverayne, how sone am I sette here so sounde!	safe
	This is the Vale of Josophat, in Jury so gente.	Josephat; Jewry
	I will steme of my stevene and sted here a stounde,	control; voice; stay; time
	For I am wery for walkyng the waies that I wente	
100	Full wilsome and wide.	desolate
	Therfore I kaste	cast (decide)
	Here for to reste;	
	I halde it beste	
104	To buske on this banke for to bide.	hasten

[**ANGELS, *singing***] *Surge proxima mea columba*
mea tabernaculum glorie vasculum vite, templum celeste.[1]

I Angelus Rise, Marie, thou maiden and modir so milde.

II Angelus Rise, lilly full lusty, thi luffe is full likand. *lily; lovely; desirable*

III Angelus Rise, chefteyne of chastité, in chering thi childe. *chief; suckling*

IV Angelus Rise, rose ripe redolent, in reste to be reynand. *reigning*

V Angelus Rise, douffe of that domesman all dedis is demand, *dove; deeds; judging*

VI Angelus Rise, turtour, tabernacle, and tempull full trewe. *turtledove*

VII Angelus Rise, semely in sight, of thi Sone to be semande. *lovely; fitting*

VIII Angelus Rise, grathed full goodely in grace for to grewe. *endowed; grow*

IX Angelus Rise uppe this stounde. *time (this instant)*

X Angelus Come, chosen childe.

XI Angelus Come, Marie milde.

---

[1] *Rise up, my dearest one, my dove, / tabernacle of glory, container of life, heavenly temple* (see explanatory note)

XII ANGELUS   Come, floure unfiled.   *undefiled*

VIII ANGELUS   Come uppe to the kyng to be crouned.

[ANGELS, *singing*]   *Veni de libano sponsa, veni coronaberis.*[1]

THOMAS   O glorious God, what glemes are glydand.   *gleams; gliding*
          I meve in my mynde what may this bemene?   *signify*
120   I see a babbe borne in blisse to be bidand   *youth (i.e., Lady); abiding (see note)*
          With aungelus companye, comely and clene.
          Many selcouth sitis in sertis have I sene,   *wondrous sights*
          But this mirthe and this melody mengis my mode.   *confuses*

MARIA   Thomas, do way all thi doutes bedene,
125   For I ame foundynge fourthe to my faire fode,   *going forth; child*
          I telle thee this tyde.

THOMAS   Who, my soverayne Lady?

MARIA   Ya, sertis I saie thee.

THOMAS   Whedir wendes thou, I praye thee?

MARIA   To blisse with my barne for to bide.   *child; dwell*

THOMAS   To bide with thy barne in blisse to be bidand!   *abiding*
132   Hayle, jentilest of Jesse in Jewes generacioun,   *lineage*
          Haile, welthe of this worlde all welthis is weldand,   *controlling*
          Haile, hendest enhaunsed to high habitacioun,   *most worthy*
135   Haile, derworth and dere is thi diewe dominacioun.   *worthy; dear; due*
          Haile, floure fresshe florisshed, thi frewte is full felesome.   *fruit; delicious*
          Haile, sete of oure Saveour and sege of salvacioun,   *seat; throne*
          Haile, happy to helde to, thi helpe is full helesome.   *incline; wholesome*
          Haile, pereles in plesaunce,   *peerless*
140   Haile, precious and pure,
          Haile, salve that is sure,   *[soul's] remedy*
          Haile, lettir of langure,   *preventer; sickness*
          Haile, bote of oure bale in obeyesaunce.   *remedy; obedience*

MARIA   Go to thi brethir that in bale are abiding   *sorrow*
145   And of what wise to welthe I ame wendande   *going*
          Withoute tarying thou telle thame this tithynge,
          Ther mirthe so besse mekill amendande.   *joy; is; (i.e., returning)*

---

[1] *Come forth Libanus [Lebanon], my spouse, come forth, thou shalt be crowned* (see explanatory note)

For Thomas, to me were thei tendande   *attending*
Whanne I drewe to the dede, all but thou.   *death*

Thomas   Bot I, Lady, whillis in lande I ame lendande,   *remaining*
151   Obeye thee full baynly my bones will I bowe.
Bot I, allas,
Whare was I thanne
When that barette beganne?   *anguish*
155   An unhappy manne
Both nowe and evere I was.

Unhappy, unhende am I holden at home,   *unworthy; regarded*
What drerye destonye me drewe fro that dede?

Maria   Thomas, sesse of thy sorowe, for I am sothly the same.

Thomas   That wote I wele, the worthiest that wrapped is in wede.   *clothing*

Maria   Thanne spare nott a space nowe my speche for to spede,[1]
162   Go saie them sothely, thou sawe me assendinge.

Thomas   Now douteles, derworthy, I dare not for drede,
For to my tales that I telle thei are not attendinge,
165   For no spelle that is spoken.   *word*

Maria   I schall thee schewe
A token trewe,
Full fresshe of hewe;
Mi girdill, loo, take thame this tokyn.   *token (sign)*

Thomas   I thanke thee as reverent rote of oure reste,   *root (basis)*
171   I thanke thee as stedfast stokke for to stande,   *stock*
I thanke thee as tristy tre for to treste,   *trust (rely on)*
I thanke thee as buxsom bough to thee bande,   *bound*
I thanke thee as leeffe, the lustiest in lande,   *leaf*
175   I thanke thee as bewteuous braunche for to bere,
I thanke thee as floure that nevere is fadande,   *fading*
I thanke thee as frewte that has fedde us in fere,   *fruit*
I thanke thee for evere.
If thay repreve me,   *challenge*
180   Now schall thei leve me.   *believe*
Thi blissinge giffe me   *give*
And douteles I schall do my devere.   *duty*

---

[1] *Then don't delay now my speaking for to prosper*

MARIA   Thomas, to do thanne thy devere be dressand,   *prepared*
    He bid thee his blissinge that beldis aboven,   *dwells*
185   And in sightte of my Sone ther is sittand
    Shall I knele to that comely with croune
    That who dispaire be dale or be doune   *whoever despairs; hill*
    With piteuous playnte in perellis will pray me;   *perils*
    If he swynke or swete, in swelte or in swoune,   *toil; sweat; sickness; swooning*
190   I schall sewe to my soverayne Sone for to say me   *sue (beg)*
    He schall graunte thame ther grace.
    Be it manne in his mournyng
    Or womanne in childinge,   *childbirth*
    All thes to be helpinge
195   That prince schall I praye in that place.

THOMAS   Gramercy, the goodliest grounded in grace,   *(i.e., Give thanks)*
    Gramercy, the lufliest Lady of lire,   *loveliest; form (body)*
    Gramercy, the fairest in figure and face,
    Gramercy, the derrest to do oure desire.   *most worthy*

MARIA   Farewele, nowe I passe to the pereles empire;
201   Farewele, Thomas, I tarie no tyde here.

THOMAS   Farewele, thou schynyng schappe that schyniste so schire,   *form; shines; brightly*
    Farewele, the belle of all bewtes to bide here,   *beauties*
    Farewele, thou faire foode,   *person (term of endearment)*
205   Farewele, the keye of counsaile,
    Farewele, all this worldes wele,   *well-being*
    Farewele, oure hope and oure hele,   *health*
    Farewele nowe, both gracious and goode.

[ANGELS, *singing*]   *Veni electa mea et ponam in te tronum meum*
    Quia concupivit rex speciem tuam.[1]

THOMAS   That I mette with this may here my mirthe is amend;   *maid*
210   I will hy me in haste and holde that I have hight,   *hurry; promised*
    To bere my brethir this boodeword my bak schall I bende   *message*
    And saie thame in certayne the soth of this sight.
    Be dale and be doune schall I dresse me to dight   *address*
    To I fynde of this felawschippe faithfull in fere,
215   I schall renne and reste not, to ransake full right.   *run; not rest; search*
    Lo, the menye I mente of I mete thame even here   *company*
    At hande.

---

[1] *Come, my chosen one, and I will place you on my throne / Because the king greatly desires your beauty* (see explanatory note)

God saffe you in feere,   *all together*
Say, brethir, what chere?

Petrus What dois thou here?
221   Thou may nowe of thi gatis be gangand.   *ways; going*

Thomas Why, dere brethir, what bale is begune?

Petrus Thomas, I telle thee, that tene is betidde us.   *sorrow; happened [to]*

Thomas Me forthinkith for my frendis that faithfull are foune.   *am sorry; found*

Jacobus Ya, but in care litill kyndnes thou kid us.   *misery; show*

Andreas His bragge and his boste is he besie to bid us,   *busy; tell*
227   But and ther come any cares he kepis not to kenne;   *if; sorrows; (i.e., wishes not to know)*
      We may renne till we rave or any ruth rid us   *continue; grief escape from*
      For the frenschippe he fecched us, be frith or be fenne.   *wood; fenland*

Thomas Sirs, me mervailes, I saie yowe,
231   What mevis in youre mynde.   *moves*

Johannes We can wele fynde
      Thou arte unkynde.

Thomas Nowe, pees thanne, and preve it, I pray yowe.   *peace*

Petrus That thou come not to courte here unkyndynes thou kid us,   *show*
236   Oure treuth has of-turned us to tene and to traye;   *(i.e., diverted); misery; suffering*
      This yere haste thou rakid, thi reuth wolde not ridde us,   *been away; grief; help us*
      For witte thou wele that worthy is wente on hir waye.
      In a depe denne dede is scho dolven this daye,   *grave; she buried*
240   Marie, that maiden and modir so milde.

Thomas I wate wele, iwis.   *am well aware*

Jacobus   Thomas, do way.

Andreas Itt forse noght to frayne hym, he will not be filde.[1]

Thomas Sirs, with hir have I spoken
244   Lattar thanne yee.   *More recently*

Johannes That may not bee.

---

[1] *It will not work to question him; he will not be polite*

THOMAS   Yis, knelyng on kne.

PETRUS   Thanne tite can thou telle us some token?   *quickly; sign*

THOMAS   Lo, this token full tristy scho toke me to take youe.   *trustworthy*

JACOBUS   A, Thomas, whare gate thou that girdill so gode?   *received*

THOMAS   Sirs, my message is mevand some mirthe for to make youe,[1]
251   For founding flesshly I fande hir till hir faire foode,   *walking bodily; person*
        And when I mette with that maiden it mendid my mode.
        Hir sande has scho sente youe, so semely to see.   *message; she*

ANDREAS   Ya, Thomas, unstedfaste full staring thou stode,
255   That makis thi mynde nowe full madde for to be.   *insane*
        But herken and here nowe:
        Late us loke where we laid hir
        If any folke have affraied hir.   *disturbed*

JOHANNES   Go we groppe wher we graved hir,   *search; buried*
260   If we fynde oughte that faire one in fere nowe.   *alive*

PETRUS   Behalde, nowe hidir youre hedis in haste;   *heed (give attention to)*
        This glorious and goodely is gone fro this grave.

THOMAS   Loo, to my talking ye toke youe no tente for to traste.   *did not attend; trust*

JACOBUS   A, Thomas, untrewly nowe traspassed we have;
265   Mercy full kyndely we crie and we crave.

ANDREAS   Mercye, for foule have we fautid in faye.   *wrongly; faulted [you] in faith*

JOHANNES   Mercye, we praye thee, we will not deprave.   *disparage*

PETRUS   Mercye, for dedis we did thee this daye.   *deeds; [to] you*

THOMAS   Oure Saveour so swete
270   Forgiffe you all,
        And so I schall.
        This tokyn tall   *good [in appearance]*
        Have I brought yowe youre bales to beete.   *assuage*

PETRUS   Itt is welcome, iwis, fro that worthy wight,
275   For it was wonte for to wappe that worthy virgine.   *enwrap*

---

[1] *Sirs, my message is intended to bring you some joy*

Jacobus Itt is welcome, iwis, fro that Lady so light,   *happy*
    For hir wombe wolde scho wrappe with it and were it with wynne.   *abdomen; wear; joy*

Andreas Itt is welcome, iwis, fro that salver of synne,   *healer*
    For scho bende it aboute hir with blossome so bright.

Johannes Itt is welcome, iwis, fro the keye of oure kynne,   *from; people*
281   For aboute that reverent it rechid full right.   *holy one; (i.e., was worn)*

Petrus Nowe knele we ilkone
    Upponne oure kne.

Jacobus To that Lady free.

Andreas Blissid motte sche be,
286   Ya, for scho is Lady lufsome allone.   *gracious*

Thomas Nowe, brethir, bese besie and buske to be bownand,   *busy; hurry; going*
    To Ynde will I torne me and travell to teche.   *India; return; teach*

Petrus And to Romans so royall tho renkis to be rownand   *men; speaking*
290   Will I passe fro this place, my pepull to preche.

Jacobus And I schall Samaritanus so sadly enserche,   *Samaria; solemnly search out*
    To were tham be wisdome thei wirke not in waste.   *warn*

Andreas And to Achaia full lely that lede for to leche,   *land (people); heal*
    Will hy me to helpe thame and hele thame in haste.   *hurry; heal*

Johannes This comenaunt accordis;   *agreement is suitable*
296   Sirs, sen ye will soo,
    Me muste nedis parte youe froo.   *part from you*
    To Assia will I goo.   *Asia*
    He lede you, that Lorde of all lordis.   *[May] he lead*

Thomas The Lorde of all lordis in lande schall he lede youe
301   Whillis ye travell in trouble, the trewethe for to teche,
    With frewte of oure feithe in firthe schall we fede youe,   *faith; woods; feed*
    For that laboure is lufsome, ilke lede for to leche.   *person; heal*
    Nowe I passe fro youre presence the pepull to preche,
305   To lede thame and lere thame the lawe of oure Lorde.   *lead; teach*
    As I saide, us muste asoundre and sadly enserche   *go apart; solemnly search out*
    Ilke contré to kepe clene and knytte in o corde   *in unity (accord)*
    Off oure faithe.
    That frelye foode   *noble one*
310   That died on rode

With mayne and moode,
He grath yowe be gydis full grath.   *cause (that); guides; diligent*

[46. THE CORONATION OF THE VIRGIN]

The Osteleres

JESUS   Myne aungellis that are bright and schene,   *shining*
    On my message take ye the waye
    Unto Marie, my modir clene;   *pure*
    That berde is brighter than the daye,   *Lady*
5   Grete hir wele haly bedene   *Greet; wholly forthwith*
    An to that semely schall ye saye,
    Off hevene I have hir chosen quene
    In joie and blisse that laste schall aye.

    I wille you saie what I have thoughte
10 And why that ye schall tille hir wende;
    I will hir body to me be brought
    To beilde in blisse withouten ende.   *dwell*

    Mi flesshe of hir in erthe was tone;   *taken*
    Unkindely thing it were, iwis,
15 That scho schulde bide be hire allone   *by herself*
    And I beilde here so high in blis.

    Forthy tille hir than schall ye fare
    Full frendlye for to fecche hir hedir;   *lovingly; bring; hither*
    There is nothyng that I love more
20 In blisse thanne schall we belde togedir.

I ANGELUS   O, blisful Lorde, nowe moste of myght,
    We are redye with all oure myght
    Thy bidding to fulfille,
    To thi modir, that maiden free,
25 Chosen cheffe of chastité,
    As is thy wille.

II ANGELUS   Off this message we are full fayne;   *glad*
    We are redy with myght and mayne   *power*
    Bothe be day and be nyght.
30 Hevene and erthe nowe gladde may be
    That frely foode nowe for to see   *worthy person*
    In whome that thou did light.   *(i.e., In whose womb)*

III Angelus   Lorde Jesu Criste, oure governoure,
    We are all boune atte thi bidding: *obliged*
35   With joie and blisse and grete honnoure,
    We schall thi modir to thee bringe.

IV Angelus   Hayle, the doughtir of blissid Anne,
    Thee whiche consayved thurgh the Holy Goste,   *conceived*
    And thou brought forthe both God and manne,
40   The whiche felled doune the fendis boste.   *put down; boast*

V Angelus   Haile, roote of risse, that fourthe brought   *branch; forth*
    That blissid floure, oure Saveoure,   *flower*
    The whiche that made mankynde of noght
    And brought hym uppe into his toure.   *tower (i.e., heaven)*

VI Angelus   Of thee allone he wolde be borne
46   Into this worlde of wrecchidnesse
    To save mankynde that was forlorne
    And bringe thame oute of grete distresse.

I Angelus   Thou may be gladde, bothe day and nyght
50   To se thy Sone oure Saveoure;
    He will thee croune nowe, Lady bright,
    Thou blissid modir and faire floure.

II Angelus   Marie, modir and mayden clene,
    Chosen cheffe unto thi childe,   *chief*
55   Of hevene and erthe thou arte quene;
    Come uppe nowe, Lady, meke and mylde.

III Angelus   Thi Sone has sente us aftir thee
    To bringe thee nowe unto his blisse;
    Ther schall thou belde and blithe be,   *dwell; happy*
60   Of joie and mirthe schall thou noght misse.

IV Angelus   For in his blisse withouten ende
    There schall thou alkynne solas see,   *every kind of solace*
    Thi liffe in likyng for to lende   *bliss; live*
    With thi dere Sone in Trinité.

Maria   A, blissid be God, Fadir all weldand,   *controlling*
66   Hymselffe wottith best what is to doo;   *knows*
    I thanke hym with harte and hande
    That thus his blisse wolde take me too.

    And you also, his aungellis bright
70   That fro my Sone to me is sente,

I am redy with all my myght
For to fulfille his comaundement.

V ANGELUS Go we nowe, thou worthi wight,
Unto thi Sone that is so gente; — *gracious*
75   We schall thee bringe into his sight
To croune thee quene, thus hase he mente. — *intended*

VI ANGELUS Alle hevene and erthe schall worschippe thee
And baynnely be at thi biddinge; — *obediently*
Thy joie schall evere incressid be,
80   Of solas sere than schall thou synge.

Cantando. — *[The angels] are to sing*

I ANGELUS Jesu, Lorde and heveneis Kyng, — *heaven's*
Here is thi modir thou aftir sente.
We have her brought at thi biddynge;
Take hir to thee as thou haste mente.

MARIA Jesu, my Sone, loved motte thou be.
86   I thanke thee hartely in my thought
That this wise ordand is for me, — *ordained*
And to this blisse thou haste me broght.

JESUS Haile be thou, Marie, maiden bright,
90   Thou arte my modir and I thy Sone.
With grace and goodnesse arte thou dight, — *adorned*
With me in blisse ay schall thou wonne. — *dwell*

Nowe schall thou have that I thee hight, — *promised*
Thy tyme is paste of all thi care: — *passed; trouble*
95   Wirschippe schall the aungellis bright, — *Worship [you]*
Of newe schall thou witte nevere more. — *annoyance; know (experience)*

MARIA Jesu my Sone, loved motte thou be. — *praised must*
I thanke thee hartely in my thoght
That on this wise ordand is for me — *ordained*
100   And to this blisse thou has me broght.

JESUS Come forth with me, my modir bright,
Into my blisse we schall assende
To wonne in welthe, thou worthi wight,
That neveremore schall it have ende.

105   Thi newis, modir, to neven thame nowe, — *annoyances; speak*
Are turned to joie, and soth it is

All aungellis bright thei schall thee bowe
And worschippe thee worthely, iwis.
For mekill joie, modir, had thou
110 Whan Gabriell grette thee wele be this   *greeted*
And tolde thee tristely for to trowe   *trustfully; believe*
Thou schulde consayve the kyng of blisse.

Nowe maiden, meke and modir myne,
Itt was full mekill myrthe to thee
115 That I schuld ligge in wombe of thine   *lie*
Thurgh gretyng of an aungell free.
The secounde joie, modir, was syne   *since (when)*
Withouten payne whan thou bare me.
The thirde aftir my bittir peyne
120 Fro dede on lyve thou sawe me be.   *From death to life*

The fourthe was when I stied uppe right   *climbed (went)*
To hevene unto my Fadir dere.
My modir, when thou saught that sight,
To thee it was a solas seere.
125 This is the fifte, thou worthy wight,
Of the jois this has no pere;   *peer*
Nowe schall thou belde in blisse so bright
Forever and ay, I highte thee here.   *promise*

For thou arte cheffe of chastité,
130 Off all women thou beris the floure,   *bears; flower*
Nowe schalle thou, Lady, belde with me
In blisse that schall evere indowre.   *continue*
Full high on highte in magesté
With all worshippe and all honnoures
135 Wher we schall evere samen be,   *together*
Beldand in oure bigly boures.   *commodious bowers*

Alle kynnys swetnesse is therin   *types of sweetness*
That manne uppon may thynke, or wiffe,   *woman*
With joie and blisse that nevere schall blynne;
140 Ther schall thou, Lady, lede thy liffe.   *lead*

Thou schalte be worshipped with honnoure
In hevene blisse that is so bright
With martiris and with confessouris,   *martyrs*
With all virginis, that worthy wight.   *person (i.e., Mary)*
145 Before all othere creatours
I schall thee giffe both grace and might
In hevene and erthe to sende socoure
To all that servis thee day and nyght.

I graunte thame grace with all my myght
150 Thurgh askyng of thi praier
That to thee call be day or nyght
In what disease so that thei are.   *misery*

Thou arte my liffe and my lekyng,   *liking (desire)*
Mi modir and my mayden schene.   *bright*
155 Ressayve this croune, my dere darlyng,
Ther I am kyng, thou schalte be quene.

Myne aungellis bright, a songe ye singe
In the honnoure of my modir dere,
And here I giffe you my blissing
160 Haly nowe, all in fere.   *Wholly; all together*

[47. DOOMSDAY]

Merceres

DEUS INCIPIT

Firste when I this worlde hadde wroght,
Woode and wynde and wateris wan   *dark*
And allkynne thyng that nowe is oght,   *all kinds [of]; extant*
Fulle wele methoght that I did thanne.
5   Whenne thei were made, goode me thame thoght.   *them*
Sethen to my liknes made I man,   *Then*
And man to greve me gaffe he noght;   *grieve [for] me; had no concern*
Therfore me rewis that I the worlde began.   *am sorry*

Whanne I had made man at my will,
10   I gaffe hym wittis hymselve to wisse,   *intelligence; direct*
And paradise I putte hym till
And bad hym halde it all as his.   *bid; (to) hold*
But of the tree of goode and ill
I saide, "What tyme thou etis of this,   *eat*
15   Manne, thou spedes thiselve to spill;   *destroy*
Thou arte broght oute of all blisse."

Belyve brak manne my bidding,   *Quickly broke*
He wende have bene a god therby;   *thought [to]*
He wende have wittyne of allkynne thyng,   *knowledge*
20   In worlde to have bene als wise as I.
He ete the appill I badde schulde hyng;   *hang [on the tree]*
Thus was he begilid thurgh glotony.
Sithen both hym and his ospring   *Thus; descendants*
To pyne I putte thame all forthy.   *suffering*

25	To lange and late methoghte it goode	*Too long*
	To catche thois caitiffis oute of care,	*rescue those; from misery*
	I sente my Sone with full blithe moode	
	Till erthe, to salve thame of thare sare.	*heal; sore (misery)*
	For rewthe of thame he reste on roode	*pity; cross*
30	And boughte thame with his body bare.	*ransomed*
	For thame he shedde his harte bloode,	
	What kyndinesse myght I do thame mare?	
	Sethen aftirwarde he heryed hell	*harrowed*
	And toke oute thois wrecchis that ware thareinne.	*those; were*
35	Ther faughte that free with feendis feele	*fought; worthy one; many*
	For thame that ware sounkyn for synne.	*were sunk in*
	Sethen in erthe than gonne he dwelle,	*did*
	Ensaumpill he gave thame hevene to wynne,	*Example*
	In Tempill hymselffe to teche and tell	
40	To by thame blisse that nevere may blynne.	*buy; end*
	Sethen have thei founde me full of mercye,	
	Full of grace and forgiffenesse,	
	And thei als wrecchis wittirly	*knowingly*
	Has ledde ther liffe in lithirnesse.	*wickedness*
45	Ofte have thei greved me grevously,	
	Thus have thei quitte me my kyndinesse;	*repaid*
	Therfore no lenger, sekirlye,	
	Thole will I thare wikkidnesse.	*Endure*
	Men seis the worlde but vanité,	
50	Yitt will no manne beware therby.	
	Ilke a day ther mirroure may thei se,	*Every; reflection*
	Yitt thynke thei noght that thei schall dye.	
	All that evere I saide schulde be	
	Is nowe fulfillid thurgh prophicie;	
55	Therfore nowe is it tyme to me	
	To make endyng of mannes folie.	*folly*
	I have tholed mankynde many a yere	*endured*
	In luste and likyng for to lende,	*remain*
	And unethis fynde I ferre or nere	*scarcely; far*
60	A man that will his misse amende.	*sin (error)*
	In erthe I see butte synnes seere;	*(i.e., everywhere)*
	Therfore myne aungellis will I sende	
	To blawe ther bemys, that all may here	*trumpets; hear*
	The tyme is comen I will make ende.	
65	Aungellis, blawes youre bemys belyve	*suddenly*
	Ilke a creatoure for to call;	*Every creature (person)*

	Leerid and lewde, both man and wiffe	*Learned; unlettered*
	Ressayve ther dome this day thei schall.	*judgment*
	Ilke a leede that evere hadde liffe,	*person*
70	Bese none forgetyn, grete ne small.	
	Ther schall thei see the woundes fyve	
	That my Sone suffered for them all.	
	And sounderes thame before my sight,	*separate*
	All same in blisse schall thei not be.	*All together*
75	Mi blissid childre, as I have hight,	*promised*
	On my right hande I schall thame see.	
	Sethen schall ilke a weried wight	*accursed person*
	On my lifte side for ferdnesse flee.	*left; fear*
	This day ther domys thus have I dight	*sentences; ordered*
80	To ilke a man as he hath served me.	

I ANGELUS Loved be thou, Lorde of myghtis moste, *Praised*
    That aungell made to messengere, *to be*
    Thy will schall be fulfillid in haste
    That hevene and erthe and helle schalle here.
85 Goode and ill, every ilke a gaste, *ghost (spirit)*
    Rise and fecche youre flessh that was youre feere, *fetch; companion*
    For all this worlde is broght to waste,
    Drawes to youre dome, it neghes nere. *judgment; comes near [in time]*

II ANGELUS Ilke a creature, bothe olde and yhing, *young*
90 Belyve I bidde you that ye ryse. *Quickly*
    Body and sawle with you ye bring
    And comes before the high justise,
    For I am sente fro hevene kyng
    To calle you to this grette assise; *court trial (judgment)*
95 Therfore rise uppe and geve rekenyng *give accounting*
    How ye hym served uppon sere wise. *in diverse ways*

I ANIMA BONA Loved be thou, Lorde, that is so schene *bright*
    That on this manere made us to rise,
    Body and sawle togedir clene *complete*
100 To come before the high justise.
    Of oure ill dedis, Lorde, thou not mene *speak not*
    That we have wroght uppon sere wise,
    But graunte us for thy grace bedene *forthwith*
    That we may wonne in paradise. *dwell*

II ANIMA BONA A, loved be thou, Lorde of all,
106 That hevene and erthe and all has wroght,
    That with thyne aungellis wolde us call
    Oute of oure graves hidir to be broght. *hither*

Ofte have we greved thee, grette and small,   *grieved*
110   Theraftir, Lorde, thou deme us noght,
Ne suffir us nevere to fendis to be thrall   *devils; enslaved*
That ofte in erthe with synne us soght.   *pursued*

I Anima Mala   Allas, allas, that we were borne,
So may we synfull kaytiffis say.   *caitiffs (reprobates)*
115   I here wele be this hydous horne;   *hear; hideous*
Itt drawes full nere to domesday.
Allas, we wrecchis that are forlorne
That never yitt served God to paye,   *please [him]*
But ofte we have his flesshe forsworne.   *body (in Eucharist) abjured*
120   Allas, allas, and welaway!

What schall we wrecchis do for drede,
Or whedir for ferdnes may we flee   *fright*
When we may bringe forthe no goode dede
Before hym that oure juge schall be?
125   To aske mercy us is no nede,
For wele I wotte dampned be we.
Allas, that we swilke liffe schulde lede   *such life*
That dighte us has this destonye.   *prepared for us*

Oure wikkid werkis thei will us wreye   *denounce*
130   That we wende never schuld have bene weten;   *thought; revealed*
That we did ofte full pryvely,
Appertely may we se them wreten.   *Openly; written*
Allas, wrecchis, dere mon we by,   *dearly may we purchase*
Full smerte with helle fyre be we smetyn.   *sharply; smitten*
135   Nowe mon nevere saule ne body dye,
But with wikkid peynes evermore be betyne.   *beaten*

Allas, for drede sore may we quake,
Oure dedis beis oure dampnacioune;   *are*
For oure mys menyng mon we make,   *sin moaning must*
140   Helpe may none excusacioune.   *Excuses will not help*
We mon be sette for oure synnes sake   *placed*
Forevere fro oure salvacioune   *[apart] from*
In helle to dwelle with feendes blake   *black*
Wher never schall be redempcioune.

II Anima Mala   Als carefull caitiffis may we ryse,   *As sorrowing*
146   Sore may we wringe oure handis and wepe.
For cursidnesse and for covetise
Dampned be we to helle full depe.   *deep*
Rought we nevere of Goddis servise,   *Took heed (Wrought)*
150   His comaundementis wolde we noght kepe,

But ofte than made we sacrafise
To Satanas when othir slepe.

Allas, now wakens all oure were.   *misery*
Oure wikkid werkis may we not hide,
155   But on oure bakkis us muste them bere;
Thei wille us wreye on ilke a side.   *denounce*
I see foule feendis that wille us feere,   *terrify us*
And all for pompe of wikkid pride.
Wepe we may with many a teere.
160   Allas, that we this day schulde bide.

Before us playnly bese fourth brought   *is forth*
The dedis that us schall dame bedene.   *deeds; condemn*
That eres has herde or harte has thoght   *ears; heart*
Sen any tyme that we may mene   *mean (speak of)*
165   That fote has gone or hande has wroght,
That mouthe hath spoken or ey has sene,   *seen*
This day full dere thanne bese it boght.   *dearly; is it purchased*
Allas, unborne and we hadde bene.   *if we had not been born*

III ANGELUS   Standis noght togedir, parte you in two,
170   All sam schall ye noght be in blisse.   *together*
Mi Fadir of hevene woll it be soo,   *wills*
For many of yowe has wroght amys.   *amiss*
The goode on his right hande ye goe,
The way till hevene he will you wisse.   *direct*
175   Ye weryed wightis, ye flee hym froo,   *accursed*
On his lefte hande as none of his.

DEUS   This woffull worlde is brought till ende,
Mi Fadir of hevene he woll it be;   *wills [that]*
Therfore till erthe nowe will I wende,
180   Miselve to sitte in magesté.
To deme my domes I woll descende,   *issue my judgments*
This body will I bere with me,
Howe it was dight, mannes mys to mende.   *put [to suffering]*
All mankynde there schall it see.

185   Mi postelis and my darlyngis dere,   *apostles*
The dredfull dome this day is dight.
Both heven and erthe and hell schall here   *hear*
Howe I schall holde that I have hight: *promised*
That ye schall sitte on seetis sere   *seats various*
190   Beside myselffe to se that sight,
And for to deme folke ferre and nere   *judge; far*
Aftir ther werkyng, wronge or right.   *works*

I saide also whan I you sente
To suffre sorowe for my sake,
195 All tho that wolde thame right repente   *those*
Schulde with you wende and wynly wake;   *joyfully*
And to youre tales who toke no tente   *attention*
Shulde fare to fyre with fendis blake.   *fire (flames)*
Of mercy nowe may noght be mente,
200 Butt aftir wirkyng, welth or wrake.   *well-being (bliss); retribution*

My hetyng haly schall I fullfille;   *promise wholly*
Therfore comes furth and sittis me by
To here the dome of goode and ill.   *hear*

I Apostolus   I love thee, Lord God allmyghty.
205 Late and herely, lowde and still,   *early*
To do thy bidding bayne am I;   *willing*
I obblissh me to do thi will   *oblige*
With all my myght, als is worthy.

II Apostolus   A, myghtfull God, here is it sene
210 Thou will fulfille thi forward right,   *plan rightly*
And all thi sawes thou will maynteyne.   *sayings*
I love thee, Lorde, with all my myght;
Therfore us that has erthely bene,
Swilke dingnitees has dressed and dight.   *Such honors; prepared*

Deus   Comes fourthe, I schall sitte you betwene,
216 And all fullfille that I have hight.

Hic ad sedem judicii cum cantu angelorum.[1]

I Diabolus   Felas, arraye us for to fight,   *Fellows, prepare*
And go we faste oure fee to fange.   *property (lit.: livestock); grasp*
The dredefull dome this day is dight;
220 I drede me that we dwelle full longe.

II Diabolus   We schall be sene evere in ther sight
And warly waite, ellis wirke we wrange,   *sneakily; work; wrong*
For if the domisman do us right   *judge*
Full grete partie with us schall gang.   *part (portion); go*

III Diabolus   He schall do right to foo and frende,
226 For nowe schall all the soth be sought.   *truth*
All weried wightis with us schall wende   *wicked*

---

[1] *Here he goes to the seat of judgment, with the song of angels*

To payne endles thei schall be broght.

    .   .   .   *[four lines missing]*

DEUS Ilke a creature, takes entent   *Everyone, pay attention*
230   What bodworde I to you bringe: *message*
      This wofull worlde away is wente,
      And I am come as crouned kynge.
      Mi Fadir of hevene, he has me sente
      To deme youre dedis and make ending.
235   Comen is the day of jugement,
      Of sorowe may ilke a synful synge.   *each sinful [one] sing*

      The day is comen of kaydyfnes,   *wretchedness*
      All tham to care that are unclene,   *misery*
      The day of bale and bittirnes.
240   Full longe abedyn has it bene,   *awaited*
      The day of drede to more and lesse,
      Of ire, of trymbelyng, and of tene,   *trembling; grief*
      That ilke a wight that weried is   *accursed*
      May say, "Allas, this daye is sene."

245   Here may ye see my woundes wide
      The whilke I tholed for youre mysdede   *suffered*
      Thurgh harte and heed, foote, hande, and hide *skin*
      Nought for my gilte butt for youre nede.   *guilt*
      Beholdis both body, bak, and side
250   How dere I bought youre brotherhede.
      Thes bittir peynes I wolde abide
      To bye you blisse thus wolde I bleede.   *purchase*

      Mi body was scourged withouten skill,   *reason*
      As theffe full thraly was I thretho,   *violently; threatened*
255   On crosse thei hanged me on a hill,
      Blody and bloo, as I was bette,   *livid; beaten*
      With croune of thorne, throsten full ill.   *thrust*
      This spere unto my side was sette,
      Myne harte bloode spared noght thei for to spill,
260   Manne, for thy love wolde I not lette.   *prevent [this]*

      The Jewes spitte on me spitously;
      Thei spared me no more than a theffe.   *thief*
      Whan thei me strake I stode full stilly, *struck; stood; silently*
      Agaynste tham did I nothynge greve.
265   Behalde, mankynde, this ilke is I   *same*
      That for thee suffered swilke mischeve;   *affliction*
      Thus was I dight for thy folye.   *put [to pain]*
      Man, loke, thy liffe was to me full leffe.   *dear*

Thus was I dight thi sorowe to slake,   *assauage*
270   Manne, thus behoved thee to borowed be.   *redeemed*
In all my woo toke I no wrake,   *vengeance*
Mi will itt was for the love of thee.
Man, sore aught thee for to quake,   *ought*
This dredfull day, this sight to see.
275   All this I suffered for thi sake.
Say, man, what suffered thou for me?

Mi blissid childre on my right hande,
Youre dome this day ye thar not drede,   *verdict; need not dread*
For all youre comforte is command,   *coming*
280   Youre liffe in likyng schall ye lede.   *lead*
Commes to the kyngdome aylastand   *everlasting*
That you is dight for youre goode dede.   *prepared; deeds*
Full blithe may ye be where ye stande,
For mekill in hevene schall be youre mede.   *reward*

285   Whenne I was hungery ye me fedde,
To slake my thirste youre harte was free,
Whanne I was clothles ye me cledde;   *clad*
Ye wolde no sorowe uppon me see.
In harde presse whan I was stedde,   *difficulties; placed*
290   Of my payns ye hadde pitee,
Full seke whan I was brought in bedde   *sick*
Kyndely ye come to coumforte me.

Whanne I was wille and werieste   *perplexed; most troubled*
Ye herbered me full hartefully,   *sheltered*
295   Full gladde thanne were ye of youre geste   *guest*
And pleyned my poverte piteuously.   *lamented*
Belyve ye brought me of the beste   *Quickly*
And made my bedde full esyly.
Therfore in hevene schall be youre reste,
300   In joie and blisse to be me by.

I ANIMA BONA Whanne hadde we, Lorde, that all has wroght,   *When was it*
Meete and drinke thee with to feede,
Sen we in erthe hadde nevere noght
But thurgh the grace of thy godhede?

II ANIMA BONA Whanne waste that we thee clothes brought
306   Or visite thee in any nede?
Or in thi sikenes we thee sought,
Lorde, when did we thee this dede?

DEUS Mi blissid childir, I schall you saye
310 What tyme this dede was to me done:
     When any that nede hadde, nyght or day,
     Askid you helpe and hadde it sone.
     Youre fre hartis saide them nevere nay,
     Erely ne late, mydday ne none,
315 But als ofte sithis as thei wolde praye,
     Thame thurte but bide and have ther bone.   *They need but endure; request*

     Ye cursid caytiffis of Kaymes kynne   *Cain's kin*
     That nevere me comforte in my care,
     I and ye forever will twynne,   *separate*
320 In dole to dwelle for evermare.
     Youre bittir bales schall nevere blynne   *sufferings; stop*
     That ye schall have whan ye come thare.
     Thus have ye served for youre synne,   *deserved*
     For derffe dedis ye have done are.   *evil deeds; previously*

325 Whanne I had mister of mete and drynke,   *need*
     Caytiffis, ye cacched me from youre yate;   *drove; gate*
     Whanne ye were sette as sirs on benke   *judges on bench*
     I stode theroute, werie and wette;   *outside, weary*
     Was none of yowe wolde on me thynke,
330 Pyté to have of my poure state.   *poor*
     Therfore till hell I schall you synke,
     Weele are ye worthy to go that gate.   *Well; way*

     Whanne I was seke and soriest
     Ye visitte me noght, for I was poure;
335 In prisoune faste whan I was feste   *incarcerated*
     Was none of you loked howe I fore.   *fared*
     Whenne I wiste nevere where for to reste,   *knew*
     With dyntes ye draffe me fro your dore,   *blows; drove*
     Butte ever to pride thanne were ye preste;   *pressed (motivated)*
340 Mi flessh, my bloode ofte ye forswore.   *body, my blood (of Eucharist)*

     Clothles whanne I was ofte and colde,   *Lacking clothes*
     At nede of you, yede I full naked,   *went*
     House ne herborow, helpe ne holde   *shelter*
     Hadde I none of you, thof I quaked.
345 Mi mischeffe sawe ye manyfolde,
     Was none of you my sorowe slaked,
     Butt evere forsoke me, yonge and alde.   *old*
     Therfore schall ye nowe be forsaked.

I ANIMA MALA Whan had thou, Lorde that all thing has,
350 Hungir or thirste sen thou God is?

Whan was thou in prisoune was,
Whan was thou naked or herberles?   *homeless*

II ANIMA MALA   Whan was it we sawe thee seke, allas;
Whan kid we thee this unkyndinesse?   *showed*
355   Werie or wette to late thee passe,   *Weary; let*
When did we thee this wikkidnesse?

DEUS   Caistiffis, als ofte als it betidde   *happened*
That nedfull aught askid in my name,   *anything*
Ye herde them noght, youre eris ye hidde: *ears; covered*
360   Youre helpe to thame was noght at hame.   *available*
To me was that unkyndines kyd;   *shown*
Therefore ye bere this bittir blame.   *bear*
To leste or moste whan ye it did,   *[the] least*
To me ye did the selve and the same.

365   Mi chosen childir, comes unto me,
With me to wonne nowe schall ye wende   *dwell*
There joie and blisse schall ever be.
Youre liffe in lyking schall ye lende.   *bliss; remain*
Ye cursed kaitiffis, fro me ye flee
370   In helle to dwelle withouten ende;
Ther ye schall nevere butt sorowe see
And sitte be Satanas the fende.   *beside*

Nowe is fulfillid all my forthoght,
For endid is all erthely thyng;
375   All worldly wightis that I have wroght
Aftir ther werkis have now wonnyng.   *dwelling [places]*
Thei that wolde synne and sessid noght   *ceased*
Of sorowes sere now schall thei syng,   *various*
And thei that mendid thame whils thei moght   *were able*
380   Shall belde and bide in my blissing.   *dwell*

Et sic facit finem cum melodia
angelorum transiens a loco ad locum.[1]

---

[1] Lines 381–82: *And thus he makes an ending, with the melody / of angels passing from place to place.*

 **EXPLANATORY NOTES**

ABBREVIATIONS: *AV*: *Authorized ("King James") Version*; ***Meditations***: *Meditations on the Life of Christ*, trans. Ragusa and Green; ***MED***: *Middle English Dictionary*; ***OED***: *Oxford English Dictionary*; **RB**: *Richard Beadle, ed., York Plays*; ***REED***: *Records of Early English Drama*; ***YA***: Davidson and O'Connor, *York Art*; ***York Breviary***: *Breviarium ad usum insignis ecclesie Eboracensis*; ***York Missal***: *Missale ad usum insignis ecclesiae Eboracensis*.
References to the ***Ordo paginarum*** are to *REED: York*, 1:16–27.

1. THE CREATION OF THE ANGELS AND THE FALL OF LUCIFER

The initial pageant in the cycle was produced by the Barkers — that is, the Tanners, thus identified in the *Ordo paginarum* of 1415 where the action of the drama is briefly summarized and its conclusion indicated as the involuntary ejection of the rebellious angels from heaven and their fall into hell. A heaven stage, on the pageant wagon, accommodated the action up to line 92, when Lucifer, illegitimately seating himself above on a throne, tumbles with his co-horts into a hellmouth on a lower level. Heaven is associated with harmony and light, and hell with cacophony, dirt, darkness, and smoke as well as, most likely, an evil odor, which the Tanners were equipped to supply.[1] The play is written in eight-line stanzas and introduces allit-eration typical of the alliterative revival of the late Middle Ages (see Introduction). It has a symmetrical pattern involving a four-part structure of scenes in heaven before and after the creation of the angels, then noisy and disordered hell, and finally heaven again. Richard Rastall notes also a division of its 160 lines according to exact principles of proportion.[2] The narrative upon which the pageant depends is traditional and appeared in English literature as early as the Anglo-Saxon *Genesis* and its accompanying illustration in Bodleian Library, MS. Junius 11.[3] A panel contemporary with the earlier years of playing the Corpus Christi plays appears in the Great East Window (1405–08) in York Minster where God is shown as the Creator while Lucifer and one of his fellow angels fall across the cosmos toward their future abode in hell.[4] Biblical sources include Isaias 14:12 ("How art thou fallen from heaven, O Lucifer, who didst rise in the morning? how art thou fallen to the earth, that didst wound the nations") and Luke 10:18 ("I saw Satan like lightning falling from heaven"). For Church Fa-thers such as Gregory of Nyssa, Lucifer's fall and transformation occurred before the creation

---

[1] See Seiler, "Filth and Stench," and Rastall, *Heaven Singing*, pp. 199–215.

[2] Rastall, *Heaven Singing*, pp. 245–46.

[3] *Caedmon Manuscript*, ed. Gollancz, p. 16.

[4] French, *York Minster: The Great East Window*, pl. 1.

of the world or any of its creatures.[5] The sponsoring craft of Barkers (Tanners) was prosperous, though not high in prestige on account of the odoriferous leather tanning process in which they were engaged. They were called Barkers because the tanning process utilized tannin derived from the bark of trees.

The opening Latin words in the playtext may not have been spoken, and are not numbered here. See Apocalypse 1:8, 21:6, 22:13.

1–8	It was a commonplace and orthodox doctrine that God is eternal, without beginning or end, uncreated and all-powerful. The Creation, on the other hand, is temporally finite in Christian tradition. As in medieval iconography, God was given a *body* in his role as the Father-Creator, for he would make man in his image and likeness (see Genesis 1:26–27).
23	*Nyen ordres of aungels.* In tradition, there initially were ten orders, with the tenth comprising those who became followers of Lucifer. The nine orders, among whom the seraphim and cherubim have speaking roles in the pageant, were popularly represented in such media as stained glass, extant examples of which appear in churches along and near the pageant route, including St. Michael Spurriergate, St. Martin Coney Street, and All Saints North Street, the latter in proximity to Barker Row (later Tanner Row), the neighborhood inhabited by members of the guild that produced this play.
24 s.d.	*Te Deum.* A portion of the *Te Deum* is sung by the angels. Since this ancient and well-known monophonic chant as included in York service books does not require great musical ability, Rastall suggests that amateurs could have been used rather than more skilled musicians from the Minster or singers from one of the more affluent parish churches (*Heaven Singing*, p. 331). Text and translations are available in Dutka, *Music*, p. 42. There is useful discussion in Sheingorn, "Te Deum Altarpiece and the Iconography of Praise."
25	*nexile.* Imagining the tripartite cosmos — heaven, earth, and hell — as wings of a building draws attention to God as a master craftsman; in a set of window panels of c.1430 now in York Minster but formerly in the church of St. Martin Coney Street, directly along the pageant route, God appears accompanied by angels who sing the *Te Deum* in his praise (Brown, *York Minster*, p. 287).
36	*Lucifer, als berar of lyghte.* Lucifer's name was conventionally glossed as the "Light bearer." His appearance demanded a splendid costume (shimmering and shining at line 69), which appeared to be changed utterly into one that is dirty and tattered after his fall. If, as in glass in St. Michael Spurriergate, he had a feather costume (*YA*, p. 20, fig. 3), it could only have then appeared nastily filthy or else already transformed into a disgusting hair coat — an effect easily performed in the play by the exchange of one actor playing the role for another who had been waiting to emerge from within hellmouth. Such was the punishment for Lucifer's pride, as the pageant makes clear, and, quite consistent with Patristic arguments, his pride is characterized by the will to power as well as sheer envy of his Creator.

[5] See Russell, *Satan*, p. 187.

40 s.d.   *Sanctus, sanctus, sanctus*. A continuation of the *Te Deum*, though these words also appear in the *Sanctus* of the Mass that was sung immediately prior to the canon.

60   *felyng of fylth*. The unfallen angels are undefiled. They maintain their pure state, in contrast to Lucifer and his companions who are consigned to a habitat that is dirty and dark, both indicative of their separation from the source of purity and light that is God. Also, it is taken for granted that they establish a kingdom that is violent, disordered, and a source of subversion to be reckoned with throughout history.

62   *stabyll in thoughte*. The good angels have willed obedience to the deity in opposition to the bending of will that is characteristic of Lucifer in his pursuit of his perceived interests. The concept of stability affects the gestures of the angels, with those who are fallen engaging in rapid and indecorous movements, as will also be typical of evil characters throughout the pageants in the York cycle.

76   *fede with the fode of thi fayre face*. There may be a subtle echo of the Eucharist here, since *seeing* the Host was considered a kind of visual communing. See Nichols, "Bread of Heaven."

89   *Ther sall I set myselfe*. The *Cursor Mundi* reports that Lucifer took his seat "In the north syde" (line 459, 1:34–35) where he expected to be reverenced by all the angels.

117   *smoke*. The Coventry dramatic records identify a fire at hellmouth in the Drapers' Doomsday play (*REED: Coventry*, p. 478), while the Anglo-Norman *Adam* directs the devils in hell to "make a great smoke [*fumum magnum*] to arise" (*Medieval French Plays*, p. 36; Butterworth, *Theatre of Fire*, p. 12). Suggestions for the design and use of hellmouth in plays such as the Barkers' pageant may be found in Meredith, "The Iconography of Hell in the English Cycles: A Practical Perspective," and see also Sheingorn, "'Who can open the doors of his face': The Iconography of Hell Mouth." The hellmouth will also be present in the *Harrowing* (Play 37) and the Mercers' *Doomsday* (Play 47).

141   *Mankynde of moulde*. See Genesis 2:7, which describes the creation of Adam from the "slime of the earth." This will not happen, as God explains in lines 142–44, until he has completed forming the earth itself and all else that is in it as a support system for humankind.

154   *The nighte even fro the day*. Separating light and darkness, the work of the first day. See Genesis 1:4.

2. THE CREATION THROUGH THE FIFTH DAY

A monologue, presented by the Plasterers, also known as Daubers. The pageant presents the Creation narrative according to Genesis 1, the first account presented in the Bible (the second follows in Genesis 2). Here the earth and all that is in it except for humans are brought into existence in five days. There is overlap with the previous play since in it the work of the first day had already been introduced. The verse form is a twelve-line stanza.

1–4   The Latin lines are immediately glossed by English translations. They are indicative of the placement of God on a higher level, with such effects of his creation as the animals, fish, and plants appearing below.

10   *Up for to trine my trone*. A reference to Lucifer's attempt to seat himself in God's throne in the previous pageant.

17   *Thare mys may never be amendid*. A theological puzzle is introduced since it would appear that God created some of the angels with a flaw in their design, but the usual explanation is that they were given a free will, which they abused of their own accord. God is utterly unforgiving, and the devils fall into their role as the opposition party and proponents of disobedience and evil throughout history as depicted by the play cycle. They are the ultimate source of conflict in the pageants and represent the absence of good.

31   *Noght by my strenkyth but by my stevyn*. The cosmos exists within God's forethought, but it is his Word that brings it into existence, not an exercise of raw power such as Lucifer wished to display — and which only led to the establishment of a kingdom of darkness in the void that is entered through hellmouth. See John 1:1: "In the beginning was the Word, and the Word was with God, and the Word was God."

41–42   *The firmament sal nought move, / But be a mene*. The cosmos has as its purpose the enclosing of the world, which will be, according to the pre-Copernican cosmology of the time, at its center. Heaven is a fixed place, unchanging and stable. See below, where the sun and moon are fixed in the pageant heavens, which are decorated with stars.

90   *Mesurid and made*. Here again God appears as a craftsman, and very possibly he actually appeared thus in this pageant, where he could have held a set of large masons' compasses, as sometimes occurs in the visual arts of the period; see above and also, for example, the fourteenth-century *Holkham Bible Picture Book*, fol. 2.

120   *sertayne signes*. Implying the signs of the zodiac, commonly appearing in association with the depictions of the seasons of the year, as on the early sculpture reset over the south porch doorway of the church of St. Margaret in York (see Halfpenny, *Fragmenta Vetusta*, pl. 24).

129   *fysch*. A panel in the Great East Window of the Minster shows the creation of fish and birds, and other panels also show other events in the creation story. In the *Te Deum* window formerly in St. Martin Coney Street, the parish church closest to the Common Hall, the Creator appears with birds, animals, and flowers, the products of his work following the creation of fish. Whales are specifically mentioned in Genesis 1:21.

154–56   *Serpentis*. The serpent is apparently flawed from its creation and thus apparently would not seem to fit the "and God saw that it was good" formula applied to all creatures in Genesis 1.

167   *wax furth*. See Genesis 1:22: "Increase, and multiply." The stanza, and the pageant, will conclude with God's blessing.

3. THE CREATION OF ADAM AND EVE

The Cardmakers, or Combsmiths, a craft that made the necessary tools for carding wool and presumably other similar items of manufacture, produced this pageant, which required that the actors who played Adam and Eve must appear in simulated nudity, probably effected with tawed leather suits as in the Cornish *Creacion of the World* which specifies suits of *"whytt lether"* (line 343 s.d.). The same type of costume would presumably have been used for other pageants in which Adam and Eve appear. The creation of Adam is shown in a panel in the Great East Window of the Minster, though this glass is heavily restored and hence should be cited with care.[6] The play was copied into the Register twice; see textual notes.

23   *Eftyr my schape and my lyknes.* Genesis 1:26 reports that God made Adam after his image (*imaginem*) and likeness (*similitudinem*). The primacy of Adam is implied in that he was first created, then Eve, and this is reinforced in the second Creation account in Genesis which has her made from one of Adam's body parts.

31–32   Death is already assumed as part of life, as if God already has foreknowledge of Adam's fall, resulting eventually in his death and the death of all humans throughout history.

35   *erthe.* In the second Creation story in Genesis, the "slime of the earth" is the substance from which Adam was made; see Genesis 2:7.

38   *lyft rybe.* While the second Creation account contains the story of Eve's creation from the rib of Adam, it does not specify the *left*. The left side was traditionally associated with the feminine, considered weaker, and in some locales in northern Europe women and children were relegated to the left side in church, the men to the right. The 1565 property list of the Norwich Grocers' play included a "Rybbe Colleryd Redd" (*REED: Norwich*, p. 53).

41   *gaste of lyffe.* The account in the second chapter of Genesis reported that God caused Adam and Eve to live by breathing life into them (2:7). Spirit (*gaste*, modern *ghost*) is identified with breath. In ancient Jewish thought, life hence begins when the newly created (and, subsequently, the newborn) takes his or her first breath.

70   *made of noght.* A return to the concept of the Creation as made out of nothing by God, but somewhat curious in this context since Adam was made from mud and Eve from his rib.

4. THE PROHIBITION OF THE TREE OF KNOWLEDGE

Although the Fullers, or Walkers, who were an integral craft essential to the cloth industry, had been involved with this pageant as early as 1415 when their participation was noted in the *Ordo paginarum*, their play was not copied into the Register until 1559 (see

---

[6] French, *York Minster: The Great East Window*, p. 49.

textual notes).[7] Their play, in ten-line stanzas, is very short and rather undramatic, though it sets forth an important view that has been maintained by some until the present day: the idea of man as in charge of the imperium. In line 16, all other creatures are recognized as man's subjects, and in lines 60–64 he is told to see himself as the master and lord of all things; see Genesis 1:29–30. A detailed discussion of gestures appropriate to the present play and subsequent plays in the Garden of Eden is contained in Natalie Crohn Schmitt, "The Body in Motion."[8]

31–36   The description of the Garden is abbreviated and general in nature. Was there an elaborate stage set with a full-scale garden setting?

68   *The frute of it negh none*. God's command denies Adam and Eve the right even to approach the fruit of the tree upon pain of death. The source is in the second Creation story (Genesis 2:17).

5. THE FALL

The *Ordo paginarum* description of this pageant is not consistent with the text, for it calls for Adam and Eve to be standing on each side of the forbidden tree as Satan deceives them — i.e., precisely the scene depicted in a panel in the Great East Window in the Minster. In James Torre's seventeenth-century description of the glass, the serpent is "twisted about a great Tree like a fair woman with his face toward Eve who is with one hand reaching to take an Apple from the Tree; And with her right hand delivering a golden Apple to Adam, who receives it with his left hand and eats it out of the other elevated to his Mouth."[9] The pageant text introduces Satan in his fallen state, having taken the form of a serpent (see line 23); his main grievance appears to have derived from his envy of God and of the power of the Creator, but clearly his thinking is confused, as he himself admits. Yet he is able to seduce Eve, who only thereafter convinces Adam to eat. According to St. Augustine, Eve's sin was less than Adam's since she was deceived, while Adam ate knowingly.[10] The pageant was produced by the Coopers, makers of casks, tubs, buckets, and similar wares. It is written in an eleven-line stanza.

3–11   The notion that Satan's envy centered on his expectation that God would assume the form and status of an angel seems curious, but it calls attention to how Lucifer was self-deceived by his appearance as the brightest of the heavenly host.

12–13   Satan is envious of God's decision to create man and his female companion as a substitute for the angels of heaven whom he has lost through their rebellion. He especially sees Eve as prey (line 18), and is certainly not the friend he claims

---

[7] The heading *Regynall* presumably indicates that the text was copied directly from the guild's original copy.

[8] See also C. Davidson, "Gesture."

[9] Torre, *Antiquities of York Minster*, p. 71.

[10] Augustine, *City of God*, 14.11.

to be. Traditionally he appears with a woman's face; see Bonnell, "Serpent with a Human Head."

26–82   An elaboration of the account in Genesis 3:1–5.

69–73   *yhe shalle be wyse . . . als wise as he.* Compare Genesis 3:5: "your eyes shall be opened: and you shall be as Gods, knowing good and evil." The York Satan adds that Eve will be God's equal in every way, "als wise as he."

104–05 Adam impulsively eats with the hope that the promise of divinity is true. Ironically, of course, it is, since this "bad bargayne" (line 119) is an essential moment in the "happy fall," *felix culpa*, that ultimately will culminate in the coming into time of Christ to effect salvation and in the promise of bliss for all humans who perform the Corporal Acts of Mercy and believe on his name — the culmination too of the cycle in the Mercers' Doomsday pageant (Play 47).

110–11 *Me shames . . . I am naked.* See Genesis 3:7; compare *Cursor Mundi*: "For shame thei stode bothe and quaked" (line 800, 1:55). In the Expulsion scene in York Minster glass in the Great East Window, Eve holds one hand over her breast and another over her genitals (French, *York Minster: The Great East Window*, p. 51). In the pageant, at her suggestion (line 131), they will cover themselves with "fygge leves," for which, on account of their unavailability in medieval York, another type of leaf would necessarily have been substituted in production.

138   *Where art thou.* A direct quote from Genesis 3:9, but in the biblical account God has been walking in the garden of paradise when he calls to Adam and Eve. In performing the play they probably were hiding like guilty children, which would be quite consistent with Genesis.

150–59 *A wikkid worme . . . ete and drynke.* God's curse on the serpent. Compare Genesis 3:14–15.

160–63 *Adam and Eve alsoo . . . we synke.* They are condemned to "swete and swynke," but no mention is made here of the travail in childbirth to which Eve and her descendants are condemned or of the rule that they should be under the domination of their husbands. These commands appear, however, in the Expulsion pageant, where they are pronounced to Adam and Eve by the angel (lines 69–74).

166–67 *Now, Cherubyn, . . . To middilerth tyte go dryve there twoo.* The Expulsion is mentioned as part of the Coopers' play in the *Ordo paginarum*, though this is in fact the subject of the next pageant.

175–76 *for sorowe and care, / Owre handis may we wryng.* A conventional gesture of despair.

6. The Expulsion from the Garden

At the conclusion of the previous pageant, Adam and Eve have already been expelled from the garden. To be sure, a different angel must play the angel of the Expulsion here. Since in this case the angel, identified in the biblical account (Genesis 3:24) as a cherubim, traditionally holds a flaming sword, as in another panel in the East Window of the Minster (French, *York Minster: The Great East Window*, p. 51), the Armorers, or Furbishers, would seem to have been a logical choice for producers of this pageant, especially since over time this craft gravitated more toward weaponry than protective gear. However, while the *Ordo paginarum* says nothing about the sword, it does have the angel supplying Adam and Eve with a spade and spindle with which they are to begin their work. The Armorers' most prosperous period was the early fifteenth century, though by 1444 they were pleading for aid for themselves and their pageant (*REED: York*: 1:62). The play is written in six-line stanzas, also including irregular stanzas of five lines.

47	*fele fandyngis manyfolde*. Middle earth, to which Adam and Eve have been banished, is a place of temptation that will mark the race from henceforth, even affecting St. Peter immediately after the Crucifixion when he denies his Lord three times.
58	*Adam, have this*. The angel hands the spade to Adam with an admonition that this will be needed for earning his living. The spade is generally taken to be Adam's identifying symbol in the iconography of the later Middle Ages; see May, "Medieval Stage Property."
70–74	*Travell herto shalle thou ta . . . To man ay be*. The point at which Eve presumably must receive the spindle from the angel. This seems verified by the following lines in which she laments that she can no longer have the kind of tranquility that she enjoyed in the garden but must work. Adam also refers to the tool that has been given him in line 77. For a typical depiction of Eve, seated outside and spinning at the left, and Adam working with his spade "in the sweat of his brow" to break up the hard ground at the right, see the *Speculum humanae salvationis* (Wilson and Wilson, *Medieval Mirror*, p. 145).
90–91	*At prime of the day. / Be tyme of none alle lost had wee*. The creation of the first parents took place at the beginning of the day (specifically at *prime*, the second of the canonical hours), and already by noon the Fall had taken place. The rapidity of the Fall is a medieval commonplace.
131	*We mon go nakid*. So in the garden, but now they cannot do this on account of their awareness of their bodies, of which they are ashamed. The biblical account has them dressed in skins (Genesis 3:21).
160	*Dede wolde I be*. A sign of despair, though in Adam's case it will not be a sickness unto death, for he will be rescued from Limbo along with Eve by the second Adam, Jesus Christ, at the Harrowing. The despair here is not the remorse of Judas but of a penitent now that he has finished his blaming of Eve for his deed. Traditional gestures are beating one's breast and wringing one's hands, which would have been appropriate for Adam and Eve as they wend forth at the end of the pageant, presumably as they set off toward the next station where the pageant will be repeated.

7. SACRIFICIUM CAYME ET ABELL

The Glovers, whose trade was in white (tawed) leather products, were joined with the manufacturers of such items in the *Ordo paginarum*. Their play, based on Genesis 4 and written in an eleven-line stanza unique in the cycle, is unfortunately incomplete in the Register, from which two leaves have been lost. The missing pages included the story of the sacrifices of Abell (a lamb) and Cayme, the latter being unsatisfactory (wheat, in the Towneley play involving the worst sheaves, which create a noxious smoke), God's reaction to the sacrifices, and Cayme's murder of Abell, traditionally in English iconography with the jawbone of an ass,[11] as in otherwise heavily restored glass at York Minster.[12] The two leaves were lost by the time of John Clerke, who added the Brewbarret episode in his distinctive sixteenth-century hand (lines 73–99). For further comment, see RB, p. 76. The biblical account does not give the reasons for the rejection of Cain's offering, and attempts at historical explanation have not been convincing. In the play prior to the loss of the leaves, the sacrifice of a lamb would have been seen as prefiguring the sacrifice of the Lamb of God, Jesus, on the cross. The angel messenger who explains the obligation of tithing — an obligation about which the medieval Church was insistent — and demands the sacrifices is not in Genesis, but a portion of the biblical account forms the basis of a responsory for Septuagesima Sunday in the *York Breviary*.[13]

14–15   *Nothynge hym thoughte was wroughte in waste . . . to bide.* The author of the play was aware of the theological problem of how God, infinitely good, could create something that could be corrupted. As Abelard remarked, "Goodness, it is evident, can produce only what is good" (qtd. Lovejoy, *Great Chain of Being*, p. 71). There is no satisfactory answer to the problem.

45   *wilde waneand.* Beadle glosses as "i.e., an evil hour" (RB, p. 530).

45–46   Cayme's hostile attitude is even more pronounced, if possible, in the Towneley *Mactacio Abel*. In the visual arts of the period such as the example cited above from the Great East Window of 1405–08 in York Minster or the somewhat earlier *Holkam Bible Picture Book*, fols. 5–6, Cain has remarkably belligerent facial expressions and body language. The *Cursor Mundi* implies that he was the son of the devil, apparently the result of Satan's seduction of Eve (1:69). His antagonism to tithing would have put him at odds with the ecclesiastical courts; the penalty for failing to tithe was intended to be excommunication, but might be a fine (see Ault, "Village Church," pp. 208–09). See the extended discussion of Cain in medieval British drama in C. Davidson, *History, Religion, and Violence*, pp. 97–123.

73–99   Oddly, Cayme sends his boy Brewbarret to obtain sheaves "of the best," and indicates he should have a drink before he goes, prior to the time when the angel appears to demand the whereabouts of Abel, who has already been killed. The angel curses Cayme in God's stead; in Genesis 4:11 God curses Cain directly. This portion of the interpolation is a not very satisfactory attempt to link up with the text that follows.

89   *Quia non sum custos fratris mei.* Adapted from Genesis 4:9.

[11] See Schapiro, "Cain's Jaw-Bone," and Guilfoyle, "Staging of the First Murder."

[12] French, *York Minster: The Great East Window*, p. 52.

[13] *York Breviary*, 1:235–36. For attention to this and other citations to the York Missal and Breviary, I am grateful to King, *York Mystery Cycle*.

109–17   Inconsistently, Cayme is destined to till the soil though unfruitfully, but also to become a wanderer and an outcast.

119   *My synne it passis al mercie.* Despair is the deeply held feeling that one is beyond salvation, and indeed Cain is frequently said to be the first permanent resident of hell and a precursor of Judas — a contrast, again, to the despair of Adam, noted above. For a useful discussion of despair leading to damnation, see Snyder, "Left Hand of God."

130   *Who that thee slees.* The murderer will be Lamech, who was believed to have been blind and to have done the deed unintentionally through the perfidy of his son. The only English dramatization appears in the Noah play in the N-Town collection, but the scene is depicted in the *Holkham Bible Picture Book*, fol. 6v; see also Woolf, *English Mystery Plays*, p. 135, and Reiss, "Story of Lamech and Its Place in Medieval Drama."

132–33   *a token . . . prentyd so in thee.* The mark of Cain, which also functions as a sign of his damnation; see Genesis 4:15. In the Cornish *Creacion*, God makes the "marcke in his forehedd; this worde: Omega" (line 1179 s.d., p. 98).

8. THE BUILDING OF NOAH'S ARK

The Shipwrights' pageant is a demonstration of the craft's skills as God orders Noah to build a ship and then informs him to go about his work. The complexity of the task seems to call for non-speaking workmen to help Noah, but in the text of the play he says, "Al be myselfe I will assaye" (line 96). As Richard Beadle suggests in "Shipwrights' Craft," the author of the play evidently was very familiar with clinker-built ship construction, and must have had close relations with the ship builders themselves. The shipwrights' occupation went into severe decline in the course of the fifteenth century when the Ouse became less navigable due to silting and the larger seagoing ships became the norm. The text of the pageant in the Register has been extensively corrected by a later hand, identified in at least in part as John Clerke's (see RB, pp. 420–21). The story of Noah and the Flood appears in Genesis 6–8, adapted from earlier Babylonian mythology after the return from exile of the Jews in Babylon in the fifth century B.C.E. It appears in the lessons and responsories for Septuagesima and Sexagesima. The eight-line stanza adopted in the play also is used in a number of other pageants in the cycle.

14–24   *synne is nowe reynand so ryffe . . . I wille al newe.* As in the biblical account, God repents that he ever made humankind on account of the wickedness of everyone except Noah, who is solemn and pure of heart (see line 33). Hence God decides to make a new beginning. Noah and his family are to be saved, the others drowned in the waters of the great Flood. This provides the motive for both the present play and the Fishers and Mariners' pageant of the Flood which follows, but there is also a common reading of their story as foreshadowing the Last Day, dramatized as the concluding pageant in the cycle by the Mercers.

50   *I am full olde and oute of qwarte.* When the ark is finished, Noah will be six hundred years of age, but his argument with God over his ability as an old man to perform the task inspires some lively dialogue.

74–80   The directions for building the ship are accurately presented. The trees must be carefully selected and squared before boards and batten are cut. It is important that the seams be masterfully joined "and naylid wele" so that they do not come apart when the boat is floated. Instead of nails in the modern sense, rivets would presumably have been used; see the diagram in C. Davidson, *Technology, Guilds,* esp. pp. 8–9, figs. 11–12.

81–86   The ark specified by God is immensely large in size. Beadle suggests that it would have "a displacement of some 40,000 tons" ("Shipwrights' Craft," p. 58). No wonder it would take a hundred years to build (see lines 114–15)!

97–111   The listing of tools suggests that these were borrowed from members of the craft. Noah begins by laying on a chalk line and pretending to work on a board, then using a tool to join it to the ark, which must of course have been prefabricated. The Cornish *Creacion* specifies "*Tooles and tymber . . . redy, with planckys to make the Arcke*" (line 2254 s.d.). Since normally the interior ribs were added last, these would not be needed. Then Noah picks up a caulking tool to cement (as if with pitch) the boards to seem to make them water-tight. In the next stanza, he explains that the boards will be held in place with rivets fitted into roves (large metal washers) and flattened; these are easily seen in depictions of clinker-built ships. A set of shipbuilders' tools from the wreck of Henry VIII's Mary Rose shows mallets, augurs, measuring sticks, and other implements of the type perhaps displayed in the York play; see C. Davidson, *Technology, Guilds,* fig. 15.

114   *A hundereth wyntres away is wente.* Diller remarks about this scene that it "is remarkable for skipping a hundred years in a single line" (*Middle English Mystery Play,* p. 92)!

127–41   *Dyverse stages must ther be . . . lyffes to laste.* In the visual arts, the ark often had three levels, which were determined by the symbolism of the vessel as a representation of the Church. Like the Church at the Day of Judgment, the ark was a providentially chosen means to safety when all the world would be destroyed.

9. THE FLOOD

Fishing and fish farming in the Ouse are well documented in the civic records, but the Fishers' craft, like that of the Mariners, also involved setting out to sea by way of Hull. Their play of the Flood, written in a fourteen-line stanza with some alliteration, required a pageant ship, perhaps fitted with animals painted on boards or some such innovation. But it is the farce involving the recalcitrance of Noah's wife which can be traced to an Eastern legend that supports the action of the first part of the play. On the one hand, Uxor may be seen as a target of medieval anti-feminism, while on the other her weakness represents all humankind in need of salvation, for she, like every one of us, is in need of rescue from destruction.[14] The Genesis account only mentions Noah's wife's boarding of the ark in 7:7 without hint of reluctance on her part. The Newcastle *Noah*, however, has the devil tempting her as a second Eve to subvert God's plan of saving Noah's family and subsequently the salvation of the race, and M. D. Anderson calls attention to a depiction of such a temptation in the *Queen Mary Psalter*.[15] Noah and his family are shown in the ark, interestingly with a mast and a sail, in a panel in the Great East Window in the Minster; the hull of the ship, however, has been restored with scraps and hence is not original.[16]

5	*worthy wiffe*. Not consistent with the view of her that appears subsequently in the pageant. Noah's piety and appreciation of his family are set against a warning from God that has already taken place (see line 12: "This world wastyd shalle be").
15–28	*My fadir Lamech . . . than was I borne*. Noah's father is not the person who was the murderer of Cain, but was a man noted for his piety. He therefore was one who already knew by "sarteyne signes" that God would take vengeance on humankind's wickedness (lines 34–40).
145	It would appear that the rain has begun. If a stage effect were involved, as is quite likely, there is no indication of how it was produced. By line 152 Uxor's "frendis" are already drowned in the Flood.
149	*modir, mende youre moode*. The first daughter encourages her mother, but the general mood of the family during the watery holocaust will generally remain solemn. Only at lines 197–98 does Uxor's mood change to one of appreciation for being saved from the Flood through God's grace, but by then the forty days and forty nights of rain are over (see line 183) and the waters are subsiding.
161	*Wendes and spers youre dores bedene*. An imbedded stage direction, implying that some openings, or at least one entry door, in the ark could be closed. Did the actors appear on the deck, or was there a large window (hardly practical) in which they could speak their lines?
171–76	The sons care for "thes catelles" and the women the "foules," most likely a common division of labor in the York region.
190	*catteraks*. From the Vulgate *cataractae caeli*, which now have been "shut up" (Genesis 8:2).
199	*caste leede*. A plumb bob was cast down to sound the depth of the water, as would have been the practice among contemporary mariners. The water is still at its full height of fifteen cubits (Genesis 7:20) but is waning (line 204).
212–16	*The raven is wighte . . . lande or tree*. Though this bird has a bad reputation, its intelligence marks it as a choice for a reconnaissance mission to see if the time

---

[14] See C. Davidson, *From Creation to Doom*, pp. 51–52.

[15] Davis, ed., *Non-Cycle Plays*, pp. 22–23 and 28–29; Anderson, *Drama and Imagery*, p. 108; Stanton, *Queen Mary Psalter*, fig. 25.

[16] French, *York Minster: The Great East Window*, p. 53.

will soon come for their departure from the ark. It will not return; according to the *Cursor Mundi*, 1:117, this is because it fed on the flesh of the creatures drowned in the Flood — and hence could not return to the ark, a symbol of the Church. In the Cornish *Ordinalia*, Noah predicts in advance that if the raven finds carrion it will not come back to him (*Ancient Cornish Drama*, 1:82–85). Thus the raven was cursed and its color changed from white to black.

237–60   *Thou doufe . . . now may we synge*. A dove is then sent out, and brings back a token; see Genesis 8:8–11. The token is an "olyve braunche," a sign that Noah and his family will "be saved."

264   *The hillis of Hermony*. Noah's first sight of land, but a pun is implied, since harmony is returning to the cosmos.

266 s.d.   *Tunc cantent Noe et filii sui*. A time for singing by Noah and his sons had been announced in line 260, with the inclusion of song by them in early performances confirmed by this late stage direction. Rastall suggests a procession by the family from the ark (*Heaven Singing*, p. 243).

278   *Dum dixit "penitet me."* Adapted from the Vulgate (Genesis 6:7).

283   *Arcum ponam in nubibus*. Genesis 9:13. The rainbow will also figure in the Mercers' Doomsday play; see *REED: York*, 1:55.

301   *be waste with fyre*. In answer to his son's suggestion that the world might last forever, Noah explains that at last — that is, at the Last Judgment — the earth will be consumed by flames. The destruction of the world by fire appears as one of the signs of Doomsday in a panel in a window in All Saints, North Street — i.e., when, according to the caption in the glass, the time will come when "sall betyde The werlde sall bryn on ilk a syde" (Gee, "Painted Glass of All Saints' Church," pls. XXIII–XXIV). The Flood is connected typologically with Doomsday in Luke 17:26–27, a passage which is part of the Gospel reading for the final day of Sexagesima in the *York Missal*, 1:42).

10. ABRAHAM AND ISAAC

The Parchment Makers were a specialized leather craft whose members appear in the list of freemen of the city after 1350, while the Bookbinders, who probably lived in the liberties controlled by the Minster rather than the city, seem never to have sought the freedom of the city. Their play, written in twelve-line stanzas used in nearly a quarter of the pageants in the cycle, is based on Genesis 22, which tells the story of the sacrifice of Isaac, with some details from previous chapters. However, it also is influenced by the *Middle English Metrical Paraphrase of the Old Testament*.[17] The story was regarded as a prefiguring of the sacrifice of Jesus Christ, the Lamb of God.[18] In demonstrating the typological relationship, the woodcut in the *Biblia*

---

[17] See *Middle English Metrical Paraphrase*, ed. Kalén and Ohlander, and Beadle, "Origins of Abraham's Preamble."

[18] See Daniélou, *From Shadows to Reality*, pp. 115–30; Mirk, *Festial*, pp. 76–78; and the surveys in Woolf, "Effect of Typology," and C. Davidson, *History, Religion, and Violence*, pp. 124–48, esp. 126–31.

Pauperum shows Abraham poised to sacrifice his son immediately to the left of a depiction of Christ on the cross. In the York pageant the point is underlined by the fact that Isaac is not a young child but of the age of Jesus at the time of his ministry and Crucifixion (line 82: "Thyrty yere and more sumdele"). In a city with a high mortality rate (church records show that over the years the pageants were played, deaths exceeded births, with a precipitous decline in population that could not be stemmed by immigration), the loss of a son would have been a potential calamity. The civic predicament was such that here especially the play would have been expected to be particularly compelling — indeed, narrating a terrifying story that, as Søren Kierkegaard would demonstrate in *Fear and Trembling*, pitted the ethical against the higher demands of loyalty to God. The play presents a very human and compelling story, made all the more so in this telling. But the outcome is happy, for Abraham is also the patriarch from whom, through Isaac, both Judaism and Christianity would spring, as indicated in the final speech of the angel that reinforces God's earlier promise. In the York lectionary, the story of Abraham appears in responsories in the days leading up to Lent.

13–20   God has told the patriarch Abraham that his progeny will be like the sands of the sea, and in Genesis 17 has made a covenant with him that includes the rite of circumcision in order to satisfy "the lawe."

14   *telde under a tree*. Compare *Middle English Metrical Paraphrase*: "Abraham was tyllyd under A tre" (ed. Kalén and Ohlander, line 554).

15–16   *my seede shulde be multyplyed / Lyke to the gravell of the see*. Compare *Middle English Metrical Paraphrase*: "Ose gravell in the se is multyplyd, / So sall I multiplye thi sede" (ed. Kalén and Ohlander, lines 476–77).

29–40   Because she was barren, Sarah gave her handmaid Agar to Abraham as a second wife, and with her he had a son Ishmael, who is only said in the pageant to be handsome. See Genesis 16.

65   *ANGELUS*. In the pageant God communicates with Abraham through the angel, his messenger, rather than directly, as in Genesis.

71   *lande of Vyssyon*. The "land of vision" will be the place chosen by God where, upon a mountain, the sacrifice, by burning, is to take place (Genesis 22:2). The three-day journey is biblical, as are the servants (line 94) who accompanied Abraham and Isaac.

151   *My sone, this wode behoves thee bere*. In iconography, as for example in the *Biblia Pauperum*, Isaac carries the bundle of wood for the sacrifice. Sometimes the wood is bundled into the shape of a cross to underline the typological connection with Christ carrying the cross to the place of his execution.

161–62   Isaac becomes increasingly concerned about the lack of a sacrificial animal, especially since clearly Abraham is becoming more and more agitated. At last, at line 188, Abraham can no longer hold back the truth that he is about to sacrifice his own son, and he will do it at God's command.

194–96   Isaac is terrified at the thought of being dismembered and burned, but he nevertheless is willing to allow himself to be sacrificed — just as Jesus, suffering the terror of his Agony in the Garden, will give himself up to his Father's will, even death on the cross. By line 270, Isaac will be deeply fearful and will report that his "flesshe waxis faynte."

212   *My force youre forward to withstande.* As noted above in the headnote to this pageant, at line 82 Isaac is described not as a child but as "sumdele" more than thirty years of age. While differing opinions concerning his age were put forward in the Middle Ages, the reason for depicting Isaac thus is that he "was fygur of Crystys passyon long er he wer borne" (Mirk, *Festial*, p. 78). See Wells, "Age of Isaac"; Woolf, "Effect of Typology," p. 811; and C. Davidson, *From Creation to Doom*, pp. 52–54. Isaac's "force" or strength is thus plausibly much greater than his aged father's.

213   *beste that ye me bynde.* In the pageant it is Isaac who suggests that he should be bound. Later, he will ask that a kerchief be placed over his eyes as well (line 288).

229   *Nowe kysse me hartely.* The son is asked to show normal reverence for a parent with a kiss, as would be expected of offspring even into adulthood. Isaac later will ask his father for forgiveness for any trespasses he may have done in speech, deeds, "or any waye" (lines 255–58).

271   *take youre swerde.* Abraham's sword is a standard item in iconography, usually shown lifted by him to strike his son on the altar. Yet there is further delay, until at last it must be raised to strike at lines 301–03, when the angel calls to him and orders him to desist. In most examples in the visual arts (e.g., the *Biblia Pauperum*, p. 96), the angel grasps his arm to prevent the sword from striking. In glass, possibly with connections to the York school of glass painting, in the Priory Church at Great Malvern, the angel appears only to be admonishing the patriarch who holds the uplifted sword, but here Abraham has his left hand on the head of Isaac, who is blindfolded and kneeling as in prayer (Rushforth, *Medieval Christian Imagery*, pp. 170–71, fig. 80).

304   *Take here a schepe.* The substitute for the son Isaac, in Christian theology mirroring the Son of God, the Lamb of God who will be a substitute for all humankind. In the pageant, the actual sacrifice of the sheep, surely not a live animal but rather a representation that Abraham and his son could pretend to burn, must have been very perfunctory, for at lines 329–32 the father and son are already prepared to return home.

365   *Rabek.* For the more complex story of Isaac's love for and courtship of Rebecca, see Genesis 25.

11. PHARAOH AND MOSES

As the play assigned to the Hosiers, makers of stockings and undergarments, this pageant was also adapted for inclusion in the Towneley manuscript. The Exodus narrative appears among the readings for Lent in the York liturgy, and is considered one of the most important of Old Testament stories. Typologically it was believed to foreshadow the Harrowing, as in the *Speculum humanae salvationis*,[19] but in its exposition of release from bondage and tyranny it surely would have resonated with people who felt they were living in this "vale of tears," the condition of post-lapsarian humankind considered normal and from which only spiritual means can effect release. The story should have been popular in its own right on account of the Red Sea scene, which presumably involved considerable ingenuity in staging; the sea may have been represented by a cloth, as indicated at Coventry by the Smiths' accounts.[20] The Hosiers, a cloth guild, would have been easily able to provide this sort of effect with the help of the Dyers. But it is another effect that is emphasized in the *Ordo paginarum*, which reports Moses' raising up of the serpent before Pharaoh, apparently in the presence of eight Jews — an act for which he is suspected of witchcraft. God also appears in the burning bush at line 101, and this would presumably demand the use of a pyrotechnic device. In iconography, through a misreading of the Vulgate, Moses appears with horns, which at Lucerne in 1583 were produced by having two hornlike curls on his head.[21] Moses has horns in a panel in the east window of York Minster that also contains a depiction of the Egyptians drowning in the Red Sea, the latter unfortunately now almost indecipherable and confused.[22] The episode of Moses and the receiving of the Ten Commandments is omitted in the York pageant. The biblical source for the pageant is Exodus 2–14. The verse form is a twelve-line stanza common in the York plays.

7	*his hayre as elde will asse*. Affirming primogeniture.
21–24	The tyrant Pharaoh is accompanied by Consolators, who are his sycophants. Consolator I echoes and elaborates his concern about those who have other allegiances than to him — in other words, the Israelites. This is their role throughout. The term *Consolators* is abbreviated throughout, only once being thus spelled out (at line 219); see discussion in RB, p. 423.
41	*Thay come of Joseph*. See Genesis 37–47. While Pharaoh describes Joseph as "worthy to prayse" (line 42) the Israelites are now unwelcome aliens in Egypt and are an oppressed minority, albeit a large one since their numbers have grown to a multitude from the time when Joseph and his brothers arrived. Their numbers are calculated in lines 55–58 as upwards of 300,000 men, aside from women, children, and servants, who are not counted.
93–96	Moses is the keeper of his father-in-law Jethro's sheep after fleeing from Pharaoh (Exodus 3). Jethro is identified as "the priest of Madian" (Exodus 3:1). Moses' self-banishment was in response to his killing of an Egyptian who was mistreating an Israelite.
105	*come noght to nere*. See Exodus 3:5: "Come not nigh hither." There is no indication that Moses should take off his shoes at this point, as in the biblical account. He is standing before God who has appeared in the burning bush, which he has first seen at line 101.

[19] Wilson and Wilson, *Medieval Mirror*, p. 194.

[20] *REED: Coventry*, p. 251.

[21] Meredith and Tailby, *Staging*, p. 135.

[22] French, *York Minster: The Great East Window*, pp. 64–65.

147–52   *wande . . . myn entent.* The magical wand or rod that becomes a serpent. For discussion of magic tricks of legerdemain, see Butterworth, *Magic*, though he does not comment on this trick specifically. Moses' rod was noted in 1500 among the possessions of York Minster, but this was probably a representation, not a relic (*Fabric Rolls*, p. 224).

154   *lepre.* An emendation since the manuscript reading of *serpent* is clearly wrong (corroborated by Towneley). This effect would have taken less skill than the rod/serpent, but similarly would have depended for its effectiveness on the reaction of those standing by, especially Pharaoh.

173   *Ego sum qui sum.* Exodus 3:14; glossed in the following line.

209   *To wildirnesse he walde thei wente.* After their liberation will come the years of wandering in the wilderness before they settle in Israel.

219   *warlowe with his wande.* Already Pharaoh sees Moses as a wizard. This is previous to the miracle of the rod/serpent in lines 231–45.

251   *God sende sum vengeaunce sone.* This line introduces the plagues of Egypt, which begin to emerge in the next speech by I Egiptius. The plagues will be rapidly reported with the drama set in motion by Pharoah's duplicity and appearance of relenting from time to time behind a hypocritical front.

261–64   *watir . . . Is turned to rede blude.* The first plague.

271   *tadys and frosshis.* Plague of toads and frogs. The second plague.

273   *myses.* Gnats. The third plague.

293   *loppis.* The word is of Scandinavian derivation, meaning "fleas"; so L. T. Smith, who was deeply conversant with Northern dialects (*York Plays*, p. 544). RB suggests "flies" (p. 505). The biblical text describing the fourth plague clearly specifies flies (see Exodus 8:24–31), and it may be presumed that *loppis* either had been adapted in Northern English to signify flies, or that the author or scribe made an error in using the word incorrectly. Fleas of course do not "flye" (line 293). Whatever the case, Towneley uses the same term (*loppys*) and also indicates flying (line 305).

295   *beestis lyes dede and dry.* The fifth plague, "very grievous murrain" (Exodus 9:3).

315   *poudre.* Powder — i.e., ashes. In Exodus 9:8–11 the ashes were taken up by Moses and allowed to be blown by the wind, causing boils.

317   *Like mesellis.* Skin affliction, implying leprosy. The sixth plague.

320   *thondour-slayne.* The effect of storm and lightning which destroy vines everywhere. The seventh plague.

339   *Wilde wormes.* Locusts, the eighth plague. See Exodus 10:4.

343–44   *thre daies . . . So myrke.* Three days of darkness. The ninth plague.

345   *grete pestelence.* Terminology reminiscent of the bubonic plague, which, along with other lethal diseases, afflicted York from time to time after 1349. The tenth plague, in Exodus 11–12, afflicting the firstborn children of Egypt.

404   The Towneley pageant has a stage direction at approximately this point: *Tunc merget eos mare* ("Then the sea shall drown them" [line 413 s.d.]).

406   *Cantemus domino*. Rastall points out that in the York rite this is the incipit of a responsory for matins at Quadrigesima and, with a slightly different text, as a tract for the Easter vigil (*Heaven Singing*, p. 237). See Exodus 15:1.

12. THE ANNUNCIATION TO MARY AND THE VISITATION

    The long opening monologue in twelve-line stanzas with interpolated Latin quotations by the Doctor serves the purpose of introducing the prophecies of the Incarnation from the Old Testament and is related to the *Ordo Prophetarum* in the liturgical drama. The quotations from the Vulgate in Latin that are included in the text are brief and are glossed in English. John Clerke's notation on the first page that "this matter is newly mayde wherof we have no coppy" perhaps refers to revisions in the Doctor's speech that were never entered in the Register. However, since no reference to the Doctor appeared in the *Ordo paginarum*, this speech hence would appear to have been added after 1415. The body of the play treats the Annunciation and the visit to Elizabeth in two scenes, written in eight-line stanzas, with a variant form chosen for the conclusion of the Visitation. These events form the Gospel readings for Wednesday and Friday of the third week in Advent. The pageant was sponsored by the Spicers, a mercantile guild, at one time joined by the metal-working craft of Founders.

15   *prophet Amos*. The quotation at line 17 has not been identified.

25   *foule fende begyled*. The Incarnation was designed to beguile the beguiler Satan and hence to trick him, thus depriving him of his right to possess all the descendants of Adam. See especially the *Temptation* pageant and explanatory notes in this edition, and additionally, for background though with qualifications, see Marx, *Devil's Rights*, pp. 114–25.

26–27   *fedd / Be tyne*. Satan's anger blinds him to the truth, and will continue to do so in the New Testament plays in which he appears.

34   *Quoniam in semine . . . etc.* Genesis 22:18.

43   *Rorate celi desuper*. The incipit of an Advent introit, from Isaiah 45:8: "Drop down dew, ye heavens, from above, and let the clouds rain the just; let the earth be opened, and bud forth a savior." See the *York Breviary*, 1:47, though it is hard to imagine that this Latin extra-metrical quote and those that follow were sung. The dew was held to represent the Holy Spirit (lines 51–52); compare the famous fifteenth-century lyric "I syng of a myden that is makeles":

> He cam also stylle ther his moder was
> As dew in Aprylle, that fallyt on the gras.
>   (Brown, ed., *Religious Lyrics*, p. 119)

59   *Propter hoc . . . etc.* Isaias 7:14.

64   *Ecce virgo concipiett . . . etc.* Isaias 7:14; compare *Liber usualis*, p. 356.

71–72 *On David sege*. As a descendant of King David, he will sit on his throne as a Great High Priest who delivers judgment and separates truth from falsehood.

73 *Zelus domini faciet hoc*. Isaias 9:7.

75–77 Jesus is the Prince of Peace, who brings reconciliation.

80–89 *Egredietur virga de Jesse . . . bees borne*. Isaias 11:1. This prophecy is the inspiration for the Jesse tree, which appears frequently in iconography, including very damaged examples in the York parish churches of St. Denys and St. Michael Spurriergate. An early fourteenth-century example in the Minster has a restored Jesse at the bottom, from whose body a vine grows; this vine is the genealogical tree illustrating Christ's lineage. In the center at the top are the Virgin and Jesus, the latter conventionally represented as a Child within the flower (*YA*, p. 33, and *Inventory of the Historical Monuments*, vol. 5, pls. 52–53 and 62).

94 *Ero quasi ros . . . lilium*. Osee 14:6. The attribution to Joel in line 90 is incorrect.

97 *lelly floure*. The lily, separating Gabriel and the Virgin at the Annunciation, is part of the standard iconography, which appears, for example, in York parish churches and in the *Bolton Hours* (see *YA*, p. 44, fig. 9). An example in York Minster glass places a crucifix on the lily, which makes the connection between the Incarnation and the sacrifice on the cross, both of which were believed to have taken place on the same day, March 25 (*YA*, pp. 39–40).

99 *hegh Haly Gaste*. In iconography the dove of the Holy Spirit often accompanies rays of light extending between heaven and the Virgin Mary, but the rather heterodox representation of Jesus' soul as a small nude child also with a cross descending appears in the *Biblia Pauperum* (p. 48) and in the miniature cited above in the *Bolton Hours*, a work associated with the rich Blackburn and Bolton merchant families at York. See lines 190–93.

104 *hir clene liffe*. Mary is a perpetual virgin, both before and after the birth of her Son; see, for example, the antiphon *Alma redemptoris mater*: "You who . . . who gave birth to your own sacred Creator and yet remained a virgin afterward as before" (trans. A. Davidson, *Substance and Manner*, pp. 21–22; and see also Raby, *History of Christian-Latin Poetry*, p. 226). *Alma redemptoris mater* is the little clergeon's song sung in Chaucer's Prioress' Tale (*Canterbury Tales* VII[B²]518ff). Mary is the *porta clausa* of Ezekiel 44:2, widely accepted as prophetic by medieval theologians, including St. Thomas Aquinas (see Gibson, "Porta haec clausa erit," pp. 143–50).

114 *Godhed, maydenhed, and manne*. Asserting Mary's role as the Mother of God (*Theotokos*), as affirmed by the Council of Ephesus in 431 C.E. See especially the discussion of the Virgin Mary by Gibson and her illustration of a devotional image of Mary that, opened, contains a Trinity with Jesus on the cross in her womb (*Theater of Devotion*, pp. 137–76; esp. p. 145, fig. 6.2).

119–20 *Non auferetur . . . est*. Genesis 49:10a. An introit or responsory.

125 *Et ipse erit expectacio gencium*. Genesis 19:10b.

134–35   *Ecce mitto angelum . . . ante te*. Mark 1:2.

140–41   *Ego quidem baptizo . . . spiritu sancto*. Matthew 3:11. Responsory verse.

157 s.d.   *Tunc cantat angelus*. Late stage direction by John Clerke, referring to the *Ave Maria* (Luke 1:28); the English paraphrase beginning in line 158 may not have been sung in earlier years. The Latin chant may have been added at some point, possibly as a replacement for the English text.

158   *Hayle*. On the gestures involved in this scene, see Palmer, "Gestures of Greeting," esp. pp. 130–34.

165 s.d.   *Tunc cantat angelus*, Ne timeas, Maria. See Luke 1:30. The English paraphrase follows. If the Latin chant was used, possibly here only a short segment would have been adopted, with the angel then speaking the remainder of the item in English.

172   *bodword*. The message that Gabriel brings concerns the gift of God's grace extended to Mary in her pregnancy with the Son of God. The Annunciation will be the first of the Five Joys of the Virgin.

190   *The Holy Gast in thee sall lighte*. Based on Luke 1:35. The moment of conception, promised above, seems to have followed at the end of this speech. The event is conventionally depicted by means of rays extending down from heaven, where the Father is positioned. In some cases pyrotechnics were used, as in the famous Florentine *Annunciation* of 1439 in which "a fire comes from God and with a noise of uninterrupted thunder passes down the three ropes towards the middle of the scaffold . . . rising up again in flames and rebounding down once more, so that the whole church was filled with sparks" (Meredith and Tailby, *Staging*, p. 245). A stage direction in the N-Town collection specifies that "the Holy Gost discendit with three bemys to oure Lady, the Sone of the Godhed nest with three bemys to the Holy Gost, the Fadyr godly with three bemys to the Sone. And so entre all three to here bosom" (ed. Spector, Play 11, line 292 s.d.). The Conception was considered a most significant event for all of history, for this was the time when the Incarnation was effected (see C. Davidson, *From Creation to Doom*, p. 68).

198–205   *Thou aungell, blissid messanger / Of Goddis will I holde me payde . . . saide*. In this speech Mary accepts the gift of the Son. The Conception has occurred.

206   The beginning of the *Visitation* portion of the pageant in which Mary visits her cousin Elizabeth, who is pregnant with John the Baptist. This scene also was popular in the visual arts as a devotional image — e.g., a fine sculpture in the Victoria and Albert Museum (Cheetham, *English Medieval Alabasters*, p. 176, no. 103) — though there is little extant evidence for York (*YA*, pp. 43 and 45).

218–21   *Blissid be thou anely . . . nere*. Derived from the *Ave Maria*.

253 s.d.   *Tunc cantat* Magnificat. The pageant ended with the singing of the *Magnificat*, or much more likely a portion of it; see Luke 1:40–55: "My soul doth magnify the Lord," etc. Technically Mary should be the singer; the actor was most likely a boy soprano.

13. Joseph's Troubles about Mary

The portion of the entry retained in the *Ordo paginarum* emphasizes Joseph's wish in his shame to send Mary away without public notice, and Gabriel's message to them (actually, in the play to Joseph only) to order them depart for Bethlehem. The text in the Register, however, makes much more of Joseph's confrontation of Mary and his accusation concerning the paternity of the child. He recounts the miraculous happening in the Temple — the flowering of the rod that he had been given — and knows about the prophecy that a virgin shall conceive, yet he cannot believe that this can possibly apply to him. The comedy involved in presenting Joseph as an old and impotent man (see line 196: "Thase games fra me are gane") emphasizes the anguish of his disbelief. In this he is much less the irascible old carpenter encountered in the Joseph of the N-Town plays. Tom Flanigan points out that, "in dramatic terms, his frustration is partially attributable to Mary's exasperating reticence."[23] But believing himself to be beguiled, he is, as Mary responds, himself "begiled" (line 214). Suggested by two biblical verses only (Matthew 1:19–20), the story of Joseph's doubts had been expanded and popularized in the *Protevangelium* and those later sources which the author would have had at hand, including the *Meditations* and chapter 5 of Nicholas Love's adaptation, *The Mirror of the Blessed Life of Jesus Christ*, that would easily have been available.[24] As the second Eve who is to play an essential role in reversing the Fall, Mary is of course exemplary in her chastity, and she was the universal object of devotion in the medieval city of York.[25] *Joseph's Troubles*, written in part in unique ten-line stanzas and, in lines 79–166, in eleven-line stanzas, was the responsibility of the Pewterers and Founders, whose craftsmanship involved the production of tin-alloy utensils and badges.[26] The Founders may also have worked in lead.

1–20	The beginning of a long lament. Joseph, returning to Mary after an absence, emphasizes how tired and weak he is. In the play, he likely was given a crutch, as frequently in iconography (e.g., the *Bolton Hours*, fol. 36). In the Coventry Shearmen and Taylors' pageant, Joseph by way of contrast simply returns, whereupon he discovers that Mary is with child and enters into a short dialogue with her prior to his vision of the angel, who will affirm her virginity. In the York play, he already knows of the pregnancy, and this informs his sour mood in the opening monologue.
21–40	Joseph's recounting of the episode in the Temple in which he is recognized as one who is chosen to marry by the miracle of the flowering rod. The scene appears in glass possibly by the York school of glass painters in a window at Great Malvern (Rushforth, *Medieval Christian Imagery*, p. 346, fig. 164).

---

[23] Flanigan, "Everyman or Saint," p. 33.

[24] James, ed., *Apocryphal New Testament*, p. 44; *Meditations*, trans. Ragusa and Green, pp. 26–30; Love, *Mirror*, pp. 34–37. For discussion, see Woolf, *English Mystery Plays*, pp. 169–73.

[25] For comparison with the same episode in the Towneley collection, see Lyle, *Original Identity of the York and Towneley Cycles*, pp. 54–56.

[26] See Blair and Ramsay, eds., *English Medieval Industries*, pp. 66–77.

43   *My yonge wiffe is with childe full grete.* According to the *Protevangelium* she is six
       months pregnant at the time of Joseph's return, but the York dramatist places
       her even later in her pregnancy. The York pageant emphasizes that this would
       be a matter of very great shame and would mark Joseph as a cuckold.

65   *why ne walde som yong man take her?* A suggestion of the old man with a young wife
       scenario of fabliaux; see Chaucer's January and May in the Merchant's Tale. The
       Meditations give Mary's age at the time of her marriage to Joseph as fourteen (p.
       14).

66–70 *over ga hir . . . mylde.* He considers abandoning her in the forest, but fears that
       "wilde bestes might sla hir." His conflicted attitude is expressed by line 70: "She
       is so meke and mylde." The *Protevangelium* had reported that Joseph was con-
       templating letting "her go from me privily," which merely echoes the statement
       in Matthew 1:19, but the idea that legal ramifications are involved was also intro-
       duced there (James, ed., *Apocryphal New Testament*, p. 44). In line 49, he had said
       "The lawe standis harde agayns me" (see Deuteronomy 22).

81   *Sho sittis at hir boke full faste prayand.* An iconographic commonplace. The prayer-
       book either rests on her lap or on a lectern in many depictions of the Annun-
       ciation; there are useful examples in alabaster carvings (see Cheetham, *English
       Medieval Alabasters*, nos. 91–98 and 100).

108   *Say, maidens, how es this?* Mary's housemaids are there to provide certainty con-
       cerning Mary's celibacy, and hence are designed to counter what might be called
       the fabliaux effect of the scene. However, the mention of the visit of the angel will
       serve to increase Joseph's doubts and to reveal his extreme anxiety as he is about
       to confront Mary herself. The handmaidens are not noted in the *Ordo paginarum*
       and thus were in all likelihood added sometime between 1415 and c. 1463–77.

257–75 The angel of the Annunciation, Gabriel, comes to Joseph in a dream (see Mat-
       thew 1:20) to explain the Incarnation and to convince him of Mary's innocence.
       In York art the scene appears in a printed Missal of 1533 (*Missale secundum usum
       ecclesie Eboracensis*, sig. B7), but this is a book that had been produced in Paris
       (see *YA*, p. 45). Gabriel orders that Joseph, as the espoused husband, should call
       the child *Jesus*. Consistent with cultural practice, the playwright's assumption
       seems to have been that the espousal ceremony had legally made them like hus-
       band and wife, verified by Joseph's taking Mary into his household to live, but
       not yet confirmed by the Church's marriage rite.

279   *Brynge hir to Bedlem this ilke nyght.* Gabriel will thus provide motivation for the
       journey to Bethlehem; nothing is said about Caesar Augustus' census that would
       require Mary and Joseph to travel to the "city of David" (Luke 2:1–5).

301   *Slike poure wede.* Emphasis on the poverty of the Holy Family is conventional,
       though representations of them in images and other media often depicted them
       wearing rich garments, even in Mary's case, for example, wearing a gown lined
       with ermine in a window of c. 1430 at All Saints, North Street (Gee, "Painted
       Glass of All Saints' Church," pl. XXXII).

14. The Nativity

The earlier history of this pageant, dramatizing the third Joy of Mary, is problematic in part on account of erasures in the *Ordo paginarum*, which in its present form also suggests a direct connection with the next pageant of the Offering of the Shepherds.[27] Were these two plays presented as a single drama in tandem, as appears to have been the case with the Masons' and Goldsmiths' Herod and Magi pageants? There is also reference in the *Ordo paginarum* to a midwife, following the *Protevangelium* a common character in earlier narratives of the Nativity but missing in the extant text. Further, the *Nativity* is based in part on the iconography introduced by the *Revelations* of St. Birgitta (Bridget) of Sweden that was prevalent only after c. 1420, as, for example, in an illustration in the *Speculum humanae salvationis*.[28] Its biblical source is mainly Luke 2:6–7.[29] That the play as it stands still was not a final version is suggested by the entry in the civic records in 1567 which specifies that John Clerke is to enter into the Register plays not previously included along with "of the Tylars the lattr part of their pageant."[30] The verse form is a seven-line stanza. The Tile Thatchers who produced the play were craftsmen involved in the building trades, specializing mainly in the tile roofs that were the norm in late medieval York.

1–28   Seeking such a desolate location for the night's lodging was necessary on account of overcrowding in the city of Bethlehem, though the biblical explanation for the lack of space in any of the inns — that is, the census allegedly ordered by the emperor — is not cited. The stable is primitive, with a broken roof, which would have appealed to the sponsoring guild, and walls that have fallen down. The scene seems very much like a Flemish painting such as the Dijon Nativity by the Master of Flemalle to which Robinson has called attention (*Studies in Fifteenth-Century Stagecraft*, p. 124 and fig. 1).

39–44   *wolde I fayne we had sum light . . . bryng.* It is "right myrke" (the traditional time is midnight), and Joseph will go for a light and will also look for a source of "fewell," presumably wood for a fire to heat the cold stable, but not to enlist the help of midwives as in earlier versions of the story. Joseph, having returned, holds a candle in the Dijon Nativity and in some other representations of the birth of Jesus such as a stained glass panel, possibly by a York glass painter, at Great Malvern (Rushforth, *Medieval Christian Imagery*, p. 278, fig. 136).

50–56   The birth of Jesus, as described by St. Birgitta (*Life and Selected Revelations*, p. 203; Cornell, *Iconography of the Nativity*, pp. 1–15). Mary would have been kneeling here with her hands held in a gesture of prayer, as suggested by St. Birgitta. She presumably remained in this posture through the recitation of the Hail lyrics that follow. The birth has been painless, for Jesus has been conceived without sin, and the Child appears as if miraculously on the ground before her. She only picks up the Child at lines 64–66, and wraps him in a "poure wede."

[27] See RB, pp. 426–27.

[28] Wilson and Wilson, *Medieval Mirror*, p. 156.

[29] See especially Robinson, *Studies in Fifteenth-Century Stagecraft*, pp. 60–80.

[30] *REED: York*, 1:351.

78 *what light is this.* Joseph's amazement at the radiance from the Child which overwhelms the light of the candle he is carrying. The source of the light is the aureole surrounding the infant, who will be the light of the world; see Birgitta, *Life and Selected Revelations*, p. 203. At Barcelona in 1453, a tableau vivant of the Nativity presented Jesus as an infant, nude and "glowing with light" (Meredith and Tailby, *Staging*, p. 72). Special lighting effects are surveyed by Butterworth, *Theatre of Fire*, pp. 55–78.

91 *this foode.* In addition to the literal meaning (i.e., the actual Child) here, King supports a "sacramental reading" that links the Child with the food of the Eucharist, particularly appropriate for a pageant presented on Corpus Christi (*York Mystery Cycle*, p. 103). A Eucharistic reading was previously suggested by Robinson, who cites the carol "Wylyam northe of York" that identified the Child as "blyesful fowde" (*Studies in Fifteenth-Century Stagecraft*, p. 77; Greene, ed., *Early English Carols*, no. 36). This would have been particularly appropriate in the play if, as King suggests, the newborn was taken up from the ground in a gesture reminiscent of the Eucharistic liturgy.

97 *a starne to be shynyng.* Conventional imagery and, as noted, consistent with prophecy (Numbers 24:17), but certainly part of the stage set.

106 *floure fairest of hewe.* Compare Isaias 11:1.

108–12 *Hayle . . . floure.* Hail lyrics, as in the Magi and Purification plays. The lines express reverence for Jesus as Creator, King, and Savior. He is the one, the *Mirour of Mans Salvacioune* explains, who at his birth was given to the world as "a soverein preste" whose flesh was like a "shelle" in which "was hidde his deitee" (lines 1078–80). Joseph's lines echo the idea, implicit in the Christmas Vigil liturgy, of the coming into time of the Redeemer who will judge the world, as King points out (*York Mystery Cycle*, p. 98), but these lyrics also are reminiscent of the texts of prayers designed to be spoken at the time of the elevation at Mass as an affirmation of God's presence (see Robbins, "Levation Prayers," and Rubin, *Corpus Christi*, pp. 155–63).

122–33 *beholde thes beestis mylde . . . warm hym with.* In Love's *Mirror*, the ox and the ass in the stable kneel down and place their mouths on the manger so as to warm the Child since they understood that on account of the cold he "hade nede to be hatte in that manere" (p. 37). These two animals are conventional in iconography (see, for example, the *Bolton Hours*, fol. 36) and are derived from the Hebrew text and the Septuagint version of Habakkuk 3:2 ("in the midst of two beasts will thou be known"), Isaias 1:3 ("The ox knoweth his owner, and the ass his master's crib"), Pseudo-Matthew, and other sources (see Schiller, *Iconography*, 1:60–61).

149 *My God, my Lorde, my Sone so free.* Robinson (*Studies in Fifteenth-Century Stagecraft*, p. 74) notes that these words echo St. Birgitta's *Revelations*: "*Bene veneris deus meus, dominus meus et filius meus*" (see Birgitta, *Life and Selected Revelations*, p. 203).

15. THE OFFERING OF THE SHEPHERDS

Like the previous play, the *Offering of the Shepherds* appears to have been rewritten after the compilation of the *Ordo paginarum* in 1415 and before the pageant was entered in the Register. In this case, however, the *Ordo paginarum* is consistent with the structure of the play aside from the missing leaf, first noticed by Beadle, which contained the angel's announcement of the newly born Child Jesus (after line 55).[31] Perhaps the most interesting aspect of the pageant, however, is the connection, not fully understood by scholars, with the *Shrewsbury Fragments*, for there are parallels with the lines of the third shepherd in the *Officium Pastorum* in Shrewsbury, MS. Shrewsbury School VI, fols. 38r–39r.[32] The biblical source in Luke 2:8–20 forms the ultimate basis for the pageant, but the story also was known through many other sources as well as from depictions in the visual arts. The one example from York that illustrates the Adoration is from the sixteenth century: a carved staircase panel from the Bar Convent.[33] There are, however, two instances of the Angel appearing to the shepherds in glass in the Minster and a fine full-page woodcut in the York *Book of Hours* printed on the Continent in 1517 which shows one shepherd falling, another on one knee, and a third shielding his face at the appearance of the angel, who holds a scroll.[34] Pamela King calls attention to the reading of a lesson recounting the event from the Venerable Bede in the York liturgy for Christmas Day.[35] The pageant, in a seven-line stanza except for the three beginning and three ending stanzas that have a common twelve-line form, was the responsibility of the Chandlers, who supplied the wax candles so very widely used in religious rites in pre-Reformation York.

5–12   *Oure formefadres . . . by borne.* The first shepherd knows the prediction of the Patriarchs and Prophets that a prince shall be born in Bethlehem, and the other two will also prove themselves knowledgeable in this respect. They are thus not ordinary shepherds but rather in a symbolic sense also representative of spiritual shepherds, the clergy, who are leaders in maintaining the adoration of the Child in the liturgy. Yet they do simultaneously maintain their identity as shepherds, including their traditional musical ability, though their singing is less competent than the angel's song. Shepherds often appear with bagpipes (see Rastall, *Heaven Singing*, pp. 349–50).

15   *A sterne shulde schyne.* The account in Luke does not include the star, which is borrowed from the Magi story, but the reference by the second shepherd to "lightfull lemes" shining in darkness (line 16) is consistent with the medieval tradition; see, for example, the star to which the angel points in the upper right of the miniature in the *Holkham Bible Picture Book*, fol. 13.

---

[31] Beadle, "Unnoticed Lacuna."

[32] See Davis, ed., *Non-Cycle Plays*, pp. 1–2.

[33] *Inventory of the Historical Monuments*, vol. 3, pl. 42.

[34] *YA*, pp. 53–54.

[35] King, *York Mystery Cycle*, p. 104, citing the *York Breviary*, 1:83.

23–24   *als clene maye / As ever she was byforne.* Again an assertion of Mary's virginity both
          before and after the birth of Jesus. King cites a processional for Christmas Day:
          "You gave birth to your Maker, and you remain a virgin eternally" (*York Mystery
          Cycle*, p. 99, quoting *York Manual and Processional*, p. 138, in translation).

31   *The force of the feende to felle in fighte.* A glance at the Last Day of history, when
          Satan will finally and permanently be overcome, but also relevant to the everyday
          struggle against temptation.

37   *Hudde.* The second shepherd is called by name.

39   *Colle.* The first shepherd also calls the third shepherd by name.

42   *swilke a sight.* This would appear to refer to the star, not yet the angel or angels,
          though a *selcouthe sight* nevertheless.

after 55 The missing leaf would have presented the coming of the angel, whose song was
          the *Gloria*, undoubtedly sung by a professional singer from one of the parish
          churches or the Minster since subsequent notice by the shepherds will be indi-
          cative of a higher level of skill. In the Shewsbury *Officium Pastorum*, the third
          shepherd comments on the "nobull noyes" made by "an angel bright" (lines
          16–17). The text of the *Gloria* is liturgical, differing from the Vulgate version in
          Luke 2:14 which has *altissimis* instead of *excelsis*, and would presumably have been
          sung from musical notation so would require an experienced church musician.
          A *Gloria*, simply represented by an incipit, from Chester in London, British
          Library, MS. Harley 2124 is reproduced in Rastall, *Heaven Singing*, pl. 7, though
          in the pageant a liturgical chant from the York service books would have been
          used. There is good reason to suspect that instruments might have been included
          since in iconography they appear frequently in representations of heavenly
          music. The first shepherd, in saying he can imitate "itt alls wele as hee" (line 60),
          is surely exaggerating his ability, though when joined by the others (as appears
          to be the case, and if so he must have been a lead singer) he is able, with their
          help, to command "a mery note" (line 65).

67   *I have so crakid in my throte.* "Crakid" may be little more than a generic term for
          singing here, but it nevertheless suggests that the shepherds sang harshly, with
          "sharp, sudden burst[s] of sound" (Carter, *Dictionary*, p. 102). The effect on the
          second shepherd's throat, suggested also by his dry lips, indicates a tight-throat
          singing technique.

78   *fynde that frely foode.* Compare Shrewsbury *Officium Pastorum*: "To fynde that frely
          fode" (line 37).

84–85   *myrthe and melody / With sange.* The shepherds sing in procession as they cross to
          where the Child and his parents are located. No indication in the York text is
          present to suggest the nature of the music, and the staging is not clarified either.

92–95   The third shepherd reveals that the angel had told them the Child should be
          found between the "two bestis tame," and this would presumably have been a
          spoken addition to his lost song on the leaf missing from the playtext.

103   *belle of tynne.* English shepherds used sheep bells to help locate their herds, but
        this must be a smaller bell, attached to a "baren" or poor brooch. Bells were con-
        sidered to be a useful defense against the devil.

112   *Two cobill notis uppon a bande.* Hazelnuts on a string, probably as a bracelet.

124   *horne spone.* A large spoon, designated as to size (large enough to hold forty peas).
        Spoons frequently appear in iconography in association with the infant Jesus; for
        discussion, see Ishii, "Spoon and the Christ Child." The third shepherd's gift to
        the Child in the Shrewsbury *Officium Pastorum* is an even larger horn spoon, which
        "may herbar an hundrith pese" (line 44). This speech (lines 39–49) and the third
        shepherd's at York are nearly identical except for Shrewsbury's "dayntese" instead
        of York's "novelté" and the addition of two final lines at York.

131   *make mirthe as we gange. Mirthe,* in this context, simply suggests singing; see Dut-
        ka, *Music,* p. 100. A partly erased addition by John Clerke, read by Beadle under
        ultraviolet light (RB, p. 428), suggests that a conclusion to the play was wanting.
        However, it is possible that Clerke was noting only a missing final song, already
        cited in the final line of text, and not any further matter.

16. Herod Questioning the Three Kings and the Offering of the Magi

In the *Ordo paginarum* of 1415 the pageant of how the three Magi, following the star,
appear in Herod's court and then present their gifts to the Christ Child is attributed to the
Goldsmiths and Masons, though in that document the guild identifications and description
of the play were at some time altered and hence are difficult to interpret. In the second list
of c. 1422 in the *York Memorandum Book A/Y*, these guilds seem to be responsible for different
plays, with further doubt introduced since the reference to the Masons is entered in a different hand and interlined. In the Register the guilds' plays are entered separately with a
portion copied twice. Lucy Toulmin Smith printed them as separate plays, but Beadle has
described how, probably in 1432 or thereabouts, they had been revised to create a single
drama that could be performed on two pageant wagons representing Herod's court and the
scene of the Holy Infant, the Masons then being given the responsibility for the former.
Beadle's argument is convincing in part also since the alliterative verse forms in the first
fifty-six lines likewise argue for composition at about this time, with the remainder utilizing
a familiar twelve-line stanza representing older strata in the text. In its present state, the
play in the Register is only representative of how it was staged between c. 1432 and not long
after c. 1470, since by 1477 the Masons were instead given responsibility for the Purification.[36] Information is lacking about the Masons' portion of the drama between 1477 and
1561, when its "pageant of Herod inquyryng of the three kynges for the child Jesu" was
given to the Minstrels; however, the earlier sponsorship was then still remembered as being
formerly "brought forth by the late Masons."[37] The Masons were much employed about
York, especially on the city churches and the Minster, until the 1530s, which more or less
marked the end of church building in York on account of the Reformation. The Goldsmiths,

[36] *REED: York,* 1:115.

[37] *REED: York,* 1:334.

who tended to live and work in the liberties, would have been uniquely able to supply the kings' crowns and other touches of gold signifying royalty, including the first Magi's gift. The Epiphany, the manifestation of the Godhead incarnate to the gentile princes of the world, is celebrated in the West on January 6; the play follows the narrative outlined in the Gospel lesson for that day (Matthew 2:1–12).

1–22   Herod reveals himself to be the typical ranting tyrant, the ridiculousness of what he says underlined by various claims such as his alleged ability to control the winds. In lines 17–18, he insists he is sixty-seven times "fairer of face and fressher on folde," which is highly unlikely to have been the way he was represented in the pageant. He seems to be directing his claim to fair appearance against those who have the right to use heraldic red, a color common in coats of arms and represented as valued beyond the financial resources of ordinary people. King calls attention to the antiphon *Herode iratus* at the feast of the Massacre of the Innocents in which Herod precipitates an overflowing of anger resulting in terrifying atrocities (*York Mystery Cycle*, p. 111, citing *York Breviary*, 1:118 and 147). To symbolize such wrath at Beverley the actor playing Herod apparently appeared in blackface (Leach, "Some English Plays and Players," p. 213), and a dark-faced Herod appears in thirteenth-century painted glass in the York Minster Chapter House (*YA*, p. 54, fig. 12). The reasons for his angry disposition are outlined in the *Stanzaic Life*, culminating in his fear that as an earthly monarch he will be destroyed by a heavenly king (pp. 63–64).

23–26   *All kynges to youre croune . . . fro light.* Herod's soldier-retainers are consummate flatterers, but here what they say has immediate meaning for the encounter with the three kings who will shortly meet with the tyrant. In the following lines Herod will assert his supremacy, threatened as he is by any challenge to his authority. He remains the villainous tyrant of the liturgical drama (for the *Officium Stellae* and Fleury *Herod*, see Young, *Drama of the Medieval Church*, 2:59–100), but since he is not restrained by the decorum of liturgical drama he can demonstrate much broader and more inappropriate gestures and loud speech. In his pride he thus serves as a foil to the gentle Mary and her infant Son, who represent peace and humility as they also are strong beyond anything that Herod can imagine, since theirs is the power that has formed the cosmos and continues to sustain all things. In stained glass in the church of St. Michael Spurriergate, Herod has been given a crown with a devil emerging from it (Skey, "Herod's Demon Crown"), an accouterment that well might also have appeared as part of his costume in this play on the feast of Corpus Christi. See also the discussion of masks for such characters in Twycross and Carpenter, *Masks and Masking*, pp. 216–20.

57–90   Beginning the Goldsmith's contribution to the pageant, the three kings are introduced as directly opposed to proud Herod. Entering from different directions, they praise God as the author of everlasting life. They are following the brilliant star stationary in the east that will stand over the place where Jesus has been born. Jacobus de Voragine's *Golden Legend*, citing Fulgentius, indicates that the star, instead of being "fixed in the firmament" was "suspended at a level of the air close to earth" and "was brighter than other stars, so bright indeed that sunlight could not dim it" (1:81). The same source mentions that when Jesus was born, the star appeared in the shape of "a most beautiful child over whose head a cross gleamed" (1:80), iconography that has been traced to the Book of Seth in the fourth century (Trexler, *Journey of the Magi*, p. 27). The Child appears in the star in the Coventry Shearmen and Taylors' pageant (line 536; *Coventry Corpus Christi Plays*, p. 99). In the York pageant, the star would have been required to be suspended at a high point above the Goldsmith's wagon stage where it would be clearly seen by the audience, and it would need also to disappear over Herod's court (see, for example, Mirk, *Festial*, p. 49). Its reappearance may have been produced, as in the York liturgical *Magi* play of 1220–25, by introducing a second star (*REED: York*, 1:1), presumably shining when the Magi depart from the tyrant's court. The kings know, if they are a little vague about it, what they are looking for, and they are grateful for their meeting so that they may travel together. Their names are not specified in the pageant, but the *Golden Legend* identifies them as Gaspar, Balthasar, and Melchior.

109   *of felashippe are we fayne.* Their meeting is fortuitous. They represent friendship, as opposed to the bully Herod who can have no real friends, and hence look forward to the sense of community that should exist among Christians — and should be reinforced by the Peace in the Mass when the pax brede or *osculatorium* is passed (see McLachlan, "Liturgical Vessels and Implements," p. 420).

119–24   *Sir Herowde is kyng . . . drede.* They will ask for "his wille and his warande" in order to travel safely — in other words, the equivalent of a modern visa. In the Coventry Shearmen and Taylors' pageant, Herod extravagantly offers a "paseporte for a hundred deyis" (line 615, p. 102).

129ff.   The action returns to Herod's court as the Magi approach. Herod reveals himself to be a sadist, torturer, murderer, and, significantly, deceiver. In this he will be encouraged by the Consolators.

157   *Mahounde, my god.* Stereotypically, Mohammed is idolatrously worshiped and in league with Satan.

189–91   *Whedirward, in the develis name . . . bune in bande.* This must have been spoken as an aside, and so too the lines of the Consolators. Similarly, lines 235–46 are asides, which the kings should not hear.

215–34   Recitation of the prophecies of Christ's coming by Balaam, Isaias, and Hosea.

215–16   *Balaham saide a starne shulde spryng / Of Jacob kynde.* Echo of the Epiphany sequence, portion sung on the second day of the season (see King, *York Mystery Cycle*, p. 114, citing *York Missal*, 1:32).

260   *Ye be bygilyd.* Spoken as soon as the kings have departed. Herod and his evil counsellors will, however, be the ones beguiled — another instance of the beguiler beguiled, an important theme in the York cycle.

268   *And playe us in som othir place.* The Masons are now free to move their pageant wagon and cast to the next station, which means that it would be placed forward, before the Goldsmiths' wagon, on the pageant route.

272 s.d. *Harrode passeth and the three kynges commyth agayn.* At this point the Masons depart, and the Goldsmiths take up the remainder of the pageant.

285 *Whame seke ye, syrs.* Spoken by Mary's handmaiden and echoing the *Quem queritis* of the Easter *Visitatio sepulchri*, which is there spoken by the angel.

303 *giftis of gud aray.* They show the gifts they have brought. Love's *Mirror* states that they "offred and leide here giftes before him" upon a cloth before his feet (p. 44).

307–08 *for honnoure and elde, / Brother, ye shall begynne.* Showing the required deference to the eldest, who will present his gift and worship the Child first. In iconography, this is usually quite obvious, with the eldest, who is kneeling, having a long beard, and the youngest, still beardless, standing where he will be seen to be the last to present his gift. For an example, see the *Biblia Pauperum*, p. 52, but the iconography is ubiquitus. Among several York examples, see the painted glass in a window in All Saints, North Street (Gee, "Painted Glass of All Saints' Church," pl. XXIIa), and the Bowet Window in the Minster (*YA*, pp. 54–55, fig. 13). The king who is kneeling and presenting a gift invariably has removed his crown, and in the Bowet Window the second king is beginning to take his off in preparation for presenting his gift.

309–20 *Hayle . . . I pray thee.* The first king speaks a set of Hail lyrics, as will the others; compare the *Nativity*, lines 107–12. Jesus has come into time to give protection from the fiend and to unbind people from sin and hell — a suggestion of the power of the keys, the ability to bind and loose sins, later delegated to St. Peter and subsequently to the Church.

313 *marc us thi men.* To be marked (sealed) as Christ's own forever, normally in the baptismal rite.

319 *golde that is grettest of price.* Traditionally the first king's gift, an appropriate tribute to a king (see Jacobus de Voragine, *Golden Legend*, 1:83). In the window at All Saints, North Street, the gift is a gold cup. Love's *Mirror*, praising Mary's devotion to poverty, says that she gave the gold and other gifts "al to pore men" (p. 45).

321 *foode that thy folke fully may fede.* The word "foode" signifies *child*, but here is a pun since the infant in this case will also become the spiritually nourishing food of the Eucharist.

328 *Als the gleme in the glasse.* As the miraculous conception has taken place, so then his birth also happens in a way that will not to disturb Mary's virginity. In depictions of the Annunciation in some Flemish paintings, the beam of light representing the coming down of the Holy Ghost passes through a glass window on its way to the Virgin (Schiller, *Iconography*, 1:49), often to her right ear, to emphasize by this means the major Epiphany theme of the Word become Flesh (Scott, *Later Gothic Manuscripts*, figs. 204, 209, 346, and 448). See also the poems cited by Gray, *Themes and Images*, pp. 100–01.

331 *Insens to thi servis.* The second gift, explained in the *Golden Legend* as symbolizing sacrifice (Jacobus de Voragine, 1:83), foreshadowing the Crucifixion but also indicative of Christ's role as the Great High Priest.

334   *For our boote shall thou be bounden and bett.* In the course of the Passion, prepar-
         atory to the actual Crucifixion. In Love's *Mirror*, the kings prepared to leave by
         kissing Jesus' feet and hand — and the infant then blessed them (pp. 44–45).
         The kneeling king kissing the Child's feet appears in Italian art (see Trexler,
         Journey of the Magi, pp. 99 and 112, figs. 22 and 28), and the infant holding up
         his hand in blessing is common (see, for example, *YA*, pp. 49–50).

341–42   *sen thy body beryed shal be, / This mirre will I giffe to thi gravyng.* Myrrh, used for
         burial, foreshadows Christ's death and burial.

357ff   *For solas ser now may we synge.* The kings possibly did engage in song as they pro-
         cessed away from the Bethlehem site, but there is no indication of what they
         sang. Processions were an important part of the Epiphany ceremonies. However,
         Rastall believes this reference to singing is merely metaphorical (*Heaven Singing*,
         pp. 45–46). Instead of then returning to Herod, the kings discover they are very
         tired, and, at the suggestion of the Third King, decide to "reste a thrawe" (line
         365). In depictions in the visual arts, the kings retain their crowns as they sleep.

369–80   The vision of the angel, whose warning against returning to Herod's court will
         be heeded; they will flee to their own countries.

17. THE PURIFICATION OF THE VIRGIN

The Purification pageant is misplaced in the Register, from which it was initially omitted,
very likely, according to Beadle, because it was not being played when the manuscript was assembled,[38] though it was to be taken up by the Masons, with financial assistance from the
Laborers, in 1477.[39] The *Ordo paginarum* supplies proof that it was being produced by the
religious guild associated with St. Leonard's Hospital in 1415, and at that time its dramatis
personae included a midwife and two of Simeon's sons not present in the pageant text as we
have it. At some time roles for the Presbyter and an angel were added. The pageant was not
to be entered until John Clerke was assigned to do so in 1567, when it was given to the Laborers.[40] Then it was copied into the Register out of order, immediately following the Emmaus
pageant. There is a reference to it, partly erased, at the location in the Register where it should
have appeared.[41] The inconsistency in the stanza forms may be attributed to changes as the
play changed hands and was passed down, finally being subjected to some modernization by
John Clerke as well. The Masons seem to have remained the principal guild producing the
pageant in the sixteenth century until when, after the 1530s, their fortunes declined on
account of the halt in ecclesiastical construction and the poverty of the city. As noted, the
Laborers had been drawn in to give support, but what role the Hatmakers played is unclear,
as Beadle observes.[42] The Purification was commemorated on Candlemas (February 2), one

---

[38] See RB, p. 435.

[39] *REED: York*, 1:115.

[40] *REED: York*, 1:351.

[41] RB, p. 436.

[42] RB, p. 437.

of the major feasts of the late medieval Church, but it is also important to remember that the "churching" of women following childbirth was a practice that was maintained as late as the 1662 Book of Common Prayer, which retained most features of the medieval English Sarum rite. The woman was expected to wear a white veil, as likely was done by the actor playing Mary in the pageant. The play essentially follows the account in Luke 2:22–38 and other sources. It conflates the Purification ritual with that of the Presentation, which in Jewish tradition was a different ceremony.[43]

1–56	The long speech by the Presbyter returns to the Creation and to the giving of the law to lapsarian humanity, and then proceeds to cite the rule on the purification of women required by Leviticus 12. Conception "having received seed" and subsequent childbearing result in a state of defilement for the woman. She will remain impure for forty days (longer for girl children), after which the purification ritual is specified. The "beistes good" (line 26) required for the ceremony were a dove and a lamb for sacrifice, or, if on account of poverty she is not able to provide the lamb, two doves may be brought to the priest of the law. Lines 53–56 indicate that the Presbyter is the one who will receive Mary and the Child at the Temple in Jerusalem. His initial speech shows signs of being patched onto the beginning of the play to identify the location at the Temple and to provide context.
5	*In nomber, weight, and mesure.* See Wisdom 11:21.
57–86	The widow and prophetess Anna, now in her eighties, has been living in the Temple and predicting the coming of the one who will be "the redempcion of Israel" (Luke 2:38, quoted in line 184). Her appearance in the story normally would come after the introduction of Simeon. Here she is the one to introduce him.
76	*The well of mekeness.* Mary is represented as a fountain, filled with grace and a conduit of grace to believers (see Gray, *Themes and Images*, p. 89). Pseudo-Matthew had placed Mary's first encounter with the angel of the Annunciation at a well (James, ed., *Apocryphal New Testament*, p. 74).
91	*I ame wayke and all unwelde.* Simeon's lament lays great stress on his age, presumably as a centenarian, and his weakness; he is only holding onto life in the hope of seeing the Messiah, as the prophets have predicted (see lines 107–18). The Holy Spirit has promised him that he will live to see the Child, a promise repeated by the angel (lines 167–70), and in the pageant he will be greatly strengthened as he performs the Temple ritual — a sign that the writer was thinking in terms of dramatic effect. In Love's *Mirror* Simeon is described as a "rightwisman," who will come to the Temple at the opportune time since he is led there by the Holy Spirit (p. 47).
113–14	*That he shulde comme with us to dwell . . . of light.* King notes that this is a paraphrase of the Candlemas antiphon *Lumen ad revelationem gentium* (*York Mystery Cycle*, p. 125, citing *York Missal*, 2:18).

---

[43] See Shorr, "Iconographic Development of the Presentation," p. 17.

119–22   *he shulde comme and harro hell . . . all on syde.* Prophetic, predicting the Harrowing, when Jesus will come like "a gyant" to break down the gates of hell, release the captives in limbo, and put down the "feyndes." In conventional iconography, Jesus at the Harrowing is depicted as much larger than the other figures, indeed like a giant.

130   *Knytt in oure kynde.* The "babb" (line 129) is of two natures, joining God and man inseparably.

137–64   *Nowe Lorde, thowe grant to me . . . owte of dowte.* These lines are mainly a prayer by Simeon asking that he might be allowed to have a sight of the holy one whom he craves to see.

166–67   *Bodworde to thee I bryng . . . of myght.* The messenger of the Holy Ghost is an angel, an intermediary who reinforces the promise that Simeon will see the Messiah.

195–222   *Here in this Temple . . . I wolde.* Mary, who has rehearsed the forty-day rule for purification, locates the holy family in Jerusalem, near the Temple to which they will proceed. In the lines which follow, they will discuss the need for the ritual, though Mary has not "conceyved with syn fleshely" (line 203). Mary will insist on fulfilling the law.

246–53   *To riche to offer bothe . . . Reddy at hand.* Their poverty is again stressed; thus they do not need to provide the lamb. The doves are ready in a basket, the conventional container that appears in iconography, as in the full-page woodcut in the Book of Hours printed at Rouen for York use in 1517 (*Hore beatissime virginis Marie*, fol. xviii; *YA*, p. 56).

263–64   Because Jesus is "the lame of God . . . / That all our syns shall take away," they have the required lamb for the ritual. These words are adapted in translation from the *Agnus Dei* in the Ordinary of the Mass.

274   *Lo, here is the Tempyll on this hyll.* The Temple must be on the pageant wagon, Mary and Joseph in the street. Their approach to it should be a short procession, perhaps holding candles as in the Candlemas ceremony; see C. Davidson, *Festivals and Plays*, pp. 20–21. Processions have been documented as early as the fourth century in commemorations of the Purification (Duchesne, *Christian Worship*, pp. 499 and 548). The *Stanzaic Life* describes the approach of Jesus and his mother to the Temple as a procession, with candles (pp. 99–100).

281–99   The holy family has arrived at the Temple, and Mary prays that their offering may be accepted. In the following lines (299–323) the priest will focus entirely on the Child, the Savior of the world, since the mother is undefiled. As the *Mirour of Mans Saluacioune* says, Mary "ne had nothing nede of purificacioune" (line 1209, p. 79), confirming the pageant's focus on the Presentation. Glass in Great Malvern Priory, perhaps by the York school of glass painters, shows Mary holding out the Child to be blessed; behind her is Anna, wearing a wimple and with a lighted taper (Rushforth, *Medieval Christian Imagery*, p. 106, fig. 38). In mid-fourteenth-century glass in York Minster, Anna has a candle in her left hand, and where there is now a patched area, her right hand had held the basket with the doves (*YA*, p. 57, fig. 14).

326 *Welcome bright starne that shyneth bright as day.* The central image of Anna's welcome in lines 324–31. The emphasis on light is appropriate to Candlemas. Jesus is the Light of the World.

338–39 *welcomme with all honour / Here in this hall.* Joseph and Mary, with the Child, are prepared to come into the Temple, though in actual Jewish rites the woman would not have been allowed to enter. The English rites of Purification were done at the church door, and only thereafter the woman was allowed to come inside (see Rastall, *Heaven Singing*, p. 260). What follows seems dramatically unworkable without a time gap for the action that Simeon is directed to do.

341–42 *Dresse thee furth in thyne array, / Come to the Temple.* Simeon must put on his vestments, which, as in the *Speculum humanae salvationis*, may have involved garments and perhaps a miter reminiscent of those worn by contemporary bishops or abbots (Wilson and Wilson, *Medieval Mirror*, p. 160).

350 *Nowe wyll I to yon Temple goo.* The Temple must be nearby, but at least on account of his newly found youthful gait he can move quickly to where he will greet Mary and the "babb." He clearly stands before her by line 358 if not before.

366 *Haill floscampy and flower vyrgynall.* Terminology applying to the Virgin Mary. She is a flower of the field, a "ryall roose" and "unfadyng" (lines 370–71). The well-known carol states: "There is no rose of suche virtue / As is the rose that bare Jesu" (J. Stevens, ed., *Mediaeval Carols*, pp. 10–11).

374 *mekly I beseke thee here where I kneyll.* Simeon has been kneeling, probably from about line 354. Compare Love's *Mirror*: "he kneled done and devoutly honourede and wirchiped him as he was in his modere armes born" (p. 47).

376 *in my narmes for to heve thee.* Simeon takes the Child in his arms (see Luke 2:28) and begins a long speech (lines 378–414) in which he asks the child to embrace him. There is no stage direction to indicate when Simeon will place the Child on the altar where he will be adored. Iconographic models suggest a freestanding square altar, with Simeon behind it and facing Mary.

415–23 *In peace, Lorde, nowe leyf thy servand, / For myne eys haith seyn that is ordand . . . For evermore.* Paraphrase of the *Nunc dimittis.* Simeon is now accomplishing that for which he has so long waited, and he can die in peace. The canticle is spoken in a paraphrase, not sung, while Simeon is still holding the Child. The *Nunc dimittis* would have been a very familiar canticle since it was sung daily for Compline, later absorbed into the service of Evening Prayer in the Book of Common Prayer of 1549. The text is from Luke 2:29–32. The *Stanzaic Life* explains that in this canticle Simeon specified three qualities of Jesus in order: "hele, light, joy of Israele" (line 2719, p. 92).

425–27 *That with thee in thy kyngdome shall dwell . . . great care.* An addition to the *Nunc dimittis*; at the Last Day, those destined for the heaven will be separated from those who will be "drevyn to hell."

441   *the sworde of sorro thy hart shal thryll.* Luke 2:35. A reference to the Seven Sorrows of the Virgin which will pierce her heart, sometimes depicted literally in Dominican iconography.

459   *God Son, thowe grant us thy blyssyng.* The baby is asked for his blessing. The infant Jesus performing a blessing at his Presentation is quite common and has been observed by Shorr as early as an illumination in the ninth-century Drogo Sacramentary ("Iconographic Development of the Presentation," p. 25, fig. 13).

18. The Flight to Egypt

The Register contains the pageant as it was at the time it was entered, but possibly not as it stood in the sixteenth century. John Clerke notes that "This matter is mayd of newe after another form" — a comment that was subsequently deleted. The play then either differed substantially, or in this case Clerke could simply have been making a hasty (and mistaken) observation based on viewing the pageants at the first station at the gates of Holy Trinity Priory. If thus altered, the play would not have been unique among the York plays. The subject matter of the flight from Herod's massacre of children is from a narrative point of view joined with the next pageant, which dramatizes that atrocity; see Matthew 2:13–21. Both were commemorated in the York liturgy, but the principal feast was of course Holy Innocents. The pageant of the Flight shows Joseph as the guardian of Mary, a traditional role, but also has less interest from the point of view of its drama than the following play. The Flight was produced by the Marshals, whose occupation involved the care of horses, so they presumably could have supplied an ass for Mary to ride upon, as the text suggests as a requirement. The verse is a unique form of twelve-line stanza, with irregularities.

1–24   Joseph begins with a lament, mainly concerning his age and his state of exhaustion, which supplies motivation for sleeping. This in turn provides the opportunity for the angel to appear and reveal to him the bad news concerning the threat represented by Herod. Joseph is not, however, rebellious, for his heart is "sette" on fulfilling the law (line 10) and on not allowing anyone to prevent him from doing so.

14   *That made me, man, to thy liknes.* See the first creation story in Genesis: "Let us make man to our image and likeness" (1:26).

29   *As thou me to thy modir chaas.* In her prayer, Mary appeals to God who has chosen her to be his mother — an essential paradox of Christianity, that the Father should choose her to bear the Son, who is part of the undivided Godhead.

37   *Wakyn, Joseph, and take entent.* This and a number of other lines are duplicated in the Towneley *Flight into Egypt.*

37–40   *Wakyn, Joseph . . . slepe no mare.* In Matthew 2:13, following the departure of the Magi, the angel of the Lord appears to Joseph in his sleep.

42   *So swete a voyce.* The angel is speaking, not singing, but has a clear, sweet voice comparable to the ideal singing voice (see A. Davidson, "High, Clear, and Sweet"). The word "shylle" is used to describe it in the next line; it is tempting

to gloss this term as *shrill*, but that word has connotations which are not applicable here. The appeal of the voice leads Joseph to know the identity of the speaker, who will be revealed to be Gabriel, the angel of the Annunication.

51–62   Gabriel's message is an expansion of the very brief biblical account of Joseph's vision that appears in Matthew's gospel, in which the angel tells Joseph to go to Egypt and to stay there until he tells him it is safe to return.

60   *Tille he be dede*. Referring to Herod, who dies, and is succeeded by Herod Antipater. There will be no dramatization of Herod's terrifying death here as there is in the N-Town play (Play 20, lines 233–85). Herod was generally thought to be, as Love insists, "the develes servant" (*Mirror*, p. 51).

84   *doughtir*. A term of endearment, appropriate for a young woman.

102   *his foo*. Joseph does not identify the foe by name until line 112. Mary will repeat "His foo" at the beginning of her speech in the next line (concatenation), but Joseph must wait until she has finished to announce that the enemy is Herod, who has chosen to slay all children under the age of two (lines 111–22).

139   *His harte*. Referring to Herod. Mary's speech (lines 135–46) is a lament over the very idea of someone wishing to kill her only son, who is of course also God's only Son.

148   *leve of thy dynne*. Indicative of the intensity of Mary's lament. Joseph will indicate that there is no time to lose, and they must be careful in their flight so that they meet no one who wishes to slay the Child (lines 153–55).

161   *such smale harnes as we have*. A reminder of the poverty of the Holy Family, for they have only a few household things to take with them.

168   *It fortheres to fene me*. While the general meaning may be surmised, the text as it stands is unclear. Bevington emends the line to read: "It fortheres [not] to fene me"; he glosses: "It's no use pretending or delaying (lit. it doesn't further matters to feign, shirk); I must bear this pack of all I'm responsible for and complain about (?)" (*Medieval Drama*, p. 434).

176   *To Egipte talde I thee*. Mary is frightened, and cannot remember what Joseph has said their destination was to be, but neither of them have a clue about where they are ordered to go. God will need to guide them.

188   *wilsom wayes make us to wende*. Love emphasizes the difficulty of travel for an old man and a young wife with a baby along "a nuyes wey and herd and diverse, that was not inhabited and also a wey ful longe" which may have taken "the travaile of two monethes and more" (*Mirror*, p. 51).

194   Bevington suggests a stage direction: "*Mary mounts an ass with her child*" (*Medieval Drama*, p. 435). This would be a convenient way to have the actors set out toward the next station. Mary mounted on an ass and holding the Child appears in a window in the choir of York Minster (*YA*, pp. 57–58, fig. 15).

19. THE MASSACRE OF THE INNOCENTS

The *Ordo paginarum* of 1415, insofar as the damaged manuscript can be read, mentions Herod, two soldiers with lances, and four weeping mothers, but probably Consolators would have been included. The text in the Register again represents the pageant in c. 1463–77 in which presumably only two mothers have speaking roles, though in regard to speech designations the manuscript here is not reliable. By John Clerke's time, the text had been revised or, more likely, replaced, for he entered the comment that "This matter . . . agreyth not with the Coucher in no poynt, it begynnyth, 'Lysten lordes unto my lawe.'" The episode of Herod and the massacre of the children of Bethlehem, deriving ultimately from Matthew 2:16, was commemorated in the liturgy in association with the feast of Holy Innocents (December 28). Iconographic evidence from York, fourteenth-century glass in the Minster, suggests that the soldiers wore armor and that they appeared to impale the infants on their spears.[44] Herod witnesses the carnage, and may even participate in it. The York pageant, written in an eight-line stanza with three stresses to the line, was produced by two manufacturing crafts, the Girdlers, makers of belts and similar items, and the Nailers.

3	*Stente of youre stevenes stoute.* Undoubtedly aimed at members of the audience, who presumably were jeering at Herod, the enemy of Christ and, by association, of all children. Herod is a worshiper of Mahounde, understood as a god, or an idol, directly opposed to the ideals of a Christian community. His evil advisors, identified as Consolators, will encourage him to act out his anger and hostility.
41–45	*I am noyed of newe . . . a swayne.* Herod is disturbed that the three kings have not returned, as they said they would — to which the Consolator in the following lines suggests that they had been wrong and hence were embarrassed to return to Herod without anything positive to relate.
57	*Tham shamys.* A dative of agency construction (now archaic) in which the subject is acted upon; i.e., a shame came to them. Compare "methinks."
63–69	This portion of Herod's speech is corrupt in the manuscript, though the gist of it is clear.
89	*boy, thou burdis to brode.* Herod accuses the messenger of jesting; it cannot be that the kings have gone on without fulfilling their promise. But in lines 103–05 the messenger will reveal the truth, which is that Herod is deceived. His response is anger, Herod's typical temperament being revealed; in iconography, as at Fairford, he is typically seen holding a child whom he is stabbing with a long sword (Wayment, *Stained Glass*, pp. 79–80, pl. XXXIX). Nevertheless, here he is somewhat less extreme than the Herod of the Coventry Shearmen and Taylors' play in which "*Erode ragis in the pagond and in the strete also*" (line 728 s.d.; *Coventry Corpus Christi Plays*, p. 105).
145	*it is past two yere.* There seems to be some confusion in the play about the length of time since Jesus was born. Later it seems to be recognized that Jesus was not yet two years of age.

---

[44] *YA*, pp. 58–60, fig. 16.

152   *knave childir kepte in clowte*. The practice was to wrap children up rather tightly in swaddling clothes in lieu of diapers and the freedom given to modern infants; two years in such a condition would not have been unusual.

193   The soldiers have now arrived at Bethlehem. The missing line following line 193 would presumably have been an addition to the first soldier's speech rather than to that of the outraged mother. In the scene which follows, the infants would have been represented by dolls or puppets since it is of course unimaginable that a real child could have been jerked, pulled, and tossed about as violently as would have been required.

203   *And me, but itt be quytte*. A stage direction is implied here to indicate that the soldier is returning the mother's blows. Still, the scene is more subdued than the massacre in the Digby play of the *Killing of the Children*, nor is there any character like the cowardly and comic Watkin of that drama.

214   *And I hadde but hym allone*. An echo of Mary's line in the *Flight to Egypt*: "And I have but hym allone" (line 146).

226–30   *Allas, that we wer wroughte / In worlde women to be . . . spill*. The women lament their state; they will see the children whom they have brought into world in the pain of childbirth now literally butchered in their sight.

240   *How so they wraste or wryng*. Hand gestures, a common sign of grief and despair. See C. Davidson, "Gesture," pp. 82 and 97.

281   *we will wende before*. Herod will lead a procession on foot to the next station where the pageant will again be presented.

20. CHRIST AND THE DOCTORS

The play of the twelve-year-old Jesus in the Temple, a dramatization of the events recounted in Luke 2:41–51 and noted in the York Missal as a lesson in the Epiphany season,[45] is unusual in the York cycle for having a text that not only was borrowed for the Towneley collection but also shared structure and language with the Chester Blacksmiths' and Coventry Weavers' plays.[46] The York pageant, in twelve-line stanzas, was produced by the Spurriers, makers and sellers of spurs, and Lorimers, who were manufacturers of harnesses, bits for horses, and, at times, also spurs. This pageant stands at the end of the Infancy series. It commemorates an event in which Jesus was separated from his parents and, as Love comments concerning the young Christ's discussion in the Temple, found "sittyng among the doctours of lawe heryng hem entently, and askyng hem questiones wisyly."[47] The description in the *Ordo paginarum* likewise describes the scene as that of a scholastic discussion or debate on a subject

[45] *York Missal*, 1:36.

[46] For a collation comparing these plays, see *Coventry Corpus Christi Plays*, pp. 175–89, but see also Greg's "Bibliographical and Textual Problems" and his chapter on the subject in his 1935 Malone Society volume (*Trial and Flagellation with Other Studies*, pp. 101–20), with corrections by Cawley, "Middle English Metrical Versions," pp. 134–40.

[47] Love, *Mirror*, p. 59.

of great sensitivity. But the incorporation of the Ten Commandments seems related to the campaign of religious education, encouraged by Archbishop Thoresby, that was the force behind the assembling and dissemination of the *Lay Folks' Catechism* and the specifying of the basic demands of laypersons' knowledge.[48]

3 *solempne sightis.* Jesus has been taken by his parents to Jerusalem for the celebration of Passover (Luke 2:41).

15–20 Beginning Mary's lament upon discovering that her child is not with them. Joseph's response in the following lines should be seen as influenced by his age and feeble health, which make him at first the more reluctant partner in returning to Jerusalem. But he will be the one to recommend the return to look for him in the city. Their search for Jesus does not appear in iconography except for their discovery of him in the Temple at the end of the story.

45 *He is but twelve yere alde.* Jesus' age is specified in Luke 2:42.

49–50 The first Magister/Doctor asks that a scholastic disputation be organized. The final lines are a sign that the author was aware of the necessity to maintain the discussion within orthodox limits; the Coventry Weavers' play, as revised in the sixteenth century, refers to the "statute of this lande" and the "perell" of standing in opposition to "any artyccull." Those who oppose are heretics to be prosecuted and "in the face of peple ooponnly slayne" (lines 855–56; *Coventry Corpus Christi Plays*, p. 138) — a glance at the statute *De heretico carburendo* (*Statutes of the Realm*, II Henry IV, c.15) perhaps.

67 *Laye fourthe oure bokes.* The Magisters will require their books; Jesus will not need to consult any. Late fourteenth-century painted glass at York Minster shows the Magisters reading at lecterns. In line 141, Jesus notes that they are "sette on rowes," which is consistent with representations in iconography. These are embedded stage directions.

93–94 *I wote als wele as yhe / Howe that youre lawes wer wrought.* The Coventry play is even more emphatic, for Jesus says he has actually been "in those placis" in which "all owre lawis furst were wroght" (lines 903–04; *Coventry Corpus Christi Plays*, p. 139). His ability to understand scripture is due to the presence with him of the Holy Spirit, as he explains in the York play (lines 101–04).

112 *Itt may falle wele in wirkyng.* An offer to test the boy Jesus.

113–16 *For David demys . . . loving.* The reference is to Psalm 8:3: "Out of the mouth of infants and of sucklings thou hast perfected praise." The Towneley play quotes the biblical text from the Vulgate.

145–50 *this is the firste bidding . . . lowde and still.* The first of the two commandments in the summary of the law in Matthew 22:37–40, but derived from Deuteronomy 6:5 and Leviticus 19:18.

---

[48] See also King, *York Mystery Cycle*, pp. 38–41.

153–56   *The secounde . . . sekirly.* To love your neighbor "Als youreselffe," Jesus says; the manuscript reading is correct since he is lecturing the priests of the Temple and it would be inappropriate to include himself. Compare the Coventry Weavers' pageant: "asse thyself" (line 963; *Coventry Corpus Christi Plays*, p. 141).

193–94   *he alleggis oure lawe / And lered nevere on boke to rede.* Jesus astonishes the Magisters, especially since he has not had formal training and ought to be illiterate. But Jesus possesses all wisdom, to the point where in the following speech the third Magister will want him sent away since he would detract from their learning and hence receive more praise than they. He will, however, be defended by the first Magister, at which point Joseph and Mary appear again, having arrived at Jerusalem to look for Jesus.

221–22   *where he sittis . . . Emong yone maistiris.* The Coventry Weavers' pageant has him sitting "aloft" (line 1022; *Coventry Corpus Christi Plays*, p. 143).

232   *They are so gay in furres fyne.* Probably ermine tippets are intended; in the example in Minster glass to which reference has been made above, the Magisters wear academic gowns and hats. Mary will refer to them in line 242 as "worthy wysse in wede," which is suggestive but not specific. For further discussion of the iconography, see *Coventry Corpus Christi Plays*, pp. 268–69.

237   *When I come there, what schall I saye?* Joseph is very class conscious and also feels shy on account of his age and debility, which will not allow him to bow or kneel before the priests. Mary will have to take control of the situation.

259–60   *My Fadir werkis . . . am I sente for to fulfyll.* See Luke 2:49: "did you not know, that I must be about my father's business?" This is beyond Mary's comprehension, and she will have to contemplate what is to follow.

21. The Baptism of Christ

The lesson from Matthew 3:13–17 recounting the Baptism of Christ was read in the York rite at Mass on the first Sunday after the Octave of Epiphany[49] — that is, one week prior to the reading of the lesson from Luke which tells the story of Christ in the Temple which formed the subject matter of the previous pageant. Further elaboration crucial to the play is found in the other gospels, especially John 1:29–34. The Baptism and John the Baptist, the saint who effected it, were popular in York. The Minster's fabric rolls reveal that it had several relics, and the saint was frequently depicted in ecclesiastical art in the city. Enough remains so that it is possible to determine how St. John was expected to appear.[50] In glass such as a panel of c. 1470 in the church of Holy Trinity Goodramgate, he is shown as he would have appeared in the desert: he wears a camel skin with head attached, with a

---

[49] *York Missal*, 1:34.

[50] *YA*, pp. 61–67 and 184.

cloak over it, and holds a roundel before him with the symbolic Agnus Dei.[51] Because the Barbers were involved in the healing arts, their sponsorship of the Baptism play, depicting the institution of a Sacrament designed to heal the spiritual defects of humankind, seems appropriate. The York playtext, representing its status at or near the end of the third decade of the fifteenth century, would probably be rewritten during the time John Clerke came to supervise the production of the cycle, as his notations in the manuscript seem to imply. The verse is in seven-line stanzas.

3–4   *yf I preche . . . of thy comyng.* John was famous as a preacher and recognized by the Christian community as a prophet; see the Baptist's words in John 1:23: "I am the voice of one crying in the wilderness, make straight the way of the Lord, as said the prophet Isaias." These words are quoted in lines 27–28 of the pageant. Modern scholarship regarding John the Baptist has cast new light on his activities and on the prevalence of ritual washing in first-century Palestine, and the question remains whether the secretive Mandaean religious minority that survived in Iraq until modern times may be traced to the cult of John the Baptist.

29–49   As King notes, John's speech here tends increasingly "to vanquish historical verisimilitude" and to rely on manuals of instruction such as the *Lay Folks' Catechism* (*York Mystery Cycle*, p. 172). The necessity of baptism for salvation is indicated.

50–71   John is told what he already in part knows, but now he is provided with specifics by the two angels. The description of the descent of the Holy Spirit along with the sound of the loud and passionate voice of the Father may be regarded as a stage direction for what is to happen at lines 149–54: a dove will descend and the voice of the Father will proclaim, perhaps in Latin, "This is my beloved Son, in whom I am well pleased" (Matthew 3:17; compare Love, *Mirror*, p. 67), omitted from the extant text of the play. The voice of the Father probably was heard without his actual presence as represented by a visible actor.

84–105   Jesus continues to explain baptism as an example (*myrroure*) for all *men* (i.e., all people) that is necessary for entering "endless blys."

101–05   *The vertue of my baptyme dwelle / In baptyme watir evere and ay . . . Haly Gaste.* Water used for baptism was considered holy even though the lengthy Continental rite of consecration was not present in English rites. Christian baptism was regarded as efficacious for the washing away of original sin and as a seal to signify being "Christ's own forever." For a brief description of the English rite, see Dudley, "Sacramental Liturgies," pp. 219–27.

120–21   *What riche man gose from dore to dore / To begge at hym that has right noght?* Proverbial, and here expressing John's reluctance to baptize Jesus. John will tremble with fear at what he has been asked to do (see lines 141–42). Woolf speaks of the "feeling of devout unwillingness" (*English Mystery Plays*, p. 219).

---

[51] *Inventory of the Historical Monuments*, vol. 5, pl. 57; Knowles, "East Window of Holy Trinity." For a survey of the iconography in relation to the York play, see C. Davidson, *From Creation to Doom*, pp. 80–85; and for England generally, Rushforth, "Seven Sacraments Compositions," pp. 89–92, and Nichols, *Seeable Signs*, esp. pp. 193–206.

149–50   *I baptise thee here in the name / Of the Fadir and of the Sone and Holy Gost.* The Trinitarian formula required in baptism, following the York Manual. Jesus would appear to be standing in the river Jordan, but there is no reason to believe that he would be nude, as in representations in glass at Holy Trinity Goodramgate or St. John Ousebridge, the latter now inserted in a window in the Minster (*YA*, pp. 66–67, fig. 17). Blue cloth might have been used to represent the water rising up to Jesus' waist, and the posture of standing as if in the water would have been retained surely. Water probably would have been poured over his head from a shell by John. The anointing with oil and chrism which appear in the Towneley play are missing here.

154 s.d.   *Tunc cantabunt duo angeli* Veni creator spiritus. Hymn for Whitsunday; see *York Breviary*, 1:503; translated by Dutka in *Music*, pp. 119–20. For York music, see *Hymni*, fols. 32v–35r; compare *Liber usualis*, pp. 885–86, for the usual musical setting, which may differ slightly from that used in the English rites. Rastall suggests that professional singing men may have been hired to sing, but the music, especially if abbreviated to the first stanza, would have been within the reach of amateurs, either from the Barbers' own guild or another (*Heaven Singing*, pp. 331–32). It is a devotional moment.

157   *The dragons poure.* Compare Psalm 73:13 (*AV* 74:13): "thou didst crush the heads of the dragons in the waters." As King observes, this passage was adapted in an antiphon for the Epiphany season (*York Mystery Cycle*, p. 43, citing *York Breviary*, 1:193). The power of the dragon has now suffered defeat through the means of the baptism of Christ since he is sinless prior to the act. Yet that defeat may not be immediately obvious, and much more will be required of Jesus — that is, his death on the cross. The Baptism may be regarded as part of the elaborate trick that God is playing on Satan through hiding Jesus under the cover of his humanity.

162–68   Jesus reminds the audience that trusting and believing in him are necessary along with the ritual of baptism in order to "come to blisse." On the other hand, those who fail "schal be dampned."

22. The Temptation in the Wilderness

The tempting of Christ by Satan in the wilderness is reported in Matthew 4:1–11, the gospel lesson for Quadragesima Sunday in the period leading up to Lent in the liturgical calendar.[52] The Smiths' play on the subject begins with a monologue by Satan, who then approaches Jesus at the conclusion of his forty days of fasting in the desert. Jesus will be tempted, as Love points out in his *Mirror*, by gluttony, "veyn joy," and a combination of avarice and idolatry. He was, says Love, "tempted in alle maner temptacion that longeth to the infirmyte of man without synne";[53] an illustration showing each of the temptations accompanies Love's text in Edinburgh, National Library of Scotland, MS. Advocates 18.1.7, fol. 49v.[54] The *Biblia*

---

[52] *York Missal*, 1:52.

[53] Love, *Mirror*, pp. 74.

[54] See C. Davidson, *Deliver Us from Evil*, p. 66, fig. 9.

Pauperum places the image of this event, with the Savior holding up his hand, palm out against an ugly horned Satan, over against a depiction of Adam and Eve with the serpent in the Garden to show that Christ's role is to reverse the effects of the Fall by resisting the tricks and false promises of Satan.[55] The play presents some challenges in staging which the sponsoring guilds were likely well-positioned to solve. In the production of the pageant the Smiths were joined in 1530 by the Locksmiths, both occupations that had a long history in the city extending back to at least to Anglo-Scandinavian York. The *Temptation* is written in six-line stanzas.

1	*Make rome.* Diabolus' appearance here suggests folk drama, or at least a tradition of impromptu playing in the streets or in houses about which we know far less than we would like. He undoubtedly made his way through the audience to the pageant wagon; one would guess that by the second stanza he was already speaking from the stage and reporting on his fall "fro heven to hell" (line 8). In his role he was clearly intended to be comic, but he also, dressed in his demonic costume, would have been potentially terrifying to members of audiences who believed in him as the ultimate source of evil in the world.
9–18	Because Christ has not yet died for the sins of the world, salvation is not yet available; all who have previously died are in limbo or in the fearful depths of darkest hell. According to the abuse of power theory that emerges frequently in the theology of the York plays, Satan still maintains the right to possess them at their death as a consequence of the Fall and the inheritance by all of original sin.
19–30	*sum men spekis of a swayne . . . and morne.* Diabolus is not unaware of the Incarnation, but typically his thinking tends to be confused. Jesus' incarnation, he believes, is a trick, which indeed it is, for it deceives Satan and as one of its consequences makes possible the release in the Harrowing of those who have lived good lives in prior times. Jesus is the second Adam who has the power to reverse the effects of the Fall, a point implicit in the Epistle to the Romans 5:12–19.
43–44	*He has fastid, that marris his mode, / Ther fourty dayes.* Forty days "withowten foode" should, he believes, have weakened Jesus' moral fiber. The space of forty days of fasting has considerable resonance, since Lent was in York as elsewhere in Western Christendom a similar time of fasting, though not so stringent, obviously, as in Jesus' case. Diabolus, who initially hopes for success through the temptation to the sin of gluttony, is of course entirely wrong about what the effect of Jesus' fasting will be.
55	*Thou witty man.* Here Diabolus approaches Jesus and flatters him.
56–57	*If thou can ought of Godhede, / Byd nowe that ther stones be brede.* Translation of Matthew 4:3; compare Luke 4:3. Jesus' answer is paraphrased in lines 74–78: man shall not live by bread alone, for "Goddis wordis are gostly fode" that spiritually nourish humans "ilkone."

---

[55] *Biblia Pauperum*, p. 65.

91   *Uppon the pynakill parfitely.* A representation of the Temple would have been required as an essential part of the stage set, though no evidence is extant to indicate the manner in which Jesus was placed on the pinnacle. It may be that the Smiths had invented a device to lift Jesus aloft and to bring him down again, or his return could have been effected by presenting him with a set of stairs by which to descend. The late stage direction calling for angels to sing *Veni creator* at this point is probably misplaced; it does not seem appropriate for the Temptation.

145   *For I have all this worlde to welde.* If Jesus will fall down before him and honor him, Diabolus, the prince of this world (so described in John 12:31), will give him all kingdoms and all countries. See Matthew 4:7–9, but Diabolus does not take Jesus up into a "very high mountain" in the play.

159   *To pyne of helle I bide thee passe.* At the end of this little drama, Jesus will perform a highly dramatic act, in contrast to the biblical account in which the devil merely leaves him. But in a thirteenth-century York Psalter (London, British Library, MS. Add. 54179, fol. 45), Christ is shown still on the roof of the temple, while the devil is falling headlong downward and into a dark hole. It indeed will be, as Diabolus says, "warre than evere it was" (line 176). The "felawschip of fendis fell" (line 173) paradoxically can hardly be characterized by any sense of either friendship or community, both primary Christian values.

181–88, 200–204 The angels, who come in the biblical text to minister to him (Matthew 4:11), are intended to express appropriate wonderment at Jesus' accomplishment in resisting the three temptations.

205–08   *My blissing have thei with my hande . . . the fende.* Conventional gesture of blessing, and directed to the audience, or at least the members of it who will "stiffely stande / Agaynste the fende" of hell.

209   *my tyme is faste command.* He is anticipating the "tyme" of his Passion when he must endure torture and death on the cross.

22A. The Marriage in Cana

Only a portion of the first speech was entered in the Register. The *Ordo paginarum*, though in imperfect condition at this point, reported a play about Jesus, Mary, the bridegroom and bride, a steward, a servant, and six containers of water to be turned into wine. The attribution to the Vintners was recorded over an erasure. In the Register the play was to have followed the *Temptation*, whereas King has pointed out that the liturgical order should have placed it after the *Baptism* — the original order of the listing in the *Ordo paginarum*.[56] The Marriage at Cana was designated as a reading for Mass at the second Sunday following the octave of Epiphany.

---

[56] King, *York Mystery Cycle*, pp. 35–36.

23. THE TRANSFIGURATION

The synopsis in the *Ordo paginarum* lists the characters, the disciples Peter, James, and John, with Jesus "ascending onto the mountain" where he is transfigured. Elijah and Moses were also presumably named before damage to the manuscript. The pageant would have required special lighting effects in order to represent the transfigured Christ; Muir points out that in the Revello Passion play a convex silver reflector was specified to direct light from the sun or, if the day was cloudy, from a candle. Other effects, recorded in Continental plays, involved having Christ drop away his outer robe so as to appear in the dazzling white garment indicated in the gospels, and sometimes he was outfitted with a gold mask to represent his face, which in the York play "schynes as the sonne" (line 98).[57] A cloud was also lowered from which the Father was to speak. The account of the Transfiguration in the gospels was read in the York rite in the first week of Lent, on Ember Saturday, from Matthew 17:1–9. The Curriers, who produced the pageant, were leather workers specializing in the processing of hides. The verse is in twelve-line stanzas.

5   *sightis seere*. Supernatural effects; in the context of the theatrical event, the term implies the use of legerdemain.

8   *to yone mountayne will I goo*. Embedded stage direction. There must be a raised space on the pageant wagon to represent the mountain, which is said in the biblical accounts to be high.

17–20   *"Shewe us thy Fadir . . . Fadir thore."* Citing John 14:8–9. The pageant makes clear that the apostles are still not able to understand the full meaning of Christ's words, for this will only be revealed to them after the Resurrection.

27–28   *Quem dicunt homines / Esse filium hominis?* Luke 9:18, glossed in the following lines.

41–42   *biddis nowe / To tyme ye have my Fadir fonne*. Smith glosses: "Bide now till ye have seen my Father" (*York Plays*, p. 186).

49   Jesus now goes up onto the mountain; the disciples look up at lines 59–60 when Jesus appears, at first alone and then with Elijah and Moses, who have come from heaven and limbo respectively to testify to his divinity as God's Son (see lines 215–16). The three figures were regarded as analogous to the Trinity; thus they reveal the triune nature of God symbolically though not literally (Elijah and Moses were never of course regarded as part of the Trinity). Moses normally appears again with horns in this scene, as in the *Biblia Pauperum* (pp. 69 and 71). The historical survey in Schiller, *Iconography*, 1:145–52, is useful.

87   *It marres my myght, I may not see*. Possibly "myght" is a mistake for *syght*, meaning here his eyesight. In any case, the *sight* must involve a brilliant effect, which would have been emphasized by having the disciples shield their eyes.

91   *Are was ther one, now is ther thre*. A comment about what they have seen, not about what is in view at this moment. See also line 187.

---

[57] Muir, *Biblical Drama*, p. 117. For possible lighting effects, see Butterworth, *Theatre of Fire*, pp. 55–78.

97   *His clothyng is as white as snowe.* See the headnote to this pageant, above.

118–20   *quyk schall we come / With Antecrist for to fyght /Beffore the day of dome.* The battle of Elijah and his brother Enoch against Antichrist at the end of history is only to be found in the Chester cycle, but other plays on the subject appear on the Continent (Muir, *Biblical Drama*, pp. 150–51). The Wycliffite *Tretise of Miraclis Pleyinge* makes reference to one such drama: "Pley we a pley of Anticrist and of the Day of Dome that sum man may be convertid therby" (pp. 101–02). The Antichrist, based on a handful of references in the New Testament, was believed to herald the end times and to appear as the reverse of the Savior — in other words, as the epitome of evil. See Jacobus de Voragine, *Golden Legend*, pp. 8–9, and the *Chester Mystery Cycle*, Play 23.

127–30   *Unto Crist come, this is the same . . . are bonne.* A reference to the Harrowing, when Adam and the others will be drawn out of the "dongeoun" of limbo by Jesus and taken to bliss.

152–56   Peter's proposal to build a tabernacle to Jesus and others to Moses and Elijah (see Matthew 17:4) demonstrates his very considerable misunderstanding on his part of Christ's nature.

169 s.d. *PATER IN NUBE.* The cloud has descended; the Father's hand, held down from it in the gesture of blessing, likely was all that was visible of him, as the usual iconography suggests. His speech reaffirms his approval of Jesus, whose "sygnes sere" reveal him to be his Son (line 174).

183   *Rise uppe and tellis me what ye see.* See Matthew 17:6 for the description of the disciples' response to the vision of God the Father in the cloud: they fall on their faces at the sight. Jesus now commands them to rise and report on what they have seen and to regain their composure. However, their act of falling down would have covered the vanishing of Elijah and Moses which could thus have appeared to happen suddenly; on sudden disappearances, see Butterworth, *Magic*, pp. 75–77.

204   *To seke all sydis seere.* In other words, the light was shining all around them, as had been the case also with the shepherds when the angel had sung to them of the birth of Christ (Luke 2:9).

205   *that noys noyed us more.* Even more than the sight that they saw with its brilliant light and the miraculous figures of Moses and Elijah joining Jesus, there was "noys." Most likely at the appearance of the cloud some music would have been performed, not impossibly vocal with organ accompaniment.

223–28   A full view of the deity will not be revealed to persons living in this life, only in the life beyond death; the Father is, however, made known through the Son and revealed in part through "Poyntes of his privité" (line 226).

233–36   *This visioun lely loke ye layne . . . than clere.* They are not to reveal what they have seen until after the Crucifixion and Resurrection; see Matthew 17:9.

23A. THE FEAST IN SIMON'S HOUSE

Not recorded by either the original scribe or John Clerke, who was ordered to enter the Ironmongers' pageant in 1567;[58] nevertheless Clerke noted its contents in his handwriting in the Register, subsequently erased. Beadle's reading, under ultraviolet light, is as follows: "This matter lakkes, videlicet: *Jesus, et Symon leprosus rogans eum ut manducaret cum eo, duo discipuli, Maria Magdalena lavans pedes Jesu lacrimis et capillis suis tergens.*"[59] Jesus, invited by Simon the Leper to eat with him in his house, came with two disciples. While at the meal, Mary Magdalen washed Jesus' feet with her tears and then dried them with her hair. The erased entry in the Register is consistent with the description in the *Ordo paginarum*, but also describes the pageant as it probably existed in the final years when the cycle was being played.

24. THE WOMAN TAKEN IN ADULTERY AND THE RAISING OF LAZARUS

The pageants are based on readings (John 8:3–11 and 11:1–44) for Lent[60] and in fact began as separate plays. In the *Ordo paginarum* of 1415, the *Woman Taken in Adultery* and the *Raising of Lazarus* were listed individually, with the Capmakers being one of the guilds responsible for the latter along with the Pouchmakers and Bottlers. The *Woman Taken in Adultery* had been presented by the Plumbers and Pattenmakers. These pageants maintain something of their original identity, with *Lazare mortus* beginning at line 99. By 1422 the producer of the *Lazarus* was the guild of Hartshorners, who dealt with harts' horns, perhaps as a medicinal substance (see *MED*, s.v. *hertes-horn*). Both appear to have been written by the same author, and retain the same twelve-line stanza. By the time the Register was compiled, the plays had been amalgamated under the sponsorship of the Capmakers, with the Hatmakers being added in the sixteenth century.[61] John Clerke noticed the missing pages in the manuscript, but it is hard to see how the play could have been mounted without their content. As Beadle has suggested, by then the play seems to have been recast, yet never entered in the Register in its new form, this in spite of an order as late as 1567 that this should be done.[62] Why the Ministry stories were so poorly represented in the cycle is hard to explain, with the present pageant being, along with the *Transfiguration*, the only extant text between the *Temptation* and the *Entry into Jerusalem*, which to be sure incorporates some further miracles. The *Woman Taken in Adultery*, based as it is on a post-Patristic addition to John's gospel, focuses on the contrast between Christian values of community and forgiveness as set forth in the new law in contrast with the old law of ancient Judaism that would set firm penalties for lapses in human behavior and crimes against established values. The *Lazarus* is a foreshadowing of the Resurrection and helps to define this event's importance for human behavior.

---

[58] *REED: York*, 1:351.

[59] RB, p. 441.

[60] See King, *York Mystery Cycle*, pp. 79–83.

[61] *REED: York*, 1:356.

[62] RB, p. 441; *REED: York*, 1:351.

9   *and he a wedded man.* An elaboration of the story as reported in the gospel that increases the seriousness of the accusation in the eyes of the Jews. In N-Town, the man runs away holding up his trousers with his hand and with boots unlaced (Play 24, line 124 s.d.).

13   *false stodmere and stynkand strye.* Name calling. The *MED* supports the emendation of the text in the Register from "stroye," which makes no sense here, to "strye." In N-Town the woman is called a "fayre yonge qwene," terms suggesting that she is a prostitute (Play 24, line 69).

20   *Sho schall be demed to ded.* Compare Leviticus 20:10: "both the adulterer and adulteress" are to be "both put to death."

48   *stoned to dede.* See John 8:5, citing the law of Moses, presumably Leviticus 10:10, as requiring stoning.

after 54 The missing leaf would have continued the accusation of the woman, including further mention of stoning as the appropriate punishment according to the old law. The suggestion is made to have Jesus weigh in on the trial as a way of entrapping him; then Jesus "bowing himself down, wrote with his finger on the ground." As the Jews continued with their line of questioning him, he "said to them: He that is without sin among you, let him first cast a stone at her" (John 8:6–7). For relevant commentary, see Gibson, "Writing before the Eye." The extant lines of the pageant which follow reveal what happened next.

57   *here will new gaudes begynne.* It is clear that the Jews are enjoying themselves; catching the couple *in flagrante* is regarded as a sport, as will be the (expected) summary execution of the woman. "Forgiveness" is not part of their lexicon. Interestingly, it is the fourth Jew who speaks, and he is supposed to be, like the third Jew, a figure of authority (see lines 25–26).

68   *Of all thy mys I make thee free.* Jesus' act of absolution. This scene is particularly appropriate for Lent, a period of penitence for one's sins, leading up to Easter, by which time one was to have confessed to a priest.

70–74   Absolution is without value without acceptance of one's guilt and making a sincere determination to maintain oneself without sin. The woman is repentant and offers praise for being released from her sinful state.

85–86   *Whoso schall othir blame, / Loke firste thamself be clene.* Proverbial. See Tilley, *Dictionary of the Proverbs,* F107.

98a   *Lazare mortus.* This is not a stage direction but rather is the beginning of the Lazarus play, announced by a heading in Latin.

107–08   *that sekeness / Is noght onlye to dede.* Conventionally, the "sickness unto death" is despair, but here death will be turned to life to show the joy of God's goodness. Love's *Mirror* follows traditional teaching in equating Lazarus prior to his death with the Lenten theme: he represents the sinful man, even the death of the soul, from which Jesus miraculously is able to resurrect him from the sleep of death (p. 125).

141   *His sisteres praye with bowsom beede*. Mary and Martha of Bethany, who pray with their rosary beads in their hands. Though they despair because the Resurrection has not yet made salvation available, they nevertheless attempt to pray for their departed brother without Christian hope. This is expressed in the laments at lines 147–70.

after 171   Missing leaf. The narrative would have included Jesus going to Bethany, where he will stand before the tomb of Lazarus. It seems to be a coffer tomb, covered with a stone that requires to be removed much as in depictions of the Resurrection tomb. In the biblical text, when Jesus saw the sisters weeping and asked the location of the tomb, he wept. This effect may have been present in the part now missing from the pageant.

184   *Lazar, veni foras*. From the Vulgate, John 11:43; said with a loud voice.

204   *to Jerusalem will I wende*. The events commemorated on Palm Sunday and Holy Week will now follow.

25. THE ENTRY INTO JERUSALEM

Heavily dependent on the Palm Sunday liturgy, the Skinners' pageant begins the portion of the cycle that dramatizes the events of Holy Week. Its importance is signaled by its length, 544 lines, with indications of music both during the approach to Jerusalem and at the end of the play, in this case suggesting singing during a procession to the next station. The *Ordo paginarum* specifies the music in the first instance as *Benedictus Etc.* ("Blessed is he who comes in the name of the Lord"), perhaps the common form used following the *Sanctus* in the Mass. A *Benedictus qui venit* also appears as a responsory in the York Processional for use on Palm Sunday.[63] The *Pepysian Gospel Harmony* reports that "Jesus entred into the cite with gret processioun."[64] Palm branches were specified, but these, not being available in northern England, would have been replaced, probably by willows. Typically, in presenting Christ as the King coming to the gates of his city Jerusalem, the influence of the Royal Entry, itself intended as a reflection of the Palm Sunday procession, has also been acknowledged. The pageant is written in seven-line stanzas.

9   *Rawnsom*. Again mention of the ransom theory of the atonement. Jesus has been sent into the world to cancel the devil's rights to people's souls, releasing from bondage those who accept that he died for them and who follow his precepts — including those who were upright though they lived before his act of sacrifice.

13   *Petir, Phelippe*. The *Ordo paginarum* lists twelve apostles, with an interlinear correction to two, as in the play.

---

[63] But see Rastall, *Minstrels Playing*, pp. 17 and 54, and comment on lines 264–65, below. For descriptions of the Palm Sunday ritual, see, for example, Rastall, *Heaven Singing*, pp. 265–71; Erler, "Palm Sunday Prophets and Processions"; and King, *York Mystery Cycle*, pp. 131–42.

[64] *Pepysian Gaspel Harmony*, p. 76.

15   *castell that is you agayne.* The Vulgate has *castellum quod contra vos* (Matthew 21:2). The Douay-Rheims translation corrects to *village*, where the ass and her colt are found that will carry the King of Kings into the city on a humble beast — that is, in a manner opposed to the pomp of earthly monarchs; see, for example, Love, *Mirror*, pp. 141–42.

26–28   *Doghtyr Syon . . . opon.* Matthew 21:5, quoting the prophecy of Zacharias (9:9).

57   *The beestis are comen.* The ass and its colt are held in common by the village; hence the disciples go there as directed by Jesus with confidence that they will have a reasonable chance of taking them.

65   *To loose thes bestis withoute leverie?* The disciples are challenged by the porter because they have not shown the documentation required for legal possession of the animals.

88   *That Lorde we lefte at Bephage.* Further locating the action in space. The disciples have traveled a short distance from Bethpage, and surely this has involved the street-level playing area. Nor can the procession which will follow have been confined to a wagon and rather must have made use of the street.

93–94   *I schall declare playnly his comyng / To the chiffe of the Jewes.* The porter offers to give advance warning of Jesus' coming into the city (his *adventus*). This he will do, thus informing the citizens of the news (see lines 120–26). There will be eight burgesses or leading citizens, presumably in livery designating their status, who, along with a group of children, will be present to represent those in attendance at the entry on the first Palm Sunday.

134   *five thowsand men with loves fyve.* Miracle story; as told in all four gospels.

136   *Watir to wyne.* At the marriage at Cana, dramatized in Play 22A, for which the text is lost; see above.

143   *new lawes.* Jesus was proclaimed to have set aside the old law and to have insti-tuted a new dispensation of grace; the concept is asserted very strongly in the Pauline epistles.

152   *Yf thei were dyme.* The laws of Moses and the writings of the ancient prophets were considered dark, not capable of explanation without reference to the new dispensation; in iconography, this is illustrated in the contrast between the Syna-gogue, blindfolded, with crown falling off, and dropping the tables of the law, and the Church, which is represented as crowned and holding a model of a church, the place where the new law of mercy is proclaimed (*YA*, p. 182, for local examples).

200–01   *And sone will bringe agayne . . . beheste.* The porter trusts that the ass will be returned when the procession is completed, for "So thai beheste."

230–31   *Emang youreselff schall come grete seele . . . verray.* Unidentified quotation, presumably from an Old Testament prophet.

260–61   *Go we than with processioun / To mete that comely.* The two processions of citizens and of Jesus' party will set out from different places and then meet, as happened

in the procession of the Host on Palm Sunday; see Erler, "Palm Sunday Prophets," pp. 63–71, and Feasy, *Ancient Holy Week Ceremonial*, pp. 67–80. The two
processions come together at the gates of the city.

262   *With braunches, floures, and unysoune.* The audience very likely may have joined
        in strewing flowers in Jesus' way. The term *unisoune* implies monophonic singing
        in tune — i.e., "in agreement and concord" (Dutka, *Music*, p. 104; see also
        Carter, *Dictionary*, p. 536).

264–65 *Our childir schall / Go synge before.* As in the actual Palm Sunday procession, chil-
        dren sing "Osanna" in praise of "the sone of David" (see Play 30, line 343), pre-
        sumably in Latin: *Hosanna filio David.* See, however, the specification in the *Ordo
        paginarum*, cited above. The Middle English *Gospel of Nicodemus* gives the mean-
        ing of *Osanna* as "Lord, save us, we thee pray" (pp. 28–29). The children probably
        were positioned not only at the head of the procession but also on the top of the
        city gates, as represented on a pageant wagon, for this seems be what is suggested
        by the Beadle in Play 30, lines 314–15. More certain is that the way was strewn
        with wildflowers and that some, representing rich men, put down *thare robes* be-
        fore Jesus (Play 30, lines 343–45).

287   The dialogue now returns to the first procession, and at line 287 the children will
        begin to sing, if they have not already started to do so. Pauper in lines 310–12
        calls attention to the second procession of the citizens who are going out to meet
        Jesus "with melodye."

334–91 The healing of the blind and the lame does not occur in the New Testament nar-
        rative during the procession on Palm Sunday, but earlier. These miracles are
        merely noted at this time; see Matthew 21:14.

392–460 Zacheus, the rich publican and a short man, will climb a sycamore tree in order
        to see Jesus. This episode also occurs prior to Palm Sunday; see Luke 19:2–28.

447   *Me schamys with synne, but noght to mende.* He is ashamed of his sin, but now he is
        not any longer ashamed of mending his ways.

448–53 *I synne forsake . . . asith agayne.* The correction of *I* to *Mi* by a later hand in line
        448 is not necessary. Zacheus is affirming his decision to forsake his sin. He will
        give half his available goods to the poor, and will make restitution to those he
        has wronged. This is the type of statement one might find in a contemporary
        will, where such charitable acts were commonly designated. Compare *Everyman*,
        lines 697–702. But in the York pageant these lines may be taken as a confession,
        leading to absolution in lines 454–57.

468   *Petir, take this asse me fro.* Jesus now dismounts; Peter will lead it away so that it
        can be returned, as promised. The porter is nearby, and Peter is able to hand it
        over to him already at lines 482–83.

470–71 *I murne, I sigh, I wepe also / Jerusalem on thee to loke.* See Luke 19:41–44, which is
        the only gospel to note Christ's tears before Jerusalem. At lines 475–79, Jesus
        predicts the fall of the city. As Love, elaborating on Luke, explains, Jesus' tears

are for Jerusalem's "detruccion therof, that came aftere, and sorowynge for heere gostly blyndnes" (*Mirror*, p. 142).

489–541   *Hayll*. Hail lyrics, exuberantly lauding the triumphant king in a profusion of praise and metaphor and ending with reference to Jesus' role at Doomsday. Related to the Hail lyrics associated with the Nativity — and to the spirit of Levation prayers at the celebration of the Eucharist.

544 s.d.   *Tunc cantant*. The singing resumes with perhaps, as Rastall suggests, *Ingrediente domino*, a responsory that was used at York for the entrance to the church on Palm Sunday (*Minstrels Playing*, p. 55).

26. THE CONSPIRACY

Attention to Judas' conspiracy and betrayal begins early, and the focus remains on this rather than on other events such as the episode of the money changers in the Temple in the period following Jesus' return to Jerusalem. The events will of course move quickly enough to the Passion, which was obviously considered the core of the cycle of plays as also in narrative accounts such as Love's *Mirror*. In the treatment of the role of Judas, there is considerable elaboration of the historical material as found in the gospels. The *Northern Passion*, for example, is typical in following the biblical linking of Judas' betrayal to the anointing of Jesus' feet by Mary Magdalen in the house of Simon, shown only in a missing play that was never entered in the Register containing the pageants in the York cycle. The *Conspiracy* as it appears in the Register shows signs of considerable rewriting of what would have been a simpler and shorter play in 1415 when the *Ordo paginarum* was compiled. An indication of this is the appearance of the alliterative line, which is evident throughout and which argues for a later date consistent with other pageants that use this verse form. In this edition, the verse is presented as in the manuscript, where, after a part of the opening speech, each alliterative half-line appears as a separate line on the page. As is the custom in this edition, the second part of each alliterative line is indented here with the first word uncapitalized. Stanzas are of fourteen lines, and, in contrast to Anglo-Saxon alliterative verse, contain rhyme.

2   *regent of rewle*. Pilate, the Roman governor of the region, has the task of preventing civil unrest — a common worry too of the authorities in late medieval England. Typically, he is concerned with his dignity, his wisdom, and the loyalty of others, the latter an important quality when viewed in light of Judas' action in the pageant. His bragging may be compared to Herod's in the Nativity plays.

14   *wyscus*. Perhaps an error for "vicious," or made up, in which case it probably means "firm, sure of himself."

20–21   Pilate's claim to be of countenance "as bright / as blossome on brere" may be ironic if he was fitted with a mask or provided with a painted face to make him appear ugly, as was usual with evil characters.

25–28   Not an offer to discuss, but a threat that all resistance will be handled severely since "all of youre helpe hanges in my hande" (line 28). Like other tyrants, his great fault is pride.

29ff.   The appearance of Caiphas and Anna in Pilate's court at this point is odd, since in the gospels Judas goes to the chief priests in the Temple. In the pageant the meeting serves to link secular authority with the ecclesiastics, who are presented as unstable and vindictive, worse than Pilate. They are fixed in their interpretation of the law, which they have internalized to the point where to question it would be to "argue with themselves."

43a   *in oure warde.* Within Pilate's jurisdiction. York was divided into wards for purposes of governance.

45–46   *But and his sawe be lawfull . . . to lende.* Pilate insists that the allegations against Jesus must be legitimate, though in the end the trial will be a charade and a demonstration of the abuse of power. Pilate makes the point concerning the necessity of a fair trial below at lines 105–07.

72–74   Reference to the overturning of the tables of the moneychangers in the Temple and Jesus' act of forcibly expelling them along with the animals to be purchased for sacrifices. This was Jesus' attack on the practices of the Second Temple that was understood as essential to his program of instituting a new law not based on the ritual practices introduced after the Babylonian captivity.

76   *appostita.* Caiphas accuses Jesus of committing perjury (line 75) and now of being an apostate, one who has rejected the truths of his religion in favor of allegedly false opinions. Caiphas wants him to be forced to submit as heretics were made to reject their heretical views in late medieval England. He will ask for the death penalty.

92b–93   *that makeles . . . full rawe.* Pilate's terminology identifies Jesus as the one who is matchless, which would have been seen as the correct designation. This is part of the author's strategy to maintain the audience's sympathy with Jesus. The high priests are guilty of allowing their imagination to be detached from reality. They are governed by their anger, which allows their reasoning faculties to wander idly and maliciously.

99   *uppon oure Sabbott day / the seke makes he saffe.* Jesus works and heals the sick on the Sabbath, and this is not permitted under a strict interpretation of Jewish law. It is a constant complaint during the trial, along with the charge that his sayings are untrue and inconsistent with Second Temple orthodoxy.

110   *than may we prophite oure pele.* Anna claims to have certified the accuracy of the allegations, and here Pilate agrees to advance the charges against Jesus.

127–54   Judas arrives on the scene and explains the connection with the meal at Simon's house when Mary Magdalen (actually an unnamed woman in the biblical account, but absorbed into the character of Mary Magdalen in late medieval tradition) was allowed to waste expensive ointment on Jesus when it should have been sold and the money given to the poor. But that is not his concern; as the treasurer of the apostles, he would have embezzled his tenth, which he has now lost. In his greed and general attitude as well as his ultimate despair he is related to Cain. Judas has come to make a bargain and thus to have his revenge.

155   *Do open, porter, the porte.* Embedded stage direction. There must be a gate and a porter on hand to guard it.

157–58   *thou glorand gedlyng . . . growe.* The porter (Janitor) provides a description of Judas, who, as in the visual arts, has a face that fails to hide his hostility. The reference to "fals face" (line 161) suggests a mask. The porter is clearly taken aback at the sight of this visitor, and in his next speech accuses him of treason, which of course is accurate. Further descriptive remarks will refer to his appearance as a sign of his disposition. What the audience sees must indeed be "uncomely to kys" (line 200).

163   *Mars he hath morteysed his mark.* Mars, as the god of war, was associated with wrath by the medieval mythographers, and his red color seems be an indicator also of the hue of Judas' face. Traditionally Judas may have red hair and a beard of the same color, though Mellinkoff reports that the only firm evidence from dramatic records she has found is from Lucerne (*Outcasts*, 1:150–53). The reference to the "mark" may suggest Cain's mark, directly opposed to the seal ceremonially given to the children of God as part of the rite of baptism. The point would have been made clearer if, as one must suspect, the character of Judas was presented as an ugly caricature.

188   *I schall buske to the benke / wher baneres are bright.* Embedded stage direction. The bench is the seat of judgment from which Pilate will be expected to issue a verdict. Banners are present during the Trial plays, where they are held by the soldiers; see Pageant 33, lines 160–83, below.

211   *be noght abayst to byde at the bar.* Literally at the bar of justice before Pilate.

215   *marchaundyse.* Jesus becomes a marketable item to be bought and sold. The *Meditations* had called Judas a "most evil merchant" (p. 325).

229b   *thirti pens and plete, no more than.* The Harleian manuscript of the *Northern Passion* explains: "oure lord Jhesu was salde / for threty penis plainly talde, / And nowther for les ne for mare" (p. 19).

247   *fales fende.* The manuscript has *frende*, but Smith (*York Plays*, p. 227), followed by Beadle, plausibly emends to *fende*. This line and the ones that follow seem confused.

254a   *of lande.* In context it is hard to see what is meant unless, though questionable, the "lurdayne" is to slip away to another "lande."

276   *take ther thi silvere.* Embedded stage direction. Oddly, it seems to be Pilate who hands over the money, but he may simply be observing the transaction.

280   *jocounde and joly I am.* So is Judas now, in contrast with his despair later.

287–91   Pilate still insists that the "sotte" Jesus might be "sakles," and hence he advises restraint in the torment to which he will be put. Nevertheless, this is insufficient to make Pilate a sympathetic character.

27. THE LAST SUPPER

The Bakers were an obvious choice for the *Last Supper* since bread was an essential requirement for the institution of the Eucharist. No event in biblical history could be of greater significance in relation to the feast of Corpus Christi, which was a celebration of the Sacrament of the Eucharist in liturgical rite and procession as well as, at York, the plays. It is thus all the more unfortunate that, due to the loss of a leaf between lines 89 and 90, the central portion of the narrative with its representation of the blessing of the bread and wine is missing. The actions performed by Jesus at the table very likely were modeled on the gestures of the priest in consecrating the elements at Mass. This is supported by the stage direction that has Jesus perform the *lavabo* rite by washing his hands after the foot washing and in preparation for the main rite of the Passover meal. King points out that the lesson for Maundy Thursday described the foot washing, and that at vespers the *York Missal* quite remarkably specifies a mimed representation of the ritual meal: "table-cloths and wafers, with wine, are to be placed before the bishop and the others sitting together by the ministers of the church, as if to dine."[65] It is hard to know how the actors were arranged for the scenes involved in the Bakers' pageant, but suggestions may be gained from entirely conventional mid-fourteenth-century painted glass in the choir of York Minster. In the Last Supper panel, Jesus is centrally placed and blessing with his right hand, while with the left he reaches out toward a dish on the cloth-covered table. The apostles are located on each side, except for Judas, who is in front of the table, as typically is the case so that he will be turned away from the viewer's gaze. A chalice and a ciborium, with hosts, stand on the table.[66] At Great Malvern, a panel shows Judas receiving the Host and simultaneously stealing a fish, which he is hiding under the table cloth.[67] The classic article on the play is by Mill, "York Bakers' Play of the Last Supper." The pageant is written in twelve-line stanzas.

4	*feeste of Paas*. The Pascal feast, Passover, which is to be hereafter rejected in favor of the new Easter feast and the regular celebration of the Mass. The Eucharist was presented by Love and others in terms of a sacramental mysticism (see *Mirror*, pp. 153–56).
7–8	*Oure lambe is roste . . . / As Moyses lawe will lely lere*. Prescriptions for the roast lamb are found in Exodus 12:3–10.
9–10	*ilke man that has / Pepill in his awne posté*. Implying the authoritarian family, with the patriarch as head of the family responsible for organizing the feast.
19	*array you all on rawe*. Perhaps the disciples took places standing by the table, but the foot washing will intervene before they actually are allowed to eat.
25–26	*Of Moyses lawes here make I an ende / In som party*. The extensive rules specified in the Old Testament are abrogated, and the new law of Christ will be substituted. For example, the lamb will no longer be required, nor the ritualistic way of eating it. But not all the old rules will be declared obsolete.

[65] King, *York Mystery Cycle*, p. 173, quoting the *York Missal*, 1:97, 101 (in translation).

[66] See *YA*, p. 71.

[67] See Rushforth, *Medieval Christian Imagery*, pp. 57–63, fig. 13.

36	*wasshed clene.* The new law will declare that persons taking communion must be cleansed through penance and absolution.
40	*Do us have watir.* Embedded stage direction. In Mark14:13–14 and Luke 22:10 two disciples are sent into the town to meet Marcellus for the pitcher of water, but there is no time for anything so time-consuming. Marcellus will also bring a towel for the foot-washing.
47–50	Peter objects to having his feet washed by Jesus, as in John 13:6–9.
60 s.d.	*Tunc lavat manus.* The foot washing is completed, and it seems that among the disciples only Peter took part in it in the pageant. Now is the preparation for the meal, which is to be an example for all future generations.
79	*To whilke of you such fare schulde fall.* The disciples have been talking inappropriately about precedence among themselves.
after 89	The missing leaf contained the Last Supper up to the moment when Jesus gives the sop to Judas. This is the detail depicted in the Great Malvern glass and very commonly in other works of visual art. In the popular *Biblia Pauperum* block books the event is aligned with Melchisedech's offering of bread and wine and with Moses in the desert who feeds himself with manna (pp. 81 and 83). In play production, as in depictions in the visual arts, it would probably have been the case that Judas was turned away from the audience so as not to make eye contact.
96	*thou sittist nexte his kne.* Spoken by James to John.
104–05	*Now is tyme to me to gang . . . of newe.* Embedded stage direction. Judas' exit is covered by the disciples seeming to be talking quietly among themselves.
116–23	Jesus' warning to the disciples. He especially has prayed for Peter, who will need to fend off the assaults of the devil — and, as indicated below in lines 132–37, will deny Jesus three times before the night is over.
142–43	*All that in worlde is wretyn of me / Shall be fulfilled.* All the ancient prophecies will be fulfilled and proven true.
144–47	*I am the herde, the schepe are ye . . . to save.* The brief parable of the shepherd and the sheep, told to the disciples by Jesus in Matthew 26:31–34 and Mark 14:27–31.
159	*on twelffe seeges sitte schall ye.* In heaven, the apostles are promised twelve thrones to sit beside Jesus at Judgment Day.
168–70	*swerdis . . . Shall selle his cote and bye hym one.* A rather confused adaptation of Luke 22:36 and 38. Andrew will report that they have two swords at line 176.
173–75	*And stones to stynte all striffe.* They are to carry stones for protection? The editor is indebted to a suggestion by Russell Peck, who wonders if this might not be an echo of the Temptation pageant in which the Fiend would tempt Jesus to turn stones into bread; here Jesus will turn bread into the body of Christ "Yoursellfe for to save" (line 174).

28. The Agony and Betrayal

The pageant falls into two parts, the first dramatizing the story of Jesus' Agony in the Garden of Gethsemane as he prays and looks forward with very human fear and apprehension to his death on the cross. The intended effect is to stimulate a sympathetic response from the audience, the feeling of devout compassion that Love insisted upon.[68] The second part builds on this sympathy as the arrest is prepared and Judas' betrayal is effected. It is clear that there were substantial changes between the compilation of the *Ordo paginarum* in 1415 and the entering of the pageant into the Register in 1463–77. In fact, as Beadle notes, "This play must have reached the main scribe in state of considerable confusion,"[69] probably due to the stages of revision to which the pageant had been subjected. The usual verse form is the twelve-line stanza, with the introduction of the long alliterative line, but with considerable irregularity and passages where the verse form thoroughly breaks down. At some time after the compilation of the Register the pageant appears to have been revised or rewritten but not re-entered in the manuscript, as a marginal note in the manuscript by a later hand explains. The Cordwainers, known from the York dramatic records to have been a troublesome craft on account of their running dispute in the final decades of the fifteenth century with the Weavers over precedence,[70] were a successful leather craft, mainly devoted to the making of shoes.

2   *My flesshe dyderis and daris for doute of my dede.* Because he is entirely human as well as entirely divine, his humanity fears the death which he must endure. As Love explains, while his reason was fully obedient, his flesh — that is, his humanity — "grucchede and dredde and wold not gladley suffre deth" (*Mirror*, p. 163). See too lines 48–49, where Jesus explicitly is filled with dread because of what he knows and fears will be the end of his life's journey as a human being.

8a   *bidis me a stounde.* Embedded stage direction, telling the disciples, who are physically tired and perplexed, to remain alert as Jesus goes away a short distance from them to a "mounte" (see line 84) or raised space on the pageant wagon where he will be alone. At line 18 the disciples sit down. They will fall asleep swiftly even though they have been advised by Jesus to pray and not to succumb so as to resist temptation — a passage which carries a suggestion of the parable of the Wise and Foolish Virgins in Matthew 25 but also has a direct source is Luke 22:40. Unfortunately, the text is defective following line 42.

50   *I swete now both watir and bloode.* See Luke 22:44. The effect was created at Revello and Lucerne with paint, applied by a hidden stage hand during Jesus' speech (Meredith and Tailby, *Staging*, p. 108). The usual iconography would dictate that Jesus should be kneeling during his prayer.

---

[68] Love, *Mirror*, pp. 153–56.

[69] RB, p. 444.

[70] See esp. *REED: York*, 1:126, 158–59, 162–65, and 166–74.

58   *if it possible be this payne myght I overpasse.* In the biblical accounts Jesus asks that "this chalice [*calicem*]" may be taken from him (e.g., Luke 22:42); the chalice is sometimes depicted literally in iconography.

71–75   *I wolde that ye wakened . . . mildely with me.* Jesus goes to the disciples for the first time to find them sleeping, as will happen two more times.

90   *Be torned fro this turnement.* For this metaphor as used to describe the Crucifixion, see the discussion in Woolf, "Theme of Christ the Lover-Knight." This motif is much stronger in the Towneley Crucifixion (Play 23, lines 89–124).

113–22   The angel is traditionally St. Michael (so identified in the *Gospel of Nicodemus*, followed by the *Meditations*, p. 323). He comes to comfort and strengthen Jesus, but not to release him from the task of becoming the sacrifice for the misdeeds of humans both before and after the Crucifixion. Afterward Jesus is promised that he will reign in bliss as monarch of heaven. This detail appears only in Luke's gospel.

127b   *I schall you sayne.* Jesus probably signs — i.e., makes the sign of the cross over his disciples, who are again sleeping — but "sayne" may also not implausibly signify "heal."

132–33   *als soon as I am tane / Than schall ye forsake me.* Jesus' prediction, which will be proven correct in spite of their protests here. They will be like sheep that have been sheared and flee away. Peter is singled out.

153   Along with the high priests, Malcus, Judas, Peter, James, John, and fourteen soldiers, the *Ordo paginarum* reported the presence of Pilate, but this is either an error or a sign that the extant text was much altered from what it had been in 1415. It is more likely that only four soldiers and four Jews were needed for production of the play as presented in the extant text.

238   *I bere light for my lorde.* Malcus is the bearer of a lantern, as in numerous depictions, including stained glass in the church of St. Martin-cum-Gregory (*YA*, p. 72, fig. 19).

248   *All hayll.* Taken to be a sign of deception as late as Shakespeare; see *Macbeth* 1.3.48–50.

250   *I wolde aske you a kysse.* This is the instant nearly always represented in the iconography, as in the St. Martin-cum-Gregory glass where Peter has already attacked Malcus. In the *Bolton Hours*, Peter at the moment of the kiss has his sword lifted high, and in the foreground the small figure of Malcus has fallen (fol. 34v). In the pageant this is delayed until lines 274–75.

258   *leme of this light.* The bright light radiating from Jesus is rare in the visual arts. The light (for possible techniques of producing it in the play, see Butterworth, *Theatre of Fire*, esp. pp. 55–78) causes the soldiers to fall to the ground. John 18:6 only has the soldiers react by falling as a result of their recognition of Jesus; the scene is depicted in the *Speculum humanae salvationis* (Wilson and Wilson, *Medieval Mirror*, p. 174). Muir suggests that the great light, which also appears in the *Semur Passion*, was borrowed from the Conversion of St. Paul (*Biblical Drama*, p. 131).

259   *whome seke ye?* John 18:4, quoted in the *Stanzaic Life*, p. 194, but also perhaps an echo of *Quem queritis*, "Whom seek ye," of the angel in the *Visitatio Sepulchri*, the liturgical Easter play.

282–90   *Of aungellis full many . . . at vayle.* Derived ultimately from Matthew 26:53–54. At the end of the speech Jesus heals Malcus' ear, for which he receives no thanks but rather a curse.

298   *Even like a theffe.* Love reports that he has "hees handes bonden byhynde hym as a thefe, girde above his kote . . . and his mantile drawen fro him, and goyng barehede and stoupyng for the grete haste and travaile that thei made him to have" (*Mirror*, p. 167).

29. The Trial before Cayphas and Anna

In this play, produced by the Bowers and Fletchers (makers of bows and arrows), Jesus now comes before the Sanhedrim: he will face the high priest, Caiphas, and Anna for the initial stage of his trial in an ecclesiastical court. The injustice effected here and throughout the trial scenes may, according to King, have been a deliberate reminder of legal irregularities in the trial of the popular Archbishop Scrope in 1405, when he was convicted of treason for his involvement in a rebellion against Henry IV and executed.[71] The play, along with the other trial plays, illustrates the law applied as an instrument of injustice and tyranny, with which the people of York were not unfamiliar. The pageant begins with a speech by Caiphas, a bully and braggart who boasts about his power over lower clergy and the people as well as about his wisdom. He begins with a call for "Pees," that is, silence, which indicates an intentionally confrontational approach to the audience, and it is clear that his pursuit of the "boy" (a pejorative designation) is vindictive and hardly a pursuit of true justice. The playtext presents considerable difficulty, especially on account of the irregularity of the verse, which more or less falls into quatrains and, after line 170, the long alliterative line within twelve-line stanzas. In its present state, the text must be seen as differing from the pageant described in the 1415 *Ordo paginarum* which appears to have focused on the Buffeting. Numerous corrections were made by later hands in the manuscript.

7   *semely in seete.* In the seat of judgment, as judge in an ecclesiastical court.

33   *I have sente for that segge halfe for hethyng.* As an unjust judge, Caiphas expects to enjoy the proceedings, which will involve the working out of a vindictiveness that will cloud all sense of partiality in his treatment of the accused. In line 41 he admits his "ire," his predominant emotion and, since it causes him to be out of control, a sign of his unsympathetic character. He is a contrast to Jesus, and must have reflected this in his gestures, surely indecorous and directly opposed to the restraint displayed by his victim.

35–50   Caiphas' charges against Jesus throughout include sorcery (he will name witchcraft outright at line 57) and sabbath-breaking in violation of the Mosaic law. He also believes that, by calling himself God's Son, Jesus is committing an act of

---

[71] King, "Contemporary Cultural Models," p. 212.

blasphemy and that, by founding a new sect, he is an apostate and heretic under
the old law.

51–56 Anna tries to contradict Jesus' claim to be the Son of God by pointing to his
       parents, Mary and Joseph, the latter an ordinary craftsman, a carpenter.

60   *To take hym with a traye.* They will use deception to catch Jesus, as in fact has already
       been done in the Betrayal scene. Legally, the case against Jesus involves malicious
       prosecution here and elsewhere in the Trial plays (see Tiner, "English Law," pp.
       145–46).

80   *Do on dayntely and dresse me on dees.* The dais, on which he is also being prepared
       for bed, serves as the location of his bishop's throne. The bed must be nearby.
       After he sleeps and Anna leaves the set, the scene moves to Peter's predicted de-
       nial of his Lord. This cannot be in the same location but rather where Jesus can
       be brought by, bound with ropes, as later he is being brought to the high priest's
       palace. A flame will be required by which Peter hopes to be warmed in the cold
       night.

130a   *youre felawschippe.* The manuscript has *oure felawschip*, but Peter remains an out-
       sider, all the more so since he has deserted his Master, as Malcus points out upon
       his recognition of him.

137a   *hurled hym hardely.* So Jesus will be treated in his captivity as, with his hands tied,
       he will be dragged from place to place and tortured. It will be Malcus who points
       out, at line 161, that Peter has thrice denied his Lord. Then Jesus will pass by for
       a short speech in which he confirms the denial, whereupon Peter must repent
       since he stands as a direct contrast to Judas, who is unable to do so. There is a
       problem with the time scheme here, since Peter's recognition of what he has done
       in denying Jesus comes at the cock crow — i.e., morning — and otherwise in this
       pageant the action is taking place in the depths of the night.

169   *full sadde sorowe sheris my harte.* Peter's sight of Jesus is stressed in the *Northern
       Passion,* which reports that at that point the apostle was "ful drery in his thoght"
       and went forth, weeping "sare" (1:75; Harleian manuscript), the stage action
       implied here. The lines that follow will be in the long alliterative line.

177   *nowe of the nyght.* Noon of the night, midnight, but again the nighttime here is
       in fact very indeterminate. The third and fourth soldiers must be outside, with
       the first and second inside the gate to the priests' palace.

247   *we myght als wele talke tille a tome tonne.* The image of an empty barrel as inappro-
       priately signifying Jesus, who is the silent one, noted for his patience. The sol-
       diers are a hardened lot, while Jesus, as frequently noted, is presented as one who
       is silent "as a sheep to the slaughter, and shall be dumb as a lamb before his
       shearer, and he shall not open his mouth" (Isaias 53:7). Woolf suggests the in-
       fluence of the *Meditations* and related writings (*English Mystery Plays,* p. 257). At
       line 248 Anna says that he thinks Jesus is "witteles." But, as Robinson notes, An-
       na's charge is premature "since Jesus has not yet been asked any questions or
       given a chance to speak" (*Studies in Fifteenth-Century Stagecraft,* p. 183).

256–57   The interrogation begins in earnest, with the listing of charges. No lawyer is allowed for the defense. The scene may not have appeared very different from that depicted in an alabaster to which attention is called by Hildburgh, "English Alabaster Carvings," pp. 77–78, pl. XVI.d; here Caiphas is seated on a throne, with hands raised as he interrogates Jesus, who has his hands tied before him. In the background are a man with a scroll of parchment and a number of others. Caiphas is wearing a miter, and is clean shaven.

266–69   One of the charges against him involves his prophecy of the destruction of the Temple, and his claim to be able to raise it up again in three days. See Matthew 26:61, Mark 14:58.

274–75   *Jesus of Jewes will have joie / To spille all thy sporte for thy spellis*. Beadle would amend to "we will have joie" (RB, p. 250), but the line is more likely ironic. Of course, as bullies the priests will have pleasure on account of what they are able to inflict on Jesus. See also line 288: "we schall have game or we goo."

286   *by Beliall bloode and his bonys*. The blood and bones are relics of a demon, Belial, and represent the reverse of the cult of relics of saints.

292   *Yf thou be Criste, Goddis Sonne, telle till us two*. See Matthew 26:61, Mark 14:58. Jesus will not fall into the snare, but now will speak briefly, answering that Caiphas has made this statement himself. He is aware of the priests' strategy to obtain a conviction and subsequently execution, as lines 312–18 demonstrate. But here the priests take his answer to be as good as a guilty plea. To Jesus' complaint about the proceedings, Caiphas will only become irate, and the first soldier, calling him a beggar, chides him for "bourd[ing] with oure busshoppe" (line 327a).

331   *Wherfore thou bourdes to brode for to bete me*. It is presumably Caiphas, not the soldier who is the deceitful witness ("wronge wittenes," line 329), so Jesus turns the charge of jesting or playing (as "to brode" — i.e., too broadly — or hastily) back upon his accuser.

336   *prelatis estatis*. The arrogance of Caiphas and Anna would have resonated from time to time with York's citizens, who frequently did not have good relations with the higher clergy associated with the Minster and the archbishop; York wills demonstrate that, as an index of their affection, citizens' bequests were very generous to parish churches, while little was usually given by them to the Minster.

340   *ye muste presente this boy unto Sir Pilate*. The decision to execute someone would need to be made by the secular authorities, just as in late medieval England. There a person could not be condemned to die by the ecclesiastical authorities, though he could be turned over to the civil government to do the deed.

344   *late men lede hym by nyght*. Injustice is best hidden, rather than exposed to the public. This is another reason for proceeding speedily through the night with Jesus' trial, in addition to the requirement imposed of reaching a conclusion before the Jewish Sabbath; see Caiphas' orders to the soldiers at lines 388–89.

355   *play popse*. A "common game" in which a person is blindfolded, then is to guess who hit him; "until he rede him that smote him, he will be blindfold stille and

hold in for the post of player" (Owst, *Literature and Pulpit*, p. 510, quoting MS. Bodley 649, fol. 82). In the Towneley *Coliphizacio* the game is called "A new play of Yoyll" (Play 21, line 498), but elsewhere it is called *Hot Cockles* (Owst, *Literature and Pulpit*, p. 510).

356–57   *stole . . . hatir.* The Buffeting. Jesus will sit on the stool, like a "foole" in this game (line 358), with the cloth (*hatir*) over his head so that he cannot see those who are hitting him with the palms of their hands in what the torturers consider a game. In this and other episodes of torture during the Passion, the iconographic evidence indicates that the tormentors surrounding Jesus should appear to be like animals, as in the *Holkham Bible Picture Book* (fol. 29v), to be consistent with Psalm 21 (*AV* 22), the psalm read in the liturgy on Good Friday: "Many dogs have encompassed me," etc. The relevance of this psalm to illustrations of the Passion is discussed by Marrow, "*Circumdederunt me multi.*" Part of the torment at this time, according to the accounts in Matthew and Mark, involved being spit upon (and so too in later redactions of the story, as in Love's *Mirror*, p. 168), and something of this may have been effected, though the text of this pageant does not specify it. For a depiction of spitting, see the *Speculum humanae salvationis* (Wilson and Wilson, *Medieval Mirror*, p. 178) and the discussion in Marrow, *Passion Iconography*, pp. 132–34.

369   *Wassaile, wassaylle.* As if raising a drink to offer a toast.

373   *Quis te percussit.* Garbled quotation in manuscript, as emended by Beadle on the basis of Luke 22:64.

376   *stode in a foles state.* The point has been missed by those who wish to speak of Christ as a "fool king," for the pageant is in fact trying make clear that it is the tormentors who are the fools, not the Christ who is keeping his silence out of "hie pacience" (Love, *Mirror*, p. 168). His wits are hardly "aweye," as the fourth soldier believes (line 375b).

395   *daunce forth in the devyll way.* Concluding Caiphas' curse. The Dance of Death, leading to that which lies beyond the hellmouth — i.e., the realm of the *fende*.

30. THE FIRST TRIAL BEFORE PILATE

The most noteworthy aspect of the dramatization of the initial trial before secular authority is perhaps the addition to the story of Pilate's wife Procula, here called Percula, derived from a single brief biblical reference (Matthew 27:19) and given extensive treatment in the Middle English *Gospel of Nicodemus*.[72] This material seems not to have been part of the Tapiters and Couchers' play at the time the *Ordo paginarum* was compiled, and the differences in versification noted by Richard Beadle and others suggest stages of composition,[73] though the presence of the long alliterative line is maintained. Thus the entire drama must be later than

---

[72] *Middle-English Harrowing of Hell and Gospel of Nicodemus*, pp. 34–37; compare James, ed., *Apocryphal New Testament*, p. 98.

[73] See especially RB, pp. 446–47.

the *Ordo paginarum*, and probably was written at least in part at about the same date as the previous pageant and others in the Passion series with similar use of the alliterative line, which here falls into nine-line stanzas but with differing rhyme. Lineation and the frequent errors in the text have necessitated considerable editorial attention, and in this the early edition of Lucy Toulmin Smith as well as the more recent work of Richard Beadle must be acknowledged. Nevertheless, the writer of the pageant has been admired for his skill in dramatizing the episodes included by him in the pageant and for making them come to life.[74] The scenes with Percula, leading up to her dream in which the devil tempts her (a parallel that quite deliberately is intended with the temptation of Eve, a connection noted by Woolf as deriving from the *Glossa Ordinaria*),[75] are particularly vivid. The trial itself likewise is a complex presentation designed to make the events believable as part of the collective memory. The trial certainly suggests considerable familiarity with the legal system and common-law criminal trials.[76] King identifies the procedure from a legal standpoint as summary justice existing outside of the usual order of statute law.[77] In general, there is careful attention to detail and argumentation, even in the monologues of Pilate and the devil, as has been noted by Hans-Jürgen Diller.[78] The guilds that produced the play also, on account of their work in making ornamented cloths and bed covers, would have been able to add substantially to the visual effect of the pageant.

1–27	The ranting introduction and self-flattery of the Roman procurator distinguishes him as a bragging tyrant, historically a brutal enforcer of Roman rule. Here he is characterized by two of the Seven Deadly Sins — i.e., Pride and Wrath — in his attitude toward potential challengers (see Mussetter, "York Pilate"). He holds up a sword, a symbol of his authority, to threaten his audience, but his tone changes abruptly at lines 25–27 when his wife appears. Other complexities in Pilate's character appear in the course of the pageant; he is anxious to maintain justice, but ultimately as a politician he will of course fail to do so under pressure. For Pilate's parentage, see also the *Stanzaic Life*, p. 219.
37–45	Percula (identified in the speech tags as Uxor or Domina) describes herself as *dame precious* and the prize of princes and thus is a parody of the vain stereotypical woman. Presented in terms familiar in medieval anti-feminist discourse, she is dressed "in richesse of robis" that would likely have been extravagant to the extreme and hence probably ridiculous. What follows is a parody of a love scene, interrupted by Bedellus. It is to be expected that she was played by a young, fair-faced boy.
59	*howe you javell jangill of Jewes.* Disappointed and angry about the interruption, Percula engages in highly indecorous conduct, in this serving as a reminder of

---

[74] For a survey of iconographic traditions upon which the dramatist has drawn, see Schiller, *Iconography*, 2:61–64.

[75] Woolf, *English Mystery Plays*, p. 245.

[76] See Tiner, "English Law," p. 144, who also calls attention to proceedings before the King's Council.

[77] King, "Contemporary Cultural Models," p. 207.

[78] Diller, *Middle English Mystery Play*, p. 144 and *passim*.

her perverse role — perverse as was Eve's in the Garden, for, as noted above, she will be seduced by the devil in her dream to attempt to prevent the sacrifice of Christ on the cross. The present scene presents her as utterly self-centered and as a sex object, suggesting the sin of Luxuria or Lechery.

73–85   The description of the sun descending toward sunset is a purple patch, leading up to the suggestion that Percula should leave her husband's court and go home to their dwelling. A curfew is specifically applied to her, here defended by the claim that she might "stakir in the strete" (line 85). Curfews were the rule in medieval York, and, with streets being dark and unlighted, it is not unreasonable that she should have been expected to be safely at home. But it will emerge that Pilate will have work to do as a judge, a role that was a male prerogative.

93b   *with wynne ye had wette yowe.* They must have a drink of wine before she leaves, suggesting another of the deadly sins, Gluttony. Indeed, the scene reaches the height of ridiculousness when Pilate praises Percula at line 109 as the "fayrest figure that evere did fode fede."

118   *telle me yf any tythyngis betyde.* Pilate is a jealous husband and wants his wife watched. This introduces another of the deadly sins, since jealousy is a species of Envy.

127–39   *to bedde that I wer broght . . . me nere.* Having "wette . . . with wyne" (line 135b), Pilate is clearly drunk and, as the preceding half-line shows, he is overweight. He will allow no noise or interruption, thus making way for a change of scene to Domina/Uxor, Percula's maid, and his son, who organize her going to bed, necessary if she is to dream.

158a   *Owte owte, harrowe!* Extrametrical, here added to the first half of line 158. A noisy entry, with the sleeping lady nearby. The devil's gestures are invariably indecorous and exaggerated.

162   *And he be slone, oure solace will sese.* Diabolus' fear is that Jesus, through his sacrifice on the cross, will take away the captives who sit in darkness in his den, which is hell. He will lose his rights to those who have died and are now in his custody. His "solace" comes from tormenting and denying solace to his prisoners.

163   *He will save man saule fro oure sonde.* Ironic, since hell is hardly a place of safekeeping.

167–75   Percula's dream, the devil speaking directly to her in her sleep. His appeal to her is directed to her wealth, position, and fear of deprivation. The deadly sins of Pride and Covetousness are invoked.

176   *I am drecchid with a dreme.* Compare the Middle English *Gospel of Nicodemus*: "I have ben dreched with dremes so / all this nyght" (p. 35, lines 197–98). She is affected, as Eve was, by the devil, and will do his bidding; she will send her lazy son, who is very unwilling to go to her husband at this time since he does not want to rise from sleep at this midnight hour.

196   *Sir Cayphas . . . this caytiffe we have cached.* Anna is speaking, and since he is a new arrival in this pageant — and a different actor than the one playing Anna in the previous pageant — he will address Caiphas by name, as the latter will also ad-

dress Anna by name in the next speech. They have Jesus in their custody when they arrive at Pilate's hall where they will charge him with capital offenses, but also they seem to be enjoying the "sporte" (see line 205) of so doing even though they are consumed by anger.

206   *I am pontificall prince of all prestis.* Caiphas' position is high priest of the Temple for the year.

214   *rugge hym in ropes.* The dragging of Jesus, passive as a lamb (for he is the Lamb of God), becomes progressively more cruel and inhumane. Marrow quotes Ludolphus of Saxony's *Vita Christi,* 2:61, concerning the way he is led to Pilate "*to be devoured* by the *wicked judge as by a mad dog* [*rabido cani*]" (*Passion Iconography,* p. 36). In line 222, the term "hurled," signifying violent action (*MED*), is used to describe the manner of dragging him, and the second soldier has indicated that they will "pulle on with pride till his poure [strength] be paste" (line 218). Anna will also use the term "drawe" (line 227b), which might have the connotation of *drawing* either to execution or to death by being pulled apart, for which usage see Play 32, lines 230–31. See also Filius' statement in line 391: "No ruthe were it to rug thee and ryve thee in ropes." In Love's *Mirror* he is said to have been "ladde as a thefe" (p. 169).

223   *he stonyes for us, he stares where he standis.* Embedded stage direction, and also one of the indications that the bullying soldiers consider him to be a fool for his passivity.

233b   *may rayse with oure rolyng.* The soldiers with Jesus make a considerable ruckus; their agitation would perhaps have been described in contemporary terms as "riot."

263a   *am I light as a roo.* Pilate has sobered up.

269   *stronge in youre state for to stande.* That is, in the dock.

275   *to the benke.* To the bench for a legal proceeding or trial, but Caiphas and Anna explain that as priests of the Temple they cannot enter a secular court (line 278). Their involvement in a capital case would be a violation of British law; see Tiner, "English Law," pp. 146 and 149 n. 28, citing William Lyndwood, *Provinciale* (1689), 3:29.

280–90   Filius arrives with his message from Pilate's wife concerning her "swevene" relating to Jesus, whom she hopes to save from execution.

312–15   The Beadle, recalling the veneration extended to Jesus on Palm Sunday, must bow and kneel and worship Jesus. This will be dismissed by Jesus' accusers and tormentors. At lines 338–46, the Beadle returns to his Palm Sunday experience, when he saw the crowd singing psalms and venerating him.

361   Pilate takes up his role as examiner, with Anna and Caiphas as accusers.

392–93   *Why falles thou noght flatte here . . . / For ferde of my fadir so free?* Jesus remains upright and does not bow, kneel, or fall down here, nor does he acknowledge Pilate's authority in any way.

402   *of a payne, and appere*. Jesus is being summoned to the bar, where he will be accused
        by the priests from the Temple. They will present the charges, which are so flimsy
        that Pilate is not impressed. As Pilate notes, their allegations have no merit.

509   *fro Galely*. Pilate's discovery that Jesus comes from Galilee allows him to evade
        making a judgment, since this is a region under the jurisdiction of King Herod
        (see Luke 23:6–8). Jesus will be passed on, again being dragged to his next loca-
        tion. In the pageant, this could have involved dragging him from one station to
        the next where this play will be repeated.

31. THE TRIAL BEFORE HEROD

The trial before Herod Antipas is told only in Luke 23:6–12, where the most significant
detail is Jesus' refusal to speak and the subsequent Mocking, after which he will be sent back
to Pilate. The story appears in expanded form in the *Gospel of Nicodemus* and the *Stanzaic Life*,
and was reputed to have been illustrated in a window in Christ Church on King's Square
along the pageant route.[79] An extant example in York glass from c. 1420–30 is present in the
choir of the Minster,[80] and the subject appears elsewhere, as in the *Holkham Bible Picture Book*,
fol. 30.[81] The play, presumably from around the same date as the other plays written in the
long alliterative line, is thus undoubtedly later than the defective and decidedly unrevealing
entry in the *Ordo paginarum*, and only in the second list, also in the *York Memorandum Book
A/Y*, is a play of the Presentation of Christ before Herod given to the "Lyttesters" or Dyers.[82]
The extant text, characterized by irregularity of the verse and stanza forms,[83] presents many
difficulties, as do the other plays written in the long alliterative line.

1–26   The ranting introduction by the tyrant, perhaps here confused with his father
        Herod the Great who was the villain of the Massacre of the Innocents, should by
        now be recognized as a familiar formula. It is again a mock challenge to the audi-
        ence. In line 4, he brandishes a sword, specified at line 255 as the curved falchion
        that would have been considered the sign of a Middle Eastern tyrant. However,
        this iconography is not necessarily typical. For example, the enthroned and
        crowned king in the *Holkham Bible Picture Book*, fol. 30v, holds a conventional
        ceremonial sword in place of a scepter, and is pointing at Jesus with his *left* hand.
        His extended index finger is a gesture signifying accusation, and his crossed legs
        suggest a figure whose personality is out of balance, as also evident in this intro-
        ductory passage in the pageant.

36   *ilke a renke . . . gone to ther reste*. Designating the time as during the night; all are
        asleep, and Herod will shortly call for his nightcap, a glass of wine, before going
        to "wynke" (line 41). He will drink after line 42, as the stage direction indicates.

---

[79] Gent, *Antient and Modern History*, p. 188.

[80] *YA*, p. 73.

[81] See also, for example, Schiller, *Iconography*, 2:63, fig. 218.

[82] *REED: York*, 1:26.

[83] See RB, pp. 447–48.

43	*unlase you.* "Points," or laces, were used for closing garments and shoes.
52–53	*Ser Satan, oure sire, / And Lucifer.* Invoked, along with Mohammed, by characters to show their moral and spiritual allegiances. Significant for understanding the dualism of medieval popular religion.
55–60	While Herod sleeps, the soldiers arrive with Jesus in the platea before a representation of a gate on the wagon stage. The Register lacks stage directions, but, as has been seen above, they are frequently embedded in the dialogue. The soldiers' purpose is to deliver Jesus so that Herod will do as expected — i.e., condemn him to death.
74	*sloppe.* Herod's loose outer garment needs adjustment; in the fifteenth century this normally reached below the knees. The garment specified here could be expected to have been colorful and to have displayed the ingenuity of the sponsoring guild.
96	*nemys hym no more.* Pilate and Herod had been in conflict, as the biblical account indicates (Luke 23:12). Note also Herod's hope that Pilate will recognize his greater authority (line 131).
109–19	Having allowed Jesus and Pilate's knights to enter, Herod is only willing to deal with Jesus if there is opportunity for entertainment. When he discovers his name, he recognizes that this man is one whom he is indeed happy to see, and he anticipates the "games" that he believes will begin. Luke's gospel indicates that Herod was anxious to see a miracle, and this aspect of the story was expanded in later accounts. *The Mirour of Mans Salvacioune* says that Herod "was fulle gladde, hoping of thee [i.e., Jesus] some mervelle to se, / Holdyng a fals wikked nygromancere thee to be" (lines 4617–18, p. 212).
142	*I hope we gete some harre hastely at hande.* Signifying Herod's wish to learn something, even something useful (actionable intelligence?).
145–46	*Saie, beene-venew . . . parle remoy.* Herod speaks in a parody of diplomatic French.
160	*bryngis ye hym nygh.* Embedded stage direction. Now Jesus will be brought directly to the king, before whom he will stand silently. This will lead to the accusation that he is a "sotte," or fool. There will be little courtesy in Herod's court. In this pageant particularly, Jesus' silence will be the source of frustration and a motive for the subsequent action: the further elaboration of Jesus as the silent sufferer being led, at first to be sure from place to place, but eventually as a sheep, in this case the *Agnus Dei*, to the slaughter.
184	*He knawes noght the course of a kyng.* Herod excuses Jesus, who has failed to kneel before him, on the basis of his presumed ignorance.
201–13	For the miracle of the five loaves and two fishes, and twelve baskets of leftovers, see Matthew 14:14–21 and Mark 6:35–44. The two dukes, as representatives of Caiphas and Anna, are the accusers.
239–46	Herod, having been frustrated by Jesus' unwillingness to kneel or otherwise acknowledge his authority, explodes into inexplicable nonsense, including words

that mimic the sound of Anglo-Norman French. Smith wrote, "There seems little attempt at sense (purposely) in this jumble of French and Latin" (*York Plays*, p. 300).

251   *it astonys hym, youre steven is so store. Store*, from Old Norse *stórr*, "great, huge." Embedded stage direction. Herod has been shouting, indeed a "byg blure" (line 253).

254   *be Mahoundes bloode.* An oath, but one not used by Englishmen! Swearing by Christ's wounds was common.

261–64   *Si loqueris . . . parantur.* Unidentified quotation.

267–68   Apparently naming the dukes as Dewcus and Udins and identifying their sovereign Herod, but otherwise a parody of French.

275–76   *as a knave cledde, / Wherto calle ye hym a kyng?* In his dress Jesus does not appear to be an aristocrat, and thus he cannot convince Herod that he is a royal and divine king, as he alleges to be. See Herod's statement in line 284: "Grete lordis aught to be gay" — i.e., impressively dressed. As he is dragged about after his arrest, he will appear more and more like a victim and less and less like one who might indeed be the Savior of the world. In lines 279–83 the notion is put forward that Jesus is intimidated by the rich array of Herod, but in no sense would he have mistaken the tyrant Herod and his men for angels!

337   *clothe hym in white.* See Luke 23:11: "And Herod with his army set him at nought, and mocked him, putting on him a white garment, and sent him back to Pilate." "White garment" (Vulgate: *vesta alba*) is a mistranslation of the Greek text, which specified "gorgeous apparel." Compare the *Northern Passion*: "He sufferd all thaire werkes ill, / And no word wald he say thar till. / Than Herod gert for grete despite / Cleth him all in clathes white" (1:101, Harleian manuscript, lines 998a–1000). At line 355 the article of clothing is called a "haterell," probably a generic term for a gown, and at line 357 a "joppon," the latter term likely to have been chosen for alliteration rather than accuracy in reporting the actual costume chosen. In any case, he will be returned to the king thus arrayed at line 369.

371a   *crye in my courte.* Crying out for anyone who knows anything against Jesus as a way of assuring fairness in the trial, such as it is.

382–83   *saie to Pilate / We graunte hym our frenschippe.* See Luke 23:12: "And Herod and Pilate were made friends that same day."

399   *We fynde no defaute hym to slee.* Ultimately Herod must admit that the charges against Jesus are inadequate to condemn him.

401   *rollis of recorde.* Tiner explains that this is "a common-law technical phrase referring to the written documents of a court" which "contain previous judgments as well as evidence touching the case at hand" ("English Law," p. 145).

411–13   *Bidde hym wirke as he will . . . motte he thee.* Herod's dismissal of Jesus.

424   *Daunce on, in the devyll way.* Compare Caiphas' similar concluding curse in Play 29, line 395.

32. THE REMORSE OF JUDAS

The 1415 description of the *Remorse of Judas* in the *Ordo paginarum* is too fragmentary to be useful except for the reference to the thirty coins as pieces of silver, as in the *Conspiracy* (Play 26, line 276) and in the biblical account. Thirty pennies, designated here in the playtext, would have been a small amount of money, by the end of the fifteenth century equivalent to perhaps a week's wages, depending on one's occupation.[84] The biblical sources are the brief accounts in Matthew 27:3–10, which includes Judas' suicide, and Acts 1:18–19. The pageant as we have it is a much expanded version of the story, again a new play or rewriting in the long alliterative line, mostly in eight-line or eleven-line stanzas and based on the elaboration of the narrative as found in the *Northern Passion*. The extant text likewise adds Pilate to the characters noted in the *Ordo paginarum*. While the second listing of pageants in the *Memorandum Book A/Y* additionally lists a *Suspensio Jude* pageant, also noted in 1432 as having Judas "burst in the middle,"[85] this play is lost. The dramatic ending of Judas' life in which a devil emerges from his bowels, though included elsewhere as at Coventry where a hook was purchased in 1578 for his hanging,[86] was never added to Cooks and Waterleaders' (or Watercarriers') drama about his remorse. The selfishness and callousness of the priests and of Pilate are emphasized, culminating in what can only be described as theft of land by these bullies that will be the field of blood from the knight who only wants to mortgage it.

16   *Nor no man to grath hym no gate.* Purvis' translation "Begin not to go on your gate" (*York Cycle of Mystery Plays*, p. 248) is speculative. The *MED*, citing this line, glosses "grath . . . gate" as "go away, set off, depart."

23   *golde wyre.* Pilate's self-flattery reveals at least that his hair color is blond.

26   *prince prevyd undir palle.* Here a generic secular gown distinguishing a man of authority, but it would have been sufficiently elaborate to identify Pilate's high status.

75   *faute in hym I fynde none.* Pilate is rejecting as legal grounds for conviction the recital once more of allegations by Anna and Caiphas. Compare Luke 23:4. He will, however, give them a chance to confront Jesus again and to accuse him by summoning him back to court (the legal term is "racleyme," in line 79).

85–87   *on the raynebowe . . . oure dedis.* Jesus has referred to the rainbow as a sign that appeared to Noah and that will again appear at the Last Day when he returns to judge the living and the dead "aftir oure dedis."

90   *wene ye be wiser than we.* Here is highlighted the contrast between the view of Jesus that Pilate and the others have of him on the one hand, and the audience's perception of him as both God and Man. The arrogance of his accusers undercuts audience sympathy for them and helps to focus attention on the suffering Savior.

---

[84] Dyer, *Standards of Living*, p. 215.

[85] *REED: York*, 1:48, trans. 2:733.

[86] *REED: Coventry*, p. 289.

Note the use of the word "sauterell," implying "babbler," in relation to Jesus in line 93.

115–16   *be Beliall bonis . . . of golde.* Swearing by Belial's bones, or relics. No bribe will be sufficient in this instance to effect Jesus' release.

129   *comaundis us to drynke.* Embedded stage direction; they drink as Judas appears in order to recite his monologue prior to greeting Pilate and the chief priests in line 153.

130–52   Judas reveals his plan to return the thirty pence, which would be his only chance of redemption, but despairs about his own spiritual condition, for he has performed such a heinous deed as to betray his innocent ("Sakles," line 142) master.

168   *we bought hym.* Caiphas insists that Jesus has been purchased like a piece of property and regards him like a slave who can be killed, if that is their wish. This is a violation of human rights as understood in the fifteenth century as clearly as today, for Judas had absolutely no legal right to sell him in the first place.

214–24   Judas' trespass is beyond redemption because he is able only to express remorse and not to be truly repentant; as the Harleian manuscript of the *Northern Passion* states, "He thoght his wikkednes was so grete / That forgifnes might he none gete" (1:87, line 856a–b). His offer to serve Sir Pilate faithfully will only be greeted with derision. Judas is indeed a celebrity (see line 212), but only as one of the prize villains of history along with Cain.

270   *Take it agayne that ye toke me.* Embedded stage direction. Judas hands over the bag of coins to Anna, who will not accept it but will pass it back quickly to the traitor (line 274).

289   *traytoure attaynte.* Caiphas regards Judas as a convicted criminal; he has accepted the fact of his guilt, the equivalent of pleading guilty in the court. Legal terms, such as would have been recognized in fifteenth-century England, are used here and subsequently by Caiphas and Judas himself.

305–06   *Me thare aske no mercy, for none mon I gete, / . . . schall fordo me.* Judas shows himself to be in the depths of despair, which is the lack of the hope of salvation and expectation of hell as a just reward. This is of course presumption, theologically speaking, since no one is beyond salvation if one uses the means of penance and absolution available to all; see Snyder, "Left Hand of God," p. 34, citing Origen, *In Matt.* 117. Despair without repentance is often depicted as leading to suicide, and is so depicted in numerous illustrations of the Vices, most famously in Giotto's representation in fresco in the Arena Chapel at Padua; for further examples, see the list in Hourihane, *Virtue and Vice*, pp. 350–52. Judas' death was particularly gruesome since his mouth had kissed Jesus and thus his soul could not leave him by that route with his last breath, as normally; instead, as the *Northern Passion* explains, his soul left "his wambe" and " went out / And his entrailes so fell him fra" (1:87, Harleian manuscript, lines 861–62).

318   *take me nowe unto my dede.* The suicide will be offstage. As Judas leaves, he flings down the money bag (see line 324). Oddly, Pilate will be the one to say that the

money shall not come into their *corbonan* (they use the Latin term from the Vulgate signifying "treasury" in Matthew 27:6 and also in the Harleian manuscript of the *Northern Passion*, 1:89, line 873).

347   *A place . . . wolde I wedde sette.* The knight's wish is to mortgage his land, not to sell it (see line 352). In the Cornish *Ordinalia*, the man who arrives to offer sale of property, for "thek-warn-ugans [thirty] sterlyn [sterling]," is the Crozier Bearer (*Ancient Cornish Drama*, 1:346, line 1554), but it is a straightforward sale, not a dishonest one in which he is cheated.

349   *fre be my fredome.* He is a freeman, able to own property, and he holds legal title to the plot of land, called Calvary.

371   *The Felde of Bloode.* See Acts 1:19; *Northern Passion*, 1:91.

33. THE SECOND TRIAL BEFORE PILATE

Concluding the series of Trial pageants, the Tilemakers' play, in spite of missing a leaf that was lost sometime after the middle of the sixteenth century, is one of the longer plays in the cycle. It was at one time two separate plays, as verified by the second list of pageants in the *York Memorandum Book A/Y*. These presented the trial as distinct from the Flagellation and Crowning with Thorns or Mocking.[87] The episodes therein dramatized were brought together by a dramatist who adopted the long alliterative line found elsewhere in the Passion series, but in this case choosing a twelve-line stanza that, as Beadle notes, is not elsewhere used.[88] Pilate's hand-washing appears commonly in iconography[89] and is depicted in a devotional woodcut inserted in a local Book of Hours of c. 1420 in the York Minster Library (MS. XVI.K.6, fol. 45). Pilate typically appears with his servant, who has a ewer and a towel draped over his shoulder. In the play a basin would also of necessity have been included. However, local spirituality focused much more on the Flagellation and Mocking, which were culminating moments in the suffering of Christ in the Trial scenes. Love stresses the importance of imagining these events "by inwarde meditacion of alle hees peynes abidyngly, and bot thou fynde thi herte melte in to sorouful compassion, suppose fully and halde, that thou hast too harde a stonene herte."[90] The pageant plausibly was regarded as an aid to such meditation since, made vivid in being staged, the sight would impress itself vividly on the memory. As Diller points out, these Trial plays are characterized by a conscious and serious effort by the York dramatist (or dramatists) to "'de-carnivalize' the Torture scenes."[91]

1   *Lordyngis.* Pilate opens with a term of polite address; see *MED*, s.v. *lording* 7b. However, he soon begins threatening and reminds his listeners that he has the power of life and death over his subjects.

---

[87] See Meredith, "*Ordo paginarum* and the Development of the York Tilemakers' Pageant."

[88] RB, p. 450.

[89] Schiller, *Iconography*, 2:64–65.

[90] Love, *Mirror*, p. 171.

[91] Diller, "Torturers," p. 62.

37	*ye prelates of pees*. Caiphas and Anna are consistently seen as bishops "of the hoold lawe," as the N-Town writer describes them (Play 26, line 164 s.d.), but peaceable they are not since they have been urging vengeance against the Prince of Peace.
46–51	Pilate has been awaiting news of the trial before Herod, and now is approached by the soldiers who have returned from his court. The first soldier in his "Hayll" greeting will parody the Hail lyrics directed to Christ, but here involving pure flattery.
55	*As his gud frende*. See also line 75, below, and comment on Play 31, lines 82–83, above. Herod and Pilate, who had previously been enemies, were cemented in friendship at this time, according to the account in Luke 23:12.
97–104	*Agayne Ser Cesar hymselfe he segges and saies . . . be slayne*. Citing Jesus' answer to those who wished to entrap him with the question "Is it lawful for us to give tribute to Caesar, or no?" (Matthew 22:17, Mark 12:14, Luke 20:22). In Caiphas' speech the charges against Jesus culminate in the accusation of blasphemy on account of his claim to be God's Son and in his insistence that he deserves execution.
112–16	*Simon, Yarus, and Judas . . . Togithere*. Caiphas' list of witnesses is adapted from the Middle English *Gospel of Nicodemus* (p. 25), which differs from the Latin original; see Craigie, "Gospel of Nicodemus and the York Mystery Plays," p. 54.
131	*youre langage so large*. That is, Anna and Caiphas would say anything to prejudice Pilate against Jesus. Pilate recognizes here that this is a case of malicious prosecution; see Tiner, "English Law."
142–45	*Uncleth hym, clappe hym, and clowte hym . . . lord badd*. Preco, the beadle, will do whatever is commanded, including torture, but here will only ask the knights to "bryng him to barre" — i.e., before the bar of justice. The soldiers are equally vicious and look forward in anticipation to the extreme torment to which Jesus will be put.
157	*stirre noght fro that stede*. Jesus is like a prisoner in the dock in an English court, but iconographic evidence only suggests that Jesus stands before Pilate, seated as judge. Jesus is said to have been brought "to barr" in the Middle English *Gospel of Nicodemus* (p. 34).
160–83	The episode of the banners in which the soldiers who hold them involuntarily lower them to show reverence for Jesus as for a king and as God's Son; see the *Gospel of Nicodemus*, in which they explain that the "schaftes" were not under their control and "lowtyd noght at oure wyttynge" (p. 33), all very much to the shock of the high priests and Pilate.
205ff.	Preco will round up "right bigg men and strange," a "company of kevellis" (lines 217–18), but, as in the Middle English *Gospel of Nicodemus* (pp. 32–35), these strong men will also not be able to prevent their banners from bowing before Jesus in spite of the stern warning that they must not allow this to happen.
258	*the cokkis has crowen*. Identifying the time of day as morning, when a cry can be made for the final stage of the trial to begin. It is subsequent to the cry that the second set of strong men, along with Pilate himself, will bow to Jesus. In an

embedded stage direction (lines 274–75), Pilate explains that he had risen from his seat, unable to "abstene / To wirschip hym" in deed and in thought. It was, he explains, "past all my powre," though he had tried very hard to restrain himself (line 278).

288   *Be his sorcery*. Caiphas' claim that Jesus is a necromancer has been taken too seriously as *the* charge against him; it is only one of a number of allegations.

300–07 Jesus finally breaks his silence, in an oblique answer to Pilate only briefly rebuking those who are speaking ill against him. As the silent sufferer who will be led to his death like a sheep to the slaughter, he otherwise will not speak, even when severely tortured. He is an exemplar of patience, like Job, understood to be an Old Testament type of Christ.

322–23 *Us falles not, nor oure felowes in feere, / To slo no man*. The ecclesiastical courts cannot act on a capital case, but they are able to turn the person over to be convicted and sentenced by the secular authority.

326–27 *He is fautles . . . his gate*. Pilate objects to the procedure on the basis of his determination that Jesus is innocent, and would prefer to let him go free. To this Caiphas brings up the charge of treason against Pilate's power (lines 329–32). This has an effect.

342   *Do wappe of his wedis*. The stripping of Jesus has a deeper typological significance, but it is doubtful that this would have been on the minds of either players or audience. Nevertheless, the act was something taken very seriously, for thereupon Jesus will stand, as Love reminds us, "nakede before hem alle" (*Mirror*, p. 170) like one in utter disgrace. He will be bound to a pillar (line 351), and the scourging, in which he patiently allows himself to be beaten bloody, will begin. His torturers again are modeled on Psalm 21 (*AV* 22), the Good Friday psalm, in which he is as if encircled by vicious attacking dogs, most vividly depicted in the fourteenth-century *Holkham Bible Picture Book*, where they use whips fitted with small pieces of metal attached to leather thongs (fol. 29v). In the *Bolton Hours* Jesus is depicted as wounded all over his body, from his head to his feet (York Minster Library, MS. Add. 2, fol. 57v). The Northern tradition associated with Richard Rolle has the number of wounds at 5,475 or thereabouts (Breeze, "Number of Christ's Wounds," pp. 87–90); the Towneley Resurrection play mentions 5,400 (Play 26, lines 291–92). He is beaten, according to Love, until "there was none semlynesse nor beutye in hym, and we helde him as foule as a leprose manne . . ." (*Mirror*, p. 171). In line 431 Jesus' *flesh* will be described as "al . . . beflapped." The description has its source in part in Isaias 1:6: "From the sole of the foot unto the top of the head, there is no soundness therein: wounds and bruises and swelling sores." For further discussion, see Marrow, *Passion Iconography*, pp. 134–41. As in the case of the Coventry Smiths' *Passion* pageant (*REED: Coventry*, p. 231), the Tilemakers' Jesus would presumably have had a white leather body garment to simulate nudity as well as to provide a surface for simulated wounds. For detailed discussion of such a violent act in drama, Jesus' nudity, and the veneration of his blood, see C. Davidson, *History, Religion, and Violence*, pp. 180–204.

380   *tarand.* If a tarandre is meant, as may be the case, this creature was chameleon-like in being able to change color; Beadle cites *OED* (RB, p. 524).

383   *He swounes or sweltes.* Previously the suffering Jesus had been accused of falling asleep; now the pain is so intense that he seems to lose consciousness.

386   *Nowe unboune is this broll, and unbraced his bandes.* Embedded stage direction; the unloosening that was begun "lyghtyly" at line 384 is now completed, though it may appear that the ropes were not entirely removed. The Mocking will follow.

389   *We will kyndely hym croune with a brere.* The crowning with thorns as a mock king; the common model for the crown was the relic at Sainte-Chapelle in Paris (see Horne, "Crown of Thorns in Art," and Réau, *Iconographie*, 2:2:457–59). It will be pushed into place at lines 400–01, so painfully that his brain "begynnes for to blede."

390–92 *but first this purpure and palle / . . . sall he were / For scorne.* A purple gown. Love called it "an olde silken mantelle of redde" (*Mirror*, p. 171).

397   *sette hym in this sete.* A mock throne, as if he were seated in the great hall of a palace.

403–05 *rede . . . For his septure.* The fourth soldier places a reed in his right hand (Matthew 27:29). Mark, however, says the reed was used to strike him on the head (15:19), while John merely reports that the soldiers "gave him blows" (19:3).

408–16 Mock reverence for the King as *rex judeorum*. The soldiers presumably kneel, as Matthew's account specifies.

420–21 Embedded stage direction. They lead Jesus back to Pilate — not an easy task because he is so sorely wounded.

434   *beholde upon hight and ecce homoo.* In John 19:13–14, Pilate, having seated himself in the judgment seat, shows Jesus to the people. In depictions in the late Middle Ages, he is shown dressed only in a loincloth, with hands still bound and consistent with Psalm 21:8: "All they that see me have laughed me to scorn: they have spoken with the lips, and wagged the head"; see Schiller, *Iconography*, 2:75–76. This was not infrequently presented as a devotional image, typically still bound and wearing the crown of thorns.

439   *In race.* Uninterpretable, appearing prior to the missing leaf which must have included the Jews' demand that Jesus be executed and that Pilate should release the criminal Barabbas; see Matthew 27:15–23. On the next extant folio, Pilate's hand washing follows in which he is attempting to deny his responsibility for the conviction of Jesus.

450–61 Pilate announces his judgment. Criminals will be hung on crosses on "aythir side" of Jesus on Golgotha.

472   *Nowe feste is he.* Jesus is more securely tied up; embedded stage direction.

474   *Drawe hym faste hense.* He will be violently led like an animal to the slaughter; the reference to "his tree" (line 481) suggests the presence of the cross, on which he

will be dragged away. But this is not consistent with the next pageant. It is indeed an evil hour, as the final line of the pageant suggests.

34. The Road to Calvary

The passing of Jesus from Pilate's palace to Calvary is a continuation of the torment and suffering experienced by him during the legal proceedings against him. Only one of the tormentors appears at the beginning of the pageant, to be joined by a second and then at line 59 by a third, who is, unusually, given a name, Wymond. The path representing the road to Calvary must utilize the ground level, the playing area or *place*. The *Ordo paginarum* described a play in which Jesus, carrying his cross, appeared "covered with blood."[92] The role of the tormentors as extreme bullies amplifies the action.[93] Love comments that Jesus "was drawene and hastede by grete violence, without reste, til he came to that foule stinkyng place of 'Calvarie,' where was set the ende and the reste of this harde bataile that we speken of."[94] The audience is asked to "make rome" for them to pass (line 16), and at the end they set off for "Calvarie," again passing through the audience. The *Meditations* cited Peter Comestor's *Historia scholastica* for the view that the cross was fifteen feet in height, and reports that Jesus, "the most gentle Lamb," took it up "patiently" and carried it.[95] But such a large cross would not have been easily brought onto the set by Wymond. Less familiar will be the playwright's use of the story of the wood of the cross that had been told in the *Northern Passion*[96] and other sources, ultimately deriving from the *Gospel of Nicodemus*. The history is complex. Grown from seed from Eden that was interred with Adam at his death, the tree was cut down for use in building Solomon's Temple, but failed to fit and was rejected. Thereafter it was used for a bridge over the brook Cedron (see line 64), and eventually a third of the wood from it was used for making the cross. A variant of this account appears in the *Golden Legend*.[97] The pageant's biblical source, which says nothing about the origin of the wood of the cross, is mainly Luke 23:26–32. Written principally in ten-line stanzas, the pageant was presented by the Shearmen, a trade that specialized in finishing wool cloth.

1–15   The first two stanzas seem to be additions to the text and are not in the ten-line stanzas in which the rest of the play mainly is written. In lines 9–11, the first soldier commands the audience not to give vocal support to the "traytoure" Jesus. This provides evidence for inherent audience sympathy for the victim and contradicts modernist views of subversive and "destabilizing" acting and widespread irreverence in response to the York mysteries. The pageant continues to present the tormentors as doglike, indecorous in their movements and barking their outbursts as they place Jesus on the cross. See the *Meditations* for reference to them as like "terrible and ferocious dogs," once more keeping Psalm 21 in

---

[92] *REED: York*, 1:21, trans. 2:717.

[93] For illuminating commentary on bullying behavior, see S. White, "Psychodynamic Perspective."

[94] Love, *Mirror*, p. 175.

[95] *Meditations*, p. 331.

[96] *Northern Passion*, 1:135, 148–67.

[97] Jacobus de Voragine, *Golden Legend*, 1:277–78.

mind (p. 319). Even porcine masks would have been appropriate for them, one would imagine.

52–54   *sties and ropes . . . nayles and othir japes.* Ladders were used in some accounts of the Crucifixion in which Jesus is attached to the cross while it is erect, though that will not be the case at York. Nails, in this case large spikes, were important objects of devotion; see their designation as *dulces clavos,* "sweet nails," in the antiphon *Crux fidelis,* sung on Good Friday; see *Hymni,* fol. 22. The nails were frequently depicted in the visual arts of a devotional nature (see the example from a prayer roll of the young Henry VIII, illustrated in Duffy, *Stripping of the Altars,* fig. 110), most usually along with other instruments of the Passion, including the ropes and hammers, also displayed in the pageant (see line 92).

65   *Men called it the kyngis tree.* The tree had flourished in King David's garden and hence came to be called the King's Tree.

67   *balke.* Compare the *Northern Passion,* 1:161 (Harleian manuscript, line 617: "A mekill balk tham bud have ane").

80–83   *I toke the measure . . . an ende.* The holes in the cross are already bored. Inevitably, however, an error has been made, not only showing the incompetence of the workmen but also proving the rightness of the prophetic passages in the Old Testament.

106–41 John's *planctus* or lament, which breaks off on account of the loss of a leaf in the manuscript following line 141. The loss unfortunately hampers understanding of the scene and possible interaction with the soldiers.

127   *Mi modir.* Anachronistic reference to the Virgin Mary as John's "modir," since only at the scene of the Crucifixion is he designated as her son, a substitute for Jesus who is dying on the cross.

160–79 *Doughteres of Jerusalem . . . and dighte.* Jesus' speech to his mother and the other Marys, based on Luke 23:28–31, is understood as a prediction of the final days of history and the Last Judgment.

183–86 *lete clense thy face . . . This signe schalle bere witnesse.* Normally an act assigned to Veronica, here transferred to the third Mary. Jesus' face makes an imprint on the cloth, which becomes a sign — and a valued relic — of the Passion. Extant examples of the "vernicle" from York appear in the *Bolton Hours,* fol. 174, and a fifteenth-century York Psalter (Cambridge, Trinity College, MS. O.3.10), fol. 11v.

190–92 *Saie, wherto bide ye here . . . stevenis steere.* Unless there has been previous interaction lost with the missing leaf, this is the first notice by the soldiers of the lamenting holy women. The first soldier insultingly calls them "quenys," or harlots.

193   *Go home, casbalde, with thi clowte.* Referring to the third Mary holding the vernicle. In lines 196–97 she responds that "This signe schall vengeaunce calle / On yowe." The word "casbalde" is a term of abuse.

200   *Lady, youre gretyng greves me sore.* In the extant text, he has not been greeted by the Virgin, though the next lines in which she asks for assistance suggest a

lacuna here. There is no indication in the stanza structure of something missing, however. That the holy women and John depart for Calvary is revealed by John in lines 203–04.

217   *oure tooles are before*. They do not have their tools in hand, but rather they will be waiting for them at the site of the Crucifixion.

225   *He swounes*. On account of being "forbledde" (line 223), Jesus is like one who is drunk and hence unable to carry the cross. For discussion, see Marrow, *Passion Iconography*, pp. 142–49. In the *Biblia Pauperum* (p. 93) and the *Speculum humanae salvationis* (Wilson and Wilson, *Medieval Mirror*, p. 184), Jesus carries his cross himself and is being led like an animal by a rope attached around his waist.

228–92   The enlisting of Symon of Cyrene to carry the cross is much expanded over the accounts in the synoptic gospels. Symon is on a journey to complete a vital business matter which is urgent and requires that he be at his destination on this day. The soldiers will be unbending and unfeeling, extremely mean and violent — once again like the "terrible and ferocious dogs" noted in the *Meditations* (p. 319, quoting Psalm 21:17).

309   *He muste be naked nede*. Jesus has been wearing his customary garments — i.e., his seamless cloak. This will now be taken from him and placed "in stoore" (line 331) until later. His blood makes the cloth stick to his sides (line 314).

341   *he is boune as beeste in bande*. Now shorn of his garment, he is led like a "sheep going to the slaughter," here made explicit. He would have projected an image of one disgustingly bruised who could hardly be an object of affection and reverence if he were not the Savior, regarded as one who is like a beloved member of one's family. Recognizing the force of such feeling is crucial to understanding the aesthetic and spiritual context of this pageant and the others in the Passion series.

35. Crucifixio Christi

The *Crucifixio Christi*, presented by the Pinners (and Painters), dramatizes the cruel placing of Jesus onto the cross by four soldiers, who would dominate the pageant if it were not for the Savior who is the silent center of the action. Their quick and impulsive gestures, movement, and speech would have been regarded as being typical of evil as opposed to the equanimity of more stable good characters. They attach Christ to the cross on the ground, as in the alternate way of doing it noted in the *Meditations* and in Love's adaptation of this work.[98] This is the manner in which the crucifying is done, for example, in a panel of painted glass now in the church of All Saints, Pavement, where, as too in the account in the *Northern Passion*, ropes are required to extend the body to fit the pre-drilled holes on the cross.[99] Jesus speaks only twice, once before being nailed to the cross, and the second time reciting a variant of very popular verses from the cross — the *O vos omnes* speech addressed

---

[98] *Meditations*, p. 334; Love, *Mirror*, p. 177. See also the discussion in Pickering, *Literature and Art*, pp. 237–48.

[99] C. Davidson, *From Creation to Doom*, pp. 125–26, fig. 11; *Northern Passion*, 1:188–89.

to those who pass by. The play, in twelve-line stanzas, represents a different style from the previous plays in the alliterative long line, and has some confusion in its speech designations. In this regard, the present text follows the edition of Beadle,[100] who in turn was guided by J. P. R. Wallis.[101]

7 *Sen we are comen to Calvarie*. Locating the scene. There is some difficulty again with imagining the pageant's action since much of it is as if on the ground; sight lines when Jesus is lying down, as he is during much of the play, are problematic even when using wagon staging. The *Ordo paginarum* specified that the crucifixion itself should be "super montem calvarie," which must have been a raised area on the pageant wagon.

25–26 *to this werke us muste take heede / So that oure wirkyng be noght wronge*. This statement has been taken as a sign that the soldiers are good workmen who are anxious to do a good job, just as craftsmen in the city of York are expected to do quality work. It is tempting to invoke the concept of the "banality of evil" introduced by Hannah Arendt (*Eichmann in Jerusalem*). The executioners in this case may be energetic, but they are certainly sadistic bullies who go out of their way to torment and cause pain — acts which they clearly enjoy in spite of their frustration with the process of attaching Jesus to the cross. The soldiers are too much like out-of-control guards at a concentration camp or similar prison facility to be sympathetic. Research such as the Stanford Prison Experiment demonstrates how ordinary human beings are capable of participating in torment and torture under circumstances in which they can see their victims as the "other" (see Zimbardo, *Lucifer Effect*). The executioners in this pageant are betrayed by circumstances and their lack of vision so that they too become like the other rabid torturers who have been observed in the previous Passion pageants in the cycle.

49–60 Jesus' prayer before being nailed to the cross may be compared to the prayer in the *Meditations* (p. 334) and also to the *Northern Passion*, 1:179.

75 *hymselffe has laide hym doune*. The *Meditations* and other sources report instead a violent action. Love wishes his readers to imagine Jesus being cast upon the cross by the soldiers, who are like mad thieves trying to pull his hands and feet so as to nail him to it (*Mirror*, p. 177); see also the *Northern Passion*, 1:179–80.

79–80 *he claymeth kyngdome with croune . . . schall hee*. Possible stage direction. He may have been given a crown here, but if so it could have been a mock crown such as was worn by a fool king in play; compare the paper crown placed on the head of the Duke of York in Shakespeare's *Henry VI, Part 3*, 1.4.93–95.

102 *a stubbe*. A short, thick nail (*MED*); see C. Davidson, *Technology, Guilds*, fig. 40 (p. 39), for an illustration, though the nail in this instance is not exactly a stub.

---

[100] RB, p. 451.

[101] Wallis, "Miracle Play of 'Crucifixio Christi.'"

107   *It failis a foote and more.* Compare the *Northern Passion*: "If the tone hand at the
             bore ware, / That other failed a fute and mare" (1:189, Harleian manuscript,
             lines 1608–09).

131–32   *A roope schall rugge hym doune / Yf all his synnous go asoundre.* All Jesus' sinews and
             bones indeed will be pulled asunder (see lines 147–48, 223–24), and this was
             regarded as having been predicted by Old Testament prophecy; see Psalm 21 (*AV*
             22), particularly verses 15 and 18. Verse 18 also says, "They have dug my hands
             and feet," predicting the driving of nails through Jesus' hands and feet. Pickering
             notes that ropes had been mentioned in connection with the Crucifixion by Hil-
             ary of Poitiers in the fourth century (*Literature and Art*, p. 244). The account in the
             Stanzaic Life is even more violent and bloody than in the pageant.

144   *foure bullis.* The suggestion that even four bulls would be ineffectual in pulling
             Jesus' limbs into place is an echo of Psalm 21:13 (*AV* 21:12): "fat bulls have be-
             sieged me."

161   *The mortaise is made fitte.* Having the cross fit into a mortise in a Passion drama may
             be reflected in a drawing of the Crucifixion in the *Carthusian Miscellany* (London,
             British Library, MS. Add. 37049, fol. 30). This therefore may be an instance in
             which art imitates the drama, a view promoted by Émile Mâle (*Religious Art*) and
             M. D. Anderson (*Drama and Imagery*), who believed that the artists were influenced
             by the stage. In general, however, a very healthy skepticism is required with regard
             to this theory.

225–26   *This fallyng was more felle / Than all the harmes he hadde.* The cross is now raised
             high. At first it will wobble until wedges are driven to stabilize it. The terrible
             pain of Jesus' torment is consistently emphasized, and in this late medieval
             writers stressed the importance of sympathizing and identifying with the pain.
             For its greater intensity and the visible signs — e.g., the flow of blood caused by
             the shock of the fall — see Mâle, *Religious Art*, 3:85.

253–64   *Al men that walkis by waye or strete . . . saules to save.* Jesus' address from the cross
             to those who pass by — i.e., in this case the audience watching the pageant. The
             words are again adapted from *O vos omnes*, the cry from Lamentations 1:12,
             chosen also as the text of an antiphon on Good Friday as well as a responsory on
             Holy Saturday, and incorporated in the Improperia. See Gray, *Themes and
             Images*, pp. 140–42. Jesus' forgiveness of his persecutors is based on Luke 23:34.

273   *Vath, qui destruit templum.* Matthew 27:40, following the Vulgate text.

293   *I rede we drawe cutte for this coote.* Compare Psalm 21:19 (*AV* 22:18): "They parted
             my garments amongst them; and upon my vesture they cast lots."

36. MORTIFICACIO CHRISTI

As the narrative and emotional climax of the Passion story, the Butchers' pageant opens
with Christ on the cross along with the two thieves, but with Pilate in front and center to tell
his version of events in his long initial speech. The play comprises both the death of Jesus and
his burial, both of which are specified for this pageant in the *Ordo paginarum* of 1415, though

since the verse adopts the long alliterative line, it is highly unlikely to have retained its early fifteenth-century form. Pilate still holds his equivocal position as one who was reluctant to kill Jesus but is compromised ethically in allowing the Crucifixion to proceed, while the high priests put forward their charges against him as vociferously as ever. Pilate is the author of the writing placed above Jesus on the cross, and he refuses to modify it. However, he must bear responsibility in spite of his effort to shift all blame to the high priests. The middle section in which the Virgin Mary and the others come onto stage is more or less consistent with the liturgical drama *Planctus Mariae*,[102] and the death of Jesus and the final Deposition scene are of course closely related to the actual Good Friday rituals performed each year in the churches.[103] If the hostile Wycliffite *Tretise of Miraclis Pleyinge* may be invoked, this pageant could have been the most *affecting* in the cycle, not unlikely moving members of the audience "to compassion and devocion, wepinge bitere teris."[104] The verse of the *Mortificacio Christi* is in thirteen-line stanzas.

25–26   *Transgressours als / On the crosse schalle be knytte*. After mentioning hanging as a punishment for felons (lines 23–24), Pilate speaks of crucifixion and perhaps points upward to the three men on crosses, with Jesus noted as being "on yone hill . . . so hye" (line 34). Depictions of the crucified Christ at York show the central figure, sometimes along with Mary and John and others but never with the two thieves. They are, for example, present in the *Speculum humanae salvationis* (Wilson and Wilson, *Medieval Mirror*, p. 188) and the *Holkham Bible Picture Book* (fol. 32r–32v), where the thieves have their arms tied over the cross-arms of their crosses and only Jesus is nailed to his cross. Also, in the latter example, Jesus' bloodied body stands in contrast with the thieves, whose clear white skin shows that they have not been tortured in the way he has been. Love reports that "stremes of that holiest blode" ran from all the "grete wondes" in his body (*Mirror*, pp. 177–78). It is not unusual, as in a panel of painted glass now in All Saints, Pavement (*Inventory of the Historical Monuments*, vol. 5, pl. 47), to see angels holding chalices to catch the streaming blood — a clear connection between the blood of Christ and the Eucharist.

82   *Thou saggard*. In late medieval art, Jesus usually hangs with arms upraised in the shape of a V to emphasize the pain, and his body most often is twisted into an S shape with the ribs clearly visible — a way of imagining the Crucifixion that became popular in the twelfth century and developed into more exaggerated forms in the later Middle Ages. See the emphasis in the pageant on the way Jesus' back is bent (e.g., in line 123). Jesus' shape approximated that of a harp, literalizing the stretching of the strings of the *cithara* of the psalms of David, with whom he was identified; in this way Jesus' act of dying on the cross could be seen as symbolically achieving harmony between this world and heaven just as his own

---

[102] See Young, *Drama of the Medieval Church*, 1:503–13.

[103] See Sheingorn, *Easter Sepulchre in England*.

[104] *Tretise of Miraclis Pleyinge*, p. 98, and, for brief commentary on the affective piety involved, pp. 132–33.

nature united the human and divine. For discussion, see Pickering, *Literature and Art*, pp. 285–98, and C. Davidson, *From Creation to Doom*, p. 126.

97–104   *To save nowe thiselffe late us see . . . trewelye, ilkone*. Reported in the synoptic gospels as a collective mocking of Jesus on the cross by the rulers, chief priests, and others. Love cites this and other similar statements by Jesus' persecutors as blasphemy (*Mirror*, p. 178), itself in the Middle Ages considered a deadly sin and deserving of very severe punishment; see *Catholic Encyclopaedia*, s.v. *Blasphemy*.

107–17   *wipe ye yone writyng away*, etc. The argument over the motto placed at the head of Jesus' cross by Pilate. The objections are only reported in John 19:20–22. The Harleian text of the *Northern Passion* reports that Pilate's text was "wretyn in the parchemyne" in Greek, Hebrew, and Latin (1:195, lines 1659–60). St. John reports that words proclaimed "This is the King of the Jews."

114   *Quod scripci, scripci*. John 19:22; see also the *Northern Passion*, 1:197.

118–30   *Thou man that of mys here has mente*. Jesus' speech is again based on the Good Friday *Improperia* or Reproaches. Jesus allowed himself to suffer on the cross thus because of his love for humankind, an emphasis that connects with the theme of Christ as a knight doing battle on the cross for his lady — i.e., the Church. See Woolf, "Theme of Christ the Lover-Knight."

131–82   The laments of Mary. Mary presumably enters, having been brought onto stage by John, either before Jesus' speech or at line 131, but there is no rubric in the manuscript to indicate the moment of her arrival. As noted above, this section roughly parallels the liturgical drama *Planctus Mariae*, but with only two short speeches for Maria Cleophe and none for Mary Jacobi, who is also specified in the *Ordo paginarum*. Mary's weeping must be seen within the context of affective piety. The reference to the sword of sorrow derives from the prophecy of Simeon in the York *Purification* (Play 17, line 441), and here she is so traumatized that she despairs and wishes to die. Jesus has just given her John to serve as a new son in his place. Mary and John are the most frequent figures to appear with the crucified Christ on roods in churches, nearly always the most prominent images at or near the high altar, but they were common in other locations. When John, addressing the Virgin Mary as "modir" (line 161), suggests that they ought to leave the site of the cross, she will object, for she wishes to stay by her Son's side until he passes away.

183–91   *With bittirfull bale have I bought . . . And treste*. Christ as sacrifice has taken on himself all of the sins of the world. His sorrow is entirely suffered "for thy sake." The *Golden Legend* quotes *Cur Deus homo* of Anselm of Canterbury: "There is nothing more painful or difficult that a man can do for God's honor than to suffer death voluntarily and not for debt but of his own free will, and no man can give himself more fully than by surrendering himself to death for God's honor" (Jacobus de Voragine, 1:208). In this way Jesus is the Great High Priest who sacrifices himself to release humankind from the powers of darkness, though, as conventional in Western tradition, not all members of the race — indeed, only a small minority — will be saved. In contrast to the belief of some early Christians such as Isaac the Syrian who believed that it would be blasphemous to impute to

God the eternal condemnation to hell of sinners, the damned are to live in that place of darkness and punishment forever.

192–95   *For foxis ther dennys have thei . . . heed for to reste*. See Matthew 8:20.

196–99   *If thou be Goddis Sone . . . for to spille*. Spoken by the bad thief, Gesmas, at Jesus' *left*; this is his traditional position. Only Luke (23:39) among the synoptic gospels records a repentant thief; the others say that both thieves reviled Jesus. The thieves' names appear in the Middle English *Gospel of Nicodemus* (pp. 63 and 65).

200–08   *Manne, stynte of thy steven and be stille . . . to thi bliss*. Spoken by the thief on Jesus' *right*, Dismas. Following Luke 23:40–41, he rebukes Gesmas and accepts his own punishment with humility. He also proclaims Jesus' innocence: "Noon ille did hee."

209–12   *to thee schall I saie . . . principall*. Jesus' forgiveness is extended to the thief on his right, who is promised a place with him in paradise "this daye."

213–15   *Heloy! heloy! . . . Lama zabatanye*. *Heloy*, from Mark 15:34, is the Aramaic word for "My God"; in *Lama zabatanye* (Vulgate: *lama sabacthani*) Jesus is quoting from the incipit of Psalm 21 (*AV* 22): "O God, my God, look upon me: why hast thou forsaken me?" The source in Psalm 21 is noticed in the *Pepysian Gospel Harmony* (p. 99).

222–25   The character identified as Garcio is conventionally named Stephaton; he appears here as a boy, who offers a sponge with vinegar and gall (line 244). Stephaton appears frequently in iconography, as in a window of c. 1339 in the west end of the Minster, where he is dressed as a soldier (French and O'Connor, *York Minster: The West Windows*, p. 79).

248–60   *Thi drinke it schalle do me no deere . . . in manus tuas*. Jesus' final speech, beginning with his rejection of the sponge offered by Garcio/Stephaton, but ending with his affirmation that his work is finished and his commendation of his "spirite" to the hands of his Father ("*in manus tuas*"), echoing Psalm 30:6 (*AV* 31:5): "Into thy hands I commend my spirit." This is the moment of his death, confirmed by his mother's moving six-line lament that follows.

272   *Lede we her heyne*. Embedded stage direction. Now that Jesus is dead, John and the Marys will leave the scene.

287   *Tho caytiffis thou kille with thi knyffe*. Pilate orders the soldiers to kill the two thieves, who are not yet dead. That Jesus died first was probably taken as a sign that the thieves were not tortured as Jesus was.

291–99   *Ser Longeus, steppe forthe . . . grounde*. Longeus, or Longinus, is given the "spere" which he is to thrust into Jesus' side to create a wound that will, along with those in his feet and hands, serve to be an object of devotion, as in an illumination that has been associated with York and local veneration in Oxford, Bodleian Library, MS. Lat. liturg., fol. 4v. See also Duffy, *Stripping of the Altars*, pp. 244–45, fig. 111. Longeus is blind, so another soldier, presumably the Centurion who speaks next, must guide the spear as he pierces the side of Jesus.

300–12   *O, maker unmade . . . markid in me.* Longeus immediately recognizes that Jesus was God, for, according to the Middle English *Gospel of Nicodemus*, he is given his sight on account of contact with Jesus' blood, which "sprent on Longeus eghen there, / And sone he sawe withouten doute" (p. 63, MS. Add., lines 629–30).

314–16   *This weedir is waxen full wan.* Compare the words of the Centurion in the Middle English *Gospel of Nicodemus*: "The sonne at his dede wex alle wanne" (p. 67, MS. Add., line 703). Jesus' death is marked by an eclipse and other marvels. The expectation would have been that these should be represented by sound and lighting effects; see, for example, Muir, *Biblical Drama*, p. 136. The Centurion is immediately inspired to believe in Jesus.

341–42   *Delyver . . . / And sewe, sir, oure Sabott to saffe.* Pilate is depicted as a Jew, which of course he was not. The rush to justice was one reason for the failure to achieve legal fairness. Now the burial must take place quickly. Joseph of Arimathea and Nicodemus will undertake that task.

370   *Nowe blemysght and bolned with bloode.* Compare Love, *Mirror*, who describes Jesus' "lovely face alle defilede with spittynges and blode, and the heres of his berde drawen awey fro his chekes, as the prophete Ysaie speketh in his persone thus, *I gaf my body to hem that smyten it, and myn chekes to hem that drowen the her aweye*" (p. 185, quoting Isaias 50:6). For discussion of the significance of Jesus' blood at the Crucifixion, see C. Davidson, *History, Religion, and Violence*, pp. 180–204.

377   *Take we hym doune us betwene.* The conventional iconography of the Deposition will pertain as they lovingly remove the nails and lower him to the ground. Love, in his adaptation of the *Meditations*, describes the process, which requires the use of ladders and pincers to remove the nails. In a painted glass panel formerly in St. Savour's Church and now in All Saints, Pavement at York, Joseph of Arimathea holds Jesus, whose hands have been released from the cross, while Nicodemus, below, pulls the nail from his feet (*Inventory of the Historical Monuments*, vol. 5, pl. 48). The holy women and John are not, however, present in the pageant as they are in the glass. In the play the two men perform an act of devotion.

381   *Late us halde hym and halse hym with hande.* Embedded stage direction. They must hold him more or less as the Virgin (who is not present) does in the *Pietà*. Because of the length of the play, this action could not have been given much time in performance.

382   *A grave have I garte.* Presumably a coffer tomb, as in another panel of glass now in All Saints, Pavement (*Inventory of the Historical Monuments*, vol. 5, pl. 48), where he is laid out. Joseph has a shroud (line 387), and Nicodemus has "oynmentis" to "anoynte" him "With myrre and aloes" (lines 400–03).

406   *on knes here I knele.* Embedded stage direction. The Burial too is an act of devotion. For extensive kneeling in the Good Friday *Depositio* rite at Durham, see Sheingorn, *Easter Sepulchre in England*, pp. 129–30.

37. THE HARROWING OF HELL

The Harrowing of Hell, detailing the story of Christ's acts between his death and resurrection from the dead, has only a slight biblical source in 1 Peter 3:19 that reports Jesus "preach[ing] to those spirits that were in prison," augmented by Old Testament predictions believed to be present in Isaias 9:2 and Psalm 23:7 (*AV* 24). The story, which is still considered of great significance by the Eastern Church and is mentioned in the Apostles' Creed, developed a full narrative in the *Gospel of Nicodemus*.[105] In England this source made the story accessible not only through the Middle English version of the *Gospel of Nicodemus* but also by means of other sources such as the *Golden Legend*.[106] As King remarks, the *Descensus* is integral to the Holy Saturday liturgy.[107] The York pageant, produced by the Saddlers, is nearly identical to the corresponding play in the Towneley manuscript, which, however, must have derived from an exemplar separate from the Register. According to the *Ordo paginarum*, the characters were twelve good spirits and six bad, but obviously the others present in the extant play could hardly have been left out. The verse form is an eleven-line stanza. Music is returned to the cycle in this play, with the singing of the patriarchs and prophets at the beginning and again especially as they are taken up into heaven by Michael. The stage set must have a typical hellmouth, at the doors of which Jesus will appear. The doors will fall before him so that he can enter to rescue the patriarchs and prophets. The iconography may be studied in glass now in All Saints, Pavement but formerly in the Church of St. Saviour.[108]

7–8   *aboute nowe woll I bee / That I have bought for to unbynde*. Jesus, or actually his soul (Anima Christi) since his "bodie bidis in grave" (line 23), will unbind those who have been in bondage in limbo on account of their lack of access to grace up to this time. With his (innocent) blood he has *purchased* those who will be released (lines 11–12) and hence in so doing he will have tricked the devil into surrendering his right to them.

36 s.d. *Tunc cantent*. The singing is ordered in a late addition to the manuscript, but no specific song is noted.

39   *Foure thowsande and sex hundereth yere*. Compare the lyric "Adam lay i-bowndyn": "fowre thowsand wynter thowt he not too long" (Brown, ed., *Religious Lyrics of the XVth Century*, p. 120).

41–42 *see I signe of solace seere, / A glorious gleme*. A bright light that in the next speech by Eve will be identified with paradise. Possible means of creating such an effect are discussed by Butterworth, *Theatre of Fire*, pp. 55–78.

[105] See James, ed., *Apocryphal New Testament*, pp. 123–42. An overview appears in Turner, "Descendit ad Inferos."

[106] *Middle-English Harrowing of Hell and Gospel of Nicodemus*, pp. 97–121; Jacobus de Voragine, *Golden Legend*, 1:222–24.

[107] King, *York Mystery Cycle*, pp. 157–58.

[108] *YA*, p. 88, fig. 25. For discussion, see especially Sheingorn, "'Who can open the doors of his face?,'" and, for practical aspects, Meredith, "Iconography of Hell."

50–54   *I, Ysaias . . . lende.* Referring to Isaias 9:2, which reports the great light shining into the darkness unto "them that dwelt in the region of the shadow of death," but with borrowing from the Middle English *Gospel of Nicodemus*, p. 99; for example: "folke in merkenes dwellande" (MS. Add., line 1193).

58   *That seede to save us nowe.* Christ is the Son descended of the Father, hence derived from his "seede."

65–68   *Lorde, late thy servaunt . . . in lande.* The *Nunc dimittis*; see the *Purification* pageant, Play 17, lines 415–27, above.

85–96   *Of that same light lernyng have I . . . fro payne.* Moses too has had previous experience of the light, at the Transfiguration when Elijah also had been present. Following his speech, the action turns to the denizens of hell.

101   *this uggely noyse.* The devils have heard the singing, and interpret the harmonious as its opposite. Devils were believed to be unmusical, capable of noise but not harmony to which they are hostile. Their shouting represents lack of restraint.

110   *sperde in speciall space.* That is, in limbo, mentioned above (line 102). Belsabub claims to be the "prince and principall" of this "space" (line 111).

119   *Lucifer, lovely of lyre.* Irony. The devils are conventionally very ugly indeed, and this is a sign that their values pertaining to physical beauty are upside down. For a fine example of the devil in the window of a York parish church (St. Martin Coney Street, located next to the Common Hall), see *Inventory of the Historical Monuments*, vol. 5, color pl. 61.

121, 123 *Attollite portas . . . eternales.* Psalm 23:7 (*AV* 24:7). Jesus traditionally holds a cross staff with banner, and has a shroud draped over his body; see, for example, Hildburgh, "English Alabaster Carvings," pp. 89–90, pl. XX. The staff would have been used to pound on the gates of hell, which do not collapse in this first instance; there is a similar use of a staff, in this case a bishop's crozier, against the door in the consecration ritual of a church or cathedral. David's speech (lines 127–32) affirms Jesus in the attack on the citadel of hell in terms of a battle. The *Golden Legend* reports that Jesus' voice was "like thunder" (Jacobus de Voragine, 1:223).

134   *All erthely men to me are thrall.* Satan is, of course, mistaken; since in the Crucifixion humans have been redeemed from their bondage to him by one who seems a most unlikely choice — a man without regular lodging, house, or hall appropriate to royalty.

140   *sette furthe watches on the wall.* Embedded stage direction; devils must be dispatched to the walls, suggesting an upper level above the hellmouth itself. Such devils, for example, appear on the walls in the Harrowing in the *Speculum humanae salvationis* (Wilson and Wilson, *Medieval Mirror*, p. 194); this illustration has flames coming from the space within hell behind them. See also C. Davidson, *From Creation to Doom*, pp. 142–43.

159   *I knowe his trantis fro toppe to taile.* But Satan indeed will be tricked: he will be the beguiler beguiled by Jesus, who has deceived him by means of his appearance in human form and his humility.

165   *I entered in Judas.* A conventional notion, but a number of inconsistencies, as also in the story of Pilate's wife, will be noted in Satan's attempt to undermine Jesus.

181–83   *Principes, portas tollite . . . rex glorie.* The second challenge based on Psalm 23:7, substituting the final portion of the verse and differing from the Vulgate reading.

187–91   *That may thou in my Sawter see.* David's reference is to Psalm 23, but see the Middle English *Gospel of Nicodemus*, p. 109, and Jacobus de Voragine, *Golden Legend*, 1:223.

194   *Opynne up and latte my pepul passe.* The third challenge, omitting Latin and echoing the Exodus theme. Now the gates must fall away, as the following speech by the first Devil indicates: "brosten are alle oure bandis of bras" (line 196). Limbo's fortifications have fallen. In the panel of painted glass at All Saints, Pavement cited above, Jesus steps forth over broken gates and chains. Glass, possibly with York connections, at Great Malvern shows metal hinges and a devil pinned under the gates (Rushforth, *Medieval Christian Imagery*, pp. 385–86, fig. 177).

229–33   *Thy fadir knewe I wele be sight . . . myght.* Satan is deceived. The substance of the debate that will follow is predicated on Satan's mistake in taking Jesus' death as a sign of his victory over him; but as earlier theologians such as Gregory of Nyssa had insisted, Satan is like a great hungry fish who will take Jesus' bait, while beneath his humanity is the hook of his divinity. Peter Lombard had spoken of the cross as a trap that had been baited by the blood of Christ, while Satan is the mouse caught therein; for discussion, see Nelson, "Temptation of Christ," p. 219; Macaulay, "Play of the Harrowing of Hell," pp. 115–19; and MacCulloch, *Harrowing of Hell*, pp. 203–04. See in particular lines 249–50: "Mi godhede here I hidde / In Marie modir myne."

255   *I schall thee prove be right resoune.* Satan is a rationalist and sceptic, fully believing that he still has the right to the souls of those in limbo. Jesus will counter with Old Testament prophecy which predicts with certainty that he will "have thame boughte with bale" (line 275).

277–88   *Nowe sen thee liste allegge the lawes, / Thou schalte be atteynted . . . in helle.* Satan tries to turn biblical texts against Jesus. The citation of Job — "he that shall go down to hell shall not come up" (7:9) — is easily confuted by another familiar passage from Job regarded as prophetic. Jesus is a divine fisherman who can "draw out the leviathan with a hook, or . . . tie his tongue with a cord" (40:20; compare *AV* 41:1).

325   *Nowe here my hande.* A handshake was a normal way of concluding an agreement, and not, as today, a common sign of greeting. Satan is happy since he believes he is promised even more victims for torment in his torture house which is hell (line 328), and he plans to *turne* — i.e., corrupt — more people as a means to this end (line 332).

339–40   The archangel Michael is designated to bind Satan; among the apocalypse scenes
          in Great East Window in the Minster painted by John Thornton in 1405–08,
          Michael, who is chaining the Devil, holds a key; see French, *York Minster: The
          Great East Window*, p. 128. In the York pageant, Satan will be confined to a "selle"
          (line 342) where he must remain seated. It will do him no good to call on Ma-
          hounde. In the *Northern Passion*, it is Jesus who binds Satan, who will be "fested
          fast / With bandes that sall ever last, / And so he sall be bunden ay / Untill it be
          domes day" (1:213).

349–80   The Extraction of Souls. Conventionally Jesus takes Adam by the forearm and
          leads him out, followed by Eve and the others. In Dante's *Divine Comedy*, Virgil
          recalls how "a Great Lord" wearing a crown of victory (*vittoria cornato*) "carried off
          the shade [*ombra*] of our first father, of his son Abel, and the shade of Noah, of
          Moses, the obedient legislator, of father Abraham, David the king, of Israel, his
          father, and his sons, and Rachel, . . . and many others" (*Inferno*, canto 4, lines
          52–61). The Extraction is shown at York in the glass in All Saints, Pavement and
          in other depictions of the scene, including a restored wall painting at Pickering in
          the North Riding (*YA*, pp. 87–89, fig. 25; Tristram, *English Wall Painting*, p. 154).
          In the Pickering example, as in the Great Malvern glass cited above, Eve holds an
          unchewed apple that she will return to Jesus as a sign of the reversal of the Fall.

374–75   *Ne derelinquas, Domine, / Animam meam in inferno*. Psalm 15:10 (*AV* 16:10).

380   *full of filthe*. In the scene dramatizing the Fall of the Angels at the beginning of the
          York cycle, hell had been shown to be a filthy place. Its smell, as for Dante, was
          presumably of excrement (see Seiler, "Filth and Stench," esp. p. 132).

384 s.d. *Tunc cantent*. Again a late rubric calling for singing, without identifying the piece
          to be sung. It appears that there will be a procession, with singing, as the souls
          are taken up by Michael into bliss.

400   *blisse us with thi holy honde*. In the *Gospel of Nicodemus*, Jesus holds out his hand
          and makes the sign of the cross, or, in a variant text of this work, makes a sign
          of the cross on Adam's forehead (*Gospel of Nicodemus*, p. 119; James, ed., *Apoc-
          ryphal New Testament*, p. 139).

408   *Laus tibi cum gloria, etc*. If this is a liturgical piece, it has not been identified. While
          it seems to be an incipit, with *"etc."* signifying the continuation of the song, Rastall
          points out that this line, integral to the stanza, seems rather to introduce an
          unspecified song at the end of the pageant (*Minstrels Playing*, p. 35), in which case
          the citation of the song here is misplaced. It thus may be that the singing noted
          in the late rubrics added at line 384 was begun only after the last line of the play
          was spoken.

38. The Resurrection

The York pageant, mounted by the Carpenters who are known to have supported their own religious guild devoted to the Resurrection,[109] incorporates material typically associated with the liturgical *Visitato Sepulchri* but embeds it in the story of the four knights chosen by Pilate to guard the sepulcher. Their narrative may be read elsewhere, as, for example, in the *Northern Passion*, and they emerge as nearly necessary depictions on representations of the Resurrection.[110] There is a strong connection in this pageant with image devotion, with a focus on seeing the rising of Jesus out of the tomb to the accompaniment of liturgical music, identified by Rastall as *Christus resurgens*, shared with the York *Elevatio* ceremony performed on Easter morning.[111] The Harleian text of the *Northern Passion* indicates that anyone who "heres or redes" (line 20) the narrative will be given Christ's blessing and a hundred days of pardon in Purgatory granted by Pope Innocent,[112] and one would imagine that a similar blessing could likely have been expected from seeing and hearing the story as staged at Corpus Christi. At some point a copy of the York *Resurrection* was borrowed by a compiler of the Towneley collection, formerly thought to be the Wakefield cycle, and the two texts even share, as Beadle has noticed, a corrupt passage (York, lines 294–98; Towneley, lines 452–58).[113] The Towneley version, which was derived from an independent copy of the play that is now lost, confirms the expected character designations for the Marys, with the first being Mary Magdalen, the second Mary the mother of James, and the third Mary Salome, and it also provides some readings that correct mistakes by the scribe who entered the play into the York Register. The York *Resurrection*, which in some ways is the climax of the York cycle, uses a six-line stanza.

1–36   The high priests have gone to Pilate and argue with him about the Crucifixion, which they claim was justified and reasonable. The Centurion will, however, contradict their assertions about its justice and even insist that Jesus "was Goddis Sone almyghty" (line 75).

86–97   In answer to Caiphas' request for some "tokenyngis trewe" (line 81), the Centurion rehearses a list of remarkable signs, including an eclipse, that occurred at the Crucifixion. These are based on Matthew 27:51–54, and represent something "outside nature" that will be accepted as such by the audience (see Twycross, "Playing 'The Resurrection,'" p. 279). Lines 93–94 are confused but refer to the arising of men from their graves in Matthew 27:52–53. Pilate, however, will dismiss the eclipse as a natural phenomenon (line 99), but more ominously Caiphas renews his charge of sorcery, for that is the only way he believes dead men could rise and walk (lines 103–04).

[109] *York Memorandum Book B/Y*, p. 254.

[110] See *YA*, pp. 91–95.

[111] Rastall, *Minstrels Playing*, p. 35; Sheingorn, *Easter Sepulchre in England*, p. 365; and see the discussion by King, *York Mystery Cycle*, pp. 158–61.

[112] *Northern Passion*, 1:249.

[113] See RB, p. 453.

123–24   *Such wondir reasouns as he redis / Was nevere beforne.* Sharply distinguishing the York Pilate from the more hostile high priests. Thereafter Caiphas and Anna will launch into a rehearsal of their charges, now including their fear that Jesus' body will be stolen from the grave (lines 147–48). Pilate agrees to guard the tomb and will appoint soldiers to do so.

183   *On ilke a side latte us sitte doune.* Embedded stage direction. The soldiers have arrived at the tomb and are taking their places at its four corners. They will sit, a convenient posture from which to show them sleeping. They are sometimes shown thus in iconography, and not infrequently take their places in niches in the tomb.

186 s.d.   *Tunc Jhesu resurgente.* Rastall points out that this stage direction, by the main scribe, refers ahead to the speech by the first Mary as "warning her not to speak until Christ has risen from the tomb and left the playing area" (*Minstrels Playing*, p. 9n14). The silence of Jesus is striking when, if the usual iconography is maintained, he steps out of the coffer tomb, perhaps onto the back of one of the sleeping soldiers. As Sheingorn notes, this involved "a significant change in content from the Latin plays" and "underscored the theme of triumph which is an inseparable part of the celebration" ("Moment of the Resurrection," p. 111). For further discussion, see C. Davidson, "Memory, the Resurrection, and Early Drama," and Twycross, "Playing 'The Resurrection.'" Whether Jesus' rising is accompanied by a "gret erthe dyn" or earthquake as the angel descends to roll back the stone (see Matthew 28:2, and the *Pepysian Gospel Harmony*, p. 102) we do not know, but it was feasible and would have been a stunning introduction to the action and the singing of the angel. The Coventry plays are known to have had a "baryll for the yerthe quake" (*REED: Coventry*, p. 474), but not for the Resurrection pageant.

    Tunc angelus cantat Resurgens. This is added in a later hand, but likely represents long-standing practice. As noted above, the item must be *Christus resurgens*, of which several possibilities are available, the most likely of which is perhaps the antiphon (see Rastall, *Minstrels Playing*, pp. 35–36). Dutka translates: "Christ having risen from the dead dies now no more: death shall have no more dominion over him. [For the life he lives, he lives with God. Alleluia, Alleluia]" (*Music*, p. 115). The first soldier, who has heard the singing in his sleep, will report that they "herde never sen we were borne / . . . Suche melodie" (lines 384–86). The angel traditionally wears an alb, taking the description in Mark 16:5 of a white garment as a prescription. The *Pepysian Gospel Harmony* describes the angel as wearing "clothes als white as snow" and having a "visage als rede as fyre" (p. 102).

187   *Allas, to dede I wolde be dight.* Beginning the laments of the Marys, leading up to their discovery at the tomb.

195–96   *he is medicyne / And bote of all.* Still the first Mary refers to Jesus as "medicyne," a medical solution to the problems of guilt and despair; see 1 Peter 2:24, which asserts, referring to Jesus' Passion and suffering on the cross, "by whose stripes you were healed." The actor playing Jesus who has just been seen by the audience will still seem to bear the wounds of his suffering, perhaps still wet, as the second Mary remembers them in the next speech.

203   *graven under the grete.* The grave, however, is almost certainly a coffer tomb, not one that is sunk into the ground.

213   *anoynementis faire and clere.* Mary I, identified in Towneley as Mary Magdalen, traditionally would have carried a jar containing ointment and spices, iconography in part conflating her (incorrectly) with the reformed prostitute who anointed Jesus' feet in the house of Simon — an act which, as we have seen, plays a role in Judas' plot to kill his Master (see Play 36, lines 129–54).

230   *The hevy stone is putte aside.* Suggesting the cover of the coffer tomb usually seen in depictions in the visual arts (see *YA*, pp. 91–92) rather than the stone which requires rolling away in Mark 16:3 and Luke 24:2, nor is it a tomb that can be entered, as in John 20:5 and in some liturgical dramas (see especially Ogden, "*Visitatio Sepulchri*: Public Enactment and Hidden Rite").

235–40 *Ye mournand women . . . . / Here in this place whome have ye sought? . . . Come nere and see.* Compare the *Quem queritis* exchange in the liturgical Easter play, the *Visitatio sepulchri*, of which, however, there is no evidence in York service books.

243   *The sudary.* Love explains that the sudary was the head wrap that Jesus wore at his burial, but also indicates that the other "clothes that he was wrapped inne" were found (*Mirror*, p. 198). The grave clothes were presented as a prime piece of evidence of the Resurrection here as in such liturgical dramas as the well-known Fleury *Visitatio* (Young, *Drama of the Medieval Church*, 1:394–95). The sudary will be shown to the audience. While Twycross suggests that the effect, in contrast with the liturgical drama, is "curiously distant" ("Playing 'The Resurrection,'" p. 293), we can hardly be sure that this was the case. It is not a relic like the Turin shroud, but it *represents* the actual cloth in which Jesus was buried and hence is likely to have had a devotional role in the drama.

260   *To Galilé nowe late us wende.* Mary II and Mary III go to inform the disciples of what they have seen.

267–88 Mary I's lament, continued after the departure of the other Marys. This is made all the more urgent when it is remembered that this is Mary Magdalen, who is represented as the repentant "Sinner" and that this is a saint with whom personal identification was often very strong among some members of the audience. She is the woman who had a special love for Jesus, a point that is exploited tastelessly in the twentieth-century musical *Jesus Christ Superstar*. When she completes her lament, she must leave the stage, and just then the soldiers, who have been sleeping throughout the previous scene, rouse themselves to find that Jesus is gone from the grave.

310–11 *Witte Sir Pilate of this affraye, / We mon be slone.* While being witnesses to the Resurrection (note especially line 293a: "Rise uppe and see"), the soldiers are primarily motivated by their fear of being executed for dereliction of duty, here presented as a capital crime. At first they consider lying, but then resolve to tell the truth — that is, that it was a supernatural event; see line 332.

339   *We dye but onys.* Proverbial. See Whiting and Whiting, *Proverbs*, D243.

348ff.   The soldiers, now back at Pilate's court, will try to explain their failure. Caiphas
              and Anna, who are also present, recognize the importance of the event but of
              course misunderstand its essential character. They will make suggestions for
              what, in the current jargon, will be a "cover-up." The knights will be bribed to
              remain quiet about the event. In Gréban's *Passion* the soldiers insist on a large
              payment "because they are selling something very rare and precious: Truth"
              (Muir, *Biblical Drama*, p. 140).

450–51   *Thus schall the sothe be bought and solde, / And treasoune schall for trewthe be tolde.*
              Pilate emerges as a politician, one more interested in himself and in public rela-
              tions affecting him, than in the truth. These words are followed by a mock bene-
              diction in which the audience is urged to hold this advice "ay in youre hartis,"
              a lesson quite at variance with the meaning of the Resurrection that the audience
              has just seen in representation.

39. THE APPEARANCE OF CHRIST TO MARY MAGDALEN

The *Ordo paginarum* indicates that in this play Mary Magdalen again appeared with her
ointment or spice jar, as she had in the previous pageant, and confirms that its subject was
her meeting with Jesus in the garden — the *hortulanus* scene. The play is a continuation of
the Carpenters' drama but also initiates the post-Resurrection appearances, however abbreviated in the York cycle. In depictions in the visual arts in the late Middle Ages, Jesus may
appear in this scene with a spade in hand like a gardener, hence accounting for the Magdalen's failure to recognize him. In other instances, such as the miniature in York Minster
Library MS. XVI.K.6, fol. 91r, he is holding a cross staff, and his red wounds are very visible.
The Magdalen typically has long blond hair. While it was presented by the Winedrawers in
the fifteenth century, there is some confusion about the sponsorship of this pageant and the
following *Peregrinus* in later years.[114]

1–27   The pageant begins with Magdalen's long lament, despairing at having lost Jesus.
              In spite of the angel's message to the holy women, she fears he cannot be found.
              Keeping in mind that, as noted above, the Magdalen is a composite figure in bib-
              lical interpretation of the time (see Malvern, *Venus in Sackcloth*, pp. 16–29), her
              role as a weeper seems to have been established in the scene at Simon's house,
              where she wept for her own sins, but her weeping, both at the tomb and at her
              unexpected meeting with the resurrected Jesus, is reported in John 20:11–15. In
              lines 38–41ff. she asks if the gardener has borne Jesus away.

62–63   *Marie, of mournyng amende thy moode / And beholde my woundes wyde.* Jesus reveals
              himself to the Magdalen. The wounds are proof of his identity.

68–69   *Trowe it wele, it turnes to goode / Whanne men in erthe ther flessh schall hyde.* The evil
              deed is actually a good thing. Line 69 seems to be a reference to the Last Judg-

---

[114] See RB, pp. 454–55, and Meredith, "John Clerke's Hand," pp. 260–61.

ment, when those who have lived in pursuit of spiritual goals will be rewarded and the others will want to hide.

70–71   *A, Rabony . . . this day.* Magdalen recognizes Jesus. The iconography here is widespread, with the Magdalen dropping down on her knees and either folding her hands or, more commonly, reaching out with her hands toward Jesus, as in the *Biblia Pauperum* (p. 108).

72   *touche me noght.* See John 20:17: *noli me tangere,* in the Vulgate rendering. This is a curious episode, since later Jesus will confirm his identity to St. Thomas by having him place his hand in his side wound. Some believe that Jesus' response to the Magdalen reflects Middle Eastern anti-feminism and an apparent prohibition against touch between the sexes. Love could not believe that there would have been no touching between two who loved each other so much; he even speculated that she would have kissed Jesus' hands and feet before the end of this meeting (*Mirror*, p. 200).

81   *Thi woundes thai are nowe wette.* The freshness of Jesus' wounds is frequently insisted upon, and is a sign of life since after the heart stops at death wounds do not actually bleed. See also lines 111–13, below, for the statement that Jesus' wounds "hath made thi body wete."

82–85   *Negh me noght . . . I stigh noght yette.* This explanation for repulsing the Magdalen's touch has long puzzled scholars; see note to line 72, above.

94–109   Jesus speaks of his armor, symbolically referring to his effort as a lover-knight on the cross. The concept of the Christian warrior derives from St. Paul's injunction in Ephesians 6:11 ff. to "put you on the armor of God," with Jesus providing the example to be followed.

142   *To Galilé schall thou wende.* Jesus sends the Magdalen to report the news about her meeting with him, and insists (line 146) that she should give a complete account.

40. THE TRAVELERS TO EMMAUS

The play is assigned to the Woolpackers and Woolbrokers in the *Ordo paginarum*, which gives the names of the disciples as Luke and Cleophas. Confusingly the running title over the pageant in the Register lists the Winedrawers, and at the head of the first page the Sledmen are noted in a later hand. In the shorter list in the *Memorandum Book A/Y*, the "Wolpakkers" are given the "Apparicio Christi peregrinis."[115] The play is based on the Gospel reading, Luke 24:13–35, for the Monday after Easter.[116] It also follows roughly the structure of the liturgical *Peregrinus*,[117] a form that was documented in England in an example from Lichfield that is contained in the *Shrewsbury Fragments*, which were somehow related to the

---

[115] For discussion, see RB, pp. 456–57.

[116] *Missale*, ed. Henderson, 1:128.

[117] Young, *Drama of the Medieval Church*, 1:471–76.

York plays.[118] The pageant's relevance to the feast of Corpus Christi, a celebration of the Eucharist, is obvious, since the central event of the pageant was the revelation of Jesus in the breaking of the bread, unfortunately imperfectly preserved in the York manuscript. F. C. Gardiner perceptively comments concerning the structure of this play, on account of what had been seen in previous pageants and will be seen in the subsequent ones, that it "assures the audience of a universe in which pilgrimage will evolve along the successive stages of an achieved transcendence."[119] The long alliterative line appears in eight-line stanzas in the first 152 lines in the York play, while in the final section the verse adopts quatrains without abandoning alliteration.

9–10   The pageant has begun with a short speech by Luke, who is now joined by Cleophas. The text demands that they should be walking, as pilgrims. The most usual marks of a pilgrim are a staff, a distinctive hat, and a scallop shell. An early fifteenth-century set of panels in York Minster Chapter House shows them also with bare feet (*YA*, p. 97). For discussion see C. Davidson, *From Creation to Doom*, pp. 158–60.

14   *Emax, this castell.* Emmaus, identified as a *castellum* in the Vulgate (Luke 24:13), a mistaken translation of the Greek text, which specifies a village.

67–69   *What are thes mervailes . . . wayes?* Jesus, pretending ignorance, joins the two disciples, who are led to believe that he is a pilgrim returning from Jerusalem. The disciples will avoid towns for good reason, for they know that, on account of their relationship to Jesus, their lives may be in danger.

112   *nowe is this the thirde daye.* Identifying the day as Sunday, Easter day. The second disciple, Cleophas, will report that news has come of a remarkable sight; this has been relayed by the holy women who have witnessed the empty tomb and the angel messenger who "tolde thame ther Lorde was alyve" (line 120).

134–36   *And also to Moyses gan he saie . . . and teched.* See Luke 24:27: "And beginning at Moses and all the prophets, he expounded to them in all the scriptures, the things that were concerning him."

154   *her is a sege.* Jesus will be seated for a meal. Depictions in the visual arts conventionally show his seat to be the place of honor. The table may already be outfitted with bread and other food and drink, or these are brought on by a servant without any delay.

157–58   *Nowe blisse I this brede . . . you to feede.* Jesus will bless the bread in a manner reminiscent of the ceremonial way in which it is done in the canon of the Mass, and will ask the disciples to eat "faithfully," again phrasing that suggests offering the Eucharistic bread in Communion. The missing segment of text at line 159 unfortunately occurs at the point when they recognize Jesus in the breaking of the bread — and the point at which he disappears. Butterworth comments on the

---

[118] Davis, ed., *Non-Cycle Plays*, pp. 4–7; see also the brief discussion in C. Davidson, *Festivals and Plays*, pp. 31–32.

[119] Gardiner, *Pilgrimage of Desire*, p. 147.

equivalent scenes in the Chester and Towneley plays, and indicates the importance of the disappearance happening like an instantaneous vanishing act to
preserve the illusion (*Magic*, pp. 75–76).

185   *Menskfully in mynde thes materes now merkis.* The sight of Jesus at the blessing of the
       bread has left a mark on their minds. The concept needs to be understood by
       means of late medieval theory of vision, which, following the classic philosophers,
       involved impressions on the memory. The memory is like wax upon which images
       are imprinted or marked. See Plato, *Theaetetus* (191c), in *Collected Dialogues*, p. 897,
       and the discussion in Carruthers, *Book of Memory*, pp. 21–22.

41. DOUBTING THOMAS

   The Scriveners' pageant is unique in that it exists in two copies, one in the Register (the
copy text for this edition) and the other, a guild copy, in the damaged Sykes Manuscript (ed.
Cawley, "Sykes MS"). Problems with the Register copy are noted by Beadle,[120] who also provides a full collation of the two manuscripts in the footnotes to his text of the play. The story
of Thomas that is dramatized is closely related to the Emmaus play, and in the liturgical
Peregrinus drama the section on his doubts was attached more or less as an epilogue to the
main action. However, the biblical account in John 20:19–31 states that the appearance to
Thomas took place one week later, and this reading was hence specified as the gospel for the
first Sunday after Easter, known as *Quasi modo* Sunday (so known from the incipit of the Introit at Mass).[121] The pageant begins with the revelation of Jesus to the disciples, who are in
the midst of eating a meal, as reported in Mark 16:14, prior to the appearance to Thomas,
at first as what appears to be an apparition that will be taken for a ghost. Jesus' appearances
and disappearances would have involved some clever effects, one would assume, since the
Bible refers to his ability to enter rooms when "the doors were shut" (John 20:19). The play
is written in six-line stanzas throughout.

5–12   The disciples' fear of the Jews, here blamed for executing Jesus, is based on
       John 20:19.

29   *Itt was vanyté in oure thought.* At first the disciples tend to dismiss the apparition as
       the result of collective hallucination or overheated imagination, forming mental
       images without basis in sense perception. In spite of the miraculous radiance that
       accompanies Jesus, they remain skeptical until his third appearance in the pag-
       eant. The radiance about him, like his sudden appearances and disappearances,
       would necessarily have involved stage effects. Evidence from iconography suggests
       that Jesus would hold a vexillum as a sign that he is the risen Christ.

35   *Itt is a sperite.* James' view is that Jesus is a spirit, or ghost, confirmed by John (line
       37). Their fear at this point seems justified, since it was believed that a spirit or
       ghost could indeed be the devil in the guise of a known person. Jesus accuses them
       of being "madmen," with thoughts distraught and at variance with reality (line 43).

[120] RB, p. 457.

[121] *Missale*, ed. Henderson, 1:139.

50   *Behalde and se myn handis and feete.* These wounds, and the one at his heart, are offered as proof. All five wounds were primary objects of devotion; see Gray, "Five Wounds of Our Lord"; Duffy, *Stripping of the Altars*, pp. 243–56, figs. 98–99; and *YA*, pp. 77–78. Jesus will allow his wounds to be touched physically to prove that he is not a ghost.

63–66 *Bringe nowe forthe unto me here / Some of youre mette . . . to ete.* This is the second proof of his physical reality. The rapidity of James' producing the honeycomb and roast fish indicates that these were on hand, probably on the table at which the disciples were eating.

75   *ye schall wanhope forgete.* They have been in despair, which is the "sickness unto death," and now they must turn aside from it and revive their hope.

93–96 *Whome that ye bynde bounden schall be . . . in hevene.* The power of the keys, given to St. Peter (Matthew 16:19); the power to forgive sins or to withhold absolution ("whatsoever thou shalt bind upon earth, it shall be bound also in heaven"). The clergy's power ("posté"), derived from the apostles, to forgive sin is the underpinning of the doctrine of Penance.

97   Thomas comes into the acting area, mourning and in despair following the suffering and death of his Master. He approaches the other disciples at lines 125–26. He will dismiss their report of seeing Jesus as tricks "Of fooles unwise" (line 136) or thereafter as "some sperit" or ghost (line 149).

158–62 *Till that I see his body bare . . . in his syde.* See John 20:25. Touching the holy wounds was to be the ultimate proof that will cure his scepticism.

175   *Beholde my woundis are bledand.* Thomas will not only touch the wounds but will have direct contact with Jesus' "blessid blode" (line 184), which was believed to have miraculous powers. Relics of his blood, as at Bruges, Westminster, or Hailes, were the objects of veneration and pilgrimage. Thomas calls it "blode of price" for its great value (line 182).

181   *Mi Lorde, my God.* Thomas' speech translates the motto, taken from the Vulgate, on a window which shows the subject in the church of All Saints, North Street: *Dominus meus et deus meus* (John 20:28). Love says that Thomas "reverently" kneeled "don with bothe joy and drede" and "touchede hees wondes as he badde and seide, *My Lorde and my God*" (*Mirror*, p. 208).

193–98 *My brethir . . . menghe.* Jesus' admonition to the disciples to go forth and preach to all countries concludes the pageant.

42. THE ASCENSION

In addition to Mary and Jesus, only four apostles — John, Peter, Andrew, and James — have speaking roles in the Tailors' pageant, but the *Ordo paginarum* indicates an early fifteenth-century cast of John the Evangelist and eleven apostles. Six angels were included — a plausible number, even if only two had speaking roles, since having four of them operate the cloud machine might have made good sense and yet have been quite consistent with traditional iconography. Jesus' ascension would have been one of the high points of the drama, and was accompanied by music, noted by John Clerke as *Ascendo ad patrem meum*, replacing the clearly erroneous stage direction calling for *Gloria in excelsys deo*, which was canceled, presumably by Clerke, in the manuscript. We might imagine the cloud machine to have some affinity with the mechanism still used in the *Assumption* performed on August 14–15 each year at Elche in Spain,[122] but it must have been more modest since it would have required technology that was manageable on a pageant wagon. The Virgin Mary also has a central role. It is usual for her to appear in the most prominent location in the grouping of apostles. The pageant is written in octaves.

1–24	The apostles remain very perplexed about Jesus' resurrection, especially since he comes and goes mysteriously. Mary then reminds Peter (lines 25–32) about his doubts immediately following the Crucifixion, though now he should have "knowyng clere." But she too would like to achieve greater understanding.
33–80	*Almyghty God . . . schall ay.* Jesus' long prayer to his Father. He has died for humankind, and now will be reunited with the Father since he has accomplished what he was sent to earth to do.
81ff.	Jesus will turn to the apostles to explain their predicament and to stress the urgency of maintaining their faith since thus the human body, subject to decay and dissolution, can transcend physicality. To do otherwise is to retain the bondage of the soul to the evil one, the devil of hell, who will supervise the "endles peyne" (line 120) to which the damned will be subjected. Finally, Jesus will return to judge those who will receive salvation and those who do not at Doomsday. The direct connection between the tree of the Garden of Eden and the cross will have been noted (lines 114–16). The speech, in which Jesus also reminds the disciples of their difficulties and martyrdoms to come, affirms the great strength that they will receive to do their work, whether it be exorcizing demons, healing the sick, speaking in tongues, handling serpents, or drinking "venym wik, withouten wene" (line 143).
93–98	*but sithen I have / Ben walkand fourty daies aboute.* King notes that the source of Jesus' argument here is a sermon by Gregory the Great which was read on Ascension Day (*York Mystery Cycle*, p. 165, citing *York Breviary*, 1:478). As seen in the two previous pageants, Jesus has appeared with the disciples and shared food with them in order to demonstrate the physicality of the Resurrection.
105–06	*Howe man by cours of kynde schall ryse / Allthogh he be roten.* Affirming the resurrection of the physical body at the Last Day.
175–76	*The Fadir blissing moste myghty / Giffe I you all that leffe here.* The *Stanzaic Life* says that Jesus "blesset hom all whit mild steven, / and befor hom alle tho / Stegh uppe into the blisse of heven" (p. 294).
176 s.d.	*Ascendo ad patrem meum.* An antiphon for Ascension Day; see *York Breviary*, 1:480. Dutka translates: "I ascend to my Father and your Father, to my God and your

---

[122] Massip, "Cloud"; C. Davidson, *Technology, Guilds*, 91–100.

God. Alleluia" (*Music*, p. 113). Rastall also cites a short responsory on this text and references modern editions of the chants in the *Liber usualis* and other sources (*Minstrels Playing*, p. 37).

179–80 *My Sone thus to be ravisshed right / In a clowde wendande uppe fro me.* Tradition says that Jesus rose triumphantly. Iconographic evidence suggests that he probably stepped into the cloud and, with the bottom of his robe and bare feet visible, was raised up, disappearing entirely into the cloud. The *Stanzaic Life* explains that Jesus' footprint remained on the "hard marbul stone" on which he was standing at the Ascension (p. 294), and this may indicate that in the play he was positioned higher than the apostles before his ascent so that his figure would stand out for the audience. While images such as a wooden roof boss (now replaced by a replica) in the nave of York Minster show the imprint of Jesus' feet after he is lifted up (J. Browne, *History of the Metropolitan Church*, pl. CXVI), this sort of detail would not have been practical in a pageant wagon production.

218 *What wondir ye to hevene lokand?* The angel's question embeds a stage direction. The apostles are all to look upward at the disappearing Jesus, as in illustrations in the visual arts such as the lost glass in the Bedern Chapel that was described by Torre, who also noted the Virgin "with hands conjoined on her breast" (O'Connor, "Bedern Stained Glass," pp. 564 and 566).

221–32 *Right so agayne come doune schall he . . . encresand ay.* Jesus will return "with woundes bledand" to judge humankind, the first angel informs them. The choice for humans will ultimately be binary, to heaven or hell. This, as the second angel says, the apostles are to preach to the world.

233–52 The speeches of James, Andrew, and Peter focus mainly on the Jews' malice and envy; they are described as false and "full of prompe and pride" so as to be impervious to Jesus' teachings even though they should be stirred to "aske mercy." This is typical of late medieval stereotyping of Jews as blind and headstrong at a time when their law was allegedly superseded by the new law of Jesus.

43. PENTECOST

Pentecost, or Whitsunday, is one of the major feasts of the Church year, along with Christmas and Easter. There are eleven apostles, all noted as present in the *Ordo paginarum*, along with the Virgin Mary and two angels. Mention is made of the dove of the Holy Spirit descending upon the disciples and Mary, and this would require a mechanical bird of some sort, as reported elsewhere in both British and Continental sources.[123] On the whole the effect in this regard might not have had the spectacular effect of the indoor Pentecost ceremony with the dove suspended from the roof of the church or cathedral such as St. Paul's in London and with incense filling the air inside.[124] But there is singing nevertheless. The two angels in the

---

[123] See C. Davidson, *Festivals and Plays*, pp. 125–26.

[124] See Young, *Drama of the Medieval Church*, 1:489.

York play will sing *Veni creator spiritus* antiphonally, as Rastall observes.[125] The play was produced by the Potters, and appears in twelve-line stanzas. The Latin passages are sometimes extra-metrical, but are included in the numbering throughout in this edition.

5–12   *we are leved alyve, ellevyn . . . seere*. Peter is concerned about the uneven number of apostles, to which no selection has yet been made to replace Judas in order to make up the original number of twelve. As a prime number, eleven has no divisible parts. Twelve, on the other hand, would enable the disciples to go out two by two, as Jesus suggested (see Mark 6:7), or by threes, fours, or even sixes, that is, "settis in parties seere" (line 12). As a superabundant number twelve is ideal for various kinds of missions, which is Peter's central concern as they go forth in groups into the wider world to testify to the risen Christ, who will return at the Last Day to judge the living and the dead.

13–14   *Nobis precepit Dominus . . . mortuorum*. Compare Acts 10:42, but quoted from the *York Missal*, 1:154. On this and other liturgical connections in this pageant, see King, *York Mystery Cycle*, pp. 167–68.

30   *He saide he schulde sette haly kirke*. Pentecost was regarded as the historical moment at which the Church was established.

37–38   *Cum venerit paraclitus / Docebit vos omnia*. Compare John 14:26, contained within the Gospel for Whitsunday (*York Breviary*, 1:487).

41, 45   *Nisi ego abiero . . . Et cum assumptus fuero*. Antiphon in the vigil liturgy of Pentecost, and also sung at the Ascension; adapted from John 16:7–8.

76   *Howe that thes mobbardis maddis nowe*. The unconverted Jews begin their accusations thus with the charge that Jesus' followers are mad. As caricatures, they are not the pious Jews of Acts 2:5, for they have been identified by the first line spoken (line 75) as followers of Mahound. This distorts the biblical story and adds a distinctly anti-Semitic twist. Further, they will be a threat to the lives of the apostles.

98 s.d.   *Veni creator spiritus*. Pentecost hymn. Translation in Dutka, *Music*, pp. 119–20, but a portion of the text and translation appear below at lines 137–40. For York music, see *Hymni*, fols. 32v–33r. Having the angels sing the hymn "betwene them two" is affirmed by line 136. Very possibly the hymn may have been introduced by the loud sound of "a mighty wind" noted in Acts 2:2; such a sound effect could have been produced in a number of ways. The *Stanzaic Life* describes it as a "sowene dyn" (*loud sound*) and as occurring suddenly (p. 342).

105   *Als lange as ye his pase pursue*. The disciples and indeed all Christians are to follow in Jesus' steps; see 1 Peter 2:21.

113–18   *I myght noght loke, so was it light . . . itt sente*. Peter comments on the intense light, for which a special effect would have been needed. Likely techniques to represent the "tongues as it were of fire" (Acts 2:3), perhaps utilizing both mirrors and flame, have been discussed by Butterworth, *Theatre of Fire*, pp. 55–78. Dublin's St.

---

[125] See Rastall, *Minstrels Playing*, p. 38, and *Heaven Singing*, p. 330.

Patrick's Cathedral apparently used "little threads" which were "employed about the Holy Spirit on the feast of Pentecost" (Fletcher, *Drama, Performance, and Polity*, pp. 78–79). It is possible that the effect at York might have used strings soaked in "burning spirit" that could safely be lighted to show flame coming down, as upon Mary and the apostles in the Paris *Resurrection* (Meredith and Tailby, *Staging*, p. 107). One would assume that the "tonges of fir" noted in the *Stanzaic Life* (p. 342) and other sources would need to be represented somehow.

119ff.   Through most of the remainder of the pageant the scribe changes to a system of numbering for the apostles. The second apostle is John, while the third is James. The fourth and fifth cannot be identified.

128   *langage nedis us none to lere*. They have received the gift of languages, both speaking knowledge and comprehension; see Acts 2:4 and 6. This will be a source of wonderment to the Jews, who serve as hostile observers (lines 157–67).

149, 151   *Tristicia implevit cor vestrum . . . Sed convertetur in gaudium*. Adapted from John 16:20, an Easter season gospel lesson. The *tristia* to *gaudium* theme is strongly presented in the post-Crucifixion pageants.

165–66   *Butt thei are drounken . . . / Of muste or wyne*. See Acts 2:13, when some of those standing about come to such a conclusion concerning the apostles. The Vulgate specifically refers to *mustus*, or "new wine." See also line 185 for Peter's answer to the charge.

188   *A gentill Jewe*. Joel, whose prophecy is invoked.

195–96   *Et erit in novissimus diebus . . . carnem*. Acts 2:17, quoting Joel 2:28. As King notes, this passage is designated for Mass on the Saturday in Whitsun week (*York Mystery Cycle*, p. 168, citing the *York Missal*, 1:161).

216   *I may no lenger with you lende*. John is now leaving and saying farewell to his adoptive mother, as Peter has directed all the apostles to do (lines 212–13). James also will graciously take his leave (lines 225–26).

44. THE DEATH OF MARY

The Drapers' Death of Mary appears to be the same play for which a character list was provided in *Ordo paginarum*, except that it has two devils instead of the one noted at the end of the pageant in the manuscript. The inclusion of a devil should be no mystery (see the rubric following line 194), since Mary begs that at death she should not see such a creature (lines 133–34). Jesus refuses, though he tells her that she will be safe and not to worry. Iconographic evidence for ordinary deathbed scenes will show the soul being threatened by one or more devils and, when merited, rescued by an angel, the latter understood to be one's guardian angel, illustrated in woodcuts in early English books on the art of dying.[126] Because of its Roman Catholic content, the play, along with the other dramas on the life of the Virgin Mary that followed, was suppressed in the period of Protestant ascendancy under

----

[126] See, e.g., Spinrad, *Summons of Death*, pp. 27–35.

Edward VI but apparently returned under Queen Mary, only to be laid aside once more when Queen Elizabeth came to the throne. The story, popularized by such sources as the *Golden Legend* of Jacobus de Voragine[127] but ultimately derived from the apocryphal *Transitus Beatae Mariae* that narrated the concluding time in the life of Mary, is illustrated in a series in painted glass of c. 1350 in the choir of York Minster; one panel shows Gabriel with the palm "oute of paradise" (line 15) coming to her, and another illustrates her death with the apostles in her presence.[128] The York Minster glass confirms a direct comparison with the Annunciation, with the Virgin reading from a prayer book when the angel arrives on the scene, and this seems to be the setting imagined by the playwright at the beginning of this pageant as well. Eight-line stanzas, marked by alliteration, are the norm, but this is not always adhered to.[129]

1–8   The announcement to Mary of her coming death, just as Gabriel in the Annunciation had addressed the very youthful Virgin with "Hayle Marie, full of grace and blysse" to tell her that she will conceive (Play 12, lines 158–61). Gabriel will specifically call her attention to the Annunciation, when he brought the "boodworde of [Jesus'] bering," in lines 22–24. Mary is sometimes said to have been sixty years of age at her death, but the *Golden Legend* suggests that she was seventy-two.

30–31   *Thyne appostelis to have in this place.* Her request to her Son, Jesus, to have the apostles at her side at her death will be granted, as Gabriel immediately announces to her (lines 33–36). As soon as Gabriel withdraws (following line 39), the disciples start appearing, beginning with John, the one with a special relationship with Mary. The *Ordo paginarum* notes the presence of eight apostles, representing the eleven of the traditional account, Thomas, in far away India, being missing.

45   *Within thre daies, iwis, / I schall be beldid in blisse.* As Gabriel has told her (lines 7– 8), she will live only for three days, which are condensed into the 194 lines of the play.

65–66   *a clowde now full clere / Umbelappid me.* In the *Golden Legend*, it is John who was taken up into a "shining cloud . . . and whisked . . . to Mary's door," and elsewhere this source explains that a great clap of thunder is heard with the disciples coming "down like a rain shower before the door of the Virgin's house" (2:78 and 90). All the disciples are amazed at the miraculous way in which they have been transported to Mary's bedside.

94   *caste some watir uppon me.* Embedded stage direction, as is also the case when the second handmaid announces that Mary is dying "in oure hende" (line 99) — i.e., as they are holding her she is slipping into a coma. There is similarly an embedded stage direction in Mary's sharp reproaches to the women for weeping (lines 103–04).

103   *thus wynly.* The *MED* suggests possible error for "wanliche."

---

[127] Jacobus de Voragine, *Golden Legend*, 2:77–80.

[128] See *YA*, p. 103.

[129] The classic study of the plays dramatizing the conclusion of Mary's life is Mill, "York Plays of the Dying, Assumption, and Coronation."

129–31   Jesus must now appear above and be seen by the audience, though he does not speak until line 151. To him Mary prays especially for those among her people who are devoted to her, and who will amend their ways. The idea of Mary as the protector and intercessor for those who extend devotion to her was a central tenet of late medieval traditional religion. Note the prayer to her of the two converted Jews (lines 119–26).

134   *The fende thou latte me noght see.* The *Golden Legend* places this request by the Virgin earlier, before her Son Jesus' Crucifixion (2:89). As noted above, the appearance of a greedy devil in deathbed scenes was conventional, but here she begs her Son that this will not occur at her death. Her request will be denied; the devil's "figoure full foule" will be present to frighten her but will not harm her (lines 154–55).

137–42   *Men that are stedde stiffely in stormes or in see.* Mary prays then for sailors, indeed for all those who venerate her and call on her in their need. For comment on the veneration of the Virgin, see, for example, Duffy, *Stripping of the Altars*, pp. 256–65.

143–50   *Also, my bliste barne . . . bringe.* Finally, Mary prays to her Son for all who call upon her name, those in trouble and in danger of being shamed, and women "in thare childing," a time of particular dread in the fifteenth century since so many women did in fact die in childbirth.

153   *Thyne asking all haly here heete I nowe thee.* Jesus is not able to resist whatever his mother requests, other than in the matter of erasing the fiend from the scene at her ending.

156   *Myne aungelis schall than be aboute thee.* The *Ordo paginarum* specified only two angels in this pageant, but four are required by the text to sing the final antiphon.

171–74   *Mi sely saule I thee sende . . . into thyne hande.* The *Golden Legend* reports in one place that "Mary's soul went forth from her body and flew to the arms of her Son" (Jacobus de Voragine, 2:80). The soul was conventionally visualized as a small doll-like figure emerging from the mouth of the dying person at his or her last breath; this could be represented in the pageant by a puppet, taken up into heaven to be received by Jesus.

194 s.d.   *Ave regina celorum.* Marian antiphon. A convenient modern edition, though not derived from York service books, is available in the *Liber usualis*, pp. 274–75. Rastall suggests a more elaborate polyphonic setting here since four angel singers are involved (*Heaven Singing*, p. 330; "Heaven: The Musical Repertory," pp. 172–73). Dutka translates: "Hail Queen of heaven, hail Lady of angels, hail holy root from whom a light for the world has risen. Hail glorious one, beautiful above all. Farewell, great in comeliness; and always [prevail upon] Christ for us" (*Music*, p. 114).

44A. THE FUNERAL OF THE VIRGIN ("FERGUS")

The Funeral of the Virgin is assigned to the Linenweavers in the *Ordo paginarum* though this guild did not take it up until much later (the name of the guild is entered over an erasure). Other records indicate that it was the responsibility of the Masons until 1431–32, when an entry in the *York Memorandum Book A/Y* notes the guild's complaint about its content (non-scriptural, with the beating of "Fergus," the Jew who attempted to overturn Mary's bier in the funeral procession and whose hand became attached to it) and audience reception ("more noise and laughter than devotion," resulting in disorder).[130] The Linenweavers were assigned the play in 1476,[131] but in fact it may have been seldom performed. The play was never entered in the Register. In general the pageant would have followed the presentation in the *Golden Legend*[132] and other sources derived from Melito's *Transitus Beatae Mariae*, and finds a parallel in the N-Town play of Mary's Death and Assumption (Play 41). It would seem that the Jews in this anti-Semitic play were particularly incensed by singing, which Sullivan believes was the chanting of Psalm 113 (*AV* 114): "Exiit Israel de Egipto, domus Jacob de populo barbaro."[133] In N-Town the incipit of this psalm is sung by Peter, followed by the apostles continuing with "Facta est Judea sanctificacio eius, Israel potestas eius," and angels adding "Alleluia" (Play 41, lines 69–70). This is the chant indicated in the *Golden Legend*;[134] Dutka translates: "Israel departed from Egypt — the house of Jacob from a foreign people. Alleluia. Judea was made his sanctuary, Israel his dominion. Alleluia."[135] Painted glass in the York Minster choir shows the Jew with his hands stuck to the bier and then severed,[136] thus providing a suggestion that sleight of hand would have been involved in the production of the play, assuming that the same iconography was maintained. The name *Fergus* is unique to York.

45. THE ASSUMPTION OF THE VIRGIN (THOMAS APOSTOLUS)

Prior to the Reformation, the Church in England celebrated the Assumption of the Virgin as a major feast on August 15. The Weavers' pageant dramatizes the legend of the apostle Thomas, absent from her death and burial, who was believed to be returning from his mission in India when he encountered the Virgin Mary being taken up into heaven. To provide him with verification that he had seen her, she removed the girdle from around her waist and gave it to him. The *Golden Legend* offers a simpler account, only saying that he again was filled with doubt, as he had been after the Resurrection, and her "girdle that had encircled her body fell intact into his hands" as proof.[137] The Assumption play at York, which appears to have been the most rich of all the York pageants in music, includes notation in the Register for *Surge proxima* and *Veni de libano sponsa* in two versions as well as two settings of *Veni electa mea*. Rastall has dated the compositions in the middle third of the

[130] *REED: York*, 1:47–48, trans. 2:732.

[131] *REED: York*, 1:110.

[132] Jacobus de Voragine, *Golden Legend*, 2:91–92.

[133] Sullivan, "Missing York Funeral."

[134] Jacobus de Voragine, *Golden Legend*, 2:81 and 91.

[135] Dutka, *Music*, p. 116. See also the commentary on the use of this psalm in N-Town in Rastall, *Minstrels Playing*, p. 119.

[136] *YA*, p. 103; Brown, *York Minster*, fig. 4.47.

[137] Jacobus de Voragine, *Golden Legend*, 2:82.

fifteenth century.[138] Since they are integral to the pageant, this would suggest a date when the play itself was rewritten in alliterative verse. If heaven is a place rich in music, as was commonly assumed, the singing and likely playing of angel instrumentalists would have been given a very high priority. Angels at York are very commonly depicted as musicians, often performing on instruments.[139] Practically speaking for polyphonic music at this time in York, the choices here would have been most likely portative organ and regals rather than the instruments played by minstrels, who were not expected to read music in score. Such instruments, along with harps, are noted in N-Town (Play 41, lines 117 s.d., 314 s.d.).[140] The York music for the Assumption involves a high level of musical sophistication, and may have been performed by twelve musicians, the number of roles for angels written into the text in the Register. This number of musicians could well have come from York Minster, though excellent musicianship may also be surmised at some of the parish churches and the monastic houses. The *Ordo paginarum*'s description of the apostle Thomas "preaching in the desert" is not a good fit with what is now present in lines 1–104; this again is indicative of the later date for the playtext as it appears in the Register. In the 1430s or thereabouts the Weavers were an extremely wealthy guild, unlike the same guild in the latter part of the century and in the following century after the migration of the industry to the West Riding.[141] The verse appears in thirteen-line stanzas, marked again by alliteration as fully as important as rhyme.

1–97   Thomas rehearses his sorrow "waylyng and weping" over the by-now-familiar events of Christ's Passion and emphasizes Jesus' rejection by the Pharisees and his torments, with a more positive note introduced when he recognizes that he has been translated to the valley of Josephat, where, though he does not know it yet, Mary has been buried. Personal engagement over the Passion was encouraged, but Thomas' tone may seem to some to be out of place here just as Mary Magdalen's lament over the Crucifixion has been viewed as out of place after the assurances of the angel at the tomb (Play 38, lines 267–87).

98–104   *I will steme of my stevene and sted here a stounde . . . for to bide.* Embedded stage direction; he is to seat himself "on this banke." The dramatic purpose is obvious, since he must remain visible through the singing of the angels and the rising of Mary from her grave. Presumably he does not look up to see the angels and Mary until his next speech, beginning at line 118.

after 104   *Surge proxima mea.* This item does not appear in any service book and, in both versions of the music, is unique to the York cycle. The second (designated the B version by Steiner in her transcriptions appended to Wall, "York Pageant XLVI") substitutes *propera* for *proxima.* As Wall notes, the words echo terms often used to

---

[138] Personal communication from Richard Rastall; he had previously suggested dating the music between 1430 and 1450 (*Heaven Singing*, p. 134).

[139] See *YA*, pp. 185–92, for discussion and a list of instruments in the parish churches, Minster, and other locations that will show the majority played by angel instrumentalists. See also Remnant, "Musical Instruments."

[140] See also Remnant, "Musical Instruments," pp. 174–75.

[141] Palliser, *Tudor York*, pp. 208–11.

describe the Virgin Mary and derived from the Canticle of Canticles (e.g., 2:10 and 13). Dukta translates: "Rise up, my dearest one, my dove, tabernacle of glory, container of life, heavenly temple" (*Music*, p. 118). The rich imagery here of dove, tabernacle, temple, even "container of life" as applied to Mary had been developed by St. Bernard of Clairvaux and was a strong presence in fifteenth-century Mariology (see the useful commentary in M. Warner, *Alone of All Her Sex*, pp. 121–33), but in fact seems more immediately to have derived from the *Golden Legend* (Jacobus de Voragine, 2:95–97). John Stevens has noted that the scribe who inserted the music into the text was "perhaps one of the cantors of the cathedral" and that "he fully understood the notation he was using, with its complicated system of ligatures and coloured notes" ("Music of Play XLV," p. 466). For a more extended discussion of the songs in the Weavers' pageant, see especially Rastall, *Heaven Singing*, pp. 121–37.

105–17   The angels then speak, in rapid fashion urging the Virgin to arise from her grave and come up with them to heaven. The terminology they use through the eighth angel's speech — rose, lily, dove especially — is again reminiscent of the Canticle of Canticles. Iconography suggests angels supporting Mary within an aureole as she ascends to the heights of heaven, where her Son is located (see *YA*, pp. 105–07, and, for Torre's description of the Virgin ascending with four angels surrounding her at the Bedern Chapel, O'Connor, "Bedern Stained Glass," pp. 564 and 567).

after 117 *Veni de libano sponsa, veni coronaberis*. The text is a direct quote from the Canticle of Canticles 4:8: "Come from Libanus [Lebanon], my spouse, come from Libanus, come: thou shalt be crowned." The reference to the crowned bride in this Old Testament passage was regarded as foreshadowing the Assumption and Coronation of the Virgin. Wall points out further connections of these words with the liturgy ("York Pageant XLVI," p. 695).

118–23   Thomas now is to look up to *see* Mary (perhaps "babbe" in line 120 should read "berde," i.e., *Lady*, as Beadle believes). Thomas sees her gleaming shape as she glides up, an indication of movement that is surely very gentle. He will also comment on the "melody" of the angels' singing, here referring to *Veni de libano*. This will lead to Mary's notice of him in the following lines and her command "do way all thi doutes" (he is still temperamentally *doubting Thomas*).

131–43   Exchanging "thy" for "my," Thomas repeats Mary's line, and then continues with a set of "Hail" verses to complete the thirteen-line stanza. These lines contain entirely conventional terminology in praise of the Virgin, regarded as most worthy of women, the second Eve, the remedy for human misery, and one who will intercede at the throne of the Most High for those who are devoted to her. She must be suspended above the earth at this time and remain so until line 200, after which she must very slowly be taken up as the dialogue continues.

166–67   *I schall thee schewe / A token trewe*. In response to Thomas' complaint in lines 164–65 that his fellow apostles will not believe him. The token will be her "girdill" (line 169), which she must toss down to him. If this is to be done effectively, he must catch it.

170–78   Mary is compared to a tree, from "reverent rote" to "floure" and "frewte." There is a hint here of Jesse tree iconography in which she emerges at the top with the fruit of her womb, Jesus.

185–91   *in sightte of my Sone ther is sittand . . . grace*. She will "knele to that comely," her Son, Jesus, in support of her followers, even when they have fallen into despair, if they beg her help. And she will prevail: "He schall graunte thame ther grace."

193   *womanne in childinge*. As noted in commentary to Play 44, lines 143–50, prayers to the Virgin were believed to be particularly efficacious and especially needed at childbirth. A relic of her girdle at Westminster was lent out to women in childbirth.

202–08   Thomas' farewells are spoken as Mary is received into heaven, and these again are laden with conventional Marian imagery.

after 208   *Veni electa mea et ponam in te tronum meum / Quia concupivit rex speciem tuam*. A liturgical text, a Matins responsory for the feast of the Assumption in the Use of York, in this case celebrating Mary's arrival in heaven; see Rastall, "Heaven: The Musical Repertory," p. 186. Dutka translates: "Come, my chosen one, and I will place you on my throne because the king greatly desires your beauty" (*Music*, p. 120). She is the elect bride of the Canticle of Canticles, the Sponsa united with the Sponsus, and, as the chosen one, will be placed on a throne beside the Sponsus who is Jesus.

218   *God saffe you in feere*. Thomas now comes to the disciples and greets them. There are four, not the eight specified in the *Ordo paginarum*. He is cheerful, but they react negatively immediately on account of their sorrow at the loss of Mary; see Andrew's charge that he is bragging and boasting (line 226). They are the ones who now need to see a physical sign, which he will finally show at line 248. Since they will require more physical evidence, they will visit the tomb and search it only to find that the "glorious and goodely is gone fro this grave" (line 262).

282–83   *Nowe knele we ilkone / Upponne oure kne*. Embedded stage direction, followed by the apostles' brief prayer to Mary in heaven, and then their departure to their various places of evangelizing, with Thomas having the final speech (lines 300–12).

46. The Coronation of the Virgin

The Coronation pageant is given to the Hostelers, or Innholders, in the Register. However, in the *Ordo paginarum* the ascription to the "Hostilers" is written over an erasure, and the second list which follows in the *York Memorandum Book A/Y* reveals that it was originally the responsibility of the "Maior etc.," meaning the Mayor and Council. The York records show that only in 1463 were the Hostelers given the play.[142] The play is short and much less dramatic than the spectacular Assumption of the Virgin play. The versification, mainly tetrameter in octaves and quatrains but with some stanzas in tail-rhyme (lines 21–32), is hardly exciting. The Assumption is reenacted, with six angels who will sing some unspecified music, but only after eighty lines. Yet this should rightfully be the climactic pageant in the Marian

---

[142] See Dorrell, "Mayor of York"; *REED: York*, 1:94.

series that begins with the Virgin's death, and so it perhaps may have been in its visual spectacle and its music before the affluent Weavers set out to outdo it with their pageant, as likely was the case. The iconography of the Coronation of the Virgin was extremely popular at York and, in spite of the effects of iconoclasm, a considerable number of images remain.[143] A common depiction was of the Trinity with Jesus crowning his mother as Queen of Heaven,[144] but in the play he seems to be alone with her among the angels of heaven. The recitation of the Five Joys of Mary (lines 113–28) and the following lines to the end of the play are clearly designed for Jesus, though in the extant text in the Register they were broken up into short segments distributed in order among the angels. This may be the way the lines were spoken in c. 1463–70, but the arrangement hardly makes logical sense and cannot have been the original intent of the playwright. An addition to the Coronation pageant, entered in the manuscript following the Last Judgment play, is not included here.[145] It dates from the sixteenth century and, as Beadle notes, "does not seem to have been framed with any particular metrical principles in mind."[146]

1–36	The scene is in heaven. Jesus speaks concerning his mother to the angels and requests that they "fecche hir hedir" (line 18). The angels then descend.
37–40	*Hayle, the doughtir of blissid Anne . . . fendis boste.* The story of the Immaculate Conception, in which Mary was conceived without physical intercourse, was a popular one, and Anne frequently appeared in local devotional images (see *YA*, p. 35).
42–43	*oure Saveoure, / The whiche that made mankynde of noght.* Referring to the tradition that the Second Person of the Trinity was also the Creator. See, for example, the *Holkham Bible Picture Book*, fols. 2–3v, in which the Creator has a cross nimbus.
57	The angels have now come before Mary, but it is not clear whether she is emerging from a tomb, as presumably should be the case.
80 s.d.	*Cantando.* The previous line suggests that it is Mary who should sing, but the late stage direction is for the angels, probably played or directed by clerks, at least in earlier times when the Mayor and Council were in control of the play. It is possible that minstrels also played in the pageant, but not necessarily in connection with the singing at this point in the pageant; see *REED: York*, 1:54, 75, 86, and 94, and Rastall, *Minstrels Playing*, p. 42. There is no information about the nature of the music, but it can be safely assumed that it would have been derived from the liturgy celebrating the Assumption and Coronation.
101	*Come forth with me.* Embedded stage direction; Mary is now to step forth onto the heaven stage, and at line 155 she will be crowned Queen of Heaven by Jesus.

---

[143] See *YA*, pp. 107–11.

[144] A good example, though damaged and lacking the original head of the Virgin Mary, is the Assumption in the east window of c. 1470 in the church of Holy Trinity, Goodramgate, in York (*Inventory of the Historical Monuments*, vol. 5, color pl. 58).

[145] The addition is printed as a "later fragment" in RB, pp. 404–05.

[146] RB, p. 462.

> That this is at a high level on the pageant wagon is specified by line 133: "Full high on highte."

113–28   As noted above, the listing of Five Joys of the Virgin, culminating in the Ascension of Jesus into heaven, and finally her own Assumption and Coronation.

142–43   *In hevene blisse that is so bright / With martiris and with confessouris.* The saints, who are translated directly to heaven without having to pass through Purgatory.

157–58   *Myne aungellis bright, a songe ye singe / In the honnoure of my modir dere.* Another song will be sung, but again it is not specified. An appropriate liturgical piece for the Coronation of Mary must be assumed. This will occur after Jesus' blessing is conferred on the audience — i.e., a *representation* of a blessing, surely with appropriate hand gestures.

47. DOOMSDAY

The final play of the cycle, the Mercers' *Doomsday*, is also the one about which the most is known with regard to production. This is so because of the discovery of a 1433 indenture between the guild and the pageant master, Richard Louth, that provides a list of stage properties used for the pageant at that time.[147] It is clear that the Mercers, who dominated the city's government, spared no expense to see that their show was a spectacle that would stand out as exemplary among the pageants in the cycle. There was a wagon with four wheels and a hellmouth, costumes for God, apostles, and devils, who were fitted with masks. Jesus wore a "Sirke [shirt] Wounded a diademe With a veserne [mask] gilted," and equipment was provided to lower him from heaven to where he would be seated as a judge on a "Rainbow of tymber" and to raise him back to heaven. The good and bad souls were differentiated, probably by color coding like those in Coventry's Corpus Christi Doomsday play.[148] Angels had trumpets for the announcement of the End Time, the required "last trumpet," as mentioned by St. Paul, which "shall sound, and the dead shall rise" (1 Corinthians 15:52). Seven large and four small puppet angels held the Instruments of the Passion — including the crown of thorns, lance, and whips mentioned in the *Ordo paginarum* as belonging to the Passion as well as other executioners' items. A set of nine smaller puppet angels, "payntid rede," were designed "to renne aboute in the heven," which was fitted with clouds and stars. In the early sixteenth century the pageant wagon was "substancialie" rebuilt by the prominent sculptor John Drawswerd, and again an inventory (from 1526) is available, though much less detailed and seemingly indicative of staging less elaborate than in 1433.[149]

The Last Judgment story as presented here does not follow the elaborate account in the Apocalypse that was drawn upon for the design of the Great East Window in York Minster, but rather the dramatization derives from Matthew 25, specifically from the verses following the parable of the talents in which the "unprofitable servant" is cast "out into the exterior

---

[147] The Mercers' indenture was brought to light in 1972 when the discovery was reported by A. Johnston and Dorrell, "York Mercers and Their Pageant of Doomsday"; for the document, see *REED: York*, 1:55–56.

[148] *REED: Coventry*, p. 237; see also Twycross, "'With what body shall they come?'"

[149] *REED: York*, 1:189, 205, and 241–42.

darkness" where there "shall be weeping and gnashing of teeth" (25:30). The test of one's worthiness to enter into bliss in the pageant is whether one has performed the Corporal Acts of Mercy, the charitable acts specified in Matthew 25:35–46. Charity was an important value for the Mercers and other mercantile guilds that were in the main in control of the city government.

There is evidence that the people of York lived in expectation of Doomsday, the final day of history, which was believed to be at least potentially at hand, as proclaimed in 2 Peter 3:10: "But the day of the Lord shall come as a thief," unexpectedly and violently. This would be the Second Advent, or Coming, of Jesus, the Son of God, into time, which then would have a stop. The early Church had hoped for the *parousia* as an event that was imminent, not just in some distant future, and this had been translated into the eschatology that pertained in the late Middle Ages when many appear to have kept alert to possible signs of the end.[150] It would not have been thought unusual for a person at York to leave a bequest to a parish church to fund a Mass that was to be continued "as long as the world shall endure." The *Pricke of Conscience*, formerly attributed to Richard Rolle and imbued with end-time theology as well as specific reciting of the Fifteen Signs of Doomsday, was one of the most widely-read books of Northern origin of the time, but see also the ever-popular *Golden Legend* and, for an example of a homily collection which emphasizes the Signs in a sermon for the first Sunday in Advent, John Mirk's *Festial*.[151] A recital of these signs appears in Play 22, lines 216–340, in the Chester Whitsun cycle. Though these signs foreshadowing the Last Judgment do not appear in the York pageant, they were known locally, for they were depicted in the Fifteen Signs window in the York church of All Saints, North Street.[152] These signs possibly figure in the additions to the York text when it was adapted and added to the Towneley collection, formerly believed to be a Wakefield Corpus Christi cycle.[153] The versification in the York play maintains an eight-line stanza.

1	*DEUS.* Here God the Father. Subsequently *Deus* will signify the Son who comes back to earth as Judge.
34	*thois wrecchis that ware thareinne.* Adam, Eve, the patriarchs, prophets, those who were worthy but not able to receive the benefits of God's grace until the Crucifixion, when they would be ransomed and released from limbo through the effects of Christ's sacrifice on the cross.
65	*Aungellis, blawes youre bemys belyve.* All people, learned and "lewd" or unlettered, will be called up by the trumpet call of the angels, traditionally one at each corner of the world. These instruments may have been props only, with actual minstrels supplying the trumpet sounds. Trumpets are noted in the 1433 indenture and again in the Mercers' records as being mended in 1461 and 1462 (*REED: York*, 1:55, 91–92, and 95; see also Remnant, "Musical Instruments," pp. 176–77).
90	*I bidde you that ye ryse.* Embedded stage direction.

---

[150] See the useful collection prepared by McGinn, in *Apocalyptic Christianity*, trans. McGinn.

[151] Jacobus de Voragine, *Golden Legend*, 1:7–9; Mirk, *Festial*, pp. 2–3.

[152] Gee, "Painted Glass of All Saints' Church," pp. 158–60, pls. XXIII–XXIV.

[153] See C. Davidson, *History, Religion, and Violence*, pp. 267–92.

91   *Body and sawle with you ye bring*. The resurrection of the body is promised, though
        for shorthand those who rise at the Last Judgment are designated simply as
        "souls." Body and soul together are again mentioned in line 99, which stresses
        the complete reunion of the two. Job 19:26 was regarded as prophetic: "And I
        shall be clothed again with my skin, and in my flesh I shall see my God." It was
        an idea that already was circulating in some Jewish circles in Jesus' time, but in
        St. Paul the concept was given a new twist in that it was to be a new and spiritual
        body, no longer subject to corruption, that was to be given life and returned to
        the soul (see 1 Corinthians 15:32–44). Additional accretions, including those
        resulting from Greek and Oriental influences, were the cause of further ambiguity
        in medieval thought about the expected event, and this was to be reflected in the
        York play, which to be sure is not a theological treatise.

95   *rise uppe and geve rekenyng*. Souls are being called to come up from their graves.
        Iconographic evidence shows that they were imagined to be rising with their grave
        clothes around them or in the nude, in order to be judged. Thereafter an exact ac-
        counting of sins and good deeds was expected, in some depictions of the Last
        Judgment including the *psychostatis* or weighing in a set of scales to achieve exacti-
        tude. The weighing of souls, however, does not appear in the Mercers' pageant.

101   *Of oure ill dedis, Lorde, thou not mene*. The expectation is that only the saints could
        live pure lives, and that one's ill deeds required forgiveness and expiation through
        the sacrament of Penance, which in turn was made effective only because of the act
        of sacrifice on the cross required to ransom humankind. But all one's sins, even
        the smallest, would be a source of anxiety. See also line 109 for the second Soul's
        statement "Ofte have we greved thee, grette and small." The good souls express
        humility, the evil ones do not.

115   *this hydous horne*. Reference to the angel trumpeters, feared by the bad souls.

129   *Oure wikkid werkis thei will us wreye*. The traditional notion that a person's evil
        deeds will testify against him or her at the Last Day, for all is written in God's
        book of Creation, good and ill.

135   *Nowe mon nevere saule ne body dye*. Punishment will be eternal, unending, and
        cruel, dwelling with "feendes blake" (line 143) without hope of ever receiving
        redemption.

146   *Sore may we wringe oure handis and wepe*. Traditional gestures of utter despair.
        Tearing one's hair was also a sign of hopelessness. Their condition is in fact
        utterly without hope, since the time of grace has passed. In contrast, the good
        souls would logically have held their hands in gestures of supplication; see C.
        Davidson, "Gesture," pp. 81–86.

151–52 *made we sacrafise / To Satanas when othir slepe*. Invoking witchcraft with specific
        reference to the witches' sabbath. Witches were reputed to worship the Devil in
        midnight ceremonies in which he celebrates the black mass, part of the ritual
        being "blessing" his followers with his left hand. Their crime is *infidelity*, con-
        sidered by authors of the *The Hammer of Witches* to be an enormous sin and the
        most serious kind of apostasy.

169   *Standis noght togedir, parte you in two.* Embedded stage direction. The dead have
             been raised from their graves and now will be separated into those on God's left
             (the bad souls) and those on his right (the good). In depictions of the Last Judg-
             ment, this orientation is maintained, as in the well-known wall painting over the
             chancel arch at St. Thomas of Canterbury in Salisbury; for a pre-restoration il-
             lustration, see C. Davidson, *Deliver Us from Evil*, p. 135, fig. 19.

177–84   *DEUS.* Now the Son rather than the Father is speaking. He announces that this
             world, this vale of tears, "is brought till ende" and prepares to descend to earth
             to sit in majesty to judge all humankind. God the Father is a separate character
             who would stay behind in heaven; Jesus refers to him in lines 233–34 as the one
             who sent him down a second time to earth.

185   *Mi postelis and my darlyngis.* The apostles will be seated on seats, six to each side of
             Jesus (see line 215). However, they will have no active part in the judgments in the
             York play that will admit some to bliss and others "to fyre with fendis blake" (line
             198). There is no role specified in the playtext for the Virgin Mary, although she
             had been noticed as a character in the *Ordo paginarum*.

216 s.d.   *Hic ad sedem judicii cum cantu angelorum.* Stage direction and rubric designating
             music. It signals the lowering of the seat of judgment along with angelic singing,
             which would be quite a logical staging effect. The song sung by the angels is not
             indicated, but it likely was a polyphonic piece, as would be appropriate for heaven-
             ly music, perhaps adding organ or regals. Following this the devils come onto
             stage with the hope of obtaining their prey. The third devil mistakenly believes
             they will be permitted to have all the souls in their power (lines 227–28).

241–44   *The day of drede to more and lesse, / Of ire . . . is sene.* Compare the sequence for the
             dead, *Dies ire, dies illa*: "Day of wrath that will dissolve this world to ash. . . . Great
             will be the fear when the Judge comes to examine all strictly. . . ."

245–76   *Here may ye see my woundes wide . . . what suffered thou for me?* Spoken directly to
             the audience as well as to the souls. It is a central moment and reminiscent of a
             devotional tableau. See, for example, the Last Judgment miniature in the *Bolton
             Hours*, fol. 208, in which Jesus' wounds in hands, feet, and side are streaming
             blood (*YA*, pp. 115–16, fig. 33). Mirk tells how Jesus, "veray God and man," shall
             "come to the dome, and all seyntys with hym, and schow all his wondys all fresch,
             and newe, and bledyng, as that day that he deyet on the crosse." The cross also
             will be shown "all blody, and all other ynstrumentys of his passyon" (*Festial*, p.
             3). In the pageant, Jesus is rehearsing the details of the Passion, the shedding
             of his blood for the salvation of humankind, many of whom have rejected him,
             and concluding with the request to know what humans have done for him (line
             276) as a lead-in to his address to those who are to be welcomed into bliss.

285–300   *Whenne I was hungery . . . In joie and blisse to be me by.* Paraphrase of Matthew
             25:34–45. Jesus gives assurance to those on his "right hande" (line 277) since
             they have performed the Corporal Acts of Mercy: feeding the hungry, giving
             drink to the thirsty, clothing the "clothles," succoring the sick and those in pris-
             on, giving shelter to the shelterless, but omitting the burial of the dead which is
             not noted in St. Matthew's gospel. As these are done to others, it is as if they are

done to the Lord Jesus. See the listing of the Corporal Acts in the influential *Lay Folks' Catechism*, p. 70.

301–08   As in Matthew 25:44, the good souls are modest and claim no credit for such deeds.

317–48   Now Jesus turns to the "cursid caytiffis of Kaymes kynne / That nevere me comforte in my care." Like Cain, they have failed utterly to do the good works expected of them. Their deeds are characterized by selfishness, pride, greed, and disregard for others. Because they kept the stranger standing in the cold and wet outside their gates, now they will be denied entrance to the gate of heaven. Their response takes a very different tone from that of the good souls as they deny Jesus' charges (lines 349–56).

365–72   Against the invitation to the "chosen childir," Jesus will turn to those on his left to consign them to "sitte be Satanas the fende" — the final disposition of the trial, which to be sure has been different from any legal proceeding in contemporary England but which, we are implicitly assured, is entirely just.

379–80   *thei that mendid thame whils thei moght / Shall belde and bide in my blissing.* Jesus concludes with a blessing, undoubtedly with the physical sign of making a cross over the good souls — and the audience.

380 s.d.   *Et sic facit finem . . . ad locum.* Rastall (*Heaven Singing*, p. 28) approves Happé's paraphrase: "And thus crossing from the place to the place, he makes an end with the melody of angels" (*English Mystery Plays*, p. 694). Unfortunately, again no suggestion is available concerning the nature of the music, though once more it may be conjectured that competent musicians would have been procured and that they would have tried to approximate what would have been reasonably convincing as heavenly. The Towneley Judgment play specifies *Te Deum laudamus*, a portion of which had also been chosen for the music of heaven at the beginning of the York cycle. Whatever the melody was at York, it must have reinforced the certitude and hope of redemption — a joining of the blessed ones with the ultimate harmony of the cosmos — that is, at the last, in Caroline Walker Bynum's words, "a concept of sublime courage and optimism" (*Resurrection of the Body*, p. 343).

❧ TEXTUAL NOTES

ABBREVIATIONS: Bevington: David Bevington, ed., *Medieval Drama* (1975); **Köbling**: E. Köbling, "Beiträge zur Erklärung und Textkritik der York Plays"; **LTS**: Lucy Toulmin Smith, ed., *The York Plays* (1885); ***MED***: *Middle English Dictionary*; **RB**: Richard Beadle, ed., *The York Plays* (1972) (incorporating numerous emendations from other sources); **RB²**: Richard Beadle, "Corrections to *The York Plays*," in Gerald Byron Kinneavy, *A Concordance to the York Plays* (1986), pp. xxxi–xxxii; **s.d.**: stage direction; **Sykes**: A. C. Cawley, ed., "The Sykes MS of the York Scriveners' Play"; **Towneley**: Martin Stevens and A. C. Cawley, eds., *The Towneley Plays*.

The base text for this edition is London, British Library, MS. Add. 35290, called the "Register" in the York civic records and here identified by the abbreviation **Reg**. Some variations in lineation from the manuscript are not noted here; see RB and Beadle and Meredith's *The York Play: A Facsimile*. In most cases the line numbering in the present text is consistent with RB. Lineation of alliterative verse throughout is based on Reg, with line numbering adjusted accordingly to account for half lines. Scribes are identified as follows: **Scribe A**; **Scribe B**: main scribe; **JC**: John Clerke; **LH**: later scribal hand (unidentified).

1. THE CREATION OF THE ANGELS AND THE FALL OF LUCIFER

This pageant was copied by Scribe A, who also entered the second pageant and the A-text of the third. He omitted the speech attribution to *DEUS* for God's first monologue, here supplied at line 1 (following LTS).

6	*hydande.* So LTS, RB; Reg: *hyndande.*
8	*Unendande.* So LTS, RB; Reg: *une dande.*
24 s.d.	Reg: stage direction, in red; faded, with the following portions unreadable: . . . *eli,* . . . *laudamus te domin.* . . .
28	*welth.* So LTS, RB; Reg: *wethth.*
34	*merour.* So LTS, RB; Reg: *morour.*
39	*welth.* Letter *l* interlined in Reg.
41 s.d.	Reg: stage direction, in red ink.
42	*A.* Interlined in Reg.
67	*es, I.* So LTS, RB; Reg: *es w I.*
129	*DEUS.* By LH, preceded by *Ihc*, also by LH. After line 144, Reg repeats *DEUS.*
130	*of mi mighte.* So RB; Reg: *of migh mighte*; LTS: *of mighte.*

2. THE CREATION THROUGH THE FIFTH DAY

1	*DEUS*. Reg: inserted following line 4.
	In. Reg: large capital letter *I*, in red.
	altissimis. Letter *i* following *m* in Reg is interlined.
11	*lengger*. So LTS, RB; Reg: *legger*.
21	*And*. Written over erasure by Scribe A in Reg.
41	*nought*. So LTS; Reg, RB: *nough*.
69	*tharon*. So LTS, RB; Reg: *tharon also*.
71	*hyng*. Corrected, letter *y* overwritten, in Reg.
77	*materis*. Reg: originally *wateris*, canceled and *materis* substituted by scribe.
95	*Two*. So LTS, RB; Reg: *Towo*.
101	*furth er*. So RB; Reg, LTS: *further*.
109	*thei*. So RB; Reg, LTS: *ye I*
117	*ye sall set*. So LTS, RB; Reg: *ye sall ye set*.
140	*dwelland*. So LTS; Reg, RB: *dewlland*.
156	*won*. So RB; Reg, LTS: *wo*.
166	*erthe*. In Reg, letter *h* extends upward, with a face looking to left drawn in.
171	*ye*. Interlined in Reg.

3. THE CREATION OF ADAM AND EVE

The Cardmakers' pageant was entered twice in Reg. The A-text is followed in this edition, with significant variant readings in the B-text listed here. Following the craft attribution in the A-text version, a later scribe, possibly JC, has written: "This is entryd afterwards."

1	*In*. Reg: large capital *I*, in red, incorporating line drawing of a man's face, facing left.
2	*ende*. So A-text; B-text: *the ende*.
4	*Methynke*. So A-text; B-text: *Me thynketh*.
14	*I no*. So A-text; B-text, RB: *I here no*.
15	*kynde and skyll*. So A-text; B-text: *kyndly skylle*.
21	*mare*. Emended to *more* by LH in Reg.
22	In Reg, *wyght* interlined by LH above *best*.
24	*me*. So B-text, followed by RB; A-text: *my*.
27	*hauttande*. So A-text; B-text: *haunttande*.
31	*hym fynde*. So B-text, RB; A-Text: *fynde hym*.
39	*nought*. So B-text; A-text, RB: *nough*.
43	*The*. So A-text; B-text, followed by RB: *This*.
44	Marginal notation by JC in both texts, indicating an omission, of which the B-text is more complete:

> And leyd your lyves in good degré.
> Adam here make I thee a man of mykyll myght;
> This same shall thy subget be,
> And Eve her name shall hight.

51	*thi.* So B-text, followed by RB; A-text: *the.*
52	*be.* So B-text; A-text, RB: *by.*
53	*all degré.* So B-text, followed by RB; A-text: *all the degre.*
55	*tyll us.* So A-text; B-text: *to us.*
72	*I have.* So A-text; B-text: *is.*
75	*ye kone.* Reg has extraneous letter between.
81	*sene.* So RB; A-text, B-text: *sone.*
82	*othir.* So B-text, followed by RB; A-text: *othithir.*
85	*DEUS.* So B-text; added by LH in A-text.
96	Marginal note added by LH, erased and faded, gives first two lines of the following play: *Adam and Eve this is [the place] / that I have grant you of my grace to have your. . . .*

4. THE PROHIBITION OF THE TREE OF KNOWLEDGE

The Fullers' pageant was entered by JC in 1559 (see *REED: York*, 1:330).

1	*Adam.* Reg: strapwork initial *A.*
35	*on haugh.* So RB; Reg, LTS: *on to haugh.*
40	*ay.* So LTS, RB; Reg: *a.*
44	Reg: line following omitted by copyist.
86	*Forwhy.* RB: *For-why*; LTS conjectures: "For-why [do my byddyng]."

5. THE FALL

This and subsequent pageants copied by Scribe B unless otherwise noted.

1	*DIABOLUS.* Added by JC.
	For. Reg: letter *F* is a large capital in red.
6	*dedyned.* So RB; Reg, LTS: *denyed.*
16	Reg: addition by LH, at right.
25b	*EVA.* Above, speech ascription at right in Reg, scribe has written *Eve.*
25c	*SATANAS.* JC has added: *Diabolus.*
43	*matere.* So LTS, RB; Reg: *materere.*
54	*SATANAS.* In Reg, written in large letters, in red, beside canceled *Eva*; below, at right, *Satanas* is written a second time.
87	*wrothe.* So LTS, RB; Reg: *wrorthe.*
119	*made.* Correction (added letter *a*) interlined by scribe.
158	*be.* Corrected (from *by*) in Reg.
159	Reg: in red, added by Scribe B.

165	*derfly*. So Bevington, RB; Reg, LTS: *defly*.
170	Reg: Line entered by JC.

6. THE EXPULSION FROM THE GARDEN

1	*Alle*. Space provided for large capital *A*, not added in Reg. This omission is a characteristic of texts entered by Scribe B.
69	Reg: added above line by JC as correction: "Eve for that thou begylyd hym so."
159	*ADAM*. This edition; LTS and RB insert speech heading for Adam at line 161 following emendation by LH.

7. SACRIFICIUM CAYME ET ABELL

7	Reg: line written at right, in red.
10	Reg: line canceled in red ink, then written again.
13	*world*. So LTS, RB; Reg: *wolrd*.
33	*ensewe*. Reg, as emended by JC; RB: *sewe*.
34–37	RB observes that these lines, having been omitted, were "added by main scribe at or immediately after rubrication" (p. 75n34–37).
70	Reg: hereafter two missing leaves, followed by lines 71–72 written over erasure by JC, a large cross indicating Brewbarret interpolation to be inserted from next page. A cue also appears: *Caret inde; Lo, maister Cayme, what shaves bryng I*.
71–99	Reg: interpolation entered by JC. Following Brewbarret interpolation, a cue gives the next line: *What hais thowe done, beholde and here*.
135	*fardir*. Corrected in Reg (medial letter *r* interlined).

8. THE BUILDING OF NOAH'S ARK

Many erasures and corrections are present in this pageant.

20	*ever*. Reg: erasure to remove *e* at end of word.
27	*above*. Reg: *a bove*, as corrected by LH.
29	*noght*. Reg: *not* written above *noght* by LH.
45	*doo*. Reg: added by LH over erasure.
59	*sownkyn*. Reg: letter *o* added in text.
74	*skwyn*. Reg: correction overwritten by LH.
75	*betwene*. Reg: corrected by LH.
81	*lang*. Reg: originally *long* (corrected).
83	*strang*. Reg: originally *strong* (corrected).
86	*do*. Reg: added, over an erasure, by LH.
99	Reg: *must* written above *bud* by LH.
101	*gynn*. Corrected by Scribe B in Reg; originally *gyn*.

102–03	Lines written in right margin in Reg; they had been erroneously entered after line 110 (deleted).
after 104	Line following is missing in Reg.
106	*ever*. Reg: erasure to remove final *e* at end of word.
110	*the bowe ther*. This edition; Reg, LTS: *ther bowe ther*; RB: *ther the bowe*.
113	*force*. Reg: an *e* was added as a correction.
119	*bowde*. Attempted emendation in Reg (to *bollde*).
120	*nere an*. Reg: corrected by LH, over erasure.
122	*yit*. Interlined by LH: *must*. Reg: correction over erasure.
124	*must*. Reg: correction over erasure.
126	*that*. Reg: interlined by LH in Reg.
	sam. Reg: a final *e* at end of word erased.
127	*must*. Reg: correction by LH, over erasure.
131	*fere*. Reg: correction, in red ink, in right margin by Scribe B.
143	*awey be*. So RB; Reg: *awey be away be* (*away be* canceled).
147	Following *helpe* in Reg, extraneous *w* deleted.

9. THE FLOOD

14	*formefadres*. LTS: *forme ffadres*; RB: *forme-fadres*; Reg: *formed fadres*.
24	*As*. So RB; Reg, LTS: *And*.
30	Reg: by LH in right margin: *for ethe*.
71	*I FILIUS*. So LTS, RB; Reg: *Filius*.
80	*fellis*. Added in Reg by LH; also, in right margin in red: *fellys*.
106	*NOE*. Reg: speech attribution added by LH.
134	*had*. Reg: interlined by LH.
204	*wate*. So LTS, RB; Reg: *watir*.
215	*wynd*. So LTS, RB; Reg: *wymd*.
221	*mayd*. Reg: corrected by LH (*d* interlined).
266 s.d.	*Tunc cantent Noe et filii sui*. Reg: stage direction inserted in right margin by LH.
270	*knwe*. So Reg, RB; LTS: *kn[e]we*.
288	*wast yt*. So RB; Reg, LTS: *wastyd*.
294	Reg: line added at right by LH, replacing misplaced *In ses* (canceled).

10. ABRAHAM AND ISAAC

15	*schulde be*. RB: *shulde be*; Reg, LTS: *schulde*.
	multyplyed. Reg: Final letter added by LH.
25	*Abram*. So LTS, RB; Reg: *Abraham*.
70	*over*. So LTS; RB: *our*.
90	Reg: following *that*, *I* interlined by LH.
95	*asse*. So RB; Reg, LTS: *Assee*.

108	*send*. Reg: emended by LH, originally *sand*.
	agayne. Reg: added by Scribe B.
145	Reg: added in right margin by LH: *Abram*.
165	Reg: in right margin, probably by JC, apparently in error: *father wold God / I shuld be slayne* (deleted).
235–38	Reg: at right, by LH: *hic*; also illegible text, erased.
268	Reg: in right margin, JC has added: *Nowe have I chose / whether I had lever etc.* Also: *My nowne swete son / to slo or greve my / God for ever.*
271	Reg: to right, *hic caret* added by LH.
272	*Methynke*. So RB; LTS: *Me thynke*; Reg: *Ye thynke*.
281–82	Reg: by LH at right: *Hic caret*.
297	Reg: added by LH in right margin: *hic*.
327	*he*. Reg: interlined, by LH, in red.
362	*lawez*. Reg: corrected by LH.
369	*Isaac*. Reg: repeated in right margin, by LH.

11. Pharaoh and Moses

1	*O pees*. Words separated in Reg by deleted letter.
2	*comaunde*. Indefinite minims in Reg.
12	*als it*. So LTS; Reg: *as it als it*; RB: *as it*.
21	*Consolator*. So RB (throughout, following line 219 in Reg; see RB, p. 423).
32	*Israell*. Reg: corrected by LH.
41	*of*. So LTS, RB; Reg: *of of* (corrected).
42	*was a prince*. Reg: letter *a* interlined by LH.
61	*qwantise*. So LTS, RB; Reg: *qwantile*.
154	*as a lepre*. So RB, following Towneley; Reg, LTS: *serpent*.
159	*send*. Reg: interlined in hand of JC.
175	*meve*. So LTS, RB; Reg: *meke*.
183	*will I fayre*. Reg: written by JC above original scribe's *fayne* (deleted).
197	*Beith*. So RB, noting alteration in Reg by LH (from ?*Beeth*); LTS: *Beeths*.
219	*Where*. So LTS; Reg, RB: *When*.
219–20	Reg: lines misassigned to *I Consolator* (ascription deleted).
240	*A*. So LTS, RB; Reg: *Al*.
255	*II Egiptius*. Reg: Originally given to *II Consolator* (corrected by Scribe B).
257	*I Consolator*. So RB; Reg: *Consolator*.
284	*Moyses*. Reg: JC's emendation over erasure.
289	*I Egiptius*. Reg: originally assigned to Moyses. JC's correction, over erasure.
291–92	Reg: Scribe B emended mistake in exchanging speech attributions.
299	*Rex*. Reg: speech attribution to *I Egiptius* corrected by Scribe B.
315	*poudre*. So RB; Reg: *poure*; LTS: *pou[d]re*.
331	*Ellis*. So LTS, RB; Reg: *Eellis*.

342	*myscheff*. Reg: two final letters added by LH crudely.
345	*pestelence*. Reg: added by LH above the line.
351	*we*. Reg: interlined by LH.
372	*us*. So RB, following Towneley; Reg, LTS: *thus*.

12. THE ANNUNCIATION TO MARY AND THE VISITATION

1	*DOCTOUR*. Speech tag in right margin by JC, who also noted: *this matter is / newly mayde wherof / we have no coppy*.
	Lord. Large capital *L* sketched in by scribe.
7	*sor*. So LTS, RB; Reg: *for*.
17	*disposuit*. So LTS, RB; Reg: *dispsuit*.
34	*Quoniam*. So LTS, RB; Reg: *Qnia*.
39–40	Line break in Reg after *ordande*.
40	*Isay*. So RB; Reg, LTS: *I say*.
	unto. Reg: syllable *un* interlined by LH.
78	*meves me*. So RB; Reg: *me meves*; LTS: *me meves he*.
88	*Jesus*. In Reg, abbreviated *Jhc*, then altered to *Jhs*.
94	*Ero*. So LTS, RB; Reg: *Ego*.
120	*donec*. So RB; Reg omits.
143	*myghtis*. So RB; Reg, LTS: *myghtist*.
154	*How*. So RB; Reg, TLS: *To*.
157 s.d.	*Tunc cantat angelus*. Reg: entered in right margin by JC.
166 s.d.	*Tunc cantat angelus*, Ne timeas, Maria. Reg: added by JC, in right margin.
169	Erasure removing *all* between *over* and *othir* in Reg.
181	Reg: line entered at right by LH.
229	*unto*. So LTS, RB, after interlined emendation by JC; originally *alway to* (*alway* deleted).
231	*grace*. So LTS, RB; Reg: *grrace*.
253 s.d.	*Tunc cantat*. Reg: added by JC; *Magnificat* in red, by Scribe B.

13. JOSEPH'S TROUBLES ABOUT MARY

1	*JOSEPH*. Reg: added by LH.
	Of. Large capital *O* in Reg.
11	*dase*. Reg: *tase*, changed by LH to *dase*.
18	*me*. So LTS, RB; Reg: *we*.
31	*I*. Added to line in Reg by LH.
47	*might*. So RB; Reg: *mght*; LTS: *may*.
80	*fra*. Altered to *fro* by LH, who also made similar changes (*a* to *o*) in Reg, as noted below.
82	*tha*. Reg: altered to *tho*.
84	*ga*. Reg: altered to *go*.
91	*yhe*. Reg: altered to *ye* by LH.

103	*Nay, nay.* In Reg, misplaced at beginning of line 104.
114	LH: *hic caret* in right margin (deleted) in Reg.
116	Reg: line added in right margin by JC.
129	*allane.* Reg: changed to *allone.*
131	*gane.* Reg: altered to *gone.*
157	*na.* Reg: changed to *no.*
188	*knawe, nane.* Reg: altered to *knowe, none* by LH.
190	*mane.* Corrected in Reg to *mone.*
193	*stane.* Reg: altered to *stone.*
196	*gane.* Reg: altered to *gone.*
218	*twa.* Altered in Reg to *two.*
219	*tham.* So RB; Reg, LTS: *that.*
220	*wa.* Reg: altered to *wo.*
after 221	Following line is missing in Reg.
222	*fra.* Reg: altered to *fro.*
224	*I.* Interlined in Reg.
	fande. So RB; LTS: *frande,* following alteration (possible interlined *r*) in Reg.
225	*swa.* Reg: altered to *swo.*
235	Reg: line written at right in a different hand.
246	Reg: in right margin, by a later scribe: *Hic deficit* (deleted).
286	*have.* So RB; omit Reg.
294	*forgifnesse.* So LTS, RB; Reg: *fo givnesse.*

14. The Nativity

1	*All.* Reg: large initial *A,* perhaps by LH.
47	*For.* So LTS, RB; Reg: *Fo;* Bevington: *Of.*
71	*what.* So LTS, RB; Reg: *what what,* with initial *what* canceled.
75–77	Reg: lines written at right; insertion by Scribe B.
154 s.d.	Added by later hands in Reg: *hic caret pastoribus* and *sequitur postea.* Another addition, visible under ultraviolet light: . . . *with haste.*

15. The Offering of the Shepherds

1	*I Pastor.* Reg: supplied by JC.
	Bredir. Reg: large initial *B* sketched in.
7	*a.* So LTS, RB; Reg: *I.*
13	*II Pastor.* Reg: supplied by JC.
20	*al.* Reg: interlined by a LH.
25	*III Pastor.* Reg: supplied by JC.
37–64	*I Pastor.* Shepherds identified in Reg by *I, II,* and *III* only; here following LTS, RB.
41–42	Reg: designated for III Pastor (deleted).

43	*III Pastor.* So LTS, RB. Reg: *II.*
55	Missing leaf follows in Reg not noted by LTS.
56	*[III Pastor.]* So RB. Presumably continuation of speech from previous page.
64 s.d.	*Et tunc cantant.* Reg: in red, by Scribe B. Added by JC in margin: *caret nova loquela* and *de pastores.*
78	*I.* Reg: interlined by later scribe.
85	*With.* At end of line 83 in Reg.
	savyour. Added to text by JC.
85 s.d.	*Et tunc cantant.* Reg: in red, by Scribe B.
87	*burgh.* So RB; Reg, LTS: *burght.*
99	Reg: additions in later hand(s) in margin: *hic caret* and *nova loquela.*
106–07	On single line, lines in reverse order in Reg.
108	Reg: addition in margin by LH: *hic caret.*
118	*askis.* So LTS, RB; Reg, Bevington: *aftir.*
120	*hic.* Reg: at left, by LH.
128	*Farewele.* So LTS, RB, citing Shrewsbury Fragment A47.
131	Reg: following but erased, visible under ultraviolet light: *Here wantes the conclusyon of this matter* (in JC's hand). Under erasure is an indecipherable writing.

16. Herod Questioning the Three Kings and the Offering of the Magi

After ascription to Masons, LH has added *Mynstrells.*

1	*Herodes.* Reg: added by LH.
6	*Listes.* So RB; Reg, LTS: *I list.*
19	*is.* Reg: interlined by LH.
56	*?hic caret.* Reg: erased and a cross.
64	*Of.* Misplaced at end of line 63 in Reg.
73	*noght.* So LTS, RB; Reg omits.
129–272	Entered in Reg in the texts of both the Masons and the Goldsmiths, of which the Masons' (abbreviated Reg/M) is presented here, with only the most substantive readings from the Goldsmiths' text (abbreviated Reg/G) included in these textual notes. For a parallel text edition, see RB (pp. 138–45).
129	At left in Reg: *sequitur postea* (erased and now indecipherable except under ultraviolet light).
131	Reg/G: *Sir, new nott is full nere this towne.*
132	*harlott.* So Reg/M; Reg/G: *losell.*
133	Reg/G: *Go bette boy and dyng tham downe.*
136	*do.* So Reg/M; Reg/G omits.
139	Reg/G: *Of one that is nowe borne.*
141	*Sir, so I say.* Misplaced in Reg/M at beginning of next line.

147	Reg/G: *Have done. Dresse us in riche array.*
151	*we.* Interlined in Reg/M.
172	*will.* Reg/G: *schall.*
175	*Forsoth.* Reg/G: *Sir.*
177	*King?* So RB, Reg/G; Reg/M: *Kingis.*
	develes name: Reg/G: *devyl way.*
178	*ye.* So Reg/G, RB; Reg/M: *thee.*
	rave. So RB, Reg/G; Reg/M: *rase.*
180	*shulde ye.* So RB; Reg/M, Reg/G: *ye shulde.*
181	*he is.* So Reg/M; Reg/G: *I am.* Reg/G omits *Filius* and assigns his speech to Herodes.
183	*he is.* Reg/G: *I am.*
187	*II REX.* So RB; Reg/G: *Lorde, we aske noght but leve.*
189	*Whedirward.* So Reg/M; Reg/G: *Whedir.*
194	*there hye wordis.* So Reg/M; Reg/G: *such wondir.*
199	*thys.* So RB, after Reg/G: *this*; Reg/M: *thy.*
	thing. Added as emendation over deleted *counsaille.*
202	*kyth.* Overwritten by LH in Reg/M.
205	*will saye.* So Reg/G; under ink blot in Reg/M.
209	*I REX.* RB, after addition by LH in Reg/G.
213	*II REX.* RB, after Reg/G.
214	*newes.* So RB, following Reg/G; Reg/M: *newe.*
217	*III REX.* RB, after Reg/G.
218	*barne.* So Reg/M; Reg/G: *sone.*
219	*contrees.* Deleted in Reg/M; JC emended to *the world.*
221	*beiths.* So Reg/M; Reg/G: *shal be.*
224	*here.* Reg/M: *her*; Reg/G: *now.*
225	*I REX.* So RB, after entry by LH in Reg/G.
227	*forsoth saide.* So Reg/M; Reg/G: *sais.*
229	*childe consayved sall.* So Reg/M; Reg/G: *barne consayved shulde.*
233	*II REX.* So RB, after late addition in Reg/G.
238	Reg/G: *This bryge shall well to ende be broght.*
245	*is.* So Reg/M; Reg/G: *was.*
250	*is.* So Reg/M; Reg/G: *it is.*
251	*grathely.* So Reg/M; Reg/G: *grathe.*
255	*than were.* So Reg/M; Reg/G: *that is.*
258	Reg/G: *Alle the soth of that childe.*
259	*we.* So Reg/M; Reg/G: *that we.*
263	*swytteron.* So Reg/M; Reg/G: *littil.*
264	*all.* So Reg/M; Reg/G omits.
272	Below in Reg/M, but erased: *Hic caret: I Rex. Alake fosoth what schall I say. We lake that syne that we have sought.* Also: *sequitur postea* (confirmed by RB). Reg/G: *Nota . . . offerynges.* Stage direction supplied in margin by JC.

295	*and se.* So RB. Misplaced in line 296 in Reg.
318	*I soght sone, I.* So RB; Reg: *soght sone I.*
329	*thow.* So RB[2]; LTS: *yow.*
336	*fro the fende to thee fette.* So RB; Reg: *free thu fende fals thee to thy fette* (*thy* canceled; obviously corrupt); LTS: *fro the fende fals thee to fette.*
371	*God hymselfe.* So RB; Reg: *God of hymselfe* (*of* deleted).

17. THE PURIFICATION OF THE VIRGIN

In JC's hand, out of order in Reg. It is, however, noted by JC in Reg at fol. 74, where the pageant, identified as *Purificacio Marie*, should have appeared: *It is entryd in the latter end of this booke next after the Sledmen, Palmers, and it begynnyth by the pr . . . "Allmyghty God in heven."* This is written over text that had been erased.

15	*he.* Reg: Interlined by scribe.
30	*Unto.* So LTS, RB; *Un-* deleted in Reg.
	as I yow tell. Corrected in Reg from *full yell.*
33	*after.* So RB; Reg, LTS: *after that.*
149	*relesse.* So RB; Reg, LTS: *reverse.*
166	*Bodworde.* So RB; Reg, LTS: *Bolde worde.*
180	*in.* So Köbling; Reg, LTS, RB: *that.*
247	*poore.* So RB, following Köbling; Reg, LTS omit.
268	*pay.* So LTS, RB; Reg: *pray.*
389	*telles.* So LTS, RB; Reg: *tell.*
407	Line added in left margin by scribe in Reg.
433–60	The remainder of the pageant is entered on a sheet (a singleton) pasted into Reg.
438	*wo.* So RB; Reg, LTS omit.
449	*gyant.* So LTS, RB; Reg: *gyane.*
460	*fyne.* So RB; Reg, LTS: *fynd.*

18. THE FLIGHT TO EGYPT

1	*Thow.* Reg has sketched in capital *T.*
	At right, in JC's hand: *This matter is mayd of new after another forme* (deleted).
3	*thin.* So LTS; Reg: *thn* (final letter unclear); RB: *this.*
12	Reg: at right, by LH: *Caret* (deleted).
33	Reg: at right, by LH: *Maria ad huc.*
34	Reg: text in margin at left deleted and illegible.
47	*What that.* So LTS, RB; Reg: *What at that.*
66	*nevere offende.* So RB; Reg: *nevere didde offende* (*didde* canceled).
137	*tharne.* So LTS, RB; Reg: *thrane.*
170	*Of all.* So LTS; Reg, RB: *Off of all.*

19. THE MASSACRE OF THE INNOCENTS

Top of previous page, in JC's handwriting: *This matter of the gyrdlers agreyth not with the Coucher in no poynt; it begynnyth, Lysten lordes unto my lawe.*

1	*HEROD.* Reg: centered above text, added in JC's hand.
90	*NUNCIUS.* So LTS, RB; Reg omits.
91	*HERODES.* So LTS, RB; Reg omits.
153	*and.* So LTS, RB; Reg: *and and.*
167	*I MILES.* So RB; Reg, LTS: *I CONSOLATOR.*
171	*boght.* This edition; Reg, LTS: *boght he*; RB: *bathe.*
173	*wathe.* RB; Reg, LTS: *waghe.*
176	*II MILES.* So RB; Reg, LTS: *II CONSOLATOR.*
193	The following line is missing in Reg.
223	*I MILES.* So LTS, RB; Reg: *II MILES.*
240–41	Lines reversed in Reg.
245	*thydingis.* So Reg (as corrected by ?LH).
274	*I CONSOLATOR.* So LTS, RB; Reg omits.
275	*than.* Misplaced in Reg at end of previous line.
276	*HERODES.* So RB; LTS: *II CONSOLATOR*; Reg omits.
279	*banne.* So LTS, RB; Reg: *bande.*

20. CHRIST AND THE DOCTORS

20	By LH, at right in Reg: *hic caret* (erased).
46–48	*JOSEPH.* RB, following Köbling; later scribe in Reg, LTS here only assign lines 47–48 to Joseph.
49ff.	Reg: speech ascriptions in this pageant are inconsistent in that they use *Magister* and *Doctor* for the same set of characters.
56	*aught.* So RB; LTS: *might.*
82	*lyve.* Corrected in Reg; scribe originally wrote *lyke.*
89	*bowrdyng.* So RB; Reg, LTS: *brandyng.*
128	*To say.* Misplaced at end of previous line in Reg.
132	*That.* So RB, following Towneley; Reg, LTS: *And.*
134	*Yitt fande.* So RB[2]; LTS: *Itt fand*; Reg: *Itt fande.*
161	*then.* Misplaced at the beginning of line 162 by scribe in Reg.
181	*forbedis.* So RB; LTS: *fo[r]bedis*; Reg: *fobedis.*
209	*we.* So LTS, RB; omit Reg.
210	*dayes thre.* This edition; LTS, RB: *ther dayes thre*; Reg: *thre dayes thre.*
221	*ye se.* This edition; Reg: *y se*; LTS: *y[e] se*; RB: *se ye.*
227	*gone.* Altered to *done* by LH in Reg.
249	*MARIA.* Initially assigned by scribe to *Jhc* (deleted) in Reg.
253	*twa.* Reg: *twa son* (*son* deleted).
254	*Son.* Added by LH in Reg.

255	*and*. Ampersand interlined by LH in Reg.
271	*or be*. Misplaced at the beginning of the following line in Reg.
275	*and he*. Erasure between words in Reg.
288	Below, Scribe B has listed *Jesu, Maria, Joseph*, and *Primus doctor, Secundus Doctor, et Tercius Doctor*.

21. THE BAPTISM OF CHRIST

1	Reg: at right, in LH: *De novo facto*.
48	*with*. So RB; Reg: *wth*; LTS: *w[i]th*.
49	Reg: mark X at left; below, at bottom of page, in JC's hand: *Her wantes a pece newely mayd for saynt John Baptiste*.
50	*I ANGELUS*. So RB; Reg, LTS: *ANGELUS*.
52	*thys day*. *Thus* entered at beginning of line 53, canceled, moved to end of line 52 and emended to *thys*. A later hand was responsible to adding *day* after *thys*.
59	*JOHANNES*. Omitted by Scribe B in Reg; Joseph later designated, corrected by ?JC.
71	Lacuna noted, as indicated by marginal note at right of line by LH in Reg: *Hic caret*.
83	Reg: later scribe wrote *Her wants a pece newely mayd for saynt John Baptiste*.
84	In right margin in Reg, probably referring to lacuna in text: *De novo facto*.
88	*The*. So RB; Reg, LTS: *By*.
94	*And*. So RB; Reg, LTS: *I*.
101	*vertue*. Reg originally read *wittnesse* (deleted); *vertue* interlined by LH.
104	*alway*. So RB; in Reg, misplaced at beginning of next line.
107	At right, *hic caret* (deleted) in Reg.
114	*Lorde*. So LTS, RB; Reg: *Lorede*.
131	*Thrughe baptyme clere*. In red at right by Scribe B in Reg.
141–44	Lines not in correct order in Reg, and lines 141 and 143 entered twice; correct order indicated by letters *a* to *d* at left in Reg in red.
154 s.d.	*cantabunt duo angeli . . . spiritus*. Stage direction, in red by Scribe B in Reg.
175	At left, in JC's hand in Reg, *hic caret finem*; below, in same handwriting: *This matter is newly mayd and devysed wherof we have no coppy regystred*.

22. THE TEMPTATION IN THE WILDERNESS

Craft assignment: *Lok-* interlined as addition to *Smythis*.

1	*Make*. Reg: large capital *M* is sketched in.
22	*Thei*. So LTS, RB; Reg: *Thi*.

91 s.d.	*Tunc cantant . . . creator.* Stage direction, for singers, added by JC in right margin in Reg.
92	*Diabolus* added in right margin by LH; this edition omits.
108	*tose.* Originally written *toce* and corrected in Reg.
154	Line misplaced following line 152 (deleted) in Reg, then written in red ink in right margin.
156	*As.* Reg: scribe began writing a lower case *a* at end of previous line (not canceled).
192	*thow leve.* Reg: deleted words, thereafter full line written in red at right.

22A. THE MARRIAGE IN CANA

Incipit for this play is only entered in handwriting of JC; subsequent folios blank, with catchword for *The Transfiguration* on page prior to its opening.

23. THE TRANSFIGURATION

5	*sightis.* So LTS, RB; Reg: *sighitis.*
13	Reg: added at right in LH: *cum Moysez et Elias.*
31	*Sum.* So LTS, RB; Reg: *sam.*
41	*and biddis nowe* misplaced at beginning of line 42 in Reg.
73	*of all welth is wele.* So RB; Reg: omits *of.*
83	*That.* So LTS, RB; Reg: *Than.*
145	*PETRUS.* Supplied in margin of Reg in LH.
168 s.d.	*Hic descendunt nubes.* By Scribe B, in red at right.
169	*Pater.* Reg: (redundant) written in right margin by LH (deleted).
171	*grayde.* So RB; Reg, LTS: *grayth.*
180	At right by LH in Reg: *Hic caret* (deleted).
185	*may.* So LTS, RB; Reg: three minims only.
238	*me.* Reg has extra minim on *m.*

23A. THE FEAST IN SIMON'S HOUSE

Reg: under erasure, in JC's hand (following RB's reading): *This matter lakkes, videlicet: Jesus et Symon leprosus rogans eum ut manducaret cum eo, duo discipuli, Maria Magdalena lavans pedes Jesu lacrimis et capillis suis tergens.*

24. THE WOMAN TAKEN IN ADULTERY AND THE RAISING OF LAZARUS

At top, guild attribution: *and Hatmakers* (added by LH, probably in 1569; see *REED: York*, 1:356).

13	*strye.* This edition; Reg, LTS, RB: *stroye.*
29	*certayne.* So LTS, RB; Reg: *certaye.*

50	Reg: at right, JC has added *Hic deficit*.
51	*hyde*. So RB, who suggests *byde* might have been intended.
54	Missing leaf follows in Reg.
after 98	*Lazare mortus*. Reg: written in red at top of page by Scribe B, preceding line 81. Placement in text after line 98 in this edition follows LTS, RB.
124	*lange*. Emended to *longe* by LH in Reg.
171	Missing leaf follows in Reg.
186	Reg: at right, by JC: *Nota quia non concordat*, and *novo addicio facto*.
189	LH has written *memorandum* and word (illegible) to right in Reg.

25. THE ENTRY INTO JERUSALEM

11	*is*. So LTS, RB; Reg: *is I*.
33	*this thyng*. In Reg, *?ki* interlined between these words.
41	*go*. So RB; Reg, LTS omit.
71	*hartely*. Letter *t* interlined in Reg.
85	*JANITOR*. Added by JC in Reg.
108	*tham*. So RB; Reg, LTS: *hym*.
162	*VII BURGENSIS*. So RB; Reg and LTS place at line 160.
204	*I say*. So RB; Reg: *I say I* (second *I* canceled).
211	*youre childer with*. So LTS, RB; Reg: *youre with*.
228	*telle*. So RB; Reg, LTS: *felle*.
247	*thought*. Reg: JC has *th* interlined above thorn (þ).
248	*latt*. Written by JC above *consayte* (canceled) in Reg.
260	*I BURGENSIS*. So RB; Reg locates at line 261.
266	*II BURGENSIS*. So RB; MS has speech ascription on previous line.
280	*this thing*. So RB; Reg, LTS: *thing*.
286	*lyst*. So RB; Reg, LTS: *lyfe*.
287 s.d.	*Tunc cantant*. Added in left margin by LH in Reg.
296–337	Lineation scrambled in Reg; text follows LTS and RB.
298	*bene of tendyr yere*. So LTS, RB; Reg: *of tendyr yere bene*.
303	*I witte*. So LTS, RB; Reg: *witte*.
320	*right*. So LTS, RB; Reg: *righ*.
332	*aghe*. So LTS, RB; Reg: *age*.
346	*syght*. So LTS, RB; Reg: *syight*.
359	Reg: in margin by later scribe: *hic caret*.
after 367	Following line is missing in Reg.
382	Reg: line written on previous page, deleted, and then added by JC, incorrectly with *my* for *myn*, at right of line 381.
after 402	Following line is missing in Reg; LTS suggested *New lawes to lare*.
429	*hid*. So RB; Reg, LTS: *it*.
431	*Wille*. So LTS, RB; Reg: *Whiche*.
448	*I*. Reg: altered to *Mi* in LH.
449	*Halve*. So RB; Reg, LTS: *Have*.

482	Reg adds *at hande* at end of line (deleted).
495	*Hayll.* So RB; Reg: *hall*, as emended by LH.
499	*bright.* So LTS, RB; Reg: *brigh*.
501	*we.* So RB; Reg, LTS: *with*.
544 s.d.	*Tunc cantant.* Added in LH in left margin in Reg.

26. THE CONSPIRACY

1	*PILATUS.* Speech identification by LH in Reg.
13	*grone.* So RB; Reg, LTS: *grume*.
34a	*thurgh.* So LTS, RB; Reg: *thurgh thurgh*.
85b	*tales.* So LTS, RB; Reg: *tales tales*.
89b	*deland.* So RB; Reg, LTS: *derand*.
117	*PILATUS.* So Reg in LH, correcting ascription to *Cayphas* by JC.
128	*Unjust.* So RB; LTS: *Un-just*; Reg: *Uncust*.
133b	*that.* So LTS, RB; Reg: *Tat*.
183b	*drawen.* So LTS, RB; Reg: *drawe*.
191	Assignment to Judas deleted in Reg.
211	*bar.* So LTS, RB; Reg: *bay*.
226a	*justified.* So LTS, RB; Reg: *justified b*.
232	*hym.* So LTS, RB; Reg: *hm*.
247	*fende.* So LTS, RB; Reg: *frende*.
250	*hastely hang.* So LTS, RB; Reg: *hastely hym hang*.
252–54	Reg: lines initially ascribed to Pilatus (deleted).
268	*faythe.* So RB; LTS: *[?faythe]*; Reg omits.
280	Reg: at right, by LH: *Caret hic*; JC has added: *Janitor* and *Judas*.
284	In LH in right margin in Reg: *Caret hic*.

27. THE LAST SUPPER

1	*JESUS.* So LTS, RB; Reg: *Deus* in JC's hand.
	Above, top right of page in Reg: *caret hic principio*.
	Pees. Reg: Large *P* sketched in.
2	Reg has *all* interlined; and *here* added by later scribe (replacing *?theryn*).
60 s.d.	*Tunc lavat manus.* Supplied by JC in right margin in Reg.
61	Reg has ascription by JC: *Deus*. This edition omits.
after 89	Missing leaf follows in Reg.
96	*I hope.* So Reg, LTS; RB: *Jhon*.
100	*is.* So LTS, RB; Reg: *is is*.
148	*slayne.* So RB; Reg, LTS: *allone*.
151	*mende.* So LTS, RB; Reg: *mened*.
173	*stones.* So Reg, LTS, RB; Kölbing: *swordes*.
177	*Us.* So LTS, RB; Reg: *Vis*.
187	At left in margin in Reg: *Hic caret*, in LH; JC has added *novo loquela*.

28. THE AGONY AND BETRAYAL

1	*JESUS.* Added LTS, RB; omit Reg.
	Reg: at right, in LH: *de novo facto.*
12	*in.* So LTS, RB; Reg: *ni.*
42	Missing leaf follows in Reg.
111–12	Reg: text erased, partially recovered under ultraviolet light; corroborated by RB: *And seis . . . yght / With rappes full rudely . . . the rode rente.*
113	*ANGELUS.* LH adds *and archangels* in Reg.
142	Following in Reg is an intruded cue for the actor: *This sothly quod Petir.*
143	Misplaced line, in Reg between lines 139 and 140.
148a	*For.* So LTS, RB; Reg: *Fo.*
159a	*se.* Interlined in Reg.
168–72	Speeches of Anna and Cayphas reversed in Reg. Lineation follows LTS, RB.
173–81	Confused lineation in Reg; text here follows RB.
181a	Reg: line originally assigned to Cayphas at end of next line.
183	*Sir knyghtis, in hy.* Part of Cayphas' speech, but originally assigned to I Miles in Reg; Reg's ascription of line 183b to II Miles altered to I Miles; so LTS, RB.
193	*armed.* Altered to *myned* by LH in Reg.
199	Reg: at right, in LH, faint: *hic caret.*
204	*he.* So LTS, RB; Reg omits.
214	*slane.* Reg: *slone,* changed to *slane* by LH.
236a	*CAYPHAS.* Speech designation added by RB. Originally assigned implausibly to Malcus in Reg.
247	*CAYPHAS.* Speech heading added RB.
249b	*ye.* So RB; Reg, LTS: *he.*
272b	Given to Malcus in RB; in Reg and LTS to Jesus.
278	*JESUS.* Inserted in LH in Reg.
295	Line incomplete in Reg.
300	*mekenes.* So Reg, LTS; RB: *merkenes.*

29. THE TRIAL BEFORE CAYPHAS AND ANNA

1	*CAYPHAS.* Entered by JC in Reg.
23b	*Tunc dicant Lorde.* Added at right by JC in Reg.
73–74	At right in Reg, *Hic caret* (deleted); also, by JC: *Hic For be we ones well wett / The better we will reste.* At left: *Hic.*
86	*MULIER.* So RB; Reg, LTS: *I Mulier.*
128a	*that.* Reg: written at end of line (deleted).
130a	*youre.* So RB; Reg, LTS: *oure.*
145	*than.* So RB, LTS; Reg: *thon.*
after 152	Line following 152 is missing in Reg.

153	Reg: at right, in LH: *Caret hic*.
176	*III MILES*. So RB; *staste* (deleted), followed by *stande* in Reg.
178b	*I MILES*. So RB, for gap in Reg.
178c	*III MILES*. So RB; Reg: *I Miles*.
198	*I MILES*. Added by RB.
199	*CAYPHAS*. Reg: main scribe had written *I Miles*, altered by later scribe.
200–07	Reg: speech designations emended by LH; initially assignments to Cayphas and Anna had been reversed.
211	*are buxom*. This edition; Reg, LTS: *have buxom*; RB: *have ben buxom*.
213b	*I* added, emendation in Reg.
214	*And felawes*. At end of previous line in Reg.
226a	Reg: *he* deleted between *to* and *take*.
241	*IV MILES*. So LTS, RB.
242	*CAYPHAS*. Originally *IV Miles*; emended by LH.
255	*tere*. So RB; Reg, LTS: *stere*.
261b	*sidis seere*. So LTS, RB; Reg: *sere sidis seere*.
262	*CAYPHAS*. Reg: speech designation entered by JC.
272	*CAYPHAS*. Reg: main scribe had written *IV Miles*; emended by JC.
275	Reg: at right, *Hic caret* in LH.
304b	*Sertis, so I schall*. In Reg written at beginning of next line.
307	Reg: at right, JC has written: *Sir my reason is not to rehers. Jesus*. Incipit of Jesus' speech at line 308, hence cue to indicate that the speeches by Jesus and Anna, which follow in lines 308–11, are reversed.
362–64	Lineation as in LTS, RB, to correct defective order in Reg.
365	Reg repeats *III Miles*; this edition omits.
372	*I saie*. So RB; Reg, LTS: *ysaie*.
373	*Quis te*. So RB, following Köbling; Reg: *In juste*; LTS: *Injuste*.
	thou. So RB; LTS: *you*.
394a	*CAYPHAS*. So RB; Scribe B: *Anna*, corrected by JC, but *Anna* retained by LTS.
395	Speech designation *Cayphas* by Scribe B; this edition omits.

30. THE FIRST TRIAL BEFORE PILATE

7	*wrekis*. So LTS, RB; Reg: *werkis*.
9	*trewys*. Reg: final *s* added by LH.
13	*plight*. So RB; Reg, LTS: *pight*.
22	*ther*. So RB; Reg, LTS: *the*.
23–24	Lines reversed in Reg.
28	*UXOR PILATI*. Entered twice in Reg; also *Uxor Pilaty* at line 30.
34	*troned*. So RB; Reg, LTS: *stonyd*.
46a	*itt may*. So RB; LTS, Reg: *itt save may*.
62–63	Lineation here follows LTS, RB.
70a	*wele*. Moved from line 70b in Reg.

75–76	As three lines in Reg. Realigned following LTS.
79	*deme*. So RB; Reg, LTS: *dome*.
after 85	Following line is missing in Reg.
90	*for thee*. This edition; LTS, RB: *forthe*.
92a	*a repreve*. So RB, following Köbling; Reg, LTS: *appreve*.
97	*Loke, nowe*. So LTS, RB; Reg: *Loke, what dose thou have done nowe*.
97–98	Lineation follows LTS, RB.
after 107	Two lines following are missing in Reg.
112	*here is*. So RB; Reg, LTS: *he this*.
115	*FILIUS*. Reg has *Filius Secundus* until line 180, subsequently *Filius Primus*.
after 127	Following line is missing in Reg.
135a	*A, sir . . . wele*. Reg: added in left margin by Scribe B.
after 135	Following line is missing in Reg.
136	*here*. Added by LTS, RB.
224	*II MILES*. Reg: in LH.
225	*lawe*. So LTS, RB; Reg: *lawne*.
227a	Following *dowtiest* in Reg: *this day* (canceled).
233a	*I MILES*. Written over erasure in Reg.
244	*batterand*. So RB; Reg, LTS: *battand*.
263a	*roo*. Corrected over erasure in Reg.
265a	*leve*. So LTS, RB; Reg: *leve i*.
271a	*there*. So LTS, RB; Reg: *thenne*.
283	*leede*. So RB; in Reg, later scribe altered to *hede*. So LTS.
296	*PILATUS*. So RB; Reg, LTS omit.
297	*soth*. So LTS, RB; Reg: *soh*.
310b	*heyned*. So RB, who questions and, following *MED*, suggests possibly *hoyned*.
351a	*Saviour*. Spelling corrected in Reg, *a* overwritten.
370	Lineation follows RB.
370d	*Alowde*. Stage direction (not so designated as such in Reg).
371a	Reg: at right, in LH: *hic caret* (deleted).
371b	*lithe*. So RB; Reg, LTS: *light*.
377	*thee*. This edition; Reg, LTS, RB: *he*.
389	*FILIUS*. Reg has *Junior Filius*.
404	*accusyng*. So LTS, RB; Reg: *accusymg*.
after 419	Following line missing in Reg.
after 431	Following line missing in Reg.
446	*dede*. So RB; Reg, LTS: *dethe*.
470	*to spede*. So LTS, RB; Reg: *to speke*.
488	*dewe*. This edition; Reg: *dewe als*; LTS, RB: *dewe of*.
497	*be and*. So RB; Reg, LTS: *and be*.
514b	*and bredde*. Reg: supplied in margin by JC. This edition omits Scribe B's *and borne* at end of line in Reg.
524	*PILATUS*. Reg, RB; LTS suggests *Anna*.

526b	*MILITES*. So RB; omit in Reg.
after 529	Line following is missing in Reg.
533	*deme*. Alteration in Reg, from *dome*.
534	*Is done*. In Reg at end of previous line; *Done* repeated at beginning of this line.

31. THE TRIAL BEFORE HEROD

1	*REX*. So LTS, RB; Reg omits.
11	*Yae*. Follows at end of previous line in Reg.
14–15	Lines reversed in Reg.
33	*to*. So RB; Reg, LTS: *in*.
42 s.d.	*Tunc bibet Rex*. Reg: stage direction added by JC.
94b	*heynde*. Corrected in Reg (*y* written over *u*).
111	*were*. So LTS, RB; Reg omits.
189	*deffis*. So RB; Reg, LTS: *dethis*.
190	Reg: *Say deynis thou not whare*. Intrusion from previous line; corrected RB.
196	*tell hyme*. Reg: interlined in hand of JC.
199	*This*. So LTS, RB; Reg: *Thus*.
	menyes. This edition; in Reg, *n* altered to *y* by LH; RB: *mennes*.
201	*II DUX*. Reg: inserted by LH.
202	*two*. Reg: added over an erasure by LH.
214	*that*. Reg: *that that*.
215	*REX*. Replaces deleted *I Dux* in Reg.
218	*light*. Alteration by LH in Reg; originally *lith*.
256–60	Lineation follows LTS.
276–77	Lineation follows LTS.
308	*droune*. So RB; Reg: *drawe*; LTS: *drawe [sonne]*.
	Reg: at left, by LH: *Nota*.
310	*roune*. So RB; LTS: *ronne*.
	Reg: at right, by LH: *Hic*.
319	Reg: at left, by LH: *Nota*.
	Reg: at right: *hic*.
329	Reg: at right, by LH: *Nota*.
	Reg: at left: *Pylatus*.
333a	*AL CHYLDER*. So RB; implied only in Reg, LTS.
334	Reg: to right, by LH: *Nota*.
347a	*AL CHILDER*. Not distinguished as speech tag in Reg, LTS.
355	*hende*. So RB; Reg, LTS: *hente*.
375	Reg: at right, by LH: *Post Rex*.
390	*rathely*. So LTS, RB; Reg: *yathely*.

32. THE REMORSE OF JUDAS

1	*Pees.* Reg: capital *P* sketched in (strapwork initial).
	me. Deleted in Reg, retained by LTS, RB.
3	*lowte me.* So LTS, RB; Reg: *lord me* (*me* deleted).
27	*to behold.* At right in Reg, misplaced at line 25, addition by JC.
46	*His.* So LTS, RB; Reg: *This.*
73	*not.* So RB; Reg, LTS: *nowe.*
91	*neven it.* So LTS, RB; Reg: *nevenist.*
110	*to hym.* So RB; Reg, LTS omit *hym.*
111	*land.* Reg: entered at end of line by JC.
123–24	Lineation as in RB.
129	Reg: in right margin, by later hands: *Hic caret; loquela de primo filio* and *et aliis.*
149	*bote myght be.* So RB; Reg: *myght be bote*; LTS suggests *loke howe beste that bote myght be.*
154–55	Reg: in left margin, by LH: *Hic caret loquela magna et diversa.*
170	*JUDAS.* Added in Reg in LH.
231	*worthi.* So LTS, RB; Reg: *wothi.*
after 239	Following line is missing in Reg; LTS suggests *I crye you sore.*
	Reg: notation at right: *caret hic* (canceled).
261	Line written at right in Reg at line 258, and also by JC at line 260 (deleted).
277	*thus.* So RB; Reg, LTS: *thu.*
after 282	Following line is missing in Reg; LTS suggests: *Nor mercy none.*
298	*talke.* In Reg, *t* and *k* are corrected (overwritten).
after 326	RB suggests a line might be missing here.
329	*PILATUS.* So RB here; LTS at line 333.
	skill. So LTS, RB; Reg: *skall.*
339	Reg: at left by LH: *Hic caret.*
363	Reg: at right by LH: *Hic caret*; JC has added *loquela.*

33. THE SECOND TRIAL BEFORE PILATE

Craft assignment to *Mylners* added by LH.

24	*hym.* So LTS, RB; Reg: *hyn.*
after 32	Following line missing in Reg; LTS suggests *and chasted.*
35	*tasted.* Reg: letter *d* added by LH.
42	*my.* So LTS, RB; Reg: *my my.*
48	*yitt.* Reg: added by LH.
49	*undre sylke on.* So RB (conjecture); Reg, LTS: *undre on.*
108	*CAYPHAS.* Reg: speech tag added by JC.
138	*PILATUS.* So RB; Reg, LTS omit.

146b	*Preco*. So RB; LTS: *Præco*; Reg omits.
146c	*I Miles*. So LTS, RB; Reg omits.
147	*this*. So RB; Reg: *ths*.
155	*name*. So RB; Reg, LTS: *named*.
159	*his*. So RB; Reg, LTS: *hir*.
175	*dastardes*. So RB; Reg, LTS: *dastard*.
191	*unfittyng*. This edition; MS, LTS, RB: *unsittyng*.
242	*barnes*. So Reg, LTS; RB: *baners*.
	of. So LTS, RB; Reg: *of of*.
263 s.d.	*They cry*. This edition.
	Oyes. Reg: added by JC.
267 s.d.	*Et Preco . . . Jesus*. Reg: stage direction entered, in red ink, in right margin by Scribe B.
293	*convyk*. So LTS, RB; Reg: *covyk*.
323	*man*. So LTS, RB; Reg: *nan*.
360	*this*. Reg: letter *t* added by LH.
361	*Swete*. Reg: original scribe had written *Swte*; missing letter added by LH.
382	Reg: line deleted in red ink (duplicated on next page).
403	*a rede*. Reg: *a* interlined by LH.
432	*as*. Reg: letter *s* added by a late hand.
after 439	Missing leaf follows in Reg.
441	*fende*. So RB; Reg, LTS: *lende*.
443 s.d.	*Tunc lavat manus suas*. Reg: stage direction added by JC.
444	Reg: line deleted, then rewritten.
465	*alone*. Reg: LH deleted *one* and substituted *alone*.

34. The Road to Calvary

after 11	Following line missing in Reg.
after 141	Following leaf missing in Reg.
142	*Maria Sancta*. This edition (conjecture).
177	*seen*. So RB; Reg omits.
198	*withalle*. So LTS, RB; Reg: *with ille*.
201	*everemore*. So RB; Reg, LTS: *nevere more*.
206	*I Miles*. Reg: added twice, in one instance in red, by later hands.
208	*Go*. So LTS, RB; Reg: *To*.
243	*III Miles*. Reg: added by LH.
336	*as*. So RB; Reg, LTS: *of*.

35. CRUCIFIXIO CHRISTI

As addition to craft ascription, by LH: *and Paynters.*

80	*hange.* So RB; Reg, LTS: *have.*
98–107	Speech identifications follow RB.
118	*suerly.* So Reg, LTS; RB: *snelly.*
154	*and.* So RB; Reg, LTS omit.
155	*Thei.* So RB; Reg, LTS: *I.*
183a	*IV MILES.* So RB; Reg, LTS: *III Miles.*
183–84	*We are redy . . . fang.* Reg: added in margin by Scribe B.
230	*morteyse.* So LTS, RB; Reg: *moteyse.*
264	Reg: addition by JC in right margin: *In welth without end / I kepe noght elles to crave.*

36. MORTIFICACIO CHRISTI

The title is written in red ink.

20	*myght.* Altered in Reg by LH; originally *myne.*
75	*CAYPHAS.* Reg: added by JC.
95	*brade.* Emended (*o* changed to *a*) in Reg.
105	*pleasaunce.* So LTS, RB; Reg: *pleasaune.*
126	*Than I.* Reg: inserted by JC at right.
133	*thou.* So Reg, LTS; RB: *he.*
155	*to.* Reg: added in text, interlined.
208	*Whan.* So RB; Reg, LTS: *What.*
241	*spare.* So LTS, RB; Reg: *sware.*
254	Reg: at right JC has added: *for why* (canceled).
259	*thee.* Altered in Reg (from *me*).
273	Reg: at right, presumably indicative of the exit of Marys: *Hic caret.*
313	*CENTERIO.* So Reg; RB: *Centurio.*
352	*NICHODEMUS.* So throughout in this edition; Reg has *Nichomedis. I.* So LTS, RB; omit Reg.
358	*we.* So RB; Reg, LTS omit.
395	*To.* So LTS, RB; Reg: *Do.*
404	*JOSEPH.* So RB; Reg: *Joshep.*
410	*mende.* So LTS, RB; Reg: *wende.*

37. THE HARROWING OF HELL

1	*JESUS.* Reg: written by LH.
10	*frewte.* Compare Towneley: *fraude.*
36 s.d.	*Tunc cantent.* Reg: stage direction by LH.

40	*this stedde*. Compare Towneley: *darknes stad*.
44	*sesse*. Compare Towneley: *slake*.
49	*ISAIAH*. So LTS, RB; Reg: *Isaac*.
58	*seede*. Possibly an error (for *?deede*).
61	*This*. This edition; Reg, RB: *Thhis*; LTS: *Yhis*.
62	*the*. So Towneley, RB; Reg, LTS: *this*.
64	*halsed homely*. Compare Towneley: *halsid hym homely*.
83	*laide*. Letter *e* altered to *a* in Reg.
97	*I DIABOLUS*. Compare Towneley: *Rybald*.
99	*II DIABOLUS*. By a different hand in Reg; compare Towneley: *Belzabub*.
135	*lad*. So Towneley; Reg, LTS, RB: *lady*.
150	*traveses*. RB, following Towneley: *travesses*; Reg, LTS: *traves*.
185	*what harlot*. So LTS, RB, interpolated from Towneley; Reg omits.
195	*I DIABOLUS*. So RB; Reg omits *I*.
	baill. Added in LH in Reg; compare Towneley: *bayll*.
196	*of*. Interlined by LH in Reg.
209	*ferde*. Compare Towneley: *flayd*.
211	At left, by JC: *nota caret nova loquela* (deleted).
228	*wonne in mirthe*. Compare Towneley: *In blys to dwell*.
242	*neyd thowe crave*. Reg: added by JC, canceling Scribe B's *thus thee I telle*; compare Towneley: *thurt thee crave*.
244	*as*. Reg: interlined by later scribe.
	knave. Reg: written over the Scribe B's *braide*.
253	Line as written at bottom of page, deleted in red ink, and rewritten on next page in Reg.
271	*servauntis*. So LTS, RB; Towneley: *servandys*.
274	*in*. Added in Reg by LH.
301	*movys*. So LTS; Reg: *monys*; RB, after Towneley: *menys*.
342	*selle*. Compare Towneley: *sete*.
347	*dolle*. This edition; Reg: *dolee*; LTS, RB: *dole*.
354	*hundreth*. So Towneley.
375	*in*. So LTS, RB, after Towneley; Reg omits.
378	*saules fro thee be*. Compare Towneley: *thi sayntys to se*.
380	*repleye*. Compare Towneley: *not fle*.
384	*OMNIS*. So RB; Reg, followed by LTS, has *Omnis* as part of dialogue (notruled off from previous speech).
384 s.d.	*Tunc cantent*. Reg: stage direction in LH.
400	*honde*. Reg: Scribe B: *hende*, corrected by LH to *honde*.
408	*etc*. Reg: added in LH at end of line.

38. THE RESURRECTION

1	*PILATUS*. Reg: entered by LH.
52	Reg: line omitted by Scribe B, inserted at right by LH.

68	At left in Reg, by LH: *Hic deficit.*
93	*tremeled, and also manne.* Compare Towneley: *tremlyd as a man.*
147	*menne.* Compare Towneley: *dyscyplys.*
158	*to.* So LTS, RB, after Towneley; Reg omits.
163	Reg adds, interlined in LH after *knightis: Lorde.*
175	*I MILES.* Added by LH in Reg.
186 s.d.	*Tunc Jhesu resurgente.* Reg: stage direction by Scribe B, in red, and, at right, JC's addition *Tunc angelus cantat* Resurgens.
188	*werke.* Compare Towneley: *warlde.*
198	*hym on.* This edition; Reg, LTS: *on hym on;* RB: *on hym.*
217	*II MARIA.* So LTS, RB; Reg: *I Maria;* compare Towneley: *Maria Jacobi.*
245	*his.* So LTS, RB; Reg: *his his.*
254	Reg: at left, by LH: *Et hic deficit* (deleted).
257	*will.* Reg: partially obscured by ink blot.
259	*lende.* So RB; Reg: *layne;* so too LTS who, however, notes *lende* must have been intended (p. 410n).
268	*Man most of myght.* This line, inserted by LTS from Towneley, replaces JC's addition in Reg: *A weryd wight.* Regarded as extra-metrical by RB.
281	*My dede . . . for slayne.* Compare Towneley: *my gylt he was fortayn.*
306	*I MILES.* So RB, after Towneley; Reg, LTS: *III Miles.*
326	*hundereth.* Compare Towneley: *thousand.*
346	*I MILES.* By LH in Reg.
383	*I MILES.* By LH in Reg.
397	*PILATUS.* Canceled but marked *stet* in Reg by LH.
432	*CAIPHAS.* Added and ruled off in Reg by JC.

39. The Appearance of Christ to Mary Magdalen

Craft attribution by JC: *Sledmen;* in another hand: *Palmers.* Also barely legible and canceled handwriting by JC that was noted by RB, indicating connection to the following *Peregrinus* play.

67	*unride.* So RB; Reg, LTS: *unrude.*
85	Reg: at left, by a LH: *Hic deficit.*

40. The Travelers to Emmaus

1	*PERIGRINUS.* So throughout in Reg.
	That. In Reg, letter *T* is sketched in as strapwork initial enclosing outline of a face.
4	Reg: at right in margin by JC: *hic de novo facto.*
6	Reg: *Hic caret* in right margin (deleted).
9	Reg: at right, in margin: *Hic de novo facto.*

11	Reg: at right, in margin: *De novo facto*.
11–12	Lineation as in LTS.
12	*brothere*. So LTS, RB; Reg: *brothe*.
18	*tales*. Reg: letter *s* added by different scribe.
20	*bales*. Reg: letter *s* added by a different scribe.
83	*Forthy*. So RB; LTS: *For-thy*; Reg: *For they*.
85	*of*. Reg: *of of*.
87–88	Reg gives lines to *I Perigrinus*; LTS, RB reassign to *II Perigrinus*.
92	*takkid*. So LTS, RB; Reg: *talkid*.
96	Reg: *thei putte hym* appears at end of line; rearranged by LTS.
107	*bolned*. Letter *l* added by LH.
109	*we*. Reg has *w* written over *h*.
111	*Israell*. So LTS, RB; Reg: *Iraell*.
132	Reg: line 134 mistakenly entered here (deleted).
136–37	Lines reversed in Reg.
151	*dowte*. So RB; Reg, LTS: *dowe*.
after 156	Two lines following are missing in Reg.
159–60	Lines reversed in Reg. LTS suggests adding to beginning of line 159: *To feed theron unterly*.
181	*wais*. Reg: letter *i* interlined by LH.
186	*preche*. Altered from *prechid* in Reg.
	it. Interlined in Reg.
193	*bringe*. RB queries whether *us* or *you* should follow this word.

41. Doubting Thomas

For a complete collation with the Sykes MS, see RB.

1	*to . . . wer*. Compare Sykes: *the . . . are*.
5	*ne*. Compare Sykes: *sens*.
8	*Of oure . . . lange*. Compare Sykes: *And wyth owr lyvys owr lath we lyff so long*.
9	*For sen . . . wrong*. Compare Sykes: *Sens that thes Jewys wroght this wrong*.
25	*oure*. RB, after Sykes: *owr*; Reg, LTS: *youre*.
27–28	Lineation as in RB.
40	*So it us*. This edition, following Sykes: *So yt us*; LTS: *Dois us*; RB: *So is us*.
44	Reg has extraneous *v* to right of line.
46	*may*. So LTS, RB, following Sykes; Reg: *nay*.
56	*Felys*. So Sykes, RB; Reg, LTS: *Folous*.
66	*ete*. Reg: corrected (crudely overwritten) by LH.
71	*here we thee*. Compare Sykes: *we wolde ye*.
83	*remenaunte sone*. Compare Sykes: *remland unto*.
85	*rayst*. So Sykes, RB; Reg, LTS: *dreste*.
90	*Releffe*. So Reg, LTS; RB, following Sykes: *Resave*.

109	*Wan was his . . . wonderus.* So RB, following Sykes; LTS: *Whan lo! as his wondis . . . wondis*; Reg: *Whan lo as wonderus . . . wondis.*
110	*skelpis.* Compare Sykes: *swapis.*
121	*So wofull wightis.* So Sykes, RB; Reg, LTS: *A blistfull sight.*
133	*JOHANNES.* Added LTS, following Sykes.
135	*a trayne.* So Sykes, RB; Reg, LTS: *attrayne.*
167	*no syne.* So RB, following Sykes; Reg, LTS: *sen ye.*
	to. So RB, following Sykes.
179	*more mistrowand.* So Reg, RB; LTS, following Sykes: *more so mystrowand.*
183	Line supplied by LTS from Sykes; Reg omits.
189	*wight.* Written over erasure in Reg.
190	*thou.* So Reg, LTS; RB, following Sykes: *they.*

42. THE ASCENSION

Supplementary ascription to Potters (canceled); indecipherable text under erasure at left.

7–8	*And lele.* Reg: deleted at end of line 7, added to beginning of next line by LH.
14	*yit any.* So RB; Reg, LTS: *it anly.*
29	*Some.* So RB; Reg, LTS: *Come.*
	schulde come is. So RB; Reg: *schulde is.*
92	*clowte.* So RB; Reg, LTS: *lowte.*
107	*same.* So LTS, RB; Reg: *sane.*
115	*One.* This edition, for roman numeral *I* in Reg; RB: *Ane.*
129	*wendand.* So RB; Reg, LTS: *weldand.*
133	*He schall.* Deletion in Reg is reinstated by LH; at left, in LH: *I am* (deleted).
176 s.d.	*Tunc cantat angelus.* Stage direction in right margin, in LH; Reg: *gloria in excelsys deo* deleted, and JC thereafter entered *Ascendo ad patrem meum.*
212	*on.* So LTS, RB; Reg: *no.*
261	*to fordo.* So RB; Reg, LTS: *for to do.*
263–64	Lineation follows LTS.

43. PENTECOST

1	*PETRUS.* Reg: speech tag omitted by Scribe B; *Deus* added (canceled) and *Petrus* inserted, both by later hands.
	Brethir. Reg: strapwork initial *B* sketched in.
13–14	Latin quotations, written in red, are extra-metrical but are numbered in this edition; *judex* interlined in Reg.
15	Reg: at right, JC has written: *Nota a newe clause mayd for the eleccion of an apostle to make the nomber of twelve.*

22	Reg: the line is imperfect (word or words missing).
37	Reg adds at right: *III APOSTOLUS*. So LTS; RB omits.
45	*cum*. So RB; Reg, LTS: *dum*.
98 s.d.	*Angelus tunc cantare*. Reg: stage direction in red ink by Scribe B; *Veni creator spiritus* a later addition, possibly by JC.
99	*MARIA*. Reg: added by LH at right.
106	*he*. So RB; Reg, LTS: *ne*.
135	*singing*. This edition; Reg, LTS, RB: *sigging*.
	LH in right margin in Reg identifies *I Apostolus* as *Petrus*.
152	*we*. So RB; Reg, LTS: *he*.
175	Reg: in left margin, added by JC: *De novo facto* (deleted).
179	Reg: at left, by JC: *Hic de novo facto* (deleted).
197	Reg: by LH, at left: *Nota*.
after 216	Following four lines missing in Reg.
227	Reg: in left margin, by LH: *Hic caret*.
228	In JC's hand in Reg: *loquela de novo facta*.
	Below, in Reg, JC has added to the text of the pageant:

> That with his grace ye may endewe
> And bryng yowe to his companye.

44. THE DEATH OF MARY

1	*Hayle*. In Reg, large capital *H* sketched in.
8	*lente*. So LTS, RB; Reg: *lentthe* (or *lent thee*).
12	*kyng*. So LTS, RB; Reg: *leyng*.
after 27	Following line is missing in Reg.
43	*hente*. So RB; Reg, LTS: *hete*.
66	*Umbelappid*. So LTS, RB; Reg: *Unbelappid*.
82	*hir*. So LTS, RB; Reg: *high*.
90	*felawschip*. So LTS, RB; Reg: *felawschp*.
	atte. Overwritten in Reg.
after 100	Following line is missing in Reg.
104	*for*. So LTS, RB; Reg: *fo*.
114	*daye*. Corrected (from *?deye*) in Reg.
122	*beseke*. So RB; LTS: *be-seke*; Reg: *besoke*.
128	*thy*. So RB; Reg, LTS: *my*.
166	Line misplaced in Reg (after line 163).
191	Misplaced line in Reg (after line 186).
194	*sing*. So LTS, RB; Reg: *see*.
194 s.d.	*Cum uno diabolo*. At right, in red, by Scribe B in Reg.
	Et cantant antiphona, scilicet. Reg: stage direction, in red, by Scribe B.

44A. The Funeral of the Virgin ("Fergus")

Heading and text missing; not entered in the Register.

45. The Assumption of the Virgin (Thomas Apostolus)

Title	*Thomas Apostulus*. Reg: written as title, but also serving to designate speaker.
40	*thei. . . ther*. So RB; Reg, LTS: *the . . . the*.
47	*were*. So LTS, RB; Reg: *we*.
62–63	Reg: added by Scribe B in left margin.
104	Music for *Surge proxima* follows in Reg.
117	Music for *Veni de Libano* follows in Reg.
132	*in*. So LTS, RB; Reg: *an*.
187	*who*. This edition Reg, LTS: *what*; RB: *who in*.
189	*swynke*. So RB; Reg, LTS: *synke*.
208	Music for *Veni electa mea* follows in Reg.
236	*has of-turned*. So RB; Reg, LTS: *of has turned*.
250	*message*. So RB; Reg, LTS: *messages*.
256	Line misplaced in Reg., which places it after line 258.
312	Reg: songs follow, with music: *Surge propera* [sic] *mea* (second version), and *Veni de Libano* (second version).

46. The Coronation of the Virgin

To right of Scribe B's craft ascription, in LH: *Inholderes*.

1	*Myne*. In Reg, large capital *M* sketched in.
	Reg: at right, above, by later hands: *caret*, and *memorandum*.
80 s.d.	*Cantando*. Reg: stage direction in red, at left; music not specified.
113–44	Lines here assigned to Jesus, following RB; assigned in Reg to angels, followed by LTS.

47. Doomsday

4	*I*. Interlined in Reg.
31	*harte*. So RB; Reg, LTS: *harte and*.
37	*erthe*. Interlined in Reg by later scribe.
87	*waste*. Reg has *s* overwritten by Scribe B.
98	*us*. So LTS, RB; Reg: *vis*.
129	Reg: at left, in different hand: *Nota*.
156	*us*. Reg: interlined by LH.

161–68	Stanza omitted here in Reg, omission marked with large maltese cross and *nota* at right, and text added by Scribe B at the end of the pageant, where it is also so marked with a cross.
169	*III ANGELUS.* Compare Towneley: *I Angelus cum gladio.*
170	*sam.* Initially written *samen* (delete *-en*) in Reg.
175	*wightis.* Compare Towneley: *saules.*
177	*DEUS.* Compare Towneley: *JESUS.*
203	Reg: at left, by LH: *What thay shall have for ther folly.*
205	Reg: at right, in JC's hand: *hic caret o soverand savyour de novo facto.*
209	Reg: at right, JC has again written *de novo facto.*
216 s.d.	*Hic ad sedem . . . angelorum.* Stage direction, by Scribe B, unseparated from Deus' speech in Reg.
228	Reg: at right, by LH: *hic caret,* and *de novo facto.*
after 228	Following four lines are missing in Reg.
229	JC has written at right in Reg: *de novo facta,* and, presumably giving incipit of missing speech, *Alas that I was borne dixit Prima Anima Mala et II Anima Mala.*
230	Reg: JC has written: *de novo facta.*
231	*wofull.* Compare Towneley: *wykyd.*
239	*bale.* Compare Towneley: *batell.*
242	*ire.* Not canceled in Reg, but interlined *care* above (so LTS); compare Towneley: *joy.*
254	*I.* So LTS, RB (after Towneley); Reg omits.
268	*liffe.* Compare Towneley: *luf.*
	to. Interlined in Reg; LTS omits, following Towneley.
289	*presse.* Compare Towneley: *prison.*
290	*payns.* Interlined over canceled *penaunce* in Reg.
309	*DEUS.* Speech designation repeated in Reg at lines 317, 324, 333, and 341.
363	*leste or moste.* Compare Towneley: *the lest of myne.*
372	Reg: at left, by LH: *nota miseremini mei etc.*
380 s.d.	*Et sic facit finem . . . ad locum.* Reg: stage direction in red ink.

APPENDIX: NOTES ON THE DIALECT OF THE YORK CORPUS CHRISTI PLAYS BY PAUL A. JOHNSTON, JR.

The forty-seven plays contained in London, British Library, MS. Add. 35290 might, at first glance, seem to be an easy set of texts in which to examine the language. For one thing, we know their provenance. They come from the city of York, and, while this is by no means a rock-solid assurance that the playwrights were residents of York (even if the actors were), it is highly likely that they were. We also know, at least approximately, in what period they were composed — that is, between the late fourteenth century and 1463–77, when the manuscript was copied.[1] This chronology, however, marks the period which signals the transition from Middle English to Early Modern English, and a number of sound changes are known to have been implemented in those years in this area — e.g., the Great Vowel Shift complex, and the monophthongization of /**ai**/.[2] We would thus expect that, like any manuscript of the period, there would be a fairly large amount of linguistic variation in the corpus, but that on the whole the plays would illustrate an identifiably Northern dialect.

To a large extent, they do, but only up to a point. As the analysis will show, the plays are written in a combination of Northern and Midland dialectal features. Some of the Midland features may be only scribal since it is not uncommon in these plays to find a Midland spelling for a word participating in a Northern rhyme. As my previous analysis of *The Worlde and the Chylde* demonstrated,[3] such "concealed spellings" can be very useful in uncovering the original dialect of a piece of verse because (allowing for the odd near- or slant-rhyme) the rhyme evidence will accord with what the author intended. The picture here, though, is not that simple, since most plays have both rhymes that would only work in a Northern dialect, and others that are exact only in a Midland variety, while the ratio varies from play to play. In any case, most rhymes in these plays could indicate either dialect. Since the syntax and morphology are predominantly Northern, the overall impression is of a series of Northern texts with Midland borrowings, not the other way around.

There are a number of reasons why such a mixed dialect should appear here. First, the North/Midland boundary was not that far away, even if it was not as close as it is in modern times.[4] The hinterland of York, though then the capital of the North, included a large number of Northeast Midland-speaking localities in the southern portion of the West Riding, Lincolnshire, and Nottinghamshire. It is likely that the audience at a major festival such as

---

[1] *York Plays*, ed. Beadle, pp. 10–11.

[2] Kniesza, "Problem of the Merger"; P. Johnston, "English Vowel Shifting," pp. 76–77.

[3] P. Johnston, "Dialect of *The Worlde and the Chylde*."

[4] Kristensson, *Survey of Middle English Dialects*, p. 238; McIntosh, Samuels, and Benskin, *Linguistic Atlas*, 1:464. Airedale was probably Northern-speaking throughout the valley, so Leeds, Bradford, and other localities in the Central West Riding were on the Northern side of the line. These were not major centers compared to York, however.

Corpus Christi in what was then England's second city included those from both Northern-
and Midland-speaking areas, and it would be logical that a stage dialect was used which was
a mixture of the two.

In addition, farther afield, York enjoyed important religious (as the seat of an archbishop),
trade, and political connections with London, especially at a time where, for twenty-four years,
the crown was in the hands of the House of York. This would have naturally led to a flow of
York-based civil servants and other professionals to the capital but also, over time, to a two-way
connection.

Thirdly, while it is too early to talk about the influence of Standard English, and Stan-
dard-based judgments concerning the nature of "proper English," there was already a largely
Midlands- and London-based movement to koinéize written English as witnessed first by the
Central Midlands Standard (CMS)[5] used by Wyclif and his followers, and later, by other writers wishing to emulate Wyclif in using a medium that would be easily understood by readers
over a wide geographic zone. Still later, we see the growth of Chancery English,[6] the direct
ancestor of Standard English and a hybrid of CMS and London norms, used first by the civil
service when they started to write records in the vernacular, then by the business community,
and also by printers such as William Caxton and Wynkyn de Worde. This reason might account for the greater incidence of Midland spellings than Midland rhymes already, since
CMS and its descendants were primarily written rather than spoken dialects at this point.

Finally, there is already evidence, even from Scotland, that the use of non-Northern forms
was associated with a more formal "high-style" tone as the prestige of London-area writers
such as Geoffrey Chaucer, John Gower, and John Lydgate was already present. The heyday
of the Scottish Chaucerians such as William Dunbar and Gavin Douglas postdates all but the
very latest emendations and additions to the play manuscript.[7] But Robert Henryson also used
Chauceresque forms, and he is very nearly contemporary with playwrights/revisers such as the
York Realist. The alliterative form in which some of the plays are written also was associated
with the Midlands, albeit the West Midlands of Langland and the *Gawain/Pearl*-poet, which has
a far more localized and distinctive dialect than the East Midlands. The reason for admixture
could be any, several, or all of these, but an exploration of the type as well as the frequency of
Midland borrowings could shed light on which of these reasons is the strongest.

1. THE TEXTS AND THEIR CLASSIFICATION

Since there is so much variation in the play cycle, a linguistic analysis theoretically could
determine which plays, or which parts of plays in several cases, might have been written by
the same author. To do this, one would have to compile full profiles of the type used in the
Linguistic Atlas of Late Middle English and compare each text to every other text.[8] However,
a smaller-scale survey, using rhyme evidence as the most likely to be authorial, will nevertheless serve to advance our knowledge, providing at least useful hypotheses about attribution that will refine or exclude previous suppositions.

---

[5] See Samuels, "Some Applications of Middle English Dialectology."

[6] Fisher, *Emergence of Standard English*, pp. 36–64.

[7] Jack, "Language of Literary Materials," p. 232.

[8] I am in fact working on a book-length study, which shall cover each play in the cycle, instead
of only a sample.

In the past, much of the interest in the York cycle has concentrated on the plays that employ the alliterative long line as the basic structural unit. There are a number of such alliterative plays in the cycle with irregular meters (by modern standards), a fact first discovered by Alex Hohlfeld, who assigned Plays 28 (*The Agony and Betrayal*), 30 (*The First Trial before Pilate*, with the Dream of Pilate's Wife), 31 (*The Trial before Herod*), and 33 (*The Second Trial before Pilate*), together with part of Play 29 (the section of *The Trial before Cayphas and Anna* having to do with Peter's denial of Christ) to a single group.[9] Charles Mills Gayley added a number of plays to this group, but the only addition subsequent researchers such as W. W. Greg or E. K. Chambers have unanimously agreed on is Play 26 (*The Conspiracy*). These were assigned to a putative playwright/reviser called the York Realist, or sometimes the Great Dramatist,[10] who worked in the second quarter of the fifteenth century, in all likelihood the latest period of composition of the plays. Some credit the York Realist with writing other material also, such as the *Hail* sequences in *Herod Questioning the Three Kings and the Offering of the Magi* (Play 16), and at the end of *The Entry into Jerusalem* (Play 25).[11] Gayley believed that he reworked all of the Passion Play sequence but *The Last Supper* (Play 27).[12]

Greg and Chambers saw other alliterative plays as belonging to a different author, entitled the Great Metrist, who worked slightly earlier than the Realist. The Metrist also often uses the long alliterative line, but often seems to use a hybrid form, utilizing extensive alliteration but with regular syllabic meters. The *Mortificacio Christi* (Play 36) is the play that is most consistently assigned to this author, but Greg added *The Creation through the Fifth Day* (Play 2), and *Doomsday* (Play 47) to this group, while Chambers added *The Travelers to Emmaus* (Play 40), *The Death of Mary* (Play 44), and *The Assumption of the Virgin* (Play 45) as well.[13] Reese points out that some of these plays are really syllabic in structure, however,[14] and that there is at least one alliterative play, Play 39, *The Appearance of Christ to Mary Magdalen*,[15] not assigned to either group. Reese also tries to separate the Metrist's and Realist's plays by frequency of types of lines with three alliterations instead of four, since the most frequent pattern is four alliterations per line for both supposed authors. He found that the alliteration sequences *xaaa* and *aaxa* are more frequent as a second choice in works attributed to the Metrist, while the Realist favors *aaax*. There is too much overlap, however, for a hard-and-fast distinction to be made, as the "Realist" Plays 26, 28, and 31 have *xaaa* as the second most-frequent pattern, while the "Metrist" Play 36 has *aaax*.

---

[9] Hohlfield, "Die Altenglischen Kollektivmisterien," p. 248; Reese, "Alliterative Verse in the York Cycle," p. 640.

[10] Gayley, *Plays of Our Forefathers*, pp. 154–60; Greg, "Bibliographic and Textual Problems," pp. 291–92; Chambers, *English Literature at the Close of the Middle Ages*, p. 29; Reese, "Alliterative Verse in the York Cycle," pp. 640 and 643.

[11] Reese, "Alliterative Verse in the York Cycle," p. 649.

[12] Gayley, *Plays of Our Forefathers*, pp. 157–58; see also Reese, "Alliterative Verse in the York Cycle," p. 642. Greg believed Play 33 to be another reworked play from the early fifteenth century ("Bibliographical and Textual Problems").

[13] See Reese, "Alliterative Verse in the York Cycle," pp. 642, 644, and 646–47; Greg, "Bibliographical and Textual Problems," p. 289n1; Chambers, *English Literature at the Close of the Middle Ages*, p. 29.

[14] Reese, "Alliterative Verse in the York Cycle," p. 649.

[15] According to my analysis, Play 39 is only semi-alliterative.

It must be noted that none of the earlier researchers founded their hypotheses on the similarity of dialect forms in the texts attributed to one author or the other. Could these features be used to test the attribution of the texts? Since all the plays mentioned but *The Creation through the Fifth Day* were copied by Scribe B, there is at least a good possibility that any other similarities and differences reflect authorial practices, or at least those of a late reviser, which the Realist is supposed to have been. To test for attribution, it is necessary to include (1) those plays assigned by any authority to either the Metrist or the Realist, even if other scholars disagree, to see if such assignments bear any weight, and (2) a control group of plays in the same area of the cycle, to make sure that such similarities and differences are not simply scribal. Table I shows the groupings which could be used to test attribution.

TABLE I: GROUPING OF PLAYS ARRANGED BY PREVIOUS ATTRIBUTION

GROUP A — GENERALLY ATTRIBUTED TO THE YORK REALIST:
Play 16(b)	"Hails" in *Herod Questioning the Three Kings and the Offering of the Magi* (lines 309–44)
Play 25(b)	"Hails" in *The Entry into Jerusalem* (lines 489–544)
Play 26	*The Conspiracy*
Play 28	*The Agony and Betrayal*
Play 29(b)	"Peter's Denial" in *The Trial before Cayphas and Anna* (lines 104–46 and 170–395)
Play 30	*The First Trial before Pilate*
Play 31	*The Trial before Herod*
Play 33	*The Second Trial before Pilate*
Play 34(a)	*The Road to Calvary* (Stanza 1, lines 1–7)

GROUP B — GENERALLY ATTRIBUTED TO THE YORK METRIST:
Play 2	*The Creation through the Fifth Day*
Play 36	*Mortificacio Christi*
Play 40	*The Travelers to Emmaus*
Play 44	*The Death of Mary*
Play 45	*The Assumption of the Virgin*
Play 47	*Doomsday*

GROUP C — OCCASIONALLY ATTRIBUTED TO THE REALIST AND/OR THE METRIST:
Play 17(e)	Repetitive sequences in *The Purification of the Virgin* (lines 320–39, 354–73, 378–93, and 438–60)
Play 34(b)	*The Road to Calvary* (remainder)
Play 35	*Crucifixio Christi*
Play 37	*The Harrowing of Hell*
Play 38	*The Resurrection*

GROUP D — CONTROL GROUP PLAYS:
Play 25(a)	*The Entry into Jerusalem* (remainder)
Play 27	*The Last Supper*

Play 29(a)	*The Trial before Cayphas and Anna* (remainder)
Play 32	*The Remorse of Judas*
Play 39	*The Appearance of Christ to Mary Magdalen*
Play 41	*Doubting Thomas*
Play 42	*The Ascension*
Play 43	*Pentecost*
Play 46	*The Coronation of the Virgin*

Upon analysis, the categories proposed in Groups A, B, and C are lacking in credibility. While previous scholars have discussed alliterative and syllabic-meter plays as if they were two discrete groups — and this division played a great role in their attribution[16] — in actual fact there is something more like a continuum. There are plays which are purely alliteratively structured, usually employing the long line and with the alliteration even being evident on unstressed syllables; most of Group A and some of Group B fall into this category. There are others that use regular alliteration, but the alliteration largely coincides with syllabic-metrical peaks, resulting in a hybrid system, with the alliteration "used as ornamentation."[17] There are syllabic plays with two and/or three alliterative syllables in most lines, illustrating some rough familiarity with the alliterative style (which I here call *semi-alliterative*), and there are others where alliteration plays no role, or next-to-no role whatsoever, and which are thus in purely syllabic verse. Yet the above categories lump together different types into the same group, and not just with the Control Group plays, which one might expect to be heterogeneous; among the Metrist plays, Plays 2, 36, and 45 are hybrids, while 40 and 44 are fully alliterative, and 47 uses only partial alliteration.

Secondly, some plays are exceedingly complex, containing several changes in line and stanza length, necessitating testing if a change from one stanza type to another correlates with a change in alliteration frequency or not. In some cases, the different parts match in their alliterative structure. This is true of Plays 40 and 44, for instance, each of which use two stanzaic types, but the material in one type of stanza is just as fully alliterative as that in the other. Play 32, on the other hand, has both fully alliterative and semi-alliterative sections, with even a burst, probably due to corruption of the text, of purely syllabic verse.[18] The small sections of Plays 16 (where most of the rest is hybrid), 17, and 29 (where it is syllabic) that are attributed to one or the other playwright have already been separated from the rest, but even here, the litany-like sections of Play 17, which are admittedly rough, are hybrid, and only the other two are fully alliterative.

According to my reckoning, the breakdown of examined texts by alliteration type results in the breakdown found below in Table II, which presents Table I attributions in the column at the right. Note that, even without considering the linguistic content of the plays but relying on the alliteration type alone, the general theories of attribution are called into question, especially where the identity of the Metrist is concerned. We are left with the possibility that either a given playwright was capable of varying their style (and why not, one may ask) or that there were multiple "Metrists" involved.

---

[16] Reese, "Alliterative Verse in the York Cycle," p. 646; *York Plays*, ed. Beadle, pp. 475–76.

[17] Reese, "Alliterative Verse in the York Cycle," p. 646.

[18] See *York Plays*, ed. Beadle, p. 449.

TABLE II: TEXTS ARRANGED BY ALLITERATION TYPE AND ATTRIBUTION GROUP

GROUP E — FULLY ALLITERATIVE PLAYS: TABLE I ATTRIBUTION

Play 16(b)	"Hails" in *Herod Questioning the Three Kings and the Offering of the Magi* (lines 309–45)	A
Play 25(b)	"Hails" in *The Entry into Jerusalem* (lines 489–544)	A
Play 26	*The Conspiracy*	A
Play 28	*The Agony and Betrayal*	A
Play 29(b)	"Peter's Denial" in *The Trial before Cayphas and Anna* (lines 118–46 and 170–395)	A
Play 30(a)	*The First Trial before Pilate* (lines 1–156)	A
Play 30(b)	*The First Trial before Pilate* (lines 157–346)	A
Play 31	*The Trial before Herod*	A
Play 32(a)	*The Remorse of Judas* (lines 1–55)	D
Play 32(b)	*The Remorse of Judas* (lines 56–129 and 335–64)	D
Play 33	*The Second Trial before Pilate*	A
Play 34(a)	*The Road to Calvary* (Stanza 1, lines 1–7)	A
Play 40(a)	*The Travelers to Emmaus* (lines 1–152)	B
Play 40(b)	*The Travelers to Emmaus* (lines 153–90)	B
Play 44(a)	*The Death of Mary* (lines 1–63, 72–182, and 187–94)	B
Play 44(b)	*The Death of Mary* (lines 64–71 and 183–86)	B

GROUP F — HYBRID PLAYS:

Play 2	*The Creation through the Fifth Day*	B
Play 17(e)	Repetitive sequences in *The Purification* (lines 320–39, 354–73, 378–93, and 438–60)	C
Play 32(c)	*The Remorse of Judas* (lines 130–283)	D
Play 36	*Mortificacio Christi*	B
Play 37	*The Harrowing of Hell*	C
Play 43	*Pentecost*	D
Play 45	*The Assumption of the Virgin*	B

GROUP G — SEMI-ALLITERATIVE PLAYS

Play 27	*The Last Supper*	D
Play 29(a)	*The Trial before Cayphas and Anna* (remainder)	D
Play 34(b)	*The Road to Calvary* (remainder)	C
Play 35	*Crucifixio Christi*	C
Play 39	*The Appearance of Christ to Mary Magdalen*	D
Play 47	*Doomsday*	B

GROUP H — PURELY SYLLABIC PLAYS:

Play 25(a)	*The Entry into Jerusalem* (remainder)	D
Play 38	*The Resurrection*	C
Play 41	*Doubting Thomas*	D

| Play 42 | *The Ascension* | D |
| Play 46 | *The Coronation of the Virgin* | D |

We see that, relying on alliterative type alone, without considering linguistic structure, the attribution of the Group A plays to a single author is still reasonable, but not the Group B plays, which include fully alliterative, hybrid, and semi-alliterative plays. The plays attributed to the Realist are all fully alliterative, although they do utilize a number of different stanzaic types. As one might expect, the Control Group is diverse, with the writers using alliteration only secondarily, if at all, while Plays 37 and 38, which Gayley believes the Realist "remodelled," probably do not belong to him. Reese, following Greg and Chambers, is probably right to reject this attribution.[19]

Concerning the Metrist plays, however, we are left with a number of interpretations. There might not be a single Metrist, but rather a number of different playwrights involved who really have nothing in common with each other. Alternatively, there may be a Metrist, possibly the person who wrote or revised Plays 40 or 44 or both; however, some of the plays attributed to him are not his. On the other hand, if there were a single Metrist, we have to suppose that he was versatile enough to write in both alliterative, or at least hybrid, verse and syllabic verse. Further linguistic analysis might tell us the answer to this.

It must be said that this breakdown is really a starting point in our search for similarities and differences. Before exploring the rhyme evidence in my final section, however, I will proceed to describe the dialectal features that are found in the spellings of the plays, both ones where the texts of the plays seem to agree, and those that are more variable. These will constitute a mini-grammar of Yorkshire dialect of the late Middle English period — a dialect which tends to be conservative syntactically (at least in poetry) and innovative morphologically and phonologically, more akin in those respects to mainstream Early Modern English than, say, Chaucerian English or pre-Chaucerian Middle English.

2. THE FEATURES OF YORKSHIRE PHONOLOGY IN THE FIFTEENTH CENTURY: NORTHERN AND MIDLAND CONSONANTAL CHARACTERISTICS

In the next two sections, I will discuss in general what the spellings reveal about the phonology of the York dialect at the time when these plays were composed. In this analysis I have been guided by the glossary in Beadle's edition of *The York Plays* along with my own observations of frequency made during my study. The statements made here refer to the corpus as a whole, unless otherwise indicated, and prominence is given to the sort of "occasional spellings" that form so much of the evidence on which traditional handbooks rely and which are, as the term implies, largely infrequent.

2.1 General Orthographical Characteristics

As usual in a manuscript from this period, <i> and <y> are virtually interchangeable, often with <y> found around letters made up of minims to break up any "forest of lines" that might appear if <i> were used. Whether used to represent consonants or vowels, <u>

---

[19] Gayley, *Plays of Our Forefathers*, p. 157; Reese, "Alliterative Verse in the York Cycle," p. 642.

and <v> obey a rule whereby the shape <v> is found initially, and usually though not invariably <u> is present medially.

The letters <þ> and <ȝ> still exist, but with restrictions. Thorn appears mostly for the initial consonant of *th-* pronominals and common adverbials — words such as *the, that, this, there, then,* and so on — and appears much less frequently in other words but never in final position. Since it is rare around the letter <y>, it is likely that thorn had its usual Northern <y>-like form with an open loop. Yogh is quite frequent for initial /j/, alternating with <y yh> and occasionally is found for /x/ in <xt> combinations (particularly in <noȝt>), but is nowhere as frequent as <gh> for this sound.

2.2 Consonantal Phonemic Inventory

In English, the consonantal system is more stable than are the vowels so that many of the consonant values shown by the orthography in the plays are similar to other dialects of English at the time, particularly Older Scots. Like that dialect, the phonemic inventory was probably the stops /**p b t d k g**/ and affricates /tʃ dʒ/; the fricatives /**f** v θ ð **s z** ʃ **h~x**/; the nasals /**m n**/ and probably /ŋ/ by this time; and the approximants /**l r j w**/, with /ʍ/ as a possibility </**xw**/>. There are, however, some traces of earlier developments that are suggestive of a strong Norse adstratum, and a few imported Southern features.

2.3 The Stops and Affricates

The stops, represented by the same spellings as those found in any Middle English dialect, have not changed much to the present day, and exhibit very few developments that require comment: stop + stop clusters such as /kt/ are sometimes simplified to /k/ (*contek, convik*), and forms like *accept* for past participle *accepted* could indicate that /pt/ > /p/, if this is not a direct importation from Latin *acceptum*. The sequences /d/.../r/ and /ð /.../r/ interchange quite freely, a situation that produced the pronunciation of Standard *father*. In York, the solution is mainly in favor of /d/ in all cases (so *mother* becomes *modir*, etc.), but there are a few counter-examples such as *elthers* for *elders*. There are a few interesting examples of <th> spellings where we would expect a <t>. The word *tidings* can give *thiding-, thithynges, tythandes* (with confusion of verbal noun and participle forms), and <t> and <th> alliterate sporadically. Shetlandic and Orcadian, both dialects spoken in old Norse territory, have /θ/ and /ð/–stopping now, as did Gallovidian at this time;[20] it is conceivable that York dialect had once had it, but was losing it.

More salient is the presence of /k/ sounds where southern dialects have /tʃ/ and a parallel /g/ for /j/, a still noticeable trait of Northern English and Scots. This is not due to sound change, however, but use of Norse cognates rather than natively-derived English words. Thus it is really a lexical phenomenon, and one can get doublets, such as *carll* and *chorle*, as well as purely Norse-influenced forms like *skell* for *shell*, *gowling* for *yowling*, and *kirke* for *church*. Again, there are a few Southern borrowings. Alongside the expected *swilke* and *slyke*, you can get *suche* as a minority form.

Apparently /kn/ is retained as a cluster since it alliterates with /k/ rather than /n/: *kende/knave/knele* (Play 26, line 124).

---

[20] P. Johnston, "Older Scots Phonology," pp. 102–03.

A final /t/ is occasionally written as <th>, as in *comforth, fruth (fruit), hurth,* and *perfyth.* It is not clear if this designates a fricative, an aspirated stop, or something else. Glottal stop is common in this position in the modern dialect, but is usually counted as a recent change.

The affricates /ʧ/ and /ʤ/ are spelled <ch> and <j> or <g> (depending on their French spelling, as in Standard English) initially, and <cch> or <tch> and <gg> or <dg> medially after short vowels, with <cch> and <gg> predominating. Besides the usual <saie>, *say* can take forms such as <segge>, which is a Southwestern or West Midland form in origin (compare Old English *secgan*), but this is the only word of this class that can. There is lexically-conditioned devoicing of /ʤ/ in words like *grucche* for *grudge,* but this is probably an extension of a more general rule applying mainly to fricatives.

2.4 The Fricatives

The fricative subsystem exhibits the most distinctively Northern forms of any subsection of the consonants, but also alternative outcomes for some of them. One typically Northern trait is /**v**/-deletion, which happens in Scots also.[21] Examples include *ene (evening), abowne, our (over),* and *nenes (names v. < nevenes).* The first three are fairly widespread in Northern England and Scotland. Still, there seem to be fewer forms reflecting this change than one would expect; perhaps, since it is mainly present in low-style poems in Scots literature,[22] it may have similar connotations here, which might be felt to be inappropriate for this kind of material. Instead, one might find spellings indicating that /**v**/ has devoiced to /**f**/ (see below). /θ/-deletion does not happen here, but /**x**/ is apparently weak and sporadically prone to disappear in /**xt**/ clusters: *dite, hytyng,* and *wyte* for more usual *dight, hyghtyng,* and *wyght* are attested. Otherwise, /**x**/ is retained, and is usually spelled <gh>, or, more rarely in /**xt**/ clusters, <ʒt>.

As in Older Scots, a morpheme-final /**v**/ or /**z**/ seems to be frequently devoiced, as spellings with <ff>, <ss> are quite common, and are responsible for many of the vowel-double consonant-e spellings of the language. This reflex of /**v**/ may compete with the voiced fricative (spelled <u>), so *give* may be *giffe* or *giue~geue.*

There is considerable variation in what spelling is used for /ʃ/ between the various plays. Some works show almost exclusively <sch> in all positions, while others may use <sh> or, medially and finally, <ssh>, which reflects Southern practice. Rarely, <(c)ch> occurs for this sound as in <fecche> = *fish* and possibly <mached>, if this represents *mashed,* which it seems to.

There is evidence of /s/–/ʃ/ interchange in a few cases,[23] certainly in Scribe A's *drynesch* for *dryness,* and perhaps in *asse* = *ask,* though *aske, ax,* and *axke* also occur. The Northern <sal(l)> for *shall* alternates with <s(c)hal(l)>, but the alliteration patterns show that the form with /s/ is the one truest to the author's intentions.

As in modern Yorkshire dialect, initial /**h**/ has seemingly disappeared, though it is mostly present in spelling. The clearest indications of this is the alliteration of /**h**/ with initial vowels; the occasional occurrence of <til> for <to>, which is more frequent before vocalic onsets, before words beginning with /**h**/, and the occasional /**h**/-less spelling.

---

[21] P. Johnston, "Older Scots Phonology," p. 104.

[22] Aitken, "Variation and Variety in Written Middle Scots."

[23] P. Johnston, "Older Scots Phonology," p. 105.

2.5 The Sonorants

Sonorants overall seem to have their modern values, though we usually cannot tell what allophony sonorant phonemes have. Where the nasals are concerned, we are in an area which is innovative as far as homorganic nasal + consonant clusters being simplified to nasals alone, as spellings showing the nasal like <lyme> (for **/mb/**), <fone> (for **/nd/** in *found*) demonstrate. Given this, probably **/ŋg/** has become a simple nasal also. Besides this, only two interesting developments involving the nasals occur: one concerns the cluster **/mn/**, where a **/p/** or, at least, some sort of stop has been inserted in between the two nasals, shown in <dampne, solempnyte>, though **/n/**-less spellings implying modern pronunciation are also found for *damn*. The other one affects **/gn/**, taken in from French, where the <g> apparently nasalized to /ɲ/, as words like *reign, deign, malign, sign*, as well as *dignity*, as revealed by <ngn> spellings. The Scots-type palatal **/n/** only is found in the word *menȝie* = <meyne>, which is sometimes spelled <menȝe, menȝhe> as it is in Scots. Given what happens to words such as *contain*, <contene>, it is more likely that the **/n/** lost its palatal timbre early, but raised the preceding vowel to /e:/.

In the North, **/l/** apparently developed a velar or velarized allophone after back vowels when final or before consonants; this generated /u/ before it, just as /x/ did a century or so earlier, and then dropped to leave a diphthong. The full-blown outcome is already shown by one word, <bowde> = *bold*, but the intermediate stage, with the diphthong preceding the /l/, is found in several examples, such as <stawllis> = *stalls*. The modern dialects of the area traditionally had clear /l/ in other positions.

York dialect is now non-rhotic, but then /r/ seems to have been pronounced except possibly before /s/, as <socery> = *sorcery* attests.

The semivowels **/j/** and **/w/** generally seem to have had their modern values, although there is some **/v/~/w/** interchange, illustrated by examples such as <wochesaff> = *vouchsafe* and <vill> = <will> (aux.). Since Old Norse **/v/** actually was pronounced as [w], we cannot blame the Norse substratum for this alternation; in fact, it is more typical of a belt from Norfolk to Sussex.[24] It may simply be scribal here, as there is a tendency to use <w> in nearly complementary distribution to <v> and <u> when the sound represented is a vowel, and it is easy to extend this to the consonant as well. More typical of Norse areas (though found as far down as Norfolk) is the simplification of **/skw/** to **/sw/** shown by *square* = <sware> and the use of a letter combination beginning with <q> to represent **/hw/**. <Qw> is the traditional spelling of this sound, occurring sporadically, but <wh> is by far the most common representation. Also there is one hyper-form which reveals that **/hw/** was becoming **/w/**, namely <whe> = *weigh*, which also shows monophthongization of the vowel.

3. THE FEATURES OF YORKSHIRE PHONOLOGY IN THE FIFTEENTH CENTURY: NORTHERN AND MIDLAND VOCALIC CHARACTERISTICS

By the fifteenth century, Northern English and Older Scots were beginning to diverge, particularly in vocabulary, syntax, and orthographical representations of local pronunciation. However, the systems are still close enough that Aitken and Macafee's classification

---

[24] McIntosh, Samuels, and Benskin, *Linguistic Atlas*, 1:549.

of vowels,[25] modified only slightly (Table III), can serve as an easy heuristic for describing the shape of Yorkshire vowel systems by assigning numbers (column 1). Pre–Great Vowel Shift values appear in column 2.

TABLE III: KEY FOR DESCRIBING NORTHERN VOWELS (MODIFIED)

VOWEL NO.	PRE-GVS VALUE	EXAMPLE	MAIN SOURCES
LONG VOWELS:			
1	/i:/	*myne* = mine	OE/ON/OF /i:/; OE/ON /y:/
2	/e:/	*sene* = seen ppt.	OE/ON/OF /e: e:o ø: æ:₁/
		felde = field	OE /ɛ/ by HL
2a	(ɪ:/)	*speyr* = speir "ask"	OE /ɪ/ by OSL
3	/ɛ:/	*lene* = lean a.	OE /æ:₂/; OF /ɛ:/
3a	(/ɛ:/)	*bene* = bean	OE /æ:ɑ/
3b	(/ɛ:/)	*ete* = eat	OE/ON/OF /ɛ œ/ by OSL
4	/æ:/ or /a:/	*bane* = bone	OE/ON /ɑ:/
4a	/a:/	*name*	OE/ON/OF /a/ by OSL
5	/ɔ:/	*cole* = coal	OE/ON/OF /ɔ/ by OSL
6	/u:/	*downe*	OE/ON/OF /u:/
7	/ʏ:/	*gude* = good	OE/ON/OF /o:/
DIPHTHONGS:			
8	/ai/	*gayne* = gain	OE /æj ɛj/; ON /ɛɪ œʏ/; OF /ai ɛi/
9	/ɔi/	*boy*	OF /ɔi/; Dutch /ɔ:j/
10	/oi/	*joyne* = join	OF /oi ui/
11	/e:i/	*dye* = die	OE/ON /e:jV/; ON /ø:jV/
12	/ɑu/	*law*	OE /aɣ/, /aw/; OF /au/; OF /aC/; OE /a/ + x OE/ON/OF /a/+/lC/
12a	/ɑu/	*knawe* = know	OE /a:w aɣV a:ɣV/
13	/ɔu/	*growe*	OE /o:w, o:ɣV/; ON/OF / ɔu/; OE /ɔx/; /ɔ/ + /lC/ (rare)
14a	/eu/	*newe* = new	OE /i:w e:ow o:w/; OF /y: eu/
14b	/ɛu/	*bewte* = beauty	OE /æ:aw/; OF /ɛu ɛau/
SHORT VOWELS:			
15	/ɪ/	*bid*	OE/ON /ɪ ʏ/; OF /i/
16	/ɛ/	*bedde* = bed	OE/ON /ɛ/; OF /e ɛ/
17	/a/	*blakkest* = blackest	OE/ON /æ a/; OF /a/

---

[25] Aitken and Macafee, *Older Scots Vowels*, p. 3.

| 18 | /ɔ/ | *God* | OE/ON/OF /ɔ/ |
| 19 | /ʊ/ | *sonne* = sun | OE/ON /ʊ/; OF /**u**/ |

3.1 The Most Salient Northern Features

Numerous phonological isoglosses separate the Northern dialect region from the Midlands. In the modern period, the most important ones involve the old long vowel system and roughly followed the line of the Humber, Wharfe, and Lune before leveling set in during the mid-twentieth century: the STANE/STONE line (Vowel 4 and 12a and related changes; the Northern limit of the early Middle English rounding and raising of /ɑː/ to /ɔː/); the SPUNE/SPOON line (Vowel 7; the Southern limit of /oː/ fronting in the thirteenth century); and the OOT/OUT line (Vowel 6; the Northern limit of /uː/ diphthongization). York was on the Northern side of all of these, and the regular developments — [ɪə] for the first two (the second via [ɪʏ] > [ɪə] in the eighteenth century) and [uː] for the last, are in evidence in the *Survey of English Dialects* data for the city.[26] We cannot tell whether diphthongization of /uː/ had taken place at the time of the plays, since both monophthongs and close diphthongs would be spelled <ou, ow>. However, for the other two, spellings implying both Northern and Midland solutions are in evidence in the plays, though for all texts the Midland spelling is much more common: <o(o)> for both vowels alternating with <a(a), ai, ay> for the first and <u> for the second.

In addition, there is another set of isoglosses separating the somewhat transitional North Midland dialects of West Yorkshire and Lindsey from the rest of the Midlands. These are the BLAW/BLOW and AULD/O(U)LD lines (Vowel 12a). Though these are really outcomes of conditioned developments of Vowel 4, they take a more southerly course than the above-mentioned group, dipping down to include Southern Yorkshire, a corner of Nottinghamshire, and the whole of Lindsey within Lincolnshire. The course of these isoglosses may reflect the high-water mark of Northumbrian Old English, as there are a number of vocabulary isoglosses, and the southern limit of a very important morphological isogloss in Middle English, *–is~-es* vs. *–ith~-eth*, is found nearby.

The LANG/LONG isogloss is also associated with Vowel 4, since here the <o> forms result from an /ɑː/ created by a late Old English process called Homorganic Lengthening (HL). Whatever the outcome, the vowel was reshortenened under influence from the inflected forms of the affected words, where the lengthening was blocked in most cases due to syllable division. The lengthening happens before /**mb**/ (*comb, womb*) and /**nd**/ (*land*) as well, but not all the /**amb**/ words reshorten. Lengthening before /**nd**/, though attested in the work of Robert Mannyng, best known for his *Handlyng Synne*, and other Lincolnshire writers, is rare in the plays, though there are a few examples of *honde* (*hand*, with a frequent umlaut plural *hende*), and *stonde* (*stand*), *fonde* (*found* pret.), and *sonde* (*message; something sent*) seem to be usual spellings. In any case, there is a considerable amount of variability in this feature.

Ironically, the change /ɑ/ > /ɔ/ before simple nasal, now as then associated with the West Midlands, was originally Northumbrian, but is only sporadic in the corpus. *Any* and *many*, frequently with <o> in Older Scots,[27] have only <a> here. <Gome> for *game*, attested once,

---

[26] Orton and Halliday, eds., *Survey of English Dialects*; York is listed as Y 19.

[27] Aitken and Macafee, *Older Scots Vowels*, p. 86.

and *tone* for *tane* may belong here, if they are not hyper-Midland spellings associated with the /ɔ:/ reflex of Vowel 4. The nearest place where this backing and rounding can be found natively is Lancashire and perhaps a few villages along the Yorkshire/Lancashire and York-shire/Derbyshire boundary.

Even more variable, even in twentieth-century York dialect, is the outcome of Vowel 11 as in *die, eye* and the inflected forms of *high*. These can either monophthongize to /**e**:/, with simple dropping of /**j**/, as is usual in Scots,[28] or develop, as in most of the Midlands, to /**i**:/, diphthongizing again in the Great Vowel Shift, as in Standard English. Occasionally encoun-tered in the material are <egh> forms for this, and for the /**e**:**xt**/ class like *right, night*, as well as the spelling *he* for *high*.

Open Syllable Lengthening, by which short vowels in open syllables became long, oper-ates in all English dialects, but the farther north one goes, the fewer constraints operate on the rule, and the differences can be quite noticeable. In York, we must assume that the low and low-mid vowels have been lengthened before an early Middle English final –*e*, which disappeared early, but there is variability in the lengthening of Vowel 15 to Vowel 2, which is not constrained by what the next syllable contains. Telltale <e> and <ei, ey> spellings appear in twenty-seven items, though many show <i> as well, and there is no way to tell this lengthening from a lowering without lengthening. However, though forms with modern /i:/ are not found in York today, they are common enough in Scots[29] to mark this change as a Northern one that has receded since the Middle Ages.

3.2 Changes Involving the Long Vowels and Diphthongs

Yorkshire is the focal area for the monophthongization of /**ai**/ to /**a**:/,[30] once thought to be an early change but now felt to be later and influenced by doublets of /**a**:/ and /**ai**/ due to either (1) English and Norse cognates of the same word, e.g., Old English *hál* vs. Old Norse *heill*, existing side by side, or (2) forms going back to earlier /**a**:**j**/ reflexes, with /**j**/ dropped between vowels when a sonorant follows (compare modern Received Pronunciation [fa:] < [faɪə] for a parallel process.[31] Most of the <aCe> spellings for /**ai**/ do indeed occur in pre-sonorant environments, which is supported by the rhymes, parallel Scots developments, and in one case, <june> for *join* (attested in *Survey of English Dialects* for East Yorkshire),[32] monophthongization is found for Vowel 12 as well as 8. It is hard to tell if the <e, ey> in words with –*tain* shows this monophthongization for mid front vowels also, or if it goes back to Vowel 3 or 2 forms in French. The much more frequent converse spellings <ai, ay> for /**a**:/ may be related to the monophthongization in part, but are more likely to reflect the use of <i, y> as a long mark, shared by Older Scots,[33] as <ey, ei> are much more frequently

[28] Aitken and Macafee, *Older Scots Vowels*, pp. 24–25.

[29] Aitken and Macafee, *Older Scots Vowels*, pp. 97–98.

[30] Kniesza, "Problem of the Merger."

[31] Aitken and Macafee, *Older Scots Vowels*, p. 142.

[32] Compare *groan* for *groin* (Orton and Halliday, eds., *Survey of English Dialects*, 1:662, for Y 11).

[33] Aitken and Macafee, *Older Scots Vowels*, p. 66.

found for both /e:/ and /ɛ:/ than any monophthongal spelling and <oy, oi> a little more rarely for Midland or Northern /ɔ:/.[34]

The spellings implying raising of long vowels, which are never in the majority, indicate that at least some Great Vowel Shift changes have taken place, a development supported by rhyme evidence (see Section 5). Surprisingly, there are few spellings supporting the raising of /a:/, since modern dialect evidence suggests that the change may have started in the vicinity,[35] but there are clear indications of the raising of /e:/ particularly before /n/, in <tyne> = *tene*, <wyne> = *ween*, and diphthongization of /i:/ in <heynd, leyffe, leythly> and perhaps <neyne> = *hind n., life, lightly* (without /x/), *nine*.[36] It is not clear if the spelling <tow> for *two*, which occurs only three times, is a transposition, a retention of Old English neuter *tú* or some sort of post-Great Vowel Shift spelling on a Midland base, but *flood* = <flowyd> (alongside <flode> and "native" <flud(d)e>) seems to show the modern West Yorkshire [ʊɪ], which is indeed a post-Great Vowel Shift reflex.

Otherwise, there is frequent interchange of the various subclasses of Vowel 3 with each other and Vowel 2 or 4, explored in detail in Section 5, since the outcome varies so much from play to play. The modern dialect has collapsed the various sources of Vowel 3 and merges it with at least 4a, but in the West Riding dialects next door, the reflexes of vowels lengthened by Open Syllable Lengthening never merge with any original vowel class except in very specific environments such as pre-rhotic position.

3.3 Changes Involving the Short Vowels

A peculiar characteristic in this land of frequent Open Syllable Lengthening involves spellings showing apparent shortening, particularly before the voiceless fricatives /f s/ (including where <ff> spellings alternate with <u> = /v/, e.g., *giffe~giue*) but also before /t d/ and even other consonants. Such shortenings are not unknown in the modern dialect where *make, take* = [mak tak][37] and shortenings of words such as *close, yoke, throat* occur in a number of Scots dialects,[38] but the items in which the vowel-double consonant-e spellings occur are a completely different group of words, *abate, bide, case, chief, (dis)ease, feet, gait, heave, life, live,* and *sweet* among them.

Spellings showing raising of both short and long vowels are attested in the plays, but as far as we know, the two sets of changes have different causes. The raising of short /a/ to /ɛ/ and of /ɛ/ to /ɪ/ is implied by spellings such as <eftyr, contek, fest, gedir, wex, blisse (bless), gytt, ryst>, where in many cases the following consonant is an alveolar or velar obstruent.

[34] One rhyme that could show either a long vowel or a diphthong is in Play 30, Stanza 4: *enioyned/perloined; perloined/troned/honed.* If the rhyme is on [ɔ:], it is a Northern one, with monophthongization; if on [ɔɪ], it is a West Yorkshire one, with diphthongization of lengthened / ɔ:/ to [ɔɪ]/.

[35] P. Johnston, "English Vowel Shifting," pp. 213–17.

[36] *Nine* could conceivably have Vowel 11, by Open Syllable Lengthening of an [ɪi] diphthong to [ei]. If so, <ey> is only a long mark spelling.

[37] Orton and Halliday, eds., *Survey of English Dialects,* 1:1010 and 1012.

[38] P. Johnston, "Older Scots Phonology," p. 85; Aitken and Macafee, *Older Scots Vowels,* p. 86.

This seems to be a favored environment for raising all over North Britain,[39] and in cases such as *after, bless,* and *gather* the raised forms can still be found.

Conversely, /ɛ/ + /r/ has a tendency to lower, giving <ar> spellings at times. This is a fairly frequent change in Old English — it is what gives us our pronunciation of words like *farm* and *barn,* after all — but in this area there was interplay at some point with a lengthening process of /**ar**/ (as in *arm*), giving doublets in Vowel 4, 16, and 17 in modern dialects. The spelling evidence suggests that the lengthening was a later process, with only lowering attested.

4. NORTHERN MORPHO-SYNTACTIC FEATURES

While it would take the space of a medium-sized monograph to do justice to the intricacies of the morphology and sentence structures exhibited in the plays, some of the more common and interesting features can be mentioned here.

Middle English was the time of decay of much of the rich inflectional morphology that characterized the old Germanic languages. The noun and adjective endings for the most part disappeared, destroying the old gender system and the case system. Verbal inflections survived better, particularly if they ended in consonants, but this led to only one ending surviving in the present tense in the North (*–is~–es*) and hence the loss of person and number cues in the verb. Since these simplifications were at least as much the product of language contact as of anything else, the North, which had been highly bilingual after the Viking invasions, was in the lead in these developments.

The result is that, where inflectional morphology is concerned, the plays are nearly at the point of Modern English, though the spellings and frequent use of final *–e* may not show that until one reads the plays and scans them. Nearly every such *–e* is silent, although it still has a tendency to appear in spelling where it once had signified something. In all the plays I examined, for instance, the infinitive overwhelmingly ends in *–e* unless the verbal stem already ends in a vowel — by this point signifying nothing.

There are a number of inflections that do survive, such as the three *–s's*: the noun plural, the possessive, and the third (and, locally, second) person singular present tense ending. The localized form for all these appears to be *–is~–ys,* as in Older Scots, but this alternates with frequent *–es.* It can also be found in other verbal contexts due to a rule called the Northern Subject Agreement Rule, whereby any noun subject, or any subject when separated from the verb, triggers the *–s* ending. One can also get *–is~–es,* a regular outcome of Old English *–as,* in plural imperatives, and occasionally, by extension, into singular ones. Both these cases display much variability, though, and it remains to be seen what conditions besides those mentioned above trigger the ending. Southern *–ith* appears in some plays sporadically.

Weak verbs can take *–id* as a past tense and past participial ending, though, depending on which consonant precedes, this can alternate with both *–t* and *–d,* particularly the latter after sonorants, and all of these alternate with *–ed.*

The present participle *–and(e)* and the verbal noun and gerundive ending *–ing(e)* and *–yng(e)* are kept apart in most cases, though the beginnings of *–ing* being used for both functions, and the confusing of the two is found in some plays.

---

[39] Aitken and Macafee, *Older Scots Vowels*, pp. 84–85.

In all cases, more study is needed to explore which plays are more conservative morphologically and which are more innovative — and whether or not there is any correlation
with increased numbers of Midland forms.

While not strictly a matter of inflectional morphology, all plays share the same personal
pronoun system, variable as to spelling only in a few cases:

> First person — singular: *I, my~mi~myn, me*; plural: *we, oure~owre, vs.*
>
> Second person — singular: *þou~þow(e)~thou~thow*; *þi~thy*; *þe*; plural: *ʒe~ye*;
> *ʒoure~ʒowre~youre~youre, ʒou~ ʒow(e)~you~yow(e)*.
>
> Third person — singular, masculine: *he, his, hym*; feminine: *scho, hir, hir*; neuter: *it, it,
> it*.
>
> Third person — plural: *þei~þai~þey~þay*; *þaire~þare~þer*; *þame~þem*. Southern *hem*
> appears at about the same frequency of other marked Southern forms.

The syntax of the plays, often convoluted because of the demands of meter, alliteration,
and end rhyme, could be the subject of an independent monograph. By way of a general re-
mark, it can be confidently said, however, that the grammar of these works contains highly
conservative Old English-like traits such as a preference for object pronouns to precede the
things of which they are objects, whether verbs or prepositions, combined with innovations
such as the progressive verbal aspect.

5. RHYME EVIDENCE FOR LINGUISTIC VARIATION AMONG THE GROUPS OF PLAYS

Section 5 builds on the previous description of word form and spelling, and focuses on
the important matter of rhyme evidence — and what rhymes can reveal about authorship
and attribution, among other things.

5.1 General Layout and Questions of Attribution

To analyze the rhymes contained within the plays under study, the procedure was first
to collect all rhymes in each play (or each part of the play, in cases where parts were assigned to different groups). These were then categorized by whether they were "general
rhymes" (i.e., those that would work in either dialect); rhymes that would work in Northern,
but not Midland varieties, regardless of what the spelling showed; the opposite, rhymes
working in Midland dialects but not Northern ones; and totally inexact rhymes that would
work in neither dialect — and in most cases, no dialect of English.

A further category, not assigned elsewhere, of "merger rhymes," involving examples
that would work if certain sound changes in progress were assumed to have been completed,
was also added. This category is an important one since one can measure where individual
playwrights or revisers stand with regard to these changes; it thus provides help in both
grouping them and dating them. Light is also shed on how these sound changes worked and
what phonological environments favored or disfavored them. A full subsection is thus devoted to looking closely at these mergers.

To test the value of basing work on attribution plus type and extent of alliteration rather
than the traditional attribution, I have arranged Table IV in two sections. The first classifies
the plays according to Table I above and lists the plays individually. The second classifies
the totals according to the main groups of Table II. The percentages of the different sorts

of rhymes are shown in Table IV, with the abbreviations N = Northern Alone, and M = Midland Alone.

TABLE IV: PERCENTAGE OF RHYME TYPES BY ATTRIBUTION AND ALLITERATION TYPE

GROUP A — GENERALLY ATTRIBUTED TO THE REALIST:

	NUMBER	GENERAL	N	M	INEXACT	MERGER
Play 16(b)	20	85.0%	0.0%	0.0%	5.0%	10.0%
Play 25(b)	24	83.3	4.2	0.0	0.0	12.5
Play 26	88	63.6	12.5	4.6	6.8	10.2
Play 28	104	68.8	11.4	5.8	1.9	12.5
Play 29(b)	73	84.9	4.1	1.4	2.7	8.2
Play 30	228	75.4	7.0	3.1	6.1	7.0
Play 31	134	76.1	6.0	5.9	2.2	11.9
Play 33	156	76.9	9.7	4.5	0.0	7.7
Play 34(a)	7	100.0	0.0	0.0	0.0	0.0
TOTAL	**834**	**75.3**	**8.2**	**4.0**	**3.4**	**9.4**

GROUP B — GENERALLY ATTRIBUTED TO THE METRIST:

	NUMBER	GENERAL	N	M	INEXACT	MERGER
Play 2	42	59.5%	11.9%	0.0%	2.4%	28.6%
Play 36	150	80.0	4.7	5.3	1.3	8.7
Play 40	96	82.3	0.0	3.1	2.1	10.4
Play 44	97	86.6	1.0	3.1	2.1	2.1
Play 45	114	78.9	0.9	3.5	1.8	10.5
Play 47	96	75.0	9.4	2.1	0.0	14.6
TOTAL	**595**	**80.1**	**3.9**	**3.4**	**1.5**	**10.6**

GROUP C — SOMETIMES ATTRIBUTED TO EITHER METRIST OR REALIST:

	NUMBER	GENERAL	N	M	INEXACT	MERGER
Play 17(e)	10	90.0%	0.0%	0.0%	0.0%	0.0%
Play 34(b)	100	81.0	8.0	9.0	2.0	3.0
Play 35	100	74.0	7.0	6.0	2.0	10.0
Play 37	135	79.3	1.5	4.4	1.4	4.4
Play 38	149	79.9	7.4	1.3	1.3	11.4
TOTAL	**494**	**79.0**	**5.7**	**4.9**	**1.6**	**6.6**

GROUP D — CONTROL GROUP:

	NUMBER	GENERAL	N	M	INEXACT	MERGER
Play 25(a)	176	80.7%	4.0%	2.3%	4.6%	9.1%
Play 27	58	67.3	13.8	3.4	5.2	15.5
Play 29(a)	113	79.6	6.2	0.9	3.5	10.7
Play 32	164	76.2	10.4	3.0	5.5	4.9
Play 39	36	75.0	5.6	0.0	2.8	19.4
Play 41	62	82.2	1.6	0.0	0.0	14.6
Play 42	70	80.0	8.6	1.4	1.4	8.6
Play 43	74	77.0	6.8	1.7	1.4	12.2
Play 46	68	88.2	3.0	1.5	0.0	5.9
TOTAL	**821**	**78.8**	**6.2**	**1.8**	**3.3**	**9.6**

By Alliteration Type (see Table II):

E	1114	76.8%	6.8%	3.7%	3.1%	8.6%
F	597	78.4	4.5	3.7	1.8	8.9
G	477	77.6	8.6	3.4	2.3	13.0
H	531	81.0	5.3	1.7	2.3	9.6

Looking first at the General Rhyme column, we see a remarkable degree of uniformity in the percentages of rhymes that would be valid in both Northern and Midland English: the average figure hovers around 75–85% of such rhymes, with only six out of the twenty-nine texts outside of this range, disregarding the two having only ten rhymes or fewer. Though one would assume that the scribe was less important in this regard than the author, it is interesting that the most deviant play is *The Creation through the Fifth Day* (Play 2), the only work among the pageants closely under study here that was copied by Scribe A, with only about 60% general rhymes. It also has both a high degree of Northern-only rhymes and no Midland-only ones, making it the most localized of the plays. As one might expect if the play is a highly vernacular example, the writer was sensitive to ongoing sound changes in progress with a truly enormous figure of 28.6% merger rhymes, which reflect completion of these sound changes. Whether the peculiar profile is scribal or authorial, in no way is it consistent with the rest of the plays ascribed to the York Metrist, or any other play analyzed here, and authorities are right to reject it as a Metrist play unless it was massively reworked.

Also interesting is the fact that Plays 26, 27, and 28 have low scores for general rhymes, if not as low as Play 2, and that they have completely different attributions. Plays 26 (*The Conspiracy*) and 28 (*The Agony and Betrayal*) present related material in the Passion plays and flank the story of *The Last Supper* in Play 27. However, the former two plays show a playwright, presumably the Realist, employing the classic alliterative long line, while Play 27 is syllabic, or rather only semi-alliterative. One can conceive of an author using more than one style, but the semi-alliterative plays look like the work of someone used to writing syllabic-metered poetry trying out alliteration, not the work of a master of the alliterative genre. Again, these plays have high proportions of Northern-only rhymes combined with high ratios of sound change rhymes. Perhaps this points to the later date usually assigned to them. They are also next to each other in the cycle, and that in itself is suspicious as one wonders whether someone, maybe before the final scribe, copied out parts of the cycle that were contiguous. We may be faced here with mere coincidence, but then we would still probably be dealing with two playwrights of similar background and different styles.

Setting aside the short extracts, we have, at the high end of general rhymes, Plays 46 (*The Coronation of the Virgin*) and 44 (*The Death of Mary*) with over 85% general rhymes. Again, we have different styles and attributions. Play 44 is fully alliterative and often ascribed to the Metrist, while 46 is totally syllabic. However, both of these are almost devoid of localized rhymes, and also have few reflecting mergers in progress, which may mark them as older plays. As we have seen, the Metrist may have been capable of utilizing different styles if all the plays usually attributed to him (except Play 2) really were his.

In fact, if one were to single out rhyme characteristics of the Metrist plays from those of the Realist, we could make a generalization that the Metrist is a better rhymer than the Realist and utilizes fewer markedly Northern or inexact rhymes. All of the Metrist plays but Play 44 have quite a noted sensitivity to the sound changes in progress, however. About 8–14% merger rhymes are shown, in fact slightly more on average than the Realist.

The question is: do we have more than one Realist, or Metrist? And where do the "maybe" plays go? Any answer to these questions depends greatly on how versatile we believe these putative playwrights/revisers to be, and for us to be absolutely certain, we would need at least a detailed study of the vocabulary and a total stylistic analysis, using both linguistic and literary methodology. It is easier to make negative than positive statements here — that is, to exclude, rather than to include. Nevertheless, there seems to be no reason at this point to exclude anything here attributed to the Realist that is usually attributed to him except perhaps Peter's Denial in Play 29, and this is highly speculative. The *Hails* are too short to judge, though particularly the sequences at the end of Play 25 "sound like" the Realist's work.

The Metrist is harder to pin down, but the syllabic Play 47, *Doomsday*, written in metrical verse, showcases neither his usual alliterative style nor his lack of localization. Its frequency of Northern rhymes is more like the Realist's, or a work such as Play 38 or 42, so perhaps we are dealing with another person here. If there was a candidate that could be added to his repertoire on the basis of what we have here, it would be *The Harrowing of Hell* (Play 37), but again, given a 4% figure of merger rhymes,[40] any conclusion would be tentative in the extreme.

There is only one linguistic feature that correlates with the extent and type of alliteration: the more alliterative the text is, the more Midland features appear in it: 3.7% for the fully alliterative texts vs. 1.7% for the wholly syllabic ones. The difference is tiny, but it makes perfect sense, seeing that the Midland dialect was the vehicle of the fourteenth-century alliterative revival. These forms may be used conventionally, just as the Scottish makars used Chaucerian language.

5.2 The York Plays and Sound Changes in Progress in the Fifteenth Century

The "merger rhymes" in the plays give a view of the cauldron of sound change that is going on not just in York but in the whole of Britain in the fifteenth century. The Great Vowel Shift is the best known component of the many transformations occurring at this time, by which process Vowel 1 diphthongized to something like [ëi], with Vowel 2 moving into the [i:] slot. Farther down in the system, Vowel 4 raised to either [ɛ:] or something like [ɛæ] (it is [ɪə] today) and Vowel 3 became [e:] or [eɛ], and Vowel 5 moved in parallel, though possibly somewhat later, to [o:] or [oɔ].[41] The gap in the low vowels is filled by Vowel 12, which monophthongizes to [ɑ:].[42] However, in contrast to Southern or Midland dialects, Vowel 7 is a front rounded vowel, and therefore does not push Vowel 6 to diphthongize, so these two nuclei stay where they are for the moment. Vowel 7 eventually does diphthongize to [ɪʊ], coming close enough to Vowel 14a, at [iu], to be able to rhyme with it, though there could not have been a true merger, as the two classes stay separate.[43]

On the whole, except for /ai/ > /a:/ and rarer examples of / ɛɪ ɔɪ **ui**/ > /ɛ: ɔ: **u**:/, the vowel change processes mentioned above do not cause mergers, at least in their first stages. Any rhyming of, say, Vowel 1 with Vowel 2 must be really a near-rhyme, of something like [ɪi] with

---

[40] See, however, Play 44, which comes in at 2.1%.

[41] P. Johnston, "Older Scots Phonology," pp. 84–85.

[42] The one spelling that seems to illustrate this principle is *haales = hauls* in Play 35, but this alternates with *haylls* and probably shows the verb *hale, haul*'s predecessor, instead.

[43] One (near) rhyme may show this diphthongization: *gome/consume* (Play 26), rhymes Vowels 7 and 14a.

[i:], and the proximity of the sounds caused them to be perceived as merged for a time until the diphthongization grew wider, at which point the rhymes of these classes die away. There may be true mergers of Vowels 4 and 3, however, due to the raising of the first, since today both vowels tend to have [ɪə].

However, by far the commonest merger shown in rhymes is of Vowel 3 with Vowel 2, an outcome made difficult to explain by the frequent interplay between the two vowels and by the multiple sources of 3.[44] First, in Anglian dialects, we must count not only /eː/ but "original" or "Germanic" /æː/ as in *needle*, *street* as an /eː/ sound, and so are cases of the French reflex of Latin /aː/ as in *clear* in this area. Second, it is not clear if the various sources of /ɛː/ have fallen together in all positions, particularly because /ɛ/ lengthened by OSL is kept apart in the West Yorkshire dialects next door, and "umlaut" /æː/, which exhibits some interplay with Vowel 2 in Older Scots to the north, with considerable allophony.[45] Traditional modern York dialect does collapse all the sources of Vowel 3 together, but merges it with 2 only before /r/, no matter what the source is. However, Vowels 3 and 2 are kept apart in other environments. Therefore, it is necessary to explore the phonetic environment, especially the consonant following the vowel, to establish what is going on.[46]

Finally, and rarely, Vowel 14a goes to /uː/ after certain consonants, notably /j/ and other palatals, but also after /r/ and occasionally after alveolars. The first two changes are common to most dialects of English now. Table V outlines the patterns of merger spellings by play, attribution group, and alliteration type. The number of spellings, however, is only shown in the group totals; in the lines for the individual plays that which appears is the symbol for the following consonant. In the Post-Great Vowel Shift (Post-GVS) column the affected vowel (V) is given instead (ENV = following consonantal environment), and any patterns by environment are discussed in the text. The symbol # = final position.

TABLE V: PATTERNS OF MERGER SPELLINGS

MERGER	4/8	EI/3	9/5	14/6	6/5	Post-GVS V	Post-GVS ENV	3/2	3a/2	3b/2
GROUP A										
Play 16(b)	-	-	-	-	-	-	-	dl	-	-
Play 25(b)	l	-	-	d	-	-	-	-	-	-
Play 26	-	-	-	-	-	iio	mn#	nr	l	p
Play 28	nn	-	-	r	-	i	n	#lnn	r	rrrr
Play 29(b)	-	-	-	-	n	e	d	l	r	r
Play 30	s	l	s	-	#n	a	k	ddklnnr	rv	rr
Play 31	l	-	-	-	#r	eao	llr	-	-	rv
Play 33	-	-	-	-	n	o (eu)	m#	nnrrrr	rrrrr	-

[44] Vowel 2 has multiple sources too, but the bulk of the native ones (Old Northumbrian /eː eːo/ and /øː/) fell together early, to be joined by French /e/ and, even later, /eː/ from /ɪ/ lengthened by OSL.

[45] Aitken and Macafee, *Older Scots Vowels*, pp. 119–20.

[46] Southern East Riding dialects do merge Vowels 3 and 2 variably, but there does not seem to be any phonological conditioning (Orton and Halliday, eds., *Survey of English Dialects*).

Play 34(a)	-	-	-	-	-	-	-	-	-	-
TOTAL	**4**	**1**	**1**	**1**	**7**	**11**	**11**	**21**	**10**	**10**

GROUP B

Play 2	n	-	-	t	#	ei	dn	#dln	-	krr
Play 36	nd	-	-	-	#n	i	#	lnr	ddr	drr
Play 40	q	z	-	-	-	-	-	dnn	rrr	dr
Play 44	-	-	-	-	-	-	-	d	-	r
Play 45	ndl	ds	-	-	-	-	-	ddnn	rr	dt
Play 47	-	-	-	-	-	ae	t#	ddddnnnr	r	trr
TOTAL	**7**	**3**	**0**	**1**	**3**	**5**	**5**	**22**	**9**	**14**

GROUP C

Play 17(e)	-	-	-	-	-	-	-	-	-	-
Play 34(b)	-	-	-	-	n	-	-	d	r	-
Play 35	l	-	-	-	#	-	-	dddr	rr	r
Play 37	Dl	-	-	-	-	-	-	dr	r	rr
Play 38	snn#	-	-	-	n	-	-	ddddnnn	dD	dD
TOTAL	**7**	**0**	**0**	**0**	**3**	**0**	**0**	**14**	**6**	**5**

GROUP D

Play 25(a)	m	-	-	-	###	n	Ee	d#	#lnn	rrrr
Play 27	-	-	-	j	-	a	r	nnnvrr	r	-
Play 29(a)	ls	-	s	-	-	o	n	n	d	d
Play 32	d	-	-	-	n	ee	##	dnr	-	vr
Play 39	-	-	-	-	-	-	-	dddr	d	rr
Play 41	s	-	-	-	-	ae	r#	tttnr	-	r
Play 42	-	-	-	-	n	-	-	lnnn	r	-
Play 43	-	-	-	-	-	-	-	ddllnrrr	-	r
Play 46	r	-	-	-	-	-	-	nn	-	-
TOTAL	**6**	**0**	**1**	**1**	**6**	**8**	**8**	**37**	**5**	**11**

By far, the most common merger pattern involves the falling together of the descendant of Old English "umlaut /æ:/" which generally is taken as a source of Middle English /ɛ:/ outside of Kentish and London dialects, and with /e:/. It is particularly prevalent in Plays 27, 38, 43, and 47, but is found to some degree in all the plays. It also exhibits noticeable conditioning, with all but five of the ninety-four examples involving positions before voiced alveolar sounds /d l n r/. Where /d n/ and probably /l/ are concerned, we are probably dealing with a raising, which may go back a long way; following /r/ tends to lower preceding vowels, however, so we are perhaps dealing with a lowering of /e:/ here. The same sort of pattern, though a little more restricted, is found in Older Scots poetry of the early sixteenth century in the work of Gavin Douglas.[47]

---

[47] Aitken and Macafee, *Older Scots Vowels*, p. 119.

The other sources of Vowel 3 show some tendency to merge before /d/, particularly in the Metrist's work, but mainly only fall together with Vowel 2 before /r/. We are therefore dealing with a merger of all instances of /ɛ:/ and /e:/ generally in pre-rhotic position, which persists into the twentieth century, as both classes give [ɪə], although there has been some restructuring and replacement of [ɪə] by [ɛə] where Received Pronunciation has this nucleus.

The Post–Great Vowel Shift spellings and those showing /ai/ > /a:/ are identical, twenty-four instances in each case, but they show quite different patterning. The Group C plays show no instances of Post-GVS rhymes, but they do show quite a few monophthongizations, particularly Play 38. The Metrist plays, if we exclude Plays 2 and 47 as suggested above, show the same pattern. Group A and some of D (25(a), 32, and 41) have more Post-GVS rhymes than ones showing monophthongization, while the rest of the D plays have few rhymes showing either change.

Monophthongization seems to be favored overall by alveolar consonants, particularly voiced ones, but also voiceless fricatives, and sonorancy of the following consonant is less of a factor than for the raising of /ɛ:/. This is interesting, because modern examples of the same change usually show monophthongization rates highest before sonorants and in final position, and also have sensitivity to voicing. Evidently, this change had different weighting constraints, and, since vowels are generally lengthened more before consonants high on the sonorancy scale, it must depend less on something like the lengthening of the first element of the diphthong as a cause of monophthongization. Aitken and Macafee mention an early monophthongization of /ai/ before anterior fricatives.[48] Unless we take the view that words such as *save* went through a /saiv/ stage from the earlier /sauv-/, there is no record of this change before /f v/, but it is plain that /s/ and the dental fricatives could foster it, and the sporadic monophthongization of other vowels occurs in the same environments as /ai/ > /a:/.

The Great Vowel Shift has been "taken apart" subsequent to the debate in the 1980s of Roger Lass vs. Robert Stockwell and Donka Minkova about whether or not it really was a chain shift, or even a series of sound changes as we usually understand them.[49] This author is on record as favoring a two-chain solution,[50] with the low- and low-mid vowels in one chain with the raising of /a:/ as the initiator, and the high- and high-mid vowels in a separate, and more co-varying chain. While there are only two plays that have the bottom-half raisings alone (Plays 27 and 30), an important though not crucial piece of evidence for the theory, the changes were favored by different environments. The raising of /a:/ takes place before /r/ or voiceless coronal stops, with the first echoing the Vowel 3/2 merger pattern. The change of /e:/ or /i:/, however, is most common in final position, before sonorants or /d:/, all positions promoting length. If the Great Vowel Shift were a unified process, there would be similarities in conditioning processes between its various stages.

Other mergers are only sporadic, except for the strangest of all, the merger of Vowel 4 with Vowel 5. This happens finally and before /n/, with one case before /r/. In the South, this would be a routine Great Vowel Shift stage, and ironically it works in modern traditional York dialect too, but due to a change that must have appeared in the late eighteenth or nineteenth century. However, it should not happen in the North, because of /o:/-fronting.

---

[48] Aitken and Macafee, *Older Scots Vowels*, p. 67.

[49] Lass, "Vowel Shifts," and Stockwell and Minkova, "English Vowel Shift."

[50] P. Johnston, "Lass's Law and West Germanic Vowel Shifts," and P. Johnston, "English Vowel Shifting," pp. 218–20.

In the Midlands, it technically could, and in any case, the Vowel 4 forms would have to be Midland ones but the modern dialects do not show it: the only word that does is *go*, which takes [uː] in much of the East Midlands and East Anglia.[51] In West Yorkshire, the two classes are separate as [ʊə] and [uː] finally, and [ʊə] and [ʊɪ] before /**n**/. We are left with various hypotheses, none of which are very satisfying: perhaps there were sociolects where, as today in Standard varieties, Middle English /**o**ː/ was never fronted, or perhaps these rhymes were eye-rhymes only, since the two classes are spelled alike for the most part.

While there is much room for further study, it is clear that the plays do furnish us with a snapshot of sorts of the York dialect of the late medieval period and suggest some ways in which other dialects were an influence on it. This implies that the speakers, or at least the literate ones, at this time did not always speak vernacular. Medieval York, which is shown not to have been an island unto itself but rather a city sustained in part by residents originally coming from outside its boundaries, had both Northern and Midland speakers. Writers took advantage of the sociolinguistic variation, though what the social meaning of using forms from each is yet something that needs to be further elucidated. We see a number of sound changes at an early enough time in their life cycle to be conditioned changes, and from examining the rhyme types, we can make some extremely tentative statements about attribution. Apparently, a Realist and a Metrist did exist, though they may not have written every play that modern authorities want to claim for them, and there may be Group C plays that one of them may have written, notably Play 37. The Metrist, in particular, was able to write in several alliterative styles. Alternatively, there seems to be a multitude of playwrights, but more variables require study before the question of which one wrote what plays can be conclusively answered.

---

[51] Trudgill, *Social Differentiation of English in Norwich*, pp. 65–66.

 BIBLIOGRAPHY

The references presented here include works cited in this edition. For an extensive bibliography of medieval drama, theater, and iconography up to 2003, see the following website: <http://www.wmich.edu/medieval/resources/edam/index.html>.

MANUSCRIPTS AND INCUNABULA

Bolton Hours. York, York Minster Library, MS. Add. 2.
Carthusian Miscellany. London, British Library, MS. Add. 37049.
Hore beatissime Virginis Mariae. Rouen: Guillaume Bernard and Jacques Cousin, 1517.
Hymni canori cum jubilo secundum. [*York Hymnal.*] ?1517.
Missale secundum usum ecclesie Eboracensis. Paris: F. Regnault, 1533.
N-Town Plays. London, British Library, MS. Cotton Vespasian D.8.
Oxford, Bodleian Library, MS. Lat. liturg.f.2. (Book of Hours)
Psalter. London, British Library, MS. Add. 54179.
Psalter. Cambridge, Trinity College, MS. O.3.10.
Skryveners [Pageant]. York, York City Archives, MS. Sykes.
Torre, James. *The Antiquities of York Minster.* York, York Minster Library, MS. L1 (7).
———. *Antiquities Ecclesiastical of the City of York.* York, York Minster Library, MS. L1 (8).
York Hours. York, York Minster Library, MS. XVI.K.6.
York Plays. London, British Library, MS. Add. 35290.

PRIMARY SOURCES (PRINTED)

The Ancient Cornish Drama. Ed. and trans. Edwin Norris. 2 vols. Oxford: Oxford University Press, 1859. Reprint, New York: Benjamin Blom, 1968.
Apocalyptic Christianity. Trans. Bernard McGinn. New York: Paulist Press, 1979.
St. Augustine. *The City of God.* Trans. Marcus Dods et al. New York: Random House, 1950.
Bevington, David, ed. *Medieval Drama.* Boston: Houghton Mifflin, 1975.
Biblia Pauperum: A Facsimile and Edition. Ed. Avril Henry. Ithaca, NY: Cornell University Press, 1987.
Biblia Sacra iuxta vulgatam versionem. Ed. Robert Weber. Third ed. Stuttgart: Deutsche Bibelgesellschaft, 1969.
Birgitta of Sweden. *Life and Selected Revelations.* Ed. Marguerite Tjader Harris. Trans. Albert Ryle Kezel. New York: Paulist Press, 1990.
Breviarium ad usum insignis Ecclesie Eboracensis. Ed. S. W. Lawley. 2 vols. Surtees Society 71 and 75. Durham: Andrews, 1880–83.
Brown, Carleton, ed. *Religious Lyrics of the XVth Century.* Oxford: Clarendon Press, 1939.
Caedmon Manuscript of Anglo-Saxon Biblical Poetry: Junius XI in the Bodleian Library. Intro. Israel Gollancz. London: Oxford University Press, 1927.
Cawley, A. C. "The Sykes MS of the York Scriveners' Play." *Leeds Studies in English* 7–8 (1952), 45–80.

The Chester Mystery Cycle. Ed. R. M. Lumiansky and David Mills. 2 vols. EETS s.s. 3 and 9. London: Oxford University Press, 1974–86.

Churchwardens' Accounts of St. Michael, Spurriergate, York, 1518–1548. Ed. C. C. Webb. 2 vols. York: Borthwick Institute, 1997.

The Coventry Corpus Christi Plays. Ed. Pamela M. King and Clifford Davidson. Kalamazoo, MI: Medieval Institute Publications, 2000.

The Creacion of the World: A Critical Edition and Translation. Ed. and trans. Paula Neuss. New York: Garland, 1983.

Cursor Mundi. Ed. Richard Morris. 7 vols. EETS o.s. 57, 59, 62, 66, 68, 99, and 101. 1874–75; reprint, London: Oxford University Press, 1961–66.

Dante Alighieri. *The Divine Comedy*. Trans. Allen Mandelbaum. 3 vols. Berkeley: University of California Press, 1980–84.

Davis, Norman, ed. *Non-Cycle Plays and Fragments*. EETS s.s. 1. London: Oxford University Press, 1970.

Dives and Pauper. Ed. Priscilla Heath Barnum. EETS o.s. 275. London: Oxford University Press, 1976.

Everyman and Its Dutch Original, Elckerlijc. Ed. Clifford Davidson, Martin W. Walsh, and Ton J. Broos. Kalamazoo, MI: Medieval Institute Publications, 2007.

The Fabric Rolls of York Minster. Ed. James Raine. Surtees Society 35. Durham: George Andrews, 1869.

Gospel of Nicodemus. See *The Middle-English Harrowing of Hell and Gospel of Nicodemus*.

Greene, Richard Leighton, ed. *Early English Carols*. Second ed. Oxford: Clarendon Press, 1977.

Happé, Peter, ed. *English Mystery Plays: A Selection*. Harmondsworth: Penguin, 1975.

Holkham Bible Picture Book. Intro. and commentary W. O. Hassall. London: Dropmore Press, 1954.

Holy Bible Translated from the Latin Vulgate. Baltimore, MD: John Murphy, 1914.

Jacobus de Voragine. *The Golden Legend*. Trans. William Granger Ryan. 2 vols. Princeton: Princeton University Press, 1993.

James, Montague Rhodes, ed. *The Apocryphal New Testament*. 1924; reprint, Oxford: Clarendon Press, 1980.

The Lay Folks' Catechism. Ed. Thomas Frederick Simmons and Henry Edward Noloth. EETS o.s. 118. London: N. Trübner, 1879.

The Lay Folks Mass Book. Ed. Thomas Frederick Simmons. EETS o.s. 71. London: N. Trübner, 1879.

Liber Usualis. Tournai: Desclee, 1959.

Love, Nicholas. *Mirror of the Blessed Life of Jesus Christ*. Ed. Michael G. Sargent. New York: Garland, 1992.

Mackay, Christopher S., trans. *The Hammer of Witches: A Complete Translation of the Malleus Maleficarum*, by Heinrich Kramer and Jacob Sprenger. Cambridge: Cambridge University Press, 2009.

Meditations on the Life of Christ. Trans. Isa Ragusa and Rosalie B. Green. Princeton: Princeton University Press, 1961.

Meredith, Peter, and John E. Tailby, eds. *The Staging of Religious Drama in the Later Middle Ages: Texts and Documents in English Translation*. Kalamazoo, MI: Medieval Institute Publications, 1982.

The Middle-English Harrowing of Hell and Gospel of Nicodemus. Ed. William Henry Hulme. EETS e.s. 100. London: Oxford University Press, 1907.

A Middle English Metrical Paraphrase of the Old Testament. Ed. Herbert Kalén and Urban Ohlander. 3 vols. Göteborg: Elanders, 1923–61.

Mirk, John. *Festial*. Ed. Theodor Erbe. EETS e.s. 96. 1905; reprint, Millwood, NY: Kraus Reprint, 1987.

The Mirour of Mans Saluacioune: A Middle English Translation of Speculum Humanae Salvationis. Ed. Avril Henry. Philadelphia: University of Pennsylvania Press, 1987.

Missale ad usum insignis Ecclesiæ Eboracensis. Ed. W. G. Henderson. 2 vols. Surtees Society 59–60. Durham: Andrews, 1874.

The Northern Passion. Ed. Frances A. Foster. 2 vols. EETS o.s. 145 and 147. 1913–16; reprint, New York: Kraus Reprint, 1971.

The N-Town Play: Cotton MS Vespasian D.8. Ed. Stephen Spector. 2 vols. EETS s.s. 11–12. Oxford: Oxford University Press, 1991.

The N-Town Plays. Ed. Douglas Sugano. Kalamazoo, MI: Medieval Institute Publications, 2007.

Ordo paginarum. See *Records of Early English Drama: York*.

The Pepysian Gospel Harmony. Ed. Margery Goates. EETS o.s. 157. 1922; reprint, Millwood, NY: Kraus Reprint, 1971.

Plato. *The Collected Dialogues, Including the Letters*. Ed. Edith Hamilton and Huntington Cairns. 1963; reprint, Chicago: University of Chicago Press, 1973.

The Pricke of Conscience. Ed. Richard Morris. Berlin: A. Asher, 1863.

Promptorium Parvulorum sive Clericorum, Dictionarius Anglo-Latinus Princeps. Ed. Albertus Way. 3 vols. London: Camden Society, 1843–65. Reprint, New York: AMS Press, 1968.

Records of Early English Drama: Chester. Ed. Lawrence M. Clopper. Toronto: University of Toronto Press, 1979.

Records of Early English Drama: Coventry. Ed. R. W. Ingram. Toronto: University of Toronto Press, 1981.

Records of Early English Drama: Norwich, 1540–1642. Ed. David Galloway. Toronto: University of Toronto Press, 1984.

Records of Early English Drama: York. Ed. Alexandra F. Johnston and Margaret Rogerson. 2 vols. Toronto: University of Toronto Press, 1979.

Sheingorn, Pamela. *The Easter Sepulchre in England*. Kalamazoo, MI: Medieval Institute Publications, 1987.

Statutes of the Realm. Ed. T. Edlyn Tomlins et al. 11 vols. London: Eyre, 1808–21. Reprint, London: Dawson, 1963.

A Stanzaic Life of Christ. Ed. Frances A. Foster. EETS o.s. 166. London: Oxford University Press, 1926.

Stevens, John, ed. *Mediaeval Carols*. Second ed. London: Stainer and Bell, 1957.

The Towneley Plays. Ed. Martin Stevens and A. C. Cawley. 2 vols. EETS s.s.13 and 14. Oxford: Oxford University Press, 1994.

A Tretise of Miraclis Pleyinge. Ed. Clifford Davidson. Kalamazoo, MI: Medieval Institute Publications, 1993.

York Civic Records. Ed. Angelo Raine and Deborah Sutten. 9 vols. York: Yorkshire Archaeological Society, 1939–78.

York Cycle of Mystery Plays, a Complete Version. Trans. J. S. Purvis. London: SPCK, 1957.

York Memorandum Book A/Y. Ed. Maud Sellers. 2 vols. Surtees Society 120 and 125. Durham: Andrews, 1912–15.

York Memorandum Book B/Y. Ed. Joyce W. Percy. Surtees Society 186. Gateshead: Northumberland Press, 1973.

York Mystery Plays: A Selection in Modern Spelling. Ed. Richard Beadle and Pamela M. King. Oxford: Clarendon Press, 1984.

The York Play: A Facsimile of British Library MS Additional 35290. Intro. Richard Beadle and Peter Meredith. Leeds: University of Leeds School of English, 1983.

York Plays. Ed. Lucy Toulmin Smith. 1885; reprint, New York: Russell and Russell, 1963.

The York Plays. Ed. Richard Beadle. London: Edward Arnold, 1982.

Young, Karl. *The Drama of the Medieval Church*. 2 vols. Oxford: Clarendon Press, 1933.

SECONDARY SOURCES

Anderson, M. D. *Drama and Imagery in English Medieval Churches*. Cambridge: Cambridge University Press, 1963.

Arendt, Hannah. *Eichmann in Jerusalem: A Report on the Banality of Evil*. Rev. ed. New York: Viking Press, 1965.

Aslan, Reza. *No God but God: The Origins, Evolution, and Future of Islam*. New York: Random House, 2005.

Ault, Warren O. "The Village Church and Village Community in Mediaeval England." *Speculum* 45 (1970), 197–215.

Barker, Margaret. *The Great High Priest: The Temple Roots of Christian Liturgy*. Edinburgh: T. and T. Clark, 2003.

Barnwell, P. S., Claire Cross, and Ann Rycraft, eds. *Mass and Parish in Late Medieval England: The Use of York*. Reading: Spire Books, 2005.

Beadle, Richard. "An Unnoticed Lacuna in the York Chandlers' Pageant." In *So Meny People, Longages and Tonges: Philological Essays in Scots and Mediaeval English Presented to Angus McIntosh*. Ed. Michael Benskin and M. L. Samuels. Edinburgh: Benskin and Samuels, 1981. Pp. 229–35.

―――. "The Origins of Abraham's Preamble in the York Play of 'Abraham and Isaac.'" *Yearbook of English Studies* 11 (1981), 178–87.

―――. "The Shipwrights' Craft." In *Aspects of Early English Drama*. Ed. Paula Neuss. Cambridge: D. S. Brewer, 1983. Pp. 50–61.

―――. "Verbal Texture and Wordplay in the York Cycle." *Early Theatre* 3 (2000), 167–84.

Beadle, Richard, and Alan J. Fletcher, eds. *The Cambridge Companion to Medieval English Theatre*. Second ed. Cambridge: Cambridge University Press, 2008.

Beadle, Richard, and Peter Meredith. "Further External Evidence for Dating the York Register (BL Additional MS 35290)." *Leeds Studies in English*, n.s. 11 (1980), 51–58.

Blair, John, and Nigel Ramsay, eds. *English Medieval Industries: Craftsmen, Techniques, Products*. London: Hambledon Press, 1991.

Bonnell, J. K. "The Serpent with a Human Head in Art and in Mystery Play." *American Journal of Archaeology*, second ser. 21 (1917), 255–91.

Brawer, Robert A. "The Characterization of Pilate in the York Cycle Play." *Studies in Philology* 69 (1972), 289–303.

Breeze, Andrew. "The Girdle of Prato and Its Rivals." *Bulletin of the Board of Celtic Studies* 33 (1986), 95–100.

―――. "The Number of Christ's Wounds." *Bulletin of the Board of Celtic Studies* 32 (1985), 84–91.

Briscoe, Marianne G. "Some Clerical Notions of Dramatic Decorum in Late Medieval England." *Comparative Drama* 19 (1985), 1–13.

Brown, Sarah. *York Minster: An Architectural History, c.1220–1500*. Swindon: English Heritage, 2003.

Browne, E. Martin, with Henzie Browne. *Two in One*. Cambridge: Cambridge University Press, 1981.

Browne, John. *The History of the Metropolitan Church of St. Peter, York*. 2 vols. London: Longman, 1847.

Butterworth, Philip. "The York *Crucifixion*: Actor/Audience Relationship." *Medieval English Theatre* 14 (1992), 67–76.

―――. *Theatre of Fire: Special Effects in Early English and Scottish Theatre*. London: Society for Theatre Research, 1998.

―――. *Magic on the Early English Stage*. Cambridge: Cambridge University Press, 2005.

Bynum, Caroline Walker. *The Resurrection of the Body in Western Christianity, 200–1336*. New York: Columbia University Press, 1995.

Carruthers, Mary. *The Book of Memory: A Study of Memory in Medieval Culture*. Cambridge: Cambridge University Press, 1990.

Carter, Henry Holland. *A Dictionary of Middle English Musical Terms*. Ed. George B. Gerhard et al. Bloomington: Indiana University Press, 1961.

Catholic Encyclopedia. Ed. Charles G. Herbermann et al. 15 vols. New York: Appleton, 1907–12.

Cawley, A. C. "Middle English Metrical Versions of the Decalogue with Reference to the English Corpus Christi Cycles." *Leeds Studies in English*, n.s. 8 (1975), 129–45.

Cawley, A. C., Jean Forrester, and John Goodchild. "References to the Corpus Christi Play in the Wakefield Burgess Court Rolls: The Originals Rediscovered." *Leeds Studies in English*, n.s. 19 (1988), 85–104.

Chambers, E. K. *English Literature at the Close of the Middle Ages*. Oxford: Clarendon Press, 1945.

Cheetham, Francis. *English Medieval Alabasters*. Oxford: Phaidon, Christie's, 1984.

Clark, Eleanor Grace. "The York Plays and the Gospel of Nichodemus." *PMLA* 43 (1928), 153–61.

Clopper, Lawrence M. *Drama, Play, and Game: English Festive Culture in the Medieval and Early Modern Period*. Chicago: University of Chicago Press, 2001.

Collier, Richard J. *Poetry and Drama in the York Corpus Christi Play*. Hamden, CT: Archon Books, 1978.

Collins, Patrick J. "Narrative Bible Cycles in Medieval Art and Drama." *Comparative Drama* 9 (1975), 125–46.

Cornell, Henrik. *The Iconography of the Nativity of Christ*. Uppsala: Uppsala Universitets Årsskrift, 1924.

Cox, John D. *The Devil and the Sacred in English Drama, 1350–1642*. Cambridge: Cambridge University Press, 2000.

Craig, Hardin. *English Religious Drama of the Middle Ages*. Oxford: Clarendon Press, 1955.

Craigie, W. A. "The Gospel of Nicodemus and the York Mystery Plays." In *An English Miscellany Presented to Dr. Furnivall in Honour of His Seventy-Fifth Birthday*. Ed. W. P. Ker, A. S. Napier, and W. W. Skeat. Oxford: Clarendon Press, 1901. Pp. 52–61.

Cross, F. L., and E. A. Livingstone, eds. *The Oxford Dictionary of the Christian Church*. Third ed. Oxford: Oxford University Press, 1997.

Crouch, David. "Paying to See the Play: The Stationholders on the Route of the York Corpus Christi Play in the Fifteenth Century." *Medieval English Theatre* 13 (1991), 64–111.

Curtiss, Chester G. "The York and Towneley Plays on *The Harrowing of Hell*." *Studies in Philology* 30 (1933), 24–33.

Daniélou, Jean. *From Shadows to Reality: Studies in the Biblical Typology of the Fathers*. Trans. Wulstan Hibbard. London: Burns and Oates, 1960.

Davidson, Audrey Ekdahl. *Substance and Manner: Studies in Music and the Other Arts*. St. Paul, MN: Hiawatha Press, 1977.

———. "High, Clear, and Sweet: Singing Early Music." In *Sacra/Profana: Studies in Sacred and Secular Music for Johannes Riedel*. Ed. Audrey Ekdahl Davidson and Clifford Davidson. Minneapolis: Friends of Minnesota Music, 1985. Pp. 217–26.

Davidson, Clifford. *From Creation to Doom: The York Cycle of Mystery Plays*. New York: AMS Press, 1984.

———. *Illustrations of the Stage and Acting in England to 1580*. Kalamazoo, MI: Medieval Institute Publications, 1991.

———. "Positional Symbolism and Medieval English Drama." *Comparative Drama* 25 (1991), 66–76.

———. "Northern Spirituality and the Late Medieval Drama and Art of York." In Davidson, *On Tradition: Essays on the Use and Valuation of the Past*. New York: AMS Press, 1992. Pp. 30–55.

———. *Technology, Guilds, and Early English Drama*. Kalamazoo, MI: Medieval Institute Publications, 1997.

———. "Gesture in Medieval British Drama." In Davidson, *Gesture in Medieval Art and Drama*. Kalamazoo, MI: Medieval Institute Publications, 2001. Pp. 66–127.

———. *History, Religion, and Violence: Cultural Contexts for Medieval and Renaissance English Drama*. Aldershot: Ashgate, 2002.

———. *Deliver Us from Evil: Essays on Symbolic Engagement in Early Drama*. New York: AMS Press, 2004.

———. "Memory, the Resurrection, and Early Drama." In Davidson, *Selected Studies in Drama and Renaissance Literature*. New York: AMS Press, 2006. Pp. 3–37.

———. "York Guilds and the Corpus Christi Plays: Unwilling Participants?" *Early Theatre* 9 (2006), 11–33.

———. *Festivals and Plays in Late Medieval Britain*. Aldershot: Ashgate, 2007.

———. "The York Corpus Christi Plays and Visual Piety." *Research Opportunities in Medieval and Renaissance Drama* 46 (2007), 25–50.

———. *Corpus Christi Plays at York: A Context for Religious Drama*. New York: AMS Press, forthcoming.

———, ed. *The Iconography of Heaven*. Kalamazoo, MI: Medieval Institute Publications, 1994.

Davidson, Clifford, and David E. O'Connor. *York Art: A Subject List of Lost and Extant Art*. Kalamazoo, MI: Medieval Institute Publications, 1978.

Davidson, Clifford, and Thomas H. Seiler, eds. *The Iconography of Hell*. Kalamazoo, MI: Medieval Institute Publications, 1992.

Diller, Hans-Jürgen. "The Torturers in the English Mystery Plays." In *Evil on the Medieval Stage*. Ed. Meg Twycross. Lancaster: Medieval English Theatre, 1992. Pp. 57–65.

———. *The Middle English Mystery Play: A Study in Dramatic Speech and Form*. Trans. Frances Wessels. Cambridge: Cambridge University Press, 1992.

Dobson, R. B. "Craft Guilds and the City: The Historical Origins of the York Plays Reassessed." In *The Stage as Mirror: Civic Theatre in Late Medieval Europe*. Ed. Alan E. Knight. Cambridge: D. S. Brewer, 1997. Pp. 91–105.

Dorrell [later Rogerson], Margaret. "The Mayor of York and the Coronation Pageant." *Leeds Studies in English*, n.s. 5 (1971), 35–45.

———. "Performance in Procession: A Medieval Stage for the York Corpus Christi Play." *Leeds Studies in English*, n.s. 6 (1972), 77–111.

Duchesne, L. *Christian Worship: Its Origin and Evolution*. Trans. M. L. McClure. Fifth ed. London: SPCK, 1920.

Duclow, Donald F. "The Virgin's 'Good Death': The Dormition in Fifteenth-Century Drama and Art." *Fifteenth-Century Studies* 21 (1994), 55–86.

Dudley, Martin R. "Sacramental Liturgies in the Middle Ages." In *The Liturgy of the Medieval Church*. Ed. Thomas J. Heffernan and E. Ann Matter. Kalamazoo, MI: Medieval Institute Publications, 2001. Pp. 215–43.

Duffy, Eamon. *The Stripping of the Altars: Traditional Religion in England 1400–1580*. New Haven: Yale University Press, 1992.

Dutka, JoAnna. *Music in the English Mystery Plays*. Kalamazoo, MI: Medieval Institute Publications, 1980.

Dyer, Christopher. *Standards of Living in the Later Middle Ages: Social Change in England, c. 1200–1520*. Rev. ed. Cambridge: Cambridge University Press, 1998.

Elliott, John R., Jr. *Playing God: Medieval Mysteries on the Modern Stage*. Toronto: University of Toronto Press, 1989.

Emmerson, Richard K., and Bernard McGinn. *The Apocalypse in the Middle Ages*. Ithaca, NY: Cornell University Press, 1992.

Epp, Garrett P. J. "Visible Words: The York Plays, Brecht, and Gestic Writing." *Comparative Drama* 24 (1990–91), 289–305.

Erler, Mary C. "Palm Sunday Prophets and Processions and Eucharistic Controversy." *Renaissance Quarterly* 48 (1995), 58–81.

Feasey, Henry John. *Ancient English Holy Week Ceremonial*. London: Thomas Baker, 1897.

Flanigan, Tom. "Everyman or Saint? Doubting Joseph in the Corpus Christi Cycles." *Medieval and Renaissance Drama in England* 8 (1996), 19–48.

Fletcher, Alan J. "The N-Town Plays." In *A Cambridge Companion to Medieval English Theatre*. Second ed. Ed. Richard Beadle and Alan J. Fletcher. Cambridge: Cambridge University Press, 2008. Pp. 183–210.

———. *Drama, Performance, and Polity in Pre-Cromwellian Ireland*. Toronto: University of Toronto Press, 2000.

Florovsky, Georges. "The Work of the Holy Spirit in Revelation." *Christian East* 13 (1932), 49–64.

Foster, Frances A. *A Study of the Middle-English Poem Known as the Northern Passion and Its Relation to the Cycle Plays*. London: Richard Clay and Sons, 1914.

Frampton, Mendal G. "The Brewbarret Interpolation in the York Play the *Sacrificium Cayme and Abell*." *PMLA* 52 (1937), 895–900.

———. "The York Play of *Christ Led up to Calvary* (Play XXXIV)." *Philological Quarterly* 20 (1941), 198–203.

French, Thomas. *York Minster: The Great East Window*. Oxford: Oxford University Press, 1995.

French, Thomas, and David E. O'Connor. *York Minster: The West Windows of the Nave*. Oxford: Oxford University Press, 1987.

Friedman, John B. *Northern English Books, Owners, and Makers in the Late Middle Ages*. Syracuse, NY: Syracuse University Press, 1995.

Gardiner, F. C. *The Pilgrimage of Desire: A Study of Theme and Genre in Medieval Literature*. Leiden: E. J. Brill, 1971.

Gardiner, Harold C. *Mysteries' End: An Investigation of the Last Days of the Medieval Religious Stage*. New Haven: Yale University Press, 1946.

Gee, E. A. "The Painted Glass of All Saints' Church, North Street, York." *Archaeologia* 102 (1969), 151–202.

Gent, Thomas. *The Antient and Modern History of the Famous City of York*. York: Thomas Hammond and A. Bettesworth, 1730.

Gibson, Gail McMurray. "'Porta haec clausa erit': Comedy, Conception, and Ezekiel's Closed Door in the *Ludus Coventriae* Play of 'Joseph's Return.'" *Journal of Medieval and Renaissance Studies* 8 (1978), 137–56.

——. *The Theater of Devotion: East Anglian Drama and Society in the Late Middle Ages*. Chicago: University of Chicago Press, 1989.

——. "Writing before the Eye: The N-Town Woman Taken in Adultery and the Medieval Ministry Play." *Comparative Drama* 27 (1993–94), 399–407.

Goldberg, Jeremy. "Craft Guilds, the Corpus Christi Play and Civic Government." In *The Government of Medieval York: Essays in Commemoration of the 1396 Royal Charter*. Ed. Sarah Rees Jones. York: Borthwick Institute, 1997. Pp. 141–63.

Grantley, Darryll. "The National Theatre's Productions of *The Mysteries*: Some Observations." *Theatre Notebook* 40 (1986), 70–73.

Gray, Douglas. "The Five Wounds of Our Lord." *Notes and Queries* 208 (1963), 50–51, 82–89, 127–34, and 163–68.

——. *Themes and Images in the Medieval English Religious Lyric*. London: Routledge and Kegan Paul, 1972.

Greg, W. W. "Bibliographical and Textual Problems of the English Miracle Cycles. III — Christ and the Doctors: Inter-Relation of the Cycles." *Library*, third ser. 5 (1914), 280–319.

——. *The Trial and Flagellation with Other Studies in the Chester Cycle*. Oxford: Malone Society, 1935.

Guilfoyle, Cherrell. "The Staging of the First Murder in the Mystery Plays in England." *Comparative Drama* 25 (1991), 42–51.

Halbwachs, Maurice. *On Collective Memory*. Trans. Lewis A. Cosner. Chicago: University of Chicago Press, 1992.

Halfpenny, Joseph. *Fragmenta Vetusta; or, the Remains of Ancient Buildings in York*. York: J. Halfpenny, 1807.

Hanks, Dorrel T. "New Sources for York Play XLV, 'The Death of Mary': *Legenda Aurea* and Vincent's *Speculum Historiale*." *English Language Notes* 14 (1976), 5–7.

Hanning, R. W. "'You have begun a Parlous Pleye': The Nature and Limits of Dramatic Mimesis as a Theme in Four Middle English 'Fall of Lucifer' Cycle Plays." In *Drama in the Middle Ages*. Ed. Clifford Davidson, C. J. Gianakaris, and John H. Stroupe. New York: AMS Press, 1982. Pp. 140–68.

Happé, Peter. "Devils in the York Cycle: Language and Dramatic Technique." *Research Opportunities in Renaissance Drama* 37 (1998), 79–98.

Hardison, O. B., Jr. *Christian Rite and Christian Drama in the Middle Ages*. Baltimore, MD: Johns Hopkins Press, 1965.

Harrison, Tony. *The Mysteries*. London: Faber and Faber, 1985.

Heffernan, Thomas J., and E. Ann Matter, eds. *The Liturgy of the Medieval Church*. Kalamazoo, MI: Medieval Institute Publications, 2001.

Hildburgh, W. L. "English Alabaster Carvings as Records of the Medieval Religious Drama." *Archaeologia* 93 (1949), 51–101.

Hill, G. F. "The Thirty Pieces of Silver." *Archaeologia* 59 (1905), 235–54.

Horne, Ethelbert. "The Crown of Thorns in Art." *Downside Review* 53 (1935), 48–51.

Hoskins, W. G. *Local History in England*. Third ed. London: Longman, 1984.

Hourihane, Colum. *Virtue and Vice: The Personifications in the Index of Christian Art*. Princeton: Princeton University Press, 2000.

Hughes, Jonathan. *Pastors and Visionaries: Religion and Secular Life in Late Medieval Yorkshire*. Woodbridge: Boydell Press, 1988.

Humphreys, K. W., ed. *The Friars' Libraries*. London: British Library, 1990.

Inventory of the Historical Monuments in the City of York. 5 vols. London: Royal Commission on Historical Monuments of England, 1962–81.

Ishii, Mikiko. "A Spoon and the Christ Child." In *The Dramatic Tradition of the Middle Ages*. Ed. Clifford Davidson. New York: AMS Press, 2005. Pp. 128–39.

James, Mervyn. "Ritual, Drama and Social Body in the Late Medieval English Town." *Past and Present* 98 (1983), 3–29.

Johnson, Stephen. "The Last Judgment." *Early Theatre* 3 (2000), 259–74.

Johnston, Alexandra F., ed. *Editing Early English Drama: Special Problems and New Directions.* New York: AMS Press, 1987.

———. "What If No Texts Survived? External Evidence for Early Drama." In *Contexts for Early English Drama.* Ed. Marianne G. Briscoe and John C. Coldewey. Bloomington: Indiana University Press, 1989. Pp. 1–19.

———. "Four *York* Pageants Performed in the Streets of York: July 9, 1988." *Research Opportunities in Renaissance Drama* 31 (1992), 101–04.

———. "*The Word Made Flesh*: Augustinian Elements in the York Cycle." In *The Centre and Its Compass: Studies in Medieval Literature in Honor of Professor John Leyerle.* Ed. Robert A. Taylor et al. Kalamazoo, MI: Medieval Institute Publications, 1993. Pp. 225–46.

———. "Traders and Playmakers: English Guildsmen and the Low Countries." In *England and the Low Countries in the Late Middle Ages.* Ed. Caroline M. Barron and Nigel Saul. Stroud: Alan Sutton, 1995. Pp. 99–114.

———. "The City as Patron: York." In *Shakespeare and Theatrical Patronage in Early Modern England.* Ed. Paul Whitfield White and Suzanne R. Westfall. Cambridge: Cambridge University Press, 2002. Pp. 150–75.

———. "The *York Cycle* and the Libraries of York." In *The Church and Learning in Later Medieval Society: Essays in Honour of R. B. Dobson.* Ed. Caroline M. Barron and Jenny Stratford. Donnington: Shaun Tyas, 2002. Pp. 355–70.

Johnston, Alexandra F., and Margaret Dorrell [Rogerson]. "The York Mercers and Their Pageant of Doomsday, 1433–1526." *Leeds Studies in English,* n.s. 6 (1972), 11–35.

Justice, Alan D. "Trade Symbolism in the York Cycle." *Theatre Journal* 31 (1979), 47–58.

Kierkegaard, Søren. *Fear and Trembling and the Sickness unto Death.* Trans. Walter Lowrie. Princeton: Princeton University Press, 1968.

King, Pamela M. "York Plays, Urban Piety, and the Case of Nicholas Blackburn, Mercer." *Archiv* 232 (1995), 37–50.

———. "Corpus Christi Plays and the 'Bolton Hours,' 1: Tastes in Lay Piety and Patronage in Fifteenth-Century York." *Medieval English Theatre* 18 (1996), 46–62.

———. "Contemporary Cultural Models for the Trial Plays in the York Cycle." In *Drama and Community: People and Plays in Medieval Europe.* Ed. Alan Hindley. Turnhout: Brepols, 1999. Pp. 200–16.

———. "The York Plays and the Feast of Corpus Christi: A Reconsideration." *Medieval English Theatre* 22 (2000), 13–32.

———. *The York Mystery Cycle and the Worship of the City.* Cambridge: D. S. Brewer, 2006.

Kinneavy, Gerald Byron. *A Concordance to the York Plays.* New York: Garland, 1986.

Kipling, Gordon. *Enter the King: Theatre, Liturgy, and Ritual in the Medieval Civic Triumph.* Oxford: Oxford University Press, 1998.

Knight, Alan. "Processional Theatre and the Rituals of Social Unity in Lille." In *Drama and Community: People and Plays in Medieval Europe.* Ed. Alan Hindley. Turnhout: Brepols, 1999. Pp. 99–109.

———. "Manuscript Painting and Play Production: Evidence from the Processional Plays of Lille." In *The Dramatic Tradition of the Middle Ages.* Ed. Clifford Davidson. New York: AMS Press, 2005. Pp. 195–202.

Knowles, John A. "The East Window of Holy Trinity, Goodramgate, York." *Yorkshire Archaeological Journal* 28 (1924–26), 1–24.

Köbling, E. "Beiträge zur Erklärung und Textkritik der York Plays." *Englische Studien* 20 (1895), 179–220.

Leach, Arthur F. "Some English Plays and Players, 1220–1548." In *An English Miscellany Presented to Dr. Furnivall in Honour of His Seventy-Fifth Birthday.* Ed. W. P. Ker, A. S. Napier, and W. W. Skeat. New York: Benjamin Blom, 1901. Pp. 205–34.

Lloyd, Megan S. "Reflections of a York Survivor: The York Cycle and Its Audience." *Research Opportunities in Renaissance Drama* 39 (2000), 223–35.

Lovejoy, Arthur O. *The Great Chain of Being: A Study of the History of an Idea*. 1936; reprint, New York: Harper and Row, 1965.

Lyle, Marie C. *The Original Identity of the York and Towneley Cycles*. Minneapolis: University of Minnesota, 1919.

Macaulay, Peter Stuart. "The Play of the Harrowing of Hell as a Climax in the English Mystery Cycles." *Studia Germanica Gandensia* 8 (1966), 115–34.

MacCulloch, J. A. *The Harrowing of Hell: A Comparative Study of an Early Christian Doctrine*. Edinburgh: T. and T. Clark, 1930.

Mâle, Émile. *Religious Art in France*. Trans. Marthiel Mathews. 3 vols. Princeton: Princeton University Press, 1976–86.

Malvern, Marjorie M. *Venus in Sackcloth: The Magdalen's Origins and Metamorphoses*. Carbondale: Southern Illinois University Press, 1975.

Marrow, James H. "*Circumdederunt me canes multi*: Christ's Tormentors in Northern European Art of the Late Middle Ages and Early Renaissance." *Art Bulletin* 59 (1977), 167–81.

———. *Passion Iconography in Northern European Art of the Late Middle Ages and Early Renaissance: A Study of the Transformation of Sacred Metaphor into Descriptive Narrative*. Kortrijk: Van Ghemmert, 1979.

Marshall, John. "'The Crowning with Thorns and the Mocking of Christ': A Fifteenth-Century Performance Analogue." *Theatre Notebook* 45 (1991), 114–21.

Marx, C. W. *The Devil's Rights and the Redemption in the Literature of Medieval England*. Cambridge: D. S. Brewer, 1995.

Massip, Francesc. "The Cloud: A Medieval Aerial Device, Its Origins, and Its Use in Spain Today." In *The Dramatic Tradition of the Middle Ages*. Ed. Clifford Davidson. New York: AMS Press, 2005. Pp. 262–74.

May, Steven. "A Medieval Stage Property: The Spade." *Medieval English Theatre* 4 (1982), 77–92.

McKinnell. John. "The Medieval Pageant Wagons at York: Their Orientation and Height." *Early Theatre* 3 (2000), 79–104.

McLachlan, Elizabeth Parker. "Liturgical Vessels and Implements." In *The Liturgy of the Medieval Church*. Ed. Thomas J. Heffernan and E. Ann Matter. Kalamazoo, MI: Medieval Institute Publications, 2001. Pp. 369–429.

Mellinkoff, Ruth. *The Mark of Cain*. Berkeley: University of California Press, 1981.

———. *Outcasts: Signs of Otherness in Northern European Art of the Late Middle Ages*. 2 vols. Berkeley: University of California Press, 1993.

Meredith, Peter. "The *Ordo paginarum* and the Development of the York Tilemakers' Pageant." *Leeds Studies in English*, n.s. 11 (1980), 59–73.

———. "John Clerke's Hand in the York Register." *Leeds Studies in English*, n.s. 12 (1981), 245–71.

———. "The Iconography of Hell in the English Cycles: A Practical Perspective." In *The Iconography of Hell*. Ed. Clifford Davidson and Thomas H. Seiler. Kalamazoo, MI: Medieval Institute Publications, 1992. Pp. 158–86.

Middle English Dictionary. Ed. Hans Kurath and Sherman Kuhn. Ann Arbor: University of Michigan Press 1952– .

Mill, Anna J. "The York Bakers' Play of the Last Supper." *Modern Language Review* 30 (1935), 145–58.

———. "The York Plays of the Dying, Assumption, and Coronation of Our Lady." *PMLA* 65 (1950), 866–76.

Mills, David. "The Chester Cycle." In *The Cambridge Companion to Medieval English Theatre*. Second ed. Ed. Richard Beadle and Alan J. Fletcher. Cambridge: Cambridge University Press, 2008. Pp. 125–51.

Montagu, Jeremy. *The World of Medieval and Renaissance Musical Instruments*. Newton Abbot: David and Charles, 1976.

Muir, Lynette R. *The Biblical Drama of Medieval Europe*. Cambridge: Cambridge University Press, 1995.

Munson, William F. "Self, Action, and Sign in the Towneley and York Plays on the Baptism of Christ and in Ockhamist Salvation Theology." In *Nominalism and Literary Discourse: New Perspectives*. Ed. Hugo Keiper, Christoph Bode, and Richard J. Utz. Amsterdam: Rodopi, 1997. Pp. 191–216.

Mussetter, Sally. "The York Pilate and the Seven Deadly Sins." *Neuphilologische Mitteilungen* 81 (1980), 57–64.

Nagler, A. M. *The Medieval Religious Stage: Shapes and Phantoms*. New Haven: Yale University Press, 1976.

Nelson, Alan H. "The Temptation of Christ; or, The Temptation of Satan." In *Medieval English Drama: Essays Critical and Contextual*. Ed. Jerome Taylor and Alan H. Nelson. Chicago: University of Chicago Press, 1972. Pp. 218–29.

Nichols, Ann Eljenholm. "The Hierosphithitic Topos, or the Fate of Fergus: Notes on the N-Town *Assumption*." *Comparative Drama* 25 (1991), 29–41.

———. "The Bread of Heaven: Foretaste or Foresight?" In *The Iconography of Heaven*. Ed. Clifford Davidson. Kalamazoo, MI: Medieval Institute Publications, 1994. Pp. 40–68.

———. *Seeable Signs: The Iconography of the Seven Sacraments, 1350–1544*. Woodbridge: Boydell Press, 1994.

Nicholson, R. H. "The Trial of Christ the Sorcerer in the York Cycle." *Journal of Medieval and Renaissance Studies* 16 (1986), 125–69.

Oakshott, Jane. "Experiment with a Long-Range Cue: York Mystery Plays, 1994." *Leeds Studies in English*, n.s. 29 (1998), 249–55.

———. "York Guilds' Mystery Plays 1998: The Rebuilding of Dramatic Community." In *Drama and Community: People and Plays in Medieval Europe*. Ed. Alan Hindley. Turnhout: Brepols, 1999. Pp. 270–89.

O'Connor, David E. "The Bedern Stained Glass." In *The Vicars Choral of York Minster: The College at Bedern*. Ed. Julian D. Roberts. York: Council for British Archaeology, 2001. Pp. 559–75.

Ogden, Dunbar H. "The *Visitatio Sepulchri*: Public Enactment and Hidden Rite." *Early Drama, Art, and Music Review* 16 (1994), 95–102.

Olson, Glending. "Plays as Play: A Medieval Ethical Theory of Performances and the Intellectual Context of *The Tretise of Miraclis Pleyinge*." *Viator* 26 (1995), 195–221.

Oosterwijk, Sophie. "'Long lullynge haue I lorn!': The Massacre of the Innocents in Word and Image." *Medieval English Theatre* 25 (2003), 3–53.

Ostovich, Helen, and Alexandra F. Johnston, eds. *The York Cycle Then and Now*. Special issue of *Early Theatre* 3 (2000).

Owst, G. R. *Literature and Pulpit in Medieval England*. Second ed. 1961; reprint Oxford: Basil Blackwell, 1966.

Oxford English Dictionary. Ed. James Murray et al. Rev. ed. 20 vols. Oxford: Clarendon Press, 1989.

Pagels, Elaine. *The Origin of Satan*. New York: Random House, 1995.

Palliser, D. M. *Tudor York*. Oxford: Oxford University Press, 1979.

Palmer, Barbara D. "'Towneley Plays' or 'Wakefield Cycle' Revisited." *Comparative Drama* 21 (1988), 318–48.

———. *The Early Art of the West Riding of Yorkshire*. Kalamazoo, MI: Medieval Institute Publications, 1990.

———. "The Inhabitants of Hell: Devils." In *The Iconography of Hell*. Ed. Clifford Davidson and Thomas H. Seiler. Kalamazoo, MI: Medieval Institute Publications, 1992. Pp. 20–40.

———. "Corpus Christi 'Cycles' in Yorkshire: The Surviving Records." *Comparative Drama* 27 (1993), 218–31.

———. "Gestures of Greeting: Annunciations, Sacred and Secular." In *Gesture in Medieval Art and Drama*. Ed. Clifford Davidson. Kalamazoo, MI: Medieval Institute Publications, 2001. Pp. 128–77.

Palmer, Barbara D., et al. "The York Cycle in Performance: Toronto and York." *Early Theatre* 1 (1998), 139–63.

Parshall, Peter. "The Art of Memory and the Passion." *Art Bulletin* 81 (1999), 456–72.

Phythian-Adams, Charles. "Ceremony and the Citizen: The Communal Year at Coventry, 1450–1550." In *Crisis and Order in English Towns, 1500–1700*. Ed. Peter Clark and Paul Slack. Toronto: University of Toronto Press, 1972. Pp. 57–85.

Pickering, F. P. *Literature and Art in the Middle Ages*. Coral Gables, FL: University of Miami Press, 1970.

Purvis, J. S. *From Minster to Marketplace*. York: St. Anthony's Press, 1969.

Raby, F. J. E. *A History of Christian-Latin Poetry from the Beginnings to the Close of the Middle Ages*. Second ed. Oxford: Oxford University Press, 1953.

Raine, Angelo. *Mediaeval York: A Topological Survey Based on Original Sources*. London: John Murray, 1955.

Rastall, Richard. "Heaven: The Musical Repertory." In *The Iconography of Heaven*. Ed. Clifford Davidson. Kalamazoo, MI: Medieval Institute Publications, 1994. Pp. 162–96.

———. *The Heaven Singing*. Cambridge: Boydell and Brewer, 1996.

———. *Minstrels Playing*. Cambridge: D. S. Brewer, 2001.

———. "The Mystery Plays 25 Years On." <http://www.leeds.ac.uk/reporter/252/mysteryp.htm> (accessed 7-2-08).

Réau, Louis. *Iconographie de l'art chrétien*. 3 vols. Paris: Presses universitaires de France, 1955–59.

Rees Jones, Sarah. "York's Civic Administration, 1354–1464." In *The Government of Medieval York: Essays in Commemoration of the 1396 Royal Charter*. Ed. Sarah Rees Jones. York: Borthwick Institute, 1997. Pp. 108–40.

Reese, Jesse Byers. "Alliterative Verse in the York Cycle." *Studies in Philology* 48 (1951), 639–68.

Reiss, Edmund. "The Story of Lamech and Its Place in Medieval Drama." *Journal of Medieval and Renaissance Studies* 2 (1972), 35–48.

Remnant, Mary. "Musical Instruments in Early English Drama." In *Material Culture and Medieval Drama*. Ed. Clifford Davidson. Kalamazoo, MI: Medieval Institute Publications, 1999. Pp. 141–94.

Robb, David M. "The Iconography of the Annunciation in the Fourteenth and Fifteenth Centuries." *Art Bulletin* 18 (1936), 480–526.

Robbins, Rossell Hope. "Levation Prayers in Middle English Verse." *Modern Philology* 40 (1942), 131–46.

Robinson, J. W. "The Art of the York Realist." *Modern Philology* 60 (1963), 241–51.

———. "The Late Medieval Cult of Jesus and the Mystery Plays." *PMLA* 80 (1965), 508–14.

———. *Studies in Fifteenth-Century Stagecraft*. Kalamazoo, MI: Medieval Institute Publications, 1991.

Rogerson, Margaret. "Living History: The Modern Mystery Plays in York." *Research Opportunities in Renaissance Drama* 43 (2004), 12–28.

Rubin, Miri. *Corpus Christi: The Eucharist in Late Medieval Culture*. Cambridge: Cambridge University Press, 1991.

Rushforth, Gordon McN. *Medieval Christian Imagery*. Oxford: Clarendon Press, 1936.

———. "Seven Sacraments Compositions." *Antiquaries Journal* 9 (1929), 83–100.

Russell, Jeffrey Burton. *Satan: The Early Christian Tradition*. Ithaca, NY: Cornell University Press, 1981.

Scarisbrick, J. J. *The Reformation and the English People*. Oxford: Basil Blackwell, 1984.

Schapiro, Meyer. *Late Antique, Early Christian, and Mediaeval Art: Selected Papers*. New York: George Braziller, 1979.

Schiller, Gertrud. *Iconography of Christian Art*. Trans. Janet Segilman. 2 vols. Greenwich, CT: New York Graphic Society, 1971.

Schmitt, Natalie Crohn. "The Body in Motion in the York *Adam and Eve in Eden*." In *Gesture in Medieval Art and Drama*. Ed. Clifford Davidson. Kalamazoo, MI: Medieval Institute Publications, 2001. Pp. 158–77.

Scott, Kathleen L. *Later Gothic Manuscripts, 1390–1490*. 2 vols. London: Harvey Miller, 1996.

Seiler, Thomas H. "Filth and Stench as Aspects of the Iconography of Hell." In *The Iconography of Hell*. Ed. Clifford Davidson and Thomas H. Seiler. Kalamazoo, MI: Medieval Institute Publications, 1992. Pp. 132–40.

Sharp, Thomas. *A Dissertation on the Pageants or Dramatic Mysteries Anciently Performed at Coventry*. Coventry: Merridew and Son, 1825.

Sheingorn, Pamela. "The Moment of the Resurrection in the Corpus Christi Plays." *Medievalia et Humanistica*, n.s. 11 (1982), 111–29.

———. "The Te Deum Altarpiece and the Iconography of Praise." In *Early Tudor England: Proceedings of the 1987 Harlaxton Symposium*. Ed. Daniel Williams. Woodbridge: Boydell Press, 1989. Pp. 171–82.

———. "'Who can open the doors of his face?' The Iconography of Hell Mouth." In *The Iconography of Hell*. Ed. Clifford Davidson and Thomas H. Seiler. Kalamazoo, MI: Medieval Institute Publications, 1992. Pp. 1–19.

Shorr, Dorothy C. "The Iconographic Development of the Presentation in the Temple." *Art Bulletin* 28 (1946), 17–32.

Skey, Miriam. "Herod's Demon Crown." *Journal of the Warburg and Courtauld Institutes* 40 (1977), 274–76.

Snyder, Susan. "The Left Hand of God: Despair in Medieval and Renaissance Tradition." *Studies in the Renaissance* 12 (1965), 18–59.

Spector, Stephen. "Anti-Semitism in the English Mystery Plays." *Comparative Drama* 13 (1979), 3–16.

Spinrad, Phoebe S. *The Summons of Death on the Medieval and Renaissance Stage*. Columbus: Ohio State University Press, 1987.

Stanton, Anne Rudloff. *The Queen Mary Psalter: A Study of Affect and Audience*. Philadelphia, PA: American Philosophical Society, 2001.

Steiner, Ruth. "Note on the Transcriptions." See Wall, "York Pageant XLVI and Its Music."

Stevens, John. "Music in Mediaeval Drama." *Proceedings of the Royal Musical Association* 84 (1957–58), 81–95.

———. "The Music of Play XLV: The Assumption of the Virgin." In *The York Plays*. Ed. Richard Beadle. London: Edward Arnold, 1982. Pp. 465–74.

Stevens, Martin. *Four Middle English Mystery Cycles: Textual, Contextual, and Critical Interpretations*. Princeton: Princeton University Press, 1987.

Sullivan, Mark R. "The Missing York Funeral of the Virgin." In *The Dramatic Tradition of the Middle Ages*. Ed. Clifford Davidson. New York: AMS Press, 2005. Pp. 150–54.

Swanson, Heather. "The Illusion of Economic Structure: Craft Guilds in Late Medieval English Towns." *Past and Present* 121 (1988), 29–48.

———. *Medieval Artisans: An Urban Class in Late Medieval England*. Oxford: Basil Blackwell, 1989.

Tilley, Morris Palmer. *Dictionary of the Proverbs in England*. Ann Arbor: University of Michigan Press, 1950.

Tillott, P. M., ed. *A History of Yorkshire: The City of York*. London: Oxford University Press, 1961.

Tiner, Elza C. "English Law in the York Trial Plays." In *The Dramatic Tradition of the Middle Ages*. Ed. Clifford Davidson. New York: AMS Press, 2005. Pp. 140–49.

———, ed. *Teaching with the Records of Early English Drama*. Toronto: University of Toronto Press, 2006.

Trexler, Richard C. *The Journey of the Magi: Meanings in History of a Christian Story*. Princeton: Princeton University Press, 1997.

Tristram, E. W. *English Wall Painting in the Fourteenth Century*. London: Routledge and Kegan Paul, 1955.

Turner, Ralph V. "*Descendit ad Inferos*: Medieval Views on Christ's Descent into Hell and the Salvation of the Ancient Just." *Journal of the History of Ideas* 27 (1966), 173–94.

Turville-Petre, T. *The Alliterative Revival*. Cambridge: D. S. Brewer, 1977.

Twycross, Meg. "'Places to hear the play': Pageant Stations at York, 1398–1572." *REED Newsletter* (1978), 10–33.

———. "The Flemish *Ommegang* and Its Pageant Cars." *Medieval English Theatre* 2 (1980), 15–41 and 80–98.

———. "Playing 'The Resurrection.'" In *Medieval Studies for J. A. W. Bennett*. Ed. P. L. Heyworth. Oxford: Clarendon Press, 1981. Pp. 273–96.

———. "Apparell Comely." In *Aspects of Early English Drama*. Ed. Paula Neuss. Cambridge: D. S. Brewer, 1983. Pp. 30–49.

———. "'With what body shall they come?': Black and White Souls in the English Mystery Plays." In *Langland, the Mystics, and the Medieval Religious Tradition: Essays in Honour of S. S. Hussey*. Ed. Helen Philips. Cambridge: D. S. Brewer, 1990. Pp. 271–86.

———. "Forget the 4:30 a.m. Start: Recovering a Palimpsest in the York *Ordo paginarum*." *Medieval English Theatre* 25 (2003), 98–152.

———. "The *Ordo paginarum* Revisited, with a Digital Camera." In *"Bring furth the pagants": Essays in Early English Drama Presented to Alexandra F. Johnston*. Ed. David N. Klausner and Karen Sawyer Marsalek. Toronto: University of Toronto Press, 2007. Pp. 105–31.

Twycross, Meg, and Sarah Carpenter. *Masks and Masking in Medieval and Early Tudor England*. Aldershot: Ashgate, 2002.

Wall, Carolyn. "York Pageant XLVI and Its Music (With a Note on the Transcriptions by Ruth Steiner)." *Speculum* 46 (1971), 689–712.

Wallis, J. P. R. "The Miracle Play of 'Crucifixio Cristi' in the York Cycle." *Modern Language Review* 12 (1917), 494–95.

Walters, Barbara R., Vincent J. Corrigan, and Peter T. Ricketts. *The Feast of Corpus Christi*. University Park: Pennsylvania State University Press, 2006.

Warner, George. *Queen Mary's Psalter: Miniatures and Drawings by an English Artist of the Early Fourteenth Century*. London: British Museum, 1912.

Warner, Marina. *Alone of All Her Sex: The Myth and the Cult of the Virgin Mary*. London: Weidenfeld and Nicolson, 1976.

Watson, Arthur. *The Early Iconography of the Tree of Jesse*. Oxford: Oxford University Press, 1934.

Wayment, Hilary. *The Stained Glass of the Church of St. Mary, Fairford, Gloucestershire*. London: Society of Antiquaries, 1984.

Wee, David L. "The Temptation of Christ and the Motif of Divine Duplicity in the Corpus Christi Cycle Drama." *Modern Philology* 72 (1974), 1–16.

Wells, Minnie. "The Age of Isaac at the Time of the Sacrifice." *Modern Language Notes* 54 (1939), 579–82.

White, Eileen. "Places for Hearing the Corpus Christi Play in York." *Medieval English Theatre* 9 (1987), 23–63.

———. "Places to Hear the Play in York." *Early Theatre* 3 (2000), 49–78.

White, Sheila. "A Psychodynamic Perspective of Workplace Bullying: Containment, Boundaries, and a Futile Search for Recognition." *British Journal of Guidance and Counseling* 32 (2003), 269–80.

Whiting, Bartlett Jere, and Helen Wescott Whiting. *Proverbs, Sentences, and Proverbial Phrases from English Writings Mainly before 1500*. Cambridge: Harvard University Press, 1968.

Williams, Rowan. *Why Study the Past? The Quest for the Historical Church*. Grand Rapids, MI: Eerdmans, 2005.

Wilson, Adrian, and Joyce Lancaster Wilson. *A Medieval Mirror: Speculum humanae salvationis 1324–1500*. Berkeley: University of California Press, 1984.

Woolf, Rosemary. "The Effect of Typology on the English Mediaeval Plays of Abraham and Isaac." *Speculum* 32 (1957), 805–25.

———. "The Theme of Christ the Lover-Knight in Medieval English Literature." *Review of English Studies*, n.s. 13 (1962), 1–16.

———. *The English Religious Lyric in the Middle Ages*. Oxford: Clarendon Press, 1968.

———. *The English Mystery Plays*. Berkeley: University of California, 1972.

Young, James M. "The York Pageant Wagon." *Speech Monographs* 34 (1967), 1–20.

Zimbardo, Philip. *The Lucifer Effect: Understanding How Good People Turn Evil*. New York: Random House, 2007.

DIALECT STUDIES

Aitken, A. Jack. "Variation and Variety in Written Middle Scots." In *Edinburgh Studies in English and Scots*. Ed. A. Jack Aitken, Angus McIntosh, and Herman Pálsson. London: Longman, 1971. Pp. 177–209.

Aitken, A. Jack, and Caroline Macafee. *The Older Scots Vowels: A History of the Stressed Vowels of Older Scots from the Beginnings to the Eighteenth Century*. Guildford: Scottish Text Society, 2002.

Chambers, E. K. See entry in previous section.

Cowling, George H. *The Dialect of Hackness, North-east Yorkshire*. Cambridge: Cambridge University Press, 1915.

Ellis, Alexander J. *Early English Pronunciation*. 5 vols. EETS e.s. 2, 7, 14, 23, and 56. London: Trübner, 1869–89.

Fisher, John H. *The Emergence of Standard English*. Lexington: University Press of Kentucky, 1996.

Gayley, Charles Mills. *Plays of Our Forefathers and Some of the Traditions upon Which They Were Founded*. New York: Duffield, 1907.

Greg, W. W. "Bibliographical and Textual Problems of the English Miracle Cycles. III — Christ and the Doctors: Inter-Relation of the Cycles." *Library*, third ser. 5 (1914), 280–319.

Hohlfeld, Alex. "Die Altenglischen Kollektivmisterien: Unter besonderer Berücksictigung des Verhältnisses der York- und Towneley-spiele," *Anglia* 11 (1889): 219-310.

Jack, Ronald D. S. "The Language of Literary Materials: Origins to 1700." In *The Edinburgh History of the Scots Language*. Ed. Charles Jones. Edinburgh: Edinburgh University Press, 1997. Pp. 213–63.

Johnston, Paul A., Jr. "Lass's Law and West Germanic Vowel Shifts." *Folia Linguistica Historica* 10.2 (1989), 199–261.

———. "English Vowel Shifting: A Great Vowel Shift or Two 'Small Vowel Shifts'?" *Diachronica* 9 (1992), 189–226.

———. "The Dialect of *A Tretise of Miraclis Pleyinge*." In *A Tretise of Miraclis Pleyinge*. Ed. Clifford Davidson. Kalamazoo, MI: Medieval Institute Publications, 1993. Pp. 53–84.

———. "Older Scots Phonology and Its Regional Variation." In *The Edinburgh History of the Scots Language*. Ed. Charles Jones. Edinburgh: Edinburgh University Press, 1997. Pp. 47–111.

———. "The Dialect of *The Worlde and the Chylde*." In *The Worlde and the Chylde*. Ed. Clifford Davidson and Peter Happé. Kalamazoo, MI: Medieval Institute Publications, 1999. Pp. 118–21.

Jordan, Richard. *Handbook of Middle English Grammar: Phonology*. Fourth ed. Trans. Eugene J. Crook. The Hague: Mouton, 1974.

Kniesza, Veronika. "The Problem of the Merger of Middle English /a:/ and /ai/ in Northern English." In *Current Topics in English Historical Linguistics*. Ed. Michael Davenport, Erik Hansen, and Hans Frede Nielsen. Odense: Odense University Press, 1983. Pp. 95–102.

———. "<ai> and <a> in Medieval Northern English Manuscripts." *Folia Linguistica Historica* 3.1 (2003), 45–53.

Kristensson, Gillis. *A Survey of Middle English Dialects 1290–1350: The Six Northern Counties and Lincolnshire*. Lund: C. W. K. Gleerup, 1967.

Lass, Roger. "Vowel Shifts: Great and Otherwise; Remarks on Stockwell and Minkova." In *Luick Revisited: Papers Read at the Luick-Symposium at Schloss Liechtenstein, 15.–18.9.1985*. Ed. Dieter Kastovsky and Gero Bauer. Tübingen: Gunter Narr, 1988. Pp. 395–410.

Luick, Karl W. *Studien zur Englischen Lautgeschichte*. 2 vols. 1898; reprint, New York: Johnson, 1964.

McIntosh, Angus, M. L. Samuels, and Michael Benskin, eds. *A Linguistic Atlas of Late Mediaeval English [LALME]*. 4 vols. Aberdeen: Aberdeen University Press, 1986.

Moorman, Frederick W. *Yorkshire Dialect Poems, 1673–1915*. 1915; electronic reprint, David Fawthrop and David Widger, 2009: <www.gutenberg.org>, ebook #2888.

Orton, Harold. *The Phonology of a South Durham Dialect: Descriptive, Historical, and Comparative*. London: Kegan Paul, Trench and Trübner, 1933.

Orton, Harold, and Wilfred A. H. Halliday, eds. *The Survey of English Dialects*. Vol. 1: *Basic Material: The Six Northern Counties and the Isle of Man*. 3 parts. Leeds: E. J. Arnold and Son, 1962.

Reese, Jesse Byers. "Alliterative Verse in the York Cycle." *Studies in Philology* 48 (1951), 639–68.

Samuels, M. L. "Some Applications of Middle English Dialectology." In *Middle English Dialectology: Essays on Some Principles and Problems*. Ed. Angus McIntosh, M. L. Samuels, and Margaret Laing. Averdeen: Aberdeen University Press, 1978. Pp. 67–80.

Stockwell, Robert, and Donka Minkova. "The English Vowel Shift: Problems of Coherence and Explanation." In *Luick Revisted: Papers Read at the Luick-Symposium at Schloss Liechtenstein, 15.–18.9.1985*. Tübingen: Gunter Narr, 1998. Pp. 355–93.

Trudgill, Peter. *The Social Differentiation of English in Norwich*. Cambridge: Cambridge University Press, 1974.

Wales, Katie. *Northern English: A Social and Cultural History*. Cambridge: Cambridge University Press, 2006.

Wright, Joseph. *A Grammar of the Dialect of Windhill, in the West Riding of Yorkshire*. 1892; reprint, London: Caffin, 2008.

———. *English Dialect Grammar*. London: Henry Frowde, 1905.

GLOSSARY

In keeping with the practice of the METS editions, the Glossary is a word-list intended for easy use. For musical terminology, see the Explanatory Notes.

Abacuc *Habbakuk*
abakke *back, away*
abaste, abayst, abasshed *afraid*
abatte, abate *abate, slacken, terminate*
abatyng *hesitation*
abedyn *awaited*
abowne *above*
aby, abie *abide, pay*
accordance, accordyng *appropriate*
accorde *agree*
actone *jerkin (as undergarment)*
adawe *to death*
adred, adreed *afraid*
adrygh *stand aside*
afferde *afraid*
affie *trust*
affraied *frightened, disturbed*
affraye, affrayse *trouble, assault*
agaste *fearful*
agayne *against*
aghe *ought*
alde *old*
algate *in all respects*
alkynne *every kind*
allegge *expound*
allone, allane *only, alone*
als *as*
amende *improve*
amisse, amys *amiss, wrongly*
an, and *if*
Ancilla *maid servant*
ane *one*
anes *once*
anlepy *solitary*

apas *apace*
aperte, appertly, appertely *openly*
appeyre *challenge*
appose, apose *question*
are, arr *ere, before*
arely *early*
arow *afraid*
array (n.) *manner, garment*
array (v.) *dress, arrange, cooperate*
arrore *error*
as armes *to arms*
asith *restitution*
aspise *consider*
assay, assaie, assaye *test, challenge, assault, undertaking*
assemeling *assembling*
assendid *ascended*
assewe *follow*
assize *assize, court session*
astonys *astonishes*
attaynte, atteynted *convict(ed)*
aughen *own*
aught *ought*
auter *altar*
avaunted *boasted*
avise *advise, consider*
avoutry, avoutery *adultery*
avowe *promise*
avoyde *gone away*
awe *ought*
awne *own*
ax, axe, asse *ask*
ay *always*
aylastand *everlasting*

ayles, eyles *ails, troubles*
aysell *vinegar*

babb *baby*
badd, bade *bade, ordered*
baile, baill, bale *custody*
balde *bold*
bale (n.) *belly*
bale, bayle, balys, baill (n.) *misery,*
   misfortune
balke *timber*
bande(s) *bond(s), rope(s)*
bandome *bondage, power*
bane (n.) *demise, slayer*
bane(s) (n.) *bone(s)*
banne *curse*
bare *bore*
bared *unclothed*
barely *to the extreme*
barenhede *time of childhood*
barett, barette *strife, anguish*
bargayne *undertaking, process*
barkis *bursts*
barne(s) *child, children, man, men*
bary *beat*
bathe *both*
batterand *battering, beating*
bay *obey*
baye *shout*
bayne *willing, obedient*
baynely *now, obediently*
bedene *altogether*
bedene, bydene *now, forthwith*
beede *prayer, prayer beads*
beflapped *beaten, bruised*
begyle(d) *beguile(d)*
beheste, beheest *promised*
behete *promise*
behewed *colored*
behoves *should, ought*
bekenne, bekende *beckon(ed), identify,*
   identified, summon(ed)
beldand(e), beeldande *supporting,*
   dwelling
belde, beelde, beilde *protect, support,*
   dwell, build, remain in a place
belder *protector*

beltid *enclosed*
belyng *bellowing*
belyve, belyffe *quickly, suddenly*
bemene(s) *signify, signifies*
bemes *beams, rays*
bende *oblige, bound*
bene *bean*
benke *bench*
bente *place*
berde *lady*
berde *beard*
bere *bier*
bere *noise*
bere(s), beris *bear(s), carry, carries*
bering *bearing, birth*
beriyng *burying*
berk *bark, shout*
berne, bernes, bernys *boy(s), knight(s),*
   people
bese, besse *be*
beseke *beseech*
besettis *assails*
besie, besye *busy*
best, beestes, beistes *beast(s)*
betake *entrust, commit*
Betannye *Bethany*
bete, bett(is), bette (v.) *beat(s), beaten*
bete, beat, beete (v.) *relieve, comfort*
bete (adv.) *quickly*
bethoughte *contrived*
betidde, betyde *happened (to)*
betyng *beating*
betyng *reward*
bewschere, bewscheris *good sir, good*
   men
bewtes, bewteis *beauties, virtues*
bib (v.) *drink*
bid, bedde, byd *bid, order, given*
bidand *abiding*
bidding *command, commandment*
bide *abide, endure, wait*
bigly *commodious, large, perfect*
binde *oblige, tie up*
birde *lady*
birrall *beryl*
bittir *cruel*
blad *blade, sword*

blak, blake *black*

blanne *stopped*

blaw, blawe *blow*

blayne *boil, sore*

bledand *bleeding*

blee *countenance, attitude*

blemysght *swollen, disfigured, fatally hurt*

blenke *radiance*

bletyng *bleating*

bliss *bless*

bliste, blyste *blessed*

blithe *happy*

blo, bloo *dark, discolored, livid*

blonderande *whirling*

blondre *dissension*

blore *boasting*

blowes, blawes, blowen *vent(s)*

blowne *vented*

blude *blood*

blur, blure *lament, bluster*

blynnande *declining*

blynne *relieve, cease, conclude, decline, end*

bodes, bodis *bodes, commands*

bodis *bodies*

bodus *forebodes*

bodword, bodeword, boodword *message*

boght, bought *purchased, ransomed*

bolned *swollen*

bolning *swelling*

bone, boone *request, reward*

bonis *bones, relics*

boone *bound, caught*

borde(s), bourde, burde *sport(s), joke(s)*

bordyng *idle talk*

bore *bore hole*

borowe(d) *redeem(ed)*

bost, boste *boast*

bostyng *boasting*

bot, bott *but*

bote, boote *help, remedy, redemption*

botht *both*

botment *remedy*

boudisch *sullen*

boundand *going*

boune (v.) *going*

boune, bon(n)e, bowne, bun(e) (adj.) *obligated, bound, tied, prepared*

bourde, bowrde *jest*

bourdeyne *burden*

bourdyng *entertainment, enjoyment*

boure(s) *bower(s)*

bowand *bowing*

bowde *very confident, bold*

bowe (n.) *bow (of a ship)*

bowe (n.) *rainbow*

bowe (n.) *bough*

bowe (v.) *bow, submit*

bowne *obliged*

bowrde, bourde *jest*

bowsom *buxom*

boy, boye *fellow (pejorative)*

boyste *box, container*

brade *broad, broadly*

bragges *large nails, spikes*

braide, brayde, brayede (n.) *attack, affliction, torment*

brake, brak *break, broke*

bralland *brawling*

brande *sword*

brasshis *blows*

braste *burst(s)*

brathe, brayth *angry, eager*

brathely *painfully*

brawle *brawler*

brawlis, brawlest *causes disorder, brawls*

brawlyng *rioting, misbehaving*

brayde (v.) *hasten*

brede *bread*

brede *breadth;* **on brede** *on every side*

breke, brekis *break(s)*

brennand *burning*

brenne, brent *burn(ed)*

brere *briar(s)*

breste (n.) *complaints*

breste, bristis (v.) *burst(s), smash(es)*

brethell *brothel, worthless fellow*

brew(e) *stir up*

briboure *briber, swindler*

brigge *conflict, situation*

brittyn(d) *dismember(ed)*
bro *brew, unsavory business*
brodyr, brethir *brother*
brokke *badger*
brosid *bruised*
brosten *burst, broken*
brothel *worthless fellow*
browls, browlys, broll(s), brolle
   brat(s), brawler(s)
broydenesse *broadness, referring to*
   space
bryme *angry, impatient*
brymly *roughly*
bune *bound*
burd *bird*
burde (n.) *board*
burde (v.) *must go*
burguns *blossoms*
bus, buse *must*
busk *bush*
buskand *going, moving*
buske *move about, hurry*
but *unless*
buxomly *humbly, eagerly*
buxsome *obedient*
by *close by*
by, bye *purchase*
byde *abide*
byhalde *behold*
bying *purchasing*
bylde *protect*

cache(d), cacche(d) *catch, drive, drove,*
   pursue(d)
cald *cold, distressing*
cant *cruel, eager*
cantely *eagerly*
care(s), caris *suffering(s), trouble(s)*
care, carre *go, went*
carefull *full of care, sorrow*
cares *comes*
carl(s), carle(s), karll, karle *slave(s),*
   churl(s)
carpand *talking*
carpe *talk, discuss*
caste, kaste *prepare, produce, attempt,*
   throw, go away

casting *applying*
catche *remove*
catel, catell *animals, property*
cautell, cautellis, kautelles *spell(s),*
   tricks
Cayme, Came *Cain*
caytyff, caysteffe, caystiff, catyf
   rascal
cele *well-being, health*
certes, sertis *certainly*
cesse, seys, seece *cease*
chaas, chase *chose*
charge (n.) *punishment*
charred *chastised*
chastye *chastise*
chatt *jabber*
cheffe, chiftan (n.) *chief*
cheffe (v.) *overtake, befall*
chenys (v.) *obliges, chains*
chere (v.) *cheer (sometimes ironic)*
chering *suckling*
chesoune *reason*
cheynes, chynes (n.) *chains*
childe (n.) *man, knight*
childe (v.) *forbid, shield*
childing, chylding *childbirth*
choppe(s) *clap, blows*
churle(s), chorl *churl(s)*
chyned *chained*
clappe, clapped *beat(en), struck*
clapped, clappid *hugged*
clatterand *chattering*
cledde *clad*
cleke *catch*
clematis *regions*
clene *clean, without sin; entirely*
clere *pure, bright*
clethe *clothe*
clipsis *eclipse*
clogh *valley*
closed *held*
clowte (n.) *cloth*
clowte, cloute (v.) *strike*
clukis *clutches*
clyme *climb*
cobill notis *hazelnuts*
comand *coming*

comande *commend*

comaunde *command*

combere(d), combred, comeres *encumber, made unhappy*

comely, comly (n.) *gracious one*

comely (adj.) *properly*

comenaunde, comenaunt *covenant*

conant, conande *wise, knowledgeable*

confessouris *confessors (saints, but not martyrs)*

conjure *engage*

connandly *knowledgeably*

connyng, conande *skill, cunning, wisdom*

consayve *comprehend, conceive*

construe, constrew *explain, expound*

contene *continue*

contraried *contradicted*

contre *country*

contynuaunce *space of time*

convik, convyk *convict, find guilty*

coote *coat, garment*

corbonan (Lat.) *treasury*

corde *agreement*

cordis *accords, agrees*

corious *curious, prying*

cors, corse, coorse *body, person*

costemes *customs*

cover *relieve*

coveyte, coveite *covet, wish for*

cowde, cowthe, couthe *could*

crabbed *of ill disposition*

crabbidly *bad-naturedly*

craftely *skillfully, wisely*

crake *break*

crepillis *cripples*

croke (v.) *bow*

cure *assist, heal*

curssis *courses*

curstely *maliciously*

curstnesse *malice*

curtaise, curtayse *courteous*

cutte *straw, (draw) straws*

cyte *city*

cytte *sorow*

dale *gift*

dale, dallys *dale(s), valley(s)*

dare, daris *fear(s)*

dared *stupefied*

darfely, derfely *cruelly*

dasshes, dasshis *blows*

daunger *subjection, dominion*

dayne *insult*

dayntely *graciously*

debate *difficulty, dispute*

ded, dede *did, performed*

dede (v.) *kill*

dede, ded *death*

dede, dedis *deed(s)*

dedis *deed (to property)*

dedyned *was offended*

deere *harm*

dees *dais*

defame (n.) *disgraceful situation*

defaute *fault, error*

defayle *desert*

deffe(s), deffis (v.) *deafen(s)*

deffe (adj.) *deaf*

deffende, defende *forbid, protect, resist*

deffie *defy*

deland *dealing, judging*

delfe, dolven *delve, delved*

delyuere *deliver, acquit, hasten*

demand *judging*

deme(d) *judge(d)*

demene(d) *condescend, endow(ed)*

demer(s) *judge(s)*

denne *grave*

denyed *denied, failed*

departid *given*

deprave *disparage*

derand *injuring*

dere (v.) *harm*

dere (adj.) *dear, precious, costly, dangerous*

dere (adv.) *dearly*

derest, derrest *most dear*

derfenes *sacrilege*

derffe *hostile, wicked*

derfly *grievous, cruelly*

dergh *length (of time)*

derk *dark*

derke *lurk, pull back*

derworth, derworthy *worthy*
dese *dais*
dette *obligation, debt*
dever(e), deyver *duty*
devoyde *stop, cease*
devyse, deuyse *devise, legal deposition, judgment*
dewe (n.) *dew*
dewe, diewe *(adj.) due, deserving*
dewly *duly*
deyd(es) *deed(s)*
dight, dyght *put, make, effected*
ding, dingne *worthy*
dingnite(s) *honor(s)*
discrie *proclaim*
disease *misery, discomfort*
dispite *malice*
disputously *cruelly*
dissever *separate*
dochard *fool*
doderon *wretch*
dole, doole, doulle *sadness, misery*
doluen *buried*
dome (n.) *judgment, verdict*
dome, dom, domme *(adj.) dumb*
domesmen *judges*
dong *struck*
doote (n.) *fool*
doote (v.) *act foolishly*
dore *door*
doughty, douty, dowty *bold, good fellow*
doulfully *sorrowfully*
doun (v.) *down*
doune(s), downe(s) (n.) *down(s), hill(s)*
doute, dowte *worry, to be distraught, fear*
douteles *without doubt*
dowte *worry*
dowtiest *boldest*
dowue, douf(f)e, doyf *dove*
draffe *drove*
drawe *pull, pull apart, as in drawing and quartering*
drawe *draw out, delay*
draye *disturbance, riot, outcries*
drecchid *tormented*

drecchyng *tormenting*
dred, drede (v.) *dread*
dredand(e) *afraid*
drede (n.) *dread*
dredles *undoubtedly*
drely *earnestly*
dremys *dreams*
dress(ed) *address(ed)*
dress(id), dreste *dress(ed), prepare(d), behave(d)*
drevyn, dreuen *driven, taken*
driffe *drive*
drofyng *riot*
drovyd *angered*
dryffe *drive*
drynesch *dry land*
dugeperes *leaders*
durdan *riot, noise*
dure *endure*
durst *dare*
dusshed *struck*
dyderis *trembles*
dygnite(s) *authority/ies*
dyme *difficult (to understand)*
dyne, dynne, dyns *noise, crying*
dyng, dynge *hit, strike, beat*
dyntes *blows*

efte *also*
eftsones *again*
egges *urges*
eghne, eghen *eyes*
eke (adv.) *also*
eke (v.) *increase, annoy*
elde, eelde *age*
ellis *else, or else*
elmys (gen.) *enemies'*
emange *among*
emell (adv.) *thus*
emell (prep.) *among*
emiddis *amidst*
enbrace, enbraste *embrace(d), surround(ed)*
encheson *reason*
encrees, encresse *increase*
encresand *increasing*
enforce(s) *attempt(s)*

enmyse *enemies*
ensampel(s), ensaumpill(is), insaumpillis *example(s), sign(s)*
enserche *search out*
entente *intent, (take) heed*
entere, entir, entirly *entirely, sincerely*
erbes, erbis, erbys *plants, vegetation*
ere, ert *are*
eres, eris *ears*
Esmael *Ishmael*
esse *ease*
estate *authority, dignity, social position*
ete *eat*
ete, ette *ate*
even (n.) *evening*
even (adj.) *equal*
everilkane, everilkone *everything*
evyn, even, ewen (adv.) *thus*
excusacioune *excuses, explanation*
exynatores *senators*
eyles *ails*
eyne, eys *eyes*
eyre *air*

faciound *fashioned*
fade *darken*
fage *deceive*
fagyng *deception*
faie *dead*
faie, fay, faye *faith*
faitour, faitor, faitoure(s), faytour *deceiver(s), liar(s)*
fales, fals *false*
fall, falle *befall*
falle *fail, separate*
fallis *befits, happens*
falsed *falsehood*
fame *reputation*
famed *made to be known*
fande, fand *found*
fandeling, fondelyng(is) *foundling(s), bastard(s)*
fandyng *temptation, difficulty*
fandyngis, fayndyngis *trials*
fang, fange *capture, take, achieve, partake of, lift up*
fanges *cares for*

fantasie *apparition, falsehood*
fantome *guile*
far, fare *far*
fare (n.) *matter, opinion, practices*
fare(n) (v.) *fare(d)*
farly, farlis, farleis, farles *wonder(s)*
fast(e) *captured, secure*
fauchone *falchion*
faute(s), fawte(s) *fault(s), lack(s)*
fauty *fallible*
fayland *failing*
faylles, faylis *fails*
faynde *strive*
fayne *gladly, willingly*
fayner *more interested*
fayre (n.) *matter, affair*
fayre (adj.) *fair*
fecche *fish*
fecche(d) *bring, fetch(ed)*
fede *eat*
fee *livestock, property*
feele *discover, perceive, hide*
feere (v.) *terrify*
feese *punish*
feetour *features*
feill *hide*
feithe *faith*
felawe, felaus *fellow(s)*
felde *field*
fele (adj.) *many*
fele, feill, felys (v.) *experience, touch(es)*
feled *perceived*
felesome *delicious*
fell (n.) *skin*
fell (v.) *overthrow, kill*
fell, fele (adj.) *cruel, wicked, evil, painful*
felle *sharply*
felle(d) *knock down, cast down, condemn, overcome, destroy*
fell(es) (n.) *hill(s)*
feloune *felon*
fende, feende (n.) *fiend*
fende (v.) *defend*
ferde *fear, afraid*
ferdest *most fearful*

ferdnes, ferdnesse *fear*
fere *frighten*
fere, feer(e), feeres *company, companion(s), together*
ferlis, ferleis, farleis *wonders*
ferly, farly *wondrous*
ferre, fer *far, afar, long*
ferse, fers *fierce*
feruent *warm*
fesid *discomfitted*
feste (n.) *feast*
feste (v.) *fasten, hold fast*
feste (adj.) *fast, incarcerated, certain*
fete *feat*
fete, fette *foot, feet*
fette *fetch(ed)*
fetys, fettis *fine*
fewele *fuel*
fewle(s), fewell, fewlys *fowl*
feyll *feel*
feylle *cover*
feyne(d), fene *feign, hold/held back, hesitate(d)*
feyth *faith*
figure, figour, figoure, figuris *figure(s) sign(s), appearance*
filde *polite*
flappe(s) *blow(s)*
flay *cause to flee*
flay(ed), flaied *punish(ed), beat(en), torture(d)*
fleme, flemyd *condemn(ed), banish(ed), (made to) escape*
flenge *fling, throw*
flesh, flessh, flesshe, flesche *body (sometimes in Eucharist)*
flesshly *bodily*
flet *swim*
flight, flyte *argue*
flittand *departing*
flitte *flit, flee*
floode(s), flod, flodde *flood(s), waters*
floure *flower*
flume *river*
flynge *strike*
fode, foode *child, person*
folde *earth*

fole *fool, idiot*
fomen *foes*
fon, fone, foune, fun, fune, funne *found, shown, discovered*
fonde, fone *attempt*
fonde, fonned *foolish, mad*
fone *few*
foo, fois, foois *foe(s)*
foode, fode *infant, child, fool, (sometimes) man;* **frely foode** *noble child*
foole *foal*
forbere *withhold*
forbledde *weak from bleeding*
force, forse, fors *strength*
fordede *favor*
fordele *advantage*
fordo *overcome, commit suicide*
fore *fared*
forfare *execute*
forfette(s) (n.) *offense(s), punishment*
forfette (v.) *offend*
forge *contrive*
formefaders *forefathers, patriarchs*
forpechyng *breathing heavily*
fors *strength*
forther *further, advance*
fortheraunce *favor*
forthi, forthy *therefore, thereby*
forthinkith *am sorry*
forwakid *sleepy, tired*
forward, forwarde *underaking, plan, agreement, promise*
fote, fette *foot, feet*
foundynge *going*
fraistyng *testing, trial*
frappe *entire crowd*
frast(e) *test, taste*
fray(es), frayis *trouble, riot(s)*
frayes *dismays*
frayne, frayne, freyne *ask, question*
frayste(d), fraist(e) *attempt(ed), discover(ed)*
free (n.) *freeman, worthy one*
free (adj.) *liberal*
freele *frail*
freke *man*

frekly *with haste*
frely *willingly, freely*
frely(e) *noble*
frendely *lovingly*
fresshely *vigorously, brightly*
frewte *fruit*
freyke, frekys *bold man, men*
freyms *frames, makes*
frithe, firthe *wood, forest*
fro *from*
frusshe *strike*
fudde *food*
fulgent *radiant*
full *great, very*
full, fuls *befoul(s), oppress(es)*
funne *found*
furth *forth*
fyle(d), file(d), fylid, fylde *defile(d)*
fyne (v.) *pass away, die*
fyne (adj.) *appropriate, fine*
fyrd *rejected*
fyre *fire, flames*

gaa *go*
gab, gabbe talk
gabbyngis *talking (idly)*
gadlyng, gedlyng(es) *rascal(s)*
gaffe *gave*
Galely, Galale *Galilee*
gales *complains*
game, gamme, gome(s), gamys *game(s), joy, mirth, proceeding*
gan *began*
gan, gon *did*
gangand *going*
gang(e) *go*
ganne, gan *began, did*
gar, garre, garte *make, made, cause*
gaste *spirit*
gate (v.) *received, conceived*
gate(s), gatte, gatis (n.) *street(s), way(s), gate(s)*
gawdes, gaudes, gaudis *tricks*
gay(e) *fashionably dressed, dressed to impress*
gayne *agreeable*
gaynesaies *contradicts*

gaynest *most direct (route)*
gaynestande *withstand*
gedy *precipitously*
generacioun *lineage*
gent(e) *gracious*
gere *gear, clothes*
gest, geste *guest, stranger, man*
gete *get, catch*
gif, giff, giffe, gyffe *if*
giffe(s), gif *give(s)*
giffyne, geffyn *given*
gilery *guile*
gilte *guilt*
glee, gle *joy*
gleme(s) *gleam(s)*
glent *deception*
glide, glyde *move*
glorand *glowering*
glydand *gliding*
glyfftyng *glaring*
gode, good(e) *good*
gollyng *chattering, shouting*
gome(s) *man, men (see also* **game***)*
gone *did*
gostly, gostely *spiritually*
gowlande *howling*
granyng *lamenting*
grath (adj.) *grave*
grath (adv.) *diligently*
grathed *made, endowed*
grathely, grath *truly, plainly, directly, courteously*
grave(d), graven *bury, buried*
gravyng *burial*
grayde, graide *formed, prepared, bestowed*
grayth *cause*
gree *suitable*
greffe, greefe *grief, grievance*
gres, gryse *grass*
gret(e), grett(e) *great*
grete, grette *weep, weeping*
grete (n.) *earth*
grete (v.) *greet*
greve(s), greves *aggrieve(s), harass(es), grieve(s)*
griffe *grief*

grissely *sorrowfully*
grith *protection*
grome(s), gromys *retainer(s)*
grope(s), groppe *examine(s),
    interrogate(s), discover(s)*
grucchand *complaining*
grucche, grucchis, grughe *grouch,
    grudge(s)*
gryll, grill *angry, fierce*
grymly *angry*
gryth, gyrth *protection*
gud, gudde (adj.) *good*
gud, gudde, goode (n.) *goods*
gudnes, goodness(e) *goodness*
gulles *red (heraldic)*
gune *did*
gwisse *certainly*
gyde, gy, gydis *guide(s)*
gynne *device, mechanism, tool*
gyrnand(e) *grimacing, snarling*
gyrnes *grins, grimaces*
gyrth *defend*

haale *pull*
haffe *have*
haftis *business*
hakke *hack, cut*
halde, haldis *hold(s)*
hale *whole*
hales *comes*
halow(e) *bless*
halse *neck*
halsed *held, fondled*
halte *lame*
haly (adj.) *holy*
haly (adv.) *wholly*
Haly Gaste *Holy Spirit*
hame *home*
happe (n.) *luck, fortune*
happe (v.) *wrap, cover*
happed *occurred*
happing *bedclothes*
hardely *fiercely, vigorously*
hardinesse *outrageousness,
    presumptuous action*
hardy *bold*
hare, hore *hair*

harle *drag*
harling *buffeting*
harlot, harlott(is), harlotte *scoundrel*
harnes *brains*
harnes, harnays, harneys *harness,
    household equipment*
harneysed *in armor*
harre *intelligence, order*
harrow *turmoil*
harrowe, harro *pull out (as from
    limbo), rob*
harstow *hear you*
hart(e), herte *heart*
hartefully *sincerely*
hartely *earnestly, great*
hartyng, hertyng *encouragement*
hastis *hasten*
hate (adj.) *hot*
hate (adv.) *severely*
hatell *person*
haterden *maliciousness*
haterell *gown*
hatir *cloth, ?hood*
hatte *hate*
hauttande *haughty*
hayre *heir*
hede, hedis *heed(s)*
hede, heed, heede, hedis *head(s)*
hedesman, hedesmen *leader(s)*
hedir, hedyr, hyder *hither*
heete *promise*
heffe *lift, heave*
hegh *high*
heild(e), heyld *fell*
helde *held, favor, incline*
hele, heyl, heel *health, well-being, hale*
heledande *falling*
helesome *wholesome*
helis, helys, helid *heals, healed*
helte *hilt*
helyng *healing*
hende (n.) *end*
hende (n.) *hand(s)*
hende (adj.) *gracious, worthy*
hendly, hendely *graciously*
heneusly *heinously*
henne *hence*

hent(e) *take, taken hold, experienced, received*

hepe, heppe *heap, crowd*

herber, herborow *dwelling, safe place*

herbered, herberd *taken in, harbored*

herberles *homeless*

herde (n.) *shepherd*

herde (v.) *heard*

here, herre *ear*

here(s), heris *hear(s)*

Hermone *Armenia*

harste *hearest*

herely *early*

herre *order*

hert, herte(s), hertis *heart(s)*

heryed *harrowed*

hete (n.) *heat*

hete, hetis (v.) *threaten(s), promise(s)*

hetyng *promising*

hething *enjoyment, mockery*

heve, hef(f)e *lift(s), grieves*

heuenyng *vengeance*

heyne *hence*

heyned *waited*

hied *hurried*

high *tall*

high *loud*

hight, hyght(e) (v.) *called, named, promised*

hight (adv.) *high*

hilded *tipped over, bowed down*

hille, hillis *cover(s)*

hing, hyng(e), hyngis *hang(s)*

hire, hyre *pay, reward*

hold (n.) *captivity*

holde, holdis *embrace(s), support(s)*

holde, halde, hylde, holden *hold/held, regard(ed), believed*

holy, whollye *wholly*

homely *affectionately*

honde *hand*

hone(d), hune *delay(ed)*

hope, hopis, hoppis *hope(s), expect(s), think(s)*

hore *hair*

horosonne *son of a prostitute*

hote *hot, heat*

hover *wait*

howsolde *household*

hurle(d) *drag(ged) violently*

hurlyng *violence*

hurth *injury, wounds*

hy, hye (v.) *go, get going (quickly);* **in hy** *come here*

hy, hye (adj.) *high*

hyde *hide, skin*

hydous *hideous*

hye *eye*

hyed *hurried*

hyne *hence*

hyne *man (lower-class), servant*

hythyn *hither*

hytist *are called*

ilkane, ilkon, ilkone *everyone, each one*

ilke *each, every*

ilke a side *every side*

ill, yll *evil*

inbrace *embrace*

indowre *continue*

ingendis *weapons*

inow, anow *very*

inowe *enough*

in soundre *asunder*

instore *restore*

intere, interly *wholly*

ire *anger*

irke *annoyed, oppressed*

Isay *Isaiah*

iwys *indeed*

japer *scoffer, deceiver, trickster*

jape(s), jappis *jests, tricks*

javell(is) *brawler(s)*

jeauntis *giants*

jente *gracious*

Jessen *Goshen*

joged *cut*

Johell *Joel*

joies, jois *joys*

jolle *jostle*

joppon *jupon, tunic*

Jude *Judea*

Jues, Juuys *Jews*
jugge, juger (n.) *judge*
juggemen, juges *judges*
june *join*
Jury *Jewry*

kacched *caught*
kantely *boldly*
kaytiffe (adj.) *miserable, unhappy*
kele *cool, detract from, assuage*
kempis *strong soldiers*
ken, kenne, kone, kende *know, believe, teach; made known, recognized, shown*
kene *sharp, malicious*
kevellis *strong men*
kid(de), kydde *known, recognized, shown*
kirke *church*
kirtill *long-sleeved gown, worn under surcoat*
knafe *boy, knave*
knotte *bargain*
knyth *afflicts*
knytte *concluded*
kynd *nature*
kynde *species, lineage, tribe, people*
kyndly *according to nature*
kynne *kin, tribe*
kyth *kinfolk, region, country*
kythe, kith(e) *make known, reveal*

laby *burden*
lach *capture, lock*
lad, ladde *person of no account*
ladde *strap*
lade *load*
laite, layte *seek*
lake, layke *game, sport, entertainment*
lame *lamb*
lame *limb*
lane *gift*
lang, lange *long, tall*
lange *belong*
langes *longs, desires*
langour *illness*

lappe, lapped, lappid *find, enclose(d), cover(ed), surround(ed), caress(ed)*
lare, lore *knowledge, lore, advice*
large *excessive*
lascchis *lashes*
lassched *lashed, scourged*
late (n.) *fuss*
late (n.) *aspect, appearance*
late, latte (v.) *let*
lathe, lath *loathe*
laugher *lower, more humble*
laughte *caught*
launce *rush*
lawe (v.) *bring down*
lawe (adj.) *low, short*
lawmere *fool*
laye *wager*
laye(s), layse *law, laws, customs*
layk(is) (v.) *play(s)*
layke *play, entertainment*
layne (v.) *conceal, remain silent*
layre *earth*
Lazar(e) *Lazarus*
leche (n.) *cure, healer*
leche, lechis (v.) *cures, heals*
ledde, led *expounded*
lede, leyd, ledis (v.) *lead(s)*
lede(s), leede (n.) *lad(s)*
leder(s) *expounder(s), leader(s)*
lee *tranquility*
leede, lede (n.) *lead (metal)*
leeffe *loved one*
leefull *lawful*
leese *lose*
lefe, leffe *dear*
leffand *living*
leffe *leave*
legge(s), ledge *allege(s), expound(s)*
legyng *expounding*
lele *loyal*
lelly *lily*
lely *truly*
lemand *gleaming*
leme, leym, lemys *beam(s)*
lemed *shone*
lemer *source of radiance*

len, lene(s), lenne(s) *lend(s), give(s), grant(s)*
lende *remain, bestow, give (including light)*
leng(e) *stay, remain*
lengand *remaining, dwelling*
lengar, lenger *longer*
lenghe *length*
lenghis *remains*
lenght, lenghe *length, space*
lente *passed, gave, given*
lepfull *baskets full*
leppe, lepe *leap, slip off, escape, go*
leprous *leper*
lere, leere, lerne *learn, teach, instruct, proclaim*
lered *learned*
lese *lies*
lesid *loosened, absolved*
lesingis *lies*
leste *least*
lesyng *lying, dishonesty*
lete, lette, latt(e), lette(n), leteyn *allow(ed)*
lett, lette, lettis *stop, refrain, prevent, hinder(s)*
lette, latte *let*
lettir *preventer*
levand, levyng, lyffand, lewyn *living*
leve (n.) *permission*
leve (v.) *believe*
leve, lefe, leffe, leyf (v.) *leave, depart*
leve, liffis, lyfis, leyf, levyd (v.) *live(s), live(d)*
levene, leuyn *lightning*
lever(e) *rather*
levis (imp.) *leave, relieve, cease*
lewde *unlettered*
lewte, lewty *truth, loyalty, faith*
leyd (n.) *man*
leyd (v.) *lead*
leyf *leaf*
leyffe *dear one*
liaunce *allegiance*
lidderon, lidrone *wicked fellow*
liddir *wicked*
liffe, lyf, lyffe *life*

lifte, lyfte *left*
ligge *lie*
light (v.) *illuminate*
light (adj.) *happy, superficial*
light(e) *brightness, light*
lightly, leythly *without effort*
likand *fair*
lilly *lily*
lire *body, appearance*
lirte *trick*
lise *lies*
list *desire*
lith, litht *limb, body part*
lith(e) *listen*
lithirnesse *wickedness*
lithre *wicked*
locus (Lat.) *place, playing area*
loffely *lovely*
loghte *seize*
lok(id), loke(d), lokis *look(ed), look(s)*
lokand *looking, gazing*
loken, lokyn *locked, shut*
longed *belonged*
longis *belongs, applies, in accord with*
longis *desires*
lorell *beggar, scoundrel, fool*
lorne *lost, destroyed*
lose(d), louse *untie(d), lost*
losell(is) *wretch(es)*
loth, lohth *loath*
lothe, lathe, lothis *loathly, despicable*
lotterell(e) *scoundrel*
lourdayne(s), lordayne, lordan *dull fellow(s), rascal(s)*
louse, lowse *loosen, untie*
loved, lovid, louyd *praised, worshiped*
loves *loaves*
lovys, louffe *praise, worship*
lowe, lowte, loute *worship, reverence, kneel, bow*
luf, loffe (n.) *love*
luffand *loving*
luffe(s), luffis *love(s)*
luffely *loved one*
luffull *praiseworthy, loving*
lufsome *beneficial, gracious*
lugg *pull*

luk, luke *look*
lurdan(s), lurdane, lurdayne(s),
   lordan *rascal(s), fool(s)*
lurkand *lurking*
lusschyd, lusshed *beat(en)*
lusshe (n.) *blow*
lusty (n.) *bold person*
lye *belie*
lyffelod *livelihood*
lygge, ligge *lay, lie (body position)*
lyghame *body*
lyk *desire*
lykand *pleasant*
lykes *pleases*
lyking *bliss*
lymbo, lymbus *limbo*
lyme, lymes, lymmys *limb(s);* **lymme**
   and lith *life and limb*
lymett *bound*
lymme *leam, light*
lyne *linen*
lyolty *truth*
lyre *body, figure, face*
lyste *listen*

ma *more*
mached *set upon*
madde, maddes *rave(s) [insanely],*
   is/are insane
Mahownd(e), Mahounde *Mohammed*
maistir(s) *master(s)*
maistrye, maystrie *mastery, important*
   deeds
make *mate*
makeles *matchless*
mallise, malles *malice*
malyngne *accuse falsely*
malysoune *curse*
mang *are confused*
mangery *meal*
manhed(e) *manhood*
manne, mane *man*
mantell *man's garment, with open sides*
mark(e) *designate, sign*
marke *measurement*
marr, marre(s), mars, merr *injure(s),*
   harm(s), obstructs

martiris *martyrs*
mase(d) *amaze(d), upset, bewilder(ed)*
mast *must*
mast *most*
may *maid*
mayne *moan*
mayne *strength*
mede, meede *reward*
medill *involve (with)*
meene *means*
meese *restrain, assuage*
meete *meat, food*
meffe, mefid, mefte *move(d)*
meke *submissive*
meke, mekis (v.) *humbles*
mekill, mykyl(l), mykill *great, greatly*
Melachiell *Malachi*
mele *time*
mell, melle(s) *mingle(s), meddle(s),*
   concern(s), consider(s), reveal(s)
mendand *mending, improving,*
   restoring
mende *restore, improve, redress*
mene, meene (v.) *think, consider, speak*
   out
mene, meene (adj.) *mean, low*
menge, mengis *unsettle(s), mate(s)*
menged *mingled, mixed*
mensk, menske, mensked, menskid
   honor(ed), worship(ed)
menskfull *exalted*
mente *intended*
menye *company, family*
merkis *marks*
mervayll(es) *marvel(s)*
mete, meete, mette (n.) *food*
mete (v.) *meet*
mete (adv.) *ready*
meve, meyve *move, speak*
meyne, menyhe, mene (n.) *company,*
   family
meyne, mene (v.) *speak, mention*
Michill, Mighill *Michael*
mirakillis *miracles*
mirre *myrrh*
mirroure, myrroure, merour
   reflection, example

misbeleve *unbelief*
mischeve *harm*
misgone *mistaken*
misseis *errors*
miste *missed*
mistir, mystir, mystris *need(s)*
mistrowand *disbelieving*
misty *dark, obscure, portentous*
mobardis, mobbardis *villainous fools*
mode *mood, disposition*
modir, modyr *mother*
moght, mowght *might*
molde, moulde *earth*
momellis *mumbles*
momelyng, momeland, mummeland *mumbling*
mon, mone *may, might*
mone, moone *moan, complaint*
mone, moone *moon*
moo *more*
moote, mote(s) *argue(s)*
mop *simpleton, puppet*
more and myn *more and less*
mornand *mourning, sorrow*
morne *mourn*
morteysed *fixed*
mott, mot, motte *might*
move(d) *urge(d)*
mowe(s) *[make] mouth(es), face(s)*
mum *whisper*
mused *conscious*
muste *new wine*
muster(es), mustir, musteris *muster(s), create(s), perform(s), manifest(s)*
mutyng *disputing*
myldely *obediently, meekly*
mynde(s) *memory, thoughts*
myre *mire, ensnare*
myrke, mirke *dark*
myrkenes, myrknes *darkness*
myron *retainer, lazy fellow*
myrroure *mirror, example*
myrthe(s), myrthis *joy, mirth, good news*
mys, mysse, misse *error, sin, evil*
mysdede, mysdedis *wrongful action(s)*

mysdone *sinned*
mysese *unhappiness, discomfort*
myslykyng, mysselykyng *sorrow, unhappiness*
mysse, mys *error, failing, sin, mishap*
mystir *need*
mytyng, mythyng *small one*

nape *ape*
nappe(d) *sleep, slept*
nare, nere *near*
narmes *arms*
natheles *nonetheless*
ne *nor*
nede *necessary*
nede, nedis *need(s)*
nedelyng, nedlyngis *necessarily*
neffes *fists*
negh(es) *near(s), come near*
neghand *coming near*
neghed *came near*
nemely *nimbly*
nemen, nemyn, nemyne, nemys *name(s), call(s)*
nere *ear*
nerre *nearer*
nerthrist *lowest*
nese *nose*
neven(e), neuen *mention, identify, name*
nevenly *plainly*
nevill *evil*
newe, newis *annoyance(s)*
newes *renews*
newly *recently, readily, soon*
newsome *problematic*
nexile *wing [as of building]*
nociens *inclinations, notions*
noddill *hit*
nodir *other*
noght *not, naught, without value*
none *noon, midnight (noon of the night)*
none *nothing, not any*
noote *matter, news, task*
notis *nuts*
nott, notis *matter(s), evidence*
novellis *marvelous things*

now *new*
nowell *owl*
nowther, nowdir *neither*
nowys *news, information*
noye, noy (n.) *annoyance*
noye(d) *annoy(ed)*
noyes *trouble*
noyse, noys *musical sounds*
noysed *heard, broadcast*
noysomemare *more noisome*

obeyesaunce *obedience*
obitte *dead*
oblissh, obblissh(e) *oblige*
offerand(es), offrand *offering(s)*
ofte sithes *oftentimes*
omys *amiss, wrong*
ones *once*
ongayne *bothersome*
ongentill *ungentle, cruel*
onthinke *reflect, consider*
oon *on*
oondis *breath*
oppen *careless*
or *ere; before*
ordan, ordand, ordande, ordayne(d) *ordained*
Osee *Hosea*
ospring *descendants*
oute tane, owtane, owte take *except*
outhir *either*
outrayes *goes subversively, injures*
overegone *reduced, passed by*
overewyn *overcome, conquered*
overhyld *adorned*
owre, oure *hour*
oyes *hear ye*

Paas *Pasch, Easter*
page(s) *boy(s), young man/men*
paie *payment, reward; please, pleasure*
paire, payre *impair, reduce*
pakald *package, burden*
palle *piece of fabric, sign of authority*
palmeres *pilgrims*
palys *palace*
panyer *basket*

pappe *breast*
parde *pardé, by God*
parfite *perfect*
parformed *made perfect*
parred *flayed*
passhed *smashed*
paste *passed, dead*
patris *patters*
paye, paie(s) *pays, reward(s), satisfy/satisfies*
payed, paied *paid, pleased*
pechyng *accusing*
peere, pere *peer*
penys *pennies, pence*
perellis, parellis *perils*
perelus, perelous *fearful*
perles, pereles *peerless, unequaled*
perte *clever, open*
pese, pece, pees *peace, calm*
pety, petie *pity*
peysed *forced*
pight *put, situated*
pilche *leather outer garment*
pine, pyne *pain*
platly *immediately*
platte *fall down*
playe, plaies *recreation, pageant(s), play(s)*
pleasaunce *good will, pleasure*
plete *argue*
plextis *wrangle*
pleyned *lamented*
pleyntes *complaints*
plye *submit*
popse *game [similar to blind man's buff]*
porte *gate*
post, poste, pooste(e), pouste *power*
postelis *apostles*
pour, poure, poors *power(s)*
poure, powre, power *poor*
powll *pull*
poynte(s) *point(s), charge(s) to be proved, acts*
praty *bright, intelligent*
pray, praye *prey*
praye, praies *pray(s), beg(s)*
preces *presses*

preche, prech(is), prechid *preach(es), preach(ed)*

prente(d) *print(ed), inscribe(d)*

presande *present, gift*

presiously *expensively*

press(e), pres *crowd, company, assembly*

presse (n.) *difficulty*

presse (v.) *repress*

prest(e) *quick, pressed*

prestly, prestely *urgently, quickly*

prevaly, pryvaly *privily, secretly*

preve(d) *prove(d), demonstrate(d)*

preyse *praise*

preysing *praising, flattering*

pris *value*

processe *progression, procession*

prokering *provoking, plotting*

propheres *offers*

prophete, prophite *prophet, profit, profitable*

prowe *credit, comfort*

pryvvyte, privite *mystery, privacy, secret*

puplisshid *proclaimed*

purchace *advantage*

purgens *purging*

purpose(d) *plan(ned)*

purpure *purple*

purveye *put forth, provide, arrange*

putry *prohibited sex*

putt *pushed*

py *magpie*

pyne, pynde *to cause pain, suffering*

pynne *nail, torment*

pynyng *tormenting*

pytefull *one who pities*

quarte, qwarte *health*

quate, qwat *what*

quell(e) *put down, condemn*

quenys *shrews, whores*

quike, quyke *living*

quilke *which*

quyte(s), quytte *requite(s)*

qwantise *tricky*

qwen *when*

qwitte *free, acquit, repaid*

Rabek *Rebecca*

racleyme (comys to) *is summoned (to court)*

radde *afraid*

radly *quickly*

raffe *rave, split, pull apart*

rafte *reft, taken away*

rakand *rushing*

rake *go, rush*

rakid *been away*

ranke *rebellious*

rankoure *rancor*

ransake *search*

rapes, rappes *ropes*

rapped *hit*

rappely *quickly*

rappes (n.) *blows*

rare, raris *roar(s)*

raryng *roaring, lamenting*

rase(d), rasid, rayse, rayst *raise(d), rose*

rasely *brutally*

rathely *quickly, fiercely*

raught *give*

rawe, rowe *row;* **on rawe** *in order*

rawnsoner *ransomer*

rawnsoune (v.) *ransom*

rawsom *ransom*

rayed *arrayed*

raykand *(idly) wandering, hurrying*

rayke(s) *rush, go(es), happen(s)*

rayst, rased *wounded*

read *advice*

rebalde(s), ribaldes, ribaldis *rascal(s), scoundrel(s), menial fellow(s)*

reche, rechid *provide(d)*

recoveraunce *recovery*

red *understood, advised*

rede (n.) *reed*

rede, reede (n.) *advisor, counselor*

rede, redde, redis, reedis (v.) *advise(s), proclaim(s), interpret(s), understand(s)*

redused *disabused*

reffuse *reject, dismiss, condemn*

reflars *rises*

refte *lost*
regally *dominion*
regne(s), regnys *reign(s)*
regynall *original*
rehete *rebuke, assail*
reke *trouble, riot*
rekeles *foolhardy person*
reken, rekenne *call up, give account of*
rekenyng *accounting*
releffe *relieve, assist*
reles *release*
releve (n.) *remainder*
releve (v.) *assist*
reme, remys *realm(s)*
remenaunte, remelaunt *remains*
remewe *go, take away*
renand *reigning*
rengne, reyne *reign*
renke, renkes, renkis, renkkis (n.) *man, men, people*
renke (v.) *reign*
renne *run*
repaire *return*
repleye *redeem*
repreve *challenge*
reproffe *disgrace*
resen, resynne *risen*
ressayve *receive*
reste, ryste *peace, rest*
reverande *revering*
reve(s), refte *deprive(s), rob(s)*
revers *turn around*
rewe(s), rewis *feel sorry for, repents*
reweles *rules, controls*
rewfull *distressful*
rewle *rule*
rewly *calm, (well) behaved*
reynand *reigning*
riall *royal*
rialte *royalty*
rid, ridde *escape from, release*
rigge *back*
right *correct*
rightwisse *righteous*
rightwisseness, rightewysnes *righteousness*
risse *branch*

robard *felon*
rode, roode *rood, cross*
rollis *parchment rolls, documents*
rolyng *agitating*
roo *peace, rest*
roo *buck*
roose *rose*
roppe, ropis *rope(s)*
rore, rooris *shout(s)*
roten *decayed, rotten*
rought *wrought*
rouk *private talk*
roune, rowne *mutter*
rownand *speaking*
rowses *boasts*
rowte *crowd*
rowted *beaten*
rowtes *blows*
roye, royis *boast, talk nonsense*
roye *king*
rude *great*
ruffe *roof*
ruffully *pitifully*
rug, rugge(d) *pull(ed) harshly, violently*
russhed *violently struck, dragged*
ruth, ruthe, rewth(e), reuth *pity, grief*
ryve (v.) *tear, split*
ryve (adj.) *abundant*
ryall *royal*
ryally *royally*
ryffe *completely, thoroughly, abundantly*
ryolest *most royal*

saande, sand(e), sandis *message(s)*
sad, sadde *solemn*
sadly *solemnly*
sadnesse *soberness*
saffe *healthy*
saffe, safe (v.) *save, set aside, observe*
sagates *thus*
saggard *one who sags, lazy fellow*
saie(s) *say(s)*
sakles, satcheles *innocent*
sale(s) *hall(s)*
sall, sal, salle, sale *shall*
salus *assails*
salve(d) *remedy/remedied, cure(d)*

salver *healer*
Samaritanus *Samaria*
same *together*
samen, samyn *together*
sande, sand, sonde *message*
sange *song*
sararre *more sorrily*
sare *sore*
sartayne, sarteyne *certainly*
satt *allowed*
sattles *sinks down*
sauffe *save, preserve*
saugh(e) *saw*
saule(s), sawle, sawlis *soul(s)*
saunteryng *babbling*
savely *certainly*
saverly *confidently*
saw(es), sawis *saying(s), word(s),
   commands*
sawen *sown*
sawntrelle, sauterell *fake saint,
   hypocrite, babbler*
sawter *psalter*
sayne (v.) *[make] sign [of cross]*
sayne (v.) *say*
scape *escape*
schaftes *banner shafts, lances*
schake *flee away*
schalke(s) *fellow(s)*
schall *shall*
schape, schappe (n.) *shape, figure*
schappe, shappis, shapist (v.)
   fashion(s), take(s) up, creates
scharid *sheared*
schath *injury*
schawe *show, appearance*
schende *injure, destroy, exhaust*
schene *shining*
schenely *brightly*
schent(e) *condemned, guilty, destroyed*
schepe *sheep*
schew(e), schewys, shewed *show(s),
   appear(s), show(ed)*
schire *brightly*
scho *she*
schogged *shook*

schone, schonnys *hesitate(s), shuns,
   object(s)*
schonte *hold back*
schope, schoppe *formed, created*
schotte *jerked*
schoures *troubles*
schowte, schoutis *shout(s)*
schrew(e) (v.) *curse*
schuke *shook*
scored *marked*
seall, seele, sale *well-being*
sees, sese *cease*
seete *seat, judgment seat*
seett *sect, party*
sege, seeges *thrones*
segge, sege, seeg(e) *man*
segger *braggart*
segges *speaks*
seggid *spoken*
seggyng(es) *speaking, saying(s)*
seke *sick*
seke, sekis, sekist *seek(s)*
sekeness(e) *sickness*
selcouth(e), selcowthe *spectacular,
   wonders*
sele, seele, seill *profit*
selle *prison cell*
sely *humble*
semand (v.) *psalming, singing psalms*
semand, semande (adj.) *appropriate,
   fitting*
sembeland, semblant *outward sign,
   appearance*
semed, semid *seemed, befitted*
semelid *assembled*
semely *handsome, lovely*
semes (n.) *seams*
seme(s) (v.) *seem(s), befit(s)*
semlys *assemble*
sen, senne, synne *since*
sene *seen*
senge *sign*
sente *assent*
senyour *senior, older man*
septoure, septure *scepter*
ser *special*

serche, sers *search, examine,*
  interrogate
sere, seere *differing, diverse,*
  independently, apart
serly *separately*
sermones *speak*
serve(d) *serve(d), obey(ed)*
served, servid *deserved*
Sesar *Caesar*
sese(d), sees, sesse, sessid *cease(d),*
  complete(d), allot(ted)
sese(d), sesid *seize(d)*
sete, seetis *seat(s)*
sethen, sethyn *since, then*
sette *set, establish, secured*
sewe(s) *pursue(s), afflict(s), sue(s)*
sex *six*
seyd *seed*
shamously *shamefully*
shappe, shoppe *form, attempt*
shende, schende *destroy*
shene *fair, bright*
shente *defeated, destroyed, overcome*
sheris *cuts, pierces*
shon *hesitate*
shrewe, schrewe *evil person*
shrewednesse, schrewdnesse *of*
  malignant disposition, wickedness,
  trickery
shynand *shining*
signe(s), sygne(s), singnes, syne,
  senge *sign(s)*
sikenes, sikenesse *sickness*
siker, seker *secure, accurate, true*
sites *sights*
sithen, sythen *since, then*
sithfull, sytfull *sorrowful*
sittand(e) *adjusted, proper, fitting*
sittis *sits [as judge]*
skantely *scantly, wrongly*
skape *escape*
skath(e), skathes *harm, malice, blows*
skatheles, scatheles *unscathed*
skaunce *deception, joke*
skelpe (v.) *whip*
skelpes, skelpys *blows*
skelpte *beat out*

skiffte *conspiracy*
skill(e), skyl, skyll *ability, reason,*
  fitting
skyfte *escape*
skymeryng *agitating*
slaa, sla, slee(is) *slay*
slake, slakis *diminish(es), slacken(s)*
slane, slayne, slone *slain*
slang *threw*
slely *slyly*
slepand(e) *sleeping*
slike, slik, slyk(e) *such*
sloppe *loose outer garment*
smore *smother*
smyte, smitten *hit*
snell *fast, wise*
soght, soghte *sought, pursued, gone*
soile *assoil, release*
solace, solys, solas *solace, favorable*
  news
solempne *splendid*
sonde *safekeeping*
sonde *message*
sondre, sondered *break/broken apart*
sone (n.) *son*
sone (adv.) *soon*
sonne, son *sun*
soper(e) *supper*
sore *pain, unhappiness*
sori *unhappy, in misery*
sorssery *witchcraft, sorcery*
sotell(e) *subtle*
sotelte(s) *subtleties*
soth(e), suth(e) *truth*
sothfastness(e) *truthfulness*
sotilly *subtly*
sott(e) *fool*
sounderes *separates*
sounkyn, sownkyn *sunken, drowned,*
  deep in
soveraynely *above all*
soveraynes, souereynes, sofferayne,
  soferans *masters*
sowme *sum, total*
space *space (of time), soon*
spare(d), sparyd *refrain(ed), hold/held*
  back

spedar *facilitator*

spede (n.) *assistance, progress, benefit*

spede, speydes (v.) *hasten(s), prosper(s)*

spell *speak*

spell(is) *discourse, saying(s), word(s)*

spence *expense*

spens *pence*

sperde *imprisoned*

spere *spear*

sperite, sprete *spirit, ghost*

spetyffull *cruel*

spille, spilte *harm, destroy, condemn, kill(ed)*

spirre, spire, spere(s), sperre, speris *ask(s), inquire(s)*

spirringes *questions*

spites *insults*

spitous *spiteful*

spitte *spat*

spoile *strip*

sporne *stumble*

stabill (v.) *hold, stabilize*

stages, stagis *stages, enclosures*

stakir *stumble*

stale *stole*

stalland *stopping*

standerdes, standerdis *banners*

standyng *(in court) place to stand*

stare *am astonished*

stark(e) *strong, prostrated*

state(s) *estate(s)*

stately *fierce, legitimately*

sted, stede, stedde (v.) *hold, placed, situated, stabilize, delay*

stede (n.) *horse*

stede, steede, steedis (n.) *place(s)*

steeles *rungs*

steere *control*

stele (n.) *steel*

stele (v.) *steal*

stem, stemmys *stop, reduce(s)*

sterand *athletic, strong*

stere *bestir, steer (control)*

stered *stirred, moved*

sterne(s) *star(s)*

stertis *starts, goes*

steven(e), stevyn (n.) *voice, command*

stevened *called*

stevenyng *shouting*

stied *went up*

sties *ladders*

stiffe *strong*

stiffely *firmly, staunchly, boldly*

stigh *ascend*

stighill *intervene*

stilly *silently*

stirre *encourage*

stodmere *prostitute, loose woman*

stok *stump*

stokyn *stock, closed in*

stole *stool*

stonyd *astonished*

stonyes *is astonished*

store (n.) *products for sale, storage*

store (adj.) *strong*

stounde *time, moment, a while*

stoure *struggle, battle*

stoutely *haughtily*

stoutnes *moving about*

strake (v.) *struck*

strake, strakis *stroke(s)*

strang, strange, straunge *strong*

straue *argued*

stremys *(light) beams*

strenghe (n.) *strength*

strenghe, strenkyth (v.) *strengthen*

streyned *attacked*

stroye *destroy*

strye *witch, hag*

stryffe, stryfe *conflict*

stryvyng *unruliness*

stubbe *short, stubby nail*

stye *path*

styll *quietly*

stynkand *stinking, foul*

stynt, stynte *stop*

stynter *suppressor*

suapped *smitten, killed*

subgette *obedient*

sudary(e) *shroud, burial cloth*

sufferand *patient*

suffirantly *patiently*

sugett, subgett *subject*

suld, sulde *should*
sum, sume *some*
suppowle *support*
surete *bond, legal obligation*
suthfast *true*
suthly *truly*
suttellte *subtlety, craftiness*
suttely, suttily *subtly, skillfully*
swa *so*
swage *stop*
swang *swung*
swappes (n.) *blows*
swappes (v.) *cut off, smote*
swarand *swear*
sware *square*
swayne *boy, young man*
sweght *weight, force*
sweltes, sweltid *is/was overcome*
swemyd *overcome*
swet(e), swette *sweat*
swetnes(se) *pleasure*
swett(e), swete, sweyt *sweet*
swetter, sweeter *sweeter*
swettyng *sweet, beloved one*
swetyng *sweating, toil*
swevene *dream*
sweying *noise*
swilk(e) *such*
swithe *quickly*
swongen *lashed (at)*
swonyng *swooning*
swyngis *whips, blows*
swynke *work, toil*
swyre *neck*
symonde *caulk*
syn, syne *since, later*
syne *sin*
syne, synge *sign*
synnous, senous *sinews*
syte, sight(e) *grief, sorrow*

tacche *attach, fasten*
tag *small piece*
takande *taking, receiving*
taken *received*
taken, takyn *token*
takis *takes*

takkid *fastened, nailed*
takyng *capturing*
talde *told*
talde *counted*
talent(e) *resolution, inclination, ability*
tales, talis *tales, stories, narratives*
tane, tone *taken*
tase *toes*
tast(e) *experience, use, test*
tastyng *touching, handling*
taynte (n.) *criminal*
taynte (v.) *convict*
taynted (adj.) *suspect*
teche, teeche *teach, inform*
telle *count*
tendande *attending*
tene, teene, teyn *trouble, suffering, difficulty, anger*
tened, tenyd (v.) *harmed, killed, grieved, angered*
tenefull *grievous*
tent, tente, tentis (give) *heed to, guard*
tent(e) *tenth*
termyne *pronounce, declare*
teynde *tithe, tenth*
teynted *convicted*
thame *them*
than, thame *then*
tharne *lose*
tharnyng *lack*
the *succeed, thrive*
theff(e) *villain, thief*
ther *where*
thergatis *in that manner*
therout(e) *outside*
tho, thois *those*
thoff *though*
thole, tholed, tholede, tholid *endured, suffered, worked*
thraldome *bondage*
thrall *captive*
thrally(e), thraly *fully, sincerely, entirely, violently*
thrang *throng, crowd*
thrange (v.) *pressed*
thrawe (n.) *throng, crowd*
thrawe (v.) *throw*

thrawe (adv.) *while;* **a thrawe** *a while*
threpyng *disputing*
threst, thraste *thrust*
threte, thrette *threaten(ed)*
thries, thryes *thrice*
thriffe *thrive*
throsten *forced down*
thrurgh, thurgh *through*
thryng *thrust, press*
thusgates *in this way*
tille *to, towards*
tille, tyll *labor*
tiraunte(s), tirrauntis *tyrant(s), villain(s), bully/bullies*
tite *quick, quickly*
tithhands, tithynge *tidings*
titill *title, legal rights*
tokyn, tokenyng(is) *sign(s)*
tole, toled *pull(ed)*
tole(s), tolis *tool(s), equipment*
tome (n.) *time*
tome (adj.) *empty*
tonne *cask*
torfoyr *calamity*
torne *act of trickery*
torne(d) *return(ed), change(d)*
touch *concern*
toune *town*
toure (n.) *tower*
toure (adj.) *excessive*
tow *two*
trace (n.) *way, course of action*
trace (v.) *seek out*
traied *betrayed*
traitoury *betrayal, treachery*
trante, trantis *trick(s)*
trasshes *ragged garments*
trast and trewe *trusted and true*
trast(e) *tested, trusted*
trast(is) *trust*
trastyng *testing, trusting, faith*
travaylle, traueylle, traueylis *effort, struggle, suffering*
traveses *attacks, contradicts*
traylle *drag*
trayne, traye *deceit, trick, deception*
tree, tre *cross*

tresorie *treasury*
tresoune *treason*
tresoure *treasure*
treuth(e) *truth*
trewys *truth, good faith*
triffilis, truffillis *trifles, idle stories*
trist (adj.) *trusted*
triste, treste (n.) *hope, trust*
triste, tristis (v.) *trust(s)*
tristely *trustfully*
tristy *trustworthy*
troned *enthroned*
trouth(e) *truth*
trow(ed) *trust(ed), believe(d)*
trowe, trowis *trust(s)*
trusse, trus *gather up, go, depart*
trye (v.) *sort*
tugge(d), tuggid *pull(ed), stretched*
tule, tulles *assail*
tulles *tools*
tulyd *attacked*
turtill, turtour *dove, turtledove*
twyes *twice*
twynne(s) *separate(s)*
twynnyng, twynnnand *separating*
tyde, tide *time*
tyght *imprisoned ones*
tyne (v.) *anger, be angry*
tyne (v.) *lose/lost, give up, waste*
tyte *quickly, sharp*
tyte *tight (in chains)*
tytle *claim, deed [to property]*
tyxste *taxed, accused, charged*

umbelappid *encircled*
umbycast *bound*
unbaynely *cruelly*
unbende *untie*
unberid *unburied*
unbraste *unbound*
unbuxumnes *disobedient*
unclene *polluted, sinful*
uncleth *disrobe*
unconand, unconnand *stupid, unwise*
uncouthe *strange*
undewe *contrary to law*
undewly *unjustly, unlawfully*

undughty *weak*
unethis *scarcely*
unfiled *undefiled, unspoiled*
ungayne *harm*
ungent *not noble (commoner or peasant)*
unhappe *misfortune, unlucky*
unhende *ungracious, unworthy*
unhendly *ungraciously, evilly*
unlappe *reveal*
unlele *disloyal*
unlely *disloyally*
unlokynne *opened*
unmeete *wrong*
unride *monstrous, cruel*
unseele *lack of well-being*
unwarly *unexpectedly*
unwelde *weak*
unwitty *unwise*
uphalde, upholde *insist, support*
uppetane *ascended*
upryse, uprysing *resurrection*
upsoght *sought out*
upstritt *rose up*

vaile *veil*
vayne *empty*
velany(e) *villainy*
very, veray, verray *very, true*
voydes *renders ineffectual*

wa, waa *woe*
waferyng *wandering*
waffe (v.) *wave*
wage *reward, bribe*
waite(s), waitis *attend(s)*
wakand(e) *awake*
wake *keep watch*
waken *incite*
wakyng *watching, as in vigil*
walde *would*
wale *choose*
walkand *walking*
wan, wanne *evil, dark*
wande(s) (n.) *rod(s), batten(s)*
wande (v.) *delay*
wanderede *wandering to point of exhaustion*

wandynge *thoughts, uncertain thoughts*
wane(s) *subside(s), recede(s)*
wangges *cheeks*
wanhope *despair*
wanne *won*
wantis *wants, lacks*
wanyand, waneand *waning [of the moon], evil time*
wappe(d) *tear/torn, wrapped*
war *worse*
war, ware, werre *was, were*
warand(e) *warrant, know*
warde *custody*
ware (v.) *were*
ware (adj.) *aware*
warely *circumspectly, surreptitiously*
waried *spoken against, cursed*
warisoune *reward*
wark(e) *deed(s), work(s)*
warlowe(s), warlous *warlock(s), wizard(s), sorcerer(s)*
warne(d) *inform(ed)*
warred *knotty, strong*
wast(e) *waste, destroy, decline, diminish;* **in waste** *futilely*
wasted *destroyed*
wathe, wathes, wothis *perilous, perils*
wave, wavyd *move(d) about, wobble(d)*
wax(e), waxen *grow(n)*
waye, wais *way, ways*
wayke *weak*
wayte *keep watch*
wayteskathe *troublemaker*
we *whee, alas*
wedde (n.) *wager*
wedde (v.) *marry [involving contract]*
wedde set *mortgage*
wede *madness*
wede, wedis *clothing*
wedir, weedir *weather*
wedlak *wedlock*
weele *well*
wegge(s) *wedges*
weldand *controlling, wielding*
welde, walde, wolde *wield, control, use*
wele *health*
well (v.) *boil, suffer*

welle, wele *well, fountain, source*
welthe, welthis *state of well-being*
wendand, weendande *going*
wende *go, wend forth*
wend(e) *thought*
wending *passing away, dying*
wene (n.) *doubt*
wene, wenys, wyne (v.) *think(s), believe(s)*
were (n.) *suspicion, doubt, confusion*
were (v.) *defend, warn, guard; perplex*
were (v.) *wear*
were (adj.) *worse*
werie *weary*
weried, wer(r)yd *wrongheaded, accursed*
wetand *knowledge*
wete, weten *thought, revealed*
wete, wette *moisten, refresh*
wetterly *entirely*
weyes *weighs*
weyke *weak*
whan(ne) *when*
whap(p) *blow*
whedir, wheder *whither*
whesid *wheezed*
whilke, wilke *which*
wiff(e) *woman*
wight *strong*
wight(e), wyte, wight(is) *person(s)*
wightly, wightely, whytely *immediately, briskly, frequently*
wightness *strength*
wik *deadly*
wile, wilis *wile(s), trick(s)*
will *well*
will, wille *perplexed*
will(is) *will, permission*
willid *gone*
willy *willing*
wilsom, wilsome (adj.) *lonely, dangerous, confused*
wirkand *working, striving*
wirke(s) *work(s), produces*
wirkyng *behavior*
wise *manner*
wisse *keep, direct*

wiste *knew*
wite, wyte *blame, inform*
witte, wytt, wate, wete, wote *know, understand*
witterly *wisely, knowingly*
wittes, wytes *wits, intelligence*
woke *week*
wol *will*
wolde (n.) *power*
wolde, walde (v.) *would*
wombe, wombis *abdomen(s)*
wone, wonne (n.) *place*
wone, wonne, wonnys (v.) *live(s), dwell(s)*
wonnand *living*
wonne (n.) *custom, belief*
wonning, wonnyng *dwelling*
wonnyd *lived*
woode, wode *wood*
woode, wode *mad*
word *world*
wordly *worldly*
wore *were*
worme(s), wormis *serpent(s)*
worthed *come*
wote, wotte, wootte *know, learn*
wraiste *twisted*
wrake, wreke *vengeance, retribution, violence*
wrang(e) (n.) *wrong, evil*
wranges (v.) *wrongs*
wraste, wrest *trick*
wraste(d) *twist(ed)*
wrathenesse *anger*
wrayste (v.) *twist*
wreke *revenge*
wrekis *disasters, vengeance*
wrekyng *punishment*
wrenchis *tricks*
wreth, wrethe, wretthe *anger, malice*
wretthid *endangered, upset*
wretyn, wreten *written*
wreye(s) *betray(s), denounce(s)*
wreyede *revealed*
wreyst *deceived*
wrie *go awry*
wright *record*

wring, wryng(e) *torture, twist (in grief)*
write, wright *carpenter*
wroken *revenged*
wroth, wrothe *anger, angry, vexed*
wrotte *wrote*
wrye *turn, avoid*
wryng *escape*
wrynkis *twistings, tricks*
wyelly *joyful*
wyghtest *strongest*
wynde *breath*
wyne *believe*
wynke *sleep*
wynly *worthily, joyfully, excessively*
wynne (n.) *joy*
wynne (v.) *flee, win*
wyshe, wysshe, wys *guide*
wyst(e) *thought*

yappely *nimbly*
yarne, yerne *yearn*
yate *gate*
yede *go forth, went*
yeme *give heed to*
yemyng *care*
yendless *everlasting*
yhere *year*
ying, yhing, yeng *young*
ylke *each*
Ynde *India*
yode, yoode *went forth*
Ysais *Isaiah*
yther *hither*

Zache *Zacheus*

Stanzaic Guy of Warwick, edited by Alison Wiggins (2004)

Saints' Lives in Middle English Collections, edited by E. Gordon Whatley, with Anne B. Thompson and Robert K. Upchurch (2004)

Siege of Jerusalem, edited by Michael Livingston (2004)

The Kingis Quair and Other Prison Poems, edited by Linne R. Mooney and Mary-Jo Arn (2005)

The Chaucerian Apocrypha: A Selection, edited by Kathleen Forni (2005)

John Gower, *The Minor Latin Works*, edited and translated by R. F. Yeager, with *In Praise of Peace*, edited by Michael Livingston (2005)

Sentimental and Humorous Romances: Floris and Blancheflour, Sir Degrevant, The Squire of Low Degree, The Tournament of Tottenham, and The Feast of Tottenham, edited by Erik Kooper (2006)

The Dicts and Sayings of the Philosophers, edited by John William Sutton (2006)

Everyman and Its Dutch Original, Elckerlijc, edited by Clifford Davidson, Martin W. Walsh, and Ton J. Broos (2007)

The N-Town Plays, edited by Douglas Sugano, with assistance by Victor I. Scherb (2007)

The Book of John Mandeville, edited by Tamarah Kohanski and C. David Benson (2007)

John Lydgate, *The Temple of Glas*, edited by J. Allan Mitchell (2007)

The Northern Homily Cycle, edited by Anne B. Thompson (2008)

Codex Ashmole 61: A Compilation of Popular Middle English Verse, edited by George Shuffelton (2008)

Chaucer and the Poems of "Ch," edited by James I. Wimsatt (revised edition 2009)

William Caxton, *The Game and Playe of the Chesse*, edited by Jenny Adams (2009)

John the Blind Audelay, *Poems and Carols*, edited by Susanna Fein (2009)

Two Moral Interludes: The Pride of Life and Wisdom, edited by David Klausner (2009)

John Lydgate, *Mummings and Entertainments*, edited by Claire Sponsler (2010)

Mankind, edited by Kathleen M. Ashley and Gerard NeCastro (2010)

The Castle of Perseverance, edited by David N. Klausner (2010)

Robert Henryson, *The Complete Works*, edited by David J. Parkinson (2010)

John Gower, *The French Balades*, edited and translated by R. F. Yeager (2011)

The Middle English Metrical Paraphrase of the Old Testament, edited by Michael Livingston (2011)

COMMENTARY SERIES

Haimo of Auxerre, *Commentary on the Book of Jonah*, translated with an introduction and notes by Deborah Everhart (1993)

Medieval Exegesis in Translation: Commentaries on the Book of Ruth, translated with an introduction and notes by Lesley Smith (1996)

Nicholas of Lyra's Apocalypse Commentary, translated with an introduction and notes by Philip D. W. Krey (1997)

Rabbi Ezra Ben Solomon of Gerona, *Commentary on the Song of Songs and Other Kabbalistic Commentaries*, selected, translated, and annotated by Seth Brody (1999)

John Wyclif, *On the Truth of Holy Scripture*, translated with an introduction and notes by Ian Christopher Levy (2001)

Second Thessalonians: Two Early Medieval Apocalyptic Commentaries, introduced and translated by Steven R. Cartwright and Kevin L. Hughes (2001)

The "Glossa Ordinaria" on the Song of Songs, translated with an introduction and notes by Mary Dove (2004)

The Seven Seals of the Apocalypse: Medieval Texts in Translation, translated with an introduction and notes by Francis X. Gumerlock (2009)

The "Glossa Ordinaria" on Romans, translated with an introduction and notes by Michael Scott Woodward (2011)

DOCUMENTS OF PRACTICE SERIES

Love and Marriage in Late Medieval London, selected, translated, and introduced by Shannon McSheffrey (1995)

Sources for the History of Medicine in Late Medieval England, selected, introduced, and translated by Carole Rawcliffe (1995)

A Slice of Life: Selected Documents of Medieval English Peasant Experience, edited, translated, and with an introduction by Edwin Brezette DeWindt (1996)

Regular Life: Monastic, Canonical, and Mendicant "Rules," selected and introduced by Douglas J. McMillan and Kathryn Smith Fladenmuller (1997); second edition, selected and introduced by Daniel Marcel La Corte and Douglas J. McMillan (2004)

Women and Monasticism in Medieval Europe: Sisters and Patrons of the Cistercian Reform, selected, translated, and with an introduction by Constance H. Berman (2002)

Medieval Notaries and Their Acts: The 1327–1328 Register of Jean Holanie, introduced, edited, and translated by Kathryn L. Reyerson and Debra A. Salata (2004)

John Stone's Chronicle: Christ Church Priory, Canterbury, 1417–1472, selected, translated, and introduced by Meriel Connor (2010)

🖋 MEDIEVAL GERMAN TEXTS IN BILINGUAL EDITIONS SERIES

Sovereignty and Salvation in the Vernacular, 1050–1150, introduction, translations, and notes by James A. Schultz (2000)

Ava's New Testament Narratives: "When the Old Law Passed Away," introduction, translation, and notes by James A. Rushing, Jr. (2003)

History as Literature: German World Chronicles of the Thirteenth Century in Verse, introduction, translation, and notes by R. Graeme Dunphy (2003)

Thomasin von Zirclaria, *Der Welsche Gast (The Italian Guest),* translated by Marion Gibbs and Winder McConnell (2009)

Ladies, Whores, and Holy Women: A Sourcebook in Courtly, Religious, and Urban Cultures of Late Medieval Germany, introductions, translations, and notes by Ann Marie Rasmussen and Sarah Westphal-Wihl (2010)

🖋 VARIA

The Study of Chivalry: Resources and Approaches, edited by Howell Chickering and Thomas H. Seiler (1988)

Studies in the Harley Manuscript: The Scribes, Contents, and Social Contexts of British Library MS Harley 2253, edited by Susanna Fein (2000)

The Liturgy of the Medieval Church, edited by Thomas J. Heffernan and E. Ann Matter (2001; second edition 2005)

🖋 TO ORDER PLEASE CONTACT:

Medieval Institute Publications
Western Michigan University
Kalamazoo, MI 49008-5432
Phone (269) 387-8755
FAX (269) 387-8750
http://www.wmich.edu/medieval/mip/index.html

Typeset in 10/13 New Baskerville
and Golden Cockerel Ornaments display
Designed by Linda K. Judy
Manufactured by Cushing-Malloy, Inc.

Medieval Institute Publications
College of Arts and Sciences
Western Michigan University
1903 W. Michigan Avenue
Kalamazoo, MI 49008-5432
http://www.wmich.edu/medieval/mip

 WESTERN MICHIGAN UNIVERSITY